Contemporary Economics

The ninth edition of *Contemporary Economics* continues to offer a clear, concise presentation of basic micro- and macroeconomic theory. Emphasizing how the discipline of economics connects to the world, the book takes a friendly and accessible tone, illustrating theory with applications.

This new edition comes with updated applications and data to reflect the changing world events and contemporary issues since the previous edition was published. With a vast range of updated applications, the handbook uses real-world, globally relevant examples that make the subject easy to understand.

Including a suite of digital resources, including instructor's manual, lecture slides, and test bank, *Contemporary Economics* is suitable for both economics students and non-majors studying economics and economic issues at the introductory level.

Robert Carbaugh is Professor Emeritus of Economics at Central Washington University, USA.

Contemporary Economics

An Applications Approach

NINTH EDITION

Robert Carbaugh

NEW YORK AND LONDON

Designed cover image: Dragon Claws/Getty Images ®

Ninth edition published 2024
by Routledge
605 Third Avenue, New York, NY 10158

and by Routledge
4 Park Square, Milton Park, Abingdon, Oxon, OX14 4RN

Routledge is an imprint of the Taylor & Francis Group, an informa business

First edition published by South-Western 2000
Eighth edition published by Routledge 2017

Library of Congress Cataloging-in-Publication Data
Names: Carbaugh, Robert – author.
Title: Contemporary economics : an applications approach / Robert Carbaugh.
Description: Ninth edition. | New York, NY : Routledge, 2024. | Revised edition of the author's Contemporary economics, [2017] | Includes bibliographical references and index.
Identifiers: LCCN 2023052443 | ISBN 9781032572574 (hardback) | ISBN 9781032572598 (paperback) | ISBN 9781003438571 (ebook)
Subjects: LCSH: Economics. | United States—Economic conditions.
Classification: LCC HB171 .C277 2024 | DDC 330—dc23/eng/20231218
LC record available at https://lccn.loc.gov/2023052443

ISBN: 978-1-032-57257-4 (hbk)
ISBN: 978-1-032-57259-8 (pbk)
ISBN: 978-1-003-43857-1 (ebk)

DOI: 10.4324/9781003438571

Typeset in Berling
by Apex CoVantage, LLC

Access the Support Material: www.routledge.com/9781032572598

Brief Contents

Contents

Figures

Tables

Preface

As a university professor, I have enthusiastically taught a Survey of Economics course to undergraduate students majoring in business, economics, and other disciplines. Most of my students are first-year students or sophomores, and they have a modest awareness of economics. They want to know more about how economics relates to their daily lives, but they do not want to read a lengthy presentation that is overwhelmed by complicated words issued from every direction. Instead, they want a presentation that is clear and concise, lively, and contemporary—one that uses fewer words and has active verbs, shorter sentences, organized ideas, and simple visuals. With these student needs in mind, it is with pleasure that I have prepared a 9th edition of *Contemporary Economics: An Applications Approach*. It is written for students at 4-year colleges and universities as well as for students at community colleges and high schools that offer an introductory course in economics.

MEETING STUDENTS' NEEDS

The first 8 editions of *Contemporary Economics: An Applications Approach* combined a clear and concise presentation of microeconomic and macroeconomic theories with an abundance of contemporary applications. To explain economic theories, the book wove them into real-world examples described in social media, television, and newspapers. The abundance of positive feedback that I have received from faculty and students indicates that my pedagogical approach makes economics relevant and interesting for students. This approach applies to the 9th edition.

Reviews of my book show that users are pleased with its theoretical structure, which has been revised and improved many times throughout its first 8 editions. Therefore, I have not significantly changed the theoretical content of the 9th edition. What I have revised in the 9th edition are the contemporary issues and applications of theory. I continue to make each chapter current by adding new economic issues, deleting outdated issues, and updating tables of data. The 9th edition thus lives up to its name, *Contemporary Economics: An Applications Approach*.

A challenge faced by instructors of an economics survey course is that some of their students will pursue more advanced courses in principles of microeconomics and macroeconomics. To be meaningful for these students, the survey of an economics course must introduce economics without duplicating the topics and rigor of principles of economics courses. The 9th edition of my textbook addresses this need by presenting a small number of theoretical tools, at a modest level of detail and sophistication, with an abundance of contemporary applications. My book tells many stories of real-world events—students like stories.

A feature that has been added to the 9th edition of *Contemporary Economics: An Applications Approach* is the inclusion of images (photos) taken from Getty Images. In many ways, seeing a colorful image printed in a chapter can add much to the topic being discussed. My images are current, and they are intended to hold the interest of students and entice them to read chapter sections.

DISTINGUISHING FEATURES

The distinguishing features of my textbook include clear and concise presentation of economic theory, integration of contemporary issues throughout theoretical presentations, the inclusion of consumer economics topics, and global coverage throughout the textbook.

Clear Presentation of Theory

Presenting economic theory in a clear and interesting manner is the foundation of this textbook. Students can easily relate to the economic theories because they are presented in terms of realistic examples chosen to appeal to students of all backgrounds and abilities. For example, demand and supply analysis is presented in terms of tuition charged by colleges and universities, the cost of production in terms of Apple iPhones, oligopoly in terms of Boeing and Airbus jetliners, and macroeconomic shocks in terms of the Covid-19 pandemic.

Student users of my textbook have commented that the presentation is user friendly, and they can remember specific examples illustrating the theories discussed throughout the textbook. Moreover, all diagrams throughout my textbook use numbers (for example, 10 automobiles at a per-unit price of $50,000) on their axes to make the examples familiar and obvious to the student. Finally, my textbook emphasizes only the economic principles that are essential to an introduction of economics: Opportunity cost, demand and supply for individual markets, production and the cost of production, profit maximization for businesses, and aggregate demand and supply for explaining the economy's output, employment, and price level.

Real-World Applications

Contemporary Economics: An Applications Approach lives up to its name by emphasizing current applications and policy issues as seen in the following examples:

- Russian Aggression Against Ukraine Brings Economic Sanctions, Ch. 1
- Famous Entrepreneurs: Steve Jobs and Jeff Bezos, Ch. 4 and 5
- Rush-Hour Horrors and Congestion Pricing, Ch. 2

- Competition Puts the Brakes on Schwinn Bicycles, Ch. 2
- Bird Flu Triggers Soaring Egg Prices, Ch. 2
- The U.S. Postal Service Hikes Rates to Boost Revenues, Ch. 3
- Dynamic Pricing of Major-League-Baseball Tickets, Ch. 3
- Should a Ceiling Be Placed on Credit Card Interest? Ch. 3
- Ford Motor Company: From Mass Production to Lean Production, Ch. 4
- The Cost of Producing an Apple iPhone, Ch. 4
- Cable Television Companies Suffer as Entry Barriers Erode, Ch. 5
- Despite Competition From Starbucks, Many Independent Coffeehouses Survive, Ch. 6
- Boeing and Airbus Rivalry for Supremacy in Commercial Aviation, Ch. 6
- Is International Outsourcing a Threat or Opportunity for American Workers? Ch. 7
- Should the U.S. Government Increase Subsidies for Renewable Power? Ch. 8
- Cap and Trade: Trading Pollution Certificates, Ch. 8
- Has Income Inequality Gone Too Far? Ch. 9
- Reforming the U.S. Social Security System, Ch. 9
- Intel's Microprocessor and the Computer Revolution, Ch. 10
- Economic Shocks and the Covid-19 Pandemic, Ch. 11
- The Federal Deficit and National Debt, Ch. 13
- Does the Penny Make Sense—Should It Be Retired? Ch. 14
- The Federal Deposit Insurance Corporation and Bank Failures, Ch. 14
- Fiscal Policy, Monetary Policy, and the Covid-19 Pandemic, Ch. 15
- U.S. Industrial Policy and the Subsidization of Semiconductors, Ch. 16
- Is China's Currency Manipulation the Problem? Ch. 17
- Market Capitalism Versus State Capitalism: Which Works Better? Ch. 18

Consumer Economics Applications

To help students become informed consumers, *Contemporary Economics: An Applications Approach* includes applications in consumer economics. Examples include features of the dollar bill, compound interest, identifying electronic codes on a personal check, understanding America's check processing system, shopping for a credit card, holds placed on checking accounts, and saving money when buying foreign currency.

For example, Chapter 4 discusses the costs of driving an automobile. Students learn about the fixed costs and variable costs of driving and how to calculate the cost of driving on a per-mile basis. These concepts provide a transition to the costs of production as discussed later in the chapter.

Global Content

No survey of economics textbook can ignore discussion of the global economy. *Contemporary Economics: An Applications Approach* addresses this issue using a two-pronged approach. First, global economic issues are woven into the textbook, Chapters 1–15. Second, the textbook includes separate chapters on international trade, finance, and development. Chapter 16, *International Trade and the Global Economy*, discusses the principle of comparative advantage and the effects of free trade and protectionism. Chapter 17, *International Finance*, introduces the U.S. balance of payments, the foreign exchange market, and the factors that determine the dollar's exchange value. Chapter 18, *Economic Systems and Developing Countries*, discusses alternative economic systems and the role of developing countries in the global economy.

SUPPLEMENTARY MATERIALS

To help students master the tools of economic analysis, Koushik Ghosh of Central Washington University has prepared an excellent online *Study Guide*. Each chapter provides a summary of important points and learning objectives, matching review questions, multiple-choice questions, true–false questions, and application exercises.

To assist instructors in the teaching of this textbook, Margaret Landman of Bridgewater State University has written an online *Instructor's Manual* with test bank. Part I contains learning objectives, lecture hints and ideas, discussion starters, and brief answers to end-of-chapter study questions and problems. Part II contains a comprehensive test bank with multiple-choice, true–false, and essay questions.

Acknowledgments

This textbook could not have been written and published without the assistance of many individuals. I am pleased to acknowledge those who provided helpful suggestions and often detailed reviews:

- John Olienyk, Colorado State University
- Darwin Wassink, University of Wisconsin—Eau Claire
- Koushik Ghosh, Central Washington University
- Chad Wassell, Central Washington University
- Cassie Koefod, Central Washington University
- Magdalena Bialic-Davendra, Central Washington University
- Shirley Hood, Central Washington University
- John Adams, Texas A&M International University
- Bruce Pietrykowski, University of Michigan—Dearborn
- Tesa Stegner, Idaho State University
- Clifford Hawley, West Virginia University
- Rolando Santos, Lakeland Community College
- Karin Steffens, Northern Michigan University
- Pam Whalley, Western Washington University
- Margaret Landman, Bridgewater State University
- Barry Kotlove, Edmonds Community College
- R. Edward Chatterton, Lock Haven University
- Dea Ochs, Jesuit College Prep, Dallas, Texas
- Z. Edward O'Relley, North Dakota State University
- Laurence Malone, Hartwick College
- Vicki Rostedt, University of Akron
- Kishore Kulkami, Metropolitan State College
- David Hammes, University of Hawaii at Hilo
- Gary Galles, Pepperdine University
- Bruce Billings, University of Arizona
- Barry Goodwin, North Carolina State University
- Wike Walden, North Carolina State University
- Joseph Samprone, Georgia College and State University
- Robert Grafstein, University of Georgia
- Mark Healy, William Rainey Harper College

- Vani Kotcherlakota, University of Nebraska
- Donald A. Coffin, Indiana University, Northwest
- Naga Pulikonda, Indiana University, Kokomo
- F. P. Biggs, Principia College
- Ken Harrison, The Richard Stockton College of New Jersey
- Donald Bumpass, Sam Houston State College
- Sandra Peart, Baldwin-Wallace College
- Michael Rosen, Milwaukee Area Technical College
- Nicholas Karatjas, Indiana University of Pennsylvania
- Ernest Diedrich, St. John's University
- Arthur Janssen, Emporia State University
- Ralph Gray, DePauw University
- Maria V. Gamba-Riedel, The University of Findlay
- Anthony Patrick O'Brien, Lehigh University
- Charles W. Smith, Lincoln Land Community College
- Paul Comoli, University of Kansas
- Walton Padelford, Union University
- David Gillette, Truman State University

It has been a pleasure to collaborate with the staff at Routledge: Taylor and Francis Group in the preparation of the 9th edition of *Contemporary Economics: An Applications Approach*. In particular, I have appreciated the help of Michelle Gallagher (Senior Editor of Economics, Finance, Accounting, and Law) and to Chloe Herbert (Senior Editorial Assistant) who orchestrated the production of this book. I also wish to recognize the efforts of Suzanne Arnold who copyedited the manuscript, Kelly Cracknell, Matthew White and Ravinder Dhindsa who worked on it during production stages, and to those who provided reviews of the manuscript. Finally, I am grateful to my students, who commented on the manuscript.

I would appreciate any comments, corrections, or suggestions that faculty or students wish to make, so that I can continue to improve this textbook in the years ahead. Please contact me! Thank you for permitting this textbook to evolve to the 9th edition.

Bob Carbaugh
Professor Emeritus
Department of Economics
Central Washington University
Ellensburg, Washington 98926

PART 1

Introduction

CHAPTER 1

Scarcity and Choice

CHAPTER OBJECTIVES

After reading this chapter, you should be able to:

1 Discuss the nature of economics and the economic way of thinking.
2 Explain how the concept of scarcity relates to the concept of opportunity cost.
3 Identify the causes of economic growth and decline.
4 Identify the opportunity cost of national security.
5 Describe the purpose and effects of economic sanctions.

DOI: 10.4324/9781003438571-2

ECONOMICS IN CONTEXT

In the years following World War II, the United States sacrificed to equip itself with a national defense that could meet the threat posed by the Soviet Union. Trillions of dollars were spent to produce jet aircraft, tanks, missiles, submarines, and other defense goods. Indeed, the resources of the United States were scarce. The production of more defense goods meant that fewer resources were available for libraries, schools, golf courses, and other civilian goods. Put simply, the United States sacrificed civilian goods to produce more military goods.

Each time the United States developed a new military system, the former Soviet Union would develop a more costly system of its own. Were it not for scarce resources, the Soviets could have produced more civilian goods *and* more military goods. Because of scarcity, however, the Soviets had to produce fewer civilian goods to fulfill the everyday needs of the people. Moreover, the Soviet Union was less efficient at producing goods than the United States and other countries. Civilian goods were thus in short supply and of poor quality in the Soviet Union, which led to bitter complaints among the people. In 1992, the Soviet Union collapsed under the pressure of its disenchanted citizens. Suddenly, the world appeared to be a calmer and more secure place to live.

That peace, however, ended dramatically when terrorists attacked the United States on September 11, 2001, prompting the U.S. military to invade Afghanistan and Iraq. To improve national security, the United States once again increased its expenditures on military goods. However, the production of more military goods meant that fewer resources would be available for the production of civilian goods, such as police and fire protection, hospitals, and highways.

The question of how an economy should use its scarce resources is a main focus of public debate for all societies. In this chapter, we will examine the economic choices that must be made in every society because of scarcity.

WHAT IS ECONOMICS?

Economics means different things to different people. To some it means making money in stocks, bonds, and real estate. To others it means understanding how to own and operate a business. To the president of the United States, it may mean developing a new federal budget or formulating plans to reform the welfare system. Although these matters are part of economics, the subject has broader dimensions. **Economics** is first and foremost the study of *choice* under conditions of *scarcity*. Both individually and as a society, we attempt to choose wisely. We are forced to do so because human and property resources are limited, and it takes resources to produce cell phones, computers, automobiles, and other goods and services that we desire.

Obtaining the greatest value from resources is the goal of economic choice. At a personal level, we have limited income to spend on the many items we want. For example,

Source: sesame/Digital Vision Vectors/Getty Images®

we might forgo purchasing a Toyota RAV4 to have funds to pay tuition at University of Wisconsin. Businesses also face alternatives. Should a company use its scarce funds to replace its photocopiers instead of buying new computers? Moreover, the government has to make choices. Should tax dollars be used to purchase additional tanks and missiles, or should these dollars be used to finance the construction of a new highway system?

The field of economics is quite broad. Its reach extends from personal concerns—why does a pound of butter cost more than a pound of margarine?—to issues of national and global importance—will an economic slump in Asia cause the U.S. economy to decline? The field of economics is generally divided into two categories—microeconomics and macroeconomics.

Microeconomics

Microeconomics is the branch of economics that focuses on the choices made by households and firms and the effects those choices have on particular markets. We can use microeconomics to understand how markets work, to make personal or managerial decisions, and to analyze the impact of government policies. Consider these microeconomic questions:

- How would a higher tax on cigarettes affect consumption by teenagers?
- Why do convenience stores often close after several years?

- How would a ban on immigrant workers from Mexico affect U.S. apple growers?
- Should I put my savings in a bank account or invest them in the stock market?
- Will an increase in the federal minimum wage help the working poor?

Macroeconomics

The other branch of economics is macroeconomics. **Macroeconomics** is concerned with the overall performance of the economy. Macroeconomics does not focus on the activities of individual households, firms, or markets; instead, it focuses on the behavior of the economy itself. It deals especially with the determination of total output, the level of employment, and the price level.

We study macroeconomics to learn how the overall economy works and to understand the controversies concerning economic policies. Among the macroeconomic topics that we will examine are the following:

- Why do some economies grow more rapidly than others?
- What causes unemployment and inflation?
- Should the government adopt policies to increase savings and investment?
- Should the government limit the outsourcing of American jobs to foreign nations?
- How does a decrease in interest rates affect the economy?

These two branches—microeconomics and macroeconomics—converge to form the field of modern economics.

THE ECONOMIC WAY OF THINKING

The practice of economics often calls for an analysis of complex problems. Although economists may differ in their ideological views, they have developed an "economic way of thinking." This methodology is based on several principles.

Every Choice Has a Cost

Because human and property resources are scarce, individuals and societies must choose how best to use them. Making prudent choices requires trading off one thing for another. At the core of economics is the notion that "there is no such thing as a free lunch." A friend may buy your lunch, making it "free" to you, but there still is a cost to someone and, ultimately, to society. This notion expresses the fundamental principle of economics: Every choice involves a cost.

The cost of any choice is the value of the best opportunity that is forgone in making it. For example, you can choose to remain in college or quit college. If you quit, you may find a job at Burger King and earn enough money to buy some Levi's jeans, rent some videos, go golfing and skiing, and hang out with your friends. If you remain in college, you will not yet be able to afford all of these things. However, your education will enable you to find a better job later, and then you will be able to afford these and many other items.

People Make Better Choices by Thinking at the Margin

Economists maintain that people make better choices by thinking "at the margin." Making a choice at the margin means deciding to do a little more or a little less of an activity. As a student, you can allocate the next hour to sleeping or studying. In making this decision, you compare the benefit of extra study time to the cost of forgone sleep.

As an example of thinking at the margin, consider how United Airlines decides how much to charge passengers who fly standby. Assume that flying a 300-seat jetliner from Seattle to New York costs the airline $90,000. Therefore, the average cost (per seat) is $300 ($90,000 / 300 = $300). You might conclude that United Airlines should always charge at least $300 per ticket. However, the airline can increase its profits by thinking at the margin. Suppose that a jetliner is going to take off with one empty seat. A standby passenger is waiting at the gate and is willing to pay $200 to fly from Seattle to New York. Should United Airlines sell them a ticket at this price? Yes, because the cost of flying one more passenger is negligible. Although the *average* cost of flying a passenger is $300, the *marginal* (extra) cost is only the cost of a can of Sprite, a bag of pretzels, and a chicken sandwich. As long as United Airlines earns revenues that are more than the marginal cost, the addition of an extra passenger is profitable.

Rational Self-Interest

Economics is founded on the assumption of rational self-interest. This means that people act as if they are motivated by self-interest and respond predictably to opportunities for gain. In other words, people try to make the best of any situation. Often, making the best of a situation involves maximizing the value of some quantity. As a student, getting high grades may be an incentive to study hard because they may help you obtain a job interview with a particular employer or get accepted into a prestigious graduate school.

Throughout this text, we will assume that economic incentives underlie the rational decisions that people make. We will assume that a firm's owners want to maximize profit to improve their well-being. Also, we will assume that households seek to maximize their satisfaction from consuming goods and services. Because income is limited and goods have prices, we cannot buy all the things we would like to have. Therefore, we should choose an attainable combination of goods that will maximize our satisfaction. Of course, self-interest does not always imply increasing one's wealth as measured in dollars and cents or one's satisfaction from goods consumed. In addition to economic motivations, people also have goals pertaining to friendship, love, altruism, creativity, and the like.

Economic Models

Like other sciences, economics uses models. In chemistry, you may have seen a model of an atom—a device with blue, green, and red balls that represent neutrons, electrons, and protons. Architects construct cardboard models of skyscrapers before they are built. Economic models are not built with plastic or cardboard, but rather with words, diagrams, and mathematical equations.

Economic **models**, or **theories**, are simplified representations of the real world that we use to help us understand, explain, and predict economic phenomena in the real world. Economic models explain inflation, unemployment, wage rates, exchange rates, and more. For example, an economic model might tell us how the quantity of phone cases that consumers purchase would change if the sellers raise the price. Other models explain how changes in interest rates in the economy affect investment spending by business. Throughout this textbook, we will use economic models to help us understand contemporary economic issues.

Positive versus Normative Economics

It is important to realize that economics is not always free of value judgments. In thinking about economic questions, we must distinguish questions of fact from questions of fairness.

Positive economics describes the facts of the economy—it deals with the way in which the economy works. Positive economics considers such questions as, why do computer scientists earn more than janitors? What is the economic effect of reducing taxes? Does free trade result in job losses for less-skilled workers? Although these questions are difficult to answer, they can be addressed by economic analysis and empirical evidence.

Normative economics involves value judgments that cannot be tested empirically. Ethical standards and norms of fairness underlie normative economics. For example, should the United States penalize India for violating U.S. patent and copyright laws? Should welfare payments be reduced to encourage the unemployed to find income-producing jobs? Should all Americans have equal access to health care? Because these questions involve value judgments instead of facts, there are no right or wrong answers. Both positive and normative economics are important and will be considered throughout this textbook.

Why do economists often appear to give conflicting advice to policymakers? Because economists do not fully understand how the economy operates, they often disagree about actual cause-and-effect relationships. Moreover, economists may have different value judgments, and thus different normative views, about the goals that economic policies should attempt to accomplish.

The first part of this chapter has given us an overview of economics and the economic way of thinking. We will now examine the economic problem of scarcity.

SCARCITY

Whether you are taking just one economics course or majoring in economics, the most important topic you will learn about is **scarcity**. Scarcity means that there are not enough, nor can there ever be enough, goods and services to satisfy the wants and needs of everyone. Consider your own situation. Can you afford the school that you would most prefer to attend or the car that you would most like to own? Do you have sufficient financial resources for all the clothes, computers, concerts, and sporting events that you want?

Societies also face a scarcity problem. Money devoted to national defense, for example, is not available for education or food stamps.

The source of the scarcity problem is that people have *limited resources* to satisfy their *unlimited material wants.* Resources, or **factors of production**, are inputs used in the production of goods and services that we want, such as phone cases and textbooks. The total quantity of resources that an economy has at any one time determines how much output the economy can produce. The factors of production are classified as follows:

1 **Land**. Land refers to all natural resources—such as raw materials, land, minerals, forests, water, and climate—used in the productive process.
2 **Labor**. This resource includes all physical and mental efforts that people make available for production. The services of professional baseball players, accountants, teachers, and autoworkers all fall under the heading of labor.
3 **Capital**. Capital, or investment goods, refers to goods that are used to produce other goods and services. This includes such things as machinery, tools, computers, computer software, buildings, and roads. Notice that economists do not consider money to be capital because it is not directly used in production.
4 **Entrepreneurship**. This factor of production is a special type of labor. An entrepreneur is a person who organizes, manages, and assembles the other factors of production to produce goods and services. Entrepreneurs seek profit by undertaking risky activities such as starting a new business, creating a new product, or inventing a new way of accomplishing something. Bill Gates (founder of Microsoft Corp.), Levi Strauss (founder of Levi Strauss Co.), and Henry Ford (founder of Ford Motor Co.) are examples of highly successful entrepreneurs.

These factors of production have a common characteristic: They are in limited supply. Quantities of mineral deposits, capital equipment, arable land, and labor (time) are available only in finite amounts. Because of the scarcity of resources and the limitation this scarcity imposes on productive activity, output will be limited.

Limited resources conflict with unlimited wants. Human wants are said to be unlimited because no matter how much people have, they always want more of something. Because not all wants can be fulfilled, individuals must choose which ones to fulfill with limited available resources. In a world of scarcity, every want that is fulfilled results in one or more other wants remaining unfulfilled.

SCARCITY AND OPPORTUNITY COST

The reality of scarcity forces us to make choices that involve giving up one opportunity in order to do or use something else. For example, the cost of going to a Chicago Bulls basketball game includes the value of what is sacrificed to attend. Economists use the term **opportunity cost** to denote the value of the best alternative that is sacrificed. Part of the cost of attending a Bulls game is the price of the ticket. This price represents the other goods and services you could have purchased with that money instead. In addition, there is the most valuable alternative use of the time devoted to watching the game. Perhaps you could have used this time to study for an upcoming economics exam. Thus, the opportunity cost of attending the game equals the ticket price plus the difference in your test score that the additional study time would have yielded. Let us consider several applications of opportunity cost.

The Opportunity Cost of Attending College

Attending college provides an example of opportunity cost. Your cost of attending college is not simply the dollar amount listed in your college catalog. The money you spend on tuition, fees, textbooks, and supplies is only part of the opportunity cost; the income that you could have earned during the years that you are spending in classes is also part of the opportunity cost.

Table 1.1 shows the total estimated, out-of-pocket costs of a year of college for the average student in 2022–2023. For example, the second column of the table shows that the cost for an average instate resident at a four-year state college is $27,940 for one year. Of this amount, the student pays $10,940 in tuition and fees, $12,310 for room and board, $1,240 in books and supplies, $1,250 for transportation, and $2,200 for personal expenses.

Is the student's opportunity cost for a year of college $27,940? No. Some of this cost must be incurred regardless of whether the student attends college. For example, you would still have to assume room and board expenses—say, by living in an apartment—even if you did not attend college. This cost would not be eliminated even if you lived at home because your family could be renting your room to someone else. The same reasoning applies to transportation and other expenses, at least the portion that you would have assumed if you were not in college. Suppose that these expenses are the same regardless whether you attend college. The opportunity cost of attending college thus consists of tuition and fees ($10,940) and books and supplies ($1,240), which total $12,180.

TABLE 1.1 Average Estimated Full-Time Undergraduate Budgets, 2022–2023

Expense	*Public Four-Year Instate On Campus*	*Private Nonprofit Four-Year On Campus*
Tuition and fees	$10,940	$39,400
Room and board	12,310	14,030
Books and supplies	1,240	1,240
Transportation	1,250	1,070
Other expenses	2,200	1,830
Total	**27,940**	**57,570**

Source: Data drawn from College Board, *Trends in College Pricing and Student Aid, 2022*, available at https://research.collegeboard.org/media/pdf/trends-in-college-pricing-student-aid-2022.pdf.

In addition, the opportunity cost of a year of college includes the amount of forgone income. Assuming that you earn $20 an hour and reduce your work hours by 30 hours a week during the 32 weeks a year that you are in college, the forgone earnings represent a cost of $19,200 ($20 × 30 hours × 32 weeks) a year. It should be noted that most students will use their education to generate future earnings that will more than offset this sum. Nevertheless, the $19,200 also represents an opportunity cost of attending college.

The opportunity cost of a year of college thus includes the payments for tuition and fees ($10,940), payments for books and supplies ($1,240), plus the $19,200 of forgone income. This sum totals $31,380. Notice that this amount is greater than the estimated $27,940 of out-of-pocket costs shown in Table 1.1.

Some students find the opportunity cost of attending college to be even higher. Suppose that you are a talented baseball player or tennis player who could play professionally after graduating from high school. The opportunity cost of a year at college could easily be millions. Tiger Woods, a professional golfer, faced this dilemma after attending Stanford University for two years between 1994 and 1996. Upon winning his third straight U.S. Amateur golf title, he chose to turn pro rather than continue his studies at Stanford. He immediately became a multimillionaire, with contracts worth more than $40 million from Nike and Titleist in hand. It is no wonder that talented athletes often consider the opportunity cost of their college education to be too high and thus drop out of school to pursue professional sports.

Opportunity Costs and Choices

Suppose that your student club conducts a fund-raiser, and each club member agrees to spend 8 hours working at a Saturday car wash. A local service station donates its parking area and water, and your club supplies the washcloths and detergent. Club members wave their signs at passing motorists in an attempt to lure business.

After washing several vehicles, the members determine that they can wash 10 compact cars or 5 minivans in an hour's time. In an 8-hour day, then, the club could wash 80 compacts (8 × 10 = 80) or 40 minivans (8 × 5 = 40).

Figure 1.1 illustrates the combinations of compacts and minivans that could be washed in an 8-hour day. Devoting the entire day to washing compacts results in 80 washed cars, shown by point *A* in the figure. Conversely, devoting the entire day to washing minivans results in 40 washed minivans, shown by point *E*. Let us connect these two combinations with line *AE*. Other combinations (*B*, *C*, *D*) are attainable on this line. Line *AE* thus shows all the possible combinations of compacts and minivans that could be washed in a day.

Sliding down line *AE*, we see that there is an opportunity cost for washing minivans. For every 10 minivans that the club washes, it must sacrifice the washing of 20 compacts. This implies that the opportunity cost for each additional washed minivan equals 2 compacts (20 ÷ 10 = 2) that are not washed. Why does this trade-off occur? Given an 8-hour day, as more hours are devoted to the washing of minivans, fewer hours can be devoted to washing compacts. The 8-hour limitation of our Saturday car wash thus forces the club to make choices concerning how much effort should be devoted to washing compacts or minivans. Tabular and graphical relationships are further discussed in "Exploring Further 1.1" at the end of this chapter.

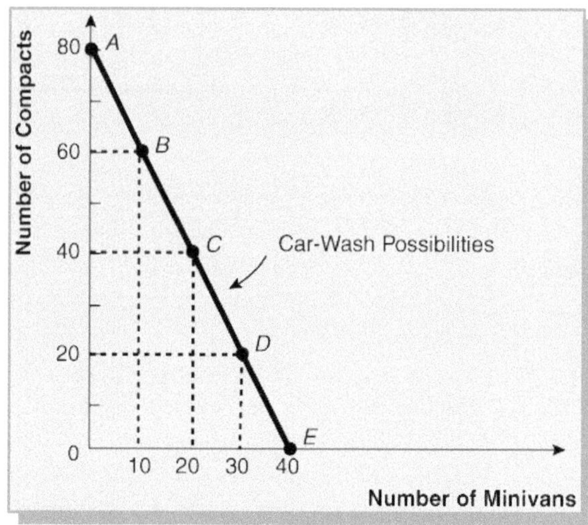

FIGURE 1.1 Opportunity Cost and Choice

In an 8-hour day, a student club can wash many combinations of minivans and compacts. Line *AE* illustrates these combinations given the assumption that the entire day is devoted to washing the two types of vehicles. The line is downward-sloping, suggesting that there is a trade-off between the number of compacts and the number of minivans that can be washed. Along line *AE*, the opportunity cost of each additional washed minivan is 2 compacts that are not washed.

CHECK POINT

1 What is economics?
2 Differentiate between microeconomics and macroeconomics.
3 Identify the major principles of the economic way of thinking.
4 How does scarcity force an individual to incur opportunity costs?
5 What opportunity cost do you face in attending college?

THE PRODUCTION POSSIBILITIES CURVE AND OPPORTUNITY COST

Just as scarcity affects the car-wash choices of a student club, it also influences the production choices of a nation. The relationship between the ideas of scarcity and choice that an entire nation faces can be illustrated by a **production possibilities curve**. A production possibilities curve illustrates graphically the maximum combinations of two goods that an economy can produce, given its available resources and technology. Several assumptions underlie an economy's production possibilities curve:

1 **Fixed resources**. The quantities of all resources, or factors of production, are held constant. This means that there are no changes in the economy's labor, machinery, and the like. Existing resources can only be transferred from the production of one good to the production of another good.

2 **Fully employed resources**. Everyone who wants a job has one, and all other resources are being used. All resources are producing the maximum output possible.

3 **Technology unchanged**. The existing technology is held fixed with no new innovations or inventions taking place.

The assumptions of fixed resources and fixed technology imply that we are looking at an economy at a specific point in time or over a very short period. Over a relatively long period, it is possible for resources to change and technological advances to occur.

Figure 1.2 illustrates a hypothetical economy that has the capacity to produce many combinations of smartphones and computers. If all resources are devoted to computer production, 6 million computers per year can be produced, denoted by point *A* in the figure. If all resources are devoted to the production of smartphones, 3 million smartphones per year can be produced, denoted by point *D*. Between the extremes of points *A* and *D* are other possible combinations of the two goods, denoted by points *B* point C. By connecting these points, we can see the economy's production possibilities curve.

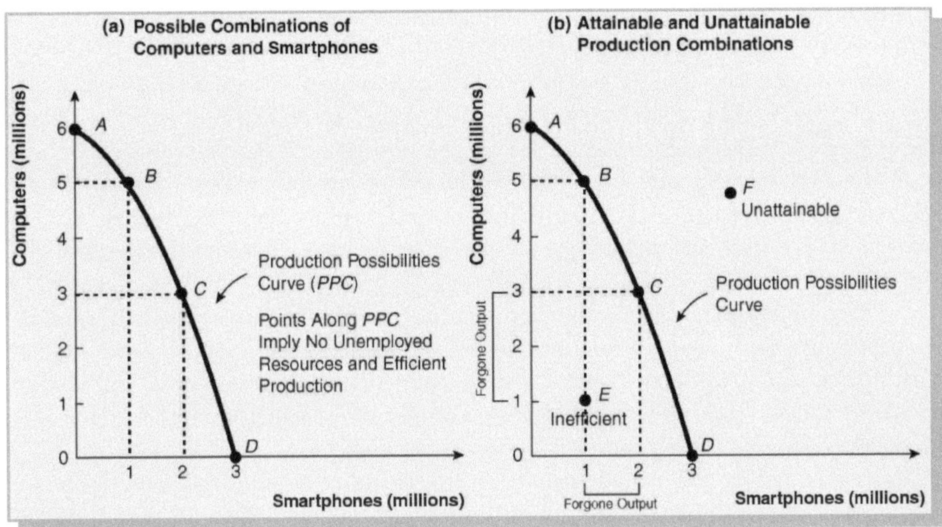

FIGURE 1.2 Production Possibilities Curve

A production possibilities curve graphically depicts the various combinations of two goods that an economy can produce with full employment, fixed resources, and fixed technology. Points inside the production possibilities curve are economically inefficient, while points outside the curve are unattainable given an economy's existing resources and technology.

The production possibilities curve in Figure 1.2(*a*) is downward-sloping because of the problem of scarcity. Resources of land, labor, capital, and entrepreneurship are limited to particular amounts at any one point in time. In a fully employed economy, if more resources are going into the production of smartphones, fewer resources will be left for computer production. To produce more smartphones, the cost will be a lower output of computers. The figure thus illustrates a basic truth of economics: All choices have opportunity costs.

Economic Inefficiency

Because all points along a production possibilities curve depict maximum output with given resources and technology, an economy realizes economic **efficiency** when it is operating along the curve. What if an economy does not employ all of its resources at their maximum capacity? For example, during economic downturns some workers probably cannot find work, and some plants and equipment may become underutilized. In this situation, the economy fails to realize the output potential of its production possibilities curve, and economic **inefficiency** occurs.

In Figure 1.2(*b*), point *E* shows an inefficient output combination for an economy that realizes unemployed labor or other underutilized resources; only 1 million smartphones players and 1 million computers are produced. With full employment, the economy can produce a larger output combination—say, 2 million smartphones and 3 million computers, shown by point C in the figure. Comparing these two points, we see that unemployment results in forgone output equal to 2 million computers and 1 million smartphones. Generalizing, the effect of unemployment is illustrated graphically by a point *beneath* the production possibilities curve. This point is attainable, but not necessarily desirable.

Even if an economy can fully employ all of its resources at their maximum capacity, certain output combinations cannot be realized. In Figure 1.2(*b*), any point outside the economy's production possibilities curve—say, point *F*—is *unattainable* because it lies beyond the economy's current production capabilities. The economy cannot achieve this output combination with its existing resources and technology. Scarcity restricts an economy to operating at points along or beneath its production possibilities curve.

Do economies operate along their production possibilities curves? Strictly speaking, no. Economies always experience some degree of unemployment and underproduction, which causes them to operate beneath their production possibilities curves. A production possibilities curve can thus be viewed as a yardstick against which an economy's production performance can be measured.

To what extent has the United States been able to utilize its industrial capacity? A measure of such utilization is the **capacity utilization rate**, which is the ratio of an industry's production to its capacity. According to this measure, an industry that is operating at full capacity has a 100-percent capacity utilization rate; a rate less than 100 percent implies that at least some plants and equipment are idle.

TABLE 1.2 Capacity Utilization Rates for Major U.S. Industries (percent of capacity)

Industry	*1972–2022 Average*	*1988–1989 High*	*2009 Low*
Total Industry	79.6	85.2	66.6
Manufacturing	78.2	85.6	63.4
Mining	86.3	86.8	78.9
Utilities	84.5	92.9	78.0
Stage of Production Process			
Unfinished Goods (Crude)	85.5	87.9	76.9
Semifinished Goods	80.1	86.5	63.5
Finished Goods	76.8	83.3	66.4

Source: Data drawn from Federal Reserve Statistical Release, G-17, *Industrial Production and Capacity Utilization*, available at www.federalreserve.gov.

Table 1.2 shows capacity utilization rates for major U.S. industries. We see that from 1972 to 2022 all U.S. industries combined operated at an average capacity utilization rate of 79.6 percent. The average capacity utilization rates for the economy's manufacturing, mining, and utilities sectors during this period equaled 78.2 percent, 86.3 percent, and 84.5 percent, respectively. The table also shows capacity utilization rates for stages of the production process.

The Law of Increasing Opportunity Cost

Figure 1.3 illustrates the production possibilities curve of our hypothetical economy as previously discussed. Notice that the production possibilities curve is bowed outward, or concave. This is because the opportunity cost of smartphones increases as more smartphones are produced. Moving from point *A* to point *B* along the curve, the opportunity cost of 1 smartphone is 1 computer; between points *B* and C, the opportunity cost is 2 computers; and between points C and *D*, the opportunity cost is 3 computers. These opportunity costs represent what occurs in the real world for most goods: Opportunity costs increase as we produce more of a good. This relationship is known as the **law of increasing opportunity cost**.

But *why* do opportunity costs generally increase as we produce more of a good? The answer is that *resources are not completely adaptable to alternative uses*. For example, some workers have skills that are more useful for producing smartphones than other workers have. When a company first starts producing smartphones, it employs workers who are most skilled at the production of smartphones. The most skilled workers are those who

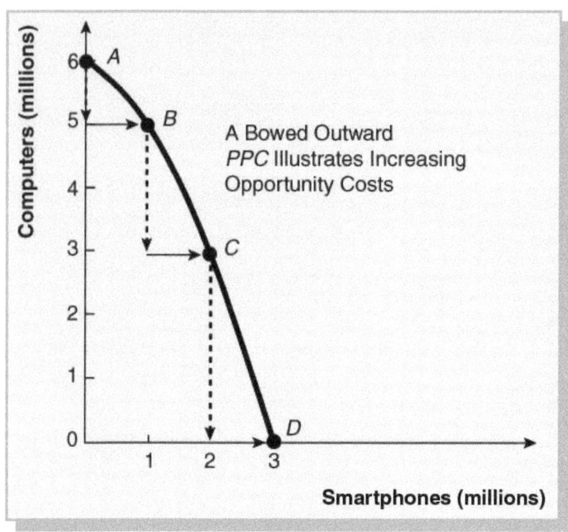

FIGURE 1.3 The Law of Increasing Opportunity Cost

In the real world, most production possibilities curves are bowed outward. This means that, for most goods, the opportunity cost increases as we produce more of them. Increasing opportunity costs occur when resources are not completely adaptable to alternative uses.

can produce smartphones at a lower opportunity cost than others. Yet as the company produces more smartphones, it finds that it has already employed the most skilled workers; thus, going forward, it must employ workers who are less skilled in the production of smartphones. These workers produce smartphones at a high opportunity cost. Whereas two skilled workers could produce a smartphone in a day, as many as five unskilled workers may be required to produce one smartphone in the same amount of time. Thus, as more smartphones are produced, the opportunity cost of producing smartphones increases.

ECONOMIC GROWTH

At any particular point in time, an economy cannot operate outside its production possibilities curve. Over time, however, it is possible for an economy to expand its output potential. This occurs through **economic growth**, which refers to the increased productive capabilities of an economy that are made possible by either an increasing resource base or technological advancement.

Economic growth entails an outward shift in an economy's production possibilities curve so that more of all goods can be produced. Figure 1.4 illustrates the significance of an outward shift in a production possibilities curve. Before the occurrence of economic growth, suppose that an economy can produce 2 million smartphones and 3 million computers, shown by point C along curve PPC_0. As a result of growth

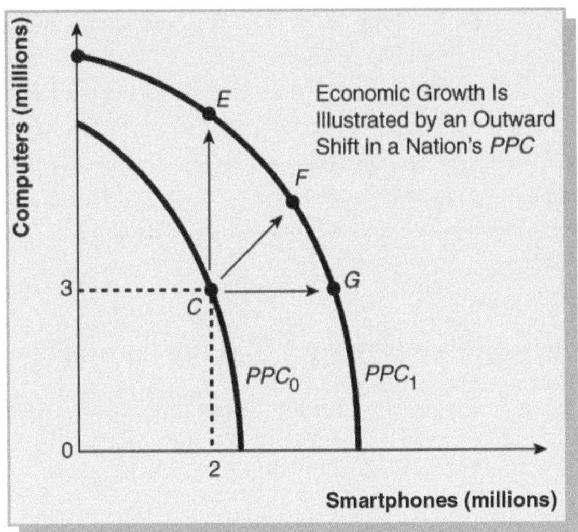

FIGURE 1.4 The Effect of Economic Growth on the Production Possibilities Curve

Economic growth shifts a production possibilities curve outward and makes it possible to produce more of all goods. Prior to growth in production capacity, point *C* was on PPC_0 and points *E*, *F*, and *G* were unattainable. After growth, shown by PPC_1, points *E*, *F*, and *G* (and many other previously unattainable combinations) are attainable.

in the economy's resource base or technological advancement, the production possibilities curve shifts outward to a higher level, PPC_1. Economic growth permits the economy to produce more computers (a movement to point *E*), more smartphones (a movement to point G), or more of both goods (a movement to point *F*). Many other previously unattainable combinations also become attainable with economic growth. In short, economic growth allows the economy to produce more of everything! However, growth does not guarantee that the economy will operate at a point along the higher production possibilities curve. The economy might fail to fulfill its expanded possibilities.

One way to increase an economy's production capacity is to gain additional resources. More (or better trained) workers or more (or improved) plants and equipment can increase a nation's output potential. Worker productivity is also facilitated by investment in infrastructure such as roads, bridges, airports, and utilities. Another way to achieve economic growth is through research and development of new technologies. Technological development allows more output to be produced with the same quantity of resources. A faster photocopier, a more smoothly operating assembly line, or a new-generation computer system are examples of technological advances.

Throughout America's history, agriculture has been a highly productive sector of the economy. In 1870, about 75 percent of Americans were farmers; in 2023, farmers constituted about 1 percent of Americans. During this period, total farm output expanded greatly. How could a declining number of farmers produce greater output?

The answer is improved technology. Whereas farmers once farmed with negligible capital equipment, today they use modern tractors, computers, pesticides, cellular phones, and the like. As a result, more food can be produced by fewer farmers. As farmers left farms, they entered manufacturing and service industries such as computers, automobiles, aircraft, accounting services, and engineering. Technological advances in farming thus made it possible to produce additional goods in other sectors of the economy. The result was an outward shift in the U.S. production possibilities curve.

Innovation and Economic Growth

As we have seen, the ability of an economy to grow rests on its resource base and technological advancement. Innovation is crucial for improving technologies that result in economic growth.

The next time that you are at an electronics store, take a close look at an iPhone. You will find that it was designed by Apple Inc. in California and likely assembled in China. Similar to Apple, the United States has often seen other industries locating abroad in the past, such as wind turbines and smartphones, which were born in the United States. Moreover, when an industry moves to another country, the United States may also lose technologies that can promote the development of future industries.

Consider the Amazon Kindle. In 2007, Amazon introduced the Kindle electronic reader, a device that allows users to download and read textbooks, magazines, and other digital media on a portable computer screen. Amazon first released the Kindle in November 2007 for $399, and it was sold out in five and a half hours. By 2023, the Kindle sold for about $140, as competition from other producers intensified.

To produce the electronic ink for the Kindle, Amazon initially partnered with E-Ink Co., an American producer. However, it turned out that E-Ink could not produce the screens due to unforeseen problems and Amazon had to find another partner. Although Amazon's search initially began in the United States, it was unsuccessful because American firms did not have the capability to produce the Kindle screen. Eventually, Amazon linked with Prime View, a Chinese company, to produce the screen. Within a short period of time, Prime View acquired E-Ink and moved ink production from the United States to China. Even though the Kindle's key innovation was invented in the United States, most of the Kindle production took place in China.

Some analysts note that as firms exit the United States, the country loses its innovation edge. They emphasize how manufacturing is a vital driver of research and development that fosters inventions which promote economic growth. The United States cannot sustain the level of economic growth it needs without a strong manufacturing sector. To promote stronger manufacturing, the United States needs investment-friendly government policies, according to these analysts.

However, others disagree. They maintain that from the perspective of America's competitiveness, all of the essential technological activities still take place in America. They also note that international trade promotes evolution in a country's industries over time. For example, the production of televisions initially began in the United States. But as technologies became standardized, television production shifted to other countries, such as Japan, with lower wages. This resulted in manufacturing costs and prices tumbling, to the benefit of consumers. Yet the question remains: How about the livelihood of Americans who formerly produced televisions? Indeed, the world economy is dynamic and the producers who have prospered have been the ones who can modify their business models to match or surpass their competitors.

BOX ESSAY 1.1 ECONOMICS IN ACTION
Adam Smith: Father of Modern Economics

Adam Smith (1723–1790) was a Scottish philosopher and is widely cited as the father of modern economics. He is the author of *The Wealth of Nations*, which is considered the first modern work of economics.

Born in a small fishing village near Edinburgh, Scotland, Smith was the only child of the village's customs officer. He studied philosophy at the University of Glasgow and University of Oxford. After graduating, Smith became a professor at the University of Glasgow. He was lured away from his professorship by a wealthy Scottish duke who gave him a pension of 300 pounds per year (10 times the average income of his day) to devote to the writing of *The Wealth of Nations*. This book was published in 1776 at the height of the Industrial Revolution, when new technologies were applied to the manufacturing of iron, textiles, and agriculture. In his later life, Smith took a tutoring position, allowing him to travel throughout Europe, where he met other intellectual leaders of the day.

The Wealth of Nations considers why some nations are wealthy and others are poor. Smith's answer to this question emphasized the importance of free markets and the division of labor. He believed that the free market is guided to produce the right amount and variety of goods by an "invisible hand." According to Smith, in a free market each participant will try to maximize self-interest. The interaction of market participants, leading to the exchange of goods and services, provides for each participant better than when simply producing for themselves. He further said that in a free market, no government regulation of any type would be needed to ensure that the mutually beneficial exchange of goods and services took place, since this "invisible hand" would guide market participants to trade in the most mutually beneficial manner.

Smith also maintained that the division of labor and specialization would result in a large increase in labor productivity. An example he used was the making of pins. He noted that one worker using hand tools might make only 20 pins per day. However, if 10 workers divided up the 18 steps required to make a pin, they could together make 48,000 pins in one day: One worker draws out the wire, another straightens it, a third cuts it, and so on. However, a large market is needed to support the division of labor. A factory employing 10 workers would need to sell more than 15 million pins a year to remain in operation.

The Wealth of Nations was a precursor to the modern study of economics. It provided a strong intellectual rationale for free trade and capitalism, greatly influencing the writings of later economists.

Sources: James Buchan, *The Authentic Adam Smith: His Life and Ideas* (New York, NY: W.W. Norton and Company, 2006); and Mark Skousen, *The Making of Modern Economics* (Armonk, NY: M.E. Sharpe, 2001).

ECONOMIC DECLINE

Just as an expanding resource base causes an economy's production possibilities to increase, decreasing resources can likewise reduce an economy's output potential. During World War II, for example, the production possibilities of Europe and Japan decreased. The war disrupted people's lives, and many people did not survive the war. Entire factories, roads, bridges, railway networks, electrical utilities, and other types of capital goods were reduced to rubble. The destructive effects of the war caused the production possibilities curves of Europe and Japan to shift inward.

The physical devastation of Europe and Japan caused by World War II yielded some paradoxical effects for these war-devastated economies. Because a large share of their stock of capital goods was destroyed by the war, these nations had to rebuild their industries from scratch. They did so with the most up-to-date factories and equipment. The result was a substantial increase in labor productivity, which allowed these economies to realize production possibilities exceeding those that had existed before the war. Conversely, nations that had been spared the devastation of the war had their prewar technologies in place and grew slower than those whose stock of capital goods was destroyed and replaced with more modern technology.

For example, the United States was the most powerful steel-producing nation in the world immediately following World War II. The U.S. steel industry came out of the war intact, accounting for nearly half of the world's steel output. Moreover, U.S. firms produced more steel than all of Europe combined and almost 20 times as much as Japan. During the 1950s and 1960s, however, the absence of foreign competition caused U.S. steel companies to become complacent. Instead of investing in new plants, they manufactured steel in outmoded plants using obsolete technologies and paid wages almost twice the average of all other U.S. manufacturing sectors. In contrast, Japan and Europe replaced the steel factories that had been devastated by the war with modern plants which used the most efficient equipment. By the 1970s, the productivity of Japanese and European steel companies was increasing relative to the productivity of U.S. companies, and the competitiveness of U.S. companies dwindled. The threat of foreign competition forced U.S. steel companies to shut down many obsolete factories in the 1980s and replace them with modern plants and equipment.

Natural disasters can also reduce an economy's output potential. For example, in 2005 the states of Alabama, Louisiana, and Mississippi were struck by two major hurricanes (Katrina and Rita) which damaged the productive capacity of the U.S. economy. These hurricanes passed through offshore areas where oil and natural gas platforms are concentrated and then struck onshore areas where petroleum is refined and natural gas is processed. In addition to the tragic loss of life and massive destruction of personal property that they caused, the hurricanes damaged energy equipment and structures. Most of this output loss was the result of the destruction of oil and natural gas operations.

ECONOMIC GROWTH: TRADE-OFFS BETWEEN CURRENT AND FUTURE CONSUMPTION

The production possibilities curve and economic growth can be used to investigate the trade-off between current and future consumption. This trade-off can be illustrated for nations producing consumer goods and capital goods.

Consumer goods are goods such as food, electricity, and clothing that are available for immediate use by households. They do not contribute to future production in the economy. **Capital goods**, such as factories and machines, are used to produce other goods and services in the future. Instead of being consumed today, capital goods are a source of an economy's economic growth potential.

A nation that sacrifices current consumption so it can invest in capital goods is forward-looking. Rather than getting instant satisfaction from the production of capital goods, the nation increases its capacity to produce consumer goods in the future. This is like students attending college. Students devote time to study that could have been spent working, earning income, and therefore engaging in a higher level of consumption. Most students decide to postpone consumption because they expect education to increase their productivity and income, allowing greater consumption in the future.

Figure 1.5 illustrates the production possibilities curves for the United States and Japan. The two axes of each production possibilities curve are designated as consumer goods (current goods) and capital goods (goods for the future). Assume that the two nations are identical in every respect except that the U.S. choice along its production possibilities curve favors consumer goods as opposed to capital goods; let this be designated by point *A* in Figure 1.5(*a*). Conversely, Japan's choice along its production possibilities curve favors capital goods and is denoted by point *A* in Figure 1.5(*b*).

The relatively large accumulation of capital goods allows the Japanese economy to grow faster than the U.S. economy. In Figure 1.5, this is illustrated by Japan's production possibilities curve, which shifts farther out to the right than the U.S. curve. Over time, Japan's faster growth rate allows it to produce more consumer goods than the United States. This increase in production, however, requires Japanese households to sacrifice current consumption in exchange for future consumption.

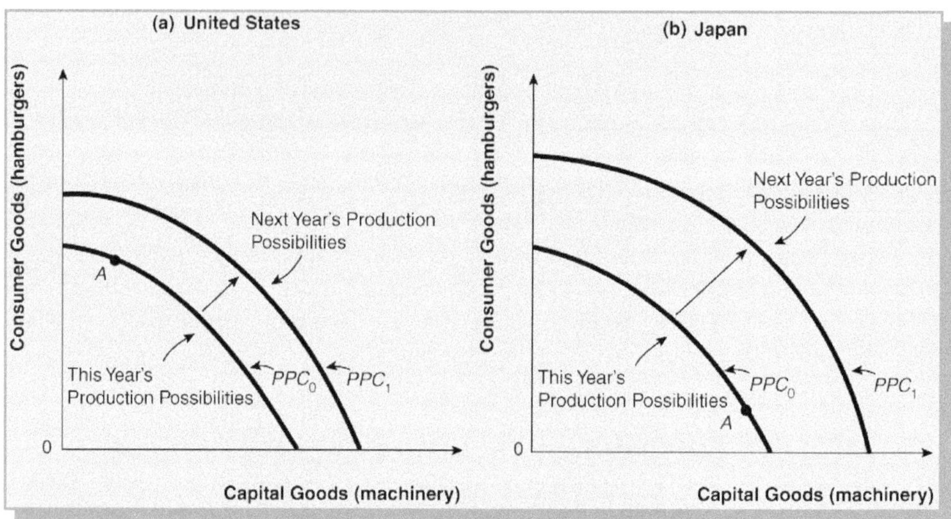

FIGURE 1.5 Economic Growth in the United States and Japan

A current choice favoring consumer goods, made by the United States in (*a*), will cause a modest outward shift in the U.S. production possibilities curve. A current choice favoring capital goods, as made by Japan in (*b*), will lead to a greater outward shift in the Japanese production possibilities curve. The extra goods, made possible by economic growth, thus result in a greater improvement in the standards of living in Japan.

TABLE 1.3 Growth in Gross Domestic Product, Annual Percent, 2014–2022

Country	*2014*	*2016*	*2018*	*2020*	*2022*
Australia	2.6	2.7	2.9	–0.1	7.8
Canada	2.9	1.0	2.8	–5.2	3.4
China	7.4	6.8	6.7	2.2	3.1
Germany	2.2	2.2	1.0	–3.7	1.7
Japan	0.3	0.8	0.6	–4.5	1.4
Mexico	2.8	2.6	2.2	–8.0	3.1
Russia	0.7	0.2	2.8	–2.7	-2.3
Singapore	3.9	3.6	3.7	–4.1	6.5
United States	2.3	1.7	2.9	–2.8	2.1

Source: Data drawn from World Bank, *World Development Indicators*, available at databank.worldbank.org.

Table 1.3 shows comparisons of selected countries' economic growth rates during 2014–2022. Notice the relatively rapid growth rate of the Chinese economy during this period. It was supported by large-scale capital investment, financed by domestic savings and foreign investment, and rapid productivity growth. Yet in recent years, China's growth rate has tapered.

PRODUCTION POSSIBILITIES APPLICATIONS

The production possibilities concept can be applied to issues pertaining to national security. Let us consider the application of the production possibilities concept to the terrorist attacks of September 11, 2001, and to the economic sanctions levied by the United States against Russia in 2022–2023.

Opportunity Cost of National Security: September 11, 2001

The September 11 terrorist attacks resulted in a tragic loss of life for thousands of innocent people. They also jolted America's golden age of prosperity and the promise it held for global growth, which had existed throughout the 1990s. Because of the threat of terrorism, Americans became increasingly concerned about their safety.

Immediately following the terrorist attacks, businesses and governments made greater efforts to improve their security. For example, Quality Carriers Inc., the country's biggest chemical trucker, rehired the night-shift security guards it had previously let go at its tanker-truck terminal in Newark, New Jersey. The company also paid employees to re-park any vehicles loaded with chemicals in plain view and under security lights. For Quality Carriers, achieving extra security required the firm to use more of its resources to protect the company from terrorists, leaving fewer resources available to transport chemicals for its customers. In like manner, security procedures were beefed up at power plants, communication companies, airports, and government buildings following the September 11 attacks.

Simply put, providing for national security entails an opportunity cost. When we employ labor, capital, and land for security, we sacrifice other things that we could have produced with them. To demonstrate this point, consider Figure 1.6, which depicts hypothetical production possibilities curves for the United States. The vertical axis denotes the annual production of security goods (for example, metal detectors and X-ray monitors) and the horizontal axis denotes the annual production of goods other than security (for example, televisions and autos) that contribute directly to our standard of living. Because of technological progress and the growth in the nation's stock of plants and equipment, the nation's production possibilities curve shifts outward, as shown by the movement from curve PPC_0 to curve PPC_1.

Assume that prior to September 11, the United States was located at point *E* along curve PPC_0. Also assume that in a typical year, economic growth would shift the United States from point *E* on curve PPC_0 to point *F* on curve PPC_1. This means that the nation

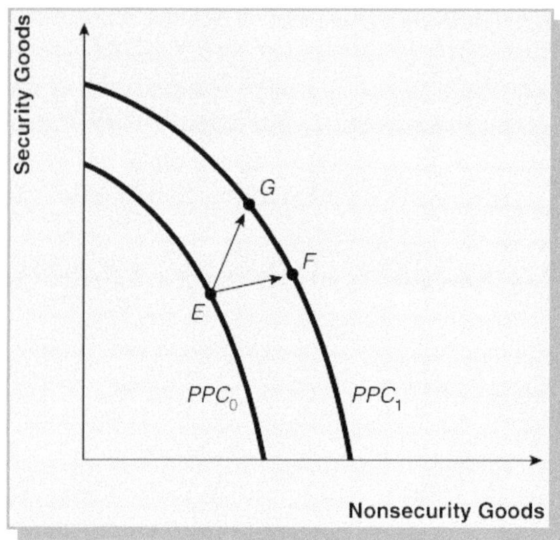

FIGURE 1.6 The Opportunity Cost of National Security

Providing for national security entails an opportunity cost. When we use land, labor, and capital to produce security goods, we sacrifice other things we could have produced with them.

would realize a modest increase in production of security goods, but most of our growth would have been used to produce additional quantities of autos, televisions, and other things we enjoy. Because of the September 11 terrorist attacks, however, we move from point *E* to point G. Notice that although we produce additional quantities of nonsecurity goods, we do not produce *as much* of those goods as we would have if the attacks had not occurred. This limits our economic well-being as measured by the quantity of nonsecurity goods available for our consumption. Therefore, providing for national security results in an opportunity cost in terms of other goods that we enjoy.

Economic Sanctions

In our world, nations often disagree with each other's policies regarding military adventures, arms proliferation, support of terrorism, drug trafficking, human rights abuses, cybersecurity, and so on. Besides military action, are there other ways to convince a foreign government to change its policies regarding these issues?

One alternative is **economic sanctions,** which are government-imposed limitations, or complete bans, placed on customary trade or financial relations between nations. The country initiating the sanctions, the *imposing country,* hopes to impair the economic capabilities of the recipient *target country.* The goal of economic sanctions is to inspire the people of the target country to force their government to modify its policies. Among the countries that the United States has levied economic sanctions against are Russia, Libya, North Korea, Iran, Cuba, Venezuela, Syria, and others. Table 1.4 provides examples of U.S. sanctions.

The imposing country or countries can levy several types of economic sanctions. *Trade sanctions* involve boycotts on imposing-country exports to the target country. The United

TABLE 1.4 U.S. Economic Sanctions

Target Country	*Year Initiated*	*Reason for Sanctions*
North Korea	1950	Human rights abuses, nuclear proliferation
Cuba	1958	Human rights abuses
Syria	1986	State sponsor of terrorism, human rights abuses
Iran	1987	Human rights abuses, nuclear proliferation
Venezuela	2019	Illegal drug trade, electronic rigging of elections, human rights abuses
Russia	2022	Russia's invasion of Ukraine

Source: Drawn from the combined lists of the U.S. Treasury Department, Commerce Department, and State Department.

States has used its status as a major producer of military hardware and high-technology goods as a lever to gain foreign adherence to its policy goals. Trade sanctions may also include restrictions on imposing-country imports from the target country. *Financial sanctions* can entail limitations on official lending or aid and the freezing of financial assets, such as bank accounts.

Figure 1.7 can be used to illustrate the goal of sanctions levied against Russia, intended to discourage it from invading neighboring countries. The figure shows the hypothetical production possibilities curve of Russia for machines and oil. Prior to the imposition of sanctions, suppose that Russia can operate at maximum efficiency, as shown by point *A* along production possibilities curve PPC_0. Under the sanctions program, the imposing countries' refusal to purchase Russian oil leads to idle wells, refineries, and workers in Russia. The unused production capacity thus forces Russia to move inside PPC_0. If the imposing countries also target productive inputs, thus curtailing equipment sales to Russia, the output potential of Russia would decrease. This is shown by an inward shift of Russia's production possibilities curve to PPC_1. Economic inefficiencies and reduced production possibilities, both of which are caused by economic sanctions, are thus intended to inflict hardship on the people and government of Russia.

The success of sanctions in modifying the behavior of a target country depends on several factors:

- The number of sanction-levying countries. A larger number of imposing countries tends to exert greater economic pressure on the target country.
- The extent to which the target country has economic and political connections to the imposing country before the sanctions are levied. Strong links to the imposing country mean the potential costs to the target country are large if it does not adhere to the desires of the imposing country.

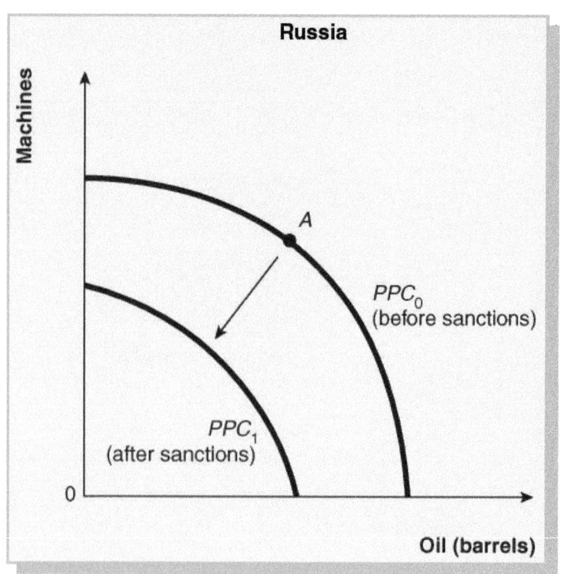

FIGURE 1.7 Effects of Economic Sanctions

Trade and financial bans placed against a target nation have the effect of forcing the nation to operate inside its production possibilities curve. Economic sanctions can also result in a leftward (inward) shift in the target nation's production possibilities curve.

- Strength of political opposition within the target nation. When the target government encounters significant domestic opposition, economic sanctions can result in powerful business interests pressuring the government to follow the imposing country's desires.
- The ability of the target country to escape sanctions. Sanctions are weakened if the target country can find alternative suppliers of embargoed goods and financial capital.

Although economic sanctions have been used by the United States and the European Union, critics maintain that they are often poorly conceived and rarely successful in changing a target country's behavior.

Russian Aggression Against Ukraine Brings Sanctions

In response to political unrest by pro-Russian supporters in Ukraine, in 2014 President Vladimir Putin sent Russian troops into the country. His military rapidly gained control of the Crimea region in Ukraine. In 2022, Putin again sent his troops into Ukraine, declaring that his goal was to demilitarize and denazify Ukraine and thus protect its people from governmental bullying and genocide. The Ukrainian government immediately protested and declared that Russia's aggression was illegal and it must stop. With military assistance from mainly the United States and Europe, Ukraine's government set out to defend itself from Russian aggression.

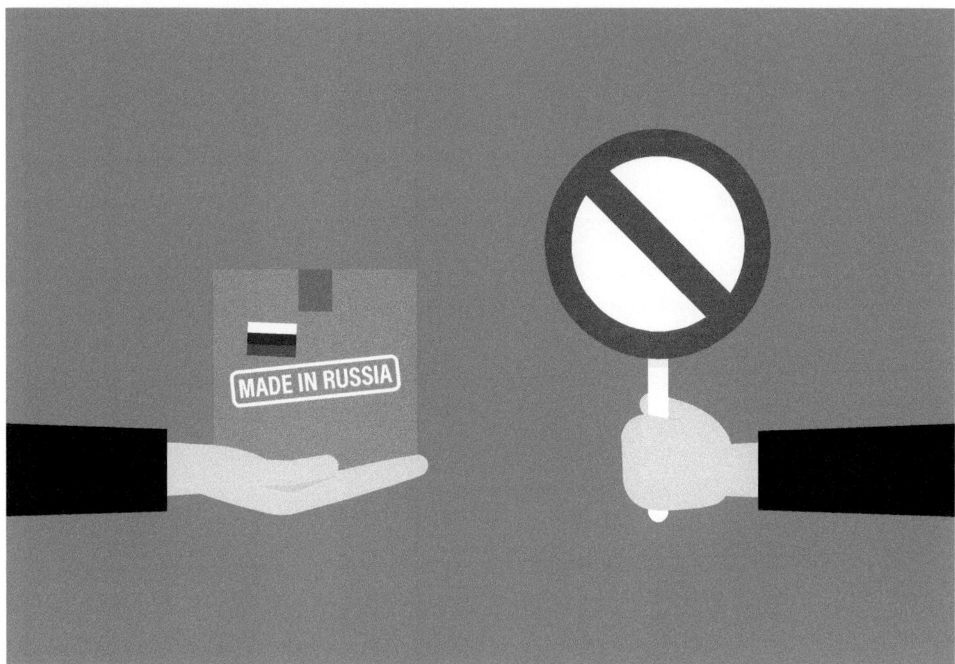

Source: tommy \ DigitalVision Vectors \ Getty Images®

To further show support for the Ukrainian government, the United States and about 30 other countries enacted a coordinated set of trade and financial sanctions covering thousands of Russian firms and individuals. The aim was to further isolate Russia from the international economy and hinder its ability to obtain the capital, materials, technology, and support that sustained its war against Ukraine. Examples of the sanctions included cutting most large Russian banks off from the global payments system, freezing financial assets of Russian oligarchs and officials and banning their foreign travel, preventing Russia from purchasing inputs ranging from chips to engines, and cutting back purchases of Russian oil.

The short-run goal of the sanctions was to make it difficult for Russia to finance the Ukraine war and thus alter Putin's incentives. In the long run, the objective was to worsen Russia's productive capacity and technological sophistication so that, if Putin decided to invade another country, he would have fewer resources at his disposal. Finally, the sanctions were meant to send a signal to other nations about the high cost of pursuing war.

At the writing of this book, the economic punishment inflicted in Russia had not stopped the pummeling of Ukraine. A limitation of sanctions is that they often take years to bite, and target countries can often find ways to evade sanctions. But sanctions did weaken Russia's standing as a world power by reducing its ability to buy what it needs, while reducing its exports to other nations. Simply put, in terms of the production possibilities analysis of Figure 1.7, the sanctions caused Russia to move inside of its production possibility curve as well as caused its curve to shift downward.

CHECK POINT

1. How can we use a production possibilities curve to illustrate opportunity cost for a nation?
2. Concerning economic growth, does it make any difference whether an economy devotes more resources to the production of capital goods as opposed to the production of consumer goods?
3. Identify the opportunity cost of national security.
4. When economic sanctions are placed on a country, how can they affect its production possibilities?

CHAPTER SUMMARY

1. The source of an economy's scarcity problem is that people have limited resources to satisfy their unlimited material wants.
2. Resources, or factors of production, are inputs used in the production of goods and services. They include land, labor, capital, and entrepreneurship.
3. The reality of scarcity forces us to make choices which involve giving up one opportunity in order to do or use something else. Economists use the term "opportunity cost" to denote the value of the best alternative that is sacrificed.
4. A production possibilities curve illustrates graphically the maximum combinations of two goods that an economy can produce, given its available resources and technology. An economy that is located along its production possibilities curve is operating at maximum efficiency.
5. As we move along an outward-bowed production possibilities curve, opportunity costs increase as more of a good is produced. Increasing opportunity costs occur because resources are not completely adaptable to alternative uses.
6. Economic growth entails an outward shift in an economy's production possibilities curve so that more of all goods can be produced. It is made possible by an increase in an economy's resource base or technological advances.
7. The terrorist attacks of September 11, 2001 forced the United States to beef up its national security. However, the devotion of additional resources to national security entails an opportunity cost in terms of other goods that Americans could consume.
8. Economic sanctions are government-imposed limitations placed on trade and financial relations between nations. The nation initiating the sanctions, the imposing nation, hopes that the economic hardship caused by sanctions will inspire the target nation to alter its political or military policies. Economic sanctions can force a target nation to locate beneath its production possibilities curve and can even cause the target nation's production possibilities curve to shift inward.

KEY TERMS AND CONCEPTS

economics
microeconomics
macroeconomics
models
theories
positive economics
normative economics
scarcity
factors of production
opportunity cost
production possibilities curve
efficiency, inefficiency
capacity utilization rate
law of increasing opportunity cost
economic growth
consumer goods
capital goods
economic sanctions
independent variable
dependent variable
direct relationship
inverse relationship
slope

STUDY QUESTIONS AND PROBLEMS

1 Suppose that you receive a weekly income of $100, which you spend entirely on pizza and deluxe hamburgers. The price of a pizza is $10 and the price of a hamburger is $5. On a diagram, draw a line that shows your consumption possibilities. What is the opportunity cost of a hamburger? Would the opportunity cost of a hamburger change if the prices of pizza and hamburgers were cut in half? Calculate the opportunity cost of a pizza and a hamburger for each of the following changes:

   a An increase in the price of pizzas to $20

   b An increase in the price of hamburgers to $10

   c A decline in weekly income to $80

   d A rise in weekly income to $120

TABLE 1.5 Production Possibilities

	Production Alternatives					
Product	*A*	*B*	*C*	*D*	*E*	*F*
Steel (tons)	0	1	2	3	4	5
Aluminum (tons)	20	18	15	11	6	0

2 Table 1.5 shows a production possibilities table for steel and aluminum.

   a Plot these production possibilities data on a diagram. On what assumptions is your production possibilities curve based?

   b What is the opportunity cost of the first ton of steel? Between which points is the opportunity cost of a ton of steel the greatest?

- c Explain how this curve reflects the law of increasing opportunity cost.
- d Label a point *G* inside the curve. Why is this point inefficient? Label a point *H* outside the curve. Why is this point unattainable?
- e Why might the production possibilities curve shift inward? Why might it shift outward?

3 How does each of the following affect the location of an economy's production possibilities curve?

- a A war leads to casualties for civilian workers
- b A new technology permits more oil to be extracted from a well
- c The economy's unemployment rate rises from 4 percent to 6 percent of the labor force
- d The economy decides to produce more CD players and fewer radios

4 In the 1990s, civil war erupted in Bosnia. The war led to the destruction of natural resources and capital and caused casualties that decreased the supply of labor for the production of consumer goods and capital goods. Illustrate the impact of the war on Bosnia's production possibilities curve for consumer goods and capital goods.

5 Draw an economy's production possibilities curve for automobiles and airplanes. Assume a technological breakthrough occurs that allows greater productivity for autoworkers but not airplane workers. Draw a new production possibilities curve. Suppose instead that the technological breakthrough allows greater productivity for airplane workers but not autoworkers. Draw a new production possibilities curve.

6 In response to Iraq's invasion of Kuwait in 1990, the United States and its allies imposed trade and financial sanctions on Iraq. Imports of Iraqi oil were terminated, as were exports of machinery, parts, and the like, to Iraq. Bank loans to Iraq and business investment in Iraq were also curtailed. Illustrate the effects of the economic sanctions on Iraq's production possibilities curve for textiles and oil. Under what conditions would the sanctions have been most likely to cause Iraq to withdraw from Kuwait?

EXPLORING FURTHER 1.1: A PRIMER ON TABLES AND GRAPHS

As you glance at this text, you will notice many tables and graphs. They are included to help you visualize and understand economic relationships. To understand how tables and graphs are constructed, let us consider an example that is familiar to you: The relationship between study time and grades in a college course.

Suppose that we conduct a survey of all students who recently completed an economics course, asking the number of hours they devoted to study each week and their course grade. The resulting information is shown in Table 1.6. According to the table, students who did not study at all received an *F* in the course. Students who studied 4 hours per week, on average, received a grade of C (2.0), and those who studied 8 hours per week received a grade of *A* (4.0). In the table, other grades are associated with other amounts of study time.

TABLE 1.6 Studying Pays Off in an Economics Issues Class

Course Grade	*Course Grade Point Average*	*Hours of Study per Week*
F	0.0	0
D	1.0	2
C	2.0	4
B	3.0	6
A	4.0	8

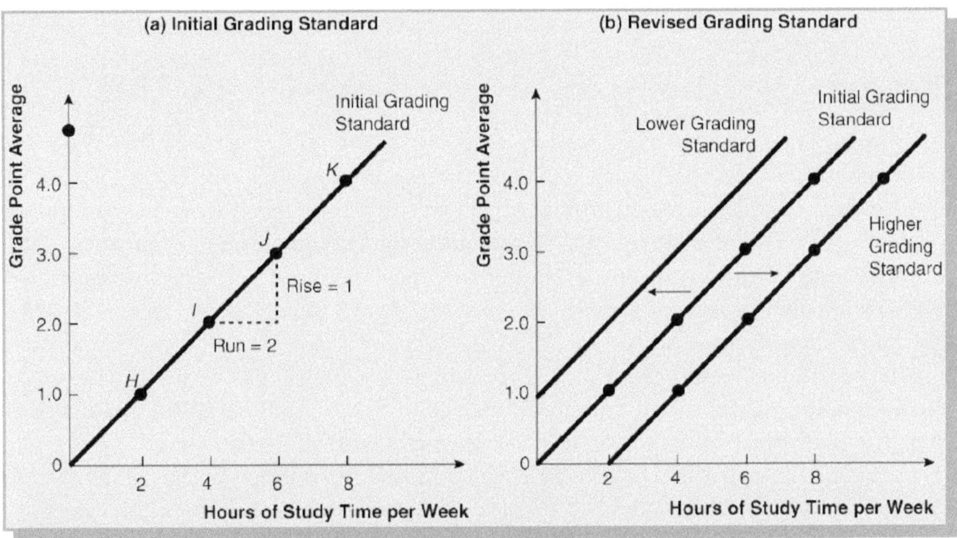

FIGURE 1.8 Study Time–Grade Relationship in an Economics Issues Class

The relationship between study time and grades is represented by this graph. Study time and grades are directly related because their values change in the same direction, resulting in an upward-sloping line. The slope of this straight line is the ratio of the vertical change to the horizontal change between any two points. When factors other than study time are allowed to change, the graph of the relationship between study time and grades will shift to a new location.

Let us now use the data in the table to construct Figure 1.8. We want to show visually how course grades change as study time changes. Study time is the determining factor, the **independent variable**, and it is placed on the horizontal axis of the figure. The course grade is the **dependent variable**—it depends on study time—and it is located on the vertical axis.

To plot pairs of study time and grades on a graph, start at the origin, where the axes meet. Count 2 units to the right on the horizontal axis, then count upward 1 unit parallel to the vertical axis, and then mark the spot. We've arrived at the point marked *H*, where 2 hours of study time yield a grade of 1.0 (*D*). To plot the next pair, we go 2 units to the right from point *H* and then upward 1 unit, arriving at point *I*, where 4 hours of study yield a grade of 2.0 (C). In a similar manner, we can plot the remaining pairs in Table 1.6, as the points *J* and *K*. Once we have plotted all the various points describing the relationship between grades and study time, we can connect them with a line (or curve). This line shows how grades are related to the time spent studying. Because the graph is a straight line, we can say that the relationship between study time and grades is *linear.*

The study time–grade line in Figure 1.8(*a*) slopes *upward to* the right, illustrating a **direct** (positive) **relationship** between study time and grades. That is, more hours of study time yield higher grades and fewer hours of study time yield lower grades. Alternatively, if higher grades were associated with less study time, the line in the figure would slope *downward* to the right. Then, we would have an **inverse** (negative) **relationship** because grades and study time would change in opposite directions.

Movements Along the Study Time–Grade Line

Referring to Figure 1.8(*a*), what causes movements from one point to another along the fixed study time–grade line? Such movements are caused by a change in the amount of time devoted to studying economics. Increases in study time result in an upward movement along this line, and decreases in study time result in a downward movement.

To illustrate such movements, as study time increases from 4 hours to 6 hours, we slide upward along the study time–grade line from point *I* to point *J*, and the grade point average increases from a 2.0 (C) to a 3.0 (*B*). Conversely, a decrease in study time from 6 hours to 4 hours would result in a downward movement along the study time–grade line from point *J* to point *I*, and the grade point average falls from 3.0 to 2.0. Put simply, a change in study time causes us to move along a fixed study time–grade line.

The relationship between study time and grades is represented by this graph. Study time and grades are directly related because their values change in the same direction, resulting in an upward-sloping line. The slope of this straight line is the ratio of the vertical change to the horizontal change between any two points. When factors other than study time are allowed to change, the graph of the relationship between study time and grades will shift to a new location.

Slope of the Study Time–Grade Line

Inspecting Figure 1.8, you will notice that each time study time increases by 2 hours, course grades increase by one letter grade, or 1.0. For example, when study time increases from 2 hours to 4 hours, the course grade increases from 2.0 (*D*) to 3.0 (C). Therefore, we conclude that the rate of change in course grades is 1 grade point for every 2-hour increase in study time.

The **slope** of the study time–grade line between any two points, say *I* and *J*, is defined as the vertical distance between the two points (the "rise") divided by the horizontal distance between the two points (the "run"). Between points *I* and *J*, grades increase by 1 grade point on the vertical axis when study time increases by 2 hours on the horizontal axis. Therefore, the slope of the line equals:

$$\text{Slope} = \frac{\text{Vertical Change}}{\text{Horizontal Change}} = \frac{1}{5} = 0.5$$

Notice that the slope of 0.5 is positive because grades and study time change in the same direction—that is, grades and study time are directly or positively related. The slope of 0.5 indicates that there will be an increase of 1 grade point for every 2-hour increase in study time. Similarly, it tells us that for every 2-hour decrease in study time there will be a decrease of 1 grade point. Because each 2 hours of additional study results in an improvement of 1 grade point, our graph is a straight line. Put simply, the slope of any straight line remains constant among all points along the line.

Alternatively, if higher grades were associated with *less* study time, the study time–grade line would slope downward to the right. Therefore, the slope of the line would have a negative value.

Shifts in the Study Time–Grade Line

So far, we have focused on relationships in which grades in an economics issues course depend on one other variable: Study time. However, we recognize that grades are affected by more factors than just study time, such as the grading standard of the instructor, the academic abilities of students, and the availability of tutors for the course. When grades are affected by both study time and some other variable, changes in that other variable generally induce a *shift* in the study time–grade line. This is because whenever we draw the line between study time and grades, we are holding constant every other variable that might possibly affect grades.

Suppose that the instructor in the economics issues course decided to raise the grading standard, making it more difficult to achieve every other grade than an *F*. To achieve a grade of 2.0 (C), a student would now have to study 6 hours per week instead of only 4 hours, as shown in Figure 1.8(*a*). Whereas students could previously receive a grade of 3.0 (*B*) by studying 6 hours a week, they now must study 8 hours to get that grade.

Figure 1.8(*b*) illustrates the effect of the higher grade standard. In the figure, we have redrawn the study time–grade line from Figure 1.8(*a*), this time labeling the line *Higher Grading Standard*. Notice that the new line lies to the *right* of the initial line. This means that the underlying relationship between study time and grades has changed: Students now must study for a greater amount of time to achieve each grade other than *F*. Alternatively, if the instructor lowered the grading standard, making it easier to achieve course grades, the study time–grade line would shift to the left, as shown by the line labeled *Lower Grading Standard*.

Recall that our study time–grade line may shift in response to factors other than changes in grading standards. For example, if the academic abilities of students increase, they could grasp economic principles in a shorter period, and the line would shift to the left. Similarly, greater availability of qualified tutors would cause the line to shift to the left.

This section has used the example of study time and grades in an economics issues class to illustrate several concepts:

- Independent and dependent variable
- Direct and inverse relationship
- Movement along a line
- Slope of a line
- Shifts in a line

Notice that these concepts also apply to economic relationships, such as supply and demand, investment, and consumption, which you will learn about as you read this text. Familiarize yourself with these concepts and be able to apply them to graphs contained in subsequent chapters.

PART 2

The Microeconomy

CHAPTER 2

Market Transactions: Demand and Supply Analysis

CHAPTER OBJECTIVES

After reading this chapter, you should be able to:

1. Identify the major factors affecting demand.
2. Identify the major factors affecting supply.
3. Explain how prices and quantities are determined in competitive markets.
4. Explain why prices sometimes decrease and sometimes increase.
5. Predict how prices and quantities will respond to changes in demand or supply.

DOI: 10.4324/9781003438571-4

ECONOMICS IN CONTEXT

LeBron James wasn't the first high school kid to jump to the National Basketball Association (NBA), but he may be the best. A three-time Mr. Ohio in high school, "King James" was highly promoted in the national media as a future NBA superstar while still a sophomore at St. Vincent–St. Mary. At just 18, he was selected as the #1 pick in the 2003 NBA draft by the Cleveland Cavaliers and signed a $90-million shoe contract with Nike before his first professional slam dunk. Since that time, James has consistently been selected as an NBA All Star, and he has helped his teams win four NBA championships. James' basketball IQ hovers at the level of genius and his physical skills are overpowering and off the charts.

Why do athletes such as LeBron James earn more than the local physical therapist? Demand and supply. Why do fresh watermelons cost 50 cents a pound in July and a dollar a pound in April? You guessed it: Demand and supply. Why did the price of CD players fall from around $800, when they were first introduced in 1983, to about $25 today? You're right again: Demand and supply. The workings of demand and supply explain many economic questions. Indeed, demand and supply are the most basic and powerful of all the economic tools that you will study in this text.

This chapter will introduce demand and supply analysis of market transactions, which shows how prices are determined by the competition among buyers for goods and services offered by competing sellers. Markets play a key role in addressing the problem of scarcity because they ration the available quantities of goods and services to buyers.

MARKETS

A **market** is a mechanism through which buyers (demanders) and sellers (suppliers) communicate in order to trade goods and services. Markets exist in many forms. The local farmers' market, espresso stand, grocery store, and barber shop are all familiar markets. Pike Place Market in Seattle, Washington, is famous for its fresh fish, fruits, and vegetables. The New York Stock Exchange is a national market in which buyers and sellers of stocks and bonds communicate with each other. At the international level, major banks such as Bank of America and Barclays Bank trade currencies in the foreign currency market. These markets link potential buyers to potential sellers.

This chapter concerns competitive markets in which many sellers compete for sales to many buyers, who are, in turn, competing with one another for available products. In such a market, each seller has a negligible effect on the market price because many other sellers are supplying similar goods. A seller has no motivation to undercut price, and if a seller charges a higher price, buyers will purchase products from other suppliers. Similarly, no single buyer can affect the price because each buyer purchases a negligible quantity. To understand how markets operate, we must first understand the principles of demand and supply.

DEMAND

How many Rolls-Royce automobiles will be bought this year? In explaining buyer behavior, economists emphasize the demand for goods and services. **Demand** is a schedule that shows the amount of a good or service that a buyer is *willing and able* to purchase at each possible price during a particular period. Just because an individual desires a Rolls-Royce does not necessarily mean that they have a *demand* for it. They also must be able to pay the $400,000 price, and they must be willing to purchase a Rolls-Royce instead of another vehicle, such as a Mercedes-Benz or a BMW.

The amount of a product that is demanded depends on many factors, such as the following:

- Price of the product
- Prices of related products
- Consumer income
- Expectations of future price changes
- Tastes
- Number of consumers

In analyzing the behavior of buyers, we will pay special attention to the relationship between the quantity demanded and the price of a good. To study this relationship, we will hold constant all other factors that affect buyer behavior.

It is helpful to distinguish between *individual demand*, which is the demand of a particular buyer, and *market demand*, which is the sum of the individual demands of all buyers in the market. In most markets, there are many buyers, sometimes thousands or millions. Unless otherwise noted, when we talk about demand, we are referring to market demand.

The Demand Curve and the Law of Demand

Figure 2.1(*a*) shows the market demand schedule for phone cases. The first column of the figure shows possible prices for phone cases. The second column shows the quantities of phone cases demanded per week at different prices, assuming that all other determinants affecting buyer behavior remain constant. The data in the demand schedule show that when the price of phone cases is $25, consumers demand 1,000 phone cases per week. At a price of $20, consumers demand 2,000 phone cases per week, and so forth.

A market **demand curve** is a graphical representation of a market demand schedule. Figure 2.1(*b*) illustrates the weekly demand curve for phone cases by plotting the data from the table. Points on the vertical axis represent price, and points on the horizontal axis represent the quantity demanded.

Notice that the market demand curve slopes downward, reflecting the **law of demand**: Price and quantity demanded are *inversely* or negatively related, assuming that all other factors affecting the quantity demanded remain the same. When the price is higher, the quantity demanded decreases; likewise, when the price is lower, the quantity demanded increases. We call the law of demand a "law" because it can be widely applied to buyer

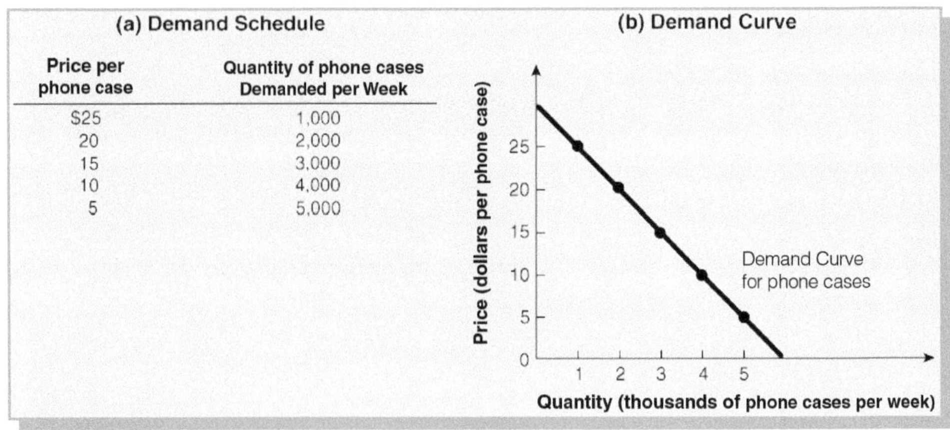

(a) Demand Schedule

Price per phone case	Quantity of phone cases Demanded per Week
$25	1,000
20	2,000
15	3,000
10	4,000
5	5,000

FIGURE 2.1 The Demand Schedule and Demand Curve for Phone Cases

The market demand schedule shows the quantity of phone cases demanded at various prices by all consumers. The market demand curve is a graphical portrayal of the data comprised by the market demand schedule. The market demand curve slopes downward, indicating that as price decreases, the quantity demanded increases. This inverse relationship between the change in the price of a good and the change in quantity demanded is known as the law of demand.

behavior. For example, when Ford finds itself overstocked with automobiles that it wants to get rid of, what does it do? It typically announces a sale, anticipating that a lower price will encourage buyers to purchase additional Ford automobiles.

The pricing of candy provides another example of the law of demand. Mars Inc. once conducted a pricing experiment for its M&Ms candy. Over a 1-year period, the price of a bag of M&Ms was held constant in 150 stores throughout the United States while the content weight of the bag was increased. With price kept constant and content weight increased, the price per ounce decreased. In the stores where the price declined, sales soon increased by 20 percent to 30 percent. As the law of demand would predict, a decrease in the price of M&Ms resulted in an increase in the quantity demanded.

For a particular demand curve, a change in price results in a movement along the demand curve. In Figure 2.1(*b*), if the price of phone cases falls from $15 to $10, consumption increases from 3,000 to 4,000 phone cases per week. We call the movement along the demand curve—which results from a change in price—a **change in quantity demanded**. Notice that a change in quantity demanded is a movement along a particular demand curve rather than a shift in the demand curve.

What Explains the Law of Demand?

For most products, consumers are willing to buy more units at a lower price than they are at a higher price. This notion of the law of demand appears to be an accurate description of consumer behavior. Economists explain this law in terms of the substitution effect, the income effect, and the law of diminishing marginal utility.

According to the **substitution effect**, when the price of phone cases falls—and all other determinants of demand remain the same—the price falls relative to the prices of all other similar goods, such as phone skins and screen protectors. Consumers have an incentive to substitute the cheaper good, phone cases, for skins and protectors, which are now relatively more expensive. The lower price of phone cases thus results in an increase in the quantity demanded.

The **income effect** also explains the law of demand. According to this principle, a decrease in the price of a phone cases results in an increase in the purchasing power of consumers' money incomes. As a result, consumers can purchase more phone cases with a given amount of money. Generally speaking, a rise in purchasing power provides consumers an incentive to purchase more of a product. In this manner, a lower price of phone cases results in an increase in the quantity demanded.

Finally, there is the principle of **diminishing marginal utility** (satisfaction). According to this principle, as a person consumes additional units of a particular good, each additional unit provides less and less additional utility. We can readily see this in the case of phone cases. A buyer's desire for a phone case when they have none may be very strong; the desire for a second case is less pronounced, and so on. Therefore, additional phone cases are "not worth it" unless the price decreases. This notion underlies the concept of the law of demand.

Changes in Demand: Demand Shifters

Recall that the relationship between the price of a good and the quantity of the good demanded over a period also depends on other determinants such as consumer tastes, prices of related goods, consumer expectations, the number of consumers in the market, and consumer income. For a particular demand curve, we assume that these other determinants remain constant. If any of these determinants change, the demand curve will shift either outward to the right or backward to the left. Therefore, we call a change in a variable that causes a shift in a demand curve a **demand shifter**. We call a shift in a demand curve caused by a demand shifter a **change in demand**.

Figure 2.2 shows a change in the demand for phone cases. Because of changing determinants of demand, if consumers become willing and able to purchase additional phone cases at each possible price, the result will be an *increase* in demand. In the figure, we can see that the demand curve shifts to the right, from *Old Demand Curve* to *New Demand Curve.* Conversely, if the determinants of demand change such that consumers are less willing and able to purchase phone cases at each possible price, the demand curve for phone cases will *decrease*—that is, the demand curve will shift to the *left.* Let us examine how each demand shifter affects the location of the demand curve.

- A favorable change in consumer tastes
- A rise in incomes if the product is a normal good; a fall in incomes if the product is an inferior good
- An increase in the price of a substitute good; a decrease in the price of a complementary good
- Consumer expectations of higher future prices
- A rise in the number of buyers served by the market

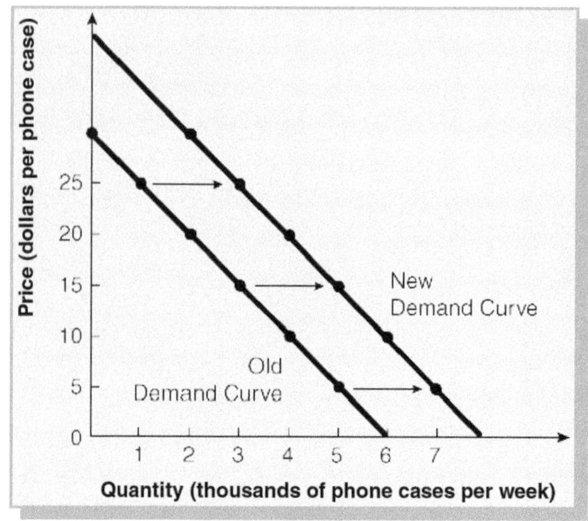

FIGURE 2.2 An Increase in Demand

An increase in demand is shown by an outward shift of the entire demand curve, indicating that more of the product is demanded at each price. An increase in demand for a product can be caused by:

- A favorable change in consumer tastes
- A rise in incomes if the product is a normal good; a fall in incomes if the product is an inferior good
- An increase in the price of a substitute good; a decrease in the price of a complementary good
- Consumer expectations of higher future prices
- A rise in the number of buyers served by the market

Consumer Tastes

Changing consumer tastes can have important effects on demand. A change in consumer tastes that makes a product more popular will shift the demand curve to the right. For example, as the popularity of Taylor Swift (an American singer–song writer) increases, consumers tend to demand more of her albums. Conversely, if the New York Yankees have a losing season and become less popular with their fans, demand for tickets to their baseball games will shift to the left.

Number of Buyers

Recall that the market demand is the sum of the individual demands of all consumers in the market. If the number of consumers in the market increases, market demand will shift to the right; a decrease in the number of consumers will cause market demand to shift to the left. In Eugene, Oregon, for example, local merchants are pleased to see student consumers attending the University of Oregon in September. This causes an increase in the demand for their products. When many students return to their homes in other cities over the December holidays, the demand for these products in Eugene decreases.

Consumer Income

College students realize that changes in income affect demand. We classify products into two broad categories, depending on how demand for the product responds to changes in income. The demand for **normal goods** *increases* as income *rises* and *falls* as income *decreases.* Most goods, such as ski trips or new cars, are normal goods. People enjoy these goods and tend to buy more of them as their income rises. In contrast, **inferior goods** are goods such as public transportation, low-quality clothing, second-hand appliances, less expensive cuts of meat, and low-quality peanut butter. The demand for inferior goods falls as income *increases*; households will switch away from consuming these inferior goods to consuming normal goods such as new cars and sirloin steak. Conversely, *decreases* in income cause the demand for inferior goods to *increase*.

Prices of Related Goods

Changes in the prices of related goods can also affect the demand curve for a particular product. When we draw the demand curve for, say, Pepsi, we assume that the prices of Coke and other colas remain constant. But suppose that we relax this assumption and allow the price of Coke to change. If the price of Coke were to fall suddenly from $5 to $4 per case, there would be an incentive for consumers to switch from Pepsi to Coke. After all, Pepsi and Coke are **substitute goods**. For substitute goods, a *reduction* in the price of one good will *decrease* the demand for the other good; conversely, an *increase* in the price of one good will *increase* the demand for the other good.

A second type of related good is a **complementary good**. Complementary goods "go together" in that they are used in conjunction with each other. Some examples of complementary goods are video games and in-game credits, peanut butter and jelly, hamburgers and French fries, cookies and milk, and spaghetti and meat sauce. If the price of video games falls, we will buy more in-game credits and, therefore, we will buy more in-game credits—so the demand for in-game credits increases. Conversely, an increase in the price of peanut butter results in a decrease in the quantity of peanut butter demanded and thus a decline in the demand for jelly. For complementary goods, a *decrease* in the price of one good will *increase* the demand for the other good; conversely, an *increase* in the price of one good will *decrease* the demand for the other good.

Expected Future Prices

The demand for gasoline may change merely because people change their expectations about tomorrow's price of gasoline. When Saddam Hussein ordered the Iraqi army to invade Kuwait in 1990, many people expected that oil supplies would be disrupted because of the war. The anticipated shortage of gasoline—and the resulting price increase—prompted many people to fill their tanks at each opportunity, thus increasing the demand for gasoline. In this manner, changes in consumer expectations can cause the demand curve for a product to change.

Another example of consumer reaction to expected future prices occurred in 2002 when smokers in Oregon purchased cartons of cigarettes by the armload before a 60-cents-per-pack increase in the state tax on cigarettes. The state tax increased from 68 cents to $1.28 after voters approved the tax hike by a two-to-one margin. Following the tax hike, a pack-a-day smoker paid $219 more a year, or $467.20, in taxes for the habit.

CHECK POINT

1 Describe the law of demand and the explanations for the law of demand.
2 Differentiate between a change in quantity demanded and a change in demand, identifying the reason(s) for each. How is each change represented graphically?
3 What factors cause a demand curve to shift? What happens to a demand curve when each of these factors changes?

DEMAND THEORY APPLICATIONS

The theory of demand has many applications. Let us consider congestion pricing for highways and the pricing of baseball tickets.

Rush-Hour Horrors: Congestion Pricing

Traffic jams. Most of us have endured them and perhaps we have even said a few choice words while sitting in them. Longer commutes cost not only time, but money, too. Congestion means reduced fuel efficiency and more wear and tear on vehicles and roads. What can we do to reduce congestion?

According to many economists, the answer lies in subjecting roads and bridges to market forces. That is, allow the price system to clear away imbalances between demand and supply. Congestion occurs when too many motorists want to use the roads, which have fixed capacity, at the same time because their price is too low. Raising the price would reduce the quantity demanded and better allocate the limited space.

Governments usually provide roads through tax dollars, which are used to pay for their construction and maintenance. Thus, motorists believe they are already paying their way for road usage through gas taxes and licensing fees. What drivers are actually paying for, however, is their direct use of roads. When a person chooses to drive, that person's activity adds an additional vehicle to the traffic flow, which increases the commute cost for all drivers.

Therefore, economists maintain that motorists should be assessed tolls to decrease the amount of rush-hour traffic, a practice called **congestion pricing**. This means that motorists are charged to drive in an area according to the level of congestion in that area. Prices are higher when roads or bridges are more congested. By making it more expensive to travel, congestion pricing encourages motorists to shift to other modes, routes, or times, which decreases congestion and improves traffic flow. Simply, put, congestion pricing is based on the law of demand, which asserts that if the price of a product increases, the quantity demanded will decrease.

Congestion pricing can be carried out by having motorists keeping pre-paid electronic metering devices in their vehicles that indicate the day and time that their vehicle traveled on a particular road or bridge. Alternatively, a picture can be taken of a vehicle's license

Source: Grafissimo/E+/Getty Images®

plate as it travels on a road, and the toll charge is sent to the motorist's mailing address or e-mail address. Tolls can be higher or lower at different times of the day, according to the level of congestion.

The use of congestion pricing for roads, highways, and bridges has been widely implemented in the United States and other countries. For example, Table 2.1 shows the toll rates on the Evergreen Point Floating Bridge, which carries motorists across Lake Washington from Seattle to its eastern suburbs. These toll rates are variable throughout the day to reflect bridge-usage patterns. The tolls are intended to help reduce congestion and provide revenue for the construction and maintenance of the bridge.

Yankees Slash Prices of Top Tickets to Fill Seats

The law of demand has other applications, including major-league baseball. In 2009 the New York Yankees were proud to open their season in their new stadium, which replaced their former stadium, built in 1923. With a capacity of 52,325 seats, the new stadium cost $1.5 billion to construct, making it the second most expensive stadium in the world.

The Yankees dramatically raised ticket prices for the new season, assuming that fans would flock to home games. The Yankees especially thought that New York's business community would be willing to spend a premium for the best sports and entertainment the region had to offer. However, the Yankees were embarrassed after their first homestand of the season, when they found that thousands of high-priced seats were unsold. The unsold tickets, some priced as high as $2,500 each, created an odd spectacle at the new

TABLE 2.1 Toll Rates on the Evergreen Point Floating Bridge, Monday–Friday, 2023 (in dollars)

Time of Day	*Good to Go Pass**	*Pay by Mail***
12 a.m. – 5 a.m.	$1.25	$3.25
5 a.m. – 6 a.m.	2.00	4.00
6 a.m. – 7 a.m.	3.40	5.40
7 a.m. – 9 a.m.	4.30	6.30
9 a.m. – 10 a.m.	3.40	5.40
10 a.m. – 2 p.m.	2.70	4.70
2 p.m. – 3 p.m.	3.40	5.40
3 p.m. – 6 p.m.	4.30	6.30
6 p.m. – 7 p.m.	3.40	5.40
7 p.m. – 9 p.m.	2.70	4.70
9 p.m. – 11 p.m.	2.00	4.00
11 p.m. – 12 a.m.	1.25	3.25

* Electronic metering device installed in your vehicle.
**A picture of your license plate is taken, and the bill is sent to your mailing address.

Source: Data drawn from Washington State Department of Transportation, *SR 520 Bridge Tolling*, available at https://wsdot.wa.gov/travel/roads-bridges/toll-roads-bridges-tunnels/sr-520-bridge-tolling.

park: While the rest of the stadium was packed during the Yankees' home games, many of the best seats closest to the field sat empty. The sight of those empty seats sparked mockery from critics who said the Yankees had badly overreached and ignored their fans, who helped build Yankee Stadium with their tax money.

Bowing to the sight of empty seats, the Yankees acknowledged their prices were too steep even by Yankees standards. Therefore, the 25-time world champions slashed their top-end prices to stimulate attendance. For example, tickets going for $2,500 were cut to $1,250 while tickets priced at $1,000 were cut to $650, and so on. So as not to alienate existing season ticket holders, who had already purchased tickets at premium prices, the Yankees provided them their choice of a refund or a credit. Also, the team doled out complimentary tickets to fill the empty seats behind home plate that are so visible on TV.

In hindsight, Yankees management realized that their outrageously high ticket prices were out of reach of many of their fans, especially during the weak economy of 2009. Simply put, the initial increase in ticket prices at the beginning of the season resulted in a dramatic decrease in quantity demanded. The result was a marketing problem for a team that traditionally provided the image that it cared about its fans. As things turned out, the Yankees continued to cut the prices of some of their most expensive seats during the 2010 season. However, prices inched upward in 2011.[1]

SUPPLY

The other side of our market model involves the quantities of goods and services that sellers would like to offer to the market. **Supply** is a schedule showing the amounts of a good or service that a firm or household is willing and able to sell at each possible price during a particular period. In economics, *supply* could refer to the number of ice cream bars that a grocery store wants to sell or the number of hours that a worker is willing to spend on the job.

The quantity of a particular good or service that suppliers plan to sell depends on many factors:

- Price of the good
- Prices of resources
- Technology
- Prices of other goods produced
- Expected future prices
- Taxes and subsidies
- Number of suppliers

In analyzing the behavior of suppliers, we will emphasize the relationship between the **quantity supplied** and the price of a good. Therefore, we will hold constant all other determinants that affect supplier behavior.

It is helpful to distinguish between *individual supply*, which is the supply of a particular seller, and *market supply*, which is the sum of the individual supplies of all sellers in the market. Unless otherwise noted, when we talk about supply, we are referring to market supply.

The Supply Curve and Law of Supply

Supply shows us the quantities that will be offered for sale at various prices. Supply refers to the schedule that relates price and quantity, and thus it is called a supply schedule or a **supply curve**. Figure 2.3(*a*) shows the market supply schedule for phone cases. The first column of the figure shows possible prices for phone cases. The second column shows the quantities of phone cases supplied per week at different prices, assuming that all of the other determinants of supply remain unchanged. We call this amount the quantity supplied. Notice that the quantity supplied refers to a single point on a supply schedule: As the price changes, the quantity supplied changes, but not the entire supply schedule. The data in our supply schedule show that when the price of phone cases is $5, producers supply 1,000 phone cases per week. At a price of $10, producers supply 2,000 phone cases per week, and so forth.

A market supply curve is a graphical representation of a market supply schedule. Figure 2.3(*b*) illustrates the weekly supply curve for phone cases by plotting the data from the table. Points on the vertical axis show price, and points on the horizontal axis show the quantity supplied. Notice that the data indicate an *upward-sloping* supply curve, which suggests a positive or *direct* relationship between price and quantity supplied. As the price of phone cases increases, the quantity supplied increases; as the price decreases, the quantity supplied decreases. We call this relationship the **law of supply**. The law of supply states

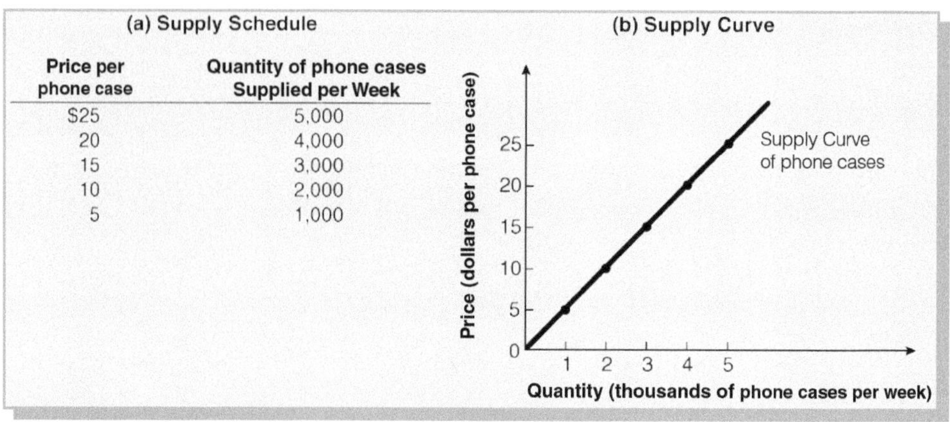

(a) Supply Schedule

Price per phone case	Quantity of phone cases Supplied per Week
$25	5,000
20	4,000
15	3,000
10	2,000
5	1,000

FIGURE 2.3 The Supply Schedule and Supply Curve of Phone Cases

The market supply schedule shows the quantity of phone cases supplied, at various prices, by all sellers. The market supply curve is a graphical portrayal of the data comprised by the market supply schedule. The market supply curve is upward-sloping, showing that as price increases, the quantity supplied increases. The direct relationship between the change in the price of a product and the change in the quantity supplied is known as the law of supply.

that, in general, sellers are willing and able to make more of their product available at a higher price than at a lower price, all other determinants of supply being constant.

The tendency for the cost of additional output to increase explains the law of supply—that is, it costs more to produce the second unit of output than the first, more to produce the third than the second, and so on. For example, to produce more phone cases, suppose a manufacturer must hire more labor. As labor becomes more plentiful relative to the fixed machinery, the added workers may have to wait to work on the machines. Therefore, each additional worker produces less added output, and the extra cost of successive units of phone cases increases. All other things being constant, phone case manufacturers would be induced to produce additional phone cases only when the price of phone cases rises. As a result, a higher price causes a greater level of output to be supplied to the market.

Changes in Supply: Supply Shifters

Recall that a supply curve refers to the entire relationship between the price of a product and the quantity supplied, when all other determinants of supply remain unchanged. When these other determinants change, the supply curve will shift either outward to the right or backward to the left. Therefore, we call a change in a variable that causes a shift a **supply shifter**. A shift in a supply curve induced by a supply shifter is called a **change in supply**.

Figure 2.4 shows the change in the supply of phone cases. Because of changing determinants of supply, if producers become willing and able to supply additional phone cases at each possible price, the result will be an *increase* in supply. In the figure, we can see that the supply curve shifts to the right, from *Old Supply Curve* to *New Supply Curve*. However, if

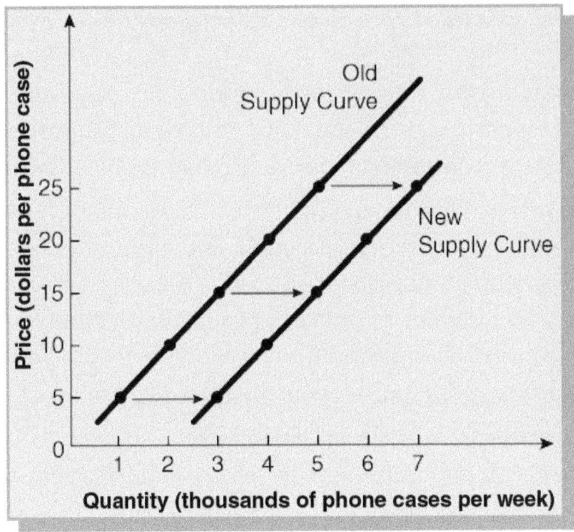

FIGURE 2.4 An Increase in Supply

An increase in supply is shown by a rightward shift of the entire supply curve, indicating that more phone cases are supplied at each price. An increase in supply of a good can be caused by:

- A decrease in the price of resources used to produce a good
- New technologies that reduce the cost of producing a good
- Expectations of future falling prices of a good may cause sellers to increase their current supply to the market
- A decrease in an excise tax on the sale of a good
- An increase in subsidies to the producers of a good

the determinants of supply change, such that suppliers are less willing and able to supply phone cases at each possible price, the supply of phone cases will *decrease*—that is, the supply curve will shift to the *left*. Let us examine how each supply shifter affects the location of the supply curve.

1 **Resource prices**. The possible profit at a particular price depends on the prices that a supplier must pay for the resources to produce a good or service. For example, a decrease in the prices of labor and materials used to produce phone cases decreases the cost of producing phone cases, resulting in a greater profit from selling a particular quantity. This increases the supply of phone cases. Conversely, increases in resource prices result in falling profitability and a decrease in supply.

2 **Technology**. Improvements in technology tend to reduce the amount of resources needed to produce a given level of output, resulting in lower costs of production and increased supply. For example, the development of a new technology by Texas Instruments has reduced the cost of producing calculators and increased their supply.

3 **Prices of other goods**. If a Ford assembly line can manufacture either minivans or pickup trucks, the quantity of minivans manufactured depends on the price of trucks, and the quantity of trucks manufactured depends on the price of minivans. Given the price of minivans, a decline in the price of trucks signals to Ford that switching to minivans with a higher relative price yields higher profit. The result is an increase in the supply of minivans.

4 **Expected future prices**. Expectations affect the current output of producers. For example, because of the 1990 Iraqi invasion of Kuwait, oil companies anticipated that oil prices would increase significantly. Their initial response was to withhold part of their oil from the market so that they could realize larger profits later when oil prices increased. Such a response shifted the supply curve for oil to the left.

5 **Taxes and subsidies**. Certain taxes, such as excise taxes, have the same impact on supply as an increase in the price of resources. The effect of an excise tax placed on the sale of gasoline imposes an additional cost on gas stations, and the supply curve shifts to the left. Conversely, subsidies have the opposite effect. When the state of Washington financed most of the construction cost of a new stadium for the Seattle Seahawks football team, it effectively lowered the cost of Seahawk football games and increased their supply.

6 **Number of suppliers**. Because market supply is the sum of the amounts supplied by all sellers, it depends on the number of sellers in the market. If the number of sellers increases, supply will shift to the right. For example, during the 2021–2022 season the National Hockey League expanded its membership to include the Seattle Kraken, thus shifting the market supply curve outward to the right.

Flat-panel TVs provide an example of change in supply. When flat-panel TVs were first introduced in the 1990s, they cost as much as $20,000. By 2023, the price of a 42-inch flat-panel TV had fallen to less than $250. The price has decreased due to an increase in supply. Factors that caused the supply of flat-panel TVs to increase included improvements in technology which reduced the costs of production, large investments in new manufacturing plants in China, Malaysia, and other Asian countries, and entry of new producers into the market. With an increase in supply came a decrease in price and thus an increase in the quantity of flat-panel TVs demanded.

Hydraulic Fracturing Squeezes More Oil and Natural Gas from the Ground

Does the law of supply apply to the production of crude oil? Yes! Major oil firms, such as Shell and ExxonMobil, realize that, as existing wells dry up, continued production requires additional drilling and more exploration to locate new oil fields. Because these activities add to a producer's cost, they require a higher market price. Unless price rises, a firm cannot realize a net gain (profit) from producing more oil. The same applies to the production of natural gas.

To increase the productivity of oil wells, producers have invested billions of dollars in new technologies that are designed to extract additional oil from a well. Conventional drilling methods tap only about 15 percent of a typical well's potential, leaving 85 percent of the oil still locked in the earth. Improved oil recovery technologies increase the amount of oil that can be pulled out of the earth—up to 80 percent of the oil from some reservoirs—thus extending the productive life of fields.

Hydraulic fracturing has become a widely used technology for increasing the productivity of oil and natural gas wells. This technique involves the injection of millions of gallons of water, sand, and chemicals at high pressure down and across into horizontally

Source: grandriver/E+/Getty Images®

drilled wells as far as 10,000 feet below the surface. The pressure causes the tight rock formation to crack. These fissures are held open by the sand particles so that oil and natural gas from the fragmented rock can flow up the well. This technology has resulted in an increase (rightward shift) of the supply curve of oil or natural gas.

Hydraulic fracturing began as an experiment in 1947, and the first commercially successful application followed in 1950. Today it is a widely used technology in the production of oil and natural gas. However, hydraulic fracturing is a controversial technology. Its proponents advocate the economic benefits of additional oil and natural gas at a lower price, and the improvement in U.S. energy security. However, critics maintain that these are outweighed by the potential environmental impacts, which include risks of ground and surface water contamination, air and noise pollution, and potentially triggering earthquakes, along with the consequential hazards to public health and the environment.

CHECK POINT

1 Describe the law of supply and explain why the supply curve normally slopes upward.
2 Distinguish between a change in quantity supplied and a change in supply, identifying the reason(s) for each.
3 What factors cause a supply curve to shift? What happens to a supply curve when each of these factors changes?

DEMAND, SUPPLY, AND EQUILIBRIUM

Buyers and sellers have different views of a product's price because buyers *pay* the price and sellers *receive* it. Therefore, a higher price is favorable for a seller but is unfavorable for a buyer. As price increases, sellers increase their quantity supplied while buyers decrease their quantity demanded. Through the interaction of demand and supply, we can find a price at which the quantity that buyers want to purchase equals the quantity that sellers will offer for sale.

Market equilibrium occurs when the price of a product adjusts so that the quantity that consumers will purchase at that price is identical to the quantity that suppliers will sell. At the point of market equilibrium, the forces of demand and supply are balanced so that there is no tendency for the market price to change over a given period.

Figure 2.5 combines the demand and supply curves introduced in Figures 2.1 and 2.3.

Referring to Figure 2.5(*a*), notice that the two curves intersect at a price of $15 per phone case. At this price, the quantity that buyers want to purchase (3,000 phone cases) equals the quantity that sellers wish to offer for sale (3,000 phone cases). Therefore, the market for phone cases is in equilibrium, implying that the price will not change unless the demand or supply curves shift. The price at which buyers' intentions are equal to sellers' intentions is called the **equilibrium price**. Notice that the equilibrium price acts to ration phone cases so that everyone who wants to purchase the product will find it available, and everyone who wants to sell the product can do so successfully.

If the market does not initially establish an equilibrium price, competition among suppliers to sell the product and competition among buyers to purchase the product will

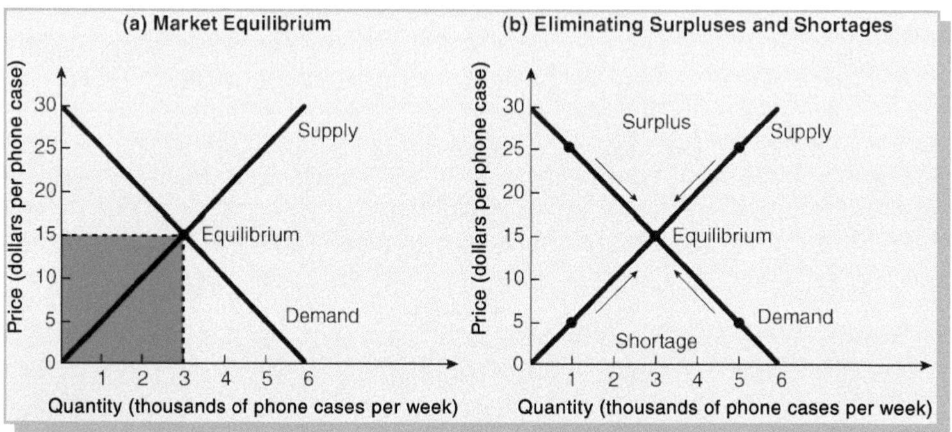

FIGURE 2.5 Equilibrium in the Phone Case Market

The demand and supply schedules represent the market for phone cases. The intersection of the market supply and demand curves indicates an equilibrium price of $15 and an equilibrium quantity of 3,000 phone cases bought and sold per week. Any price above $15 will result in a weekly surplus of phone cases, and pressure pushing the price downwards. Similarly, any price below $15 will result in a weekly shortage of phone cases, and pressure pushing the price upwards. By influencing the supply and demand, adjustments in price serve to promote market equilibrium.

cause the price to move to an equilibrium level. Figure 2.5(*b*) shows the same supply and demand curves we have examined in Figure 2.5(*a*), but this time the initial price is $25 per phone cases. At this price, we refer to the supply curve and find that suppliers are willing to sell 5,000 phone cases per week; referring to the demand curve, we find that buyers are willing to purchase 1,000 phone cases per week. The amount by which the quantity supplied exceeds the quantity demanded—4,000 phone cases—is called a **surplus**, or excess supply. However, the surplus in the market will not be permanent. To clear the market of their unsold phone cases, sellers will reduce the price. The price reduction will result in a decrease in the quantity supplied and an increase in the quantity demanded, thereby eliminating the surplus. The weekly surplus in the phone case market will be eliminated when the price falls to $15, the point at which the supply and demand curves intersect.

Just as a price above the equilibrium price results in a surplus, a price below the equilibrium price entails a **shortage**. Referring to Figure 2.5(*b*), suppose that the initial price is $5 per phone case. At this price, we refer to the supply curve and find that sellers are willing to supply 1,000 phone cases per week; referring to the demand curve, we find that buyers are willing to purchase 5,000 phone cases per week. The amount by which the quantity demanded exceeds the quantity supplied—again, 4,000 phone cases—is called a shortage, or excess demand. When a shortage occurs, competitive bidding among buyers pushes the price upward. A rising price causes an increase in the quantity supplied and a decrease in quantity demanded until the equilibrium price is restored at $15 per phone case.

We have seen how adjustments in price coordinate the decisions of buyers and sellers. If the price rises above the equilibrium level, excess supply will set in motion forces that cause price and quantity to return to their equilibrium levels. If the price falls below the equilibrium level, excess demand will cause price and quantity to return to their equilibrium levels. By regulating the quantities supplied and demanded, adjustments in price serve to promote market equilibrium.

SHIFTS IN DEMAND AND SUPPLY CURVES

Market equilibrium is the combination of price and quantity at which the plans of sellers and buyers synchronize. Once a market attains equilibrium, that combination of price and quantity will remain unchanged until a shifter (determinant) of supply or demand changes. A change in a determinant will cause a shift in the supply curve or demand curve; the result will be a change in the equilibrium price and quantity.

Figure 2.6 illustrates the effects of changes in the demand and supply of phone cases. In the four cases illustrated, the original equilibrium occurs at the intersection of the market supply curve (S_0) and the market demand curve (D_0). At the equilibrium price of $15 per phone case, 3,000 units are demanded and supplied per week.

First, let us consider the effects of a change in demand, assuming that supply is constant. Referring to Figure 2.6(*a*), suppose that the rising popularity of phone cases results in an *increase* in market demand from D_0 *to* D_1. When demand increases, the price that makes the quantity demanded equal the quantity supplied is $20 per phone case. At this price, 4,000 phone cases are bought and sold each week. Therefore, an increase in the demand for a product causes both its equilibrium price and equilibrium quantity to increase.

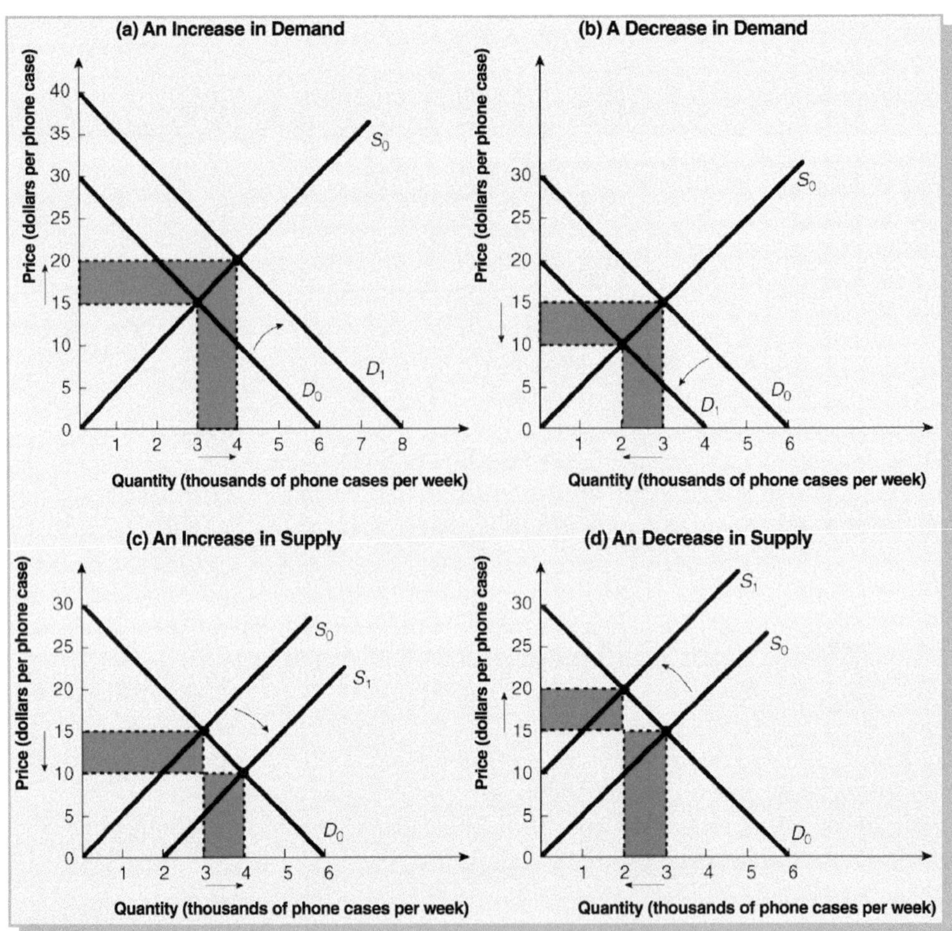

FIGURE 2.6 Changes in Demand and Supply: Effects on Price and Quantity

A change in demand or supply changes the equilibrium price and quantity in the market. Panels (*a*) and (*b*) show the effects of an increase and decrease in demand; panels (*c*) and (*d*) show the effects of an increase and decrease in supply.

Conversely, suppose that the declining popularity of phone cases results in a *decrease* in market demand from D_0 *to* D_1 as seen in Figure 2.6(*b*). Because of the decrease in demand, the equilibrium price falls to $10 per phone case, and the equilibrium quantity declines to 2,000 phone cases per week. Therefore, a decrease in the demand for a product causes both its equilibrium price and equilibrium quantity to fall.

Let us now consider the effects of a change in supply, assuming that demand is constant. Referring to Figure 2.6(*c*), assume that new cost-saving technologies are introduced in phone case manufacturing plants, causing the market supply of phone cases to increase from S_0 to S_1. Following the increase in supply, the new equilibrium price is $10 per phone case, and the equilibrium quantity is 4,000 units. Therefore, an increase in supply causes the equilibrium price to fall but equilibrium quantity increases.

Finally, suppose that rising wages prompt the market supply of phone cases to shift from S_0 to S_1 as in Figure 2.6(*d*). With the new market supply curve, the equilibrium price is $20 per phone case, and the equilibrium quantity is 2,000 units. Therefore, when supply decreases, the equilibrium quantity declines, and the equilibrium price rises.

We can now make the following predictions, all other factors remaining constant:

- When demand increases, both the equilibrium price and the equilibrium quantity increase.
- When demand decreases, both the equilibrium price and the equilibrium quantity decrease.
- When supply increases, the equilibrium price falls and the equilibrium quantity rises.
- When supply decreases, the equilibrium price rises and the equilibrium quantity falls.

In each of the preceding examples, only one side of the market changed while the other side remained constant. In reality, however, complicated changes involving changes in both demand and supply shifters often occur. For example, both the demand and supply of natural gas might decrease at the same time. Although simultaneous changes in demand and supply are not illustrated in this chapter, try applying your graphing skills to the examples in Table 2.2. See whether you can verify the conclusions of each example.

TABLE 2.2 Impacts of Changes in Both Demand and Supply

Change in Demand	*Change in Supply*	*Impact on Equilibrium Price*	*Impact on Equilibrium Quantity*
1. decrease	decrease	indeterminate	decrease
2. increase	increase	indeterminate	increase
3. decrease	increase	decrease	indeterminate
4. increase	decrease	increase	indeterminate

* Indeterminate suggests that price (quantity) might increase, decrease, or stay the same.

CHECK POINT

1. Explain how the forces of supply and demand push the price toward equilibrium.
2. Draw a diagram that shows how shortages cause the price to rise toward equilibrium and surpluses cause the price to fall toward equilibrium.
3. What happens to the equilibrium price and quantity in a competitive market in each of the following cases: (*a*) Supply increases; (*b*) Supply decreases; (*c*) Demand increases; (*d*) Demand decreases?

CONTEMPORARY APPLICATIONS OF DEMAND AND SUPPLY

Now that we have learned about the effects of changes in demand and supply, let's apply our principles to some real-world situations. Consider the following applications.

Bike Competition Puts the Breaks on Schwinn

The Schwinn Bicycle Co. provides an example of how increasing competition can result in a decrease in demand for a firm's product. Established in Chicago in 1895, the Schwinn Bicycle Co. grew to build bicycles that became the standard of the industry. Although the Great Depression forced most bike companies out of business, Schwinn survived by manufacturing high-quality bikes that were sold by dealers who wanted to promote the brand. Schwinn emphasized constant innovation, adding features to its bikes such as balloon tires, built-in kickstands, head and tail lights, and chrome fenders. By the 1960s, the Schwinn Sting-Ray was viewed as the bike that virtually every child wanted. Celebrities such as Ronald Reagan and Captain Kangaroo were seen on television commercials proclaiming that "Schwinn bikes are the best."

Although Schwinn dominated the U.S. bike industry from the 1940s to the 1960s, the market was changing. Bikers desired something other than the heavy, durable bikes which had always been Schwinn's hallmark. Competitors arose such as Trek, which produced mountain bikes, and Mongoose, which built bikes for BMX racing. These firms aggressively marketed their bikes at discounted prices to attract customers away from Schwinn. At the same time, tariffs on imported bikes motivated Americans to buy them from low-cost companies in Taiwan, South Korea, Japan, and eventually China.

As competition escalated, Schwinn relocated its production to a plant in Greenville, Mississippi in 1981. Like other U.S. businesses, Schwinn moved its production to the South in order to hire non-union workers at lower wages. Schwinn also acquired components manufactured by low-wage workers in foreign countries. However, production in the Greenville plant was hampered by inefficiency and uneven product quality; and the bikes that it built were no better than the ones imported from abroad. As its losses piled up, Schwinn filed for bankruptcy in 1993.

Eventually Schwinn was bought by the Pacific Cycle Co., which outsourced the manufacturing of Schwinn bikes to low-wage workers in China. Today, most Schwinn bikes are produced in Chinese factories and are sold by Walmart and other discount merchants. And under Pacific's ownership, bikers do pay less for a new Schwinn. It may not be the premier bike that was the old Schwinn, but it sells for about $180, about one-third of the original price in today's dollars.

Analysis. Referring to Figure 2.7, assume that Schwinn is a typical firm operating in a competitive bike market. Suppose that consumers view the bikes sold by Schwinn and other firms to be substitutes and that the price of a Schwinn bike is $400. As other firms cut the price of their bikes, cyclists demand greater quantities of them. The demand curve for Schwinn bikes thus decreases from D_0 to D_1, resulting in falling sales for Schwinn. To improve its competitiveness, Schwinn decreases its costs by replacing high-wage union workers with non-union workers at lower wages, causing its supply curve to increase from

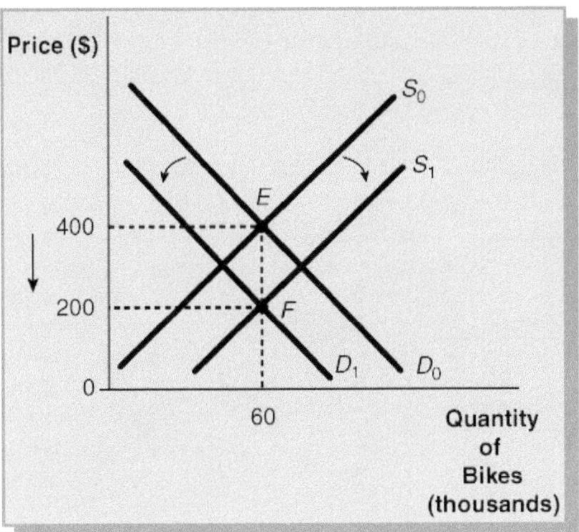

FIGURE 2.7 The Market for Schwinn Bikes

S_0 to S_1. This allows the firm to reduce price and increase sales, although not by enough to avoid bankruptcy.

Rising Health Care Costs Harm Households

The high costs of health care illustrate another application of demand and supply. Although Americans are living longer, healthier lives, the share of the nation's income that is devoted to health care has grown rapidly.

Health care services have become more expensive because the market demand curve for health care has increased more rapidly than the market supply curve. Figure 2.8 shows the market for health care services. Assume that the equilibrium price for these services is $200—the point at which the supply curve (S_0) intersects the demand curve (D_0). Suppose that the supply curve of health care services increases to S_1, but the demand curve increases by a larger amount to D_1. Because the increase in demand pulls the price of health care services up by a larger amount than the increase in supply pushes price down, the price of health care services increases to $250. Let us examine the characteristics that underlie the demand curve and supply curve of health care services.

Concerning the demand for health care services, consumers tend to be relatively insensitive to changes in the prices of health care services, such as doctors' and hospitals' services. This is because there are not good substitutes for health care services and these services are necessary to many people for daily life. A lack of consumer resistance to price changes partly explains why doctors and hospitals have incentives to raise prices.

Also, the demand curve for health care has shifted to the right over time, putting upward pressure on price. Increases in the demand for health care services can be explained by rising household incomes, the aging population (thus requiring more medical attention), and that many people have health insurance which protects them from the full cost of illness or injury.

Source: JazzIRT/E+/Getty Images®

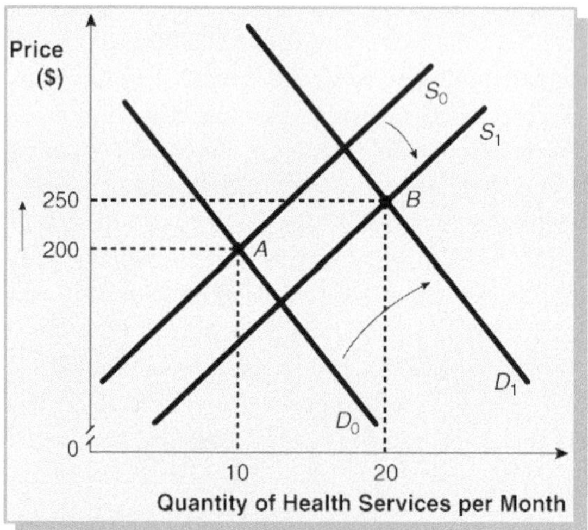

FIGURE 2.8 Increasing Cost of Health Care

In the figure, the increase in the demand curve for health care services is larger than the increase in the supply curve. Because the increase in demand pulls the price of health care up by a larger amount than the increase in supply pushes prices down, the price of health care increases.

Sluggish increases in the supply of medical services have also contributed to higher prices. For example, considerable financial resources and time are needed to train doctors. Also, critics have maintained that the American Medical Association has willingly kept admissions to medical school—and thus the supply of doctors—artificially low to give doctors greater ability to increase the price of their services. Moreover, the health care industry has been characterized by slow productivity growth. For example, how can you noticeably raise the productivity of nurses in the birthing room of a hospital?

Simply put, that health care services have become more expensive reflects the demand curve for services increasing more rapidly than the supply curve.

Bird Flu Triggers Soaring Egg Prices

The year 2022–2023 was a tough period for American consumers of eggs as prices jumped by about 70 percent. In December 2022, wholesale prices of large Midwestern eggs hit a record high of $5.46 per dozen, then they fell to $2.25 a dozen, which was still higher than $1.30 a year earlier. Retail prices showed a similar trend, although at higher levels than wholesale prices. Why the jump in egg prices?

Since the start of 2022, a highly contagious Avian influenza had resulted in the deaths of about 58 million chickens in 47 states. It was the deadliest outbreak on record, exceeding the outbreak of 2015 when 50 million chickens were culled. The chicken virus, which usually occurs during migration in spring only to disappear in a few months, did not come and go in 2022, and it showed no signs of slowing.

Therefore, U.S. chicken inventories were about 29 percent lower near the end of 2022 than the previous year. The lower-than-usual egg inventories, combined with a rising demand for eggs stemming from the holiday baking season, resulted in several weeks of record high prices. Egg prices also increased as part of overall food inflation driven by rising costs of feed, labor, packaging, and transportation.

The demand for eggs usually declines after the holiday season, a period when people bake more and eat warmer breakfasts. The decline in 2023 was especially steep as the surging prices caused shoppers to purchase less eggs. U.S. retailers sold about 12 percent fewer eggs in January 2023 compared to the same period the previous year.

Analysts attributed the rapid spread of Avian influenza to wild birds carrying it to farms as they migrate. To limit the spread of the virus, whole poultry flocks were killed after the injection was confirmed. The disease has a mortality rate of nearly 100 percent in chickens, often causing death within 48 hours. The outbreak was expected to keep the overall supply of eggs tight until the national egg-laying chicken flock was replenished. Most chickens don't start laying until between 18 and 22 weeks of age and take the winter off laying.

American consumers were squeezed by the sharp rise in prices as there aren't many substitutes for eggs. Because eggs are a staple product for consumers, many grocers tried to hold prices down. Some retailers reported that they sacrificed some profits on eggs for months to keep prices as low as possible. However, there was much uncertainty about how long the outbreak would continue. Amid such unpredictability, prices tend to be sticky, which means that they increase quickly, but take much longer to come down.

Analysis. Figure 2.9 shows the U.S. market for eggs. The market price initially equals $2 per dozen eggs, shown at the intersection of supply curve S_0 and demand curve D_0.

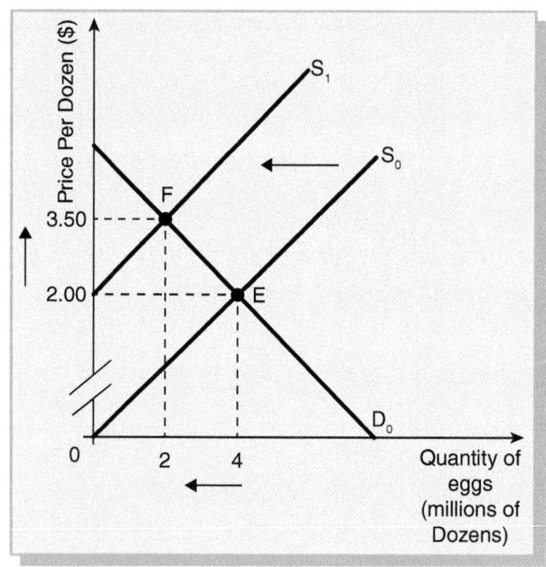

FIGURE 2.9 The U.S. Market for Eggs

The Avian influenza resulted in the death of many chickens, which caused the supply of eggs to decrease and the price to increase.

Due to the Avian influenza, the population of chickens falls, which results in the supply curve of eggs decreasing to S_1. Given the demand curve for eggs, the scarcity causes the price to rise to $3.50 per dozen and the quantity demand decreases from 4 million dozen to 2 million dozen.

What Drives Gasoline Prices?

Watching the numbers on the gas pump tick ever higher can cause blood pressure to rise and make one ponder: Why are gasoline prices so high? It is too simplistic to say that demand and supply determine gas prices. The answer goes far beyond the local pump to gas stations in China, to speculators throughout the world, to the Organization of Petroleum Exporting Countries (OPEC), to U.S. environmental legislation, and the like.

The price of a gallon of gas is based on the combination of four costs: That of crude oil, refining gas, distribution and marketing, and taxes. As seen in Table 2.3, in January 2023, crude oil accounted for about 55 percent of the pump price, refining accounted for 20 percent, distributing and marketing accounted for 10 percent, and federal and state taxes averaged 15 percent.

The most important factor that determines the price of a gallon of gas is the price of crude oil, which is used to make gasoline. The top five crude oil producers and their percentage shares of world crude oil production in 2021 were the United States (14.5 percent), Russia (13.1 percent), Saudi Arabia (12.1 percent), Canada (5.8 percent), and Iraq (5.3 percent). Also, crude oil is produced in 32 states of the United States. The top-five producing states and their percentage shares of U.S. production in 2021 were

TABLE 2.3 What We Pay for a Gallon of Gasoline and Diesel, January 2023 (in percentages)

	Regular Gasoline (retail price: $3.34 per gallon)	*Diesel (retail price: $4.58 per gallon)*
Taxes (federal, state, local)	15%	13%
Distribution and marketing	10	19
Refining	20	28
Crude oil	55	40
Total	**100**	**100**

Source: U.S. Energy Information Administration, *Gasoline and Fuel Update*, March 13, 2023, available at https://www.eia.gov/petroleum/gasdiesel.

Texas (42.4 percent), New Mexico (11.1 percent), North Dakota (9.9 percent), Alaska (3.9) percent, and Colorado (3.7 percent).[2]

Refining crude oil is the next step in the process. Gasoline is extracted from crude oil and additives such as detergents and lubricants are added. When producers sell crude oil to a refiner, they generally agree to a price set on an exchange, such as the Chicago Mercantile Exchange. After the oil is refined into gasoline, it is sold by the refiner to a distributor, at a price tied to the wholesale price of gasoline on an exchange. Finally, gas station owners set their own pump prices based on how much they paid for their previous shipment, how much they will have to pay for their next shipment, and how much their competitor is charging. Gas stations often realize little profit on the sale of gasoline. They want to entice motorists into their convenience stores to purchase snacks, beer, and soft drinks.

Moreover, retail gasoline prices vary in certain states or regions throughout the country, as seen in Table 2.4. Besides taxes, there are other factors that contribute to regional and even local differences in gasoline prices. For example, pump prices tend to be higher the farther gas is sold from the source of supply: Ports, refineries, and pipeline and blending terminals. This helps explain why pump prices tend to be higher in New England states than the Gulf Coast states. Also, pump prices are often highest in locations with few gasoline stations. Even stations located close together may have different traffic patterns, rents, and sources of supply, which influence their pricing. Moreover, some areas of the country, such as California, are required to use special reformulated gasoline with additives to help reduce carbon monoxide, smog, and toxic air pollutants. This boosts the pump price of gas.

The Rationing of Gasoline

The rationing of products has sometimes been used by governments as a way of minimizing the impact of scarcity. For example, when Vladimir Putin sent his troops to occupy Ukraine in 2022, he announced the tightening up of natural gas exports to the European

TABLE 2.4 U.S. Regular Gasoline Prices, Dollars Per Gallon*

Region	*March 2023*	*March 2022*
United States	$3.46	$4.32
East Coast	3.32	4.27
Midwest	3.31	4.09
Gulf Coast	3.09	4.03
Rocky Mountain	3.73	4.14
West Coast	4.40	5.15
California	4.73	5.59

* Prices include all federal, state, and local taxes.

Source: Data drawn from U.S. Department of Energy, *Gasoline and Fuel Update*, March 13, 2023, available at https://www.eia.gov/petroleum/gasdiesel.

Union. The European Union then asked its member states to ration natural gas by about 15 percent as part of a wider plan to deal with decreased supplies from Russia.

Another rationing example occurred during World War II, when the U.S. government implemented rationing programs for gasoline, rubber, sugar, and other products. The two most direct ways to ration a product are an excise tax or a government coupon system. Let us consider the merits of these programs as applied to gasoline.

Excise Tax Rationing. When we go to a gas station and fill up our vehicle, the gasoline that we purchase is subject to an excise tax. As of 2022, the federal excise tax of gasoline was 18.4 cents per gallon. State governments also impose excise taxes on gasoline, as seen in Table 2.5.

An excise tax is directly paid to the government by the gasoline-station owner, who then attempts to pass it on to consumers through a higher pump price. Besides providing revenue for the government, an excise tax can be used to discourage consumption of a product.

Figure 2.10 shows the hypothetical market for gasoline. Assume that the equilibrium pump price is $4 per gallon and the quantity is 100 gallons, shown at the intersection of supply curve S_0 and demand curve D_0. Suppose that the U.S. government wants to reduce the consumption of gasoline to 80 gallons.

Referring to Figure 2.10(a), assume that the government levies an excise tax of $2 per gallon of gasoline. We can view the tax as an increase in the incremental cost of gasoline. Therefore, the tax shifts the supply curve upward (leftward) as shown in the figure, where S_1 is the with-tax supply curve. The equilibrium pump price thus rises from $4 to $6. Note that the equilibrium quantity decreases from 100 gallons to 80 gallons because of the tax hike and the higher pump price it imposes on consumers. Simply put, an excise tax rations gasoline through the price system. It reduces the quantity demanded by providing consumers the incentive to decrease purchases as the price rises.

TABLE 2.5 Selected State Excise Taxes on Gasoline, 2022 (cents per gallon)*

High Excise-Tax States	*Low Excise-Tax States*
Pennsylvania 61¢	Alaska 9¢
California 54	Connecticut 15
Washington 49	New Mexico 17
Illinois 42	Mississippi 18
Florida 35	Oklahoma 19
Maryland 42	Texas 20
New Jersey 42	Louisiana 20
North Carolina 41	Missouri 22
Ohio 39	New Hampshire 22

*State taxes on gasoline also include sales taxes. The federal excise tax on gasoline was 18.4 cents per gallon in 2022.

Source: Data drawn from American Petroleum Institute, *Motor Fuel Taxes*, January 2022, available at https://www.api.org/oil-and-natural-gas/consumer-information/motor-fuel-taxes.

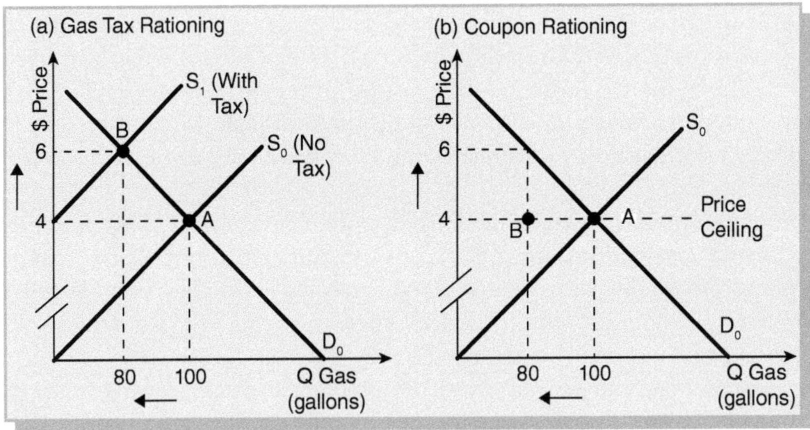

FIGURE 2.10 The Rationing of Gasoline

The rationing of gasoline can occur in response to the imposition of an excise tax on gasoline, which results in a decrease in the supply curve of gasoline, a higher price of gasoline, and a decrease in the quantity demand. Gasoline rationing can also occur if the government prints a limited number of coupons which motorists must use when they purchase gasoline.

The case for an excise tax is supported by the fact that it is relatively easy to collect, its implementation comes at a low cost to the government, and because most Americans drive, few can avoid the tax (in the absence of electric vehicles). Also, excise-tax rationing gives buyers the freedom to decide how much gas will be purchased. Gasoline goes to those who want the product badly enough to pay the price, this being dependent on a buyer's tastes or need for gasoline and on the buyer's income,

However, critics maintain that the quantity demanded of gasoline is relatively insensitive to changes in price because there are not good substitutes for gasoline and gasoline is necessary to many people for daily life. Therefore, the price of gasoline would have to increase dramatically to cause a significant reduction in quantity demanded. For example, economists estimate that to reduce the consumption of gasoline in the short run by 20 percent, the price would have to increase by about 100 percent. Such an increase in price might be viewed as too burdensome on consumers, especially the poor, and thus the imposition of an excise tax on gasoline is not a good policy option. Apparently, this was a factor that resulted in the U.S. government's decision to not implement gasoline-tax rationing during World War II.

Coupon Rationing. A coupon rationing system is another method of forcing Americans to conserve gasoline. During World War II, the federal government defined a target consumption level of gasoline, and it gave each household a limited number of nontransferable coupons (stamps). To purchase gasoline legally, the buyer had to surrender to the gas station not only the regulated pump price but also a stipulated amount of ration coupons. By printing a limited number of coupons, the government restricted purchases of gasoline.

To visualize the operation of coupon rationing, refer to Figure 2.10(*b*). Suppose the goal of the federal government is to reduce the consumption of gasoline from 100 gallons to 80 gallons. The government then would impose a ceiling on the pump price of gasoline, say, at $4 per gallon, and print 80 coupons which drivers would receive at local U.S. Post offices. Drivers would then pay the regulated pump price of gas and give the gas station one coupon for each gallon purchased. Therefore, the consumption of gasoline would be limited to the 80-gallon target of the government. Unlike excise-tax rationing, coupon rationing does not ration gasoline through the price system. Instead, it rations gas according to a government limit on the quantity of gas that can legally be purchased.

Rationing with nontransferable coupons has the advantage of allowing the government to meet a consumption target as well as not burdening lower-income people with higher pump prices. But it also has disadvantages. For example, during World War II, the coupon rationing program of the federal government suffered from the stealing and counterfeiting of coupons. Also, an expensive government bureaucracy was needed to run the program, and bureaucrats faced the problem of deciding how much gasoline should be allocated to a particular consumer. Should the allocation be based on registered owners of vehicles, on driver's licenses, or on special needs such as a doctor who travels long distances to serve a patient? By the end of the war, most Americans were disenchanted with coupon rationing.

By the 1970s, discussions of possible rationing programs included the notion of allowing coupons to be legally transferrable from one party to another. People who do not use all of their gas allotment during a month would have excess coupons and could sell them to others experiencing shortfalls. Therefore, the true price of a gallon of gas would be the pump price plus the price of coupons. Also, the antiquated coupons of World War II would be replaced with digitally updated debit ration cards.

CHAPTER SUMMARY

1 A market is a mechanism through which buyers and sellers communicate in order to trade goods and services. Through the price system, markets link potential buyers with potential sellers.

2 Demand is a schedule that shows the amount of a good or service that buyers are willing and able to purchase at each possible price during a particular period. A demand curve is a graphical representation of the data comprised by a demand schedule. A movement along a demand curve, resulting from a change in price, is called a change in quantity demanded.

3 According to the law of demand, price and quantity demanded are inversely related, assuming that all other factors affecting the quantity demanded remain the same. Economists explain the law of demand in terms of the substitution effect, the income effect, and the principle of diminishing marginal utility.

4 A demand shifter is a variable that causes a shift in a demand curve. Among the most important demand shifters are consumer tastes, the number of buyers, consumer income, the prices of related goods, and expected future prices. When a demand shifter causes an increase in demand, the demand curve shifts to the right; a decrease in demand causes the demand curve to shift to the left.

5 Supply is a schedule or curve showing the amounts of a good or service that firms or households are willing and able to sell at various prices during a particular period. The quantity supplied refers to a single point on a supply curve. Changes in quantity supplied are caused by changes in the price of the product.

6 According to the law of supply, sellers are willing and able to make more of their product available at a higher price than a lower price, all other determinants of supply being constant. The tendency for the cost of additional output to increase explains the law of supply.

7 A supply shifter is a variable that causes a shift in a supply curve. Among the major supply shifters are resource prices, technology, the prices of other goods, expected future prices, taxes and subsidies, and the number of suppliers. When a supply shifter results in an increase in supply, the supply curve shifts to the right; a decrease in supply shifts the supply curve to the left.

8 In a competitive market, equilibrium occurs when the price of a product adjusts so that the quantity that consumers will purchase at that price is identical to the quantity that suppliers will sell. The price at which buyers' intentions are equal to sellers' intentions is called the equilibrium price. A surplus of a product causes the price to fall to its equilibrium level; a shortage of a product causes the price to rise to its equilibrium level.

9 The following predictions can be made about the demand and supply curves when all other factors remain constant:

- When demand increases, both the equilibrium price and the equilibrium quantity increase.
- When demand decreases, both the equilibrium price and the equilibrium quantity decrease.

- When supply increases, equilibrium price falls and equilibrium quantity rises.
- When supply decreases, equilibrium price rises and equilibrium quantity falls.

KEY TERMS AND CONCEPTS

market
demand
demand curve
law of demand
change in quantity demanded
substitution effect
income effect
diminishing marginal utility
demand shifter
change in demand
normal good
inferior good
substitute good, complementary good
supply
quantity supplied
supply curve
law of supply
supply shifter
change in supply
market equilibrium
equilibrium price
surplus
shortage

STUDY QUESTIONS AND PROBLEMS

1 When personal computers were first introduced in the 1980s, their price exceeded $5,000. Since then, the price has decreased dramatically. Use demand and supply analysis to explain the price reduction of computers. What effect did the price reduction have on the quantity of computers demanded?

2 By the 1970s, postwar baby boomers had reached working age, and it became more acceptable for married women with children to work outside the home. Using demand and supply analysis, explain how the increase in female workers likely affected the equilibrium wage and employment.

3 Suppose a decrease in the demand for the Boeing 777 jetliner results in a sharp decline in the demand for Boeing engineers. Use demand and supply analysis to explain the impact on salaries paid to engineers and on the amount of their labor supplied.

4 In 1994, a severe frost destroyed about 25 percent of Brazil's coffee crop. Using demand and supply analysis, explain the impact of the frost on the price of coffee, and on the quantity of coffee demanded.

5 The tastes of many U.S. consumers have shifted away from beef and toward chicken. Using demand and supply analysis, explain how this change affects the equilibrium price and equilibrium quantity in the markets for chicken and beef.

6 Suppose that the implementation of the North American Free Trade Agreement (NAFTA) permits low-cost shirts, manufactured in Mexico, to enter the shirt market of the United States. Draw a graph showing the likely effects of their entry on the price and quantity of shirts supplied by U.S. firms.

7 Which of the following goods are likely to be classified as normal goods or services?

a Snow skiing

b Foreign travel

c Lima beans

d Computers

e Used cars

8 Which of the following goods are likely to be classified as substitute goods? Complementary goods?

a Cookies and milk

b Pizza Hut pizza and Domino's pizza

c Automobiles and batteries

d E-mail and first-class mail

e Wheaties and Cheerios

9 Assume that one of the following events occurs. How will each event affect the quantity demanded or demand curve for gasoline?

a The market population decreases

b The price of gasoline falls

c Buyers' incomes decrease

d Buyers expect that the price of gasoline will fall in the future

e The price of automobiles increases

f The price of gasoline rises

10 Assume that one of the following events occurs. How will each event affect the quantity supplied or supply curve of phone cases?

a The price of phone cases increases

b The prices of the resources used to produce phone cases increase

c Manufacturers expect that the price of phone cases will fall in the future

d New cost-saving technologies are developed to manufacture phone cases

e The number of phone cases manufacturers increases

f The price of phone cases decreases

11 Construct a market demand curve and market supply curve for computers based on the data in Table 2.6.

a What is the equilibrium price and the equilibrium quantity of computers?

b Find the price at which there would be a surplus of 40 computers and plot it on your diagram. How would the forces of demand and supply push the price back to equilibrium?

c Find the price at which there would be a shortage of 60 computers and plot it on your diagram. How would the forces of demand and supply push the price back to equilibrium?

TABLE 2.6 Supply and Demand Schedules of Computers

Price	*Quantity Demanded per Week*	*Quantity Supplied per Week*
$400	90	10
800	80	20
1,200	70	30
1,600	60	40
2,000	50	50
2,400	40	60
2,800	30	70
3,200	20	80

d Suppose that new cost-saving technologies allow manufacturers to supply 20 additional computers at each price. Construct a new supply curve to depict this situation. What is the new equilibrium price of computers and the new equilibrium quantity?

e Suppose instead that rising prices for the resources used to produce computers force manufacturers to supply 20 fewer computers at each price. Construct a new supply curve to depict this situation. What is the new equilibrium price of computers and the new equilibrium quantity?

f Suppose instead that rising incomes cause buyers to demand 20 additional computers at each price. Construct a new demand curve to depict this situation. What is the new equilibrium price of computers and the new equilibrium quantity?

g Suppose instead that worsening preferences cause buyers to demand 20 fewer computers at each price. Construct a new demand curve to depict this situation. What is the new equilibrium price of computers and the new equilibrium quantity?

NOTES

1 Matthew Futterman and Darren Everson, "Yankees Slash Prices to Fill Costly Seats at New Park," *The Wall Street Journal*, April 29, 2009, pp. B1–B2; Richard Sandomir, "Yankees Slash the Price of Top Tickets," *New York Times*, April 28, 2009, available at www.nytimes.com/2009/04/29/sports/baseball/29tickets.html.

2 U.S. Energy Information system, *Oil and Petroleum Products Explained: Where Our Oil Comes From*, 2021, available at https://www.eia.gov/energyexplained/oil-and-petroleum-products/where-our-oil-comes-from.php.

CHAPTER 3

Demand and Supply Applications

CHAPTER OBJECTIVES

After reading this chapter, you should be able to:

1 Explain how the quantity demanded responds to a change in price.
2 Describe how a firm's total revenue is influenced by price changes.
3 Explain the nature and operation of dynamic pricing.
4 Assess the advantages and disadvantages of governmental price ceilings and price supports on individual markets.

DOI: 10.4324/9781003438571-5

ECONOMICS IN CONTEXT

Economists have maintained that "there is no such thing as a free lunch." Even if the lunch is on the house, someone must pay for the resources used to grow, prepare, and serve the food.

Although the residents of the state of California are among the richest in the nation, for many years they have demanded cheap electricity, low rents, and free college. To obtain these goods, they have elected government officials who have ignored the laws of demand and supply and kept prices low—below market equilibrium levels. By 2001, however, Californians were paying the price for this defiance in the form of electricity shortages, which resulted in businesses shutting down and darkened homes.

Government officials in California have traditionally attempted to ensure cheap electricity for state residents by mandating ceilings on the retail price. Yet in 2001, a robust economy and unseasonably cold weather caused the demand for electricity to rise faster than supply could respond. California's utility companies thus had to purchase power from out-of-state utilities at high prices and then sell it to consumers at the low, state-controlled prices. Without the price ceiling, the shortage of electricity would have caused power prices to rise until demand and supply came into balance. Businesses and households would have voluntarily responded to the higher prices by reorganizing production, turning down thermostats, and shutting off lights. With the price ceiling, however, shortages prevailed, imposing more hardship on Californians.

The previous chapter introduced demand and supply analysis of market transactions. We learned that competitive markets can guide the allocation of resources to produce the goods and services that people demand. This chapter will broaden our understanding of demand and supply analysis. We will consider how sensitive buyers or sellers are to a change in price. We will also examine whether a seller's revenue rises or falls following a change in price. Finally, as an application of demand and supply principles, we will analyze the potential effects of government price ceilings and floors on individual markets.

PRICE ELASTICITY OF DEMAND

Suppose that you are the ticket manager for the Los Angeles Lakers, a professional basketball team. You are contemplating an increase in the price of your tickets, and you wonder how your fans will react. According to the law of demand, an increase in price will result in a decrease in quantity demanded. But how much will the quantity demanded fall in response to the price hike? The answer to your question depends on the price elasticity of demand.

The **price elasticity of demand** shows how responsive, or sensitive, buyers are to a change in price: It measures the percentage change in quantity demanded relative to the percentage change in price. The elasticity formula is

$$E_d = \frac{\text{Percentage change in quantity demanded}}{\text{Percentage change in price}}$$

where E_d is the elasticity coefficient.[1]

Suppose that attendance at the Lakers' games decreases by 10 percent when the price of tickets increases by 5 percent. Thus, the price elasticity of demand is 2:

$$E_d = \frac{\text{10 percent change in quantity demanded}}{\text{5 percent change in price}} = 2$$

The value of the elasticity coefficient, 2, suggests that game attendance changes 2 percent for each 1-percent change in the price of a ticket.

You may have noticed that instead of 2, the value of E_d should be −2. This is because price and quantity demanded are inversely related according to the law of demand. In our example, the increase in ticket prices causes the numerator in the formula to be positive (+10 percent), while the decrease in game attendance causes the denominator to be negative (−5 percent). As a result, E_d will have a negative value. By convention, economists drop the negative sign when calculating the price elasticity of demand, realizing that price and quantity demanded move in opposite directions.

Depending on the response of buyers to a change in price, demand is characterized as elastic, inelastic, or unit elastic.

- **Elastic**. Demand is elastic when the percentage change in quantity demanded is greater than the percentage change in price, meaning that E_d is greater than 1. Example: A 20-percent reduction in the price of Pepsi causes a 30-percent increase in the quantity demanded. Specifically, E_d is 1.5 in this case (30 / 20 = 1.5).
- **Inelastic**. Demand is inelastic when the percentage change in quantity demanded is less than the percentage change in price, meaning that E_d is less than 1. Example: A 30-percent increase in the price of Levi's jeans causes a 10-percent decrease in quantity demanded. Specifically, E_d is 0.33 in this case (10 / 30 = 0.33).
- **Unit elastic**. Demand is unit elastic when the percentage change in quantity demanded equals the percentage change in price, meaning that E_d equals 1.0. Example: An 8-percent decrease in the price of Timex watches causes an 8-percent increase in the quantity demanded (8 / 8 = 1.0).

Table 3.1 shows the estimated price elasticities of demand for selected products. When making such estimates, economists distinguish between a period during which consumers have little time to adjust (the short run) and periods during which consumers have time to fully adjust to a price change (the long run). From the table, we see that the short-run price elasticity of demand for medical care is 0.3, which means that the demand for medical care is inelastic. Our elasticity estimate suggests that if the price of medical care were to change by, say, 10 percent, the quantity demanded would change by 3 percent. The table also shows that in the short run the price elasticity of demand for automobiles is 1.9, suggesting that the demand for automobiles is elastic. Our elasticity estimate implies that

TABLE 3.1 Estimated Price Elasticities of Demand

	Elasticity Coefficient	
Item	*Short Run*	*Long Run*
Airline travel	0.1	2.4
Medical care	0.3	0.9
Automobile tires	0.9	1.2
Gasoline	0.2	0.7
Housing	0.3	1.9
Automobiles	1.9	2.2
Movies	0.9	3.7
Natural gas	1.4	2.1

Sources: Data drawn from Robert Archibald and Robert Gillingham, "An Analysis of the Short-Run Consumer Demand for Gasoline Using Household Survey Data," *Review of Economics and Statistics*, November 1980, pp. 622–628; and Hendrik Houthakker and Lester Taylor, *Consumer Demand in the United States* (Cambridge: Harvard University Press, 1970), pp. 56–149.

a 10-percent change in the price of automobiles would result in a 19-percent change in quantity demanded.

DETERMINANTS OF PRICE ELASTICITY OF DEMAND

As Table 3.1 indicates, the demand for automobiles is elastic, whereas the demand for housing and gasoline is inelastic. What factors account for differences in the price elasticity of demand?

Availability of Substitutes

The demand for a product is more elastic if many substitutes are available for it. If there are numerous substitutes available for a product, consumers can easily switch their purchases to substitutes when there is a price hike for that product. For example, suppose that the price of Shell gasoline rises. Because there are many substitutes for Shell gasoline, such as Conoco, Arco, and Texaco, motorists will turn to the readily available substitute gasoline as the price of Shell gasoline rises. We would expect the quantity demanded of Shell gasoline to decrease significantly in response to the price hike.

If a good has few substitutes, its demand tends to be more inelastic. Medical care has no close substitutes, for example. The short-run price elasticity of demand for medical care is estimated to be about 0.3. It is very inelastic.

Many companies hire celebrities to advertise their merchandise. For example, Michael Jordan, a retired basketball star, advertises Nike shoes. What message is he trying to convey? He is suggesting that, for Michael Jordan, Nike shoes are the "only" shoes worth having, and all other shoes are clearly inferior. If consumers accept Jordan's message and desire to be like him, they will also feel that there are no good substitutes for Nike shoes. As a result, the demand for Nike shoes will become more inelastic.

Owners of professional basketball teams price their tickets with the elasticity of demand in mind. In 1997, for example, fans encouraged by the Miami Heat's victory in Game 2 of the Eastern Conference playoffs against the New York Knicks were shocked when they lined up to buy tickets for the next home play-off game. The cheap seats at AmericanAirlines Arena, which had gone for $20 in Games 1 and 2 out of the best-of-7 series, jumped unexpectedly to $50 for Game 5. Moreover, the $90 seats jumped to $130. The Heat's management defended the price hikes, arguing that winning Game 5 was a necessity for the future success of the team. The management apparently felt that because Heat fans could not get along without attending Game 5, they would tolerate a price hike. As things turned out, AmericanAirlines Arena was filled in spite of the higher ticket prices.

Proportion of Income

Most consumers spend a large proportion of their income on automobiles and housing. A 10-percent rise in the prices of these goods would result in price increases of perhaps $6,000 and $50,000, respectively. These price hikes would likely substantially reduce consumers' ability to purchase these goods and significantly decrease the quantity demanded. The demand for goods on which a large proportion of personal income is spent therefore tends to be quite elastic.

However, a 10-percent rise in the price of a ballpoint pen means a price increase of perhaps 5 cents. This increase represents an insignificant fraction of consumer income, and it is unlikely to result in significant decreases in the quantity demanded. The demand for goods on which a small fraction of income is spent thus tends to be more inelastic.

Time

Suppose that Puget Sound Energy Co. announces an increase in the price of natural gas. How will households in Washington State react? The answer depends partly on how much time we allow for a response. If we consider the household reaction to the price increase by tomorrow, the response will likely be very small. Households have their existing gas-burning furnaces and stoves and cannot significantly reduce their quantity demanded as the price increases.

If we give households a year to react to the price hike, however, their response will be greater. Some households will switch from furnaces burning natural gas to heat pumps; others will switch from stoves burning natural gas to electric stoves. In general, demand tends to be more elastic with time because consumers can find more substitutes for goods over longer periods. This explains why the short-run elasticity coefficient of natural gas in Table 3.1 is less elastic at 1.4 than the long-run elasticity coefficient of 2.1. The same line of reasoning applies to the other goods shown in Table 3.1.

CHECK POINT

1 What is the price elasticity of demand?
2 How is the price elasticity of demand measured?
3 Differentiate among elastic demand, unit elastic demand, and inelastic demand.
4 Why is demand more elastic for some products and more inelastic for others?

PRICE ELASTICITY OF DEMAND AND TOTAL REVENUE

The price elasticity of demand can also help the managers of a business decide whether to change prices in order to increase sales revenues. For example, in 1991, Apple Computer Inc. cut the prices on some models of its Macintosh computers by as much as 50 percent in an attempt to stimulate the quantity demanded. The market reaction to the price reduction was extraordinary. At the end of the year, Apple announced that the sales of its Macintosh computers had increased by 85 percent and that its revenues had skyrocketed. In 1992, Apple again slashed prices, which resulted in rising sales and increased revenues. Clearly, these price reductions benefited Apple.

Determining the impact of a price change on a firm's **total revenue** is crucial to the analysis of many problems in economics. Total revenue (TR) refers to the dollars earned by sellers of a product. It is calculated by multiplying the quantity sold (Q) during a period by the price (P):

$$TR = P \times Q$$

For example, suppose that the Dell Inc. charges \$3,000 for a computer, and 10,000 computers were sold last month. Total revenue on the sale of computers equals \$30 million (\$3,000 × 10,000 = \$30 million). This amount also equals the total expenditures by consumers over this period.

Suppose that Dell reduces the price of its computers by 10 percent. Although the quantity demanded will increase, will the firm's total revenue rise? The problem in determining the effect of a price change on the total revenue of computers is that a change in price and a change in quantity would move in opposite directions. A decrease in price will result in an increase in quantity demanded, and an increase in price will cause the quantity demanded to decrease. However, total revenue is calculated by multiplying price and quantity. It is not clear how Dell's total revenue will react to the opposing forces of price and quantity.

To determine the impact of a price change on Dell's total revenue, we need to know how consumers will respond to the change in price. This response is measured by the price elasticity of demand. Consider the following situations:

- **Elastic demand**. Suppose that the elasticity of demand coefficient for Dell computers is 2. If Dell reduces computer prices by 10 percent, the quantity demanded will increase by 20 percent. Because the percentage increase in the quantity demanded is greater than the percentage decrease in price, the firm's total revenue will rise following the price cut. Conversely, a price increase of 10 percent would result in a 20-percent decrease in the quantity demanded and thus a decline in the firm's total revenue. In general, total revenue will move in the opposite direction of the price change when demand is elastic.

- **Inelastic demand**. Suppose that the elasticity of demand coefficient for Dell computers is 0.5. If Dell slashes computer prices by 10 percent, the quantity demanded will rise by only 5 percent, and total revenue will decrease. Conversely, a 10-percent price hike will cause the quantity demanded to fall by 5 percent, resulting in an increase in total revenue. In general, total revenue will move in the *same* direction as the price change when demand is *inelastic*.
- **Unit elastic demand**. Suppose that the elasticity of demand coefficient for Dell computers is 1.0. If Dell reduces computer prices by 10 percent, quantity demanded will increase by 10 percent, and total revenue will remain unchanged. Likewise, a 10-percent increase in price will leave total revenue unchanged. In general, a change in price will *not* induce a change in total revenue when demand is *unit elastic*.

All businesses face the question of what price to charge for their product. The answer is not always obvious. Increasing the price of a product often has the effect of reducing sales as price-sensitive consumers seek alternatives or simply do without. For every product, the extent of that sensitivity is different. Indeed, pricing is a tricky business. It requires a clear understanding of the demand curve and elasticity, as seen in the following examples.

Cigarette Tax Raised to Increase Government Revenue

The taxation of cigarettes has a long history in the United States. In 1862 the U.S. Congress passed excise taxes on many items including tobacco. This was the result of the U.S. government's increasing debt and need for additional revenue during the American Civil War. After the war, many of these excise taxes were repealed, but the tax on tobacco remained.

The U.S. government currently imposes an excise tax of $1.01 on a pack of cigarettes (20 cigarettes). Also, the 50 states and the District of Columbia all tax cigarettes but at varying rates, as seen in Table 3.2. Some counties and cities also add their own taxes. In Chicago, for example, the combined federal, state, county, and city taxes are $7.17 per pack, the highest in the nation. New York City ranks second, with a combined tax of $6.86 per pack.

Part of the motive behind raising the cigarette tax has been to reduce cigarette consumption to improve public health. However, the main motivation has been to increase the tax revenue of the government. Researchers have estimated the price elasticity of demand for cigarettes to be about 0.4 (inelastic).[2] This means that a 10 percent increase in the price of cigarettes causes the quantity demanded to decline about 4 percent. The more inelastic the demand for cigarettes, the easier it is for the government to increase revenue through a tax increase.

TABLE 3.2 State Cigarette Excise Tax Rates Per Pack (20 cigarettes), 2019*

High Tax States	*Low Tax States*
District of Columbia $4.50	Missouri $0.17
New York 4.35	Georgia 0.37
Connecticut 4.35	North Dakota 0.44
Rhode Island 4.25	North Carolina 0.45
Maryland 3.75	Idaho 0.57
Massachusetts 3.51	South Carolina 0.57
Oregon 3.33	Wyoming 0.60
Hawaii 3.20	Virginia 0.60
Vermont 3.08	Tennessee 0.62

*Average state cigarette tax: $1.91 per pack.

Source: Data drawn from U.S. Department of Health and Human Services: Centers for Disease Control and Prevention, *The Tax Burden on Tobacco*, 1970–2019, April 21, 2021, available at https://chronic-data.cdc.gov/Policy/The-Tax-Burden-on-Tobacco-1970-2019/7nwe-3aj9.

For example, from 1990 to 2000, cigarette taxes were raised in 30 states. Although cigarette sales decreased in each state following a tax increase, total cigarette tax revenue increased. Inelastic demand contributed to this increase. Table 3.3 provides examples of the impact of cigarette tax increases on tax revenues.

Colleges Hike Tuition Used to Offset Cutbacks in State Aid to Higher Education

After decades of growth, total state funding for higher education dropped as the U.S. economy dived into recession during 2007–2009. The cuts continued even after the economy bottomed. As the economy shrank and tax revenues declined for state legislatures, they decreased their appropriations to colleges. The decline in state funding was even sharper when considering increases in enrollment, meaning schools had thousands of dollars less to spend on each student. The business model of public colleges and universities was thus changing. Formerly, most funding came from the state. Now students and their families provide most of the funding to state schools.

College administrators have weighed how far they could raise tuition fees to balance their budgets without driving away students. Administrators noted that if the price of tuition did not increase, revenue shortfalls would trigger substantial layoffs of faculty and staff. This would result in a decline in the number of courses offered to students, which

TABLE 3.3 State-Level Sales and Cigarette Excise Tax Revenue in Response to Cigarette Tax Increases

State	*Year*	*Tax Increase (per pack)*	*New Tax (per pack)*	*Percentage Decrease in Quantity Transacted*	*Percentage Increase in Tax Revenue*
Arizona	1994	$0.40	$0.58	2.1%	221.6%
Michigan	1994	0.50	0.75	20.8	139.9
California	1999	0.50	0.87	18.9	90.7
Utah	1997	0.25	0.52	20.7	86.2
Oregon	1997	0.30	0.68	8.3	77.0
New York	2000	0.55	1.11	20.2	57.4
Maryland	1999	0.30	0.66	15.3	52.6
Wisconsin	1997	0.15	0.59	6.5	25.8

Source: Drawn from Matthew Farrelly, Christian Nimsch, and Joshua James, *State Cigarette Excise Taxes: Implications for Revenue and Tax Evasion*, RTI International, May 2003, available at https://untobacco-control.org/taxation/e-library/wp-content/uploads/2019/10/Excise_Taxes_FR_Report.pdf.

would delay their graduation from college. Therefore, many schools responded by jacking up tuition, which fueled public anger and inflated student debt levels. Schools also reduced their costs by increasing class sizes, teaching more online classes, and using more adjunct professors. Simply put, higher education was becoming more of a private good for which individual students (and their families) would have to pay to receive their own education. Does an increase in tuition necessarily result in an increase in total tuition revenue? How high can tuition be raised?

Analysis. Figure 3.1 illustrates the effect of a tuition increase on the total tuition revenue for, say, the University of Washington (UW). Referring to Figure 3.1(a), let us consider the effect on total revenue of an increase in tuition from $10,000 to $12,000 per year when demand is inelastic. In this case, the decline in attendance caused by the tuition hike does not offset the increase in tuition revenue per student. The net result is that total tuition revenue increases from $300 million to $336 million when tuition is raised.

But when tuition increases, some students may question whether attending UW is worthwhile. They may switch to a private university or drop out of school to seek full-time employment. Therefore, a relatively large decrease in attendance may occur following a tuition hike, suggesting that demand is elastic. Referring to the elastic demand curve shown in Figure 3.1(b), when tuition increases from $10,000 to $12,000 the decrease in attendance more than offsets the increase in tuition per student. Thus, total revenue decreases from $300 million to $288 million. The attempt to increase total revenue by raising tuition backfires when demand is elastic.

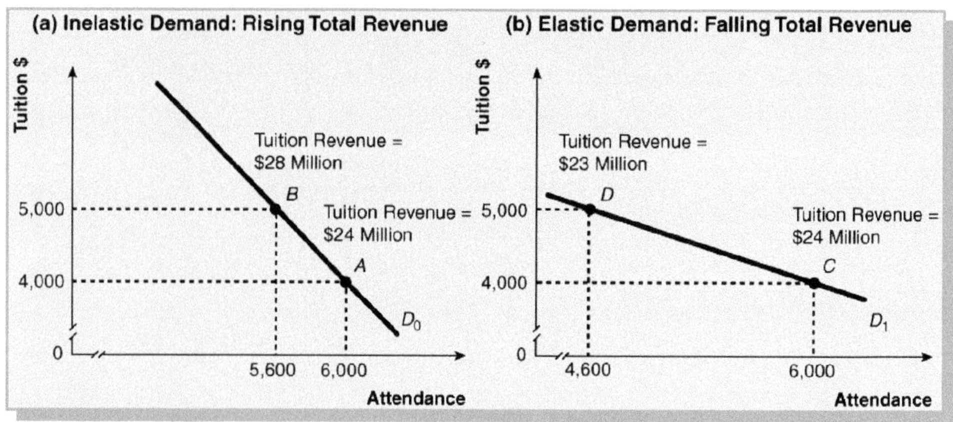

FIGURE 3.1 Raising Tuition and Total Tuition Revenue

For the University of Washington, whether a tuition hike will increase total tuition revenue depends on the students' elasticity of demand. If demand is inelastic, a tuition increase results in increased total revenue. But if demand is elastic, an increase in tuition results in declining total revenue.

U.S. Postal Service Boosts Rates to Increase Revenue

It is no secret that the U.S. Postal Service (USPS) is in financial difficulty. For many years, it has suffered huge deficits in the face of declining demand for letter mail and increasing costs of running the Postal Service. Alternatives such as e-mail, faxes, and cell phones increasingly have substituted for hard-copy letters, thus reducing mail deliveries by the USPS.

To generate additional revenue to cover rising operating costs, the USPS has raised rates on mail delivery, such as the increase in the price of a first-class Forever stamp from 60 to 63 cents in January 2023. Rates on other mail services, such as priority mail, parcel post, and periodicals, were also raised. Whether the revenue of the USPS rose or fell depended on the response of users to the rate hikes—that is, the price elasticity of demand.

Consider Bear Creek Corp. of Medford, Oregon. Before the USPS rate hike of 2001, the firm sent about 900,000 packages of gourmet cheesecakes, pears, and other specialty items by priority mail, the USPS's most economical way to mail packages for delivery in as little as two or three days. Following the rate hike, however, households could not count on the USPS to bring them cinnamon swirls and chocolate truffles. Why? Bear Creek maintained that priority mail was less attractive than its private-sector competitors, FedEx and United Parcel Service. Because of the rate hike, Bear Creek expected its catalog retailers to ship 20 percent fewer priority mail packages. The manager of Bear Creek noted that there were many alternatives, and his company was not dependent on the USPS to deliver his products.

Analysis. The purpose of a rate hike is to increase the revenue of USPS, as illustrated in Figure 3.2. Suppose that the price of a letter (Forever stamp) is 60 cents, and the quantity demanded is 1 million letters. The revenue of the USPS thus totals $600,000 ($0.6 x 1,000,000 letters = $600,000).

Source: mcdomx \ E+ \ Getty Images®

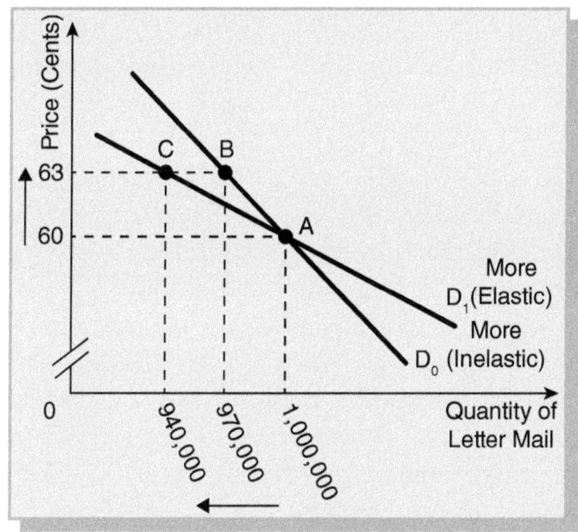

FIGURE 3.2 U.S. Postal Service: Price Elasticity of Demand and Total Revenue

If the demand for letter mail is inelastic, an increase in the price of mail will result in increased total revenue for the USPS. If the demand for letter mail is elastic, an increase in the price of mail will result in falling total revenue for the USPS.

Suppose the demand for USPS mail delivery is inelastic, shown by demand curve D_0 in the figure. In response to the increase in a letter's price from 60 cents to 63 cents, the quantity demanded falls from 1 million letters to 970,000 letters. Therefore, USPS revenue will rise from $600,000 to $611,100 ($0.63 x 970,000 letters = $611,100). We would expect the USPS revenue to increase if demand is inelastic, suggesting a

TABLE 3.4 Price Elasticity of Demand for Mail Services of the U.S. Postal Service

	Elasticity of Demand	
Mail Classification	*Traditional Estimate*	*More Recent Estimate*
First-class letters	0.31	0.85
Periodicals	0.17	2.2
Parcel post	1.19	3.5
Bound printed matter	0.23	2.01
Media mail	0.14	3.5

Sources: Postal Rate and Fee Changes, 1997. *Testimony of George Tolley to the U.S. Postal Commission*, July 1997, Docket No. R1997–1, available at http://www.prc.gov. Select "Contents," "Docketed Cases and Matters," "Rate," and then locate the testimony of George Tolley. Margaret Cigno, Elena Patel, and Edward Pearsall, *Estimates of U.S. Postal Price Elasticities of Demand Derived From a Random-Coefficients Discrete-Choice Normal Model*, 2012, U.S. Postal Regulatory Commission.

relatively small decrease in quantity demanded as the price increases. This means that few substitutes exist for USPS mail delivery, and it is a necessity for the lives of many Americans.

However, suppose the demand for USPS mail delivery is elastic, shown by demand curve D_1 in the figure. The increase in price from 60 cents to 63 cents will reduce the quantity demanded from 1 million letters to 940,000 letters. Therefore, USPS revenue will fall to $592,200 ($0.63 x 940,000 = $592,200). The revenue reduction is due to elastic demand, which means that there is a relatively large reduction in quantity demanded as the price rises. This means there are good substitutes for USPS mail delivery, such as cell phones and e-mail.

What is the evidence about the price elasticity of demand for USPS mail delivery? As seen in Table 3.4, the price elasticity of demand has traditionally been estimated to be less than 1.0, suggesting that the demand for these services is inelastic. Therefore, we would expect the revenue of the USPS on these services to increase following a rate hike.

However, more recent estimates suggest that the demand for USPS mail delivery may be more elastic than previous estimates indicated—see column 3 of Table 3.4. To the extent that more recent estimates more accurately measure elasticity, the ability of the USPS to increase revenue by raising rates will be lessened (if demand is elastic and rates increase, total revenue will fall).

DYNAMIC PRICING

Most Americans are used to paying a fixed price for the goods that they purchase. When you go to the grocery store, you will likely pay a price that will remain unchanged for perhaps days, weeks, or longer. But this practice has changed in recent years. To maximize revenue per sale, many merchants have adopted a pricing strategy called dynamic pricing.

Dynamic pricing is a scheme in which product prices continuously adjust, sometimes in a matter of minutes, in response to real-time changes in demand and supply. For example, a merchant might increase price when demand strengthens and then decrease price as demand weakens, all within the same day. Among the factors that determine a dynamic price are the level of demand, time of day or night, day of the week, customer location, and competitor pricing.

Amazon is one of the largest retailers that has adopted dynamic pricing, and it changes many of its prices daily, sometimes every ten minutes. As the firm's inventories of a particular product decrease, you will quickly see a rise in price. Also, Uber will raise price if the demand for its ride-share service increases during rush hour, rain or snow, or at the end of a sporting event. And anyone looking for a hotel in Seattle during a conference will pay a high price compared to days when there are no events occurring in the city. Finally, a commuter airline flight from New York City to Detroit will be more expensive at 6p.m. on a Friday than it might be on a Tuesday afternoon because more people will travel home after work on a Friday afternoon.

The idea behind dynamic pricing is that not all people want to pay the same price for a product. Some people may be willing to pay more while others want to pay less. By understanding the nature of each consumer's price elasticity of demand, a merchant can determine the optimal price. This means that a merchant will charge a higher price to relatively inelastic customers and a lower price to relatively elastic customers.

Setting up a dynamic pricing strategy requires a business to analyze mountains of customer and competitor data. Almost no firm has the time to manually assess every single piece of data to offer the best pricing. Therefore, firms rely on computer software and statistical methods to do the brunt of the work, often provided by data analytics companies. The software will automate the process, which allows a firm to set prices in real time and make decisions quickly.

Dynamic Pricing of Major-League-Baseball Tickets

The San Francisco Giants provide an example of the dynamic pricing of tickets to major-league baseball games. Under the Giants' system, because not all games are considered equally attractive, the same price is not charged for all. Instead, higher ticket prices are charged for those games where demand is stronger and more inelastic as compared to games where demand is weaker and more elastic. Therefore, we would expect that ticket prices against prestigious teams like the New York Yankees and the Chicago Cubs would be higher than prices against lower profile teams like the Minnesota Twins. Also, ticket prices for popular weekend games are higher than for less enticing weekday games.

Table 3.5 shows the prices for selected Giants games, as quoted on March 13, 2023. Dynamic ticket prices can fluctuate in accordance with evolving won–lost records of teams, whether a team is no longer a contender for the playoffs, pitching matchups, injuries to key players, and the weather. So, if you buy a Giants ticket right before game time, you may be paying a different price than if you bought that ticket two weeks ago.

TABLE 3.5 Dynamic Ticket Pricing of the San Francisco Giants, Oracle Park, March 13, 2023

Opposing Team	*Lexus Dugout Club*	*Premium Club Infield*	*View Reserved Centerfield*
Kansas City Royals			
Friday, 4-7-23 (opening day)	$874	$273	$54
Sunday, 4-9-23	361	94	20
Los Angeles Dodgers			
Monday, 4-10-23	443	129	28
Wednesday, 4-12-23	443	122	28
New York Yankees			
Thursday, 4-20-23	331	83	18
Friday, 4-21-23	445	120	25

Source: Data drawn from San Francisco Giants, *2023 Giants Dynamic Ticket Pricing* at mlb.com/giants/tickets/pricing.

To implement its dynamic pricing strategy, the Giants subscribe to the services of Qcue, Inc., a data analytics company. Using computer software and statistical analysis, Qcue estimates how much value Giants fans place on a particular game and recommends prices for seats throughout the stadium. This information is then presented to the Giants management, who decide what prices to charge. The Giants management typically meets three to four times a week throughout the season to adjust ticket prices.

For the Giants, ticketing is an important revenue stream. By using dynamic pricing, the team has maintained a balance between maximizing revenue and attendance while keeping fans happy.

CHECK POINT

1. What conclusions can be drawn about the price elasticity of demand when a firm's price and total revenue move in opposite directions? In the same direction? What if total revenue remains unchanged following a change in price?
2. Will an increase in tuition result in higher tuition revenue for a college or university?
3. What factors explain an increase or decrease in the total revenue of the U.S. Postal Service following a rate increase?
4. How do the San Francisco Giants practice dynamic pricing of tickets to baseball games?

PRICE CEILINGS AND FLOORS

Having learned about the reaction of consumers to price changes, let us next consider the issue of fairness of prices. Occasionally, government officials maintain that the forces of demand and supply result in prices that are unfairly low to sellers or unfairly high to buyers. Government officials may enact price controls to address these problems. When a **price ceiling** is imposed on a product, it establishes the maximum legal price a seller may charge for that product. Conversely, a **price floor** prevents prices from falling below the legally mandated level. Let us consider the effects of price controls on individual markets.

Rent Controls Make Housing More Affordable

Rent controls have been used in more than 200 U.S. cities, including New York, Boston, San Francisco, and Washington, DC. The objective is to protect low-income households from escalating rents caused by perceived housing shortages and to make housing more affordable to the poor.

The economic effects of rent controls are illustrated in Figure 3.3. Assume initially that the equilibrium rent for a 2-bedroom apartment in New York City equals $600 per month, shown by the intersection of the market supply curve (S_0) and the market demand curve (D_0). To protect renters from the possibility of escalating rents, suppose that the municipal government passes a rent-control law that freezes the monthly rent at $600. Because the ceiling rate equals the market equilibrium rate, the ceiling does not affect the market.

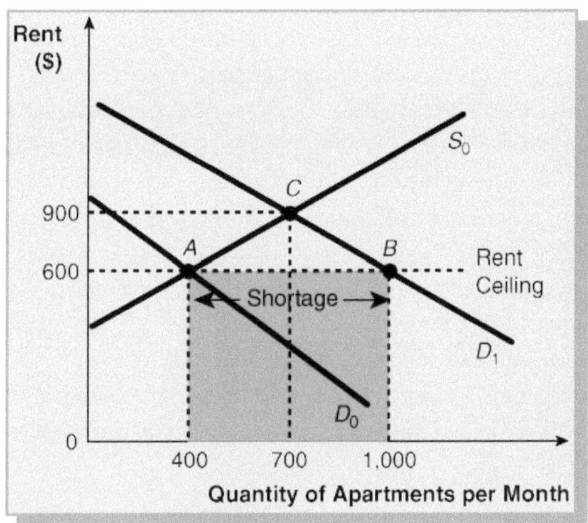

FIGURE 3.3 Rent Ceilings and Housing Shortages

When the equilibrium rent for apartments is equal to, or lower than, its legal maximum limit, a rent ceiling has no effect on the market. This occurs when the rent ceiling is $600 and the demand and supply curves for apartments are D_0 and S_0, respectively. When the equilibrium rent is above its ceiling, the ceiling takes effect and a shortage occurs. This situation occurs when the rent ceiling is $600 and the demand and supply curves are D_1 and S_0, respectively.

Because of the rising population in New York City, suppose that the market demand curve for apartments shifts to D_1. Prices try to rise to $900, the price that would occur in a free market, but are prevented from doing so by the rent ceiling. Renters who already have apartments are protected from the government-placed lid on rent because they pay $600 rather than $900 per month.

Although the rent ceiling protects current renters from rising prices, it results in adverse side effects. Because the $600 ceiling is set below the equilibrium level, people would like to be able to rent 1,000 apartments. However, landlords are willing to supply only 400 apartments at the ceiling price. Thus, when the rent ceiling is set below the free-market equilibrium price, there is a shortage of 600 apartments.

Initially, if the ceiling on rent is not far below the equilibrium price, the adverse effects of rent control may be hardly perceptible. As time passes, however, these effects will grow, yielding the following results:

- **The future supply and quality of rental apartments will diminish**. Because rent ceilings reduce the profitability of apartments for landlords, they serve as a disincentive to the construction of new rental housing. Potential investors in apartments may find it more profitable to invest in shopping malls or office buildings that are not subject to rent controls.
- **Under-the-table markets may develop**. When landlords cannot increase rent, they often adopt other means to collect income. Landlords may require a renter to make under-the-table payments just to get a key ("key money") to the apartment. Other renters may have to purchase the landlord's furniture at outrageous prices to obtain an apartment.
- **Discrimination may occur in the rationing of apartments**. Because price no longer serves its rationing role under rent ceilings, landlords may ration available apartments to people according to other criteria such as race or religion.
- **Rent controls will benefit the wealthy**. Because rent controls pertain to units of apartments and are not based on the income of renters, they can benefit the rich. For example, wealthy individuals such as singers and politicians have taken advantage of living in New York City, where rent ceilings hold down the cost of apartments.

In spite of these problems, rent controls have their proponents. Supporters argue that eliminating controls wouldn't spur the construction of any low-income rental housing, just more luxury housing. The low-income people who benefit from the current regulations, they say, would be displaced. Because current renters benefit from rent controls, whereas landlords and future renters suffer, the political lines are clearly drawn in the rent-control debate.

SHOULD A FEDERAL CEILING BE IMPOSED ON CREDIT CARD INTEREST?

Do consumers pay too much interest on their Mastercard and Visa balances? This has been a topic of much controversy. If you are a cardholder carrying a balance, it is in your

Source: sdominick \ E+ \ Getty Images®

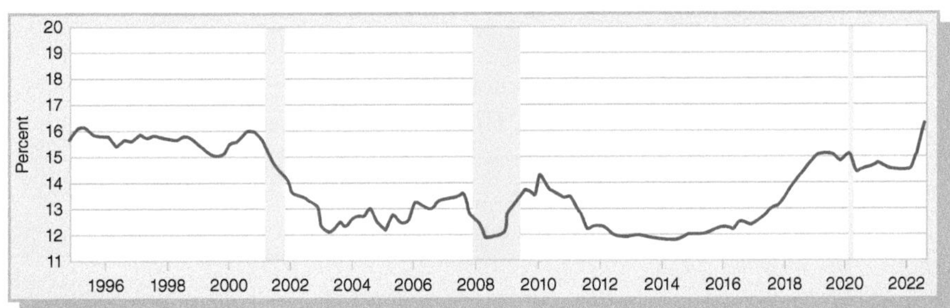

FIGURE 3.4 Commercial Bank Interest Rates on Credit Card Plans, All Accounts, 1996–2022*

*Shaded areas denote U.S. recessions

Source: Figure adapted from Federal Reserve Bank of St. Louis, *FRED Economic Data*, January 9, 2023, available at https://fred.stlouisfed.org/series/TERMCBCCALLNS.

interest to monitor the finance charges you are paying your card issuer. Credit card rates can be 15 percent or more, as seen in Figure 3.4.

There is no federal regulation on the maximum interest rate that your credit-card issuer can charge you. While many states have usury laws that restrict interest rates that lenders can charge, these laws don't generally apply to credit card loans.

Critics of banks that issue credit cards have complained that there is a wide gap between card rates and the interest rates that banks pay their depositors. They note that banks may pay, say, 2-percent interest to attract savings deposits and use this money to lend to credit card borrowers at 16-percent interest. As a result, banks can earn large profits on their credit card operations. Such high charges on credit card balances are often characterized as excessive and unfair to consumers, especially those with low incomes.

However, banks that issue credit cards argue that the high interest rates reflect the realities of pricing a complex product in a competitive market. Bankers note that the cost of obtaining deposits to fund credit card operations typically represents less than 40 percent of a bank's total cost of operating a credit card plan. Other costs, such as various processing and billing expenses and fraud and credit losses, are significant. Also, many individuals have rewards credit cards which offers them cash back, points, or travel miles for every dollar they spend, usually up to certain limits. These rewards are costly for a credit-card-issuing bank.

To protect consumers from high costs of credit-card loans, some members of Congress have called for the U.S. government to impose a nationwide ceiling on credit-card interest. For example, Rep. Alexandria Ocasio-Cortez and Sen. Bernie Sanders sponsored a bill known as the Loan Shark Prevention Act of 2019. It would impose a mandatory 15 percent ceiling on credit-card interest. Also, the Act would authorize states to set their own ceilings lower than the federal one. It remains to be seen if this bill will be enacted into law.

To visualize the operation of a ceiling on credit card interest, refer to Figure 3.5, which shows market for loanable funds (credit). The supply of loanable funds (S_0) is based on banks that issue credit cards, while the demand for loanable funds (D_0) is based on households who use credit cards. The interest rate is the cost of borrowing money—a higher interest rate makes borrowing a given amount of money more expensive.

Assume the market equilibrium rate on credit-card loans is 18 percent, shown by the intersection of S_0 and D_0.To protect households from excessively high costs of credit, suppose the government imposes a ceiling at 15 percent. The advantage of the ceiling is that it makes credit cards more affordable for borrowers. Yet a disadvantage is that it results in a shortage of loanable funds because the quantity of funds supplied ($6 million) is less than the quantity of funds demanded ($12 million). Thus, not all households will receive the amount of credit that they want to receive.

Because the interest-rate ceiling would make the issuance of credit cards less profitable for banks, they would have the incentive to cut costs or find other sources of revenue. For example, banks might tighten credit standards for borrowers to decrease

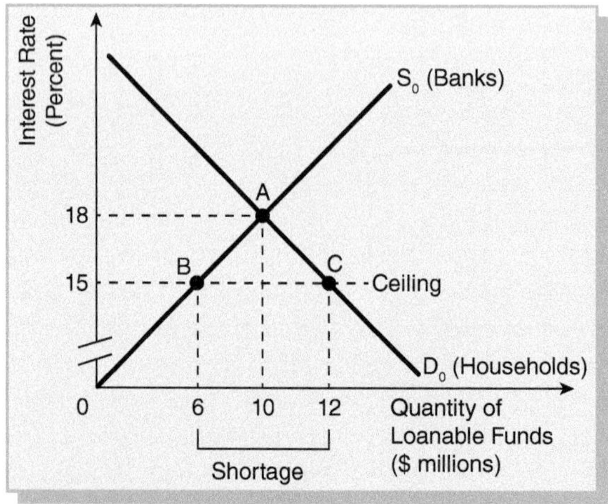

FIGURE 3.5 Ceiling on Credit Card Interest Rate

A below-equilibrium price ceiling will cause the quantity of loanable funds demanded to exceed the quantity of loanable funds supplied, resulting in a shortage of loanable funds.

collection costs, reduce rewards offered with credit cards, or increase the annual fee or late-payment fee charged to cardholders. Although an interest-rate ceiling on credit cards would help households in terms of their monthly interest bills, it could impose other burdens on them.

Farmers Reap Subsidies from the Government

We have previously examined the effects of imposing governmental price ceilings on the sale of a product. Let us now consider the effects of a price floor (support).

During the Great Depression of the 1930s, prices for agricultural products such as milk, wheat, and corn fell so low that it was hard for farmers to afford to grow their crops. So, the U.S. government stepped in and implemented price support programs to ensure that farmers received a minimum price for their goods. With price support, production levels would be more stable because farmers would have a steady source of income to pay for planting and harvesting their crops. Therefore, food production would continue for consumers.

Since the 1930s, agricultural support programs have evolved over time. Many different price support programs have been tried by the U.S. government, but they all tend to have similar effects. We will focus on the main elements of elements of these programs, to stabilize prices and incomes for farmers.

Figure 3.6 shows how a price support works for wheat. With a competitive market, the intersection of the market supply curve (S_0) and the market demand curve (D_0) establishes

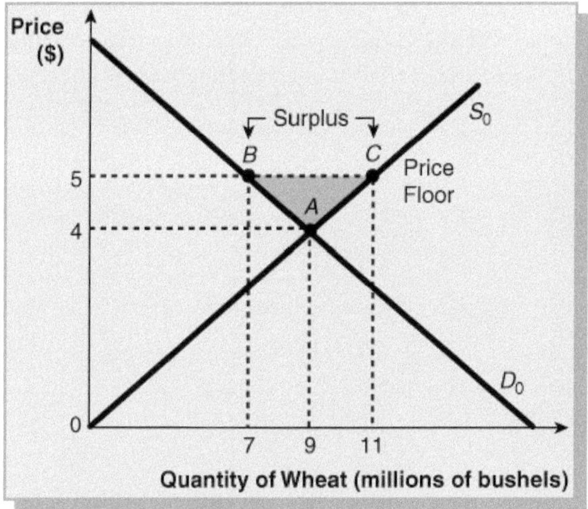

FIGURE 3.6 Effect of Price Support for Wheat

The agricultural support price of $5 per bushel is above the market equilibrium price of $4 per bushel. The support price results in an increase in quantity supplied and a decrease in quantity demanded, causing a surplus of 4 million bushels per year. To prevent the price from falling below the support level, the government purchases the surplus and stores it. The cost to taxpayers of purchasing the surplus is $20 million.

the equilibrium price at $4 per bushel. A total of 9 million bushels are produced and sold per year at this price, yielding an income of $36 million for farmers.

To support the incomes of wheat farmers, suppose the government sets a price floor of $5 per bushel. The higher price induces farmers to increase production to 11 million bushels, but consumers demand only 7 million bushels. As a result, there is a surplus of 4 million bushels. To prevent the surplus from causing the price of wheat to fall, the government purchases the surplus and stores it. In this manner, farmers can sell 11 million bushels of wheat at a price of $5 per bushel, thus realizing an income of $55 million. This amount exceeds the income that farmers would earn in a free market, $36 million.

One result of agricultural price support is the transfer of money from consumers and taxpayers to farmers. This transfer works in two ways. First, for each bushel of wheat that consumers purchase, they pay a higher price ($5) than they would have paid without a price support ($4). Second, when the government purchases the 4-million-bushel surplus at a price of $5 per bushel, it comes at a cost of $20 million to taxpayers. Simply put, households pay higher prices for wheat, as well as higher taxes to subsidize farmers.

A key argument against agricultural price support is that it results in the oversupply of agricultural products because farmers get paid to produce more. The farmers that receive subsidies will produce as much output as they can to maximize profits. This floods the market with agricultural goods.

Critics have questioned whether the incomes of farmers should be subsidized by other taxpayers. Farmers' incomes tend to be higher than that of the average American household. Also, farmers often earn income from sources other than farming, making them less vulnerable to decreases in the price of farm products.

This chapter has broadened our understanding of demand and supply by considering contemporary applications of these principles. The next chapter will consider the role of production and the costs of production in influencing business decisions.

CHECK POINT

1 Why does government sometimes impose price controls on individual markets?

2 What are the advantages and disadvantages of a legal price ceiling imposed on the sale of a product? How about a legal price floor?

3 As explained in this chapter, which of the following are price ceilings? Price floors?

   a Rent controls

   b Controls on credit card interest rates

   c Agricultural price controls

CHAPTER SUMMARY

1 The price elasticity of demand measures how sensitive buyers are to a change in price. Depending on the response of buyers to a change in price, demand is characterized as elastic, inelastic, or unit elastic.

2 Demand tends to be more elastic for some products and less elastic for others. The major determinants of the price elasticity of demand are the availability of substitutes, the proportion of buyer income spent on a product, and the time period under consideration.

3 If a firm's price and total revenue move in opposite directions, demand is elastic. If the firm's price and total revenue move in the same direction, demand is inelastic. If the firm's total revenue does not respond to a change in price, demand is unit elastic.

4 Occasionally, the government will impose price controls on individual markets in which prices are considered unfairly high to buyers or unfairly low to sellers. When the government imposes a price ceiling on a product, it establishes the maximum legal price that a seller may charge for that product. Conversely, the government may establish a price floor to prevent prices from falling below a legally mandated level.

5 Although price controls on individual markets attempt to make prices more "fair" for buyers and sellers, they interfere with the market's allocation of resources. Price ceilings that are set below the equilibrium price level result in market shortages of a product. Price floors that are set above the equilibrium level entail market surpluses.

KEY TERMS AND CONCEPTS

price elasticity of demand
total revenue
elastic demand
inelastic demand
unit elastic demand
price ceiling
price floor
rent controls

STUDY QUESTIONS AND PROBLEMS

1 Suppose that researchers estimate that for every 1-percent change in the price of computers, the quantity demanded will change by 2.5 percent. Describe the price elasticity of demand for computers. What if researchers estimate that the quantity demanded for computers will change by 0.5 percent in response to a 1-percent change in price?

2 Economists estimate the short-run price elasticity of demand for airline travel to be 0.1, 0.3 for housing, 1.5 for glass, and 1.9 for automobiles. What is the meaning of these elasticity coefficients?

3 Why is demand relatively inelastic for medical care and gasoline but relatively elastic for movies and automobiles?

4 An advertisement appears in the *Seattle Times*: "Wanted, two Seahawks tickets for next week's game against the Broncos. Will pay any price. Phone Joe at 271–4597." If Joe really means what he says in his ad, what could you infer about his price elasticity of demand for tickets?

5 How will the following changes in price affect a firm's total revenue?

- a Price rises and demand is inelastic
- b Price falls and demand is elastic
- c Price rises and demand is unit elastic
- d Price falls and demand is inelastic
- e Price rises and demand is elastic
- f Price falls and demand is unit elastic

6 Suppose that the U.S. Postal Service implements an increase in the price of first-class mail in order to generate additional revenue. What can you infer about the price elasticity of demand for first-class mail?

7 Suppose that the Grand Central Movie Theater reduces the price of popcorn by 20 percent, but consumers purchase only 10 percent more of the product. What does this indicate about the price elasticity of demand, and what will happen to total revenue as a result of the price reduction?

8 Assume that the price elasticity of demand for corn is 0.6 and that farmers have a record harvest—corn production is higher than ever. What will happen to the total revenue received by farmers?

9 Suppose that the price elasticity of demand for airline travel is 0.4 in the short run and 2.2 in the long run. If airlines raise the price of tickets, what will happen to their total revenue over these time periods?

10 Assume that the price elasticity of demand for labor is 0.2. If a labor union succeeds in negotiating an 8-percent increase in hourly wages, what effect will this have on its members?

11 Table 3.6 shows the demand schedule and supply schedule for apartments.

- a Draw the supply curve and demand curve for apartments from the data given in the table. What is the equilibrium rent? What is the quantity of apartments rented?
- b Suppose that the government imposes a legal rent ceiling at $400 per month. How many apartments will be demanded and supplied? What will be the size of the shortage?
- c How will landlords likely cope with the rent ceiling?

12 Table 3.7 shows the demand schedule and supply schedule for milk. Quantities are in gallons.

- a Draw the supply curve and demand curve for milk from the data given in the table. What is the equilibrium price? How much milk will be produced and sold? How much revenue will farmers receive from the sale of milk?
- b Suppose that the government imposes a price floor on milk equal to $2 per gallon. How much milk will be produced and purchased? What will be the size of the surplus?
- c If government maintains the floor price by purchasing all the unsold milk from farmers, how much will the government pay? How much revenue will the farmers receive, from consumers and the government, from the sale of milk? What might the government do to dispose of the surplus?

TABLE 3.6 The Market for Apartments

Rent (monthly)	*Quantity Supplied*	*Quantity Demanded*
$700	1,000	200
600	800	400
500	600	600
400	400	800
300	200	1,000

TABLE 3.7 The Market for Milk

Price	*Quantity Supplied (gallons)*	*Quantity Demanded (gallons)*
$0.50	5,000	9,000
1.00	6,000	8,000
1.50	7,000	7,000
2.00	8,000	6,000
2.50	9,000	5,000

NOTES

1 The midpoint formula is used to calculate the elasticity between two points on a demand curve (or supply curve). This formula uses the averages of the two quantities and the two prices under consideration as reference points. According to the midpoint formula, the percentage change in quantity equals the change in the quantity divided by the average of the two quantities; the percentage change in price equals the change in price divided by the average of the two prices. Therefore, the price elasticity of demand equals:

2 In 2011, the International Agency for Research on Cancer (IRAC) conducted a review of the literature for the price elasticity of demand for cigarettes based on hundreds of studies. Estimates from the IRAC review imply that a 10 increase in cigarette price decreases overall cigarette consumption by between 2 and 6 percent. However, the use of an average price elasticity of demand may yield misleading predictions about consumption and revenue as there is a large variation in cigarette prices across countries, states, and municipalities. For example, a 10-percent change in a low-price state may have a different impact on cigarette consumption than a 10-percent change in a high-price state. See IARC Handbooks of Cancer Prevention, Tobacco Control, Vol. 14: *Effectiveness of Tax and Price Policies for Tobacco Control*, 2011: Lyon, France.

CHAPTER 4

Production and the Costs of Production

CHAPTER OBJECTIVES

After reading this chapter, you should be able to:

1 Distinguish between the short run and the long run and between a fixed input and a variable input.
2 Describe how the law of diminishing returns relates to the productivity of a variable input in the short run.
3 Identify the costs of production that a firm realizes in the short run.
4 Explain how economies of scale and diseconomies of scale affect the long-run average total cost curve of a business firm.
5 Distinguish between accounting profit and economic profit.

DOI: 10.4324/9781003438571-6

ECONOMICS IN CONTEXT

For years, McDonald's has attempted to maximize the output of its existing resources. At every McDonald's restaurant, some workers specialize in taking orders, while others prepare food, or serve customers at the drive-through window operation. Many McDonald's restaurants have installed automated machines to prepare French fries and take orders, thus increasing labor productivity. Moreover, McDonald's' sophisticated cash registers are user friendly. They merely require an employee to touch a key with a picture of, say, a Big Mac to record the price rather than enter the dollar price of the hamburger on the cash register. This saves time and money for the firm.

Because McDonald's operates in thousands of locations, it can standardize operating procedures and menus, further adding to the company's efficiency. Moreover, McDonald's trains its managers at its Hamburger University, and the firm can spread the cost of its advertising over thousands of individual restaurants. These procedures result in cost savings for the firm.

However, McDonald's does face challenges. Because the firm's menu is standardized across the nation, if customers in some parts of the nation do not like a product, it is generally dropped from the menu despite its popularity elsewhere. McDonald's' McRib sandwich, for example, was not popular with some consumers and therefore was dropped from the national menu. Another problem with McDonald's' geographically uniform menu is that the ingredients must be available nationwide and cannot be subject to shortages or sharp price fluctuations.

In today's economy, business managers face pressure to reduce costs while maintaining or improving product quality. Competition has forced firms such as McDonald's, Boeing, Intel, and General Motors to incorporate the latest technologies in order to fulfill these objectives. Moreover, employees of these companies must undergo retraining programs to increase their productivity. It turns out that for most goods and services, cost and output are closely related, implying that the theory of production is intertwined with the theory of cost. In this chapter, we will learn about production and its costs.

THE SHORT RUN AND LONG RUN

The time frame in which a company plans its operations influences the production techniques that it selects. In general, a firm's production may take place in the short run or the long run. These periods are not defined in terms of days, weeks, or months; rather, they are defined conceptually.

The **short run** is a period during which the quantity of at least one input is fixed and the quantities of other inputs can be varied. A **fixed input** is any resource for which the quantity cannot be varied during the period under consideration. For example, the productive capacity of large machines or the size of a factory cannot easily be changed over a short period. In agriculture and some other businesses, land may be a fixed resource. There are also **variable inputs** whose quantities can be altered in the short run. Typically, the variable inputs of a firm include labor and materials. In response to a change in demand, a firm can employ more or fewer variable inputs, but it cannot alter the capacity of its factory.

The **long run** is a period during which *all* inputs are *variable* in amount: There are no fixed inputs in the long run. Over the long run, firm managers may contemplate alternatives such as constructing a new factory, modifying an existing factory, installing new equipment, or selling the factory and leaving the business. How long is the long run? That depends on the industry under consideration. For Burger King or Pizza Hut, the long run may be 6 months—the time required to add a new franchise. For General Motors or Ford, it may take several years to construct a new factory.

BOX ESSAY 4.1 ECONOMICS IN ACTION
Steve Jobs: A Great Innovator

In market economies, whenever a new opportunity appears, innovators quickly find a way to profit from it. Because innovators are free to pursue their self-interests as they see fit, they also profit from ancillary opportunities that are undreamed of by most. Consider the case of Steve Jobs.

The next time you use an iMac computer, listen to music on an iPhone, or purchase music online from iTunes, remember the name Steve Jobs. He is the innovator who brought these technologies to the masses. Born in Los Angeles in 1955, Jobs cofounded Apple Computer in 1976 with Steve Wozniak and became a multimillionaire before the age of 30.

An adopted child, Jobs gained an early appreciation for technology. At the age of 12, Jobs landed an internship at Hewlett-Packard Co. There he attended electronics lectures after school and worked during the summer. During his internship, Jobs met Steve Wozniak ("Woz"), an engineering hotshot who had dropped out of the University of California, Berkeley, and had a mania for inventing electronic gadgets.

After dropping out of Reed College in Portland, Oregon, in 1974 Jobs worked as a video game designer at Atari Inc. He attended meetings of Wozniak's computer club and soon convinced Wozniak to help him build a personal computer. Wozniak and Jobs designed a computer in Jobs' bedroom and they constructed the prototype in his garage.

Encouraged by their efforts, Jobs and Wozniak founded Apple Computer Inc. To raise funds for their startup, they sold their most valuable possessions: Jobs sold his Volkswagen bus and Wozniak sold his Hewlett-Packard scientific calculator, raising $1,300. With that money capital and credit obtained from local electronics suppliers, they established their first production line. Jobs thought up the name of the new company, Apple, in fond memory of a summer he had spent as an orchard worker near Portland.

In 1976, Jobs and Wozniak built their first computer, called the Apple I. They sold it at a price of $666 and earned revenues totaling $774,000. The following year, Jobs and Wozniak put together the Apple II, the first personal computer to hit it big. Though the power of computing previously had been available only to "techies," the Apple II could be delivered to offices, classrooms, and dens. Then came Apple's Macintosh computer in 1984, the first personal computer to feature a mouse, icons, and computer graphics.

Since his early years at Apple, Steve Jobs continued to develop breakthrough products. In 2001, Jobs rocked the music business with Apple's iPod music player, and iTunes Music Store in 2003, the first time anyone had convinced all the major record companies to market their songs online. In 2003, Jobs was diagnosed with cancer, which led to his death in 2011. Today, few doubt the innovation and marketing abilities of Steve Jobs.

Source: Laurie Rozakis and Dick Smolnski, *Steven Jobs: Computer Genius* (Rourke Enterprises, Vero Beach, FL, 1993) and Alan Deutschman, *The Second Coming of Steve Jobs* (Random House, New York, 2001).

THE PRODUCTION FUNCTION

The transformation of resources into output does not occur haphazardly. When Toyota Motor Corporation produces automobiles, for example, it takes resources (land, labor, capital, and entrepreneurship) and, using a technological production process, transforms them into output. **Production** refers to the use of resources to make outputs of goods and services (for example, steel, locomotives, and banking services) available for human wants.

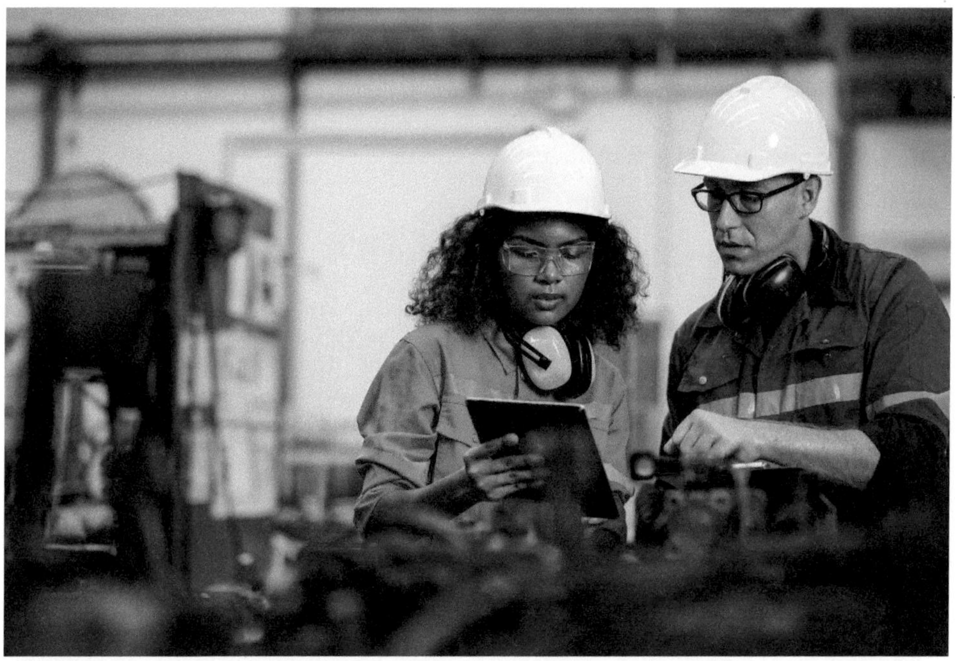

Source: Nitat Termmee/Moment/Getty Images®

TABLE 4.1 A Production Function for Chocolate Chip Cookies

1 cup butter or margarine, softened
2 ¼ cups flour
½ cup brown sugar
1 cup white sugar
2 eggs
½ teaspoon salt
1 teaspoon vanilla extract
1 teaspoon of baking soda
1 package (12 oz.) chocolate chips
Mix butter with white sugar, brown sugar, eggs, and vanilla. Add flour, baking soda, and salt. Blend into creamed mixture. Add chocolate chips. Drop by teaspoon onto ungreased baking sheets. Bake at 375 degrees for nine minutes. Makes approximately 6-dozen, 2-inch cookies. For variety, add one cup of raisins or chopped nuts.

The relationship between physical output and the quantity of resources used in the production process is called a **production function**. For example, a production function might tell us that with one lathe, a machinist can produce a maximum of 20 axles per day. With one lathe and an assistant, a machinist might produce up to 30 axles per day. The production function specifies the *maximum* amount of output that can be produced with a given number of resources.

The next time you make a batch of chocolate chip cookies, consider that the recipe you are using is an example of a production function. The recipe provides the types and amounts of resources and the processes that are required to produce a particular number of cookies. The resources include the ingredients shown in Table 4.1—brown sugar, white sugar, eggs, butter, and the like—as well as the kitchen equipment and the labor of the cook. The recipe also includes instructions for combining the various resources to produce cookies. Similarly, production functions in industry and agriculture specify the level of output and resources used in the production process.

SHORT-RUN PRODUCTION

To illustrate the production function, consider a simple case with one fixed resource and one variable resource. Figure 4.1 shows the short-run production function of Denver Block Co., a manufacturer of cement blocks used in the construction of buildings. Assume that the essential resources in the production of blocks are capital (a factory that includes a block machine, cement mixer, and forklift) and labor. Also suppose that the factory is already constructed and has a fixed capacity. For simplicity, suppose that the only resource that we can vary is labor, even though the production of cement blocks requires other resources such as water, cement, sand, and gravel. As expected, using more workers with the machinery generally results in more blocks being produced; using fewer workers produces fewer blocks.

The purpose of a production function is to tell us how many blocks we can manufacture with varying amounts of labor. Refer to Figure 4.1(*a*), which shows a production function relating the total number of blocks produced (second column) to the amount of labor (first column). Employing zero workers results in no blocks being produced. A single machine operator can produce 1,000 blocks a day; adding a second operator increases output to 2,200 blocks per day, and so on. Figure 4.1(*b*) shows this **total product** (*TP*) schedule graphically.

We are also interested in how many additional blocks can be produced for each additional worker employed. The **marginal product** (*MP*) of labor is equal to the change in output that results from increasing the amount of labor by one unit, holding all other inputs fixed.

$$MP = \Delta\text{Total product}/\Delta\text{Labor}$$

Where Δ, the Greek letter *delta*, denotes the change in a variable.

The marginal product of labor is calculated in Figure 4.1(*a*). When Denver Block Co. increases labor from zero to one worker, total output rises from zero to 1,000 blocks per day. The marginal product of the first worker is thus 1,000 blocks. Employing a second

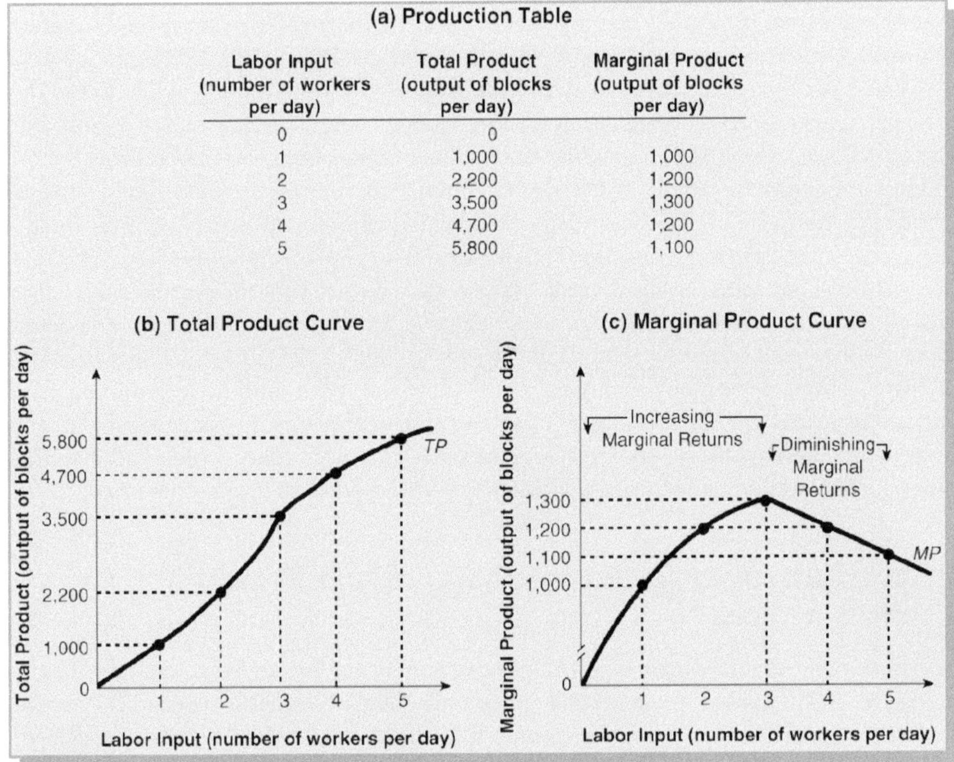

(a) Production Table

Labor Input (number of workers per day)	Total Product (output of blocks per day)	Marginal Product (output of blocks per day)
0	0	
1	1,000	1,000
2	2,200	1,200
3	3,500	1,300
4	4,700	1,200
5	5,800	1,100

FIGURE 4.1 Short-Run Production Function of Denver Block Company

The production table shows the maximum number of cement blocks that the firm can produce when it uses one block machine and different amounts of labor. The total product curve and the marginal product curve are based on these data. The law of diminishing returns accounts for the shape of the firm's product curves in the short run.

worker causes total output to rise from 1,000 blocks to 2,200 blocks, and thus the marginal product of the second worker equals 1,200 blocks. Similar calculations generate the remainder of the marginal product of labor. The marginal product curve is illustrated graphically in Figure 4.1(*c*).

Inspecting the marginal product curve, we see that the marginal productivity of labor rises for a while when the amount of labor used is low. Eventually, however, the marginal productivity of labor decreases. The principle that explains the decline in the marginal product curve is the **law of diminishing marginal returns**: After some point, the marginal product diminishes as additional units of a variable resource are added to a fixed resource.

In Figure 4.1(*c*), the marginal product of labor increases for the first three workers hired. Beginning with the fourth worker, however, the marginal product declines. Diminishing returns therefore begin with the fourth worker employed in block manufacturing.

It is easy to understand the reasons for the shape of the marginal product curve in Figure 4.1(*c*). If Denver Block Co. employs just one worker, that person must perform all of the aspects of block manufacturing: Mixing concrete, operating the block machine, and driving the forklift. If the firm hires a second person, the two workers can specialize in different aspects of block manufacturing. Therefore, two workers can produce more than twice as much as one worker. The marginal product of the second worker is thus more than the marginal product of the first worker, and the firm realizes **increasing marginal returns**. As the firm continues to add workers to the machinery, however, some workers may be underutilized because they have little work to do while waiting in line to use the machinery. Because the addition of ever more workers continues to increase output, but by successively smaller increments, the firm realizes **diminishing marginal returns**.

Here's a familiar example of the law of diminishing returns. Suppose that the total learning in your economics course depends on the quality of this textbook, your intelligence, the effectiveness of your professor, and the time you devote to study. Assume that the first three variables are fixed, implying that they do not vary throughout the course. Now let us include hours of study time per day over the duration of the course to determine the increased course learning. Will the second hour devoted to studying economics increase learning by as much as the first hour? How about the third hour, and so on? You will probably find that diminishing returns to learning will eventually occur as successively more hours are devoted to studying economics each day. In other words, the marginal product of an additional hour of study will decrease, and eventually become zero.

Improvements in Technology Shift Product Curves Upward

In discussing the general shapes of a firm's product curves, we assumed that the state of technology, quality of human resources, and amount of capital equipment remained constant as the firm changed its use of a variable resource. But what happens when these factors change? These factors are *shifters* that cause entire product curves to shift upward or downward.

Recall that technology consists of society's pool of knowledge concerning production in industry and agriculture. An important aspect of technology is that it sets restrictions on the amount and types of goods that can be produced from a given amount of resources: A firm cannot produce more than the existing technology will allow. Referring to Figure 4.1, a technological change that increases productivity *shifts* the whole total product curve and the marginal product curve upward. This means that each worker can produce more output so that diminishing returns are delayed to a higher level of output per worker. In this way, technological improvements can overcome the adverse effects of the law of diminishing returns. As long as technology improves, diminishing returns can be avoided.

In addition to technological improvements, education, training, and capital investment can also induce upward *shifts* in a firm's total product curve and marginal product curve. For example, increased education results in smarter workers, and vocational training provides specific job skills. Moreover, capital investment relieves strains on production capacity and increases output per worker. This is why economists advocate education, training, investment, and research and development as important factors that increase worker productivity and living standards. Let us consider how improvements in technology and work rules have boosted product curves in the fast food and iron ore industries.

New Technologies Make Drive-Through Lanes Faster

The effect of technological improvements on productivity can be seen in fast-food restaurants such as Wendy's, McDonald's, and Burger King. These firms know that every second waiting represents lost business at their drive-through windows, which account for about 65 percent of their sales revenue. Industry analysts estimate that by increasing drive-through productivity by 10 percent, the average fast-food restaurant can increase its sales by $55,000 or more per year.

To beef up speed, fast-food restaurants have implemented new technologies such as windshield transponders that are scanned when the driver passes the menu board; purchases are billed to customers' monthly accounts, thus allowing them to bypass the cash window. Restaurants have also constructed separate kitchens in which meals are prepared for drive-through customers. The griller keeps 25 square burgers sizzling on the grill and, within 5 seconds of a customer's order, puts one on a bun. Once the meat hits the bun, the griller sends it to the sandwich makers, who have no more than 7 seconds to complete each customized creation. To help customers promptly exit the drive-through window, restaurants have developed see-through bags that allow customers to quickly verify that they have received all their items.

One cost of speed, however, can be the low morale among workers, who sometimes complain that they cannot keep pace with the fast service goals of the restaurant. Indeed, demanding productivity increases from drive-through workers, who are paid low wages and have high turnover rates, can be tricky. Perhaps you have encountered these problems when you worked for Wendy's, McDonald's, or Burger King.

Do New Technologies Always Increase Worker Productivity?

Proponents maintain that technological innovations increase worker productivity, reduce production costs, and improve people's standards of living. They note that innovations such as the light bulb and cell phone caused a profound break with previous patterns, resulting in major changes in people's lives. However, do new technologies always increase worker productivity?

New technologies can require time to translate into higher economic productivity as people must figure out how to best use them. For example, the electric motor first appeared in the 1880s, but it did not result in major productivity improvements until the 1920s, when the mass-production assembly line reorganized work around the technology. Also, the first microchip was created in 1958 by an electronics engineer at Texas Instruments Inc., and it was used in Air Force computers and the Minuteman Missile. It took years for microchips to be present in personal computers, smartphones, and other electronic devices we use. Finally, the personal computer revolution began in the 1980s, but it was not until the late 1990s that worker productivity surged as computers became more powerful, cheaper, and connected to the Internet.

The impact of technological advancement on the lives of workers is an area of concern. Consider robotics, which assist in a wide range of manufacturing industries ranging from beverage to automotive to electronics. In automobile manufacturing, robots help human workers assemble vehicles to automate the process and make it more efficient, thus reducing the labor content of a vehicle. While there are many benefits associated with robotics, there are also concerns that robotics and automation may replace human beings in jobs. Workers thus face the challenge of improving their education to become part of this transformation.

Skeptics argue that today's innovations cannot always be expected to have as large an economic impact as those of the past, such as electricity and the internal combustion engine. They also note that some technologies can have adverse side effects that harm productivity. For example, new digital technologies may require people to learn new skills, adapt to new systems, and change their behavior. However, some workers may have difficulty in learning the necessary skills, and others may be slow learners. Also, the development of today's digital technologies can raise security challenges, as viruses, cyberattacks, and other security breaches impose costs on businesses, offsetting some of the technology's productivity-increasing features.

Simply put, our microeconomic model suggests that a technological improvement will cause the total product schedule and marginal product schedule to shift upwards. However, conducting this process can require time, and it may yield adverse side effects that harm productivity.

Artificial Intelligence: Transforming the World

When people hear the term "artificial intelligence," they often think of robots. That may be due to movies that deal with human-like machines that threaten to destroy humanity. But this is not what artificial intelligence represents.

Although there is no universally agreed-upon definition, **artificial intelligence** (AI) is generally described as a set of technologies that makes computers or machines as intelligent as human beings. AI is based on the concept that human intelligence can be expressed so that a machine can copy it and perform tasks, from the simplest to the most complicated. AI thus allows computers and machines to perform a variety of functions, such as the ability to reason, learn, analyze data, make decisions, and more. One of the reasons for the increasing role of AI is the opportunities for increases in productivity and economic development that it presents.

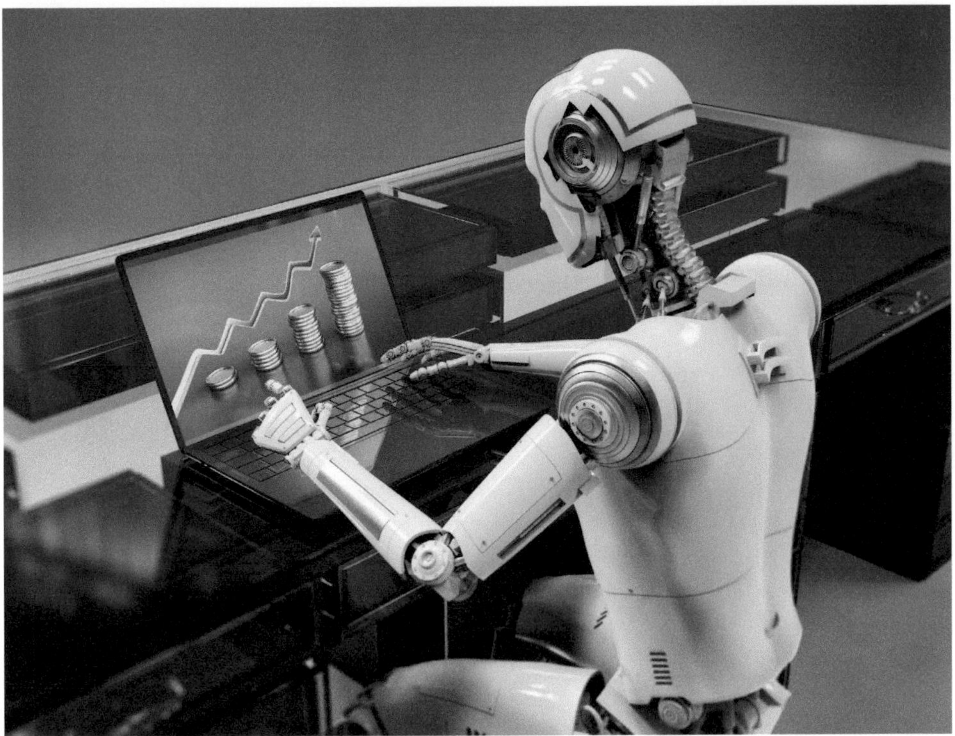

Source: Kateryna Kon/Science Photo Library/Getty Images®

The field of AI dates to the 1940s, when the programmable digital computer was invented, a machine based on mathematical reasoning. This device inspired computer scientists to direct their efforts at building an electronic brain. At a workshop held at Dartmouth College in 1956, those who attended became leaders in AI research for decades, and they were granted millions of dollars to make an intelligent machine. By the early 2000s, AI technologies were transforming every walk of life.

The applications for AI are endless. For example, the technology is used in the banking industry, where it helps a bank process loan applications and determine fraud, such as unusual credit card usage. It is also used in the health care industry for identifying medical treatments and drug dosages, as well as aiding in surgical procedures in the operating room. In the trading of securities, AI makes trading more efficient by matching demand and supply, and making pricing of securities easier. Moreover, AI is used for self-driving automobiles that require a computer to analyze external data so an automobile can operate in a manner that prevents collision. Finally, AI technology helps manufacturing firms like Tesla streamline production operations, improve product quality, reduce repetitive jobs, and decrease unit costs.

Although AI is altering the world, it poses questions for society. Some people fear that machines will become so sophisticated that humans will fall behind. Also, machines may be able to hack into people's privacy and threaten their security. Furthermore, there is apprehension about how AI will affect human employment by creating intelligent machines that make people's skills obsolete and causing them to become unemployed. Finally, AI technology can be very expensive to develop and implement, and it requires sophisticated technical expertise and qualified workers to build and operate AI tools.

Indeed, advances in AI technologies have not only promoted an increase in productivity, but provided new markets and business opportunities. Before the recent wave of AI, it would have been difficult to envision using computer software to link riders to taxis in cities like Boston and San Francisco, but Uber became a pioneer in the transportation industry by doing just that. Moreover, AI has become integral to many successful companies, such as Amazon, Apple, and Microsoft, where AI technologies are used to advance operations and outpace competitors.

SHORT-RUN PRODUCTION COSTS

If you ask managers about the competitiveness of their firms, their answers are likely to bring up costs. Costs are an extension of the production process. To illustrate, assume that General Motors pays its workers $40 an hour and that 30 hours of labor are required to assemble a vehicle. The cost of assembly totals $1,200 per vehicle ($40 × 30 = $1,200). Suppose that improving technology results in a 10-percent increase in labor productivity—only 27 hours of labor are now required to assemble a vehicle. Assembly costs now total $1,080 ($40 × 27 = $1,080) per vehicle. In this manner, higher worker productivity results in lower production costs that can lead to increased profits for General Motors. Higher productivity can also result in increased wages for General Motors workers if they could capture some of the productivity gains as higher wages.

Total Fixed, Total Variable, and Total Costs

Let us consider HP Inc., formerly known as the Hewlett-Packard Company. The firm manufactures computer printers, and it realizes costs in the short run when it employs fixed inputs and variable inputs.

First, we will consider the hypothetical fixed costs of HP. **Total fixed cost** is the sum of all costs that do not vary with output. Managers often refer to fixed costs as *overhead costs.* They include such things as the cost of machinery, lease payments on some equipment, rent on a building, property taxes, and interest payments on a loan. The monthly value of HP's fixed inputs represents its monthly fixed cost. We see in column 2 of Table 4.2 that the firm's total fixed costs are $50. In Figure 4.2(*a*), total fixed cost is shown by the horizontal line at $50. Fixed costs remain constant no matter how many printers are produced.

The production of printers also results in variable costs for HP. **Total variable cost** is the sum of all costs that change as the rate of output varies. They include payments for most labor, materials, storage and warehousing, shipping, electricity, and fuel. As HP produces more printers, more variable inputs are employed, and thus its total variable cost increases. Total variable cost therefore depends on weekly or monthly output. Total variable cost is shown in column 3 of Table 4.2, and it is translated into a total variable cost curve in Figure 4.2(*a*).

TABLE 4.2 Hypothetical Cost Schedules for HP Printers in the Short Run

Quantity Produced per Day	*Total Fixed Cost*	*Total Variable Cost*	*Total Cost*	*Average Fixed Cost*	*Average Variable Cost*	*Average Total Cost*	*Marginal Cost*
0	$50	$0	$50	$–	$–	$–	$–
1	50	80	130	50.00	80.00	130.00	80
2	50	150	200	25.00	75.00	100.00	70
3	50	210	260	16.67	70.00	86.67	60
4	50	260	310	12.50	65.00	77.50	50
5	50	320	370	10.00	64.00	74.00	60
6	50	390	440	8.33	65.00	73.33	70
7	50	470	520	7.14	67.14	74.28	80

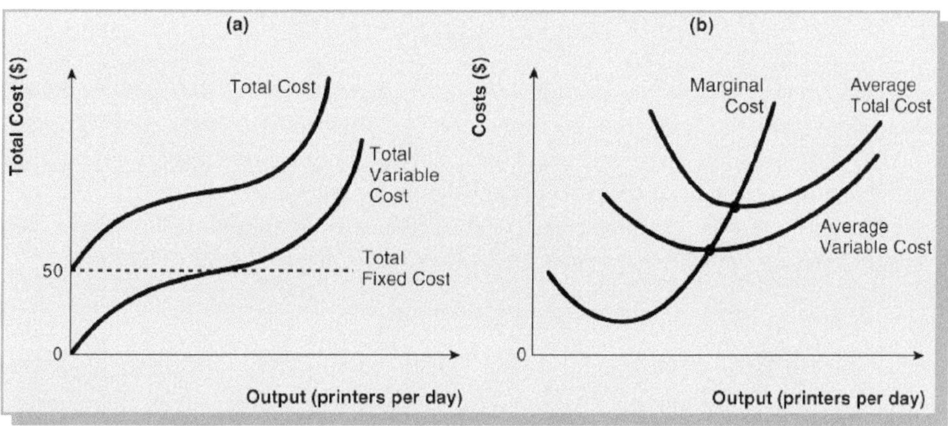

FIGURE 4.2 Short-Run Cost Curves for HP

Total cost includes both fixed and variable costs. Fixed costs must be paid even if no output is produced. Average total cost is the sum of average fixed cost and average variable cost. Marginal cost is the addition to total cost resulting from the production of one additional unit of output.

The rate at which total variable cost rises as more printers are produced depends on the capacity limitations imposed by fixed inputs. In general, total variable cost rises more slowly at low levels of output and then increases ever more rapidly. This aspect of variable costs is attributable to the principle of diminishing marginal productivity in the short run. As diminishing marginal productivity is encountered, each additional worker adds fewer units to the firm's output, yet the firm pays the same wage to each worker. As a result, total variable costs rise faster and faster.

Total cost represents the sum of the value of all resources used over a given period to manufacture computer printers. Thus, total cost is calculated as the sum of total fixed cost and total variable cost:

$$TC = TFC + TVC$$

The total cost of HP is shown in column 4 of Table 4.2, and it is translated into a total cost curve in Figure 4.2(*a*). Notice that total fixed cost is represented by the vertical distance between the total cost curve and the total variable cost curve.

Average Costs

Besides caring about total costs, HP managers care about *per-unit*, or *average*, costs. In the calculation of per-unit profit, average cost data are compared against price, which is always stated on a per-unit basis. **Average fixed cost**, **average variable cost**, and **average total cost** make up the per-unit cost schedules of a firm, as shown in columns 5–7 of Table 4.2.

Let us begin with average fixed cost, or *AFC*, which is the total fixed cost per unit of output. Average fixed cost equals total fixed cost divided by output (Q), or

$$AFC = TFC / Q$$

Because total fixed cost remains the same no matter how many units are produced, average fixed cost steadily declines as output increases. You can see by inspecting column 5 of Table 4.2, average fixed cost decreases continually. To keep Figure 4.2(*b*) as uncluttered as possible, the average fixed cost curve is not shown.

Next, we look at average variable cost, or *AVC*, which is the total variable cost per unit of output. Average variable cost equals total variable cost divided by output, or

$$AVC = TVC / Q$$

Column 6 of Table 4.2 shows the average variable cost of HP, which we translate into an average variable cost curve in Figure 4.2(*b*). According to this schedule, HP's average variable cost first decreases but eventually begins to increase as the firm produces more printers. Because a typical average variable cost schedule is shaped like the letter *U*, economists refer to this curve as U-shaped.

Finally, average total cost, or *ATC*, is the total cost per unit of output. Average total cost equals total cost divided by output, or

$$ATC = TC / Q$$

This can be rewritten as

$$ATC = (TFC / Q + TVC / Q)$$

In other words, average total cost equals average fixed cost plus average variable cost, or

$$ATC = AFC + AVC$$

Marginal Cost

Businesses make decisions "on the margin." When the managers of HP consider a profit-maximization strategy, they are interested in whether the revenue earned from selling an additional printer will more than offset the cost of producing an additional printer. Because marginal means "additional," the managers are interested in **marginal cost**.

Marginal cost (MC) refers to the change in total cost when one more unit of output is produced, or

$$MC = \Delta TC / \Delta Q$$

Marginal cost is easy to calculate: Just measure how much total cost increases as each additional unit of output is produced. Column 8 of Table 4.2 shows the marginal cost of HP printers. As the firm increases output from zero printers to one printer, total cost rises from \$50 to \$130, and thus marginal cost equals \$80. Producing a second printer increases total cost from \$130 to \$200, and thus marginal cost equals \$70, and so on. We translate this marginal cost data into a marginal cost curve in Figure 4.2(*b*). Notice that a firm's marginal cost curve is typically U-shaped: As output expands, marginal cost decreases, eventually reaches a minimum, and then increases.

The law of diminishing returns accounts for the U-shaped marginal cost curve. Recall that in the short run, as additional units of labor are added to machinery, the rate at which total output increases initially tends to rise. Assuming that the firm pays the same wage to workers as output expands, as each additional worker adds more to total output than the previous one, the cost of each additional unit of output decreases. This extra cost is the marginal cost. Therefore, as more units are produced, the marginal cost initially falls. This will not occur indefinitely, however. As more labor is applied to machinery, the marginal productivity of labor will eventually diminish. As a result, the marginal cost of production will increase. The U-shaped nature of the marginal cost curve is thus a reflection of diminishing marginal productivity in the production process.

Shifts In Cost Curves

In discussing the general shapes of a firm's cost curves in both the short run and long run, we assumed that certain other factors—technology, resource prices, and taxes—remained constant as the firm changed its level of output. These factors are *shifters* that cause cost curves to shift upward (downward), suggesting that a given level of output can be produced at a greater (smaller) cost.

- **Technology**. As we have learned, a technological change that increases productivity shifts the total product curve and the marginal product curve upward. Because a better technology allows the same output to be produced with fewer resources, a firm's cost curves *shift downward*. For example, computers and robots reduced the number of labor hours needed to produce automobiles, and printing presses reduced the number of labor hours required to produce books and newspapers, thus resulting in lower costs.
- **Resource prices**. A decrease in the price of resources, such as materials and labor, will reduce the cost of producing each output level. Therefore, a firm's cost curves will *shift downward*. In 1997, for example, the starting price for a personal computer smashed

through the $1,000 barrier as manufacturers lowered the prices of chips used to produce personal computers. Lower-priced chips meant that firms such as Dell and Gateway could produce computers at a lower cost, allowing them to slash their computer prices.

- **Taxes.** Taxes are another component of a firm's costs. Suppose that the federal government reduces the excise tax from 25 cents to 20 cents on each gallon of gasoline sold by service stations. This policy lowers the cost of doing business for a service station, which causes the firm's cost curves to *shift downward*.

BOX ESSAY 4.2
How Much Does It Cost to Drive?

How much does it cost to drive? Let us apply the notion of economic cost to driving. Some of your driving costs depend on the number of miles driven. These costs are the operating (variable) costs, including fuel, maintenance, repair, and tires. Other costs are the ownership (fixed) costs, such as insurance, license, and depreciation.

TABLE 4.3 The Cost of Driving a New Vehicle in 2022 (20,000 miles)

	Medium Sedan	*Subcompact SUV*	*Medium SUV (4 WD)*
Operating Costs Per Mile			
Fuel	12.51¢	15.20¢	18.89¢
Maintenance, repair, tires	8.87¢	9.84¢	10.20¢
Cost per mile	21.38¢	25.04¢	29.09¢
Total operating cost (20,000 miles)	$4,275	$5,008	$5,818
Ownership Costs			
Insurance	$1,618	$1,527	$1,529
License, registration, taxes	$440	$507	$715
Depreciation	$3,702	$4,254	$6,063
Finance charges	$392	$460	$665
Total ownership costs	$6,152	$6,748	$8,972
Total cost	$10,427	$11,756	$14,790
Total cost per mile	52.1¢	58.8¢	73.9¢

Gasoline costs based on $2.77 per gallon of regular gasoline.

Finance charges on a loan at 10 percent down and 6 percent interest for 5 years.

Source: Data drawn from American Automobile Association, *2022—Your Driving Costs: Fact Sheet*, available at https://newsroom.aaa.com/wp-content/uploads/2022/08/2022-YourDrivingCosts-FactSheet-7-1.pdf.

Each year the American Automobile Association (AAA) estimates the cost of driving a new vehicle. The table below shows the AAA estimates for individuals who purchased selected 2022 vehicles and drove 20,000 miles per year. We see that the cost of driving medium sedans averaged 52.1 cents per mile, subcompact SUVs averaged 58.8 cents per mile, and medium SUVs averaged 73.9 cents per mile.

As you read Table 4.3, notice that the costs pertain to variable (operating) costs and fixed (ownership) costs. You should be able to apply these concepts to the production costs that are discussed in this chapter.

CHECK POINT

1 In general, a firm's production may take place in the short-run or the long-run period. Distinguish between these two periods.
2 Distinguish between a firm's total product and its marginal product.
3 As a firm adds more of a variable input to a fixed input in the short run, what happens to the marginal product and the total product? What accounts for this behavior?
4 Classify the following as fixed costs or variable costs per unit of time: wages, rental payments on a factory building, insurance premiums, electricity and water expenses, property taxes, transportation expenses, and advertising expenditures.
5 Why is the marginal cost curve U-shaped?
6 What causes a firm's cost curves to shift upwards or downwards?

COST OF PRODUCTION APPLICATIONS

Minimizing production costs is an important strategy for businesses. We will now learn about how production costs change in response to evolving market forces.

The Cost of Producing an iPhone

Apple Inc. is one of the most popular companies in the world, and it produces a leading smartphone. Founded by Steve Jobs and Steve Wozniak in 1976, Apple is headquartered in Cupertino, CA. Most of the company's iPhones are assembled in China by Taiwanese companies, such as Foxconn.

China provides a plentiful supply of low-wage assembly workers for Apple. In 2022, the average wage for an assembler was about $10 an hour, but wages went up to $27 an hour for the top earners. China also provides a flexible manufacturing site that permits Apple to adjust production in response to changing demand conditions and to make last-minute changes to the iPhone just before it is launched.

However, Apple does not produce the iPhone alone. It relies on many different tech companies to produce components for the iPhone: They are located in Japan, South Korea, China, the United States, and other countries. Some of these tech companies even come from competing smartphone manufacturers like Samsung. Apple must make sure that its components are compatible with other components, as well as the iPhone's operating system.

According to Apple officials, the main reason to produce in China is not because of lower labor costs. If this were the situation, Apple could manufacture iPhones in even cheaper locations like Vietnam or Cambodia. The main reason to produce in China is the skill needed in tooling engineering that is widespread in China, but not in the United States. Also, China has the advantage of housing seven of the world's largest ten ports, which makes it easy to ship goods around the globe. If Apple were to produce the iPhone in the United States, it could only build a small amount a year at a substantially higher cost.

Apple has maintained the largest market share of any smartphone producer, having a market share of 22 percent in 2022, followed by Samsung at 19 percent. Also, Apple has realized large profits by maintaining a sizable markup on its smartphones. Table 4.4 shows the estimated production cost, retail price, and profit margin of Apple and other firms in 2022.

Dell Computer Cuts Costs to Remain Competitive

The personal computer (PC) business has many rags-to-riches stories. One such story is the rollercoaster ride of Dell, which makes laptop computers, desktop computers, and other products.

As a 19-year-old student at the University of Texas, Michael Dell started a computer company in 1984 with capital of $1,000 that was borrowed from his family. Using stock

TABLE 4.4. The Cost of Making Smartphones, 2022*

Smartphone	*Production Cost ($)*	*Retail Price at Launch ($)*	*Profit Margin (percent)*
Apple iPhone 14 Pro Max	501	1,099	54
Apple iPhone 12	373	829	55
Samsung Galaxy S4	244	579	58
Samsung Galaxy Note 3	232	699	67
Google Pixel XL	286	769	63
Google Pixel 6 Pro	486	899	46

* Costs include materials and assembly. They do not include costs of marketing, research and development, distribution, staff, and other costs.

Source: Data drawn from Tuan DO, *The Real Costs of Smartphones*, Techwalls, February 7, 2023, available at https://www.techwalls.com/production-costs-of-smartphones.

components, he assembled computers in his dormitory and sold them to local customers. Upon realizing much success, he dropped out of college to focus full-time on the business.

The first Dell computers were advertised in national magazines and were sold directly to customers to eliminate the middleman, thus making Dell computers less expensive than competing brands. Dell developed an innovative strategy of making computers only after they were ordered. After a customer placed an order through the Web or over the phone, the company's factories assembled the required components, installed PCs with software, and shipped them in a matter of hours. This system allowed Dell to decrease idle inventory and avoid marketing expenses associated with selling through retail channels. What made Dell PCs even more attractive was that customers could configure their PCs when ordering, thus providing customizable options. By the 1990s, Dell's direct-sales model expanded by offering computers via the Internet, where computers could be purchased and paid for online. By 1999, Dell became the largest seller of PCs in the United States.

However, the rise of big-box retailers like Costco and Best Buy eventually posed a growing competitive threat to Dell. Also, Dell's lack of investment in research and development resulted in other brands like Acer and Hewlett-Packard (HP) surpassing Dell in terms of innovation, with more features and better hardware than similar Dell computers. Moreover, Dell's direct-sales model meant that it could not exploit increasing consumer interest in retail computer sales. Finally, Dell fell behind on its ability to compete on price as competitors such as HP and Apple attained cost savings by entering into agreements with other firms to make their PCs in low-wage countries such as China and Malaysia. As computer prices dropped from thousands to hundreds of dollars, Dell was not making as much profit from each sale. By 2006, Dell lost its title of the largest PC manufacturer to rival HP.

Failing to stay attuned to consumer desires after early success, and carrying too much debt, Dell was forced to downsize its operations in 2013 to remain competitive. To cut costs, the company eliminated bonuses, laid off employees, and made fewer products, while concentrating on ones with higher projected profit margins. Things eventually got better for Dell. Today, the company is one of the most popular PC brands in the world, and it is a prominent player in the industry.

Rising Wages Hamper China's Competitiveness

An abundance of cheap labor has long supported the competitiveness of China's business firms. Chinese workers have toiled for a tiny fraction of the cost of their European or American competitors.

However, as China's economy has grown, finding more workers has become harder, especially on the coasts where most of China's factories are located. For example, China's one-child policy has resulted in a decrease in the population of young adults, promoting labor scarcity; this policy was implemented in the 1970s and lasted until 2016. Also, although the country's inland villages house millions of potential workers for its coastal factories, China's land policies and household registration system make it hard to migrate to the cities. Therefore, the supply of cheap factory workers is limited in China's coastal areas.

Also, the average hourly wage rate of Chinese factory workers has more than tripled in the past decade. Chinese factory workers earned about $6 an hour in 2021. This wage rate is several times higher than factory wages in India, Cambodia, and Bangladesh, and China is now on par with countries such as South Africa and Portugal. With Chinese workers becoming more expensive, some firms have been taking their business elsewhere, especially in apparel. This means that China could increasingly lose jobs to other low-wage developing countries. Thus, "Made in China" is no longer as cheap as before, and China will have to rely on labor skills, productivity, technology, and infrastructure as sources of competitiveness.

LONG-RUN PRODUCTION COSTS

So far, we have examined how costs vary in the short run as the rate of output expands for a firm of a given size. In the long run, however, all inputs under the firm's control can be varied: A firm has sufficient time to replace machinery and increase the size of a factory. Because no inputs are fixed in the long run, there are no fixed costs. Therefore, all costs are variable in the long run. In this section, we will examine how altering factory size, and all other inputs, influences the relationship between production and costs in the long run.

A useful way to look at the long run is to regard it as a planning horizon. When operating in today's market, HP must plan and determine its strategy for the long run. For example, even before HP decides to manufacture a new type of computer printer, the firm is in a long-run situation because it can choose from a variety of types and sizes of equipment

Source: Monty Rakusen/DigitalVision/Getty Images®

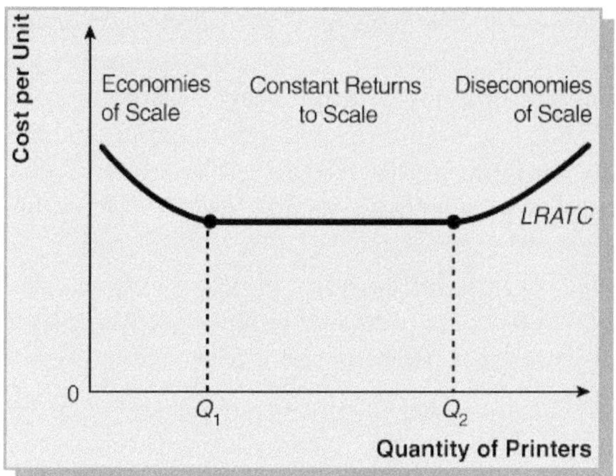

FIGURE 4.3 Long-Run Average Total Cost Curve for HP

The long-run average total cost curve shows the minimum cost per unit of producing each output level when any desired size of factory can be constructed. The long-run average cost curve above is U-shaped, reflecting economies of scale in the decreasing portion and diseconomies of scale in the increasing portion. The curve also has a flat bottom as a result of an extended stage of constant returns to scale after economies of scale are exhausted.

to manufacture the printer. Once HP makes this decision, it is in a short-run situation because the type and size of the equipment that it owns are, for the most part, frozen.

The **long-run average total cost curve** (*LRATC*) shows the minimum cost per unit of producing each output level when any desired size of factory can be constructed; this means that the firm can adjust its scale of operation (production capacity) in the long run. Figure 4.3 shows a hypothetical *LRATC* curve of HP. Notice that this curve typically decreases with increases in output up to a certain point, reaches a minimum, and then increases with further increases in output. This U-shaped appearance of the *LRATC* curve is determined by economies of scale and diseconomies of scale, which exist simultaneously at many different levels of output.

Economies of Scale

When a firm realizes **economies of scale**, the *LRATC* curve slopes downward: An increase in scale and production results in a decline in cost per unit. Economies of scale can result from the following factors:

- **Specialization of labor and management**. As a firm becomes larger, it may be able to benefit from greater specialization of labor and management. At Pizza Hut, for example, some workers specialize in taking orders, others make pizza, and others wash dishes.
- **Efficient capital**. Smaller firms may not be able to acquire large, specialized machinery. For example, Walmart employs sophisticated computer systems to track inventories and provide sales information to management.

- **Design and development**. The next time you purchase printed textbooks, compare the prices of a 2-semester introductory text and a 1-semester advanced text. To your surprise, you may find that the principles text does not cost much more than the advanced text. This is true even if the principles text has 250 more pages and is produced in a multicolor format compared to a black-and-white format for the advanced text. Economies of scale are present in this situation. Publishing introductory and advanced texts requires costs for development and advertising that are approximately the same per page. For introductory texts, these costs are distributed over large levels of output—say, 50,000 copies, compared to only 10,000 copies for an advanced text. This results in a lower cost per copy and a relatively lower price per copy for the introductory text.

When you use a prescription drug you also benefit from the principle of decreasing long-run average cost. It costs about $985 million to bring a typical new prescription drug to the market.[1] And that's just for the first pill. Making the second pill costs about a penny. Assuming $985 million in research and development costs and a 1-cent marginal production cost thereafter, the average total cost falls from about $985 million to produce 1 pill to $9,850 to make 100,000 pills, to $9.85 to make 100,000,000 pills. Therefore, the price per pill declines as the research and development cost ($985 million) is spread over a larger number of pills produced by pharmaceutical companies, as shown in Table 4.5.

Automatic teller machines (ATMs) provide another example of economies of scale. Located in banks, gas stations, convenience stores, and shopping malls, ATMs dispense cash, accept deposits, and transfer funds between accounts. Although buying and installing an ATM is expensive, a single machine is very productive and can perform hundreds of transactions per day. The average cost per transaction declines considerably as the purchase and setup cost is spread over a large volume of transactions. The cost per transaction is estimated to be about one-fourth the cost of a human teller at a bank. As a result, many banks have replaced tellers with lower-cost ATMs.

For example, the average total cost of a banking transaction is about $1.07 for a teller and 27 cents for an ATM. Given these costs, why don't small banks and credit unions lay

TABLE 4.5 Average Total Cost of a Prescription Drug

Quantity of Pills	*Average Total Cost (dollars)*
1	985,000,000
100	9,850,000
10,000	98,500
100,000	9,850
1,000,000	985
100,000,000	9.85

off their tellers and install ATMs? The reason is scale. Realizing the cost advantages of an ATM requires a large number of transactions, which small banks and credit unions do not have. Because of their relatively small scale, these financial institutions achieve their least-cost method of serving customers by employing tellers rather than ATMs. Simply put, the least-cost method is not necessarily the one that uses the most advanced technology.

From Mass Production to Lean Production

Henry Ford (1863–1947) was a noted pioneer of American industry. In 1903, Ford organized the Ford Motor Co. At first, the company manufactured only expensive automobiles, just as its competitors did. However, Ford came from modest, rural roots. He thought that the people who built cars ought to be able to afford one so that they too could go for a spin on a Sunday afternoon. Ford soon began developing a simple, sturdy vehicle that many people could afford. This car became known as the Model T, which appeared in 1908.

Ford maintained that if he paid his factory workers a living wage and produced more cars in less time for less money, everyone would buy them. To make his Model T affordable, Ford paid his workers $5 a day, double the industry standard. However, he was criticized for his generous pay scale: *The New York Times* dismissed Ford as being "distinctly utopian," and *The Wall Street Journal* accused him of employing "spiritual principles" where they do not belong.

In producing the Model T, Ford realized the importance of economies of mass production. He pioneered assembly-line methods to slash the costs of producing automobiles. In 1908, the Model T sold for $850, which was not cheap in those days. In 1913, Ford installed moving assembly lines in his factories. The frame of the car moved through the plant on a conveyor belt. Workers on each side assembled the car by adding parts that had been brought to them by other conveyor belts. In 1914, Ford workers could assemble a Model T in little more than 1½ hours.

Building the earlier Model T had taken about 12½ hours. The large savings slashed Ford's production costs. In 1916, the Model T could be sold at a profit for $400, the lowest price of any automobile. Not surprisingly, by 1921, Ford's Model T, which remained largely unchanged for 19 years, had more than 50 percent of the market. It was at this time that Ford made his famous announcement that "Any customer can have a car painted any color that he wants so long as it is black." Indeed, standardization, specialization, and mass production were the keys to Ford's low manufacturing costs, and constant price reduction was the key to attracting additional customers.

By the 1970s, however, U.S. auto manufacturers were challenged by lower costs and higher-quality products from foreign firms. Japanese manufacturers such as Toyota changed the rules of production from mass production to lean production. Toyota realized that it could not catch up to Ford and General Motors by using traditional mass production methods. Instead, Toyota adopted "lean manufacturing," which places greater emphasis on flexibility and product quality.

Instead of mass-producing large numbers of identical vehicles, Toyota produces batches of similar vehicles. Toyota's goal is to have parts arrive just as they are needed, and these parts can be used interchangeably in its various models. This has allowed Toyota to manufacture higher-quality vehicles at lower costs and to introduce new models quickly. Toyota's success with lean manufacturing has placed great pressure on American auto firms to improve their manufacturing operations in order to compete in the global auto industry.

Diseconomies of Scale

Economics of scale are only part of the story. If they were the entire story, the question would then have to be asked: Why not manufacture automobiles in even larger enterprises? If Ford and General Motors merged, wouldn't they be able to manufacture autos more cheaply and thus realize additional profit per auto than if they produced them separately? Likely not. As a firm gets larger, the opportunities to realize economies of scale are eventually exhausted. As a firm grows, it is likely to encounter **diseconomies of scale**, which cause unit cost to increase and the *LRATC* curve to turn upward.

We can trace diseconomies of scale to the problems of managing large-scale operations. Beyond some scale of operation, the daily production routine becomes removed from the firm's top executives as additional layers of bureaucracy are added to the management team. The paperwork burden grows, and managers must control many business activities—finance, transportation, accounting, sales, research and development, personnel, and so on. The red tape and bureaucratic problems of running a large-scale operation contribute to inefficiencies and increased cost per unit.

Although Ford Motor Company benefits from economies of scale, its large size also poses problems. For example, during the 1970s, Ford constructed a factory in Flat Rock, Michigan, to manufacture blocks for 8-cylinder engines. Ford followed the principle that large-scale production brings lower costs per unit of output. The firm spent $200 million to build a 4-story factory designed exclusively to manufacture engine blocks in the fastest, most efficient way possible. By 1981, however, Ford had shut down the factory and shifted production to a much older plant in Cleveland. The reason? The Flat Rock plant was too big and inflexible. It had been constructed to make engines at very large volumes, but it could not be converted to produce the 4- and 6-cylinder engines that became popular as gasoline prices rose. In effect, the Flat Rock plant was viewed as an inefficient dinosaur that could not keep pace with the rapidly changing economy.

There may also be an intervening range of output over which a firm realizes **constant returns to scale**. This occurs when a firm's output changes by the same percentage as the change in all inputs. For example, a 20-percent increase in all inputs causes a 20-percent increase in the firm's output. As a result, the cost per unit remains constant, and the *LRATC* curve is horizontal. This situation is consistent with many U.S. industries. For example, over an intermediate size range, smaller firms can be as efficient as larger ones in such industries as publishing, shoes, lumber, and apparel.

Economies of Scope Cut Costs for Producers

Besides benefitting from economies of scale that reduce long-run average total cost, a firm can benefit from economies of scope. **Economies of scope** are cost savings gained by producing two or more distinct products, when the production cost is less than the cost of producing each good separately. Therefore, economies of scope result from product variety.

A train illustrates the concept of economies of scope. A single train can transport both freight and passengers more cheaply than two separate trains, one only for freight and the other for passengers. In this situation, the single train that has separate cars dedicated to freight and passengers is less costly, and it may lead to lower tonnage or ticket costs for the train's customers.

The production of computers provides another example of economies of scope. Suppose that Toshiba Corporation wishes to expand its product line, and it remodels its manufacturing building to make a variety of personal computers, including desktops, laptops, and tablets. By spreading the cost of operating the building across several computers, the average total cost of production declines. Therefore, the cost of producing each computer in separate buildings would be larger than the cost of using a single building to produce a variety of computers.

In the aerospace industry, The Boeing Company is the only producer of large commercial jetliners in the United States. The company also makes other products, such as military aircraft and rockets for space travel. Because of economies of scope, Boeing can produce some of its of aerospace products at a lower cost than producing each product separately.

For example, Boeing can spread some of its research and development costs over commercial and military jets, thus decreasing the average total costs of each. Also, some inputs can be reused by other products without being redesigned, thus lowering development costs. Moreover, different variants of the company's leading commercial jet, the 737, go down the same assembly line, thus reducing capital expenditures. However, they require many specialized tools for each variant.

Because productive inputs, such as labor and capital, often have more than one use, economies of scope may come from common inputs that are used in the production of a variety of goods. For example, The Procter and Gamble Company makes hundreds of household items, ranging from Tide laundry detergent to Crest toothpaste. Many of the same inputs that go into making one product, such as labor and capital, are also used to produce another. This means that the company can employ marketing experts and graphic designers, for example, who use their talents across many of the company's product lines. Each extra product that they work on reduces the average total cost because of economies of scope.

Bath & Body Works, Economies of Scope, and Reshoring

Bringing production closer to home is known as "reshoring," and it has recently become a priority for many American companies. Supply-chain disruptions from Covid-19, trade wars between China and the United States, geopolitical tensions with Russia and China, and stuck ships at ports have often left American consumers without products they desire. The solution: Relocate production close to your American market. Let us consider the case of Bath & Body Works, LLC.

Bath & Body Works (BBW) is an American retail store chain that makes and sells soaps, lotions, fragrances, and candles. Founded in New Albany, Ohio, in 1990, BBW has since expanded across six continents, and it has become the largest bath shop chain in America. With a predominately U.S. supply chain, BBW sells its products through company-owned stores, franchises, and digital channels.

As a young company, BBW primarily relied on a global supply chain for its products. For example, a bottle of the company's foaming hand soap used to take three months to produce as its components had to travel some 13,000 miles from suppliers in China, Canada, and Virginia to the company's Ohio distribution center. But BBW needed to get its products to American consumers faster.

So, in 2008 BBW started persuading skeptical companies throughout its supply chain to move production facilities from China and other developing countries to BBW's manufacturing campus in Columbus, Ohio. Because land, labor, and compliance with zoning and environmental laws cost more in Columbus than in China, BBW sweetened its offer by providing production volume guarantees for a set number of years. In turn, the supplying companies offset higher American labor costs by investing in increasing automation in their Columbus factories.

Concerning the production of foaming hand soap at the Columbus manufacturing campus, one factory produces the foaming pump device, another produces the bottle, a third produces the label, and a fourth produces the soap, fills the bottle, fastens the label, and attaches the lid. A fifth puts the bottles into packages. Getting a bottle of foaming soap to distribution only requires 21 days and a few miles, rather than 3 months and 13,000 miles. Most of BBW's products are now made on the Columbus site.

By producing a variety of products, BBW has been able to reduce the average total cost of its production. This is known as economies of scope, and it means it is cheaper for, say, two products to share the same resource inputs than for each of them to have separate inputs. With BBW's suppliers located together, they can share raw materials and employees to make hand sanitizer and other popular products. Also, locating corporate executives just a short drive away from manufacturing plants allows problems to be solved and new products to be developed quickly.

For example, the firm uses a campus transportation service to quickly send product samples in the next production stage or to a company executive for approval, no overnight transportation needed. BBW can thus churn out about 7,000 new scented products a year as new products are launched every four to six weeks.

In an environment where global supply chain issues have been a problem for many retailers, BBW has avoided many of them by decreasing dependence on foreign suppliers and shippers. Also, the streamlined production model allows the firm to take advantages of economies of scope and quickly react to sudden changes in market conditions.[2]

COSTS AND PROFIT

An essential characteristic of the cost schedules we have observed is that they include the market value of all the resources used in the production process: Land, labor, capital, and entrepreneurship. To calculate this cost, we simply identify all the resources used in production, determine their value, and then add things up.

Explicit Costs and Implicit Costs

Economists define the total cost of production as the sum of explicit costs and implicit costs. **Explicit costs** are payments made to others as a cost of running a business. For a local

Pizza Hut franchise, explicit costs would include wages paid to labor, the cost of materials and electricity, telephone and advertising expenses, rental charges for the restaurant, health insurance for employees, and the like.

Implicit costs are the costs that represent the value of resources used in production for which no monetary payment is made. For Pizza Hut, implicit costs might include the forgone salary of the restaurant owner who uses their time to run the business. It might also include forgone interest because the owner invests their funds in the firm rather than depositing them into a savings account. If the owner uses their own building to house the restaurant, they also sacrifice rent that they could receive from other tenants. With implicit costs, no money changes hands. They represent the imputed value that the firm's resources could command in their best alternative uses.

Accounting Profit and Economic Profit

Consider now what the term **profit** means. Most people think of profit as the difference between the amount of revenues a firm takes in (total revenue) and the amount it spends for wages, materials, electricity, and so on (total cost). If costs are greater than revenues, we call such "negative profits" **losses**. Although this description seems clear enough, accountants and economists have different views concerning the types of costs that should be included in total cost. As a result, they have different notions of profit.

To an accountant, the following formula describes profit:

$$\text{Accounting profit} = \text{Total revenue} - \text{Explicit costs}$$

We know this definition of profit as **accounting profit**. When preparing financial reports, accountants are concerned only with costs that are payable to others, such as wages, materials, and interest.

Besides caring about explicit costs, economists are interested in a firm's implicit costs, such as forgone salary, rent, and interest. **Economic profit** is total revenue minus the sum of explicit and implicit costs:

$$\text{Economic profit} = \text{Total revenue} - (\text{Explicit costs} + \text{Implicit costs})$$

Economists thus subtract the full cost of all resources from revenues in order to obtain a definition of profit.

Because accounting practice does not recognize the implicit costs of owner-supplied inputs, accounting costs, as we've discussed, *underestimate* economic costs. As a result, accounting profits based on accounting costs *overestimate* profits by underestimating costs. What does zero economic profit imply? In economics, a firm that makes zero economic profit is said to be earning a **normal profit**. It represents the minimum profit necessary to keep a firm in operation. In other words, normal profit occurs when total revenue just covers explicit costs and implicit costs.

Should the owner of a company worry if it has made only a normal profit for the past year? The answer is no. Although a normal profit may appear unattractive, the owner has realized total revenues sufficient to cover both explicit and implicit costs. If, for example, the owner's implicit cost is the forgone salary of $50,000 for managing the business of someone else, then realizing a normal profit suggests that they have done as well as they could have in their next-best line of employment.

This chapter has considered the role of productivity and costs of production in influencing business decisions. In the next chapter, we will learn how a firm goes about maximizing economic profit. We will consider how a firm maximizes profits in a competitive market and under a monopoly.

CHECK POINT

1. How do economies of scale and diseconomies of scale relate to a firm's long-run average total cost curve?
2. How do economies of scope differ from economies of scale?
3. Distinguish between explicit costs and implicit costs.
4. Why does the calculation of profit differ for an accountant as opposed to an economist?
5. Why do economists regard normal profit as a cost?

CHAPTER SUMMARY

1. In general, a firm's production may take place in the short run or the long run. The short run is a period during which the quantity of at least one input is fixed and the quantities of other inputs can be varied. The long run is a period during which all inputs are considered to be variable in amount.
2. The relationship between physical output and the quantity of resources used in the production process is called a production function. A production function shows the maximum amount of output that can be produced with a given amount of resources.
3. According to the law of diminishing marginal returns, as a firm adds more of a variable input to a fixed input, beyond some point the marginal productivity of the variable input diminishes.
4. A firm that produces goods in the short run employs fixed inputs and variable inputs. Fixed costs are payments to fixed inputs, and they do not vary with output. Variable costs are payments to variable inputs, and they increase as output expands.
5. We can describe a firm's costs in terms of a total approach: Total fixed cost, total variable cost, and total cost. We can also describe them in terms of a per-unit approach: Average fixed cost, average variable cost, and average total cost.
6. Marginal cost refers to the change in total cost when another unit of output is produced. The short-run marginal cost curve is generally U-shaped, reflecting the law of diminishing marginal returns.
7. The long-run average total cost curve shows the minimum cost per unit of producing each output level when any size of factory can be constructed. Economies of scale and diseconomies of scale account for the U-shaped appearance of this cost curve.

8 In discussing the general shapes of a firm's cost curves in the short and long run, we assume that technology, resource prices, and taxes remain constant as the firm changes its level of output. Changes in any of these factors will cause a firm's cost curves to shift upward or downward.

9 Economists define the total costs of production as the sum of explicit costs and implicit costs.

10 According to accounting principles, profit equals total revenue minus explicit costs. Besides caring about explicit costs, economists are interested in a firm's implicit costs. Economic profit thus equals total revenue minus the sum of explicit costs and implicit costs.

11 A firm that makes zero economic profit is said to earn a normal profit. It represents the minimum profit necessary to keep a firm in operation. In other words, the firm earns just enough revenue to cover its explicit costs and implicit costs.

KEY TERMS AND CONCEPTS

short run
fixed input
variable inputs
long run
production
production function
total product
marginal product
law of diminishing marginal returns
increasing marginal returns
diminishing marginal returns
total fixed cost
total variable cost
total cost
average fixed cost
average variable cost
average total cost
marginal cost
long-run average total cost curve
economies of scale
diseconomies of scale
constant returns to scale
economies of scope
explicit cost
implicit cost
profit
losses
accounting profit
economic profit
normal profit

STUDY QUESTIONS AND PROBLEMS

1 As the manager of a restaurant, you estimate the total product of labor used to cook meals, as shown in Table 4.6. Use these data to calculate the marginal product of labor.

  a In a diagram, plot the total product and marginal product schedules.
  b What effect does the law of diminishing marginal returns have on these schedules?
  c What underlies the law of diminishing marginal returns?

TABLE 4.6 Productivity Data

Quantity of Labor	*Total Product*	*Marginal Product*
0	0	
1	20	
2	45	
3	65	
4	80	
5	90	

2 Taylor & Francis has maintained data on the labor input and production of economics textbooks, as seen in Table 4.7.

a Use these data to calculate the marginal product for each quantity of labor hired. Assume that when no workers are hired, output is zero.

b Using two figures, plot the total product curve and the marginal product curve.

c Identify the number of workers hired when total product is at a maximum.

d At which level of employment does the law of diminishing marginal returns begin?

TABLE 4.7 Producing Textbooks

Labor Input (workers)	3	5	1	2	4	6	7
Output of Textbooks (total product)	380	600	100	220	520	620	580

3 Hanson Electronics Co. has fixed costs of $2,000 and variable costs as shown in Table 4.8. Complete the table.

a In a graph, plot total fixed cost, total variable cost, and total cost. Explain the shapes of these curves in relation to one another.

b In another graph, plot average fixed cost, average variable cost, average total cost, and marginal cost. Explain the shapes of these curves in relation to one another.

c How does the law of diminishing marginal returns explain the shape of the marginal cost curve?

TABLE 4.8 Hanson Electric Company's Cost of Production (in dollars)

Output	*Total Variable Cost*	*Total Cost*	*Average Fixed Cost*	*Average Variable Cost*	*Average Total Cost*	*Marginal Cost*
1	$1,000					
2	1,600					
3	2,000					
4	2,600					
5	3,400					
6	4,800					

4 Wassink Instruments has compiled output and cost data, shown in Table 4.9, on its production of microscopes. Use these data to compute total fixed cost, total variable cost, average fixed cost, average variable cost, average total cost, and marginal cost for each output level shown.

TABLE 4.9 Cost Data for Microscopes

Output	*Total Cost*
0	$400
1	700
2	900
3	1,000
4	1,200
5	1,500
6	1,900

5 Your dry-cleaning firm currently cleans 300 shirts per day. Fixed costs for the firm are $400 per day. Variable costs are $1 per shirt. Calculate the total cost and the average total cost at the existing output level. Calculate the average fixed cost. What price would your firm have to charge in order to realize a normal profit at the current level of output?

6 Your shoe manufacturing company estimates that whenever it triples machinery, labor, and any other inputs in the long run, its output also triples. Assuming that input prices remain constant as your firm expands, construct the firm's long-run average total cost curve.

7 Some people are concerned about the decline of the small family farms and their replacement by large corporate farms. Explain how economies of scale might be a cause of this trend.

8 As a result of increasing student population at the University of Wisconsin the nearby Pizza Hut restaurant is realizing record sales. It is considering adding a new oven to bake additional pizzas. However, the daytime supervisor recommends simply employing more workers. How should the manager decide which course of action to take?

9 How will rising steel prices affect the average total cost curve and marginal cost curve of ABC Construction Inc., a builder of skyscrapers?

10 The introduction of the personal computer has decreased the number of hours required to type and edit a manuscript. How has this improvement in technology affected the average total cost curve and marginal cost curve of a publishing company?

NOTES

1 Oliver Wouters, Martin McKee, and Jeroen Luvten, "Estimated Research and Development Investment Needed to Bring a New Medicine to Market, 2008–2018," *Journal of the American Medical Association* (JAMA), March 3, 2020, pp. 844–853.

2 Austen Hufford, "A Soap Maker Cracks the Code to Made in America," *The Wall Street Journal*, July 25, 2023; West Coast Fundamentals, *Why I See Long-Term Upside for Bath & Body Works*, June 18, 2022, available at https://seekingalpha.com/article/4519088-bath-and-body-works-long-term-upside.

CHAPTER 5

Competition and Monopoly: Virtues and Vices

CHAPTER OBJECTIVES

After reading this chapter, you should be able to:

1. Explain the nature and operation of a perfectly competitive firm.
2. Explain how a perfectly competitive firm achieves economic efficiency in the long run.
3. Identify factors that contribute to monopoly.
4. Describe how a monopoly goes about maximizing profits.
5. Assess the advantages and disadvantages of a perfectly competitive firm and a monopoly.

DOI: 10.4324/9781003438571-7

ECONOMICS IN CONTEXT

The aircraft carrier has been dubbed "97,000 tons of diplomacy." But in the early 2000s, the U.S. Navy was being anything but diplomatic in its sharp criticism of Newport News Shipbuilding Inc. Newport News, whose sprawling shipyard has hugged the James River in southern Virginia since it turned out its first tugboat in 1891, has long been the government's only producer of aircraft carriers. Navy officials have expressed frustration with the company's failure to deliver promised cost savings.

The situation, Navy officials maintained, highlights what occurs in the absence of healthy competition. As a single producer, Newport News does not have to worry about staying ahead of its rivals to earn profits. Therefore, it lacks an incentive to organize production to minimize costs. Excess costs can result from the ineffective supervision of employees, the use of outdated equipment, the payment of large bonuses to management, and the like.

However, the situation cannot easily be remedied because the nature of the work that goes into building nuclear-powered warships makes it virtually impossible for a competitor to emerge. A typical carrier takes five years to build, stands 20 stories high including its tower, and carries more than 80 heavy fighter jets on a deck that covers 4½ acres. The investment outlay required to construct another shipyard would be mammoth, a fact that discourages others from building a shipyard to compete against Newport News. Indeed, the Navy faced a difficult problem: How to pressure Newport News into making carriers at a reasonable cost when no alternative supplier exists.

Millions of businesses operate in the U.S. economy; each behaves differently in terms of its control over product price, the types of non-price policies it uses, and its ability to realize the necessary profit to remain in business over time. Some firms have substantial control over product price, whereas others have little or no price-making ability. Some firms spend millions of dollars on product development or advertising, while others spend only negligible amounts on these activities. Some firms realize large economic profits over the long run while others, no matter how well they are managed, have no such potential.

The degree of competition in a market determines a firm's ability to control the price it charges for its product and its potential to realize continuing economic profits. As we will see, as market competition *increases*, a firm has less control over product price and is *less* likely to earn continuing economic profits.

Economists have formulated four market classifications to illustrate different competitive situations: Perfect competition, monopolistic competition, oligopoly, and monopoly. With perfect competition, competition is strongest; in contrast, competition is nonexistent in a pure monopoly. In the middle is monopolistic competition, which is closer to perfect competition, and oligopoly, which is closer to monopoly.

In this chapter, we will examine the virtues and vices of perfect competition and monopoly. The next chapter will consider monopolistic competition and oligopoly.

PERFECT COMPETITION

Let us begin with **perfect competition**, the most competitive market structure. New firms can enter a market if it appears profitable or exit if they expect losses. For example, lawn maintenance is an easy market to enter. To enter the market, one needs only a lawnmower, an edger, and perhaps an ad in the local newspaper. A perfectly competitive market is characterized by the following:

- **Many sellers and buyers**. Each firm sells or purchases only a negligible share of the total amount exchanged in the market.
- **A standardized product produced by firms in the industry**. For example, the wheat grown by one farmer is identical to the wheat grown by another farmer. As a result, brand preferences and consumer loyalty are nonexistent.
- **Perfect information**. All sellers and buyers are fully aware of market opportunities. That is, they know everything that relates to buying, producing, and selling the product.

Perfect competition is rare in the United States because most markets do not fulfill all of these assumptions. The usefulness of this market structure is that it serves as an important ideal against which real-world markets can be judged. Some markets, however, come close to fulfilling the assumptions of perfect competition and thus provide an approximation that is characterized by ease of entry and exit. Examples include agriculture, the

Source: Pencho Chukov/Moment/Getty Images®

fishing industries, stock markets (such as the New York Stock Exchange), and the foreign exchange market.

THE PERFECTLY COMPETITIVE FIRM AS A PRICE TAKER

In a perfectly competitive market, each seller or buyer is small relative to the size of the market, and so its decision to supply or purchase a particular quantity of a product does not affect the market price. A perfectly competitive firm is called a **price taker** because it must "take," or accept, the price that is established by the market.

Figure 5.1 illustrates the hypothetical case of Puget Sound Fishing Co., which operates in a perfectly competitive market. In Figure 5.1(*a*) the market price of fish is $7 per pound, as determined by the intersection of the market demand curve and the market supply curve. Once the market price is established, Puget Sound Fishing Co. can sell all the fish it wants to at that price because it supplies an insignificant share of the market output. In Figure 5.1(*b*), the demand curve, as it appears to Puget Sound Fishing Co., is drawn as a *horizontal line* at the market price. This demand curve is also a *price line* for the firm. Note that the firm's output is much smaller than the market output. For example, hundreds of fishing firms might operate in the market, producing a combined output many times greater than that supplied by Puget Sound Fishing Co.

Why won't Puget Sound Fishing Co. raise its price above $7? The reason is that in a perfectly competitive market, many other firms are also selling fish at $7 per pound. If Puget Sound Fishing Co. set its price above $7, it would sell no fish. Conversely, the firm will not set its price below $7 because it can sell all the fish it wants to at the market price; thus, a lower price would decrease its revenue.

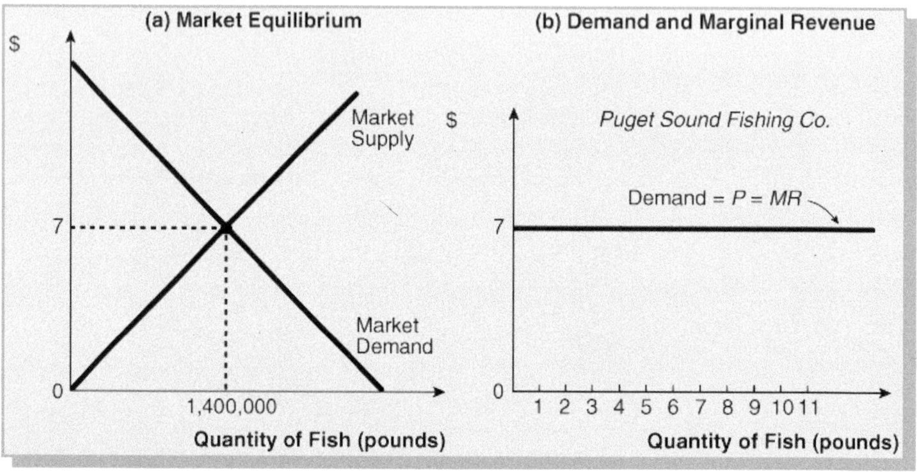

FIGURE 5.1 Demand and Marginal Revenue of a Perfectly Competitive Firm

As a price taker, Puget Sound Fishing Co. sells additional units of output at a price that is determined by the market. The firm's demand schedule appears horizontal and coincides with its marginal revenue schedule.

For a perfectly competitive firm, **total revenue** (*TR*) is simply the price per unit (*P*, $7 in this example) multiplied by the output level (Q), or $TR = P \times Q$. The rate of increase in total revenue is especially important. It represents the increase in total revenue resulting from the sale of another unit of output. We call this rate of increase **marginal revenue** (*MR*). Mathematically, this is expressed as $MR= \Delta\ TR/\Delta Q$.

For Puget Sound Fishing Co., total revenue is zero when no fish are sold. The sale of the first pound of fish increases total revenue from zero to $7 ($7 × 1 = $7), so the marginal revenue is $7. The second pound increases total revenue from $7 to $14, so the marginal revenue is again $7. Marginal revenue is therefore a constant, $7, because total revenue increases by this fixed amount as each additional pound of fish is sold.

What is the relationship between price and marginal revenue for a perfectly competitive firm? In Figure 5.1(*b*), we see that, as a price taker, Puget Sound Fishing Co. sells fish at a constant price of $7 per pound. We also see that the firm's marginal revenue equals $7 for each pound sold. Therefore, in perfect competition, price (*P*) equals marginal revenue, or $P = MR$.

PERFECT COMPETITION: PROFIT MAXIMIZATION IN THE SHORT RUN

We have just learned about the demand and revenue schedules of a perfectly competitive firm. The next step is to combine information about the firm's revenues and costs to find the output that will maximize profits in the short run.

Marginal Revenue Equals Marginal Cost Rule

Recall that *MR* represents the addition to total revenue from the sale of another unit of output, and marginal cost (*MC*) represents the addition to total cost of producing another unit of output. If *MR* exceeds *MC*, total revenue will increase more than total cost as output rises. Because total profit is the difference between total revenue and total cost, the production of additional units that add more to total revenue than to total cost will increase total profit. Conversely, if *MC* exceeds *MR*, decreasing output will result in increased total profit. Profit maximization thus occurs at that output where $MR = MC$. In economic jargon, this is the **marginal revenue = marginal cost rule**: Total profit is maximized when marginal revenue is equal to marginal cost. This rule applies to all firms, whether they operate in perfectly competitive markets, monopolistic markets, oligopolistic markets, or monopolistically competitive markets.

With perfect competition, the $MR = MC$ rule can be modified. Because price and marginal revenue are identical for a perfectly competitive firm, profit maximization occurs at that output where price equals marginal cost, or $P = MC$. This is simply a special case of the $MR = MC$ rule.

Perhaps you can benefit from the price = marginal cost rule the next time you purchase an automobile. Auto dealers want to get a price that at least covers all of their costs, including both variable costs and fixed costs. They might, however, be willing to sell you an automobile for only its marginal cost—that is, the wholesale price that they paid for it plus a little labor for dealer preparation of the vehicle. If the price exceeds the marginal cost, the dealer will add to total profit by selling the vehicle. If you are a skilled bargainer, you may be able to buy an auto at a price that is less than the average total cost.

Profit Maximization

Figure 5.2 shows the revenue and cost curves of Puget Sound Fishing Co., which operates in a perfectly competitive market. As expected, the average total cost curve and marginal cost curve are U-shaped. The demand curve is horizontal, which means that price equals marginal revenue at all levels of output.

In Figure 5.2, Puget Sound Fishing Co. maximizes total profits by selling 2,500 pounds of fish, where $MR = MC$. The firm's price equals \$7 per pound and its total revenue equals \$17,500 (\$7 × 2,500 = \$17,500). Because the average total cost for 2,500 pounds of fish equals \$6 per pound, the total cost for all 2,500 pounds is \$15,000 (\$6 × 2,500 = \$15,000). The firm's total profit is \$2,500 (\$17,500 – \$15,000 = \$2,500). This amount is denoted by the shaded area in the figure.

An alternate way to calculate total profit is to multiply *profit per unit* by output. Profit per unit equals price minus average total cost ($P - ATC$). In Figure 5.2, at the profit-maximizing output of 2,500 pounds, the price is \$7 and the average total cost is \$6. Profit per unit thus equals \$1 (\$7 – \$6 = \$1). Multiplying this amount by 2,500 pounds gives us a total profit of \$2,500.

Notice that Puget Sound Fishing Co. does not attempt to maximize profit per unit, the point at which price exceeds average total cost by the greatest amount. What matters is *total* profit, not the amount of profit per unit. This is the age-old problem of selling, say, cookies at a school fund-raiser. Perhaps you can maximize profit per unit by selling one box for \$5, but you would make more total profit if you sold 100 boxes at a per-unit profit

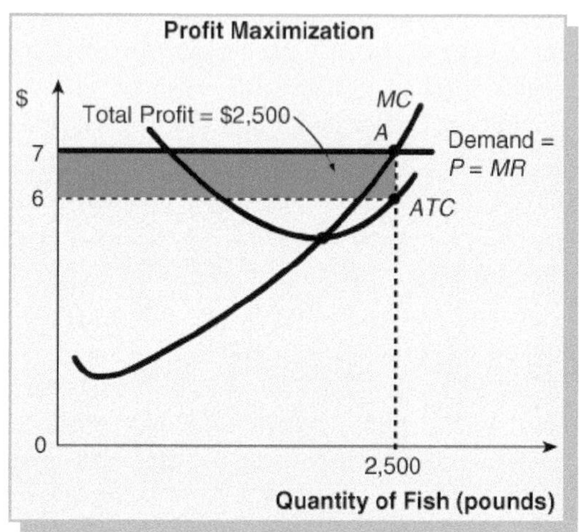

FIGURE 5.2 Profit Maximization for a Perfectly Competitive Firm

The total profit of Puget Sound Fishing Co. is maximized at 2,500 pounds of fish, where marginal cost equals marginal revenue at point *A*. Total profit (\$2,500) equals profit per unit (\$1) multiplied by the profit-maximizing output (2,500 units).

of only 25 cents each. The increase in volume would more than offset the reduction in profit per unit, resulting in a higher total profit. For Puget Sound Fishing Co., total profit is at its maximum when marginal revenue equals marginal cost.

However, Puget Sound Fishing Co. is not guaranteed a profit. For example, a downturn in the economy may cause the firm to realize losses. Loss minimization for a perfectly competitive firm is discussed in "Exploring Further 5.1" at the end of this chapter.

PERFECT COMPETITION: LONG-RUN ADJUSTMENTS AND ECONOMIC EFFICIENCY

To the owner of a business, profits are good and losses are bad. From the viewpoint of the overall economy, however, profits and losses play equally important roles in allocating scarce resources efficiently. Although a market economy is often referred to as a profit system, it is really a profit and loss system. Losses are important for the efficiency of the economy because they tell businesses when to stop producing, as explained below.

An important characteristic of perfect competition is the long-run behavior of firms in this market structure. Although the number of firms in a competitive market is fixed in the short run, freedom of entry and exit applies to the long run. Because it is easy to enter and exit from a market, perfectly competitive firms operate at the *lowest possible cost,* charge the *lowest price* that they can without going out of business, and earn *no economic profit.* These characteristics are ideal from the consumer's perspective.

Let us consider again the case of Puget Sound Fishing Co. Assume that the firm's cost curves are identical to all other firms in the fish market. This assumption allows us to analyze a *typical* or *average* firm, realizing that all other firms are similarly affected by any long-run adjustments that may occur.

Figure 5.3 shows the long-run position of Puget Sound Fishing Co. Notice that the firm produces at point *A*, where its demand curve just touches the lowest point on its long-run average total cost curve. The firm thus produces 500 pounds of fish at $5 per pound. Any other output level would result in a loss for the firm because its demand curve would be below its long-run average total cost curve.

Also notice that point *A* is the *minimum* point on the firm's long-run average total cost curve. This means that the firm produces at the lowest possible cost per unit in the long run. Competition forces the firm to use the least costly—and thus the most economically efficient—production techniques. Efficient production is an important objective for society because the fundamental problem of economics is scarcity; efficiency counteracts the scarcity problem by allowing a greater amount of output to be produced with a given number of resources. What accounts for this long-run position of a perfectly competitive firm? Freedom of entry into and exit from the market is the basis for the position of the average perfectly competitive firm in the long run.

Effects of Market Entry

Let us first consider the effect of entry of sellers into a perfectly competitive market. Referring to Figure 5.3(*a*), suppose the equilibrium price in the fish market is $6 a pound,

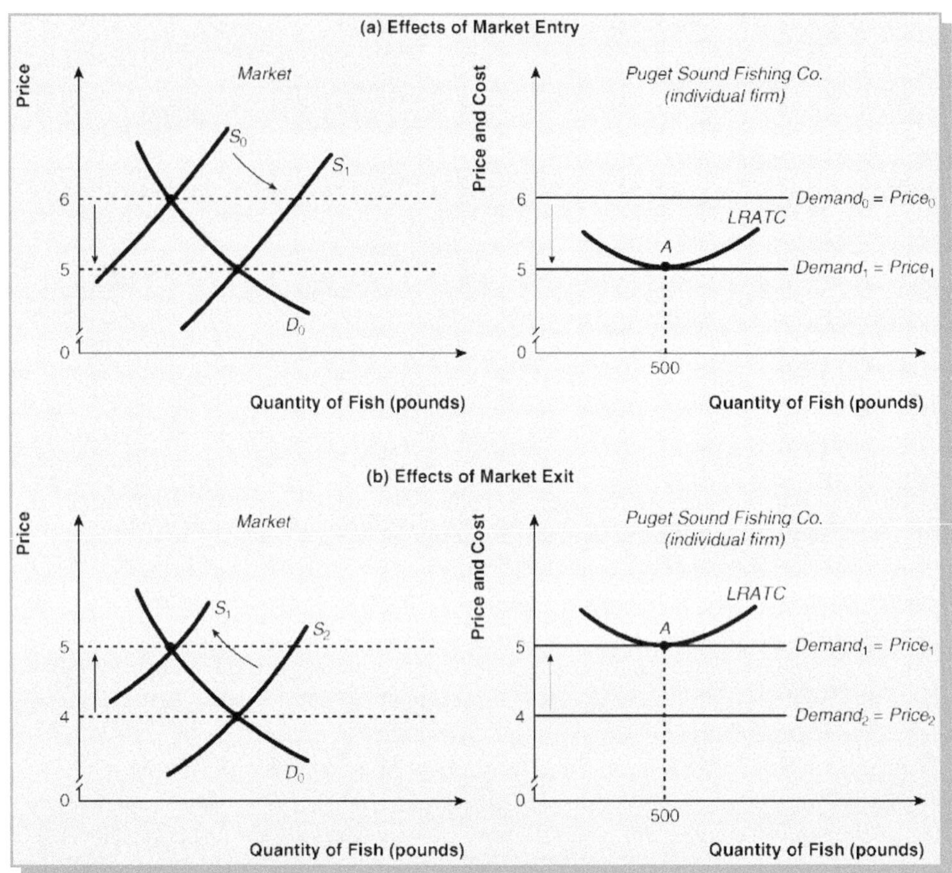

FIGURE 5.3 Long-Run Adjustments for a Perfectly Competitive Firm

In the long run, competitive prices will equal the minimum average total cost of production because short-run profits result in new firms entering a competitive industry until those profits have been competed away. Conversely, short-run losses will hasten the exit of firms from the industry until product price barely covers average cost. At the point of long-run equilibrium, price equals minimum average total cost, which allows just a normal profit.

shown at the intersection of the market supply curve (S_0) and the market demand curve (D_0). With a market price of $6 per pound, the demand curve of Puget Sound Fishing Co. is located at *Demand*$_0$. The firm realizes an economic profit because its demand curve lies above its long-run average total cost curve. Over time, however, economic profits attract new competitors into the market. The resulting increase in market supply causes a decrease in market price and a decline in economic profits. Entry continues until the market supply reaches S_1, the price falls to $5 per pound, and economic profits fall to zero for Puget Sound Fishing Co. Once economic profits disappear, entry ceases.

The personal computer (PC) industry provides an example of market entry and decreasing prices. When the first PC was introduced by International Business Machines Inc. (IBM) in 1981, there was negligible competition. IBM charged prices as high as $7,000 for a PC and it realized huge economic profits. This attracted other firms, such as Compaq and

Dell, to develop PCs that were of the same quality as those produced by IBM. As these firms entered the personal computer market, market supply increased, prices declined, and economic profits decreased for the average firm. Today buyers can purchase a PC that is much more powerful than its 1981 ancestor at a price of $400 or less. Note that although IBM does not fulfill all of the assumptions of perfect competition, it illustrates the long-run adjustments that occur in industries with relative freedom of entry.

Effects of Market Exit

Now we will examine the effect when sellers exit a perfectly competitive market. Referring to Figure 5.3(*b*), suppose the equilibrium price in the fish market is $4 per pound, shown at the intersection of the market supply curve (S_2) and the market demand curve (D_0). At this price, the average firm realizes a loss because the cost of supplying each fish exceeds the price. Lower profits would cause some firms to close their doors and exit the market. This results in a decrease in market supply and an increase in price. The exodus of firms continues until the market supply reaches S_1 and the price rises to $5 per pound, at which point zero economic profits accrue for the remaining firms. Easy entry into and exit from the market thus causes a perfectly competitive firm to operate so that price equals the minimum average total cost, which allows only a normal profit.

Although production under perfect competition occurs in the long run at minimum average total cost, this result does not imply that perfectly competitive firms necessarily are more efficient than firms in other types of market structures. However, it does mean that, given the technology available to the firm, economic forces in perfect competition require producers to minimize the per-unit cost of production.

International Harvester Inc. was a firm that provided an example of the effects of market exit during the 1980s. For decades, International Harvester was famous as a manufacturer of farm equipment, such as tractors and combines. As International Harvester encountered strong competition from other firms, however, it realized declining revenues and economic losses. In the mid-1980s, International Harvester exited the farm equipment market. Today it manufactures trucks, school buses, and engines under the name of Navistar International Corporation. Note that although International Harvester did not fulfill all of the assumptions of perfect competition, it illustrated the long-run adjustments that occur in industries with relative freedom of exit.

CHECK POINT

1 Identify the assumptions of a perfectly competitive market.
2 Why is a perfectly competitive firm a price taker?
3 How does a firm determine its profit-maximizing output?
4 Why does a perfectly competitive firm produce at the lowest point on its average total cost curve in the long run? Why does the firm realize zero economic profits in the long run?

BOX ESSAY 5.1 ECONOMICS IN ACTION
Jeff Bezos: American Entrepreneur

Jeffrey Bezos is an American business magnate, investor, and commercial astronaut. He is the founder and former Chief Executive Officer of Amazon.com., an online merchant of books and later a wide variety of products. Under his leadership, Amazon became the world's largest online sales company.

Born in Albuquerque, New Mexico in 1964, Bezos founded the Dream Institute while in high school, a center that fostered creative thinking in young students. In 1986, he graduated summa cum laude from Princeton University with degrees in computer science and electrical engineering. He first took a job at a telecommunications startup and then transitioned into investment banking.

In 1994, Bezos moved to Seattle, Washington, to open a virtual bookstore. Working out of his garage with a few employees, he started developing software for the site. Named after the South American river, Amazon began selling books in 1995.

Amazon soon became a leader in e-commerce. As more companies moved into Internet sales, Bezos saw the necessity for diversifying. By 2005, Amazon offered a vast display of products, such as hardware, apparel, and consumer electronics. It quickly expanded into other arenas, including video and audio streaming, cloud computing, and artificial intelligence.

Besides Amazon, Bezos founded a spaceflight company in 2000, called Blue Origin. In 2020, he bought *The Washington Post* and affiliated companies, making him the richest person in the world.

Sources: Jeff Bezos: American Entrepreneur, Britannica, December 3, 2023, at Britannica.com/biography/Jeff-Bezos and Jeff Bezos, Biography, May 23, 2023 at biography.com/business-leaders/jeff-bezos.

MONOPOLY

If you attend a college, the firm that sells food in your school cafeteria is usually granted an exclusive franchise to do so by your college. Moreover, if you have visited a national park or a ski resort and had lunch at one of its restaurants, you were probably purchasing food from a firm granted an exclusive franchise. As we shall learn, when a firm does not face competition, it can charge a higher price and produce output of lesser quality than if there were more competition in the market. Let us consider markets in which competition is severely restricted by barriers to entry, a situation that is known as **monopoly**.

A monopoly is a market structure that is characterized by a single supplier of a good or service for which there is no close substitute. With monopoly, the firm (the monopolist) and the industry are one and the same. For many years, the suppliers of local electricity, natural gas, water, and phone service were examples of local monopolies; however, competition has increased in these industries during the past two decades.

Do you know that every time you pay for an item with paper currency, say, a dollar bill, you are using a product that comes from a near monopoly? Since 1879, virtually all the paper purchased by the U.S. Treasury Department's Bureau of Engraving and Printing has come from one supplier: Crane & Co., Inc., of Dalton, Massachusetts. The U.S. reliance on a single source for currency paper is not unique; most other industrial nations also rely on a single domestic supplier for their currency paper.

How does a firm become a monopoly? The first requirement is to produce a good or service that has *no close substitutes.* If a good has close substitutes, even though one firm may produce it, the firm faces competition from other firms that produce the substitute goods.

Note, however, that technological change and innovation can create new products and thus weaken a monopoly's control of the market. For example, the development of e-mail and smartphones has eroded the U.S. Postal Service's monopoly on first-class letter mail. Also, the development of satellite dishes has diminished the monopoly of local cable television firms.

BARRIERS TO ENTRY

Another characteristic of monopoly is the existence of barriers that make it difficult or impossible for new firms to enter an industry. **Barriers to entry** are impediments created by the government or by the firm or firms already in the market, that protect an established firm from potential competition.

In the airline industry, established firms benefit from several barriers to entry. First, restricted access to takeoff and landing slots at many large airports has greatly deterred entry of competing airlines. These slots are allocated by federal legislation aimed at limiting the number of takeoffs and landings during peak traffic periods. Also, new entrants often have limited access to airport facilities such as gates, ticket counters, and baggage handling and storage. Furthermore, established airlines often enact aggressive price-cutting policies to discourage new competitors from entering the market. Major airports dominated by only a few airlines tend to have higher airfares than those having intense competition among airlines.

However, barriers to entry can break down over time, and monopoly positions can erode, as seen in the case of Motorola, Inc., a telecommunication company. In 1989, Motorola introduced the MicroTAC, the smallest and lightest cell phone at the time, and made headlines and rave reviews across the globe. It seemed as if the company's monopoly edge would continue for some time. But in a moment, Motorola faced a flood of competing, lower-cost cell phones from Asian firms. Motorola's supply chain efficiencies and brand name appeal were of little help in a massive industry upheaval enabled by new information technology. Motorola was bought by Google LLC in 2012.

Legal Barriers

Many legal barriers are created by government policy. *Patents*, for example, help prevent entry by giving an inventor the exclusive right to produce a particular good. *Copyrights* refer to exclusive rights granted to a composer or author of an artistic, musical, literary, or dramatic work. *Licenses* regulate entry into particular occupations, such as medicine, law, and architecture. Finally, *public franchises* give a holder the sole legal right to supply a good or service. The U.S. Postal Service, for example, has the exclusive right to deliver first-class letter mail.

Control over Essential Inputs

Sole control over the entire supply of raw materials and other inputs is another way to prevent potential competitors from entering an industry. From the early 1900s until the end of World War II, Alcoa (Aluminum Co. of America) monopolized the U.S. aluminum industry through its ownership of most of the bauxite mines in the world (bauxite is used to manufacture aluminum). Likewise, the International Nickel Co. of Canada once owned nearly all of the world's nickel. In professional sports, it is virtually impossible to compete with the National Hockey League, the National Football League, and the National Basketball Association. Why? These teams have contracts with the best players and leases with the best arenas and stadiums. Moreover, Nintendo weakened its rivals by prohibiting game developers from designing games for anyone else, and Topps Chewing Gum established a 14-year monopoly on baseball cards by signing players to exclusive contracts.

Economies of Scale and Natural Monopoly

Economies of scale also can serve as a barrier to entry. For Apple Inc., economies of scale occur when increased output of smartphones results in lower average total cost. However, a new startup company, with relatively low output, will find it difficult to compete because its average total cost will be higher than Apple's, which benefits from economies of scale. The prospect of higher average total cost may deter entry into an industry.

Economies of scale also relate to what economists call a natural monopoly. A **natural monopoly** is a type of monopoly that occurs because of conditions where high startup costs and substantial economies of scale result in only one firm being able to efficiently produce the output of an industry. This means that one firm can supply a product to the entire market at a lower cost per unit than could be achieved by two or more firms each supplying only some of it. The monopolist can reduce average total cost, taking advantage of economies of scale over the entire range of market demand.

Figure 5.4 illustrates the hypothetical case of Northern States Power Co., a natural monopoly that supplies electricity to the residents of St. Cloud, Minnesota. Suppose the market demand for electricity equals 5 million kilowatt hours (kwh). Given the firm's average total cost curve, *ATC*, we observe economies of scale—that is, decreasing average total cost—throughout the relevant range of production. As a single producer, Northern States Power Co. can service the entire St. Cloud market at a cost of 7 cents per KWH, resulting in a total cost of $350,000 ($0.07 X 5 million kwh = $350,000).

Instead of having a monopoly serve the St. Cloud market, suppose that the market is divided evenly among five competing firms. Assume that each firm realizes a cost curve shown by *ATC*. With each firm producing 1 million kwh, unit cost equals 11 cents. The total cost for each firm thus equals $110,000 ($0.11 x 1 million kwh = $110,000), resulting in a total cost for the market of $550,000.

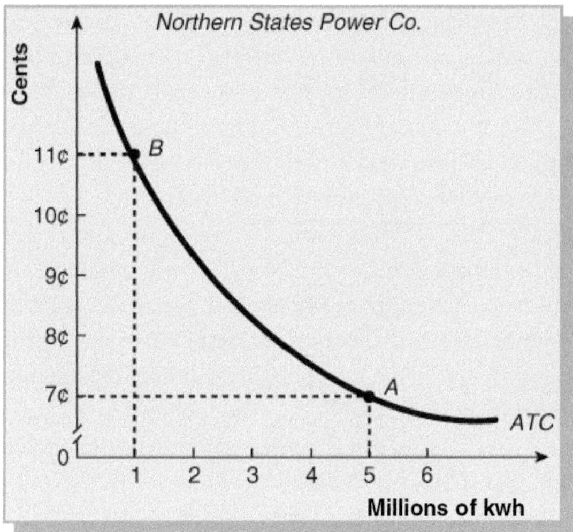

FIGURE 5.4 Economies of Scale and Natural Monopoly

Because of economies of scale, average total cost may decrease over the entire range of market output. In this situation, one firm can serve consumers at lower costs than two or more firms. This describes a natural monopoly.

Comparing the cost of serving the St. Cloud market for Northern States Power Co. and the five competing firms, we conclude that, with economies of scale, the lowest cost of servicing the market occurs under monopoly. Northern States Power Co. can provide 5 million kwh of electricity at a cost of $350,000, whereas the cost of the five competing firms is $550,000 for the same level of service. Clearly, economies of scale serve as a barrier to entry that protects Northern States Power Co. from competition, assuming that the firm is the first to operate in the market.

Many public utilities, such as natural gas, water, electric, cable television, and local telephone companies, have traditionally been regarded as natural monopolies. The government grants an exclusive franchise to these firms in a geographic area. With economies of scale, the firms can drive down average total cost by producing large amounts of output. The government then regulates the monopolies to ensure that the cost savings are passed on to the public in the form of lower prices.

BARRIER TO ENTRY APPLICATIONS

We have learned that effective barriers to entry can enhance a firm's monopoly power. Let us next consider some contemporary applications of barriers to entry.

New York City Taxicabs Aided by Government Licenses

Taxicabs provide an example of legal barriers that shut out competition. In New York City, the government restricts the number of taxicabs to one cab for every 600 people.

As a result, about 13,500 yellow cabs service the city. To operate a taxi, one must obtain a license and place an official medallion on the taxi's hood as proof of legality. Licenses are auctioned off to the highest bidder, who have paid up to $1 million for a license. Why? Restricting competition decreases the supply of taxis, drives up fares, and allows the remaining taxis to expand their market share. The increased profits realized by cab drivers come at the expense of travelers and excluded competitors.

But the taxi monopoly eroded when Uber Technologies, Inc. arrived in New York City in 2011. Uber is a ridesharing company that hires independent contractors as drivers. Despite unsuccessful legal challenges from taxicab companies, Uber pulled riders away from taxicabs, and it characterized the taxi industry as inefficient, corrupt, and greedy. Uber succeeded in becoming a viable competitor to New York City's taxicab companies.

In 2022, the transportation rivals reached a truce when Uber teamed up with two New York City taxicab companies and allowed passengers to use their smartphones to obtain a taxicab on the Uber app. The fare is based on Uber's pricing policies, including surge pricing, which can increase at peak travel times.

Do Patents Encourage Innovation?

A patent is an exclusive right granted by a government to an inventor for a limited period in exchange for public disclosure of an invention. Nations of the world have agreed on a uniform patent length of 20 years from the time of application. Patents have fostered the development of industrial giants, such as Google, Microsoft, Kodak, AT&T, and General Electric.

Proponents maintain that patents serve the public good. In return for registering and publishing your idea, you get a temporary monopoly on using it. This provides an incentive to innovate because it assures the innovator of some economic profit if the innovation is commercially successful. It also provides a mechanism whereby others can innovate, because the publication of good ideas increases the speed of technological advance as one innovation builds upon another.

However, critics argue that the evidence concerning the public good aspect of patents is weak. They note that patent lawyers are good at leaving out as much detail as possible in patent applications, and thus obscuring how the patented idea works from even experts in the field. This limits the ability of others to innovate. Also, license fees can be very expensive, and patents are often filed merely to hinder rivals from engaging in product development.

Economists Michele Boldrin and David Levine have questioned whether patents are effective in promoting innovation. They found that, during the 1800s–1900s, countries without patent systems were no less innovative than those which had them. They also found that when the rate of innovation does change, it does not appear to be related to patents.[1]

However, this does not mean that patents provide no advantages, especially to parties lacking capital but having good ideas. But in many sophisticated manufacturing industries, such as jetliners, control of the underlying intellectual property is only a portion of what is required to create a competitive product. If that were not the case, China's producers of jetliners, which have been given access to Western technology, would be competing with European and American rivals such as Airbus and Boeing. They are not.

Cable Television Companies Suffer as Barriers to Entry Erode

Cable television is a method of delivering video content to consumers using coaxial and fiber-optic cables. It first appeared in 1948 to make television signals better in more remote areas, then it spread to urban areas. The owners of cable television companies have often benefited from a legal barrier to entry in the form of an exclusive franchise to serve a particular community. This franchise is provided by state or local governments who regulate the prices and services provided by cable television companies.

Cable television companies have traditionally justified their monopoly status on the grounds that cable television is a natural monopoly, much like water and electric utilities. The central issue is one of high fixed costs. What would be the payback for a competitor to build an additional cable plant in a city? The infrastructural costs of wires and other technology are enormous. Therefore, many communities decided that having more than one cable system was inefficient. Most cable television companies are thus granted a monopoly franchise over the market they serve.

However, advances in technology have changed entire industries and eroded traditional barriers to entry. For example, technological innovations have allowed companies to provide cable programming without the need for stringing or laying cable throughout a city. These technologies include direct broadcast satellite, wireless cable, and the use of common carrier lines. Also, local telephone companies can provide cable to consumers in their jurisdictions.

By the 2000s, cable television companies encountered competition from substitute providers, such as Netflix, Amazon Prime, Hulu, Apple TV, and other digital channels and streaming services. With growing numbers of people switching to competitors, cable companies came under pressure to hold down rates and offer more services, such as free movies and video clips, to attract customers. Also, cable television companies started providing Internet services to increase profitability.

Cable television companies have traditionally offered an array of popular channels that customers buy as packages. The bundling of channels has been justified in that it allows customers to purchase a combined package which costs less than buying each channel separately. However, with streaming services such as HBO and Apple TV offering premium shows, the interest in traditional cable television has declined. Therefore, cable television companies are under pressure to unbundle packages to remain competitive, thus providing consumers freedom to purchase only the channels they want. It remains to be seen how the cable television industry will evolve in the years ahead.

De Beers: The "Gift of Love"

The diamond industry provides our last example of how barriers to entry can break down over time. Let us consider the case of De Beers, the former diamond monopoly. Throughout much of the 1900s, De Beers Consolidated Mines of South Africa was one of the world's most famous near-monopolies. Although De Beers mines accounted for approximately 15 percent of the world's diamond production, the firm monopolized the sale of diamonds by purchasing for resale a large share of the diamonds produced by other mines throughout the world. De Beers was thus able to sell about 85 percent of the world's diamonds to a select group of manufacturers and dealers.

De Beers controlled the price of diamonds to maximize its profits. This was accomplished by limiting the sale of diamonds to an amount that would yield prices that exceeded the cost of production. In good times, De Beers' profits surpassed 60 percent of revenues.

When the demand for diamonds decreased and prices fell, De Beers reduced sales to maintain price. The firm also advertised on television and in magazines to bolster demand. You may have seen these ads, which promote the giving of diamonds for engagements, anniversaries, and other occasions as a "gift of love" and "diamonds are forever." Conversely, when the demand for diamonds strengthened, De Beers increased sales by delving into its inventory of diamonds and selling them on the market.

To defend its monopoly position, De Beers attempted to prevent competing firms from selling diamonds. De Beers maintained an inventory of diamonds that could be dumped on the market to reduce prices and thus drive competing sellers out of business. In the early 1980s, for example, Zaire attempted to sell diamonds independently of De Beers. As a result, De Beers flooded the market with diamonds, causing the price of diamonds to decrease. Zaire thus stopped competing against De Beers, and it sold its diamonds to De Beers for resale on the world market.

At the turn of the century, however, events weakened the monopoly power of De Beers. New diamond discoveries in Angola and Canada resulted in an increasing flow of diamonds onto the market outside De Beers' control. Australian diamond producer Argyle pulled out of the De Beers consortium. Moreover, the discovery of diamonds in Siberia led to additional production, which further undermined the monopoly power of De Beers. By 2020, De Beers controlled only about 23 percent of the world's diamond production.

De Beers has given up on its efforts to control the world supply of diamonds. It has declared that it will alter its structure from a diamond consortium to a company selling high-quality diamonds under the De Beers label. Therefore, it will decrease its stockpile of diamonds and adopt a policy of increasing overall demand for diamonds through sales promotion. With its large share of the diamond market and ability to control its own production levels, De Beers will likely have a significant impact on the price of diamonds in the years ahead. However, the De Beers monopoly turned out to be temporary. Competition finally came to the diamond business.

Swiss Watches and Technological Change

The Swiss watch industry provides an application of the effects of technological change. The Swiss watch industry started in Geneva in the 1500s when jewelers began producing the world's first mechanical watch and mechanical clock. Swiss producers were recognized for outstanding craftsmanship, and they exported about 60,000 watches per year by the early 1800s.

In the early 1900s, the mass production of Swiss watches started. The division of labor, product standardization, and interchangeable components led to higher productivity and falling unit costs, which allowed Swiss producers to improve their competitiveness in the world market.

During World War II, the political neutrality of Switzerland permitted its manufacturers to produce mechanical watches for consumers, while warring nations of the

Source: clu/E+/Getty Images®

world transferred production to timing devices for military applications. Thus, the Swiss watch industry enjoyed considerable market leverage as it prospered without significant competition.

By the 1960s, watch manufacturing was a mature industry for the Swiss, who benefited from a centuries-old world market and proven methods of manufacturing and marketing. Swiss watch makers accounted for about 50 percent of the world's mechanical watch market before the 1970s. Despite having comparatively high wages and production costs, Switzerland was the home of some of the leading firms in the watch industry.

However, the competitiveness of Swiss watch manufacturers began to decline in the early 1970s, when Japanese firms such as Seiko and Casio launched new techniques for mass-producing mechanical watches that were high quality and affordable. Watch exports from Japan surged during the 1970s and surpassed those of Switzerland in the early 1980s.

Also, new technologies resulted in the introduction of electronic quartz watches, which kept more accurate time and had a lower price than the mechanical watches of Switzerland. Electronic watch producers in Japan, Hong Kong, and the United States soon became competitors of the Swiss watch companies.

Despite technological advances, the Swiss were hesitant to embrace quartz watches, as mechanical watchmaking was a huge aspect of the Swiss identity and because moving into electronic watches was considered unneeded. Yet other nations believed in the benefits of quartz technology, and by 1978 quartz watches surpassed mechanical watches in popularity, throwing the Swiss industry into crisis. Swiss watch sales declined, exports fell, watch manufacturing businesses were closed, and watch workers lost their jobs. With the development and mass marketing of quartz watches, Swiss mechanical timepieces became generally regarded as functionally obsolete.

Because of quartz technology and foreign competition, the Swiss had to reorganize their watch business. Many of the remaining Swiss firms consolidated under the umbrella of several large watchmaking producers. Also, mass production methods were launched to reduce labor input and therefore decrease unit costs. Moreover, the production of some watch components was outsourced to countries with lower wage rates. Finally, Swiss watch manufacturers retreated to the higher end of the market, where mechanical watches were desired for their glamorous design, elaborate craftsmanship, and aesthetic appeal. Despite these adjustments, Swiss watch sales continued to plummet.

By the early 2000s, smart watches (a wearable computer in the form of a watch) significantly increased their share of the world watch market, especially after the launch of the Apple Watch in 2015. The popularity of smart watches has resulted in apprehension of a new type of technology that may further threaten the Swiss watchmaking industry.

PROFIT MAXIMIZATION FOR A MONOPOLIST

In the previous section, we learned that De Beers was able earn substantial profits by controlling most of the world's diamond production. Let us now consider how a monopolist goes about achieving a combination of price and output that yields maximum profits.

Price and Marginal Revenue

Recall that a perfectly competitive firm is a *price taker* that is at the mercy of the market in which it operates. The firm faces a horizontal demand curve for its product at a price that is established by market demand and supply. Because each additional unit of the firm's output sold adds a constant amount (price) to total revenue, its marginal revenue is constant and equals product price.

In contrast, a monopolist is a *price maker* that can decide its own product price. Why? A monopolist is the sole producer of a product for which there are no close substitutes, and thus its output decisions necessarily affect product price. The firm's price will rise only if output falls; output will rise only if the price falls. A monopolist, unlike a perfectly competitive firm, thus faces a downward-sloping demand schedule for its product.

Note that a monopolist is not completely immune from market forces in deciding price and output. Although a monopolist can charge any price it wishes, it knows that at higher prices, less output will be sold. Therefore, a monopoly faces a downward-sloping demand curve instead of a perfectly horizontal demand curve.

Table 5.1 shows the demand and revenue conditions for De Beers, which is assumed to be a monopoly in the sale of diamonds. Referring to columns 1 and 2 of the table, as De Beers reduces the price of diamonds, the quantity demanded increases. For example, De Beers can choose a price of $3,600 and count on customers demanding one diamond, or it can reduce the price to $3,200 and sell two diamonds. Figure 5.5 translates this

TABLE 5.1 Demand and Revenue Schedules for De Beers as a Monopolist

Quantity of Diamonds	*Price*	*Total Revenue*	*Marginal Revenue*
0	$4,000	$0	
1	3,600	3,600	3,600
2	3,200	6,400	2,800
3	2,800	8,400	2,000
4	2,400	9,600	1,200
5	2,000	10,000	400
6	1,600	9,600	–400

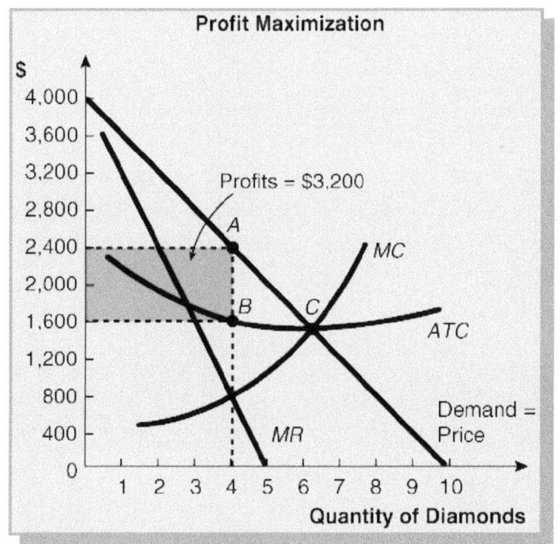

FIGURE 5.5 Profit Maximization for a Monopolist

The figure shows De Beers maximizing profits by producing four diamonds, the output corresponding to the intersection of its marginal revenue and marginal cost curves. At this output, price ($2,400) exceeds average total cost ($1,600) and profit per unit equals the difference ($800); the firm's total profits ($3,200) are calculated by multiplying the profit per unit times the profit-maximizing output.

information into graphical form. The figure shows a downward-sloping demand curve for De Beers.

Column 3 of Table 5.1 shows De Beers' total revenue, which is calculated by multiplying the market price by the quantity of diamonds ($TR = P \times Q$). Changes in both price and quantity demanded thus result in changes in the firm's total revenue. For example, if the price of diamonds falls from $3,600 to $3,200 per diamond, thus resulting in an increase in quantity demanded from one diamond to two diamonds, total revenue would rise from $3,600 to $6,400.

Column 4 of Table 5.1 shows the marginal revenue schedule of De Beers. Recall that marginal revenue is the addition to total revenue when another unit of output is sold. In the table, as De Beers increases sales from, say, one diamond to two diamonds, total revenue rises from $3,600 to $6,400. The marginal revenue of the second diamond is thus $2,800 ($6,400 – $3,600 = $2,800). Note that as De Beers lowers the price to sell additional diamonds, its marginal revenue on each additional unit sold is less than the price. Translating this information into the graphical representation of Figure 5.5, the monopolist's marginal revenue schedule is downward-sloping and lies beneath its demand curve.

Maximizing Profits

Although De Beers cannot dictate how many diamonds people will demand at different prices, it can select a particular price and quantity combination that will result in maximum profits. How does the firm find this combination? According to the profit-maximizing rule, as discussed earlier in this chapter, a firm will maximize total profit by selling that output where marginal revenue equals marginal cost.

Figure 5.5 shows hypothetical revenue and cost schedules of De Beers. The firm would maximize total profit by selling four diamonds—the output at which marginal revenue equals marginal cost. Having determined its profit-maximizing output, De Beers must now decide what price to charge for diamonds. To set product price, De Beers uses its demand curve and finds the highest price at which it can sell the profit-maximizing output. In De Beers' situation, the highest price at which it can sell four diamonds is $2,400 per diamond, shown by point *A* in Figure 5.5. Multiplying price ($2,400) by output (4), we calculate De Beers' total revenue to be $9,600. At the profit-maximizing output, the firm's average total cost is $1,600. Multiplying this amount by four units, we calculate total cost to be $6,400. The firm's total profit thus equals $3,200, found by subtracting total cost ($6,400) from total revenue ($9,600).

There is another method for computing total profits. First, subtract average total cost ($1,600) from product price ($2,400), which gives profit per unit ($800). Then multiply this amount by the profit-maximizing output (4) to compute total profit ($3,200).

Notice that De Beers does not charge the highest possible price for diamonds. Because De Beers is a price maker, it could have charged a price higher than $2,400 and sold fewer than four diamonds. However, any price higher than $2,400 does not correspond to the intersection of the firm's marginal revenue and marginal cost curves, which establishes the profit-maximizing output. The fact that De Beers has a monopoly does not guarantee profits. Decreasing demand for diamonds can result in losses for the firm, as discussed in "Exploring Further 5.1" at the end of this chapter.

Continuing Monopoly Profits

Recall that with perfect competition, economic profits are unattainable in the long run. Because of low barriers to entry, the existence of economic profits will induce firms to enter a competitive industry until those profits have been competed away.

Sizable economic profits, however, can persist under monopoly if the monopolist is protected by barriers to entry and the demand for its product is strong. With blockaded entry, a monopolist can charge the price that will maximize its short-run profit and still attract no rivals. The attainment of long-run economic profits is thus possible under monopoly.

Remember, however, that barriers to entry are rarely complete and thus detract from the ability of a firm to realize persistently high profits. As technologies change and new products are developed, the monopolies of today will evolve into firms operating in the competitive industries of tomorrow. For example, throughout the 1960s and 1970s, Boeing accounted for more than two-thirds of the noncommunist world's production of jetliners. Because of the rise of Europe's Airbus, Boeing's market share has fallen to around 50 percent in recent years.

THE CASE AGAINST MONOPOLY

From what we have seen so far, monopoly isn't *all* bad. At times, a monopoly can fully take advantage of the economies of scale that occur under natural monopolies. Moreover, some innovative firms, such as IBM and Xerox, once had monopolies simply because each was the first to enter its industry. Why, then, do people often dislike monopolies?

Imagine an industry that is made up of many identical competitive firms. Suppose that a single firm then purchases all competing firms and creates a monopoly. Given identical cost conditions, a monopolist is likely to charge a *higher* price and earn *higher* profits than a competitive industry, which harms consumers. The monopolist attains excess profits by consciously *restricting* output and increasing price above the competitive level. The output restriction comes at the expense of society, which would have preferred additional output and thus additional resources devoted to the production of the good.

Figure 5.5 shows the effect of restricted output for De Beers as a monopoly. In the figure, we see that De Beers maximizes profits by producing four units of output, at which point marginal revenue equals marginal cost. At this output, the firm's average total cost is at point *B*. However, average total cost is at a minimum at point C. By restricting output, De Beers fails to operate at the lowest point on its average total cost curve. In contrast, firms in a competitive industry operate at the minimum point on their average total cost curves.

A monopolist also lacks the incentive to organize production to reduce cost. Recall that competition serves as a major source of disciplinary pressure on firms, which hold down costs in order to survive. But a monopolist is insulated from the rigors of competition by barriers to entry, and thus does not have to produce at minimum average total cost or use inputs in the most efficient manner irrespective of the rate of output. Excess costs can be the result of the ineffective supervision of employees, the payment of large bonuses to management, the provision of company perks such as jet planes and vacation lodges, and the like.

Moreover, high-quality service is not always a characteristic of monopoly. Have you ever been frustrated trying to force, with both hands, a letter into a drive-by mailbox that is completely filled with other letters? (This author has.) Have you ever been annoyed with the local cable TV company—the only one in town—because of its agonizingly slow repair service? The phrase "The customer is always right" does not necessarily apply when barriers to entry protect a firm from the discipline of competition.

Monopoly may also promote inequality in the distribution of income. To the extent that a monopolist charges a higher price than a competitive firm with identical costs, the monopolist levies a "tax" on consumers that goes into economic profits. These profits, however, are not uniformly distributed among members of society because corporate stock tends to be largely owned by the wealthy. The distribution of income is thus altered in favor of the wealthy.

Finally, government grants of monopoly, such as exclusive franchises to serve a market, allow firms to waste resources in the attempt to secure and maintain them. Indeed, business executives often spend vast sums on political contributions and the hiring of lobbyists to convince government officials that their firm should become or remain a legal monopoly. From the perspective of economic efficiency, such expenditures are wasteful because they do not contribute to increased output.

Keep in mind, however, that monopoly may have some advantages. Recall that with natural monopoly, economies of scale are best fulfilled when one firm produces the entire market output. Also, a monopolist can eliminate certain types of duplication that are unavoidable for several small, independent firms—for example, a few large machines may replace the many small pieces of equipment used by competitive firms, or one purchasing agent may do a job that formerly required many buyers.

Monopolies have an advantage in pursuing research and development activities, which can result in new products, improving technologies, and decreased unit cost. The vast resources (profits) of monopolies can finance expensive research and development programs. Moreover, because monopolies are sheltered from competition, they do not have to be preoccupied with day-to-day decisions regarding costs and revenues. Instead, they can take the longer view that is necessary for successful research and development.

However, the research and development argument does not consider monopoly *incentives.* Just because a monopoly has the potential to conduct research and development does not necessarily mean that it will. Instead, a monopoly may prefer to rely on existing products and technologies and earn sizable profits merely because of its monopoly power. The firm may conclude that research and development is not essential for its survival. In contrast, a competitive firm cannot continue to earn profits unless it stays ahead of its rivals; this pressure results in incentives to produce better products at a lower cost.

CHECK POINT

1 Identify the major barriers to entry that foster monopoly.

2 Compare the price-making ability of a monopoly with that of a perfectly competitive firm.

3 Discuss the strategy of profit maximization for a monopoly.

4 Evaluate the cases for and against monopoly.

MONOPOLY APPLICATIONS

We have learned how a monopolist strives to maximize total profits and its effect on the allocation of society's resources. Let us next turn to some applications of monopoly.

The U.S. Postal Monopoly and Universal Service

The story of the United States Postal Service began in 1775 when the Continental Congress named Benjamin Franklin the first American Postmaster General. Franklin and his fellow patriots saw a robust mail system as critical to the nation's development. In the past two centuries, Congress has clung to this belief despite the huge losses that the Postal Service has realized in recent years.

The mission of the Postal Service is to provide the American public with universal postal service at affordable prices. This means that the Postal Service is obligated to serve all Americans, regardless of geography, at a uniform price and quality. Therefore, if you live in rural America, you pay the same price for a letter as if you live in an urban center.

To enable the Postal Service to provide universal service at reasonable prices, Congress gave it a legal monopoly over the delivery of first-class letter mail. Also, the Postal Service has a legal monopoly over the use of your mailbox. Federal law prohibits the delivery of unstamped mail into mailboxes, thus granting the Postal Service exclusive access to mailboxes.

Proponents justify the Postal Service's legal monopoly on several grounds. A monopoly is necessary to ensure that the Postal Service has sufficient revenue to carry out its universal service mandate without taxpayer subsidies. Also, as a single mail carrier, the Postal Service can operate at a lower cost to the nation than multiple suppliers can. This is because mail delivery fits the economic model of a natural monopoly—unit cost per delivery decreases as mail volume increases. Finally, without protecting the Postal Service with a legal monopoly, private carriers would siphon off high-profit delivery routes, leaving only money-losing routes to the Postal Service.

However, critics argue that the Postal Service's legal monopoly is not warranted. Because the Postal Service does not face the threat of competition, it lacks incentives to control costs and maintain high quality. Also, it is questionable that the Postal Service is a natural monopoly that realizes large economies of scale—most of its costs come from labor costs, which are variable costs, rather than fixed costs, where cost per unit declines as mail volume increases.

Critics also note that although the Postal Service is a legal monopoly in the delivery of first-class letter mail, private firms like FedEx Corporation and United Parcel Service (UPS) realize a profit on the delivery of urgent (overnight) mail, 2-day and 3-day letters and parcels, and unaddressed advertising circulars and periodicals. Together, these groups compete on a local, national, and international basis for portions of markets previously served only by the Postal Service.

Since 2009, the U.S. Government Accountability Office has included the Postal Service on its "high risk" list. It maintains that the Postal Service has not been able to reduce costs fast enough to offset the decline in mail volume and revenue, as online communication and payments have expanded. The Postal Service needs to restructure to address its long-term financial viability, according to the U.S. Government Accountability Office.

So, what should be done about the Postal Service? Some analysts recommend an end to the Postal Service's monopoly status and the auctioning of the Postal Service to a private-sector owner who would operate it on a for-profit basis. Germany, Japan, and the United Kingdom are among the countries that have privatized mail delivery.

It is argued that the resulting cost savings and quality improvements from privatizing mail delivery would promote reasonable prices for consumers. However, would there be a buyer for the Postal Service given the universal service constraint it faces from Congress? Would rural customers have to pay higher prices for mail than they do under the current system? Would mail be delivered 6 days a week? At the writing of this textbook, the future of the Postal Service remains in question.

Reducing Monopoly Power: Generic Drugs Compete Against Brand-Name Drugs

Not only have barriers to entry broken down in the delivery of mail, they have also broken down in the prescription drug industry. Our monopoly model predicts that when barriers to entry break down and competition appears, the result is declining price, rising output, and increasing efficiency. Consider the case in which generic drugs come into the market to compete against brand-name drugs.

For decades, the U.S. government has established competing policy goals regarding the pricing of prescription drugs. On the one hand, it desires to ensure that brand-name drug companies have sufficient incentives to invest in the research and development of innovative drugs. To achieve this goal, a drug company is given patent protection for 20 years from the time of the patent approval by the Food and Drug Administration, thus providing the firm a temporary monopoly for its product. During this period, the firm can charge a price for its brand-name drug that is high enough to cover its costs of discovery and development, and to earn an economic profit. Thus, the firm has an incentive to invent new products that benefit consumers. Without patents, many new drugs would be easily and quickly duplicated by other firms, preventing the innovator from obtaining enough reward to justify its investment.

However, the government wants to discourage the firm from charging excessively high prices for its brand-name drugs. To meet this goal, it allows generic drugs to compete against brand-name drugs. A generic drug is a copy that is identical to the brand-name drug in active ingredients, dosage, and performance. Because generic drugs are copies rather than original formulations, they are not patentable. Also, generic drugs are usually sold under their chemical name rather than under a brand name. For example, the generic version of Paxil is paroxetine and the generic equivalent of Lipitor is atorvastatin. When the patent expires on the brand-name drug, generic producers enter the market as competitors.

In general, generic drugs are less expensive than brand-name drugs because generic firms do not have the development costs that the producer of a new brand-name drug has. Also, producers of generic drugs tend to engage in price competition with each other, partly because they sell identical products. Although the list prices of brand-name drugs do not usually decrease after generic competitors enter the market, some brand-name producers offer discounts and rebates to some purchasers, and those discounts tend to be larger when generic versions of the drug are available. Moreover, competition from generic firms has prompted brand-name firms to produce copies of their own drugs, which they then sell under generic names at reduced prices in order to capture a share of that market. Simply put, the performance of the prescription drug industry is consistent with the competitive model: When competition is introduced into a market, price declines, output rises, and efficiency improves.

Is Google a Monopoly? Should It Be Broken Up?

When the Internet first emerged in the 1990s, users found that they could publish text and images that could be read for free by any other user. However, there was no search engine that could be used to find what you were looking for. Google cracked that problem by inventing the first effective search engine.

Google began in 1995 as a research project by Larry Page and Sergey Brin, Ph.D. students in computer science at Stanford University. They focused on the problem of finding out which web pages link to a given page. Working in a garage in Palo Alto, CA, Page and Brin built a search engine that allowed people to easily locate what they were looking for on the Internet.

In 1998 Google became a legal corporation, Google Inc.; the firm's name is now Google LLC. Google quickly grew and by 2023 it had 89 percent of the market for Internet searches in America and more than 93 percent in many European countries. Yet this meant that anyone who wished to conduct searches on the Internet was becoming increasingly reliant on Google.

Similar to Amazon and Facebook, Google benefits from so-called "network effects," in which the popularity of a service attracts more users and thus becomes self-perpetuating. Google collects more data than any other search-engine firm, and it is better at fashioning that data for insights. Once people begin using Google's search engine (and its maps, e-mail, and digital storage), they rarely switch to other platforms. Small advertisers generally find switching to other platforms too troublesome to bother. Therefore, network effects and economies of scale have resulted in Google becoming the dominant search engine.

But does this mean that Google is an illegal monopoly? Let us briefly examine both sides of this debate.

The case against Google is that as a dominant firm, it claimed about 60 percent of global search advertising revenues in 2022, which amounted to more than $150 billion. Also, there are numerous complaints in the United States and Europe that Google has used its search monopoly to exclude actual and potential rivals, big and small. How? Manipulating clicks by decreasing competitors' rankings in Google searches is one way. Another is locking up critical content, like video and books, so that rival search engines are discouraged from providing their users with access to that content. As a result, Google has deprived any rival of the queries and advertisers necessary to create alternatives for users.

However, defenders of Google note that complaints about the firm have been far removed from what the antitrust laws require for a monopolization case: (1) the existence of monopoly power and (2) predatory conduct undertaken to attain or maintain that power.

For example, although Google has the dominant share of the search-engine market, it faces competition from a variety of means of finding information on the Internet, including general search engines like Bing, specialized search engines like Amazon, eBay, or Zillow, and social networks like Facebook and Twitter. Moreover, there are mobile applications that provide competition for Google. As courts have indicated, marketplace success based on skill, foresight, and industry is what the antimonopoly laws are supposed to promote. It is not difficult to recognize that Google's success is due to its innovative products delivered at no cost to consumers who find them invaluable for finding information on the Internet.

Moreover, a high market share is of little concern to antitrust authorities unless it continues over time, and is protected by barriers that insulate it from competition. Critics argue that Google is protected by the popularity of its products, which yields data that allows Google to make its products even better. However, Google's defenders note that product improvement is a good thing, not an illegal barrier to competition, and nothing prevents consumers from switching to another search engine if they don't like Google's services. Moreover, Google's share of the market has fluctuated over time. Finally, the lesson of recent decades is that technology monopolies may be dominant for a while, but they eventually crumble when they fail to adapt with the times, or when new technologies expand the market in unexpected ways, exposing them to new rivals.

Would Vouchers Improve the U.S. Education System?

> Vouchers don't work. Smaller class size and proven academic programs do, and they are doable tomorrow. Let's do what's right and what works.
>
> American Federation of Teachers

> Competition and the profit motive must be reintroduced into education so that teachers and school administrators will once again have a powerful incentive to meet the needs of the children and parents they serve.
>
> Andrew Coulson, Scholar at the Washington, DC-based Education Policy Institute

For decades, many frustrated parents have challenged one of America's near-monopolies, public education. These parents are concerned about the poor quality of the U.S. elementary and secondary education system, evidenced by high numbers of school dropouts and declining reading and math skills. They ask whether it is fair to tax families, compel their children's attendance at schools, and then give them no choice between teaching methods, religious or secular education, and other matters. The question is, how can we make our educational system more productive?

One method would be to reform the structure of elementary and high school education by giving parents vouchers (a stipulated amount of money) to spend on their children's education. This would enable children to attend the public or private school of their choice. Although some states and cities have limited voucher programs, the only federally funded program is in Washington, DC.

Proponents maintain that the competition attributable to vouchers would offer new paths to learning. New methods of teaching would replace the old, and costs would go down. Students would benefit from an improvement in the quality of their education, and good teachers would benefit from a wider market for their services. Government schools would have to meet the competition or close.

However, the teachers' unions that control government schools do not relish that competition. They see it as a threat to the pay and job security of their faculties. Moreover, teachers' unions fear that a voucher system would be ineffective at improving quality, especially in communities with less-educated parents, who would be less able to make informed decisions and be less effective at influencing school policies than would more highly educated parents. Finally, any voucher system would siphon off money from the nation's public school system, leading to reductions in quality.

CHECK POINT

1 Why does the U.S. Postal Service have a legal monopoly on the delivery of first-class letter mail? Explain why critics of the U.S. Postal Service argue that privatization of mail delivery would result in a more efficient allocation of resources for the nation. Do you agree?

2. What has been the effect on prescription drug prices when generic drugs compete against brand-name drugs?

3 Is Google an illegal monopoly? Summarize the case for and case against Google.

4. Should a system of vouchers be provided to students attending public schools?

CHAPTER SUMMARY

1 A perfectly competitive market is characterized by many sellers and buyers, firms that produce a standardized product, perfect information among buyers and sellers, and easy entry into and exit from a market.

2 Because a perfectly competitive firm supplies a negligible share of the market output, it must "take" or accept the price that is determined in the market.

3 Given favorable demand conditions, a firm will maximize total profit by selling that output where marginal revenue equals marginal cost.

4 If total revenue exceeds total variable cost, a firm will minimize short-run losses by producing output where $MR = MC$ rather than shutting down. As a result, losses are less than the fixed-cost losses that would be realized if the firm shut down.

5 Because of easy entry into and exit from a market, perfectly competitive firms operate at the lowest possible cost, charge the lowest price they can without going out of business, and earn no economic profit. These characteristics are ideal for the consumer.

6 Barriers to entry are impediments, created by the government or by the firm or firms already in the market, that protect an established firm from potential competition. The

major barriers to entry are legal barriers, control over essential resources, and economies of scale.

7 A monopoly differs from a perfectly competitive firm in that the monopoly's demand curve and marginal revenue curve are downward-sloping rather than horizontal. Like a perfectly competitive firm, a monopolist will maximize total profit by operating at that output where marginal revenue equals marginal cost.

8 Given identical costs, a monopolist will find it profitable to produce a smaller output and charge a higher price than a perfectly competitive firm. Moreover, a profit-maximizing monopoly will not operate at the minimum point on its average total cost curve in the long run. However, economies of scale may make lower average total cost more attainable for a monopoly than for a competitive firm. Moreover, a monopolist generally has greater financial resources for research and development programs than a competitive firm, making it possible for the monopolist to achieve a lower cost per unit.

KEY TERMS AND CONCEPTS

perfect competition
price taker
total revenue
marginal revenue
marginal revenue = marginal cost rule
barriers to entry
monopoly
natural monopoly
shut-down rule

STUDY QUESTIONS AND PROBLEMS

1 Suppose that a perfectly competitive firm sells 300 batteries at $10 each. At this output, the firm's total variable cost is $1,800 and its total fixed cost is $600. Calculate the firm's profit per unit and total profit from this information.

2 Eddy's Pizza Parlor receives $15 per pizza and sells 100 pizzas to maximize profits. Assuming that the firm's variable cost is $8 per pizza and total fixed costs are $500, what is the profit per unit on a pizza at the profit-maximizing level of output? What is the firm's total profit?

3 Suppose that a monopolist can sell nine diamonds at $500 each. To sell 10 diamonds, the firm must reduce the price to $475. Calculate the marginal revenue of the 10th diamond.

4 Assume that a monopolist finds that at existing output and price levels, marginal revenue is $20 and marginal cost is $15. The firm would maximize profits or minimize losses with _____ price and _____ output.

5 Table 5.2 shows the revenue and cost conditions for Johnson Electronics Inc.

   a Graph the information contained in the table.

   b In what market structure does this firm operate? Why?

   c What level of output will maximize the firm's total profit? What price will be charged?

   d Compute the firm's maximum total profit.

TABLE 5.2 Revenue and Cost Conditions of Johnson Electronics Inc.

Output	*P = MR*	*ATC*	*MC*
10	$10	$20.80	
20	10	12.40	$4.00
30	10	9.92	5.00
40	10	9.00	6.20
50	10	8.80	8.00
60	10	9.00	10.00
70	10	9.56	13.00
80	10	10.50	17.00

6 Table 5.3 shows the revenue and cost data for Smith Technologies Co.

a Graph the information contained in the table.

b In what market structure does this firm operate? Why?

c What level of output will maximize the firm's total profit?

d Compute the firm's maximum total profit.

TABLE 5.3 Revenue and Cost Data of Smith Technologies Co.

Output	*Price*	*MR*	*ATC*	*MC*
0	$35.00			
1	32.00	$32.00	$48.00	$48.00
2	29.00	26.00	30.00	12.00
3	26.00	20.00	23.34	10.00
4	23.00	14.00	21.00	14.00
5	20.00	8.00	20.00	16.00

7 Table 5.4 shows the short-run revenue and cost data for a television manufacturer that sells in a perfectly competitive market.

a Graph the information contained in the table.

b Assuming that the market price is $280 per television, determine the firm's profit-maximizing output and total profit.

TABLE 5.4 Cost Data for a Perfectly Competitive Firm

Quantity of Televisions	*AFC*	*AVC*	*ATC*	*MC*
1	$600	$200	$800	$200
2	300	150	450	100
3	200	140	340	120
4	150	146	296	160
5	120	160	280	220
6	100	180	280	280
7	86	206	292	360
8	76	238	312	460
9	66	276	342	580
10	60	320	380	720

- **c** Assuming that the market price is $580 per television, determine the firm's profit-maximizing output and total profits.
- **d** Assuming that the market price is $160 per television, will the firm continue to produce or should it shut down? Why? What if the market price is $120 per television?

8 Figure 5.6 shows the short-run cost conditions faced by a perfectly competitive firm.

- **a** If the product price equals $35 per unit, the firm would maximize profits or minimize losses by producing and selling ______ units of output. At this level of output, the firm's total revenue equals ______, total cost equals ______, and total profit (loss) equals ______.
- **b** If the product price equals $20 per unit, the firm would maximize profit or minimize losses by producing and selling ________ units of output. At this level of output, the firm's total revenue equals ________, total cost equals ________, and total profit (loss) equals ________. Why would the firm prefer to continue to produce rather than shut down?
- **c** If the product price equals $10 per unit, the firm would maximize profits or minimize losses by producing and selling ________ units of output. Why?

9 Figure 5.7 shows the demand and cost conditions faced by a monopolist. To maximize profits or minimize losses, the firm should produce and sell _______ units of output and charge a price of _______ per unit.

- **a** At the profit-maximizing (loss-minimizing) level of output, the firm's average total cost equals ______ and profit (loss) per unit equals ______.
- **b** At the profit-maximizing (loss-minimizing) level of output, the firm's total revenue equals ______, total cost equals ______, and total profits (losses) equal ______.

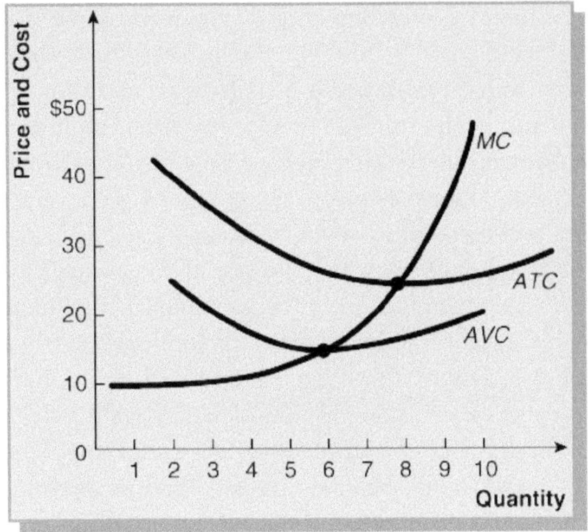

FIGURE 5.6 Short-Run Cost Conditions Faced by a Perfectly Competitive Firm

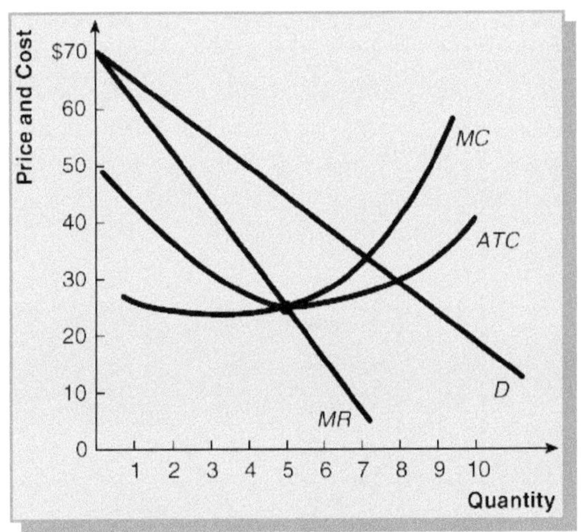

FIGURE 5.7 Demand and Cost Conditions Faced by a Monopolist

EXPLORING FURTHER 5.1: LOSS MINIMIZATION AND THE SHUT-DOWN RULE

Suppose that a temporary decrease in demand depresses the price of product below the average total cost curve of a firm. Faced with losses at all levels of output, how will the firm respond to this situation? It could temporarily produce at a loss or shut down production until the price rises. Let us first apply this situation to Puget Sound Fishing Co., a perfectly competitive firm.

If Puget Sound Fishing Co. shuts down, not only does it earn zero revenue, but also it must still pay any interest on borrowed money, insurance premiums, license fees, and other fixed costs that it incurs even when output is zero. Simply put, if a firm shuts down, its losses equal its total fixed costs. If, however, the firm stays in operation, it earns revenue that can be applied first to its total variable costs (wages) and then to its total fixed costs. Which situation will result in the smallest loss for Puget Sound Fishing Co.?

The following **shut-down rule** serves as a guide for a firm that realizes *losses* in the short run: If *total revenue exceeds total variable cost*, the firm should continue to produce because all of its variable costs and some of its fixed costs can be paid out of revenue. If the firm shuts down, all of the fixed costs must be paid out of the owner's pocket. By producing output where $MR = MC$, the firm's loss will be *less* than its total fixed cost. Conversely, a firm should shut down if total variable cost exceeds total revenue.

Referring to Figure 5.8, assume that Puget Sound Fishing Co. has a total fixed cost of $3,728,[2] and that the price of fish is $4 per pound. Because the price lies below the firm's average total cost curve, all levels of output result in *losses*. Which output should the firm choose? The logic of the $MR = MC$ rule, as discussed previously, applies in this situation. At 1,600 pounds of fish, corresponding to the intersection of the firm's marginal revenue and marginal cost curves, the firm's revenues total $6,400 ($4 × 1,600 = $6,400). Moreover, average total cost equals $5.33 per pound at this output, resulting in total costs of $8,528 ($5.33 × 1,600 = $8,528). Puget Sound Fishing Co. thus loses $2,128, the difference between total revenue and total cost. Conversely, the firm would lose $3,728 in fixed costs if it shut down.

According to the shut-down rule, Puget Sound Fishing Co. should continue to operate because total revenue exceeds total variable cost. Referring to Figure 5.8, because the firm's average variable cost is $3 at 1,600 units of output, total variable cost equals $4,800 ($3 × 1,600 = $4,800). Because total revenue ($6,400) exceeds total variable cost

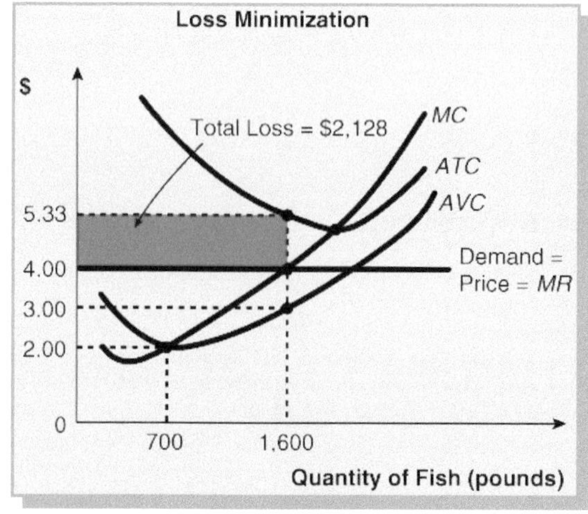

FIGURE 5.8 Loss Minimization for a Perfectly Competitive Firm

Since average total cost always exceeds price, the firm suffers a loss at every level of output. The firm would minimize short-run losses by continuing to operate as long as the price at least covers average variable cost, because some of this revenue can be applied to fixed costs.

($4,800), the difference ($1,600) can be used to pay off some of the firm's fixed costs. The firm thus loses a smaller amount ($2,128) by producing than by shutting down ($3,728). Keep in mind, however, that a firm cannot stay in operation when it is continually losing money; over the long run, it must at least break even.

Besides applying to a perfectly competitive firm, the shut-down rule applies to other market structures including monopoly, monopolistic competition, and oligopoly (discussed in the next chapter). For example, suppose that a temporary decrease in demand depresses the price of a product below the average total cost curve of a monopolist. If the firm can charge a price that exceeds average variable cost, it will minimize short-run losses by producing a level of output where $MR = MC$ rather than shutting down.

NOTES

1 "Intellectual Property: A Question of Utility," *The Economist*, August 8, 2015, pp. 49–52; Michele Boldrin and David Levine, *The Case Against Patents*, Federal Reserve Bank of St. Louis, Working Paper 2012–035A.

2 Total fixed cost can be calculated from the data of Figure 5.8. First, compute average fixed cost at some level of output—say 1,600 pounds of fish; the difference between the average total cost ($5.33) and average variable cost ($3) gives the average fixed cost ($2.33). Next, multiply $2.33 times 1,600 pounds of fish, which gives a total fixed cost of $3,728.

CHAPTER 6

Imperfect Competition

CHAPTER OBJECTIVES

After reading this chapter, you should be able to:

1 Distinguish between monopolistic competition and oligopoly.
2 Identify the goals and effects of advertising.
3 Explain how a seller successfully practices price discrimination.
4 Discuss the major theories of oligopolistic behavior.
5 Distinguish between a horizontal merger, a vertical merger, and a conglomerate merger.
6 Explain how the threat of potential competition encourages firms to produce high-quality products and sell them at reasonable prices to consumers.

DOI: 10.4324/9781003438571-8

ECONOMICS IN CONTEXT

America's early colonists needed tools, such as hammers, hoes, and knives to build homes, plant crops, and hunt. Iron tools were in demand, but it wasn't until the 1800s that technological advances reduced cost and increased the quality of steel. By the late 1800s, steel production switched from using charcoal to coal in iron ore smelting, and large integrated steel mills were built to conduct all the steps of steelmaking.

Following World War II, U.S. steel producers dominated the world by exporting large amounts of steel, while steel imports by the United States were virtually zero. U.S. Steel, Bethlehem Steel, Republic Steel, and National Steel evolved to become the four largest companies in the industry. Together, they accounted for about half of industry production in 1970. They had significant market power and some ability to use price as a competitive weapon.

However, America's steel industry became increasingly competitive as the result of import competition from countries like South Korea and Japan. By 1997, the share of the domestic market held by the top four American steel companies fell to 39 percent, and 29 percent when imports were considered. Increased competition placed pressure on American steel companies to increase productivity and decrease unit cost. They also had less control over price, and their profit rates declined.

America's integrated steel companies faced additional competition in the 1990s when steel mini-mills appeared, such as Nucor Corp. Instead of extracting iron from iron ore, mini-mills get most of their iron from scrap steel that is recycled from automobiles and other equipment. Electric furnaces melt scrap, which is then used to produce steel. As of 2022, there were more than 100 mini-mills in the United States, which accounted for over half of total domestic steel production. Nucor was America's largest steel company in 2022, with a market share of about 18 percent, followed by U.S. Steel with a market share of 11 percent.

In this chapter, you will learn about imperfectly competitive markets, which fall into two categories. Monopolistic competition is a market structure in which many firms compete by offering similar but slightly differentiated products. Monopolistic competition involves a considerable amount of competition and a small dose of monopoly power. The other market structure is oligopoly, in which a small number of firms compete. Oligopoly is characterized by more monopoly and less competition.

CONCENTRATION RATIO

Economists use **concentration ratios** to measure how close an industry comes to the extremes of competition and monopoly. A concentration ratio typically refers to the percentage of an industry's sales (output) that are accounted for by the four largest firms in that industry.

Concentration ratios range from zero to 100 percent. A low concentration ratio suggests a high degree of competition: The four largest firms account for a small portion of industry output and therefore compete with many other firms in the industry. Conversely, a high concentration ratio implies an absence of competition. In the extreme case of monopoly, the concentration ratio is 100 percent—the largest firm accounts for the entire industry output.

The top-four concentration ratio provides an approximation of whether an industry is monopolistically competitive or oligopolistic. When the four largest firms control 40 percent or more of industry output, the industry is generally regarded as oligopolistic. When the four largest firms control less than 40 percent of industry output, the industry approximates **monopolistic competition** or perfect competition, depending on how low the concentration ratio is.

Table 6.1 shows the top-four concentration ratios for selected U.S. manufacturing and service industries in 2017. Column 1 shows examples of low-concentration industries that approximate the characteristics of monopolistic competition. Column 2 shows high-concentration industries that approximate the characteristics of oligopoly.

Be wary, however, of relying on concentration ratios alone to identify industry concentration. Most importantly, they do not consider foreign competition and competition from substitute domestic products. For example, the U.S. automobile industry is quite concentrated. Yet it faces significant competition from foreign manufacturers. Because concentration ratios consider only domestic sales by U.S. firms, they overstate the monopoly power of U.S. auto companies.

TABLE 6.1 Top-Four Concentration Ratios for Selected U.S. Manufacturing and Service Industries, 2017 (in percentages)

Low-Concentration Industries (Monopolistic Competition)	*High-Concentration Industries (Oligopoly)*
Dairy Products 39%	Tobacco 91%
Crude Petroleum Extraction 27	Motorcycles 85
Brick and Stone 26	Breakfast Cereal 82
Poultry Products 26	Outdoor Power Equipment 76
Air and Gas Compressors 25	Pulp Mills 75
Funeral Homes 17	Soap and Detergents 74
Fabricated Wire 14	Ship Building 65
Engineering Services 12	Electric Lamp Bulbs 65
Machine Shops 3	Distilleries 57

*Measured by sales, value of shipments, or revenue in 2017.

Source: Data drawn from United States Census Bureau, *Explore Census Data: Concentration Ratios*, November 2020, located at https://data.census.gov.

TABLE 6.2. Ten Largest Car Manufactures in the United States, 2020–2022, Market Share (percent)

Manufacturer	*2022*	*2021*	*2020*
General Motors	16.1%	14.7%	17.5%
Toyota Motor Co.	14.5	15.5	14.5
Ford Motor Co.	13.4	12.6	13.9
Stellantis*	12.1	11.8	12.5
Hyundai–Kia	10.2	9.9	8.4
Honda	7.3	9.8	9.2
Nissan	6.3	7.2	6.8
Subaru	3.9	3.9	4.2
Volkswagen Group	3.8	4.3	3.9
Tesla Motors	4.0	2.1	1.5

*Merger between Fiat Chrysler Autos and PSA Group in 2021.

Source: Data drawn from Bart Demandt, *U.S. Car Sales Analysis, 2021*, Carsalesbase.com, and Maria Gatea, *Top 10 Largest Car Manufacturers in the U.S.*, Storage Cafe, January 26, 2023.

For example, increased foreign competition has caused U.S. firms to lose their control of the American automobile market. During the 1960s, General Motors (GM) sold half of the new cars purchased by Americans and, together, the "Big Three" U.S. automakers (GM, Ford, and Chrysler) accounted for more than 90 percent of sales—and GM was the industry's dominant firm and price leader. However, GM's market share decreased to about 16 percent of the domestic market in 2022, as shown in Table 6.2. The decline of GM was accompanied by growing competition in the U.S. market from Japanese automakers, which accounted for about 32 percent of U.S. auto sales in 2022.

Because of global competition, U.S. companies have been forced to design more technologically advanced and fuel-efficient automobiles. Also, pricing vehicles competitively has required U.S. automakers to cut overhead expenses, limit wage increases, and increase output per worker. Indeed, global competition has led to an improvement in the quality of the autos sold to American buyers and has decreased the ability of the U.S. Big Three to tacitly increase prices.

MONOPOLISTIC COMPETITION

The market structure that is closest to perfect competition is monopolistic competition. This market structure is based on many firms that each have a relatively small share of the total market. Although monopolistic competition typically does not involve hundreds, or thousands, of firms, as in perfect competition, it does involve a relatively large number of firms, say 30 or more.

With a high degree of market competition, monopolistically competitive firms do not consider the reactions of their rivals when forming their product price and output policies. Moreover, the ability to cooperate to reduce competition is all but impossible given the large number of sellers in the market. Monopolistic competition also assumes that there is relative freedom of entry into the market and exit from the market.

Monopolistic competition differs from perfect competition in one important aspect: It assumes that the product of each firm is not a perfect substitute for the product of competing firms. Product differentiation is thus a fundamental characteristic of monopolistic competition. This gives each firm some power to control the price of its product.

For example, people who believe that Nike shoes are more comfortable than other athletic shoes may be willing to pay a higher price for Nikes. Similarly, people who like the look and feel of Levi's jeans will be willing to pay more for them than for other jeans. Even with product differentiation, however, a monopolistically competitive firm does not have unlimited control over price. Because many other firms produce similar goods and services, a firm that excessively increases its price risks losing many of its customers.

Similar to the demand curve for a monopoly, the demand curve for a monopolistically competitive firm is downward-sloping. If a firm increases its price, it will lose some—but not all—of its sales. Conversely, price reductions result in increased sales. Because a monopolistically competitive firm faces competition from substitute goods sold by rivals, its demand curve is more sensitive to price changes (more elastic) than the demand curve for a monopoly, which does not face competition from close substitutes. This implies that if a monopolistically competitive firm raises the price of its product, it will lose a relatively large number of sales to competitors.

Monopolistic competition can be found in industries in which many small retailing firms compete. Restaurants tend to compete in monopolistically competitive markets. In most towns, there are many restaurants, each offering slightly different meals. Each restaurant has competitors, including other restaurants, fast-food outlets, and frozen-food cases at local grocery stores. Other examples of monopolistic competition are supermarkets, gasoline service stations, accounting and law firms, barbershops, auto repair shops, and shoe stores.

Profit Maximization in the Short Run

Figure 6.1 shows the hypothetical revenue and cost schedules for Fraggini's Pizza Parlor, a typical firm in the local pizza business. Fraggini's competes with Domino's, Pizza Hut, and many other firms in a market that has relative freedom of entry and exit. Notice that Fraggini's demand curve is downward-sloping, which suggests that Fraggini's product is sufficiently superior to some of its customers that a price above those of its competitors will not reduce sales to zero, at least over a small range of prices. As a result, Fraggini's marginal revenue curve is downward-sloping and lies beneath the demand schedule. To sell more pizzas, Fraggini's must reduce its price, and thus the marginal revenue from additional units will be less than the price.

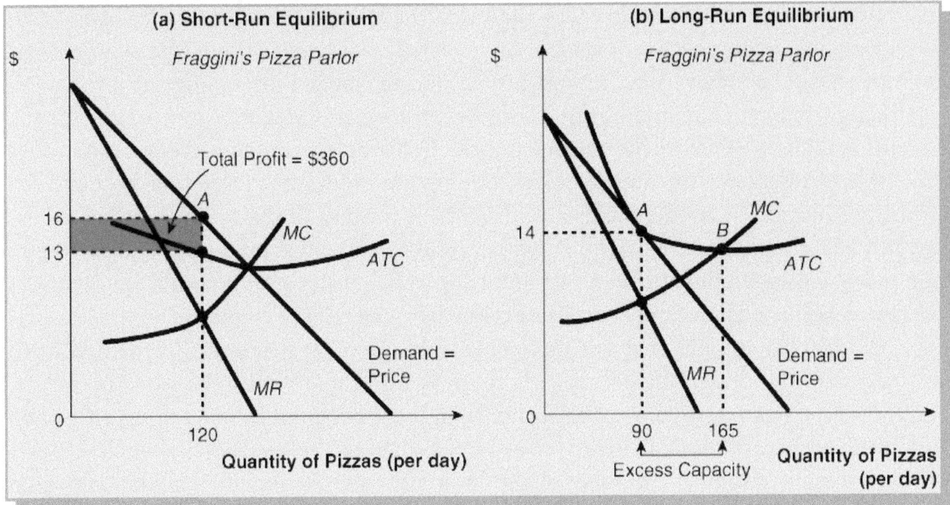

FIGURE 6.1 Market Outcomes Under Monopolistic Competition

Given favorable demand conditions, a monopolistically competitive firm will maximize total profit in the short run by operating at that output where marginal revenue equals marginal cost. Over the long run, the existence of profits in a monopolistically competitive industry will attract new firms. At entry, a decrease in the demand curve and marginal revenue occurs, which eventually results in zero economic profit for the firm. The firm does not increase production to the output for which average total cost is at its lowest point, because it would lose money by doing so.

Refer to Figure 6.1(*a*). Given the marginal revenue curve, *MR*, and the marginal cost curve, *MC*, Fraggini's will maximize total profit by selling 120 pizzas per day, the output where marginal revenue equals marginal cost. Fraggini's demand curve indicates that the firm will charge a price of $16 per pizza to sell this quantity. Looking at the firm's average total cost curve, we see that Fraggini's cost per pizza is $13 at the profit-maximizing output. Fraggini's thus earns a profit of $3 per pizza, or a total daily profit of $360 ($3 × 120 = $360). Assuming that Fraggini's is open every day, this amounts to yearly profits of $131,400.

The Long Run: Normal Profit and Excess Capacity

Realizing the economic profit earned by Fraggini's, competitors will be interested in entering the pizza business. Suppose that firms enter the market and sell similar but not identical pizzas. With entry, the available supply of substitute pizzas increases. For Fraggini's, this results in a decrease in its demand and marginal revenue curves, a decline in the price at which it sells pizza, and a reduction in profits. Entry continues until Fraggini's economic profits are competed away. We conclude that because of easy entry, monopolistically competitive firms tend to earn only a *normal profit* in the long run.

Figure 6.1(*b*) illustrates the market position of Fraggini's in the long run. At the output where marginal revenue equals marginal cost, 90 pizzas, the average total cost curve is tangent to the demand curve. Because the price ($14) just covers the average total cost ($14), Fraggini's economic profit is zero. At any smaller or larger output, the average total cost curve would be above the demand curve, causing Fraggini's to operate at a loss.

Although the long-run equilibrium position of Fraggini's yields zero economic profit, the firm produces *less* than the output at which it would minimize average total cost. The difference between the output corresponding to minimum average total cost and the output produced by a monopolistically competitive firm in the long run is called **excess capacity**. Referring to Figure 6.1(*b*), Fraggini's long-run equilibrium output equals 90 pizzas per day. However, the firm's average total cost would be at a minimum if the firm sold 165 pizzas per day. Therefore, Fraggini's excess daily capacity is 75 pizzas.

Excess capacity implies that monopolistically competitive markets are crowded, with each firm using an underutilized plant. In other words, there tend to be more pizza parlors or gasoline service stations at the corner than those required for maximum efficiency. Underutilized plants result in rising costs and higher prices for the consumer. Notice, however, that an advantage of monopolistic competition is product differentiation, which allows consumers to choose from a wide range of types, styles, brands, and quality variants of a product.

MONOPOLISTIC COMPETITION APPLICATIONS

We have learned that monopolistically competitive firms encounter significant amounts of competition in their quest for economic profits. Let us next consider some applications of monopolistic competition.

Despite Competition from Starbucks, Many Independent Coffeehouses Survive

Starbucks Corporation is the world's largest coffeehouse chain, and it is headquartered in Seattle, Washington. Its story begins in 1971 at Seattle's historic Pike Place Market. It was there that the company opened its first store, offering fresh-roasted coffee beans, tea, and spices. The name "Starbucks" was motivated by the classic saga, "Moby Dick," which emphasized the seafaring tradition of early coffee merchants. In 2022, Starbucks' share of America's coffee market was about 37 percent.

The rise of Starbucks shocked many independent coffeehouse owners, who feared that the company would steal their patrons and wipe out their businesses. However, many independent coffeehouses have continued to operate. They have often found proximity to Starbucks to be an advantage. Analysts maintain that Starbucks increases the overall market and attracts new customers to gourmet coffee shops who then patronize the independent café next door.

Critics of Starbucks often compare it with Walmart Stores. Yet, Starbucks doesn't enjoy the advantages that have made Walmart the curse of many Main Street retailers—lower

Source: Karen K / 500px/Getty Images®

prices, wider selection, and longer hours. The Starbucks menu isn't cheaper or broader than the independents', and the chain's hours are often shorter. This may be why independents still flourish in the industry.

An important reason for the success of independent coffeehouses is product differentiation: They are less like restaurants and more like neighborhood taverns, a concept that coffeehouse chains do not threaten. Customers often come alone to an independent café in search of conversation and friendship. There they are served by familiar employees, sit in an intimate room with upholstered chairs and antique tables, and enjoy poetry readings, jazz performances, and films. Moreover, the emergence of Starbucks has inspired independents to upgrade their cafes and broaden their menus.

Many independents are probably not as profitable as Starbucks shops. The size of its gourmet coffee orders means that Starbucks receives purchasing discounts that fatten its profit margins. But the profit margins on gourmet coffee drinks are so high that independent cafes can prosper even without volume purchasing discounts.

Concentration Keeps the Beer Industry Foaming

Brewing beer in America dates back to the English and Dutch settlers in the 1600s. However, the industry didn't take off until the 1800s, when beer became mass-produced. By the late 1880s, breweries increased the scope of their operations by using the growing railroad system, and they shipped beer throughout the country. Pabst Brewing in Milwaukee and Anheuser-Busch in St. Louis became the largest breweries in the country.

The period following World War II witnessed consolidation in America's beer industry, as the number of breweries declined, and the share of the market held by leading breweries increased. Between 1950 and 2000, the four-firm concentration ratio for beer producers increased from 22 percent to 95 percent, and Anheuser-Busch's share of domestic output surged from 6 percent to 54 percent.

What led to the evolution of America's beer industry from low concentration to high concentration? On the supply side of the market, technological advances increased the speed of bottling and canning lines. A modern production line can produce 1,100 bottles or 2,000 cans of beer per minute. Also, automated brewing and warehousing allow brewers to decrease unit labor costs. Moreover, plant construction costs per barrel are about one-third less for a 4.5-million-barrel plant than for a 1.5-million-barrel plant. Finally, mergers among breweries contributed to increased market concentration.

Changes on the demand side of the market have also promoted market concentration. First, consumer tastes switched from the stronger-flavored beers of many small breweries to the light products of the larger breweries. Indeed, Bud Light and Miller Light became popular brands for many consumers. Second, the consumption of beer moved away from taverns and into homes. The significance of this change was that taverns were usually supplied with kegs from local brewers. However, the acceptance of aluminum cans for home consumption made it possible for large distant brewers to compete with the local brewers.

Advertising has also served as a barrier to entry in the beer industry. Large breweries that sell national brands realize advertising cost advantages over smaller breweries that sell regional and local brands. National television advertising tends to be less costly per viewer than local advertising.

Since the early 2000s, small regional breweries and local craft breweries have rebounded, and they have captured some of the market share of large breweries. Small brewers typically produce less beer than large breweries, and they have new flavors and varied brewing techniques that appeal to local consumers. Nevertheless, the U.S. beer industry remains concentrated. As of 2022, the small brewers had a combined share of 13 percent of America's beer market while the large breweries had an 87-percent market share.[1]

ADVERTISING

Product differentiation is the hallmark of many imperfectly competitive firms. Such firms often engage in advertising either to make buyers aware of the unique features of their products or to convince them that their product really is different from those of their competitors, or both. Advertising constantly surrounds us—in magazines and newspapers, online, and on radio, television, and billboards. Table 6.3 shows the world's largest advertisers in 2021.

Many imperfectly competitive markets are characterized by brand names, continual product development and improvement, and product promotion. For example, the brand name Prestone has become a synonym for antifreeze, while Pennzoil is synonymous with motor oil. As a result of the acceptance of these brands by consumers, the manufacturers of Prestone and Pennzoil charge higher prices for their products than those charged for competing brands. Indeed, the market value of product brands can amount to billions of dollars.

TABLE 6.3 The World's Largest Advertisers, 2021 (billions of dollars)

Company	*Industry*	*Advertising Expenditures*
Proctor and Gamble (U.S.)	Household products	$11.5
Amazon (U.S.)	Internet retailing	10.9
L'Oreal (France)	Cosmetics	9.9
Samsung Electronics (South Korea)	Electronics	8.6
Alibaba Group (China)	E-commerce	8.4
Unilever (Great Britain)	Consumer goods	8.1
Nestlé (Switzerland)	Food and drink	7.8
Comcast (U.S.)	Cable television	6.7
Louise Vuitton (France)	Luxury fashion products	5.8
Google (U.S.)	Technology	5.4

Source: Data drawn from Marketing Mind, *World's Largest Advertisers in 2021*, December 22, 2021, available at https://www.marketingmind.in/worlds-largest-advertisers-in-2021.

A Diagrammatic Analysis of Advertising

The objective of nearly all advertising is to increase the demand for a firm's product. Consider the Coca-Cola Co., which engages in extensive advertising. By persuading consumers that Coke really is better than Pepsi and other rivals, Coca-Cola can expect to increase the amount of soda that it can sell at each price. In Figure 6.2(*a*), this is shown by a rightward shift in the firm's demand curve. Without advertising, the Coca-Cola Co. sells 6 million cases at a price of $5 per case, denoted by point *A* on demand curve D_0. As a result of persuasive advertising, the firm's demand curve may shift to D_1. At the $6 price, the firm can now sell 10 million cases.

Besides increasing the demand curve of Coke, persuasive advertising can make demand less sensitive to price changes (less elastic). By successfully generating brand loyalty through advertising, Coca-Cola Co. convinces consumers that there exist fewer substitutes for its product. By allowing the firm to charge higher prices with a smaller loss of sales, advertising enhances the price-making ability of the Coca-Cola Co. Profits rise when advertising increases the firm's revenue more than the cost of advertising.[2]

Persuasive advertising also affects the long-run average total cost of Coke, as shown in Figure 6.2(*b*). Without advertising, the Coca-Cola Co.'s average total cost curve is denoted by ATC_0. At a price of $5, the firm sells, say, 6 million cases of Coke. The firm's unit cost is $3 per case, shown by point *A*. To increase its market share, suppose the Coca-Cola Co. decides to advertise. The advertising expenditures result in an upward shift in the firm's

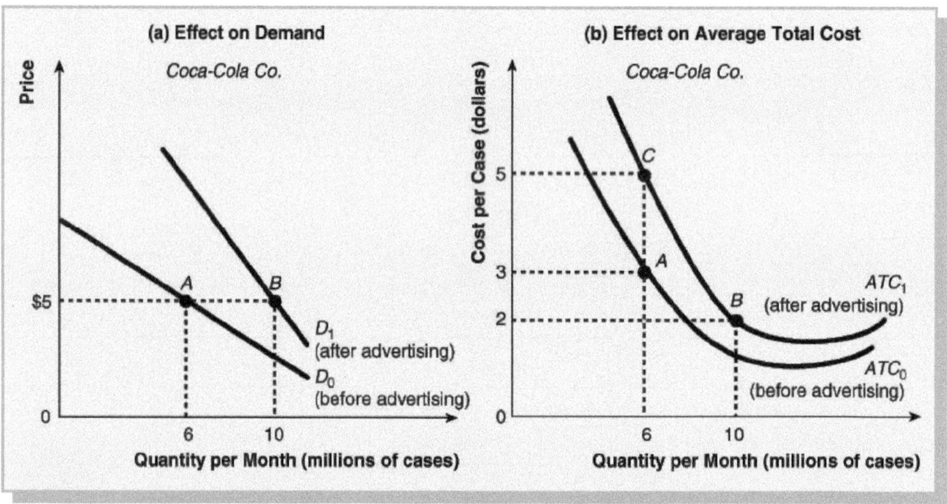

FIGURE 6.2 The Effect of Advertising on Demand and Average Total Cost

The purpose of nearly all of advertising is to increase the demand for a firm's product and to make it less sensitive to price changes (less elastic). As a result, the firm's market share increases, as does its price-making ability. By fostering an increase in market share and production, advertising can help a firm more fully realize economies of scale and decreases in unit costs.

cost curve to ATC_1. Through successful advertising, suppose Coke's sales increase to, say, 10 million cases. By producing additional cases of Coke, the firm can take advantage of economies of scale that decrease unit cost to $2, shown by point *B*. The reduction in unit cost, made possible by economies of large-scale production, more than outweighs the increase in unit cost, resulting from advertising. Thus, consumers can purchase Coke at a lower price with advertising than they would without.

On the other hand, what if PepsiCo, Inc. initiates an advertising campaign that offsets the demand-increasing effects of Coke's advertising campaign? In this case, the market share of each firm remains unchanged as the result of advertising. For the Coca-Cola Co., advertising results in an increase in its cost curve from ATC_0 to ATC_1. Because the firm's sales remain at 6 million cases, however, unit cost rises to $5 per case (point C). The consumer thus faces a higher price because of advertising. Critics of advertising argue that this is the typical case rather than the reduction in unit cost from point *A* to point *B*. Instead, they argue that advertising expenditures could be used for hospitals, education, or other useful products that might better improve the well-being of society.

PRICE DISCRIMINATION

We have learned that imperfectly competitive firms seek to determine the price that will maximize their total profits. Sometimes, the firm may charge more than one price for a particular good. For example, golf courses often charge senior citizens a lower price than other adults to play a round of golf. Movie theaters often give discounts to students to see a movie. In these *cases*, the firm charges different prices to different customers for what is essentially the same product or service. These practices are known as **price discrimination**—that is, charging some customers a lower price than others for an identical good even though there is no difference in the cost to the firm for supplying these consumers.

To engage in price discrimination, a seller must have price-making ability and thus operate in an imperfectly competitive market. It also must prevent significant resales of products from the lower-priced to the higher-priced market. If buyers can resell a product, price discrimination is unlikely to succeed. Finally, the seller must divide its customers into groups, each having a different willingness and ability to pay. Price-sensitive buyers (those with *more elastic* demand schedules) will pay a *lower* price than buyers who are not as sensitive to price (those with less elastic demand schedules).

Price Discrimination in the Airline Industry

Airline carriers provide an example of price discrimination. Consider a recent United Airlines flight from its hub at O'Hare International Airport in Chicago to Los Angeles. If any of the passengers had compared notes, they would have found that they had paid 27 different fares. One paid nothing, using frequent flyer miles; another who bought a first-class ticket on the day of departure paid $1,249; and one who bought a coach ticket on the day of travel paid $108. In general, the people who bought their tickets earlier paid less, but not always.

Although this pricing strategy may seem chaotic, its purpose is to squeeze as many dollars as possible out of each seat and mile flown. That means trying to project just how many tickets to sell at a discount without running out of seats for the business traveler, who usually books at the last minute and therefore pays full fare. According to the airlines, "You don't want to sell a seat to a guy for $79 when he's willing to pay $450."

Airlines use price discrimination to increase their revenues. For airline travel, the key distinction among travelers is between leisure travel and business travel. Leisure travelers have relatively elastic demand because they can plan ahead and are flexible in their schedules. To encourage these price-sensitive customers to fly on their planes, airlines will charge them relatively low prices and, of course, do so in a manner that prevents them from reselling their tickets to less price-sensitive passengers. Business passengers, however, have less elastic demand because they often must travel on short notice, do not stay over weekends, and are insensitive to ticket fares. As a result, airlines charge higher fares to business travelers, who are a primary source of airline profits.

To preserve their fare structures, airlines generally make their tickets nontransferable. Otherwise, vacationers might purchase tickets when they are cheap and resell them to other travelers closer to departure, when fares are much higher. Or vacationers might purchase cheap tickets and sell them to business travelers who would normally have to pay a higher fare for a ticket. Such behavior would create competition for the airlines in the high-price segment of the market and undermine their price discrimination policy. Travelers can fly at a later date on their unused tickets by applying the value of the ticket to an alternate trip after subtracting change fees, which can run as high as $150 on a domestic flight and $250 on international flights. But most airlines require the new ticket to be in the original passenger's name. Industry analysts estimate that about 2 to 3 percent of all tickets expire unused. In 2009, that translated into about $2 billion-worth of tickets thrown away.

Colleges also use price discrimination. In 1995, for example, Johns Hopkins University began offering aid according to the student's price elasticity of demand for attending the university.[3] Johns Hopkins wanted to attract academically gifted students who would major in humanities but might attend other universities. These students had relatively elastic demand curves for education at Johns Hopkins, given the availability of substitute universities. By granting them an extra $3,000 in aid, the university was able to increase enrollment in that group by 20 percent.

However, Johns Hopkins did not worry about losing prospective pre-med students, whose demand curves for education at Johns Hopkins were relatively inelastic. Because most of these students were already hooked on its pre-med program, a price increase would not knock many out. Johns Hopkins cut this group's aid by $1,000 per student and still increased net revenue. Today, this pricing strategy is being tried out at colleges and universities all over the nation. Perhaps your relatively elastic demand for the college you are attending contributed to your receiving a scholarship.

CHECK POINT

1 Identify the characteristics of an imperfectly competitive market structure.
2 How do concentration ratios attempt to measure how closely an industry comes to the extremes of competition and monopoly?
3 Explain how monopolistic competition involves a considerable amount of competition and a small dose of monopoly power.
4 How does a firm successfully practice price discrimination?

OLIGOPOLY

Oligopoly is another form of imperfect competition. In oligopoly, a small number of firms compete, and each firm has significant price-making ability. Oligopoly embodies a range of market situations. It includes a situation in which two or three firms dominate an entire market, as well as one in which seven or eight firms share, say, 75 percent of the market (while a competitive fringe of remaining firms accounts for the remainder). Oligopoly also includes firms that produce standardized products as well as differentiated products. The steel and pharmaceutical industries are generally regarded as oligopolistic.

The quantity sold by an oligopolist depends not only on that firm's product price but also on the other firms' prices and quantities sold. Therefore, each firm must consider the impact of its own actions on the actions of other firms.

To understand the interaction between prices and sales, consider the following example. Suppose that you operate one of three grocery stores in a small town. If you reduce your prices and your rivals do not reduce theirs, your sales will increase, but the sales of your two rivals will decrease. In this situation, your rivals are likely to cut their prices as well. If they reduce prices, your sales and profits will decline. So before deciding to decrease your prices, you attempt to predict how your rivals will react, and you try to estimate the impact of those reactions on your profit.

Why are some industries dominated by a few firms? We can provide some partial answers here:

- **Barriers to entry**. Oligopolistic industries may be fostered by barriers to entry such as product differentiation and advertising, patents, and the control and ownership of key resources. Historical control of raw materials explains the dominance of Alcoa (Aluminum Co. of America) in the aluminum industry. The high costs of obtaining needed plant and equipment may also deter entry. The aircraft and cigarette industries are characterized by high investment requirements.
- **Economies of scale**. With economies of scale, a firm's average total cost declines as output expands. Smaller firms in this situation tend to be inefficient because their

average total costs will be greater than those realized by a larger firm. With economies of scale, a firm may be able to drive its smaller rivals out of the market and prevent potential competitors from entering the market. Economies of scale are noticeable in the cement and rubber industries.

- **Mergers**. Another reason that oligopoly occurs is that firms combine under a single ownership or control, a practice known as **merger**. The merged firm is larger, and therefore it may realize economies of scale as output expands, and it usually has a greater ability to control the market price of its product. In the beer industry, for example, giants such as Anheuser-Busch and Miller have grown through the acquisition of competing breweries.

OLIGOPOLISTIC RIVALRY

Concerning oligopoly, one may get the impression that because there are only a few sellers in the market, there is little, if any, rivalry among them. In reality, firms often fight for market share through vigorous price competition, product promotion, and improvements in product quality. Let us consider two cases of oligopolistic rivalry: (1) between the Coca-Cola Co. and PepsiCo, Inc. in the soft drink industry and (2) between Kodak and Fuji in the photographic equipment industry.

Rivalry in the Soft Drink Industry

Historically, the Coca-Cola Co. has dominated the soft drink industry. Sales and profits have generally risen ever since Coke was first introduced to the market. Prior to the 1950s, no second-place firm was even worth considering. Consumers generally regarded Pepsi, Coke's closest competitor, to be an inferior drink.

During the 1950s, PepsiCo embarked on a strategy to increase its market share. The company improved the taste of its soft drink by using less sugar in its formula and establishing uniform control over local bottlers, who had previously added varying amounts of carbonated water to the syrup so that Pepsi's taste varied throughout different regions of the country. It also offered consumers a 12-ounce bottle that sold for the same price as Coke's famous 6½ ounce bottle. To enhance its image, PepsiCo adopted advertising campaigns featuring young women and men drinking Pepsi in high-income surroundings. The campaigns featured Pepsi as "the light refreshment," implying indirectly that Coke was "heavy." PepsiCo also adopted promotional efforts to increase sales in grocery markets where Coke was comparatively weak. Moreover, Pepsi attacked Coke in the vending machine and cold-bottle segments of the market by offering financing to local bottlers who were willing to buy and install Pepsi vending machines.

As Pepsi's market share increased, the Coca-Cola Co. launched retaliatory advertising campaigns. Using slogans such as "The really refreshed" and "No wonder Coke refreshes best," these campaigns picked up Coke's sales. In return, PepsiCo initiated two new advertising campaigns—"Be sociable" and "Think young." These campaigns especially caught on with teenagers, who account for the highest per-capita consumption of soft drinks. The youth theme suggested that Coke was an old-fashioned drink. The Coca-Cola Co. countered with its new advertising theme of "Things go better with Coke."

By 1980, the Coca-Cola Co. decided that it needed to compete more directly with Pepsi, which had a sweeter flavor than Coke. The firm developed a new formula for its soft drink and called it "New Coke." In spite of heavy advertising, public acceptance of New Coke was at best lukewarm and, at worst, disastrous. Several months after its introduction, the Coca-Cola Co. was forced to bring back "Classic Coke," which was based on the original formula used by Coke. It is estimated that the fiasco cost the firm's shareholders up to $500 million.

As of 2023, Coke and Pepsi continued to dominate the soft drink market. It remains to be seen how their competitive struggle will play out.

Rivalry in the Photographic Equipment Industry

Eastman Kodak Company, commonly known as Kodak, is widely known as a producer of photographic film products and cameras. During most of the twentieth century, Kodak maintained a dominant position in the photographic equipment market. By 1976 it accounted for 90 percent of American film sales and 85 percent of camera sales. However, Kodak's near-monopoly position led to its managers becoming complacent: They were reluctant to change their business model as global competition appeared.

In the 1980s, Fuji Photo Film Co. of Japan entered the U.S. market with lower-priced film and supplies. Fuji established a film manufacturing plant in the United States and through aggressive marketing and price reductions it began cutting into Kodak's sales. By 1995, Fuji accounted for 17 percent of the photo film sold in America and Kodak's sales slipped to 75 percent of the market. Moreover, Kodak was not able to significantly increase its sales in Japan, the second-largest market for its photo film and paper after the United States. Clearly, Kodak failed to appreciate how formidable a competitor Fuji had become.

The development of digital cameras and smartphones (which operate as cameras) also contributed to Kodak's descent. It is ironic that Kodak was a pioneer in the development of digital technology in the 1970s. However, because Kodak's rivals did not yet have access to this technology, Kodak lacked the incentive to produce and market digital cameras. Instead, Kodak continued selling cheap, film cameras to customers who purchased lots of its expensive film. All of this changed in the 1990s as rivals like Nikon launched their digital cameras. This forced Kodak to move into digital cameras. By 2005, Kodak ranked at the top of the digital camera market in America. However, despite high growth, Kodak failed to anticipate how fast digital cameras became "commodities," with low profit margins, as more companies entered the market. Kodak's digital camera sales were soon undercut by Asian rivals who produced their cameras more cheaply. Kodak also failed to appreciate the nature of emerging markets. It hoped that the new Chinese middle class would purchase lots of its film. They did for a while, but then switched to digital cameras that did not use film.

Kodak provides a vivid example of a company that was weakened by global competition and advancing technology. With profits turning into losses, Kodak declared Chapter 11 bankruptcy in 2012, under which it went reorganization under the supervision of a bankruptcy court judge. Kodak ceased making pocket video cameras, digital cameras, and digital picture frames. Also, the company sold off many of its patents and businesses that had made it famous, thus emerging as a smaller and leaner business. Today, Kodak continues to compete on commercial print and advanced materials and chemicals.

Airbus and Boeing Rivalry for Supremacy in the Commercial Jetliner Industry

Source: Sean Gladwell/Moment/Getty Images®

The commercial jetliner industry provides another example of oligopolistic rivalry. Consider the competitive battle between Boeing and Airbus.

Although the Europeans developed the first commercial jetliner in the 1950s, Boeing learned from the Europeans' mistakes and leapfrogged ahead. European manufacturers were concerned that competition from Boeing would wipe out their weak and divided aviation industry. Hence, the governments of France, Germany, Spain, and the United Kingdom exercised the only option they felt was available to them: Pooling their resources to establish a company that could compete against Boeing. This led to the formation of the Airbus Co. in 1969.

When Airbus was first created, analysts generally doubted whether it could compete against Boeing, which enjoyed a near monopoly in the sale of jetliners. Maintaining that they were nurturing an "infant industry," the governments of Europe granted jetliner development subsidies to Airbus. By the 1980s, Airbus had become a strong competitor against Boeing, and by the early 2000s it accounted for about half of the world market for large jetliners.

As Airbus grew, Boeing complained that Airbus's success was primarily the result of unfair subsidies from the European governments, and that they placed Boeing at a competitive disadvantage. Boeing maintained these subsidies allowed Airbus to set unrealistically low prices, offer concessions and attractive financing terms to airlines, and write off development costs.

Airbus defended its subsidies on the grounds that they prevented the United States from holding a worldwide monopoly in commercial jetliners. Airbus also argued that Boeing benefited from development subsidies and tax breaks from federal and state governments.

After a lengthy investigation, in 2019–2020 the World Trade Organization (WTO) ruled that both producers received illegal subsidies from their governments. At the writing of this text, it remains to be seen how compliance with the WTO's findings will be resolved.

Today, Boeing and Airbus make up about 99 percent of the world's large aircraft orders. The two companies have negligible competition other than between themselves. Boeing and Airbus benefit from barriers to entry, including the high costs of developing jetliners and substantial economies of scale. These barriers present a great challenge to Russian and Chinese aircraft producers who are attempting to crack the world market.

GAME THEORY AND OLIGOPOLY BEHAVIOR

A feature of oligopoly is that firms must weigh the impacts of their decisions on other firms and anticipate how those other firms will react. Basically, the conduct of an oligopoly can be viewed as a high-stakes game in which the goal is to earn economic profits by outguessing your competitors. In the real world, Boeing and Airbus have been rivals in the commercial jetliner market, as have Coca-Cola and PepsiCo, Inc. in the soft drink market; Anheuser-Busch, Miller, and Coors in the beer market; Ford, General Motors, and Chrysler in the auto market; and General Mills, Post, and Kellogg's in the breakfast cereal market. These firms tend to form their price policies based on the price policies of their rivals.

We can gain important insights into oligopolistic markets by examining a method of analysis called **game theory**. Game theory examines oligopolistic behavior by examining a series of strategies and payoffs among rival firms. A strategy is a course of action, say, to charge a high price or a low price—and the payoff is the economic profit that results from that strategy.

Consider a hypothetical market with two competing airline firms, American and United, whose goals are to increase their economic profits by price changes. Each firm makes its pricing decisions independently, without knowing in advance what its rival will do. Figure 6.3 shows the profit–payoff matrix for these firms. Each cell in the matrix shows the yearly profit that each of the two firms can expect to earn depending on its own pricing strategy and that of its rival. The top portion in each cell shows the profit of United, and the bottom portion shows American's profit.

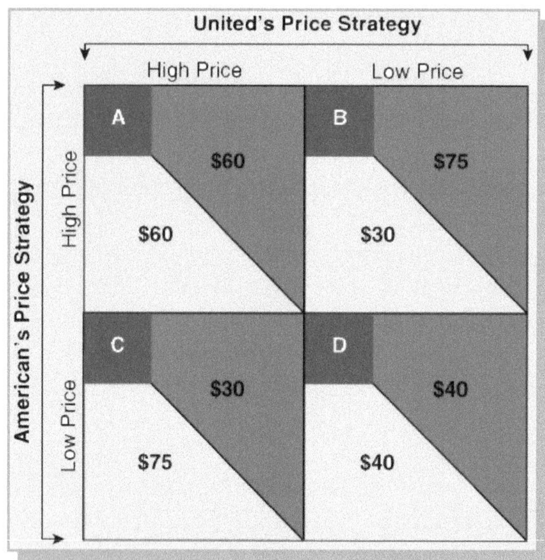

FIGURE 6.3 Game Theory and Oligopoly Behavior

United and American would earn the largest profits if they both selected a high-price strategy. If they behave independently, either firm might realize higher profits by selecting a low-price strategy against its rival's high-price strategy. However, such rivalry tends to cause both firms to gravitate to a low-price strategy.

Competitive Oligopoly and Low Prices

As shown in Figure 6.3, the option that is available to each firm is to charge either a high price or a low price, and the payoff matrix shows the profit that each firm can expect to earn, given its own pricing choice and that of its competitor. For example, if both firms charge high prices (cell *A*), each will earn a profit of $60 million. Instead, suppose that United charges a low price and American charges a high price (cell *B*). United will then attract customers from its rival and earn a profit of $75 million; American will earn a modest profit of $30 million. Conversely, if American charges a low price and United charges a high price, American will earn a profit of $75 million, while United will earn a profit of only $30 million.

As the payoff matrix shows, each firm will realize additional profits if both firms charge a high price. However, the maximum payoff for a firm will be achieved when its rival charges a high price while it alone charges a low price, thereby attracting customers from its rival. The minimum payoff for a particular firm will be achieved when it charges a high price while its rival charges a low one, because then it will lose many sales to its rival.

The outcome of this game yields a tendency toward a low-price strategy for competitive oligopoly. If United or American charges a low price, it is doing the best that it can do, given the behavior of the other firm. Thus, once United and American reach cell *D* in the figure, neither firm will desire to alter its price. The market thus gravitates toward a low-price strategy for each firm. Simply put, fear of what the rival firm will do is what causes each firm to offer a low price. The low price is good for consumers, but it is not good for the firms, which realize a profit of only $40 million rather than the $60 million that each would have earned if both had charged high prices (cell *A*).

Cooperative Behavior and Cheating

How can United and American avoid the modest profits associated with cell *D*? The answer is to cooperate with each other and decide how to set prices. For example, the managers of the two firms might strike an agreement that each will charge a high price. This action will cause the firms to locate at cell *A* in the figure, where each earns profits of $60 million instead of $40 million.

Although cooperative behavior can increase the profits of each firm, the profits are not at a maximum. Therefore, each firm may be enticed to cheat on this pricing agreement and charge a low price while its rival maintains a high price. For example, if United agrees to charge a high price, but secretly charges a low price, the outcome will move from cell *A* to cell *B*, where United earns a profit of $75 million. Similarly, if only American cheats, the outcome will move from cell *A* to cell C, and the firm will earn a profit of $75 million. Therefore, there is a tendency for cooperative price-fixing agreements to break down.

COLLUSION AND CARTELS

Source: Anton Petrus/Moment/Getty Images®

Recall that game theory considers the possibility that oligopolistic firms may form collusive agreements with each other rather than behaving as competitors. Let us further examine how oligopolies form collusive agreements, known as cartels.

A **cartel** is a formal organization of firms that attempts to act as if there were only one firm in the industry (monopoly). The purpose of a cartel is to reduce output and increase the price to increase the joint profits of its members.

A widely known cartel is the **Organization of Petroleum Exporting Countries (OPEC)**, a group of nations that sells oil on the world market. Although OPEC has generally disavowed the term *cartel*, its organization consists of a secretariat, a conference of ministers, a board of governors, and an economic commission. Most of the countries that belong to OPEC are located in the Middle East, including countries such as Saudi Arabia, Iran, Kuwait, and Qatar, though some are elsewhere, such as Venezuela. OPEC has assigned production controls among its members to make oil scarce, thus supporting prices higher than would exist under more competitive conditions. The world's top oil-producing countries and oil-consuming countries are shown in Table 6.4 and Table 6.5.

In response to decreasing oil prices caused by increases in U.S. shale oil output, in 2016 OPEC reached an agreement with 10 other oil-producing countries to coordinate

TABLE 6.4 The 10 Largest Oil Producers and Share of World Oil Production in 2022*

Country	*Million Barrels Per Day*	*Share of World Total (percent)*
United States	20.21	20
Saudi Arabia	12.14	12
Russia	10.94	11
Canada	5.70	6
China	5.12	5
Iraq	4.55	5
United Arab Emirates	4.24	4
Brazil	3.77	4
Iran	3.66	4
Kuwait	3.02	3
Total, Top 10	73.36	73
World Total	99.89	

*Oil includes crude oil, all other petroleum liquids, and biofuels.

Source: Data drawn from U.S. Energy Administration, International Energy Statistics, Total Oil (Petroleum and other Liquids) Production as of May 1, 2023, available at https://www.eia.gov.

TABLE 6.5 The 10 Largest Oil Consumers and Share of Total World Oil Consumption in 2021*

Country	*Million Barrels Per Day*	*Share of World Total (percent)*
United States	19.89	21
China	14.76	15
India	4.79	5
Russia	3.67	4
Japan	3.41	4
Saudi Arabia	3.35	3
Brazil	2.96	3
South Korea	2.58	3
Canada	2.26	2
Germany	2.13	2
Total, Top 10	59.80	62
World Total	96.66	

*Oil includes crude oil, all other petroleum liquids, and biofuels.

Source: Data drawn from U.S. Energy Administration, International Energy Statistics, Total Oil (Petroleum and other Liquids) Production as of May 1, 2023, available at https://www.eia.gov.

and unify prices. The enlarged group became known as **OPEC+**. Among the 10 other countries was Russia, the world's third-largest oil producer behind the United States and Saudi Arabia.

After operating in obscurity throughout the 1960s, OPEC captured control of oil pricing in 1972–1981, when the price of oil skyrocketed from $3 to more than $35 per barrel in 1981. During this era, OPEC's success at increasing oil prices was largely attributable to strong consumer demand for oil and insensitivity to price increases (inelastic demand). Moreover, OPEC accounted for half of the world's oil production and about two-thirds of the world's oil reserves throughout this era.

Since the early 1980s, the global oil market has undergone a series of upswings and downswings. When oil has been in surplus, OPEC has levied production quotas to shove prices upwards. For example, surplus oil conditions resulted in the Declaration of Cooperation in 2016, with OPEC members and 10 non-OPEC oil-producing countries coming together to reduce production and support stable prices. During the Covid-19 pandemic, the global demand for oil went into a freefall. This resulted in OPEC members and non-OPEC oil-producing nations cutting production to stabilize the oil market.

What Determines Cartel Profitability?

Although a cartel attempts to maximize the profits of its members, several obstacles may limit its success. Recall from our discussion of game theory that, once a cartel is established, incentives arise for individual member producers to leave the cartel and operate independently. If a single producer were to charge a price below the cartel price, this would attract additional sales to that producer, at the expense of other cartel members, possibly increasing its profits above what they would be under the cartel. However, if other cartel members follow suit and reduce their prices, all firms will receive both lower prices and profits than they enjoyed under the cartel arrangement. Because of the incentive for individual members to leave the cartel and establish prices independently, the life span of cartels is often short.

Besides the problem of cheating, other obstacles to forming and maintaining a cartel can arise. Among the obstacles that cartels face are:

- **Number of sellers**. Generally speaking, the larger the number of sellers, the more difficult it is to coordinate price and output policies among cartel members.
- **Cost and demand differences**. When cartel members' costs and demands differ greatly, it is more difficult to assign production controls and agree on price.
- **Potential competition**. The increased profits that occur under a cartel may attract new competitors, thus restricting the cartel's control of the market.
- **Economic downturn**. As market sales dwindle in a weakening economy, profits decline, thus undermining the success of a cartel.
- **Government policy**. In the United States, cartels are illegal. Business executives who are found guilty of engaging in collusion can be fined and sent to jail. This does not mean that firms do not engage in collusion. However, it is usually done secretly and is difficult to prove.

MERGERS AND OLIGOPOLY

An examination of the history of American business reveals that many firms grew as the result of mergers, thus attaining oligopolistic power. A **merger** is the combination of the assets of two firms to form a single new firm. By combining their assets, the acquiring firm and the acquired firm hope to become more profitable than they were before the merger. Classic examples of mergers creating oligopolies include steel companies, oil companies, railroads, grocery store chains, and wireless carriers. Table 6.6 shows the largest merger deals in U.S. history.

There are three types of mergers: A **horizontal merger** occurs when one firm combines with another firm that sells similar products in the same market. The historic merger of Jones & Laughlin Steel and Republic Steel to form LTV Steel is an example of a horizontal merger. A **vertical merger** is a merger between firms that are in the same industry, but at different stages in the production process. For example, Bridgestone (tires) has acquired rubber plantations in Indonesia and Malaysia, and the Campbell's Soup Co. has acquired mushroom farms throughout the United States. Finally, a **conglomerate merger** brings

TABLE 6.6 Largest Merger Deals in the United States

Rank	*Date*	*Acquiror*	*Target*	*Value ($ billions)*
1	2000	American Online	Time Warner	$164.7
2	2013	Verizon Communications	Verizon Wireless	130.3
3	1999	Pfizer	Warner-Lambert	89.2
4	2016	AT&T	Time Warner	85.4
5	1998	Exxon	Mobil	78.9
6	2006	AT&T	Bell-South	72.7
7	1998	Travelers Group	Citicorp	72.6
8	2001	Comcast	AT&T Broadband & Internet	72.0
9	2014	Actavis	Allergan	68.4
10	2009	Pfizer	Wyeth	67.3

Source: Data drawn from Institute for Mergers, Acquisitions, and Alliances, *United States-M&A Statistics*, available at https://imaa-institute.org/mergers-and-acquisitions-statistics/united-states-ma-statistics.

together two firms producing in different industries. The merger of Greyhound (bus service) and Armor and Co. (meat products) is an example of a conglomerate merger.

Of these types of mergers, the federal government looks most carefully at proposed horizontal mergers. The reason is that horizontal mergers can unite firms that formerly competed against one another, thus reducing competition and increasing the monopoly power of the newly formed firm. However, horizontal mergers can contribute to cost savings and other efficiencies. For example, the newly formed firm might (1) add to industry output and promote additional competition, (2) enter markets that neither merging firm could have entered individually, or (3) realize cost reductions that would have been unavailable if each merging firm had performed the same function separately. Such cost reductions could be the result of economies of scale, integration of production facilities, plant specialization, and lower transportation costs. In deciding whether a horizontal merger should be approved, the federal government weighs the benefits of increased efficiencies versus the costs of increased monopoly power.

CHECK POINT

1. Oligopoly involves a considerable dose of monopoly and a small dose of competition. Explain.
2. How does game theory illustrate the mutual interdependence of firms in oligopoly?

3 Why are cartels difficult to form and operate?
4 Distinguish between a horizontal merger, a vertical merger, and a conglomerate merger.
5 Why do government regulators especially scrutinize proposed horizontal mergers?

CHAPTER SUMMARY

1 Imperfect competition exists when more than one seller competes for sales with many other sellers, each of which has some price-making ability. Imperfect competition comprises the market structures of monopolistic competition and oligopoly.

2 Economists use concentration ratios to measure how closely an industry comes to the extremes of competition and monopoly. A low concentration ratio suggests a high degree of competition, and a high concentration ratio implies a low degree of competition.

3 Monopolistic competition is characterized by a large number of sellers, each having a relatively small share of the total market, relative freedom of entry into and exit from the market, and product differentiation among sellers. Although monopolistically competitive firms tend to earn zero economic profits in the long run, they suffer from the problem of excess capacity.

4 The goal of persuasive advertising is to shift a firm's demand curve to the right and make it less sensitive to price changes. Advertising results in an upward shift in a firm's cost curve. However, the economies of large-scale production made possible by increased sales volume because of advertising may lead to lower unit costs than would occur without advertising.

5 Price discrimination is the practice of charging some customers a lower price than others for an identical good or service, even though there is no difference in the cost to the firm for supplying these consumers. A firm that practices price discrimination will charge a lower price to buyers with more elastic demand and a higher price to buyers with less elastic demand.

6 In oligopoly, a small number of firms compete with each other, and each firm has significant price-making ability. Oligopolistic markets are characterized by high barriers to entry, economies of scale, and mergers. Because uncertainty about the interaction of competing firms in oligopoly makes it virtually impossible to formulate a single theory of oligopoly behavior, a number of different theories exist. However, game theory can be used to illustrate the mutual interdependence of firms in oligopolistic markets.

7 Rather than engage in cutthroat competition, oligopolies may decide to collude and form a cartel. The purpose of a cartel is to restrict output and drive up price, thus maximizing the joint profits of its members.

8 Oligopolies are characterized by horizontal mergers, vertical mergers, and conglomerate mergers. Of these three types of mergers, government regulators monitor proposed horizontal mergers most closely. The reason is that horizontal mergers can unite firms that formerly competed against one another, which may increase the monopoly power of the newly formed firm.

KEY TERMS AND CONCEPTS

concentration ratios
monopolistic competition
product differentiation
excess capacity
price discrimination
oligopoly
merger
game theory
cartel
Organization of Petroleum Exporting Countries (OPEC)
OPEC+
horizontal merger
vertical merger
conglomerate merger

STUDY QUESTIONS AND PROBLEMS

1 What is the meaning of a top-four concentration ratio of 20 percent? 85 percent?

2 Suppose that Don's Texaco is a typical gas station in a monopolistically competitive market. Draw a diagram showing the market position of the firm in the long run. Will the firm encounter the problem of excess capacity? Why or why not?

3 Figure 6.4 shows the short-run position of Hal's Electronics, a typical firm selling radios in a monopolistically competitive market.

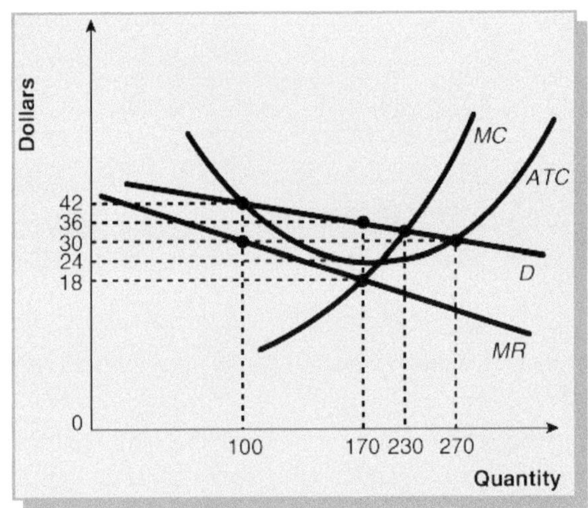

FIGURE 6.4 Short-Run Position of a Monopolistically Competitive Firm

a Hal's profit-maximizing output, price, and total revenue will be ________, ________, and ______.

b At the profit-maximizing output, Hal's average total cost and total cost will be ______ and ______.

c Hal will earn an economic profit of ______.

d Suppose that firms enter this industry, attracted by short-run economic profits. In the long run, what will be the effect on Hal's demand curve, marginal revenue curve, and economic profits?

4 Draw a diagram that shows how persuasive advertising affects a firm's demand curve and average total cost curve. Under what conditions will advertising result in lower cost per unit? How would you modify your diagram if advertising were assumed to be informative rather than persuasive?

5 Suppose that Delta Airlines practices price discrimination in the sale of tickets to business travelers and tourists. Discuss how price discrimination can result in higher revenues and profits for the firm than those that would occur in the absence of price discrimination.

6 Assume that Nike and Reebok are the only sellers of athletic shoes in the United States. They are contemplating how much to charge for similar basketball shoes. The only two choices are a high price and a low price. Table 6.6 shows the payoff matrix for these firms, with profits stated in millions of dollars per year.

TABLE 6.7 Hypothetical Profit–Payoff Matrix for Nike and Reebok

		Nike	
		High-price	*Low-price*
	High-price	Nike = $600	Nike = $750
Reebok		Reebok = $600	Reebok = $150
	Low-price	Nike = $150	Nike = $150
		Reebok = $750	Reebok = $150

Note: prices stated in millions of dollars per year.

a Use the payoff matrix to discuss the interdependence that characterizes these firms.

b In the absence of cooperative behavior, what will be the likely pricing strategy for each firm?

c Why might cooperative behavior be beneficial for these firms? Why might there be an incentive to cheat on a price-fixing agreement?

NOTES

1 Kenneth Elzinga, "Beer," in Walter Adams and James Brock, editors, *The Structure of American Industry* (Upper Saddle River, NJ: PrenticeHall, 2001), pp. 85–113. See also Philip Van Munching, *Beer Blast* (New York: Random House, 1997) and Douglas Greer, "Beer: Causes

of Structural Change," in Larry Duetsche, editor, *Industry Studies* (New York: M.E. Sharpe, 1998), pp. 28–64.

2 However, not all advertising is persuasive. Sometimes, advertising can be informative. Advertising is judged to be informative when it provides trustworthy information about the quality and price of a good or service or the location of suppliers. Such advertising results in greater price elasticity of demand and less price-making ability for firms.

3 "Colleges Manipulate Financial-Aid Offers Shortchanging Many," *The Wall Street Journal*, April 1, 1996, pp. Al and All.

CHAPTER 7

Labor Markets

CHAPTER OBJECTIVES

After reading this chapter, you should be able to:

1 Explain how a firm determines the quantity of workers demanded.
2 Explain why even if U.S. wages are higher than foreign wages, U.S. labor can still be competitive if it is more productive than foreign labor.
3 Identify the advantages and disadvantages of a minimum wage law.
4 Describe the methods that unions employ to increase the wages of their members and the factors that give a union strength.
5 Explain why domestic workers are sometimes fearful of international trade and liberal immigration policies.

DOI: 10.4324/9781003438571-9

ECONOMICS IN CONTEXT

In 2023, Theresa Johnson was treated like royalty. She was flown around the country on all-expenses-paid trips to Los Angeles, Phoenix, St. Louis, and Miami and was wined and dined at the finest restaurants. Such benefits used to accrue to individuals applying for high-profile professions, such as computer engineering and consulting. But 28-year-old Theresa Johnson was part of a group of job seekers, students with PhDs in accounting, who wanted to teach college students.

Traditionally, the job search for these assistant professors was a long battle that resulted in modest pay and an ill-equipped office. At the turn of the century, however, an increase in the number of students desiring to learn about accounting and a scarcity of PhDs in accounting resulted in job seekers being treated like big shots. Accounting graduates were receiving lucrative packages in 2023, with many colleges offering salaries more than $170,000. What explains the high salaries of those holding PhDs in accounting?

In this chapter, we will learn about the theory of wage determination. In particular, we will learn why some workers receive higher wages than others and what methods workers can use to increase their wages without losing their jobs.

LABOR MARKET EQUILIBRIUM

Like other markets in the economy, labor markets are influenced by the forces of demand and supply. In labor markets, households are the sellers and business firms are the primary buyers. We call the price of labor the wage rate.

We can analyze a labor market and the factors that determine the wage rate and quantity in that market by using the model of demand and supply. Figure 7.1 refers to the market for apple pickers in Mt. Pleasant, Michigan. In the figure, the market demand curve for apple pickers is labeled D_0.

Notice that the demand for apple pickers exists because there is a demand for the apples that apple pickers help to produce. The demand for apple pickers is therefore a **derived demand**: It is derived from the demand of consumers for apples. An increase in the demand for apples will inspire growers to plant additional apple trees and hire more apple pickers; thus the demand for apple pickers will increase. Conversely, a decrease in the demand for apples results in a reduced demand for apple pickers.

We would expect that apple growers would be willing to hire more apple pickers at lower wages than at higher wages. There are two reasons why fewer apple pickers will be needed as their wages rise: (1) producers will switch to substitute resources, such as machinery; and (2) consumers will purchase fewer apples as they become more expensive because of the higher wages being paid to apple pickers, suggesting that fewer apple pickers will be needed to produce apples. "Exploring Further 7.1" at the end of this chapter further discusses the factors underlying the demand for labor.

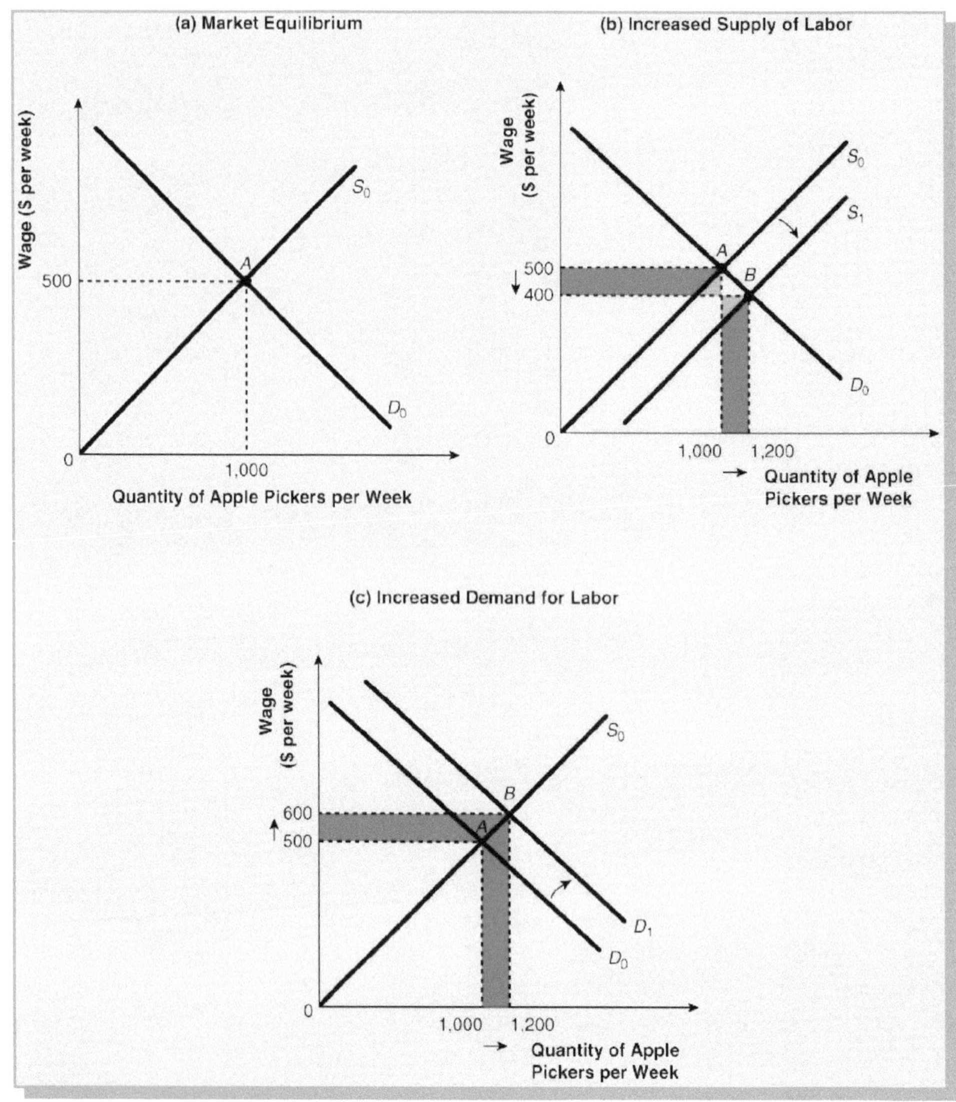

FIGURE 7.1 Market for Apple Pickers

The market demand curve for labor is downward-sloping, showing that a lower wage results in an increase in the quantity of labor demanded. The market supply for labor is upward-sloping, implying that higher wages cause the quantity supplied of labor to increase. The point of intersection between the labor demand and labor supply curves determines the equilibrium wage and employment level. An increase in the market supply of labor results in a fall in the wage rate and an increase in the amount of labor employed. An increase in the market demand for labor causes a rise in the wage rate and an increase in the amount of labor employed.

Figure 7.1 also shows the market supply curve of apple pickers, labeled S_0. As wages rise, other things remaining the same, additional workers will be drawn into the labor force, thus increasing the quantity supplied.

Referring to Figure 7.1(*a*), the point of intersection of the labor demand and labor supply curves determines the equilibrium wage and employment level: 1,000 workers are hired at a wage of $500 per week. Any wage above $500 per week would result in a surplus of apple pickers and eventually decrease the wage to $500. Any wage below $500 per week would cause a shortage of apple pickers and impose upward pressure on the wage.

In any labor market, certain changes can occur that will result in increases or decreases in the labor supply curve or the labor demand curve. When these changes take place, the equilibrium wage rate and quantity of workers demanded are affected.

Referring to Figure 7.1(*b*), suppose that the number of teenagers in the population rises, resulting in more workers available to pick apples. Therefore, the supply curve of labor shifts to the right, to S_1. As supply increases, the equilibrium wage falls from $500 per week to $400 per week, and the number of apple pickers employed increases from 1,000 to 1,200.

Let's now consider the effect of a change in the demand curve for labor. Referring to Figure 7.1(*c*), suppose that the market demand for apples increases. Because the demand for apple pickers is derived from the demand for apples, the demand for apple pickers shifts to the right—say, to D_1—in the figure. As demand increases, the equilibrium wage rate rises from $500 per week to $600 per week, and the number of workers employed rises from 1,000 to 1,200.

We will next apply the theory of labor markets to some contemporary labor issues—the minimum wage law, labor unions, international outsourcing, and immigration.

CHECK POINT

1. Explain how the demand for labor is derived from the product that labor helps produce.
2. How is equilibrium determined in the labor market?
3. What factors cause the market demand curve for labor and the supply curve of labor to increase or decrease?
4. What effect does an increase in the market supply curve of labor have on the wage rate and the quantity of labor demanded? How about an increase in the market demand curve for labor?

DO MINIMUM WAGE LAWS HELP WORKERS?

To help the working poor during the Great Depression, Congress passed *The Fair Labor Standards Act* in 1938. This law established a federal **minimum wage**, the smallest amount of money per hour that an employer can legally pay a worker. Congress set the first federal minimum wage at 25 cents per hour, and periodically increased it to $7.25 per hour by 2012. The federal minimum wage applies nationwide. Employers may not pay workers less than $7.25 per hour unless they or their occupation are specifically exempt from the minimum wage under state or federal law.

Besides the federal legislation, most states have passed their own minimum wage laws. In any state where the minimum wage exceeds the federal minimum wage, the employee is entitled to receive the higher wage. However, federal minimum wage law supersedes state minimum wage laws where the federal minimum wage is greater than the state minimum wage. Table 7.1 provides examples of states with minimum wages.

To government officials, raising the minimum wage is an attractive method of reducing poverty because it does not require an increase in government welfare payments or an accompanying tax increase. Proponents maintain that a national standard for wages is essential to restore wages to the barest minimum and to prevent any further cuts below it. However, opponents note that the government doesn't guarantee jobs by increasing the minimum wage. It guarantees only that those who get jobs will be paid at least that minimum wage. By requiring this, critics argue, the government destroys jobs.

Chris Dussin, owner of the Old Spaghetti Factory in Portland, Oregon, provides an example of increasing the minimum wage. He felt that he could only raise prices so much before he would start chasing customers away, even in a prosperous economy. In 2002, Oregon increased its minimum wage from $6 to $7.50 per hour. From 2002 to 2006, costs at Dussin's three Oregon restaurants increased by $300,000, more than the increase in revenues. Mr. Dussin saw his bottom line eroding and his profit margin decreasing to only 2 to 3 percent of sales. Although he was able to increase prices on some items, he had

TABLE 7.1 Selected State Minimum Wage Rates, 2023 (dollars per hour)

High Minimum Wage States	*Low Minimum Wage States*
Washington $15.74	Alabama $7.25
Massachusetts 15.00	Wisconsin 7.25
New York 14.20	Idaho 7.25
New Jersey 14.13	Kansas 7.25
Arizona 13.85	North Dakota 7.25
Maine 13.80	Georgia 7.25
Maryland 13.25	Montana 9.95
Vermont 13.18	Ohio 10.10
Rhode Island 13.00	Minnesota 10.59
New Mexico 12.00	Alaska 10.85

2023 Federal minimum wage, $7.25

Source: Data drawn from LaborLawCenter, *State Minimum Wage Rates*, 2023, available at https://www.laborlawcenter.com/state-minimum-wage-rates.

to decrease the number of hostesses and increase the number of tables assigned to each server. Moreover, higher labor costs forced him to abandon plans to open an Old Spaghetti Factory in Bend, Oregon. However, he opened another restaurant in Boise, Idaho, which had a minimum wage of $5.15 and, unlike Oregon, allowed employers to pay less to workers who collect tips.[1]

A Diagrammatic View of the Minimum Wage

To understand the arguments for and against the minimum wage, consider Figure 7.2. It illustrates the competitive market for low-skill workers, a group whose equilibrium wage rate is likely to be below the minimum wage. Suppose that the equilibrium wage equals $4 per hour, shown at the intersection of the market supply curve (S_0) and the market demand curve (D_0). At the equilibrium wage, workers supply 8 million hours of labor per week, and businesses demand 8 million hours of labor per week.

Suppose that the federal government imposes a minimum wage of $6 per hour—a rate that is higher than the market equilibrium wage. What are the effects of this wage floor? First, consider the impact of the wage hike on the quantity of labor demanded. Recall that a profit-maximizing employer will hire a worker only if the value of the output the worker produces is greater than the wage. Assuming that a legislated increase in the price of labor does not increase workers' productivity, the quantity of labor demanded will decrease in response to a wage increase.

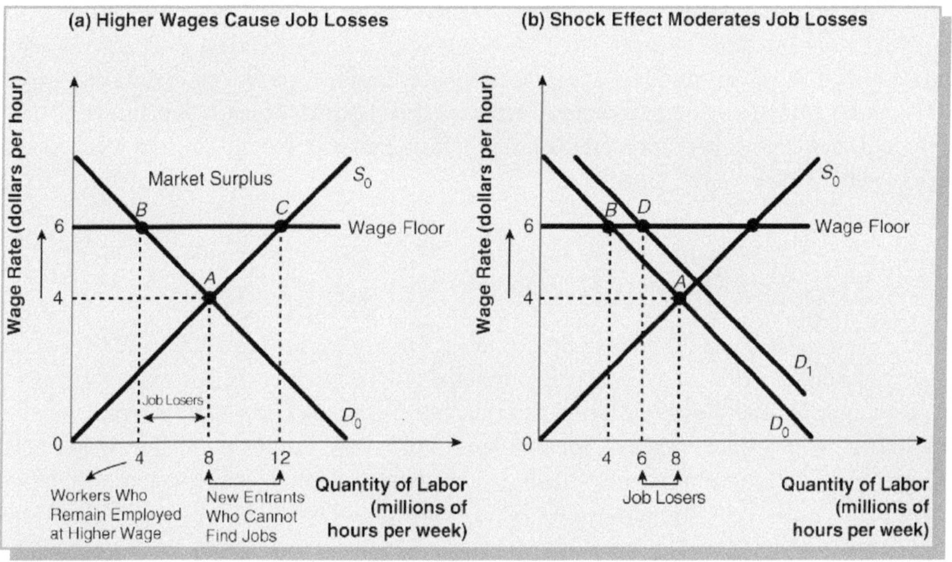

FIGURE 7.2 Effects of a Minimum Wage

By raising the wage rate above the market equilibrium wage, a minimum wage increases the quantity of labor supplied but decreases the quantity of labor demanded. Some workers realize higher wages, but others remain or become unemployed. If a wage hike causes the marginal productivity of labor to increase, the demand for labor would increase and unemployment would decline.

In Figure 7.2(*a*), as the wage rises from $4 to $6 per hour, the quantity of labor hours demanded falls from 8 million hours to 4 million hours. Put simply, raise the wage, and workers are priced above the value they can add. An excessive price for labor yields a reduced quantity of workers demanded—the least-productive ones will lose their jobs.

Also, notice what happens on the supply side in Figure 7.2(*a*). The rise in wages from $4 to $6 per hour attracts people into the labor market. As a result, the quantity of labor supplied rises from 8 million hours to 12 million hours per week. Everybody prefers one of those higher paying jobs. At the minimum wage of $6 per hour, there is a *surplus* of labor equal to 8 million hours per week (12 million–4 million = 8 million). In other words, there are 8 million hours of labor that people wish to provide at the minimum wage, but are unable to provide. With more job seekers than jobs, *unemployment* results.

The minimum wage benefits workers who are fortunate enough to find work at a wage level that exceeds the market equilibrium wage. However, it harms many workers, including teenagers and young adults, who seek employment at the higher wage, but cannot find jobs. Critics maintain that the minimum wage law says to the potential worker, "Unless you can find a job paying at least the minimum wage, you may not accept employment." For those who lose their jobs because of the minimum wage, it is hard to understand why they would think such a law is a good idea.

The minimum wage tends to have its greatest impact on unskilled workers, especially teenagers. Because teenagers are often the least experienced and least skilled members of the labor force, their market equilibrium wage is low. Teenagers, especially minorities, are therefore the most likely to lose jobs because of increases in the minimum wage.

Numerous studies have sought to quantify the effects of raising the minimum wage on employment. The debate focuses on how sensitive, or elastic, the demand for labor is in response to changes in the wage rate. The preponderance of empirical evidence suggests that increases in the minimum wage do result in decreases in employment, but this effect is likely to be small. On average, studies estimate the elasticity of labor demand to be 0.2. This means that a 10-percent increase in the minimum wage would result in a 2-percent decrease in employment.[2]

The Shock Effect (Efficiency Wage Theory)

However, some economists argue that increasing the minimum wage may yield some benefits to employers that can potentially offset the rise in labor costs. For example, higher wages might reduce worker turnover and thus lower training costs. Also, workers may be motivated by increased wages to become more productive. Moreover, higher wages may shock firms into upgrading their technology, improving their management, and using labor more efficiently. These benefits would likely cause the demand for labor to shift to the right, thus lessening the employment-reducing effects that a higher minimum wage might cause. This so-called **shock effect** is illustrated in Figure 7.2(*b*), where we assume that the minimum wage leads to an increase in the demand for labor, from D_0 to D_1. The increase in the demand for labor moderates some of the unemployment that otherwise would have occurred; the quantity of labor demanded declines by only 2 million hours per week rather than by 4 million hours.

Such a shock effect occurred in 1914 when Ford Motor Co. offered to double the wages of its employees from $2.50 to $5 per day. At that time, the prevailing wage in manufacturing was only $2 to $3 per day. The offer to increase wages was motivated by the high rates of absenteeism and turnover among workers at Ford's factories. Ford apparently hoped that an increase in wages would improve the morale of workers and encourage them to work harder in order to keep their high-paying jobs. As a result, Ford believed that labor productivity would increase. Immediately following the wage hike, more than 10,000 workers applied for employment with Ford. According to analysts, Ford's tactic was successful. Employees remained on the job and worked harder, resulting in labor productivity gains exceeding 50 percent.[3]

ARE WORKERS BETTER OFF WITH LABOR UNIONS?

Source: exxorian/DigitalVision Vectors/Getty Images®

Throughout this chapter, we have assumed that individual workers actively compete in the sale of their services. Yet in some markets, workers form **unions** to sell their services collectively. Unions exist because workers realize that acting together provides them with more bargaining power than they would have if they acted individually—putting them at the mercy of their employers. You are probably familiar with unions such as the United Auto Workers, the United Steel Workers, and the Teamsters.

In 1970, about 25 percent of the U.S. labor force belonged to unions. Only about 12 percent are members today, as seen in Table 7.2. With the declining role of manufacturing

TABLE 7.2 Union Membership, 1985–2022

Union Membership	*1985*	*2005*	*2022*
Number of union workers (millions)	17.0	15.7	16.0
Union workers as a percentage of total wage and salary workers	18.0%	12.5%	11.6%
Public-sector union workers	35.7%	36.5%	36.8%
Private-sector union workers	14.3%	7.8%	6.8%

Source: Data drawn from Bureau of Labor Statistics, *Union Members Summary*, January 19, 2023, available at https://www.bls.gov/news.release/union2.nr0.htm.

jobs in the workforce, continued union success hinges on penetrating the service sector. That's very difficult to organize. Service workers tend to work in many different locations, and many jobs in the service sector are transient.

The aim of a labor union is to improve the wages, jobs, and working conditions of its members. Unions act on behalf of workers to bargain with employers on matters relating to employment, a process known as **collective bargaining**. This process allows one negotiator to act as the workers' agent rather than having each worker negotiate their own labor contract.

Most disagreements between labor and management involve wages, hours, or other conditions of employment. If labor and management cannot settle their differences, they may receive outside help called **mediation**. If the two parties still cannot agree, they may submit to a process known as **arbitration**. A person called an arbitrator listens to both sides of a dispute and makes a decision that is binding on both sides. **Strikes** may also occur when workers feel that stopping work is the best way to pressure their employer into granting their demands. Before a union calls a strike, it must put the question to a vote by its members. Generally, a strike cannot be called unless a majority of the voting members support it.

Increasing Union Wages

To increase the wages of their members, unions use several strategies: (1) increase the demand for labor, (2) restrict the supply of labor, or (3) impose an above-equilibrium wage floor on the market. Let us consider each of these strategies.

Increase the Demand for Labor. From the perspective of a labor union, the most preferable technique for increasing wages is to increase the demand for labor. As seen in Figure 7.3(*a*), an increase in the demand for labor causes an increase in both the wage rate and the quantity of labor demanded. Employment and incomes thus rise for union members, a most favorable outcome.

Unions adopt several strategies to increase the demand for the labor of their members:

- **Increase the demand for the good they help produce and thus the derived demand for their own labor services**. One way to increase product demand is to advertise and persuade the public to purchase only those goods manufactured by union workers.

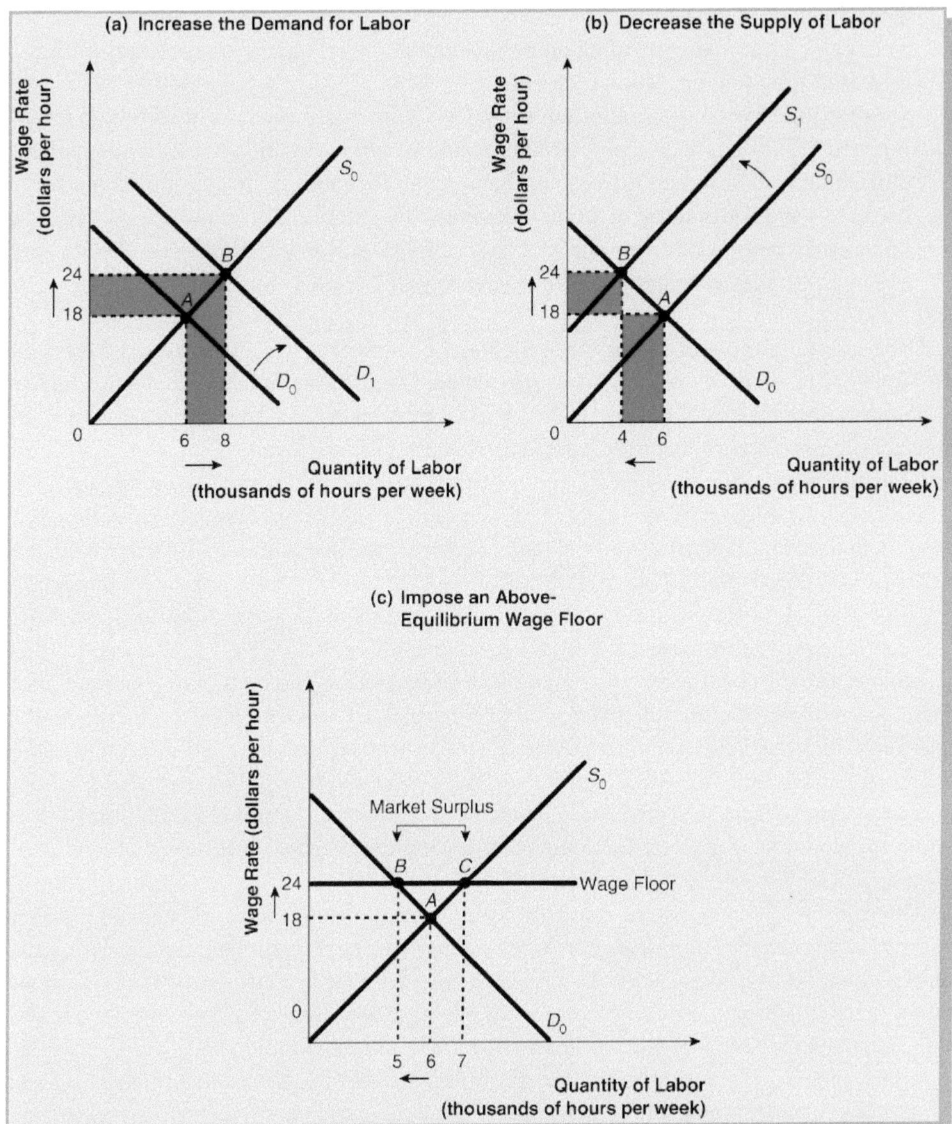

FIGURE 7.3 Union Methods of Increasing Wages

From the perspective of a union, the preferred method for increasing wages is to increase the demand for labor. An increase in the demand for labor causes an increase in both the wage rate and the quantity of labor demanded. Another way to increase wages is to restrict the supply of labor. Those workers who keep their jobs receive higher incomes, but fewer workers will be employed. A successful industrial union will impose an above-equilibrium wage floor on the market for its members. Although the wage hike increases the incomes of those members having jobs, some members may be priced out of the market.

Another approach might be to pressure Congress to impose restrictive tariffs or quotas on, say, steel imported from South Korea, so that U.S. consumers will demand more steel produced by U.S. workers. Moreover, teachers' unions often lobby for increased government spending on public education, and aerospace workers push for increased spending on national defense.

- **Support increases in the minimum wage laws to increase the cost of unskilled labor.** A rise in the wage rate of unskilled labor results in a decrease in the quantity demanded of unskilled labor and an increase in the demand for more skilled, union workers.
- **Increase the productivity of union members.** By establishing grievance procedures, unions may reduce turnover and promote stability in the workforce—conditions that enhance workers' productivity, thus increasing the demand for union workers.

Decrease the Supply of Labor. Another way of promoting wage increases is to restrict the supply of labor. As seen in Figure 7.3(*b*), a decreased supply of labor results in a higher wage rate, although it reduces the quantity of labor demanded. Those workers who keep their jobs receive higher incomes, but fewer workers are employed.

Craft unions, such as bricklayers and electricians, often adopt restrictive membership policies such as high initiation fees, long apprenticeship programs, and limitations on union membership. *Professional associations*, such as the American Bar Association or the American Medical Association, are like craft unions in terms of their restrictive impact on the supply of labor. Entry into a profession is limited through certification requirements and control over professional schools.

Impose an Above-Equilibrium Wage Floor. Rather than organizing the workers of a particular occupation, an *industrial union* represents all workers in a specific industry, regardless of their skills or craft. Examples of industrial unions are the United Auto Workers (UAW) and the American Postal Workers. Similarly, public employee unions represent the workers in a profession, such as teaching. The National Education Association, for example, is a powerful union that represents teachers throughout the United States.

The purpose of an industrial union or a public employee union is to bring all workers in an industry into a union, thus putting them in a strong bargaining position. Industrial unions must also organize workers at most of the firms in an industry. Otherwise, non-union firms might gain a cost advantage by paying lower wages to their employees and thus undersell the union-organized firms. In practice, industrial unions may fail to organize an entire industry. In automobiles, for example, the UAW has organized Ford, General Motors, and Chrysler—the "Big Three" of the U.S. auto industry—as well as several foreign firms with assembly plants in the United States. However, workers at other foreign assembly plants have chosen not to affiliate with the UAW.

Figure 7.3(*c*) shows the impact of the UAW on the market for autoworkers. The competitive wage and employment levels are $18 per hour and 6,000 hours of labor demanded per week, respectively, as seen at point *A* in the figure. Suppose that the UAW organizes the U.S. Big Three auto companies and bargains for a wage rate of $24 per hour. The bargained wage rate has the effect of imposing an above-equilibrium wage floor on the labor market. Although the wage hike results in increased incomes for those workers who remain employed, the quantity of labor demanded falls from 6,000 to 5,000 hours per week. The push for higher wages thus prices some workers out of a job. Generally, unions adhere to the policy of "last hired, first fired." Workers with the least amount of seniority are the first ones to lose their jobs. Also, the higher wage increases the quantity supplied of labor to 7,000 hours per week, resulting in a surplus of labor equal to 2,000 hours per week.

What Gives a Union Strength?

Not all unions are able to increase the wages of their members. What factors allow unions to obtain large wage increases while suffering only modest reductions in employment?

If non-union workers are good substitutes for union workers, an employer may turn to these substitutes and reduce its demand for union labor as it becomes more costly. Higher union wages will therefore price union workers out of the market, resulting in a sharp decline in their employment. For this reason, unions lobby against liberal immigration policies and the importation of goods produced by foreign workers. Unions have also attempted to obtain contracts with a **union shop** provision. This provision requires that all employees join the recognized union within a specified length of time (usually 30 days) after their employment with the firm begins. Each state has the option to accept or reject union shops.

Besides substituting non-union for union labor, firms may substitute other factors of production for union workers as their wages are pushed upward. For example, General Motors may automate some production operations, replacing people with robots. When machines are good substitutes for labor, the bargaining power of labor declines.

The strength of a union also depends on the number of substitutes that are available for the product that its members help produce. For example, during the 1980s the U.S. trucking industry was deregulated in an attempt to foster additional competition and the more efficient use of resources. Unionized firms in the trucking industry therefore began to compete with non-union firms having lower labor costs. The labor-cost advantage allowed many non-union trucking firms to slash prices in order to win a larger share of the market. The result was a decline in the market share of unionized trucking firms and a loss of more than 100,000 jobs for Teamsters' members. The sharp decline in employment eventually led the union to agree to a 30-percent cutback in wages and fringe benefits in an attempt to save jobs.

The experience of the U.S. auto industry illustrates how non-union workers can threaten the employment levels and wage structures of union workers. For decades, the UAW has represented workers at the Big Three, whose factories are located in the northern states where the UAW is strong. Being an effective bargainer, for decades the UAW pushed its members' wages above the levels of the average American manufacturing worker. By the 1980s, however, non-union Japanese companies had established automobile assembly plants in the southern part of the United States, where unions are not strong. Lower wages combined with more efficient workers have given the Japanese a labor-cost advantage in the production of automobiles. This has allowed them to capture an increasing share of the U.S. auto market, causing fewer sales for the U.S. Big Three and job losses for UAW members. As the number of non-union workers in the auto industry grows, the UAW's power to set wages and working conditions is weakened.

Right-to-Work Laws

The security of a labor union is influenced by whether a state has a right-to-work law. A **right-to-work law** guarantees that no person can be compelled, as a condition of employment, to join or not to join, nor to pay dues to a labor union. The law is intended to regulate agreements between labor unions and employers that would prohibit the employer from hiring non-union workers. As of 2023, 26 states had right-to-work laws.

Right-to-work laws were first adopted in the southern states decades ago as part of an attempt to attract factory jobs from the heavily unionized northern states; those laws, in conjunction with other pro-business policies, were quite successful. Right-to-work laws eventually spread to the western states and, more recently, to the industrialized midwestern states that have strong ties to unions. Right-to-work laws are strongly opposed by unions because they do not want to see their membership and influence decline.

Proponents of right-to-work laws point to the Constitutional right to freedom of association and the common-law principle of private ownership of property. They contend that workers should be free to join unions and to refrain from joining, and that it is unfair for a union to require employees to pay dues or fees as a condition of employment. Proponents also argue that businesses will be more likely to set up shop in a right-to-work state, resulting in more jobs and better jobs. However, critics maintain that right-to-work laws allow employees the right to be free riders by benefitting from collective bargaining without paying for it. Therefore, union workers may end up subsidizing non-union workers. Critics also argue that weakening union power will result in lower wages and a race to the bottom—that is, right-to-work laws allow firms to pay workers less rather than more.

Which side is right? Unfortunately, assessing the validity of each side's argument is difficult because it is hard to isolate the direct effect of right-to-work laws on a state's economy—each state has various business-friendly policies, of which right-to-work laws are only one. Therefore, the evidence is mixed concerning the effects of right-to-work laws.

Caterpillar Bulldozes Canadian Locomotive Workers

The ability of a union to successfully bargain for its members decreases when the employer can hire substitute workers. Consider the case of the locomotive industry.

Caterpillar Inc. is a global producer of heavy machinery such as tractors, construction and mining equipment, and diesel engines. In 2012 Caterpillar closed a 62-year-old plant in London, Ontario, that made railroad locomotives. As a result, about 450 manufacturing jobs were lost.

The Canadian Auto Workers (CAW) union, which represented most of the workers, characterized the closure as rotten and greedy behavior on the part of Caterpillar's management. The CAW noted that upon announcing the closure of the Ontario plant, Caterpillar immediately announced the opening of a new locomotive plant in Muncie, Indiana, where workers have the right, but are not compelled, to join a union. Caterpillar made it clear that it wanted to avoid any union representation at the Muncie plant. Why?

By locating in Muncie, where unemployment was high and non-union workers were abundant, Caterpillar could hire workers with wages about half the Ontario level. Caterpillar offered jobs ranging from $12 to $18.50 per hour, in contrast to wages averaging

$35 (U.S. dollars) at the Ontario plant. Viewing the Ontario plant's cost structure as unsustainable, Caterpillar demanded a 50-percent wage cut to reduce costs, but this was unacceptable to the CAW. However, the CAW stated that it would be willing to make concessions such as reduced vacation time. After 10 months of unsuccessful negotiations, Caterpillar decided that its bargaining gap with the CAW was too wide to resolve. Therefore, Caterpillar locked out its Canadian workers and closed the locomotive factory. The firm gave its laid-off workers severance payments based on longevity of employment at Caterpillar. Besides moving to Muncie, Caterpillar increased its production in Brazil and Mexico, where wages are lower than in Canada or the United States.

Did Restrictive Work Rules Cream Twinkies and Ding Dongs?

For about a century Hostess Brands was an acclaimed wholesale baker and distributor of bakery products in the United States. When was the last time you ate some of its Twinkies, Ding Dongs, or Wonder Bread? The company was started by Ralph Nafziger in a church basement in Kansas City in 1905. As a result of numerous acquisitions, Hostess Brands became the largest commercial bakery in the United States.

Hostess eventually became weighed down by increasing debt, management and labor turmoil, rising labor costs, and the changing tastes of Americans that resulted in declining sales for Hostess's sugary products. In 2012 Hostess decided that it could no longer continue as a bakery and it closed its doors. What went wrong for Hostess?

Hostess blamed its lack of competitiveness on large pension and medical benefit obligations stemming from the aggressive bargaining of the Bakers union and Teamsters union. Hostess also noted that the high costs of distributing its baked goods from production facilities to the shelves of retail stores contributed to its losses. These costs were due to restrictive work rules of the Teamsters union, which prevented its drivers from helping to load their trucks with Hostess products. Also, a separate worker arriving at a retail store in a separate vehicle had to be employed to shift goods from a delivery truck to a retailer's shelf. Moreover, the same delivery truck could not be used to transport Wonder Bread and Twinkies, thus adding to distribution costs. These work rules resulted in Hostess losing money on many of its delivery stops, although the company's bakery production lines were relatively efficient. Increased costs for ingredients and fuel and the U.S. recession also weakened Hostess.

However, Hostess's unions maintained that work rules and obligations for pensions and medical benefits were not the problem. Instead, the firm was poorly run by its management. For example, according to its unions, the firm did not invest enough in new products and trucks or upgraded software. Also, even as Hostess was falling toward bankruptcy, it was granting its executives raises ranging between 35 percent and 300 percent.

As Hostess approached bankruptcy, it appealed to its workers to accept cuts in wages and benefits and to modify work rules. Although the proposed cuts were reluctantly accepted by the Teamsters union, they were rejected by the Bakers union, which launched a strike in November 2012. This was the last straw for Hostess, and it shut down its 33 bakeries and 565 distribution centers and fired about 18,500 employees with the hope of auctioning off its product lines.

In March 2013, bankrupt Hostess sold its Twinkies and other snacks to Apollo Global Management and Metropoulos & Company, two investment firms with a shared history of corporate turnarounds. The new owners agreed to inject $60 million in capital investments into the bakeries and to hire at least 1,500 workers. But they would not be represented by unions, including the one whose strike triggered Hostess's decision to shut down in 2012. It remains to be seen how the bakery industry will evolve.

Is Walmart Good for America?

Given Walmart's presence around the country, it would be surprising to find someone who has not shopped at a Walmart store or does not recognize the name "Walmart." Today, Walmart is widely recognized as one of the most powerful companies in U.S. business history. Although the company has been praised as a model of economic efficiency, Walmart has also been condemned as a bad bargain. Is Walmart good for America?

Let us begin by looking at Samuel Walton (1918–1992), the founder of Walmart Inc., and the factors that contributed to his company's success. Born in Kingfisher, Oklahoma, Samuel Walton stumbled into retailing. He first learned how to compete playing high school football and basketball. As a student at the University of Missouri, Walton waited tables, managed newspaper routes, and worked as a lifeguard. After earning an undergraduate degree in economics in 1940, he contemplated pursuing an MBA degree, but could not afford it. So he accepted an offer to be a management trainee with J.C. Penney Co.

When discount retailing emerged in the 1960s, Walton became wealthy, operating some 15 variety stores in Arkansas, Oklahoma, and Missouri. They were traditional small-town stores that charged relatively high price markups. As a student of retailing, Walton saw that discount stores had great potential. Walton opened his first Walmart Discount City in Rogers, Arkansas in 1962. That same year, rivals Kmart and Target got their start. Discount retailing had entered the American way of life.

Once committed to discount retailing, Walton developed a business model that he held to for the rest of his life: To remove costs from the merchandising system wherever they existed—in retail stores, in the manufacturers' profit margins and with the wholesalers—all with the goal of driving prices down. His stores also provided a wide assortment of good quality merchandise, guaranteed satisfaction on all purchases, friendly and knowledgeable service, and free parking.

Using that model, Walton slashed his profit margins to the bone, making it necessary for Walmart to increase sales at a rapid pace. It did, and Walton hit the road to open stores wherever he saw profitability. He would buzz towns in his low-flying airplane, surveying the lay of the land. When he had calibrated the proper intersection between a few small towns, he would purchase a piece of farmland there and open another Walmart store.

To Walton's great delight, Walmart became the world's number one retailer, surpassing the profitability of its competitors such as Sears and Kmart. Walton's extraordinary leadership skills inspired hundreds of thousands of employees to believe in Walmart's success, and many rode the firm's stock to wealth. Walton's cost-cutting techniques have been emulated by Home Depot, Barnes & Noble, and other retailers.

However, not everyone admires Walmart's business success. Critics maintain that because of Walmart's efforts to cut costs, the company has become hostile to labor unions, and that the company has a long history of trying to squelch unionization efforts. Some employees are scared that their store will be closed if they vote for a union, according to critics of Walmart.

CHECK POINT

1. Explain why an increase in the minimum wage may be beneficial to some workers but harmful to others.
2. How might an increase in labor productivity offset the adverse effects of a higher minimum wage?
3. Identify the methods that labor unions use to increase the wages of their members. Which method is most preferable to a union?
4. What factors underlie the ability of a union to increase the wages of its members?

INTERNATIONAL OUTSOURCING: THREAT OR OPPORTUNITY FOR U.S. WORKERS?

Source: Nitat Termmee/Moment/Getty Images®

In discussions about jobs, attention often focuses on international trade and terms such as "outsourcing." The concern is that jobs may leave the United States, going to Malaysia, India, and other countries where workers command lower wages.

Outsourcing is the contracting out of tasks that once were done in-house. When a car manufacturer in Michigan buys brake pads from a supplier in Ohio rather than producing them in-house, that's domestic outsourcing. Also, American firms may practice international outsourcing by purchasing inputs from a foreign provider. For example, firms in Mexico supply seat covers and wiper blades to Detroit automakers.

The practice of outsourcing is subject to controversy. Proponents maintain that it is an effective business strategy for firms seeking a competitive advantage in finding low-cost labor; it helps firms to increase profits and pass lower costs on to consumers. Also, outsourcing can improve efficiency because it allows another more efficient producer to perform tasks rather than the outsourcing firm itself. However, critics argue that outsourcing has caused the loss of domestic jobs and lower wages, especially in U.S. manufacturing industries.

Boeing, Outsourcing, and Labor Unions

Boeing provides an example of a company that engages in the outsourcing of jetliner production. Although the company assembles jetliners at its plants in Seattle, Washington and Charleston, South Carolina, it obtains components from producers throughout the world.

It doesn't make sense for Boeing to allocate resources to designing and manufacturing all components for its jetliners. There are too many disciplines involved. Although Boeing produces some components, it is more efficient for it to rely mostly on specialist suppliers to produce components for Boeing. About 65–70 percent of the content for a given Boeing jetliner is procured from domestic and international suppliers, which can number in the thousands.

For example, Boeing farms out a big chunk of machined and sheet metal components as well as engines, windows, communication systems, and other components. Australia, Canada, Japan, Italy, and China are among the component-supplying countries for Boeing. The suppliers must meet Boeing's performance specifications, quality standards, and delivery schedules at the agreed cost. To complete the production of a jetliner, Boeing is supported by a giant global logistics operation to send the components located around the world to its American assembly plants.

Although outsourcing can create efficiencies for Boeing, it can also cause concerns for its workers, as illustrated by Figure 7.4. In the figure, curve S_0 shows the supply of machinists who work at Boeing, while curve D_0 shows Boeing's demand for machinists. At equilibrium point A, 700 machinists are hired at a wage rate of $25 per hour. To reduce labor costs, suppose that Boeing outsources some of its component production to machinists in China. Therefore, the demand curve for Boeing machinists will decrease to D_1, which results in a decrease in equilibrium employment and the wage rate. However, as more work is outsourced to China, Chinese machinists will start demanding higher wages, which will reduce China's competitive low-wage advantage.

Of course, the Boeing machinist union will try to resist the effects of falling wages and employment for its members. Also, if Boeing machinists realize that their jobs may be

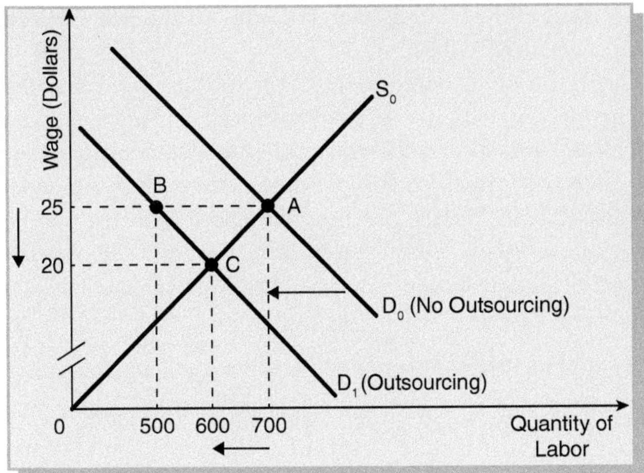

FIGURE 7.4 Effect of International Outsourcing on the Domestic Labor Market

With international outsourcing, the demand for American workers declines, resulting in falling employment and wages.

outsourced to cheaper Chinese workers, they may lose confidence in Boeing and become discouraged and less productive. Moreover, some machinists may seek employment elsewhere if they decide that they are being treated unfairly by Boeing.

However, Boeing maintains that if it cannot locate some work abroad, it will become less competitive as its rival, Airbus, will reduce costs and prices by outsourcing. This will result in Boeing losing sales to Airbus, thus threatening the jobs of even more Boeing workers.

But what happens if there are no more cheap labor regions for Boeing to tap? Will the company turn to technology and industrial robots to replace workers, causing higher levels of unemployment?

What Prevents U.S. Jobs from Being Outsourced Abroad?

That wage rates are lower in foreign countries is often cited as a reason for international outsourcing by American companies. However, can we be sure that jobs will flow to foreign countries with lower wages?

Suppose that you are the manager of El Paso Radio Co., a firm located in the United States. Wouldn't you want to locate your assembly plant in Mexico, where labor is cheaper? The answer is that firms are interested in more than just the wages that they must pay to workers. They are also interested in the productivity of labor.

For example, suppose that a typical radio assembler in the United States earns $25 per hour, and a radio assembler in Mexico earns $15 per hour. Also assume that the productivity of the U.S. assembler is 20 radios per hour, and that the productivity of the Mexican assembler is 10 radios per hour. Therefore, we have higher productivity in the United States but lower wages in Mexico. Where will El Paso Radio Co. locate its assembly plant?

It will locate its plant in the United States because more radios are produced per dollar paid to labor than in Mexico. To illustrate, with a marginal product of 20 radios and a wage rate of $25 per hour, the U.S. workers assemble 0.8 radios per dollar that they are paid (20 / 25 = 0.8). In contrast, with a marginal product of 10 radios and a wage rate of $15 per hour, the Mexican workers assemble 0.67 radios for each dollar that they are paid (10 / 15 = 0.67). Because the firm receives more output for each dollar spent on assemblers in the United States than in Mexico, the firm will find it less costly to hire U.S. workers rather than Mexican workers. The conclusion is that even if U.S. wages are higher than Mexican wages, if U.S. labor is more productive than Mexican labor, U.S. labor can still be competitive.

IMMIGRATION AND THE LABOR MARKET

Immigration of foreigners also affects the domestic labor market. Historically, the United States has been a target for international migration. Because of the vast flow of immigrants, the United States has been described as the "melting pot" of the world. Immigrants are motivated by better economic opportunities and by noneconomic factors, such as politics, war, and religion. Table 7.3 shows the number of immigrants coming to the United States during 1821–2020.

Although immigration can enhance America's productivity, some people prefer harsher restrictions on immigration. They argue that immigration has reduced their employment opportunities and wages.

Figure 7.5 shows the economic effects of Mexican workers migrating to the United States. Referring to Figure 7.5(*a*), suppose that the equilibrium wage rate is $20 per hour in the United States, found at the intersection of the U.S. supply curve of labor, S_0, and the U.S. demand curve for labor, D_0. Referring to Figure 7.5(*b*), Mexico's equilibrium wage

TABLE 7.3 U.S. Immigration, 1821–2020

Period	*Number (thousands)*
1821–1840	743
1861–1880	5,127
1901–1920	14,531
1941–1960	3,551
1981–2000	16,433
2001–2020	20,759

Source: Data drawn from U.S. Department of Homeland Security, Office of Immigration Statistics, *Yearbook of Immigration Statistics*, 2022, available at https://www.dhs.gov/immigration-statistics/yearbook.

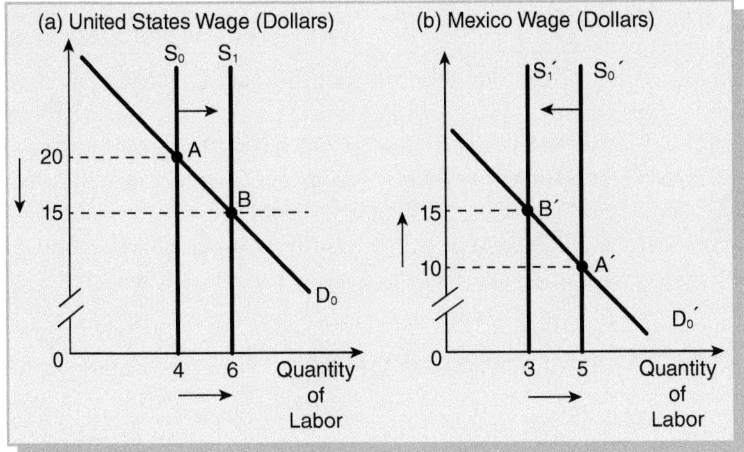

FIGURE 7.5 Effects of Labor Migration from Mexico to the United States

Before labor migration, the wage rate in the United States exceeds that of Mexico. In response to the wage differential, workers in Mexico will migrate to the United States. This results in a decrease in Mexico's supply of labor and an increase in the U.S. supply of labor, thus causing wage rates to rise in Mexico and fall in the United States until they equalize.

rate is \$10 per hour, found at the intersection of the Mexican supply curve of labor, $S_{0'}$, and the Mexican demand curve for labor, $D_{0'}$.

Suppose that workers can move freely between Mexico and the United States, that labor markets are competitive, and that migration occurs solely in response to wage differentials. Responding to higher wage rates, Mexican workers will migrate to the United States. The result is a decrease in Mexico's supply of labor to curve $S_{1'}$ and an increase in the U.S. supply of labor to S_1, as shown in the figure. Therefore, wage rates will rise in Mexico and fall in the United States until they equalize at \$15 per hour.

The migration of labor harms affected native workers in the United States by causing their wage rates to fall, as there are more people looking for jobs, and it helps native workers in Mexico by causing their wage rates to rise. U.S. labor unions often support restrictions on immigration because competition from foreign workers can reduce their members' jobs and wages.

However, immigration can also increase the demand for workers and thus create new jobs. For example, immigrants purchase goods and services, thus increasing demand. Employers may expand production in sectors where immigration permits them to hire more people or use more labor-intensive production methods. Therefore, immigration may increase competition for existing jobs in some occupational sectors, but it can also create new jobs. This is because the economy does not have a fixed number of jobs.

The United States has reaped a bonanza of highly educated newcomers who enhance the competitiveness of its firms. America's high-tech industries, from biotechnology to semiconductors, depend on immigrant scientists, engineers, and entrepreneurs to remain competitive. Moreover, immigrants help revitalize America by establishing new businesses and generating jobs, profits, and taxes to pay for social services.

Even the less-skilled immigrants contribute to America's economy by working in jobs many native Americans do not want, such as cleaning offices, cooking in restaurants, and agricultural work. Also, the infusion of immigrants into the United States includes highly educated newcomers who establish new businesses and develop new technologies ranging from biotechnology to semiconductors, thus providing jobs for native Americans.

The Immigration and Nationality Act of 1965, as amended, eliminated America's country-specific quota system, and it established a limit on the total number of immigrants allowed into the United States. Also, priority is given to those who immigrate for the purpose of family reunification and those possessing exceptional skills.

Canada's Immigration Policy

Like the United States, Canada is one of a handful of countries where immigration has been an important factor shaping society and culture. With its small population and vast tracts of unsettled land, Canada's open immigration policy was initially fueled by a desire for expansion, with most immigrants settling in rural, frontier areas. Today, Canada remains a country that actively solicits immigrants from a wide variety of countries. Although China, India, and the Philippines are the three major contributors of Canada's immigrants, the country receives its immigrant population from more than 200 countries of origin. Immigration population growth is concentrated in or near large cities such as Vancouver, Toronto, and Montreal.

In Canada there are three categories of immigrants: closely related persons of Canadian residents living in Canada, skilled workers and business people who fit labor market needs, and people accepted as immigrants for humanitarian reasons or who are escaping persecution or unusual punishment in their homelands. To determine whom it should allow in, Canada uses a point system. You do not even need a job or employer, just skills. Applicants are awarded points for proficiency in languages, education, and job experience.

While the United States has struggled with its own immigration policies, Canada has been very receptive to immigrants. Just why does Canada accept immigrants with open arms? Because it needs to: Canadians understand the positive economic benefits of immigration, including business development and the creation of jobs for native-born Canadians. This is because a large proportion of Canadian immigrants are highly skilled people who are net contributors to the economy. Also, with a sparse population and low birth rate, Canada needs immigrants for population growth and economic development. About two-thirds of Canada's permanent visas are granted for Canada's economic needs, including the filling of labor holes; in contrast, about two-thirds of U.S. green cards are granted for family reunions. Moreover, Canadians see multiculturalism as an important component of their national identity.

Canadians maintain that people who are exposed to different viewpoints and cultures are more likely to cooperate with one another or reach a compromise when differences exist as well as become more productive by learning from others. Therefore, Canadians see immigration as adding to the social fabric of the country. Finally, Canada has little reason to worry about illegal immigration. Although Canada and the United States share a long border, there are not millions of Americans desiring to move to Canada. To put it another way, the United States serves as a buffer zone for unauthorized immigration to Canada.

Simply put, Canada emphasizes open immigration policies that accept talented foreigners who have the skills the country requires and the motivation to succeed. Canada has transformed itself into an immigrant country, with a foreign-born population (20 percent) that exceeds that of the United States (13 percent). This infusion of talent has contributed to the economic vitality of Canada.

However, by 2013 Canada was modifying its immigration program. The goal is to remedy the increasing economic division between locals and many of the immigrants who entered Canada under the former immigration system, in which immigrants have lagged behind locals in terms of wages. The new system considers whether immigrants have employment arranged in Canada and whether they have specific skills in demand, such as computer programming. Also, Canada considers worker flexibility, which includes factors such as time spent previously in Canada. The future of Canada's immigration program remains in question.

CHECK POINT

1. What methods do labor unions use to improve the economic well-being of their members?
2. What factors underlie the strength of a labor union?
3. Does outsourcing benefit American workers? Why are some workers fearful of outsourcing?
4. Although the United States has been described as the "melting pot" of the world, many Americans are fearful of liberal immigration policies. Why?

CHAPTER SUMMARY

1. As in other markets, the forces of demand and supply underlie labor markets. The point of intersection of the labor demand and labor supply curves determines the equilibrium wage and level of employment. The demand for labor is derived from the demand for the product that labor helps produce.
2. In a competitive market, a firm will maximize profits by hiring workers up to the point at which the **value of the marginal product of labor** equals the wage rate. Moreover, the value of the marginal product curve of labor constitutes a firm's **demand curve for labor**.
3. Even if U.S. wages are higher than Mexican wages, if U.S. labor is more productive than Mexican labor, U.S. labor can still be competitive.
4. An increase in the market supply curve of labor causes the equilibrium wage to decrease and the quantity of labor demanded to increase. As the market demand curve for labor increases, both the equilibrium wage and the quantity of labor supplied increase.

5 To help the working poor, in 1938 Congress established a federal minimum wage, the smallest amount of money per hour that an employer may legally pay a worker. The minimum wage benefits workers who can find work at a wage level that exceeds the market equilibrium wage. However, it harms workers who seek employment at the higher wage, but cannot find jobs. To the extent that a higher wage causes labor to become more productive, the demand for labor increases, thus offsetting the unemployment effects caused by the minimum wage.

6 Labor unions use several strategies to increase the wages of their members: Increase the demand for labor, restrict the supply of labor, and impose an above-equilibrium wage floor on the market. The ability of a union to increase the wages of its members is threatened by non-union labor, by other factors of production (machinery) that may be substituted for labor, by the availability of good substitutes for the product that members help produce, and by a high labor share of production costs.

7 In the discussion about jobs, much attention has focused on outsourcing. The concern is that a free-trade environment allows good jobs to drain from the U.S. economy, sending them to China, India, and other countries where workers command much lower salaries.

8 Although the migration of foreign workers into the United States can enhance the nation's productivity, many Americans prefer restrictions on immigration. They argue that open immigration tends to reduce their employment opportunities and wages.

KEY TERMS AND CONCEPTS

derived demand
minimum wage
shock effect
unions
collective bargaining
mediation
arbitration
strikes
union shop
right-to-work law
outsourcing
marginal product of labor
value of the marginal product of labor
demand curve for labor

STUDY QUESTIONS AND PROBLEMS

1 Draw a figure showing how the intersection of the market demand curve for labor and the market supply curve of labor determines the equilibrium wage rate and employment level. How are the equilibrium wage rate and employment level affected by:

   a An increase (decrease) in the market supply curve of labor?

   b An increase (decrease) in the market demand curve for labor?

2 Explain how U.S. labor can be competitive with Mexican labor, even if U.S. wage rates are higher than Mexican wage rates.

3 Table 7.4 pertains to the hiring decision of Youngquist Strawberry Co., which hires workers and supplies strawberries in competitive markets.

- **a** Complete the remaining columns of the table.
- **b** Draw a figure showing the firm's demand curve for labor.
- **c** If the wage rate is $560 per week, how many workers will the firm hire? What if the wage rate is $400 per week?

TABLE 7.4 Labor Data for Youngquist Strawberry Co.

Labor Input (workers per week)	*Total Product (boxes of berries per week)*	*Marginal Product of Labor (boxes of berries per week)*	*Product Price*	*Value of the Marginal Product of Labor*
0	0		$0	$
1	100		8	
2	190		8	
3	270		8	
4	340		8	
5	400		8	
6	450		8	

4 Table 7.5 shows the market for less-skilled workers.

- **a** Draw a figure plotting the market demand curve for labor and the market supply curve of labor. Find the equilibrium wage rate and the level of employment.
- **b** Suppose that the government enacts a minimum wage of $6 per hour. How much labor will be supplied and demanded at this wage rate? Will the level of employment be higher or lower than the employment level that exists in the absence of a minimum wage? By how much?
- **c** Suppose that the minimum wage inspires workers to become more productive. Draw a new demand curve for labor that results in the same level of employment as that which occurs in the absence of a minimum wage.

5 Draw a figure showing the market supply curve of labor and the market demand curve of labor. What techniques do labor unions use to raise their members' wages? Assuming these techniques succeed in raising wages, what effect do they have on the quantity of labor demanded? Show the effects graphically. Which technique is most favorable for a union?

6 What factors underlie the extent to which the UAW will, or will not, increase its demand for higher wages?

TABLE 7.5 Market for Less-Skilled Labor

Wage Rate (dollars per hour)	*Quantity of Labor Supplied (thousands of hours)*	*Quantity of Labor Demanded (thousands of hours)*
$1.00	10	70
2.00	20	60
3.00	30	50
4.00	40	40
5.00	50	30
6.00	60	20
7.00	70	10

7 Draw a figure showing the market supply curve and the market demand curve of autoworkers. Assume that the UAW organizes U.S. auto firms. In your figure, show the effects of the following situations:

a The UAW imposes an above-equilibrium wage floor on the market for autoworkers.

b Japanese firms export additional autos to the United States, which causes a decrease in the demand for domestic autos and also a decrease in demand for members of the UAW. Concerning jobs and wages, what options does the UAW have to minimize the adverse effects of the decreased demand for its members? What is the limitation of each option?

8 Explain verbally, and show graphically, why domestic workers may be apprehensive about liberal immigration policies.

EXPLORING FURTHER 7.1: A FIRM'S HIRING DECISION

Concerning a firm's demand curve for labor, consider how the Mt. Pleasant Apple Co., a typical apple producer, chooses the quantity of workers demanded. Suppose that the firm sells apples in a competitive market and thus cannot affect the price it gets for the sale of apples. Also assume that the firm hires workers in a competitive market and therefore has no influence on the wages it pays to apple pickers. Finally, assume that the firm is a profit maximizer—that is, it cares only about the difference between the total revenue obtained from the sale of apples and the total cost of producing them.

When hiring apple pickers, Mt. Pleasant Apple Co. must know how much workers contribute to its output. Figure 7.6 gives a numerical example. Referring to Figure 7.6(*a*), the first column of the table shows the number of apple pickers. The second column shows the amount of apples harvested each week by the workers. The firm's production

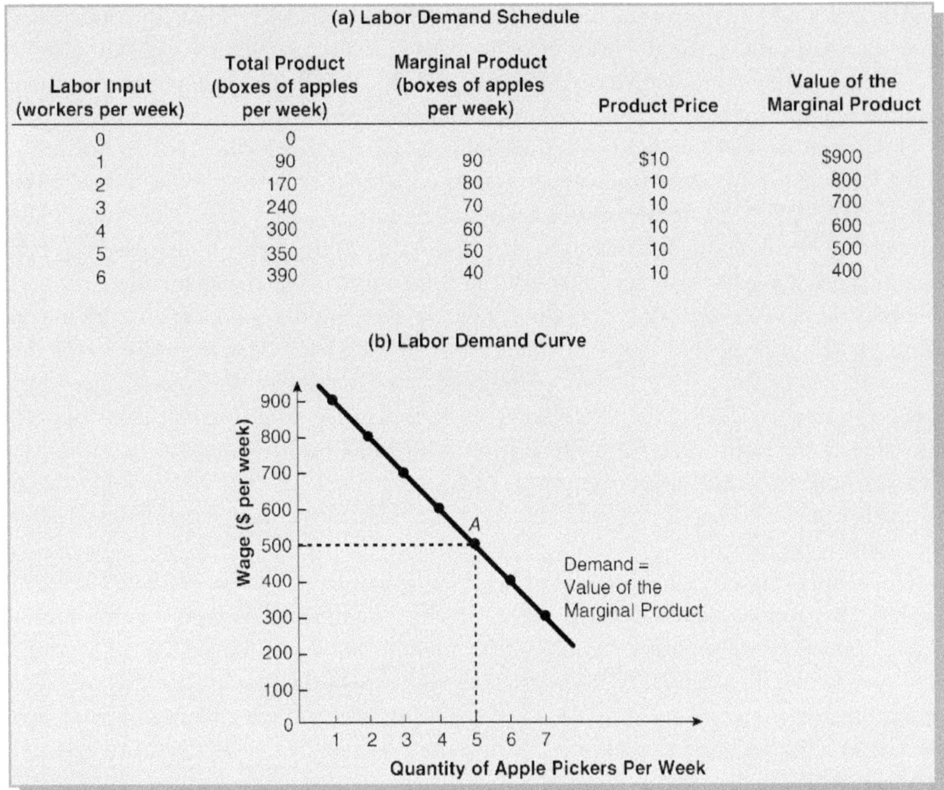

(a) Labor Demand Schedule

Labor Input (workers per week)	Total Product (boxes of apples per week)	Marginal Product (boxes of apples per week)	Product Price	Value of the Marginal Product
0	0			
1	90	90	$10	$900
2	170	80	10	800
3	240	70	10	700
4	300	60	10	600
5	350	50	10	500
6	390	40	10	400

FIGURE 7.6 Mt. Pleasant Apple Company's Demand Schedule for Labor

A firm's demand schedule for labor is based on its value of marginal product schedule, which decreases as extra workers are employed.

data suggest that one worker can harvest 90 boxes of apples per week, two workers can harvest 170 boxes, and so on. The third column in the table gives the marginal product of labor, the *additional* output from hiring each worker. When the firm increases the number of workers from, say, one to two, the amount of apples harvested *rises* from 90 boxes to 170 boxes. The marginal product of the second worker is thus 80 boxes (170–90 = 80). Similarly, the marginal product of the third worker is 70 boxes of apples (240–170 = 70), and so on. Consistent with the law of diminishing returns (discussed in Chapter 4), the marginal product decreases as the firm hires more workers. In this example, diminishing marginal productivity sets in with the first worker hired.

Besides needing to know about the amount of apples harvested by each additional worker, the Mt. Pleasant Apple Co. needs to know each worker's contribution to revenue. The value of the marginal product of labor is the increase in revenue that results from hiring an additional worker. In other words, the value of the marginal product is the dollar value of a worker's contribution to production.

We calculate the value of the marginal product by multiplying the marginal product of a worker by the price of apples. Referring to Figure 7.6(*a*), suppose that the price of apples is $10 per box. The value of the first worker's product equals $900, found by multiplying their marginal product by the price of apples (90 × $10 = $900). Similarly, the value of the second worker's productivity is $800 (80 × $10 = $800). The value of the marginal product schedule of labor is illustrated graphically in Figure 7.6(*b*).

How many workers should the Mt. Pleasant Apple Co. hire? The firm will hire additional labor if it adds more to revenue than to cost—that is, as long as the value of the marginal product is greater than the wage rate. The firm will stop hiring labor only when the two are equal. Suppose that the market wage is $500 per week. In this case, the first worker is profitable because the dollar value of their output ($900) is greater than the cost of hiring the worker ($500). Hiring the second worker, the third worker, and the fourth worker is also profitable because the dollar value of their additional outputs exceeds the wage rate. Hiring stops with the fifth worker because the value of their marginal product equals the wage rate. After the fifth worker, additional hiring is unprofitable. For example, the value of the sixth worker's marginal product is $400, but the wage rate is $500. Mt. Pleasant Apple Co. thus maximizes profits by hiring five workers. The conclusion is that a firm will hire workers up to the point at which the value of the marginal product of labor equals the wage rate.

The value of the marginal product of labor curve constitutes the firm's demand curve for labor. Recall that a labor demand curve shows the number of workers that the firm is willing to hire at each possible wage rate that might exist. The firm makes its hiring decision by selecting the quantity of labor at which the value of the marginal product of labor equals the prevailing wage. Therefore, when the wage rates and the amounts of labor that the firm is willing to hire at each rate are plotted in a graph, we have the firm's demand curve for labor.

NOTES

1 "Weighing Minimum Wage Hikes," *The Wall Street Journal*, November 3, 2006, p. A–4.

2 Alice Sasser, *The Potential Economic Impact of Increasing the Minimum Wage in Massachusetts*, Federal Reserve Bank of Boston, NEPPC Research Report Series, No. 06–1, January 2006.

3 Daniel Raff and Lawrence Summers, "Did Henry Ford Pay Efficiency Wages?" *Journal of Labor Economics*, October 1987, pp. 557–586.

CHAPTER 8

Government and Markets

CHAPTER OBJECTIVES

After reading this chapter, you should be able to:

1 Explain why markets sometimes fail to allocate resources efficiently.

2 Describe the nature and operation of antitrust policy.

3 Assess the advantages and disadvantages of economic regulation versus social regulation.

4 Explain why public utilities, such as electricity and cable television, have traditionally been provided an exclusive franchise to serve a local community.

5 Identify the factors that contribute to the failure of the market system.

DOI: 10.4324/9781003438571-10

ECONOMICS IN CONTEXT

For decades, individuals have made tape recordings of live musical performances or musical performances sold on records, tapes, or CDs. These recordings were often copied and traded with friends and other collectors. However, taped copies were of a lower quality than the original, thus reducing the possibility for widespread copying of music files as an alternative to purchasing music from recording companies. By the late 1990s, however, technological improvements made it possible to record music files from the Internet. As a result, musical recordings could be compressed into compact files that could be played back at near-CD quality.

In 1999, Shawn Fanning, a freshman at Northwestern University, introduced the Napster program and music service. Using the Internet, Napster allowed users to swap music files with other users of this service. Napster provided the software that users would need to locate and download music files and Napster maintained a central directory containing the addresses of computers that contained such files.

However, a significant share of the music traded through Napster involved illegal transfers of copyrighted music. In 2000, the Recording Industry Association of America initiated a lawsuit against Napster, claiming that the service was engaged in copyright violation. According to the music industry, Napster had no rights to its recordings and therefore was preventing the music industry from making money on its recordings.

In rebuttal, Napster argued that its service allowed new musicians to distribute music to a wide audience at virtually no cost. Napster also argued that the existing system of music distribution provided the recording companies with a monopoly over the distribution of a given artist's music. This resulted in high prices and profits for these companies, but only limited rewards to most musicians. Moreover, Napster contended it was difficult for new artists to break into the market under the existing system.

Agreeing with the music industry, the court ruled against Napster, shutting down the free distribution service that it provided. Despite the Napster trial, the online distribution of music became a low-cost alternative to the existing system of selling music on CDs and cassette tapes. The recording industry thus faced the challenge of developing a business model that would allow it to take advantage of the low-cost distribution mechanism provided by the Internet while remaining profitable.

Apple's iTunes Music Store, launched in 2003 and became a viable business model. Although the iTunes Music Store was initially successful, subscription-based streaming services like Spotify soon became competitors. In 2019 Apple thus announced that iTunes Music Store would no longer be included in new versions of its Mac operating system. Although the era of pay-per-song downloads may be over, iTunes Music Store changed the way people obtained digital audio and video content.

In this chapter, we will examine the role of government in the market economy. As we will see, in some cases unregulated markets may not provide the best answers to the fundamental economic questions of society. Whenever that occurs, government intervention is needed to temper the market's operation and to make it conform to the interests of society.

MARKET FAILURE

The U.S. economy relies mainly on the market system to determine what goods and services are produced, in what quantities, and at what prices. Americans have generally accepted the market system as the most effective way of allocating resources to meet the needs and wants of households and families.

The market system provides firms with incentives to produce the goods that consumers want at the lowest possible cost and to find innovative ways of meeting consumer demands. Firms that efficiently produce the goods that consumers desire will prosper; others will be driven out of business, and the resources they employ will be reallocated to more highly valued uses.

The interaction among many producers and many consumers results in the production and consumption of an ideal quantity of each good. Markets are also flexible and accommodate change well. Changes in technology and consumer demands are quickly registered in the market, rearranging the types, prices, and quantities of goods and services that are offered for sale. The quest for profits encourages firms to develop new products and cheaper ways of producing existing products.

Some markets, however, fail to allocate resources efficiently—a situation called **market failure**. When a monopoly serves a market, for example, it makes output artificially scarce and sets the price higher than would occur in a more competitive market in order to maximize profits. In other markets, some people who are affected by the production or consumption of a good are not able to influence those choices.

For example, a steel mill may ignore the pollution problems that it creates, or a toy manufacturer may not provide full information about the risks of using its product—information that consumers may need to make the best decision. Such market failures provide a legitimate reason for governments to consider intervening in the private sector through such means as regulation. Sources of market failure include the following:

- Monopoly power
- Spillovers or externalities
- Public goods
- Inadequate information
- Economic inequality

Let us consider the nature of these problems and then see why government intervention is desirable in each situation.

MONOPOLY POWER

Although competition generally results in the most efficient use of a nation's resources, an individual firm would prefer to conduct business in an environment that is more akin to monopoly. If allowed, some competing firms may attempt to create a monopoly environment by colluding with rivals, merging with rivals, or driving rivals out of business.

Recall that a monopoly tends to produce much less desirable outcomes than a competitive market. Given the same costs, a monopoly maximizes profit by selling a smaller output and charging a higher price than would a competitive market. Also, substantial barriers to entry may shelter a monopoly from the pressure of competition, meaning that the monopoly's costs are above their lowest possible level. The lack of competition also suggests that there is no external pressure for advancements in technology in a monopoly. Simply put, monopoly results in market failure because the monopoly uses too few resources in order to produce goods at an artificially higher price.

Antitrust Policy

What can the government do to counteract monopoly power? One approach is to adopt a rigorous **antitrust policy**. Antitrust policy is the attempt to foster a market structure that will lead to increased competition and to curb anticompetitive behavior that harms consumers. Antitrust laws are designed to prevent unfair business practices that restrain trade, such as price-fixing conspiracies, corporate mergers that are likely to reduce the competitive vigor of particular markets, and predatory acts designed to achieve or maintain monopoly power.

By the late 1800s, large corporations had begun to dominate many U.S. industries, including oil, railroads, and banking. These firms were run by the so-called robber barons, who attempted to drive competitors out of business, monopolize markets, and gouge consumers. They realized their monopoly power by forming *trusts*, the 19th-century name given to cartels and other business agreements intended to restrain competition. In the oil industry, for example, Standard Oil of New Jersey acquired small, competing firms and eventually accounted for 90 percent of sales in the domestic market. In tobacco, American Tobacco controlled up to 90 percent of the market for tobacco products.

Concern about the growing monopoly power of these firms prompted the federal government to intervene in the private-sector economy in order to prevent the acquisition and exercise of monopoly power and to encourage competition in the marketplace. These efforts culminated in the passage of the **Sherman Act of 1890**, the cornerstone of federal antitrust law. This act prohibits contracts and conspiracies in the restraint of trade as well as monopolization and the threat of monopolization of an industry. For example, conspiracies such as collusive agreements among competing sellers to fix prices and control markets are outlawed. Firms that are found in violation of the Sherman Act may be broken up, and the parties responsible for illegal conduct can be fined and imprisoned. Moreover, the parties harmed by illegal monopoly behavior can sue for three times the amount of monetary injury inflicted upon them.

Although the Sherman Act attempted to provide a solid foundation for government action against business monopolies, its vague language allowed the courts wide latitude in interpreting its meaning. The **Clayton Act of 1914** was enacted to make explicit the intent of the Sherman Act. The Clayton Act outlaws price discrimination, certain types of mergers, and tying (exclusive) contracts between a supplier and a buyer that substantially lessen competition. It also prohibits interlocking boards of directors among competing companies.

The U.S. Department of Justice and the Federal Trade Commission enforce the antitrust laws. The Justice Department is exclusively responsible for enforcing the Sherman Act and, with the Federal Trade Commission, it is responsible for enforcing the Clayton

Act. The majority of antitrust cases initiated by these agencies are settled by an agreement between the government and the defendant. This saves the federal government time and money.

Is Microsoft a Monopoly?

Microsoft provides an example of a firm that has violated the antitrust laws. The U.S. government's antitrust case against Microsoft was one of the largest and most carefully watched cases in history. Let us consider this case.

Microsoft Corporation, also known as Microsoft, is a U.S. technology company that manufactures, licenses, and sells computer software, computer electronics, and personal computers and services. Its best-known software products are the Microsoft Windows line of operating systems, Microsoft Office suite, and Internet and Edge web browsers. Microsoft is the world's largest software maker measured by revenues and is one of the world's most valuable companies.

In 1975, Microsoft was founded by Bill Gates and Paul Allen, childhood friends with a passion for computer programming. The company rose to dominate the personal computer operating system market in the 1980s. However, Microsoft's market dominance and business practices attracted widespread condemnation. The company has been accused of engaging in unlawful monopolistic practices such as locking vendors and consumers into its products.

In 1998 the U.S. government filed an antitrust suit that accused Microsoft of being a monopoly and engaging in abusive practices contrary to the Sherman Antitrust Act of 1890. Focusing on predatory strategies and market barriers to entry, the government alleged that Microsoft abused monopoly power on Intel-based personal computers in its handling of operating system and web browser sales. The key issue of the case was whether Microsoft was allowed to bundle its Internet Explorer web browser software with its Microsoft Windows operating system.

Microsoft stated that the merging of Microsoft Windows and Internet Explorer was the result of innovation and competition, that the two were the same product and were inextricably linked together, and that consumers were getting all the benefits of Internet Explorer for free. Also, Microsoft noted that its 95-percent share of the software market was temporary due to rapid improvements in technology that would occur soon. The government countered that Microsoft's browser was a distinct and separate product which did not need to be tied to its operating system, since a separate version of Internet Explorer was available for Mac computers.

In 2000 the court ruled that Microsoft was guilty, not because of its dominant market position, but because it used illegal methods of preserving its monopoly position: In particular, the company had taken actions to crush threats to its monopoly, including Apple, Java, and other firms. Among these practices were contracts that Microsoft forced commercial users of its operating system to sign which penalized them for promoting operating systems that competed with Microsoft's product. Under the court's ruling, Microsoft had to pay more than $1 billion in fines to the government and payouts to firms that were adversely affected by its illegal business practices.

This ruling eventually resulted in the government's reaching an agreement with Microsoft to settle the case. Under the terms of the agreement, Microsoft could not enter into licensing agreements with personal computer manufacturers that restrict them from working with other software developers. It also required Microsoft to provide other software makers access to elements of its Windows source code, which are necessary for them to make their applications work under the Windows operating system. However, it did not impose any restrictions on the features Microsoft is allowed to incorporate in its Windows operating system, which was at the heart of the government's case against the company.

Economic Regulation and Deregulation

Is the best approach to improving the performance of markets the vigorous enforcement of the antitrust laws? Or should we consider more extreme intervention in the marketplace? If market forces fail to establish prices that are equal to the cost of production, why not enact direct government regulation and mandate that prices be set this way?

Besides using antitrust laws to regulate business conduct, the federal government can enact **economic regulation** to control the prices, wages, conditions of entry, standards of service, or other important economic characteristics of industries. Industries that have been subject to economic regulation have included airlines, trucking, railroads, banking, communications, and energy.

Industries were originally made subject to economic regulation for many varied reasons. For example, the natural monopoly enjoyed by industries with large economies of scale made meaningful competition impossible. In other instances, fear of "destructive competition" provided the primary rationale for regulation. Extending the scope of service was yet another aim behind government intervention.

By the late 1970s, however, the tide of opinion was turning against economic regulation. It became obvious that the growth of the economy and technological progress had eroded many former natural monopolies, converted nascent industries into mature ones, and created conditions conducive to reliable competitive services. Because the existing economic regulations were applicable to outdated economic conditions, it was time for a change.

Recognizing the problems of economic regulation, in the late 1970s the federal government dismantled regulations in several industries in which the existing regulations were perceived to have outlived their usefulness—airlines, trucking, railroads, energy, telecommunications, and banking. The purpose of such **deregulation** was to increase price competition and provide incentives for companies to introduce new products and services.

Public-Utility Regulation

Economic regulation involves the regulation of public utilities such as electricity, gas pipelines, telephones, and cable television. Rather than promoting competition in these industries through the use of antitrust laws, the U.S. government has traditionally allowed public utilities to operate as private monopolies subject to government regulation of price and output policies. Some nations have tried government ownership as an

Source: mgstudyo/E+/Getty Images®

alternative; but with few exceptions, these have proved to be less effective than private ownership and regulation.

Usually, the reason that governments resort to regulating a monopoly rather than promoting competition through antitrust policy is that the industry in question is believed to be a *natural monopoly*—an industry in which product demand can be supplied most efficiently by a single firm. In such cases, the judgment may be made that competition is not workable and that the market is best served by a single monopoly firm that can fully exploit the advantage of economies of scale, but would be prevented from exercising monopoly power over customers by price regulation.

Figure 8.1 shows the hypothetical cost and revenue curves for Dallas Power and Light Co., an assumed natural monopolist in the electricity industry. As an unregulated monopolist, Dallas Power and Light Co. would maximize profits by applying the familiar $MR = MC$ rule. Referring to Figure 8.1(*a*), the firm's price and output of electricity would thus be 10 cents per kilowatt hour (kwh) and 6 million kwh, respectively. Because price exceeds average total cost at 6 million kwh, the firm realizes an economic profit.

Suppose that the legislature decides to impose public-utility regulation on Dallas Power and Light Co. In addition to overseeing service and entry into and exit from the industry, public-utility regulation determines the price of the monopolist. Legislatures have traditionally allowed regulated firms to receive a **fair-return price**—that is, the firm can charge a price that is just high enough to cover its average total cost. In our example, Dallas Power and Light Co. will set its price at the point where its demand curve intersects its average total cost curve; the fair-return price is thus 7 cents per kwh. Recall that average

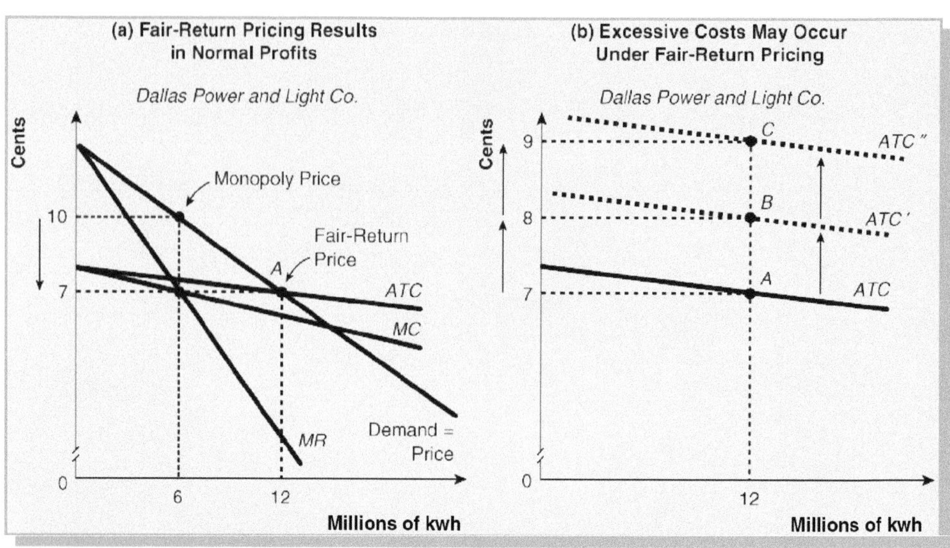

FIGURE 8.1 Public-Utility Regulation of Natural Monopoly

As an unregulated monopolist, Dallas Power and Light Co. would maximize profits by charging 10 cents per kilowatt hour of electricity. Public-utility commissioners would typically require the firm to charge a price equal to 7 cents, the fair-return price. Although this eliminates excess profit, the firm can still earn a normal profit for its stockholders. Critics of fair-return pricing contend that it reduces incentives for public utilities to innovate or to contain costs because the firm realizes essentially the same profits regardless of its efforts.

total costs include a "normal" or "fair" profit. Although fair-return regulation eliminates the excess profit for Dallas Power and Light Co., it allows the firm to earn a fair profit for its stockholders.

But what type of costs should be included in the average total cost of Dallas Power and Light Co.? When economists construct average total cost curves, such as the one in Figure 8.1(*b*), and conclude that, for 12 million kwh of electricity, it costs 7 cents per unit to provide electricity, they are referring to only the least possible cost. It is possible to produce 12 million kwh at 8 cents or 9 cents—as shown by points *B* and C in the figure.

Cost curves are drawn as they are because we usually assume that profit-seeking firms will use the most efficient methods available. In situations in which public-utility regulators set rates that cover average total cost, however, the incentive to hold costs down may be weak. What is to prevent the managers from awarding themselves large salaries and forcing the customers to foot the bill? Should the utility be allowed to charge prices that cover obviously foolish expenditures such as the purchase of fuel from one supplier at a price twice as high as other suppliers? In short, fair-return regulation tends to reduce the incentives for public utilities to innovate or to contain costs, because the firm realizes essentially the same profits regardless of its efforts.

Although the regulation of public utilities can result in economic inefficiency, so can deregulation, as seen in the case of California's electricity market.[1] For decades, government officials in California regulated the price and output policies of electric utilities.

However, critics maintained that because the utilities could easily pass on costs to customers, they lacked incentives to produce electricity cheaply. Paying 50 percent more for power than their counterparts in other states, California businesses pushed for the deregulation of electric utilities as a way of providing market incentives to reduce cost. In 1996, California restructured its electricity industry, allowing consumers to obtain power from out-of-area (often out-of-state) suppliers. As a result, many local utilities sold their power-generation plants, purchased power on the wholesale market from other suppliers, and resold it to their retail customers. By breaking the power-generation monopoly of local utilities, state officials anticipated decreases in electricity costs.

However, California's policy had a flaw: It resulted in only *partial* deregulation rather than the complete deregulation of electric utilities. Although state officials tried to provide consumers with access to cheap electricity by freezing the retail price, the wholesale price was not regulated; it varied according to changing conditions in the national market. When rising electricity costs pushed the wholesale price above the frozen retail price, many California utilities suffered losses. Simply put, California's partial deregulation of electricity was not generally viewed as a success.

Peak-Load Pricing: Buying Power by the Hour

Another aspect of public-utility pricing involves peak-load pricing. For decades, power economists have recognized that consumers do not have an incentive to conserve electricity at times when they should conserve. To promote the conservation of electricity, many utilities have enacted a variable pricing system called **peak-load pricing** or time-of-use pricing. To understand how peak-load pricing works, let us first consider the costs of producing electricity.

Producing electricity entails fixed costs and variable costs. Fixed costs mainly consist of the costs of electric power generators, the costs of the plants that house them, and the costs of transmission lines. These costs do not vary with changes in electricity production. Variable costs include the costs of labor, coal, natural gas, and diesel fuel. As more power is produced, more of these inputs are needed to operate the generators.

For a typical utility, fixed costs are very high relative to total costs in electricity production. Also, power plants generally operate most of the time with a large amount of excess capacity. Therefore, customers who buy power during the peak periods cause electric companies to incur very high costs—the cost of constructing and operating generators that are used only during the peak period and that stay idle at other times.

Moreover, the variable costs of producing electricity change substantially throughout the day. During the night, the demand for electricity is smallest, and the variable costs of producing electricity are lowest because the utility uses very efficient plants that operate 24 hours a day. These plants use coal or nuclear fuel to boil water to turn the electrical turbines, which take a long time to rev up. As demand climbs, say around mid-afternoon on a summer afternoon, additional plants—which are more expensive to operate—are called into operation to supply power for people's air conditioners. These "peak-load" plants usually use gas turbines that run on exhaust gases instead of boiling water. Although they can be brought online almost instantly, they use expensive fuels (diesel and natural gas).

The variable costs of providing peak service are thus greater than those of providing off-peak service.

Apparently, those who purchase electricity during the middle of the night should pay a lower price per kwh than those who purchase electricity during the afternoon. But often, they do not. Most of us pay a constant price per kwh regardless of whether we use expensive hours or cheap ones. Thus, we have no reason to conserve power during hours of high demand. Peak-load pricing changes all of this.

With peak-load pricing, prices reflect the difference in the cost of providing electricity during peak hours and off-peak hours. Therefore, consumers are charged more for electricity during peak demand periods when it costs more to provide power. The higher price encourages consumers to switch part of their usage to the cheaper off-peak periods. The shift in demand is achieved in several ways. For example, people may purchase timers that operate air conditioners, water heaters, and space heaters only during off-peak periods. Similarly, they may avoid using washing machines, clothes dryers, and dishwashers during peak periods. The effect of such consumption shifts is that a utility can serve its customers with much smaller generating capacity.

Wisconsin Public System provides an example of peak-load pricing for electricity. This regulated utility serves customers in Wisconsin and Michigan. In 2023, Wisconsin households had the option of buying all their electricity during a week at a fixed price of 13.6 cents per kwh hour. They could also buy electricity under a peak-load option. From Monday through Friday during the summer season, the price of electricity bought during the off-peak period (7 p.m. to 9 a.m.) was 7.8 cents per kwh; a price of 24.9 cents per kwh was charged for purchases during the peak period (9 a.m.to 7 p.m.). The off-peak price was also applied to weekend consumption of electricity. The large differential between the peak and off-peak prices provided motivation for households to shift consumption to the off-peak times of the day. When customers participate in a peak-load pricing system, they obtain a special meter that measures electricity use during peak-usage hours and off-peak-usage hours.

CHECK POINT

1 How does monopoly power contribute to market failure?

2 How do the Sherman and Clayton Acts attempt to combat monopoly power?

3 Why have public utilities traditionally been granted an exclusive franchise to serve a local community? Identify the problems of public-utility regulation.

4 How does peak-load pricing attempt to spread the available power around throughout the day?

5 Evaluate the argument for increasing federal government subsidies for renewable energies.

SPILLOVER EFFECTS

We have learned that monopoly power can result in market failure. Another source of market failure involves what economists refer to as spillover effects.

A **spillover**, or **externality**, is a cost or benefit imposed on people other than the producers and consumers of a good or service. For example, if a smelter pollutes the air or water, and neither the firm nor its customers pay for the harm that pollution causes, the pollution becomes a **spillover cost** for society. In some cases, however, spillovers can be desirable. For example, the development of laser technology has had beneficial effects far beyond whatever gains its developers captured, improving products in industries as diverse as medicine and telecommunications. Laser technology is an example of a **spillover benefit**.

How does the market system fail when the production of a good or service entails spillover effects? When the production of some good results in spillover *costs*, *too much* of it is produced and resources are *overallocated* to its use. Conversely, *underproduction* and *underallocation* of resources arise from spillover *benefits*. Let us show these conclusions graphically.

Spillover Costs

How can spillover costs cause failure in a market for chemicals? Referring to Figure 8.2, the market demand curve for chemicals is shown by D_0, and S_0 denotes the market supply

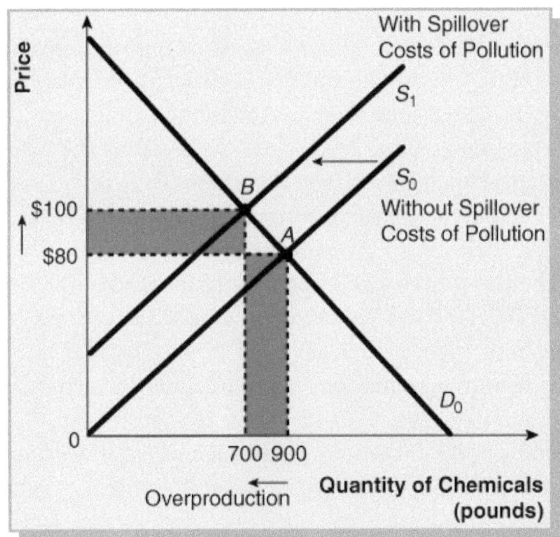

FIGURE 8.2 Correcting for Market Failure: Spillover Costs

In the case of pollution, market failure occurs because the firms fail to take into account the spillover costs. As a result, too much output will be produced at too low a price. To correct this market failure, government could require firms to install pollution-abatement equipment or pay a tax on pollution.

curve. Notice that the market supply curve includes the firms' private marginal costs of producing chemicals, such as labor and material costs. In equilibrium, 900 pounds of chemicals are sold at a price of $80.

Now suppose that the production of chemicals results in toxic wastes. If firms can dump these wastes into the waterways and thus pass their pollution costs on to the public, their private marginal costs of producing chemicals are lower. Referring to Figure 8.2, market supply curve S_0 includes only the firms' private marginal costs of producing chemicals. Therefore, it lies too far to the right of a supply curve that includes all costs (both private costs and spillover costs of pollution). This means that the equilibrium output, 900 pounds, exceeds the optimal output of 700 pounds. Simply put, the market supply curve does not reflect all of the costs resulting from the production of chemicals. Therefore, the market produces too many chemicals and thus overallocates resources to their production.

How can the government force the market to decrease its pollution? One approach involves **command-and-control regulations** that impose restrictions on the amount of the polluting activity that can occur, as well as stipulate how the goal will be fulfilled. Clean air and water laws restrict the amount of pollutants that firms can place into the air, rivers, and lakes. Moreover, toxic-waste legislation specifies special procedures and dump sites for the disposal of contaminated solvents and soils.

By mandating that chemical firms be responsible for pollution abatement, such laws increase the firms' private marginal cost of production. In Figure 8.2, the market supply curve thus shifts from S_0 to S_1. The price of chemicals rises from $80 to $100, and the equilibrium output falls from 900 pounds to 700 pounds. In this manner, the overallocation of resources to chemical production is corrected.

Another way to reduce spillover costs is to establish **incentive-based regulations**, which set an environmental objective but are flexible because producers can find different ways to achieve the objective. Companies that are unable to fulfill the objective pay penalties in the form of taxes, but they are not rewarded for exceeding the objective.

For example, the government may levy a **carbon tax** (excise tax) on the production of chemicals in order to encourage firms to reduce pollution. This tax sets the price that polluters must pay for each ton of greenhouse gas emissions they emit. Facing this tax, firms must decide whether to pay it or expend additional funds to develop new methods to reduce pollution. In either case, the tax will increase the private marginal cost of producing chemicals, again shifting the market supply curve from S_0 to S_1 in Figure 8.2. Any tax revenue resulting from the regulations could be used to compensate those harmed by the pollution.

Economists generally favor incentive-based regulations over command-and-control regulations. The main problem with command-and-control regulations is that regulators lack the detailed knowledge of individual production facilities and processes and of alternative production and abatement methods that would be necessary to implement an efficient regulatory program through command and control. It can also be costly to monitor and enforce the regulations. However, incentive-based regulations make it profitable for firms to develop the most efficient techniques to reduce pollution.

Cap and Trade: Trading Pollution Permits

The trading of pollution permits (emissions certificates) provides an example of incentive-based regulations on the environment. Companies can trade the permits—some purchase them to comply with air-quality regulations, whereas others sell them for a profit.

Known as a **cap and trade system**, the trading of pollution permits is a market-oriented solution to the problem of greenhouse gas. Under this system, the Environmental Protection Agency (EPA) sets a cap on the total amount of greenhouse gas it will allow in the air. This amount is divided into units. The EPA then issues a limited number of permits, each permit giving the holder—say, an electric utility—the right to produce a unit of pollution. Such permits are sold by the EPA at auction.

The permits are tradeable, so companies that find ways to emit less greenhouse gas than they are entitled to can sell some of their permits to others. The EPA auction and the private resale market thus establish a price on the emission of greenhouse gas into the environment. The more greenhouse gas a company emits, the more permits it must buy, thus raising its costs of production. Therefore, polluting companies have the incentive to reduce their levels of pollution. The program does not tell companies how to reduce pollution; rather, they are free to choose the most cost-effective method for achieving reductions.

Figure 8.3 helps us visualize the operation of a cap and trade system. The demand for pollution permits is shown by curve D_0. It shows that as the price of polluting the environment decreases, more firms will choose to pollute more. The supply of pollution permits, shown by curve S_0, is vertical because the quantity of pollution is fixed by the number of permits allowed by the government. The equilibrium price of pollution permits

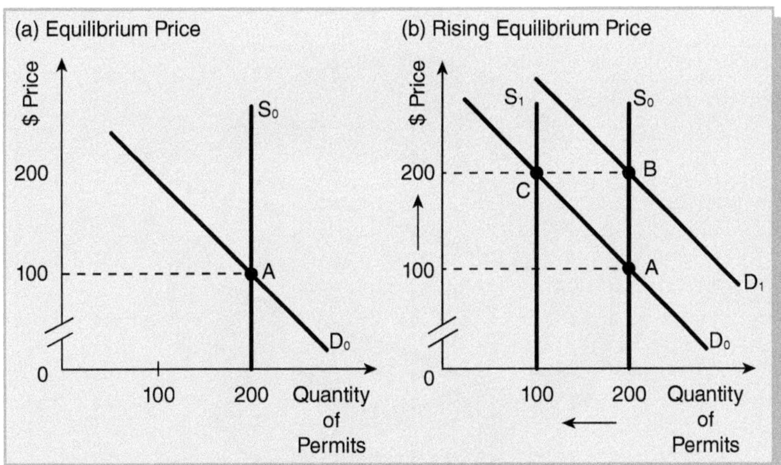

FIGURE 8.3 Cap and Trade: The Market for Pollution Permits

The equilibrium price of pollution permits occurs at the point of intersection of the supply and demand curves for permits. The equilibrium price of permits will increase in response to an increase in the demand for permits or a decrease in the supply of permits.

occurs at the intersection of the supply and the demand curves for pollution, as shown in Figure 8.3(*a*).

Changes in the equilibrium price of pollution permits will occur in response to a change in the demand or supply of permits, as shown in Figure 8.3(*b*). If companies want to emit more greenhouse gas into the environment, the demand for pollution permits will increase to curve D_1 in the figure. As the price of pollution permits increases, polluting the environment becomes more expensive for companies. Also, if the EPA reduces the amount of pollution that companies can legally emit, the supply curve of pollution permits will decrease to curve S_1 in the figure, and the price of the permits will increase. Simply put, the cap and trade system promotes conservation by increasing the price of goods whose production harms the environment.

Concerning the United States, the cap and trade system has been used by states such as California, Connecticut, Virginia, and Maryland. The program is also used in Europe as well as in Australia and New Zealand.

However, a cap and trade system is not without problems. For example, regulatory agencies run the risk of issuing too many pollution permits, which can result in a price on the permits that is too low. This reduces the incentive for polluters to cut back on their emissions. Conversely, issuing too few permits can result in an excessively high price on permits. Moreover, the revenues from auctioning emission permits goes to the government. These revenues could, for example, be used for research and development of sustainable technology for a cleaner environment.

Spillover Benefits

Source: filo/DigitalVision Vectors/Getty Images®

Recall that in the case of spillover costs, the market supply curve understates the total costs associated with the production of a good. Now we will see that the market demand curve understates the total benefits associated with the purchase and consumption of a good that entails spillover benefits.

Assume that a new drug, called "Cold Free," is developed; this drug cures the common cold. In Figure 8.4(*a*), the market demand curve, D_0, shows the price that private individuals would be willing to pay for Cold Free to receive the benefits of having fewer colds. The market supply curve, S_0, shows the quantity of Cold Free that is offered for sale at different prices. At equilibrium point *A*, 50 packages of Cold Free are sold at a price of $6.

Because of spillover benefits, however, this equilibrium point fails to achieve an optimum allocation of resources. Why? When buyers take Cold Free, other people who do not purchase the drug also benefit because the virus is less likely to spread. For society in general, taking Cold Free results in a healthier population, yielding widespread output and income benefits.

The market demand curve, D_1, represents the private benefits from using Cold Free plus the extra, or spillover, benefits accruing to society in general. With market demand curve D_1, the optimal equilibrium at point *B* is established, shown by the intersection of D_1 and S_0. We conclude that with spillover benefits, the actual equilibrium output, 50 packages, is less than the optimal output, 70 packages. The market fails by not producing enough Cold Free and thus underallocating resources to its production.

How could the government prevent market failure in this instance? One approach would be for the government to require all citizens to purchase and use Cold Free each year. In Figure 8.4(*b*), such a policy would shift the market demand curve to the right, from D_0 to D_1. This explains why all children must receive diphtheria, tetanus, pertussis,

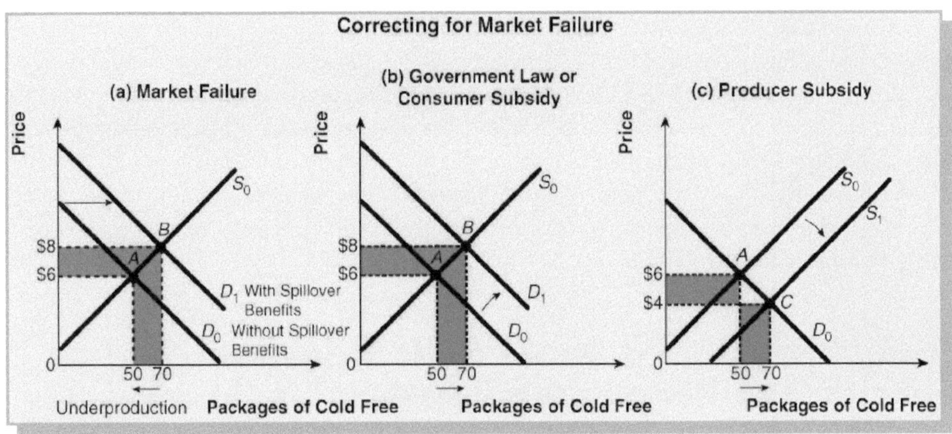

FIGURE 8.4 Correcting for Market Failure: Spillover Benefits

With spillover benefits, market failure occurs because the market demand curve does not reflect the spillover benefits of a good. As a result, the good is underproduced and underconsumed. Government could correct this market failure by requiring consumers to purchase additional units of the product, granting subsidies to consumers to finance purchases of the product, or subsidizing producers so that they could supply additional units of the product at a lower price.

polio, and other vaccines before entering primary school. Another solution would be for the government to provide subsidies to individuals to help them pay for the cost of Cold Free, again shifting the market demand curve to the right.

Alternatively, the government might grant subsidies to the producers of Cold Free. Such a subsidy would lower the producers' cost of production so that the market supply curve would increase from S_0 to S_1 in Figure 8.4(*c*). Producers could thus offer more Cold Free to consumers at a lower price.

In practice, subsidies are often granted for activities that yield spillover benefits. Education, for example, receives large subsidies. Students in public schools, from kindergarten through high school, receive an education that is virtually free. Moreover, the cost of a student's education at a state college or university is only partially paid for by student tuition and fees—the remainder comes from government tax dollars. The government also provides subsidies for public television, mass transit and medical programs, as well as for the construction of stadiums for professional sports.

Subsidies for the Covid-19 Vaccine

The Covid-19 pandemic illustrates the use of government subsidies to promote the development and distribution of a critical vaccine. On January 30, 2020, the World Health Organization declared the outbreak of novel coronavirus to be a pandemic, which soon led to the illness and death of many people. Just one year after the first case of Covid-19 was detected, the first Covid-19 vaccine doses were distributed throughout the United States.

To help finance the research and development of the Covid-19 vaccine, the U.S. government provided a massive grant to Moderna Inc., and Pfizer Inc., two leading pharmaceutical companies. Then the government spent $25 billion to buy vaccines at an average price of about $21 a dose, and it made them available to the public at no cost.

When the Covid-19 national emergency program ended in 2023, and government supplies of the vaccine were used up, Moderna and Pfizer announced that they would market vaccines at a list price of up to $130 a dose, subject to discounts which could vary depending on health systems, pharmacies, federal health programs, and other potential buyers. Also, the pharmaceutical companies announced a patient assistance program to provide the vaccine free to uninsured or underinsured people. However, the announcement fueled criticism from some lawmakers, who noted that the companies were charging an excessively high price for the vaccine.

Should the United States Shift More Energy Subsidies to Renewable Power?

When discussing energy policy, we typically think of two types of energy. Renewable energy is energy that comes from natural resources such as sunlight, wind, tides, biomass, and geothermal heat, which are naturally replenished. Conventional energy includes coal, natural gas, and oil. These energies come from fossil fuels that are not naturally replenished.

Since the 1970s, U.S. energy policy has been directed at two broad goals. First, policymakers have attempted to reduce energy import dependence and enhance national security. Second, environmental concerns about conventional energies (air pollution, water pollution) have resulted in government's promotion of clean, renewable energies.

Given the importance of abundant amounts of energy for Americans, the federal government tends to subsidize all forms of energy development. These subsidies result in a lower price of energy paid by consumers and a higher price received by producers. Federal subsidies to energy producers include capital grants, low-interest or preferential loans, preferential tax treatment, and the like. Historically, most energy subsidies have gone to developing conventional energy resources and reserves to encourage more domestic energy production. That is, we started subsidizing fossil fuels a long time ago and we still have them today. However, energy subsidies are also granted to producers of renewables, as seen in Table 8.1. Should the pendulum swing towards renewables?

Increasing subsidies for renewables are justified on the grounds that renewable energy is a developing industry in its infancy. It cannot currently compete with conventional energies, a mature industry that has enjoyed government support for many years. Proponents of renewables contend that the fossil fuel industry is mature enough to fund its own research and development and thus needs little or no additional help from the government. They also maintain that it will take years for renewables to attain the economies of scale and learning efficiencies that can occur with increased market share. The idea is not to prop up clean energy industries forever. It is to get them to a point where they can stand on their own.

However, critics question whether renewable energy can be counted on for the future. For example, they note that wind and solar are unreliable sources of energy because their production can occur only if weather conditions are right, or it is the right time of the day. Therefore, wind and solar energies require backup power generation, a dual setup

TABLE 8.1 Federal Subsidies for U.S. Energy Production, 2010–2016 (millions of dollars)

Energy	*2010*	*2013*	*2016*
Natural gas	$24,105	$28,220	$32,652
Crude oil	11,512	15,370	18,797
Coal	21,657	20,223	14,807
Nuclear	8,318	8,099	8,352
Biomass	4,358	4,680	4,963
Hydroelectric	2,588	2,582	2,482
Wind	863	1,557	2,038
Solar	88	205	533
Geothermal	207	215	209

Source: U.S. Energy Information Administration, *Direct Federal Financial Interventions and Subsidies in Energy in 2016*, April 24, 2018, available at https://www.eia.gov/analysis/requests/subsidy.

that entails additional costs. They also maintain that the data shows that future economies of scale and learning efficiencies are unlikely for renewables unless, perhaps, future technological advances are made. Will this really occur? Moreover, they cite examples of government subsidies that have been granted to clean energy companies that have gone bankrupt, such as producers of solar panels and electric-car batteries. Should the government be in the business of attempting to pick winners and losers?

Should Government Subsidize Professional Sports?

Source: Noam Galai/Moment/Getty Images®

Are governmental subsidies of new sports stadiums a good investment? Many professional sports teams insist that public subsidies are necessary if they are to operate in the community. Table 8.2 gives examples of public funding for sports stadiums.

The subsidy begins with the federal government, which permits state and local governments to issue tax-exempt bonds to help finance sports stadiums. Tax exemption decreases interest on debt and therefore decreases the amount that cities and teams must pay for a stadium. State and local governments also pay subsidies to help cover the cost of sports facilities.

Often, subsidies are justified on the grounds that attracting or retaining sports teams more than offset the cost through increased local tax revenue by creating new jobs and more spending. Also, local officials often view a downtown stadium project as an important part of the revitalization of the central city's urban core.

However, critics argue that the promised stadium-driven booms often turn out to be disappointments. At best, they have a tiny, and sometimes even a negative, impact on local

TABLE 8.2 Public Funding for Professional Sports Stadiums

City	*Sport*	*Public Funds as a Percent of Stadium Cost*
Cincinnati	Baseball	91%
Pittsburgh	Baseball	85
San Antonio	Basketball	84
Milwaukee	Baseball	77
Denver	Football	75
Seattle	Baseball	72
Pittsburgh	Football	70
Seattle	Football	70

Source: Drawn from Eric Bull, *Top 10 Biggest Federal Subsidies for Pro Stadiums*, The Brookings Institution, September 9, 2016, available at https://www.brookings.edu/blog/brookings-now/2016/09/09/top-10-biggest-federal-subsidies-for-pro-stadiums-hint-the-yankees-are-1.

employment. Whatever good may be achieved is more than canceled out by the cost of taxes levied to subsidize them.

Why? Subsidies for sports stadiums mean that taxes must rise or that government must reduce other spending. Those funds could have been used to dredge a harbor, fund education, or provide more police, all of which would make the economy more productive. Also, subsidized stadiums use taxpayer money to generate more wealth for owners and players, who do not usually spend a large portion of their income in the local area. Meanwhile, the new facility siphons money away from other local establishments. When more people fill the seats in an expanded stadium, fewer dollars are spent on other entertainment, such as bowling, golf, or theater.

Yet proponents of subsidies contend that the critics miss a basic issue: Professional sports teams add to the quality of life of residents in cities that host teams. People root for local athletes, look forward to reading about their success or failure in the newspaper, and share in the joy when the home team wins a championship. If people benefit from having a pro sports franchise in their community, they are presumably willing to pay for it—if not directly through the purchase of tickets, then indirectly through higher taxes. Thus, residents should think of a pro sports team in the same way they think of a new art museum or new symphony hall that receives public subsidies.

Simply put, subsidy proponents maintain that professional sports yield spillover benefits that are similar to quality-of-life benefits such as clean air and scenic views. If the value of these spillover benefits is large enough, they alone might justify the subsidies that taxpayers grant to teams. However, measuring these spillover benefits is difficult and subject to criticism.

SOCIAL REGULATION

We have learned that government implements economic regulation by setting standards for prices, wages, conditions of entry, and standards of service in particular industries. Since World War II, the government has assumed an ever-increasing role in regulating the *quality of life* for society. **Social regulation** is intended to correct a variety of undesirable side effects in a market economy that relate to health, safety, and the environment—effects that markets, left to themselves, often ignore. Markets do not respond well to these problems, primarily because only a small fraction of the benefits gained from lessening these problems accrues to those who produce the side effects. Incentives to take action or to collect information leading to health, safety, and environmental improvements are thus lacking in the private business sector.

Whereas economic regulation governs the conditions of doing business in a particular industry, social regulation addresses the conditions under which goods are produced in a variety of industries. Social regulation applies to a particular issue (such as environmental quality) and affects the behavior of firms in many industries (such as automobiles, steel, or chemicals). Consider the following examples of social regulation:

- The Environmental Protection Agency regulates the amount of pollutants that firms can discharge into the air, lakes, and rivers.
- The Consumer Product Safety Commission removes dangerous products from the marketplace. It can also establish standards for product safety, such as controls that automatically shut off the engine of a lawnmower when the operator lets go of the handle.
- The National Highway Traffic Safety Administration requires that automobiles be equipped with seat belts and brake lights.
- The Food and Drug Administration approves the sale of both prescription and non-prescription drugs.
- The Occupational Safety and Health Administration establishes standards that are intended to decrease workers' exposure to injury and to health risks, such as those associated with asbestos.

As with other types of government regulation, not everyone agrees on the merits of social regulation. Some people claim that compliance with social regulations results in higher operating costs for the firms striving to meet them. These higher costs are similar to a tax. Suppose that the imposition of health and safety regulations increases a firm's costs by $10 per unit. The firm's supply curve therefore shifts upward by that amount, which results in higher prices and a decrease in output. Like other taxing situations, the consumer absorbs part of the regulatory tax in the form of a higher price, while a firm's revenues are reduced by the remainder of the tax.

Proponents of social regulation, however, contend that although the costs are high, the benefits are even higher. They may claim, for example, that government regulations on asbestos lead to 2,000 fewer people dying from cancer each year; highway fatalities would be 30 percent higher in the absence of auto safety features required by regulation; and that mandated childproof lids result in 85 percent fewer child deaths caused by the accidental swallowing of poisonous substances. Although social regulation results in higher consumer prices, is this too much of a burden when compared to an improved quality of life for society?

Although social regulation based on a careful balancing of costs and benefits can sometimes improve market performance, policymakers often ignore the fact that the government is an imperfect regulator. Critics of social regulation, for example, claim that regulators often lack accurate information about an industry and cannot always predict the effects of specific regulations. Although the decision to regulate may be well intentioned, the regulations themselves can have adverse and unintended consequences.

Do Corporate Fuel-Economy Standards Promote Fuel Conservation?

The U.S. government's fuel-economy standards for automobile companies provide an example of the problems of social regulation. The Arab oil embargo of 1973–1974 and the resulting tripling of the price of crude oil brought into sharp focus the fuel inefficiency of U.S. automobiles. New car fleet fuel economy had decreased from 14.8 miles per gallon (mpg) in 1967 to 12.9 mpg in 1974. In search of ways to reduce the U.S. dependence on imported oil, automobiles were an obvious target. It was apparent that decreasing U.S. reliance on imported oil would be difficult without imposing a large price increase on gasoline to promote conservation or increase the efficiency of the automobile fleet in use.

In 1975, the U.S. government enacted standards for **corporate average fuel economy (CAFE)** that apply to all cars and light trucks sold in the United States. For model years 2024–2026, the standards require an industry-wide fleet average of 49 miles per gallon for passenger cars and light trucks. Manufacturers whose average fuel economy falls below this standard are subject to fines. However, manufacturers are allowed to earn CAFE credits in any year in which they exceed the fuel-economy requirements, which they may use to offset deficiencies in other years.

Proponents of CAFE maintain that high fuel-economy standards are necessary to conserve gasoline. They argue that without governmental regulation, auto companies lack the incentive to engage in the costly research and development activities that are necessary to produce fuel-efficient vehicles. By mandating a system of fuel requirements, CAFE helps the United States conserve gasoline, reduce its dependence on foreign oil, decrease air pollution, and combat global warming.

However, CAFE is subject to criticism. According to American auto companies, meeting the CAFE standards requires an increase in the cost of producing automobiles, which will be passed on to consumers in higher prices. Also, meeting the CAFE standards results in the production of smaller, lighter-weight vehicles that can be less safe on highways.

Critics also argue that CAFE creates a motivation for motorists to drive more, not less. When a vehicle's miles per gallon rise, it costs less per mile to drive that vehicle. From the motorist's viewpoint, a rise in gasoline economy is equivalent to a reduction in the price of gasoline. This means that price-sensitive motorists will drive their gasoline-efficient vehicles more than they would have driven a less gasoline-efficient vehicle.

One way of reforming CAFE would involve a market-oriented solution to boost fuel economy. Auto manufacturers would be allowed to trade fuel-economy credits, similar to the trading of pollution permits discussed earlier in this chapter. Under a credit-trading system, firms that exceeded one of the CAFE standards would generate credits that they could sell to firms falling below that standard. The selling and buying of credits would be voluntary. Such a policy would allow manufacturers to concentrate production in their area of cost competitiveness, whether it be small, fuel-efficient vehicles or large, inefficient ones. This would allow firms to choose the means of complying with CAFE standards that is least expensive for them, resulting in aggregate cost savings.

PUBLIC GOODS

So far, we have analyzed market failure in terms of monopoly power and spillover effects. Another source of market failure is public goods. Let us consider the nature of **private goods** and public goods and see why the latter contribute to market failure.

Private goods, which are produced through the market system, are *divisible* in that they come in units that are small enough to be purchased by individual consumers. For example, we can go to McDonald's and buy one or several Big Macs and a small, medium, or large Coke. Private goods are also subject to the *exclusion principle*, the notion that only those who have the ability to pay can purchase the good, whereas those who do not possess the ability to pay are excluded from consumption. Moreover, the *principle of rival consumption* applies to private goods. When I eat a Big Mac, you cannot eat the same one. Thus, you and I are rivals for that hamburger. In general, the market system works well in producing private goods in accordance with the needs of consumers.

An entire class of goods is not considered private goods and thus is not provided by the market system. These are called **public goods** and include things such as national defense, highways, lighthouses, and air-traffic control. These goods are *indivisible* because they cannot be produced and sold very easily in small units. For example, you cannot go down to the local store and purchase $10-worth of national defense. Moreover, the exclusion principle does not pertain to public goods. For example, all households are protected by national defense even if they don't have the money to pay for it. Finally, more people can use public goods at no extra cost. Once money has been spent to construct a lighthouse, the benefit you receive does not lessen the amount of protection received by anyone else.

The reason the market system fails to supply public goods efficiently is that the exclusion principle does not apply. Consider the snow removal system of Buffalo, New York. Such a system is justified if the benefits of improved transportation exceed the costs of buying and operating snowplows, dump trucks, and the like. However, the benefit received by each individual motorist would not justify the cost of such a large and indivisible product. Once the snowplows clean the streets, there is no practical method of excluding certain motorists from their benefits. As a result, why should any motorist voluntarily pay for benefits received from clean streets? Clean streets are available for everyone, and a motorist cannot be excluded from driving on them if he decides not to pay.

Economists call this the **free-rider problem**: It is impossible to exclude you from the consumption of a public good whether or not you pay for it. Of course, if everyone behaved in this manner, no money would be spent on public goods, and entrepreneurs would have no incentive to supply them to the market. We conclude that the market system fails by *underproducing* public goods!

Because of the free-rider problem, citizens still look to the government to provide public goods through the use of tax financing. Of course, there is no guarantee that public goods, such as national defense and pollution control, will be provided in optimal amounts.

INADEQUATE INFORMATION

Another source of market failure is inadequate information, a less visible type of market failure than monopoly power, externalities, and public goods. This inefficiency occurs when either sellers or buyers have incomplete or inaccurate information about the price, quality, or another aspect of a good or service. Without adequate information, markets may give false signals, incentives may get distorted, and sometimes markets may simply not exist. In such cases, government may decide to step in to correct the market failure.

Lack of information often arises in the sale of used cars. The sellers of used cars know the flaws of their cars, whereas buyers often do not. Because the owners of the worst cars are more likely to sell them than the owners of the best cars, car buyers may be fearful of purchasing a "lemon." Therefore, many people refuse to purchase cars in the used-car market.

Let us examine market failure by considering how inadequate information about sellers and their goods can disrupt the operation of the gasoline market. Suppose there were no government inspection of gas pumps, no system of weights and measures established by law, and no laws against false advertising. Each gas station could announce that its gas has a minimum octane rating of 87 when in actuality it is only 80. Moreover, the gas station could calibrate its pumps to show that they are pumping, say, 10 gallons of gas, when in fact they are pumping only 9 gallons. In this situation, the cost to the motorist of obtaining reliable information would be very high. Each motorist would have to purchase samples of gas from various stations and have them analyzed to determine the level of octane. Motorists would also have to pump gas into, say, five-gallon containers to make sure that a station's pump is calibrated correctly. Because of the high costs of obtaining information about the seller, many motorists might prefer to opt out of this chaotic market. More realistically, government might step in to correct the failure of the market. It could pass legislation against false advertising, hire inspectors to check the accuracy of pumps, and establish a system of weights and measures.

Inadequate information about sellers disrupts the efficient operation of a market, but so can inadequate information about buyers. In the labor market, an employer has several economic incentives to provide a safe workplace. A safe workplace fosters higher worker productivity by reducing job accidents, thus decreasing the costs of training new workers. It also entails lower insurance premiums for a firm that, by law, must provide insurance against job injuries. These factors would reduce a firm's costs and thus increase its profit. Conversely, providing safe equipment and protective gear results in additional costs, which reduce the firm's profit. When deciding how much safety to provide, a firm must consider the extra benefits and extra costs associated with a safe workplace.

In a competitive market, if workers have complete information about the workplace safety of firms, they will be reluctant to work for those firms with unsafe workplaces. The supply of labor to those firms will decrease, forcing the firms to increase their wages in order to attract additional labor. The increased wages reduce the firm's profits and give it an extra incentive to provide a safe workplace.

Instead, suppose that workers are unaware of the safety at various workplaces. Because of inadequate knowledge, the employer will not have to pay higher wages in order to attract additional workers. The incentive of the employer to eliminate safety hazards is diminished, and society does not receive the desirable amount of workplace safety. Indeed, market failure can impose hardships on workers.

How can government intervene to correct the problem of inadequate information in the labor market? It can require that firms give information to workers about known workplace dangers and it can mandate standards of workplace safety that are enforced by inspection and fines. The government can also give information to workers about the workplace safety records of firms.

ECONOMIC INEQUALITY

As we have learned, monopoly power, spillover effects, public goods, and inadequate information all cause market failure. When these phenomena occur, the market system fails to produce the optimal mix of output for society. Besides being concerned about what goods to produce, we also care about whom output is produced for. Does the market system result in a distribution of output that is fair to all members of society?

In a market economy, output is disproportionately distributed to people with the most income. Although this may be efficient, it is not necessarily equitable. Persons who are disabled or elderly, for example, may not be able to earn as much income as young, healthy individuals. However, they are still considered "worthy" of receiving goods and services.

In some situations, society may desire to modify the way in which the market system distributes goods. Rather than relying exclusively on the individual's ability to pay for these goods, society provides income transfers. Such transfers are payments from the government to households and firms for which no goods or services are currently rendered. Transfer payments include payments such as unemployment compensation, food stamps, Temporary Assistance for Needy Families, Medicare, and business subsidies. They are intended to supplement the income of those for whom the market system provides too little. Recipients of transfer payments can therefore obtain a greater share of the nation's output.

To finance the costs of its transfer payment programs, the government enacts graduated taxes on households and businesses and channels these funds to the needy. Through this system of taxation and transfer payments, income is redistributed from the wealthier to the less wealthy.

This chapter has discussed the role of government in the market economy. The next chapter will broaden our understanding of government by considering the mixed economy of the United States.

CHECK POINT

1 Explain how the market system fails to allocate resources efficiently when the production of some good entails spillover costs or spillover benefits. What can the government do to correct for market failure in these situations?
2 What is the purpose of social regulation? Identify some government agencies that are involved in social regulation. Why are people sometimes critical of social regulators?
3 How does the market system fail to allocate resources efficiently in the case of public goods? How about when society experiences economic inequality?
4 How does inadequate information cause market failure?

CHAPTER SUMMARY

1 In some cases, unregulated markets may not provide the best answers to the fundamental economic questions of society. Whenever that occurs, government intervention is needed to temper the market's operation and to make it conform to the interests of society.
2 Some markets fail to allocate resources efficiently, a situation called market failure. The main sources of market failure are monopoly power, spillovers or externalities, public goods, inadequate information, and economic inequality.
3 Antitrust policy is the attempt to curb anticompetitive behavior and to foster a market environment that will lead to increased competition. The Sherman Act of 1890 and the Clayton Act of 1914 are the foundations of federal antitrust policy.
4 Besides using antitrust laws to regulate business behavior, the federal government sometimes enacts economic regulation to control the prices, wages, conditions of entry, and standards of service of an industry. Industries that have been subject to economic regulation have included airlines, trucking, railroads, banking, communications, and energy. By the late 1970s, however, it was generally agreed that many economic regulations were no longer suited to prevailing economic conditions. As a result, the federal government initiated steps to dismantle many economic regulations, a process known as deregulation.
5 Public utilities have traditionally been subject to economic regulation on the grounds that they are natural monopolies. In return for being granted an exclusive franchise to serve a local market, the utility is subject to price regulation according to the fair-return principle. Although fair-return pricing allows a utility to realize a price that covers its average total cost, it does not provide an incentive for a utility to minimize its costs.
6 A spillover is a cost or benefit that is imposed on people other than the producers and consumers of a good or service. When the production of some good results in spillover

costs, too much of it is produced, and resources are overallocated to its use. Conversely, underproduction and underallocation of resources arise from spillover benefits.

7 Social regulation attempts to correct a variety of undesirable side effects in a market economy that relate to health, safety, and the environment—effects that markets, left to themselves, often ignore. Federal government agencies involved in social regulation include the Environmental Protection Agency, the Consumer Product Safety Commission, the Food and Drug Administration, and the Occupational Safety and Health Administration.

8 Public goods, such as national defense, are indivisible and are not subject to the exclusion principle. As a result, the market system fails to supply public goods efficiently.

9 Without adequate information, markets may give false signals, incentives may get distorted, and sometimes markets may simply not exist. In such cases, government may decide to step in to correct the market failure.

10 Because an unregulated market may fail to provide a fair distribution of income and output for society, government modifies the distribution of income through taxation and transfer payment programs.

KEY TERMS AND CONCEPTS

market failure
antitrust policy
Sherman Act of 1890
Clayton Act of 1914
economic regulation
deregulation
fair-return price
peak-load pricing
spillover
externality
spillover cost
spillover benefit
command-and-control regulations
incentive-based regulations
carbon tax
cap and trade system
social regulation
corporate average fuel economy standards (CAFE)
private goods
public goods
free-rider problem

STUDY QUESTIONS AND PROBLEMS

1 Table 8.3 shows hypothetical demand and cost data for New England Power and Light Co., a monopolist that sells electricity in Massachusetts.

a Draw a figure that illustrates the firm's demand curve, marginal revenue curve, marginal cost curve, and average total cost curve.

b As an unregulated monopolist, the firm would maximize economic profits by producing ____units of electricity and selling them at a price of $____. The firm's total revenue equals $ _____, total cost equals $ _____, and total profit equals $_____.

TABLE 8.3 Hypothetical Demand and Cost Data for New England Power and Light Co.

Quantity of Electricity	*Price*	*Marginal Revenue*	*Average Total Cost*	*Marginal Cost*
0	$52.50			
1	48.00	$48.00	$72.00	$72.00
2	43.50	39.00	45.00	18.00
3	39.00	30.00	35.00	15.00
4	34.50	21.00	31.50	21.00
5	30.00	12.00	30.00	24.00
6	25.50	3.00	29.25	25.50

c Suppose that the legislature imposes public-utility regulations on the firm and sets the price of electricity according to the fair-return principle. Such regulations result in the firm producing ______ units of electricity and selling them at a price of $_____. The firm's total revenue equals $_____, total cost equals $______, and total profit equals $_______.

d Why might fair-return regulation result in inefficiencies for the firm?

2 Under what conditions do unregulated markets fail to allocate resources efficiently?

3 How do the antitrust laws attempt to combat the problem of monopoly power?

4 By the late 1970s, many economic regulations were being removed in industries such as trucking, airlines, and communications. Comment on the advantages and disadvantages of such deregulation.

5 By the 1990s, deregulation was spreading to the electricity and cable television industries. Explain why this occurred.

6 Why does the government regulate markets that generate spillover costs and spillover benefits?

7 Compare and contrast social regulation versus economic regulation. Give examples of each.

8 Why does the market system provide goods such as Pepsi, while the government provides goods such as highways and lighthouses?

9 How does the government attempt to correct the failure of markets resulting from economic inequality?

NOTE

1 From "Power Struggle," *Fedgazette*, Federal Reserve Bank of Minneapolis, January 2001, pp. 1–3.

PART 3

The Macroeconomy

CHAPTER 9

The Mixed Economy of the United States

CHAPTER OBJECTIVES

After reading this chapter, you should be able to:

1 Identify the personal distribution of income and the possible sources of income inequality.
2 Identify the major sources of revenue and expenditures of the federal government, state governments, and local governments.
3 Evaluate various proposals for reforming the Social Security system.
4 Assess the strengths and weaknesses of the U.S. tax system.
5 Identify the merits of a flat-rate income tax, a value-added tax, and a national sales tax.

DOI: 10.4324/9781003438571-12

ECONOMICS IN CONTEXT

At the turn of the century, the nation's economy was performing at peak levels. The number of workers employed was at an all-time high, the unemployment rate was at a 30-year low, and inflation-adjusted wages were increasing after years of stagnation. Single women with children, immigrants, and minorities, whose economic status had not improved in decades, were experiencing progress. Besides spreading the benefits of economic growth more widely, the robust economy generated other benefits. It contributed to a decrease in welfare caseloads, allowing the government to focus more resources on designing and implementing welfare reform. Moreover, low unemployment and a rise in average wages contributed to a reduction in crime.

By 2008, the economy was headed into a pronounced downturn. As consumers and business owners became increasingly pessimistic about their future incomes, they cut their expenditures to "save for a rainy day": Such cash withdrawals pulled the economy down even further. Therefore, President Barack Obama cut household and business taxes and increased government spending in 2009 to help prop up the economy. According to Obama, the private sector of the economy needed the help of the government to reduce the hardship caused by the economic downturn. This topic will be discussed further in subsequent chapters.

In previous chapters, we have emphasized the private sector of the economy, which includes households and businesses. By adding the role of government to our discussion, we will now examine the mixed economy. In the mixed economy of the United States, the private sector consists of the millions of households and businesses in the nation. The public sector comprises the federal, state, and local governments. These two sectors illustrate pertinent factors concerning our mixed economy.

HOUSEHOLDS AS INCOME RECEIVERS: INCOME INEQUALITY

Everyone knows that there are many rich and many poor people in our society. How do individual households share the nation's income? This issue is addressed by the **personal distribution of income**, as seen in Table 9.1. The table indicates the share of before-tax annual money income received by each one-fifth of American families, ranked from lowest to highest. In 2021, for example, the poorest 20 percent of all families received 2.9 percent of total money income; if income were equally distributed, these families would have received 20 percent of the total. Conversely, the richest 20 percent of families received 52.6 percent of total money income. The richest one-fifth of all families thus received about 18 times more of the before-tax money income than the poorest one-fifth.

TABLE 9.1 Distribution of Income in the United States, 1980–2021*

Shares of Total Household Income (Percent) *Shares of Total Income by Percentile*	*1980*	*2000*	*2021*
Lowest 20 percent	4.2	3.6	2.9
Second 20 percent	10.2	8.9	8.0
Middle 20 percent	16.8	14.8	13.9
Fourth 20 percent	24.7	23.0	22.6
Top 20 percent	44.1	49.7	52.6
	100.0	100.0	100.0

*The data of this table provide snapshots of the income distribution at points in time. They ignore the possibility for upward mobility of income which can occur over time. The frequency that people can move to a higher income bracket is of crucial concern in the debate about income inequality.

Source: Data drawn from U.S. Department of Commerce, U.S. Census Bureau, *Income in the United States, 2021*, Table A-3, available at https://www.census.gov/library/publications/2022/demo/p60-276.html.

Note, however, that the distribution of income is not the same thing as the distribution of wealth. A complete account of a family's wealth would also include things such as bank savings deposits, houses, land, cars, pensions, Social Security, and stocks and bonds.

Over a period of years, economic growth has increased the incomes of Americans. However, Table 9.1 shows that over the period 1980–2021, the poorest four-fifths of Americans saw their share of total money income decrease, while the richest one-fifth realized an increasing share. In relative terms, the rich became richer, while the poor became poorer. Is this good for the country?

Some societies value equality of outcome while others value equality of opportunity. For example, Europeans tend to believe that in a fair society there should be no major income gaps among people. To achieve this outcome, Europe has relied on generous jobless benefits, child subsidies and income support, and other welfare programs. Conversely, Americans have tended to place more emphasis on equality of opportunity. They believe that a society with income gaps can still be fair if people can move up the economic and social ladder. Therefore, America was faster than Europe to invest in education as a means of reducing income inequality. Starting in the early 1900s, America made large investments in public high schools in pursuit of universal secondary education. After World War II, the GI bill offered all returning soldiers the opportunity of higher education.

Most Americans agree that a perfectly equal distribution of income is not optimal. They recognize that some degree of income inequality is necessary to provide incentives to work, invest, and undertake entrepreneurial risks that promote economic growth. In the extreme, if government imposed a 100 percent tax on income and distributed the tax revenue equally to Americans, would we have the incentive to work, invest, and undertake business risks?

However, critics ask if we really need the degree of income inequality that exists in the United States? They also contest income inequality on the grounds of fairness. Moreover, critics maintain that too much income inequality can be destructive to economic growth. They note that when physical capital (machines and factories) mattered most in the development of the U.S. economy, savings and investments were fundamental. Then it was important to have a large contingent of rich people who could save a larger share of their income than the poor and invest it in productive capital. But now human capital is scarcer than machines, and widespread education has become vital for economic growth. And broadly accessible education is hard to attain unless a society has a relatively even distribution of income. Therefore, undue income inequality can harm growth. What's more, high and increasing levels of income inequality can translate into growing inequality of opportunity for the next generation and thus declining social mobility.

Sources of Income Inequality

Why do some people earn more income than others? Among the most important determinants of income differences are age, differences in productive resources, investment in human capital, inheritance, and discrimination.

Age is a determinant of income because, generally, with age comes more education, more training, and more experience. Income is usually lower when people start working at age 18; it rises to a peak at around age 45 to 50, then gradually decreases as people approach retirement age. When individuals begin working at a young age, they usually have little work-related experience and earn less than older workers with more experience. As workers become older, they develop additional work skills, become more productive, work longer hours, and develop seniority, and thus they earn a higher income. At the age of 45 to 50, the productivity of workers usually peaks. As workers reach retirement age, the number of hours they work usually declines, along with their stamina and strength. These factors detract from the income-earning ability of older workers.

Other determinants of income are the quantity and quality of resources that an individual possesses. In a market economy, those who use their human and physical resources to produce many things that are highly valued by others have high incomes. The connection between personal reward and productivity provides individuals with a strong incentive to use their resources efficiently and to figure out better ways of doing things.

People are not born with equal amounts of potential raw talent or intelligence. However, inherited differences in people can be magnified or offset by acquired skills. Sharpening one's productive talents or acquiring new skills is called investment in **human capital**. People invest in their education, training, and health care for self-improvement that leads to higher productivity and higher income.

Inheritance also affects income. It is not unusual for people to inherit cash, stocks, bonds, homes, or land that generates profit, interest, or rental income. Such gifts represent the benefits of someone else's labor or investments rather than the benefits of one's own labor or investments.

Finally, discriminatory labor markets can influence income. Economic discrimination occurs whenever female or minority workers who have the same education, training, abilities, and experience as white male workers earn lower wages or receive less access to jobs or promotion.

Trends in Income Inequality

When the United States was in its infancy, household incomes in the original 13 colonies were more equal than virtually any other place on earth. However, during the industrial revolution (1750–1850) income gaps widened within the country. For example, manufacturing workers were more productive and earned more than farm workers. Also, the great industrialists attained the rewards of building steel mills, railways, and other productive technologies. Their success was also reinforced by monopoly power and crony capitalism in which success in business depends on close relationships between businesspeople and the government. By the early 1900s, President Theodore Roosevelt's antimonopoly policies weakened America's powerful industrialists and bankers, and legal changes began to boost workers' rights. Union power soared and minimum wages increased, thus narrowing the income gap between American workers and managers, especially during the 1930s and 1940s.

After several decades of stability, income inequality has grown since the 1970s in the United States. During the 1980s–1990s, the least-educated Americans fell increasingly behind those in the middle. As the computer revolution increased the demand for skilled workers and old manufacturing industries crumbled, those with a high-school degree or less saw their relative earnings sink. Meanwhile, incomes at the top rose smartly during this period: A rising skill premium rewarded those with lots of education.

The recession of 2007–2009 temporarily upended this upward trend. America's wealthiest fared poorly during this period, largely because the tanking stock market ravaged their bonuses and dividends. However, the federal government's safety net programs prevented an income collapse at the bottom.

The top 1 percent includes the people who earn the very highest salaries in the U.S. economy, like sports and entertainment stars, investment bankers and venture capitalists, corporate attorneys, and CEOs. The bottom half of the income distribution includes many people who have at most a high school diploma. Simply put, the rising tide was raising a few boats hugely and most other boats not nearly as much.

Has Income Inequality Gone Too Far?

Do widely unequal societies operate efficiently? Are their economies stable and sustainable in the long run? The answer to these questions is no, according to economist Joseph Stiglitz, who received the Nobel Prize in Economics in 2001. Stiglitz argues that taken to the extreme, and this is where he thinks the United States currently is, income inequality can harm a country and its economy. Stiglitz especially blames the finance industry for the growing divide between the rich and poor in America. The remainder of this section summarizes some of his ideas regarding income inequality.[1]

It is not uncontrollable technological change or globalization that has produced an unequal society in America, but the exercise of political power by moneyed interests over the legislative and regulatory processes. While there may be underlying economic forces at work, politics have altered the market to benefit the top at the expense of the rest. Those with political power use it to insulate themselves from competitive forces by obtaining favorable tax treatment, government-protected market share, and the like.

There is nothing wrong if someone who has invented a new technology that is beneficial for all receives a large income. However, many of those in America's financial sector became wealthy by economic manipulation. They exploited the poor and uninformed and they made huge amounts of money by preying upon these groups with predatory lending. They sold them costly mortgages while hiding fee details in fine print. Why didn't the government stop this behavior? The reason is that the financial elite support the political campaigns with huge contributions and thus purchase the rules that allow them to make the money. Much of the inequality that exists today is a result of government policies.

A free and competitive market is highly beneficial to society at large, but it requires government regulation and oversight to remain functional. Without constraint, dominant interests use their leverage to make gains at the expense of the majority. Concentration of power in private hands can be just as harmful to the operation of markets as excessive regulation and political control.

Excessive inequality can be likened to sand in the gears of capitalism, resulting in lower growth and less efficiency. Lack of opportunity means that America's most valuable asset, its people, is not being fully used. Many at the bottom, or even in the middle, are not living up to their potential, because the rich, needing few public services and worried that a strong government might redistribute income, use their political influence to cut taxes and curtail government spending. This leads to underinvestment in infrastructure, education, and technology, hindering the engines of growth.

So, what is the solution to inequality? Transferring money from the top to the bottom is only one possibility. Even more important is helping the economy grow in ways that benefit those at the bottom and top, and ending the crony capitalism in which success in business depends on close relationships between businesspeople and the government.

HOUSEHOLDS AS SPENDERS

Besides receiving income, householders are also spenders. Part of household income flows into consumption expenditures, while the rest is used to pay taxes or goes into savings.

Table 9.2 illustrates the disposition of household personal income during 1980–2022. For example, the table shows that in 2022, about 82 percent of household income was used for consumption expenditures. Consumer purchases include durable goods, such as computers and automobiles; nondurable goods such as food and clothing; and services such as the work done by doctors and lawyers for consumers. The U.S. economy is service oriented, with more than half of all household consumption expenditures paying for services in 2022.

TABLE 9.2 Disposition of Personal Income, 1980–2022

Year	*Personal Income (billions of dollars)*	*Personal Taxes (percent of personal income)*	*Personal Outlays* (percent of personal income)*	*Personal Savings (percent of personal income)*
1980	2,323.6	12.9	77.5	9.6
1990	4,913.8	12.1	80.5	7.4
2000	8,655.9	14.3	81.6	4.1
2010	12,594.5	9.8	84.5	5.7
2020	19,832.3	11.3	73.6	15.1
2022	21,806.3	14.7	82.2	3.1

*Personal consumption expenditures, personal interest payments, and personal transfer payments.

Source: Data drawn from *Economic Report of the President*, March 2023. Table B-17, available at https://www.whitehouse.gov/wp-content/uploads/2023/03/ERP-2023.pdf.

Besides spending money as consumers, households allocate a portion of their income for taxes, of which the federal personal income tax is the most important component. As seen in Table 9.2, about 14 percent of household income was used to pay taxes in 2022.

The amount of household income that is not used for consumption expenditures or to pay taxes is saved. In 2022, the household saving rate was 3 percent of personal income, as seen in Table 9.2. Household savings are put into bank accounts, stocks and bonds, insurance policies, and the like. The motivation to save is usually driven by a desire to create a nest egg for unforeseen adversities, education savings for children, or retirement. People also save for speculation. For example, an individual might purchase stock in Boeing Inc. with the hope of selling it in the future at a higher price, thus realizing a handsome profit.

THE BUSINESS SECTOR

Business is the second component of an economy's private sector. A business is an organization that is established to produce and sell goods and services. In the United States, there are more than 24 million businesses. Many are small firms, such as local gas stations or grocery stores. Others are large firms such as automobile and computer manufacturers.

A business firm can be organized in one of three ways: as a sole proprietorship, a partnership, or a corporation. The structure that is chosen determines how the owners share the risks and liabilities of the firm and how they participate in decision making. Although sole proprietorships are numerically dominant, corporations account for the largest share of total sales.

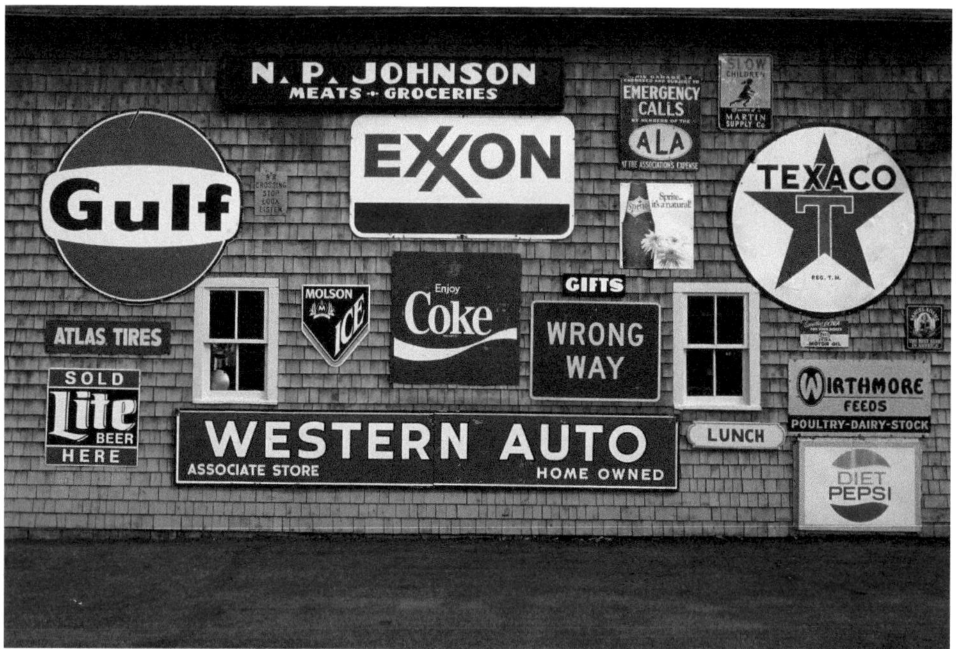

Source: Joseph Sohm/Corbis Documentary/Getty Images®

A **sole proprietorship** is a firm that is owned and operated by one individual. These establishments are typically small, such as a local espresso stand or pizza business. A sole proprietorship is relatively easy to organize and operate, and its owner is not responsible or answerable to anyone. The size of a sole proprietorship, however, is limited by the proprietor's wealth and credit standing, as well as by business profits. The greatest disadvantage of a sole proprietorship is the proprietor's unlimited liability—that is, the personal assets of the owner are subject to use for payment of business debt. Almost everything that a proprietor owns, such as an automobile or a home, may be sold to pay the firm's debts if it fails or is held liable for damages in a lawsuit.

A **partnership** business organization is an extension of the sole proprietorship. Rather than being owned by one individual, a partnership has two or more owners who pool their financial resources and business skills. Many doctors, for example, form partnerships. This allows them to share office expenses and reduces the need to be on call 24 hours a day, seven days a week. Lawyers and accountants also tend to organize partnerships. In a partnership, each partner has unlimited liability. One partner's poor business decisions may impose significant losses on the other partners, a problem that sole proprietors need not worry about. Also, decision making is usually more cumbersome in a partnership than in a sole proprietorship because there are more people involved in making decisions. Moreover, a partnership is usually terminated when one partner dies or voluntarily withdraws from the business.

A **corporation** is a "legal person" that conducts business just as an individual does. Corporations can produce and sell output, make contracts, pay fines, and sue and be sued. General Motors, IBM, Boeing, and Microsoft are examples of corporations that have become household names.

Corporations are owned by stockholders, who receive profits in the form of dividends. Large corporations, such as Apple Inc., may have hundreds of thousands of stockholders; however, some smaller corporations have only a few stockholders. The stockholders vote, according to the amount of stock they own, for a board of directors. The board, in turn, appoints officers to run the corporation according to the guidelines established by the board.

One advantage for the stockholders of a corporation is limited liability. When a corporation declares bankruptcy, a stockholder can lose only the money used to purchase the firm's stock. Moreover, corporations can obtain funds by selling shares of stock or by borrowing money. Corporations borrow by issuing bonds to investors or by obtaining loans directly from banks and other financial institutions. In contrast, sole proprietorships and partnerships can only obtain outside funding through loans. Finally, corporations are efficient at transferring ownership. When stockholders of a corporation wish to give up their ownership rights, they can sell their stock to other investors.

However, corporations also have several drawbacks. The first is the double taxation of income. The profits of a corporation are first subject to corporate income taxes. Then, if any of the after-tax profits are distributed to stockholders as dividends, those payments are taxed as personal income. Corporate profits are thus taxed twice under our current tax system; the profits of sole proprietorships and partnerships are taxed only once as personal income.

Corporations can also suffer from the problem of separation of ownership and control. The stockholders of a corporation often have little to do with its actual operation. Instead, officers, who may own little or no corporate stock, manage the firm. The objective of the stockholders is to maximize the dividends they receive from their stock ownership in the firm. Unless the officers receive compensation in corporate stock, their motivations may differ from those of stockholders. For example, officers may reward themselves with extravagant salaries or lavish offices, neither of which is necessary for the efficient operation of the company. Such luxuries increase the cost of doing business and decrease the dividends of stockholders.

CHECK POINT

1 What is meant by the personal distribution of income?
2 Identify the determinants of an individual's income and how income is spent.
3 Describe the advantages and disadvantages of the three legal forms of business organization—sole proprietorship, partnership, and corporation.

GOVERNMENT IN THE MIXED ECONOMY

The activities of government have a major influence on our lives. In a **mixed economy**, the government provides an appropriate legal and social framework, promotes competition, alters the distribution of income by taxing income away from some people and giving it away to others, provides public goods such as national defense, encourages businesses to produce goods entailing spillover benefits (such as public television), discourages companies from polluting the environment, and initiates policies to promote price stability and high employment for the nation. These functions require government expenditures that are financed through the taxes paid by households and businesses.

Government expenditures, or outlays, consist of purchases and transfer payments made by the federal, state, and local governments. **Government purchases** are expenditures on goods and services. They include such items as street lighting, sewage systems, city playgrounds, national parks, county roads, police cars, fire trucks, tanks, computers, and jet planes. Governments also purchase the labor services of engineers, teachers, accountants, and lawyers to produce goods ranging from highway construction to college education. When a government purchases goods and services, fewer resources are available to produce goods and services used in the private sector.

Government expenditures also include **transfer payments**, which are payments of income from taxpayers to individuals who make no contribution to current output for these payments. Transfer payments thus provide a *safety net* of income security for the poor and needy.

The public assistance programs of the U.S. government make use of transfer payments. These programs are financed by general tax revenues and are thus regarded as public charity, or welfare. Also, these programs are known as **entitlement programs** because all eligible people can legally receive the income support that the programs provide. The major public assistance programs include the following:

- **Supplemental nutrition assistance** (formerly known as food stamps) provides vouchers to low-income persons that can be used to purchase food.
- **Supplemental security income** payments are made to the disabled, blind, and elderly who are unable to work and who do not qualify for Social Security assistance.
- **Temporary assistance for needy families** provides payments to surviving spouses with small children and also to single-parent families. These families are usually headed by women who cannot work because they must care for their young children.
- **Medicaid** provides health care payments to low-income families and to the blind, elderly, and disabled.
- **Earned-income tax credits** supplement the income of poor wage earners. The credit decreases the federal income taxes that wage earners owe or provides them with cash payments if the credit is greater than their tax liabilities.

The United States has devised a system of taxes and transfer payments to alter the distribution of income in favor of the poor—in other words, economically advantaged "Peter" is taxed to help economically disadvantaged "Paul." Critics of the system, however, maintain that many transfer payments are doled out without concern for need. Moreover, the welfare system has historically contained powerful disincentives against work and personal responsibility, thus promoting continued welfare.

SOCIAL INSURANCE

Besides granting public assistance to the poor, the federal government partially replaces income that has decreased because of retirement, disability, or unemployment. The U.S. social insurance programs include Social Security, Medicare, Medicaid, and unemployment compensation. Social insurance is regarded as an entitlement program.

Unemployment compensation provides temporary income support for workers who become unemployed through no fault of their own. The amount an unemployed worker receives each week and the number of weeks an unemployed worker is allowed to receive benefits vary among the states.

Social Security is the largest retirement and disability program in the United States. Social Security was created in 1935 as a means of providing income security upon retirement to people who would not otherwise have that form of security. The Social Security system provides cash benefits to retired and disabled workers and to their dependents and survivors.

In 1965, the federal government added a health insurance program, **Medicare**, to the Social Security system. Its objective is to reduce the financial burden of illness on the elderly. Medicare covers physician fees, hospitalization, outpatient care, and skilled nursing at home. Also added in 1965 was **Medicaid**, a program that provides health insurance for people with limited income. The program is partially funded and managed by state governments, but the federal government sets baseline standards for Medicaid eligibility and benefits and provides a large portion of the funding.

The Social Security Program

Social Security is a *pay-as-you-go* system that is financed by payroll taxes. In 2023, employees paid a flat tax of 6.2 percent for old-age, survivors, and disability insurance, on their wages up to $160,200, with an equal match by their employers; the self-employed paid a tax of 12.4 percent. In addition, employees and employers each paid a 1.45-percent tax on all wages to finance Medicare. Social Security taxes flow into the U.S. Treasury, and each program's share is credited to separate trust funds–one for retirement and survivors, another for disability, and two others for Medicare. Social Security and Medicare contributions are mandatory for most wage earners.

Contrary to popular belief, the Social Security trust funds do not themselves hold money to pay benefits. They are simply accounts that are located at the U.S. Treasury. These balances, like those of a bank account or a government savings bond, represent a promise (IOU) from the government. It pledges to obtain resources in the future, equal to the value of the trust-fund accounts, if funds are needed to pay Social Security benefits. Any surplus of taxes in the Social Security system is used to purchase U.S. Treasury securities.

The federal government then uses these funds as part of its operating cash, which is used to pay for any of the many functions of government, such as national defense. Simply put, the government borrows from the Social Security trust fund to pay for other government programs.

For more than three decades after Social Security was created, the system's income routinely exceeded its payout, and its trust funds grew. Beginning in the 1970s, however, the trust funds started to decline. This was largely the result of benefit increases. Not only was the number of beneficiaries growing, but also benefits were being periodically adjusted to keep pace with inflation. By the 1980s, Social Security benefits were being automatically raised each year to reflect inflation. These cost-of-living adjustments, or **COLAs**, also contributed to revenue shortfalls.

Another concern regarding Social Security is that the number of workers paying into Social Security taxes has declined relative to the number of Social Security beneficiaries. An aging post-World War II baby boom generation, falling birth rates, and increasing life expectancies have all contributed to this decline. In 1945, for each worker collecting benefits, there were 46 workers paying payroll taxes. In 2023, there were only 3 workers for every beneficiary. Estimates suggest that there will be only 2 workers for every beneficiary by 2050. The bottom line is that, in the future, there will be relatively fewer people of working age to support a growing elderly population.

The declining ratio of young to old foretells serious solvency problems for Social Security. Economists estimate that the Social Security system's trust funds will run dry in 2033, and unless Congress takes action to shore up the program, beneficiaries would receive about 77 percent of their scheduled benefits after that point. And Medicare is even worse, with the program estimated to be unable to pay for full benefits in 2031.

From the 1940s to the 1980s, Social Security recipients received a good deal for the taxes they paid to support the system. Most recipients received more than the value of the taxes they paid. However, because Social Security tax rates have increased over the years and the eligibility age for full benefits has risen, it is becoming increasingly apparent that Social Security will not be such a good deal for many future recipients. Workers who earned average wages and retired at age 65 in 1980 recovered the value of the retirement portion of the combined employee and employer shares of their payroll taxes plus interest in 2.8 years. For their counterparts retiring at age 65 in 1996, it took 14 years. For those retiring in 2025, it will take a projected 23 years.

But returns alone do not fully explain the value of Social Security, which has features that are not available in typical private-sector retirement plans. Spouses can get benefits even if they never earned wages. Children can get benefits if they have a working parent who dies. People who are too disabled to work can get benefits for life.

Concerns about Social Security's financing problems and survival have led to proposals to reform the system. One option that has been proposed is to increase the Social Security tax rates paid by current employees. However, wage earners may resist future increases. Because Social Security is a pay-as-you-go system, not a penny of the tax goes into the accounts of those who make the contributions. To these workers, Social Security may be viewed as a program that offers little in return. Instead of raising the payroll taxes of current wage earners, why not decrease the benefits of the elderly? Consider these options:

- **Remove the income cap**. As of 2023, workers paid Social Security taxes on only the first $160,200 they earned in a year. So those who earn millions a year pay the same tax as a worker who earns only $160,200 a year. Removing the income cap would create more tax revenue without further taxing strained paychecks.
- **Raise the retirement age**. Congress did so. But the retirement age could be further raised to 70 or higher, reflecting the increased life expectancy of the future generations.
- **Decrease the COLA**. Social Security benefits are increased annually to reflect inflation, as measured by the change in the consumer price index. The formula could be revised downward.
- **Fully tax Social Security benefits**. Rather than taxing Social Security benefits only partially, treat them as ordinary income subject to full taxation.

None of these options is politically popular with senior citizens. Many of them lived through the Depression and World War II, and they believe the wolf is always at the door. Their generation took care of their parents and frequently lived with and supported them in extended families. Why shouldn't the next generation do the same? Given the voting power of senior citizens, it is not difficult to see why the president and Congress have been reluctant to cut Social Security benefits.

However, critics see Social Security as an anachronism, built on Depression-era concerns about high unemployment and widespread dependency among the aged. They see the prospect of reform today as an opportunity to modernize the way society saves for retirement. Believing that government-run, pay-as-you-go systems are unsustainable in aging societies, they prefer a system that would let workers acquire wealth by investing for their own retirement, rather than the current system, which must impose tax hikes on future workers to meet promised benefits.

Should Social Security Be Privatized?

In his second inaugural address in 2005, President George W. Bush proposed that workers under 55 be allowed to divert 4 percentage points of their 12.4 percent annual Social Security payroll tax into personal investment accounts. This approach would allow participants to take advantage of the superior growth prospects offered by the stock market. Today, the promised benefits of Social Security work out to about a 2 percent annual return on payroll taxes. The same funds invested in a balanced portfolio of stocks might earn a greater amount.

Private investment accounts have several advantages. They would allow retirement plans to be tailored to individual needs and preferences. Individuals who can bear more risk, perhaps because they own their houses outright, might prefer to hold retirement portfolios that are more heavily weighted with stocks. Private accounts would also allow healthy persons who like their jobs to work past the usual retirement ages without having to sacrifice a part of their retirement incomes. Simply put, private accounts would allow individuals to be able to save for retirement with their preferred mix of stocks and securities, and they would also choose their own best time to retire.

However, critics of private investment accounts argue that the funds going into them would be removed from the social insurance system. Therefore, they would no longer be available to pool risk and transfer income between high- and low-wage workers, between families with and without children, and between the able and the disabled during retirement. Rather than offering a guaranteed government benefit, Social Security payments to individual workers would depend on asset values, interest rates, and investment strategies as well as lifetime earnings.

Critics also note that adding private accounts to Social Security doesn't absolve us of the promises still outstanding to retirees. Maintaining existing benefits would entail just as high a cost to a privatized Social Security system as it would the current system. For example, suppose a privatized program places 4 percent of your Social Security tax into a private investment account. The rest continues to pay current beneficiaries, except now there's less revenue to cover the same bill. The money has to come from somewhere, so taxes must be increased, money borrowed, or benefits cut.

Finally, there is the cost of changing from the existing social security system. If workers shift, say, 4 percentage points of payroll tax into their individual retirement accounts, the government would have to find some other money to pay benefits to current retirees by raising taxes or borrowing money.

GOVERNMENT FINANCE

We will now compare the expenditures and receipts of the federal, state, and local units of government. Indeed, the preparation of the federal government's annual budget is a complicated process, as seen in Figure 9.1.

Table 9.3 gives a breakdown of the federal budget for fiscal year 2022. It may be surprising that the largest component of federal spending was not national defense. Instead, it was *income transfer programs* such as Social Security, Medicare, and income security assistance to the poor and disabled. These items made up 45.2 percent of federal expenditures in 2022. The next largest expenditure in that year was *public health*, which accounted for 14.6 percent of federal spending, followed by *national defense*, which accounted for 12.2 percent of federal spending.

Another category of federal expenditures is *interest on the public debt*. In the past, the federal government often incurred a budget deficit, which is the amount by which expenditures exceed tax revenues. The national or *public debt* is the total accumulation of the federal government's combined deficits occurring over many years. To finance its debt, the federal government sells securities (U.S. savings bonds) to investors. When a security matures, investors are paid its face value plus the accumulated interest. Expenditures for interest on the public debt stood at 7.6 percent of federal expenditures in 2022. As the government uses more tax dollars to pay for interest on the public debt, fewer tax dollars are available for public education, police and fire protection, and other governmental programs.

Where does the federal government obtain its funds? Table 9.3 gives a breakdown of federal government receipts in fiscal year 2022. We see that the largest share of revenue

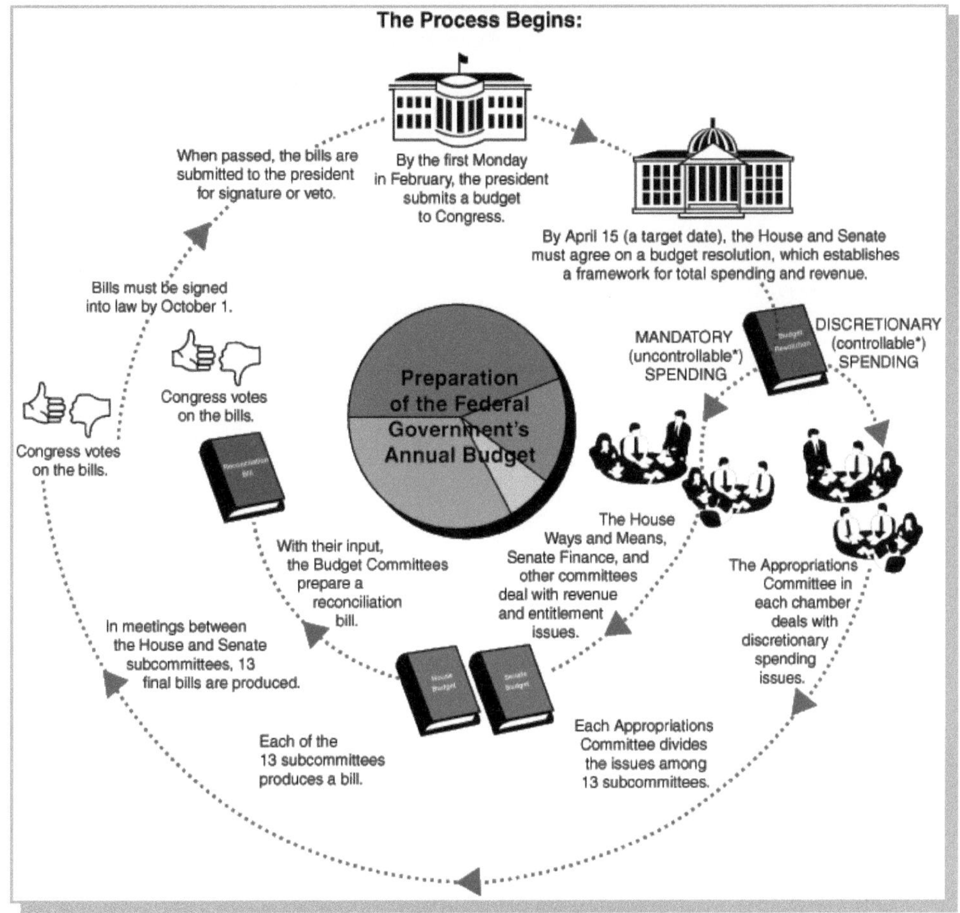

The Process Begins:
By the first Monday in February, the president submits a budget to Congress.
By April 15 (a target date), the House and Senate must agree on a budget resolution, which establishes a framework for total spending and revenue.
MANDATORY (uncontrollable*) SPENDING
DISCRETIONARY (controllable*) SPENDING
The House Ways and Means, Senate Finance, and other committees deal with revenue and entitlement issues.
The Appropriations Committee in each chamber deals with discretionary spending issues.
Each Appropriations Committee divides the issues among 13 subcommittees.
Each of the 13 subcommittees produces a bill.
In meetings between the House and Senate subcommittees, 13 final bills are produced.
With their input, the Budget Committees prepare a reconciliation bill.
Congress votes on the bills.
Congress votes on the bills.
Bills must be signed into law by October 1.
When passed, the bills are submitted to the president for signature or veto.
Preparation of the Federal Government's Annual Budget

FIGURE 9.1 Preparation of the Federal Government's Annual Budget

came from the *personal income tax* (53.7 percent), which is paid by households, sole proprietorships, and partnerships. This was followed by *Social Security* contributions, or payroll taxes (30.2 percent). The federal government also levied *corporate income taxes* on corporate profits (8.1 percent), consumption taxes taking the form of excise taxes or sales taxes on goods such as gasoline, tobacco, and alcohol, and other miscellaneous taxes consisted of death and gift taxes, customs duties, and licenses (8 percent).

The expenditures and receipts of government vary among the different governmental units. Referring to Table 9.3, we see that state and local governments allocated 32.3 percent of their expenditures to *public education* in 2020. *Public welfare* was the second most important expenditure of state and local government (22.7 percent), followed by expenditures on highways (5.8 percent). On the revenue side, state and local governments relied on *sales and excise taxes* (18 percent) and *property taxes* (16.5 percent) in 2020. Personal income taxes accounted for 11.7 percent of state and local revenues while corporation income taxes accounted for 1.7 percent. This is unlike the federal government, which

TABLE 9.3 Government Receipts and Outlays, Percent of Total

Federal Government (2022)			
Receipts (percent)		*Outlays (percent)*	
Individual income tax	53.7	Social Security, Medicare, Income Security	45.2
Social security tax	30.2	Health	14.6
Corporation income tax	8.1	National defense	12.2
Other	8.0	Net interest	7.6
Total	100.0	International affairs	1.1
		Other	19.3
		Total	100.0
State and Local Government (2020)			
Receipts (percent)		*Outlays (percent)*	
Sales taxes	18.0	Education	32.3
Property taxes	16.5	Public welfare	22.7
Individual income taxes	11.7	Highways	5.8
Corporation income taxes	1.7	Other	39.2
Revenue from federal government	25.1	Total	100.0
Other	27.0		
Total	100.0		

Source: Data drawn from *Economic Report of the President*, March 2023. Tables B-47 and B-50, available at https://www.whitehouse.gov/wp-content/uploads/2023/03/ERP-2023.pdf.

relies primarily on the personal income tax as its main revenue source. Besides collecting tax revenues, state and local governments receive grants from the federal government, which amounted to 25.1 percent of state and local receipts in 2020.

How does the tax burden of the United States compare to that of other nations? Table 9.4 presents total tax receipts at all levels of government as a share of gross domestic output for eight nations. This measures the size of the tax burden in each nation relative to its economic output and it is equivalent to an average tax rate for the nation as a whole.

TABLE 9.4 Tax Revenue as a Percent of Gross Domestic Product for Selected Nations

Country	*2000*	*2021*
Denmark	46.9%	46.9%
Sweden	50.0	42.6
Germany	36.4	39.5
Canada	33.2	34.7
Japan	25.3	33.2
Israel	34.1	32.2
South Korea	20.9	29.9
United States	25.8	28.3
Ireland	30.8	21.0
Mexico	11.5	16.7

Source: Data drawn from Organization of Economic Cooperation and Development, *Revenue Statistics*, 2022, available at https://www.oecd.org/tax/tax-policy/revenue-statistics-highlights-brochure.pdf.

As can be seen in the table, U.S. citizens had a lighter tax burden than many other people living in the industrialized world in 2021.

TAXATION PRINCIPLES: BENEFITS RECEIVED AND ABILITY TO PAY

Much of the public debate regarding taxation, as reported in the press, concerns the issue of equity. Are taxes fair? People are generally more likely to comply voluntarily with tax policies if they believe that the policies are reasonable and equitable. A fair tax system is usually regarded as one that is based on people's ability to pay taxes, although some have contended that taxes should instead be based on how much people benefit from public expenditures.

According to the **benefits-received principle** of taxation, taxes should be paid in proportion to the benefits that taxpayers derive from public expenditures. Just as people pay private dollars in proportion to their consumption of private goods, such as food and clothing, an individual's taxes should be related to their use of public goods, such as parks or roads. From this viewpoint, the ideal tax would be a *user charge*, such as a fee that you pay each time that you cross a toll bridge.

The *gasoline tax*, for example, is consistent with the benefits-received principle. Gas taxes are used to finance the construction and maintenance of roads and other transportation systems. The number of gallons of gas that an individual buys is an indicator of the amount of transportation services used; the larger the number of gallons bought, the greater the tax paid. Also, *taxes on airline tickets* are used to finance air-traffic control, airport operations, and airport security. Frequent flyers obtain greater benefits from the airline transportation system and thus pay higher taxes to fund its operation. Moreover, if the construction of a new bridge is financed by tolls on the bridge, this payment method follows the benefits-received principle because drivers pay for the bridge only if they use it.

Difficulties arise, however, when we attempt to apply the benefits-received principle to many important categories of government spending, such as national defense, police and fire protection, and public education. How could we calculate the benefit that particular individuals get from these goods, and the amount of tax they should have to pay? We cannot make such a calculation! Moreover, it is even more difficult to apply the benefits-received principle to programs that redistribute national income. For example, it would not make sense to force unemployed workers, who receive unemployment compensation, to pay all the taxes to finance their welfare benefits. Although there are many situations in which the benefits-received principle applies, it has historically played a minor role in the development of the U.S. tax system.

The **ability-to-pay principle** contrasts with the benefits-received principle. Ability-to-pay taxation is founded on the notion that people with greater income and wealth should be taxed at a higher rate because their ability to pay is presumably greater. Most people would find it reasonable for Bill Gates, the founder of Microsoft Corp. and one of the wealthiest people in the United States, to pay more taxes than those with modest income; he should also pay a higher proportion of his income in taxes. As we will see in the next section, progressive income taxation incorporates the ability-to-pay concept.

A limitation of the ability-to-pay principle is that there is no precise way to calculate one's fair ability to pay taxes. How much higher should the tax rate be for those with higher incomes? The answer seems to be based on guesswork and on the government's need for revenue.

PROGRESSIVE, REGRESSIVE, AND PROPORTIONAL TAXES

Recall that governments raise revenues from a variety of taxes, such as income taxes, property taxes, Social Security taxes, and sales taxes. These taxes fit into one of three types of taxation systems: *proportional* taxation, *progressive* taxation, and *regressive* taxation. Taxes are proportional if they take a constant fraction of income as income rises; progressive if they take a larger fraction of income as income rises; and regressive if they take a smaller fraction of income as income rises.

Table 9.5 shows the average tax rate and **marginal tax rate** under these tax systems. Column 1 shows different levels of total income earned by an individual. Column 2 shows the total taxes due at various levels of income. Column 3 shows the average tax rate, which is equal to total taxes due divided by total income:

TABLE 9.5 Progressive, Proportional, and Regressive Taxes

Progressive Tax

Total Income	*Total Taxes Due*	*Average Tax Rate*	*Marginal Tax Rate*	
$0	$0	–	–	In a progressive tax system, the average tax rate and marginal tax rate rise as income increases.
100	5	5%	5%	
200	20	10	15	
300	45	15	25	

Regressive Tax

Total Income	*Total Taxes Due*	*Average Tax Rate*	*Marginal Tax Rate*	
$0	$0	–	–	In a regressive tax system, the average tax rate and marginal tax rate fall as income increases.
100	30	30%	30%	
200	50	25	20	
300	60	20	10	

Proportional Tax

Total Income	*Total Taxes Due*	*Average Tax Rate*	*Marginal Tax Rate*	
$0	$0	–	–	In a proportional tax system, the average tax rate and marginal tax rate remain the same as income increases.
100	10	10%	10%	
200	20	10	10	
300	30	10	10	

$$\text{Average tax rate} = \frac{\text{Total taxes due}}{\text{Total Income}}$$

Column 4 shows the marginal tax rate, which is the fraction of additional income paid in taxes:

$$\text{Marginal tax rate} = \frac{\text{Changes in taxes due}}{\text{Change in Income}}$$

Let us first calculate the average tax rate under a *progressive* tax system. Referring to the upper portion of Table 9.5, at an income of $100 the average tax rate is 5 percent ($5 / $100 = 0.05); at an income of $200, the average tax rate is 10 percent ($20 / $200 = 0.10); at an income of $300, the average tax rate is 15 percent ($45 / $300 = 0.15). As these figures show, this tax system is progressive because the average tax rate increases as income rises.

Now we will compute the marginal tax rate under a progressive tax system. Referring to Table 9.5, as income increases in the first bracket from $0 to $100, taxes due rise from $0 to $5. The marginal tax rate of the first bracket thus equals 5 percent ($5 / $100 = 0.05). Moving to the second bracket, as income rises from $100 to $200, taxes due increase from $5 to $20, and the marginal tax rate equals 15 percent ($5 / $100 = 0.15). As income increases by another $100, taxes due rise by $25, and the marginal tax rate equals 25 percent. Our current tax system is progressive because the marginal tax rate increases as an individual moves to higher brackets of income. We conclude that in a progressive tax system, both the average tax rate and the marginal tax rate rise as income increases. Progressive taxation is thus consistent with the ability-to-pay principle of taxation.

Next, we consider a *regressive* tax. With regressive taxation, a smaller fraction of income is taken in taxes as income increases. Refer to the regressive tax shown in Table 9.5. As income increases, taxes due also rise. The tax is regressive, however, because the average tax rate and the marginal tax rate fall as income increases. A regressive tax thus imposes a relatively larger burden on the poor than on the rich and thus contradicts the ability-to-pay principle of taxation.

Finally, there is the *proportional* tax, also called a *flat-rate* tax. Proportional taxation means that as an individual's income rises, taxes due rise by the same fraction. Refer to the proportional tax shown in Table 9.5. As income rises, the average tax rate is 10 percent for each tax bracket, and the marginal tax rate turns out to be 10 percent as well.

What is the relationship between a proportional tax and the ability-to-pay principle of taxation? Consider a 20-percent tax that collects $2,000 from Joe Smith, who earns $10,000 a year, and $20,000 from Helen Miller, who earns $100,000 a year. Although everyone pays an identical tax rate of 20 percent, the tax imposes a greater burden on Joe than on Helen. After paying the tax, Joe has little income left to buy groceries for his family; Helen, however, can live comfortably after paying her tax. One could argue that Helen is not paying a fair share of her income in taxes according to the ability-to-pay principle.

THE U.S. TAX STRUCTURE

Let us now try to understand the principles on which the U.S. tax system is constructed. What can be said about the progressivity, regressivity, or proportionality of the major taxes in the United States?

Federal Personal Income Tax

The most important tax in the U.S. economy is the federal personal income tax. All U.S. citizens, resident immigrants, and most others who earn income in the United States are required to pay federal taxes on all taxable income. Taxable income is gross income minus exemptions, deductions, and credits:

Gross Income (wages, salaries, tips, bonuses, and so on)
– **Exemptions** (an allowance for each household member)
– **Deductions** (home mortgage interest payments, business expenses, charitable contributions, medical expenses, and certain state and local taxes)
– **Credits** (child care, elderly and disabled, low-income allowance)

Taxable Income

Table 9.6 shows the federal income tax rates for a single taxpayer in 2022. The federal income tax is *progressive* because the average tax rate and the marginal tax rate increases as an individual moves into higher brackets of taxable income, as seen in the table.

TABLE 9.6 Federal Income Tax Rates for a Single Taxpayer, 2022

Tax Bracket (dollars)		*Taxes Due (dollars)**	*Average Tax Rate*	*Marginal Tax Rate*
Over	*Up To*			
0	10,275	1,027.50	10.0 %	10%
10,275	41,775	4807.50	11.5	12
41,775	89,075	15,213.60	17.1	22
89,075	170,050	34,647.50	20.4	24
170,050	215,950	49,335.50	22.8	32
215,950	539,900	162,718	30.1	35
539,900	no limit			37

*Computed at the top of the six taxable income brackets.

Source: Data drawn from Internal Revenue Service, *2022 Tax Rate Schedules*, available at www.irs.gov.

Federal Corporate Income Tax

After a corporation has determined its annual income and met all its expenses, it must pay part of its income to the federal government. As of 2022, the federal corporate income tax was 21 percent at all levels of taxable income, as seen in Table 9.7. Taxable income for a corporation is gross income less cost of goods sold and other allowable tax deductions. Besides being taxed at the federal level, corporate income is subject to taxes of most states and some localities, which averaged about 3 percent in 2022.

Social Security Tax

As of 2023, the Social Security tax was imposed on an individual's wage income up to \$160,200. The Social Security tax (excluding Medicare) equaled 12.4 percent, split evenly between employee and employer (6.2 percent each).

The Social Security tax is largely a *proportional* tax because it taxes a fixed percentage of wage earnings. It does have some *regressive* features, however, because the tax rate is higher on low wages than on high wages. For example, in 2023, a worker's Social Security tax rate was 6.2 percent, applied to the *first* \$160,200 of wage income. A worker earning exactly \$160,200 would pay a Social Security tax of \$9,932.4 (0.062 x \$160,200 = \$9,932.4). However, a worker who earns twice as much, \$320,400, would also pay a Social Security tax of \$9,932.40, resulting in a tax rate of only 3.1 percent

TABLE 9.7 Federal Corporate Income Tax Rates Around the World, 2012, 2022

Corporate Income Tax Rate (percent) *Country*	*2012*	*2022*
Germany	30%	30%
Japan	34	30
Mexico	30	30
Canada	28	26
France	35	26
China	25	25
United States*	35	21
Russia	20	20
Ireland	12	12

* U.S. state and local corporate tax rates averaged 3 percent in 2022.

Source: Data drawn from Christina Enache, *Corporate Tax Rates Around the World*, 2022, The Tax Foundation, December 13, 2022 and Scott Hodge *On the U.S. Having the Highest Corporate Tax*, The Tax Foundation, March 30, 2012.

($9,932.40 / $320,400 = 0.031). We conclude that the Social Security tax becomes regressive once wage income exceeds $160,200.

The regressivity of the Social Security tax is magnified when we consider nonwage income such as dividends and interest, which tend to be received more by higher-income individuals. In the previous example, suppose our worker with wage income of $320,400 also received dividends of $100,000, so that their total income was $420,400. The Social Security tax would then amount to only 2.4 percent ($9,932.40 / $420,000 = 0.024) of total income.

Sales, Excise, and Property Taxes

States obtain most of their revenues from general sales taxes on goods and services. In addition, states usually add their own excise taxes to the federal excise taxes on gasoline, liquor, and cigarettes. As for local governments, most of their revenue comes from property taxes.

Sales taxes are *regressive* because lower-income families generally spend a larger fraction of their income to purchase consumption items that are subject to sales and excise taxes. Higher-income families, however, generally save a portion of their income and thus devote a smaller fraction of their income to consumption goods that are subject to sales and excise taxes.

Assume, for example, that the state of Wisconsin imposes an 8-percent sales tax on all purchases. The Miller family earned $30,000 during the last year while the Jefferson family earned $100,000. The Millers, with a $30,000 income, spend their entire income on food and other necessities, whereas the Jeffersons, with a $100,000 income, spend $40,000 on food and other necessities and save the remainder. Because each family pays an 8-percent sales tax, the lower-income Millers pay taxes of $2,400 (0.08 x $30,000 = $2,400), which is about 1/12 of their income. The higher-income Jeffersons, however, pay taxes of $3,200 (0.08 x $40,000 = $3,200), which is about 3/100 of their income. Although the wealthier Jeffersons pay more taxes than the poorer Millers, the sales tax is regressive because the Jeffersons' average tax rate is lower than that of the Millers.

Excise taxes, such as those on cigarettes, are also *regressive*. Cigarettes are widely recognized as an inferior good—that is, consumption decreases as income increases. Individuals with lower incomes thus tend to spend more on cigarettes than those with higher incomes. The cigarette taxes paid by low-income people account for a larger fraction of their incomes than do cigarette taxes paid by high-income people.

Property taxes are levied mainly on real estate—buildings and land. Each locality establishes an annual tax rate that is applied to the assessed value of property. Economists generally agree that property taxes on real estate are *regressive* for the same reasons that sales taxes are regressive: As a fraction of income, property taxes are higher for the poor than the wealthy because the poor must spend a larger share of their income on housing.

Overall U.S. Tax System

As we have seen, the federal tax system (especially the personal income tax) is somewhat progressive. However, state and local governments rely mainly on sales, excise, and property taxes, which are regressive. Most economists argue that when federal, state, and local taxes are combined, the overall effect is roughly *proportional*. The overall tax system itself does not significantly affect the distribution of the nation's income, because the rich and poor alike pay roughly the same fraction of their income as taxes.

Although the U.S. tax system does not substantially redistribute income from the rich to the poor, the U.S. system of transfer payments does decrease income inequality. Transfer payments to the poorest one-fifth of American families are almost four times as much as their combined incomes. The U.S. tax-transfer payment system is therefore more progressive than the U.S. tax system by itself.

IS THE U.S. TAX SYSTEM FAIR?

Source: Nora Carol Photography/Moment/Getty Images®

Billionaire investor Warren Buffett once stated that it is unfair for rich people, like himself, to pay less in federal taxes, as a percentage of income, than middle-class Americans. He drew attention to the fact that he paid a lower tax rate than his secretary. Buffett also noted that many millionaires paid a smaller percentage of their income in taxes than a significant proportion of middle-class families. To restore fairness to the U.S. tax system, Buffet called for a minimum tax rate of 30 percent on individuals making more than a million dollars a year. The revenue generated by the higher tax could be used to help pay down the U.S. deficit and invest in the things that help our economy grow and keep the country safe, such as education, research and technology, and a strong military. However, critics labeled Buffet's proposal as class warfare and also argued that it would negatively affect job creation and investment.

TABLE 9.8 Share of Federal Personal Income Tax Paid by Various Income Groups

Percentage of Federal Personal Income Tax Paid			
Percentiles Ranked by Adjustable Gross Income	*2020*	*2010*	*2000*
Top 1%	42	38	37
Top 5%	63	59	56
Top 10%	74	70	67
Top 25%	89	87	84
Top 50%	98	98	96
Bottom 50%	2	2	4

Source: Data drawn from Tax Foundation, *Summary of the Latest Federal Income Tax Data, 2023 Update, available at https://taxfoundation.org/publications. See also Internal Revenue Service, Statistics of Income, Individual Income Rates and Tax Shares*, November 3, 2022, available at *https://www.irs.gov/statistics/soi-tax-stats-individual-income-tax-rates-and-tax-shares.*

One argument deployed against tax hikes for the rich is that the burden of taxation is already biased, since the poorest half of Americans paid only 2 percent of the federal income tax in 2020, as seen in Table 9.8. On the other end of the spectrum, the top 1 percent of income earners paid 42 percent of federal income taxes, while the top 10 percent of income earners paid 74 percent.

However, proponents of a tax system that protects the less fortunate note that they are very poor or they are protected by tax breaks that benefit children and the elderly. For example, low-income Americans (protected by the tax system's standard deduction and personal exemptions) account for about half of the people who do not pay federal income taxes. Also, America's tax system provides preferences for low-income families, especially with children.

Moreover, the federal income tax is only one of several types of taxes that individuals pay, both over the course of their lifetimes and in a given year, and it makes little sense to treat it as though it were the only tax that matters. Millions of Americans pay Social Security taxes, estate taxes, and other federal taxes such as excise taxes on gasoline. They also pay state and local taxes, which tend to be regressive and undo a sizable share of the federal income tax system's progressivity. When all taxes are considered, the American tax system is only mildly progressive, which moves it away from a fairness principle based on the ability to pay.

So, should the top 1 percent of income earners pay more than 42 percent of the federal income tax? Should low-income earners who pay no federal income tax be asked to pay at least something? Obviously, there is no definitive answer to this question. What do you think?

CHECK POINT

1 Distinguish between government expenditures and transfer payments.
2 Identify the major sources of revenue and expenditures of the federal government as well as state and local governments.
3 Which of the following taxes is consistent with the ability-to-pay principle, and which is consistent with the benefits-received principle: federal income tax, gasoline tax, tolls used to finance the construction of a bridge?
4 Define a proportional tax, a progressive tax, and a regressive tax. Classify the major federal, state, and local taxes, according to these tax systems.

SHOULD THE U.S. INCOME TAX SYSTEM BE REFORMED?

Because the distribution of income in the United States is quite unequal, many people look to the federal income tax to redistribute income. Recall that the federal income tax is designed to be *progressive*, bearing down harder on the rich than on the poor. It fulfills this objective by defining brackets of taxable income and taxing each at progressively higher rates.

However, federal tax burdens are not so progressively distributed. Legal tax rates pertain only to taxable income. Much income is nontaxable because of tax loopholes established by Congress. Tax loopholes include exemptions, deductions, and credits, as previously discussed. Because tax loopholes reduce the income that is subject to tax, the tax rates that everybody pays are higher than they would otherwise have been to raise the same amount of revenue.

Critics of the federal income tax system maintain that it is unfair and inefficient. They contend that the federal income tax favors the rich, who can shelter much of their income by using tax loopholes. For example, although the deduction of mortgage interest to encourage home ownership is generally viewed to be a good thing, it helps higher-income people more than lower-income people. Why? Higher-income people tend to have more expensive houses. Second, critics argue that the federal income tax system is costly for taxpayers, who must keep records and fill out tax forms. Given the complexity of the federal regulations, an estimated 40 percent of all taxpayers pay for professional help devoted to legal tax avoidance. Such costs could be avoided with a simpler tax system. Finally, the tax system violates the principle that people with the same income pay the same taxes. Depending on the composition of a particular taxpayer's household, Americans with identical incomes may pay wildly different taxes.

Also, progressive tax rates are inefficient because they discourage saving and investment, which are needed for economic growth. Why? Under an income tax, people who spend their wages immediately are taxed only once—they pay the tax on their wages. However, the income tax entails more severe treatment to people who save their wages and then spend their savings and interest at a future date. These people pay tax on their wages and also pay tax on the interest they earn on savings. Therefore, they get hit with a larger percentage tax burden than those who spend their wages up front.

These concerns have prompted proposals for reforming the federal income tax system. Any reasonable reform would reduce loopholes, lower rates, and abolish the tax bias against saving and investment. The result would be a simpler system that is easy for taxpayers to figure out and one that is transparent, so that the cost of government services would be readily visible. Three of the most widely discussed reforms that have been proposed are the flat-rate income tax, the value-added tax, and the national sales tax. It should be noted that reforming a tax system is difficult because it will create winners and losers. The losers tend to be much better at identifying themselves and organizing to oppose it than the potential winners. Therefore, it is hard to mobilize support for tax reform.

Flat-Rate Income Tax

In its purest form, a **flat-rate income tax** system would junk the existing array of tax rates on personal income and replace them with a single tax rate. In addition, all exemptions, deductions, and credits would be abolished. By eliminating tax loopholes, all income, regardless of its source, would be taxed at the same rate, ending complaints that many taxpayers, especially the rich, are able to shelter much of their income by using tax loopholes. A flat tax system would also be designed to generate the same revenue as the current progressive income tax. It is estimated that a flat tax of about 20 percent would yield identical revenue.

As seen in Figure 9.2, replacing the progressive income tax with a flat-rate tax would have a dramatic impact on the distribution of the U.S. tax burden. Holding tax revenue

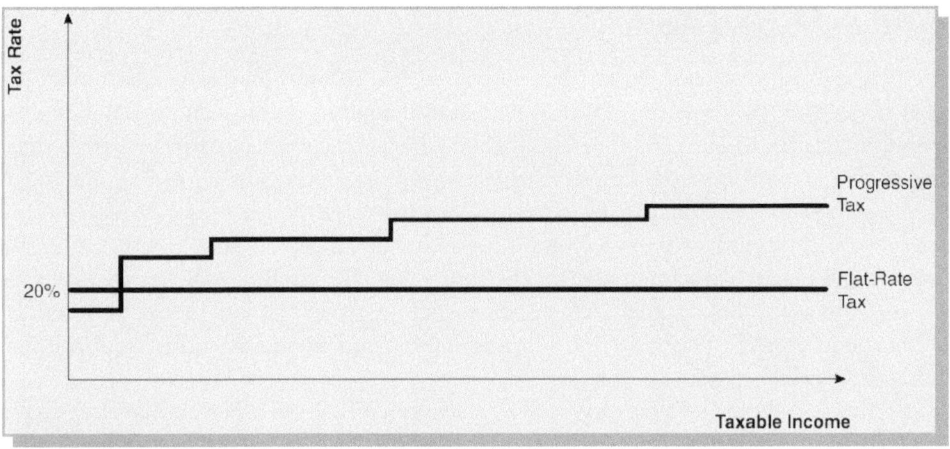

FIGURE 9.2 Replacing the Progressive Income Tax With a Flat-Rate Tax

Replacing the progressive income tax with a flat-rate tax of 20 percent would decrease the tax burdens of higher-income individuals while increasing the tax burdens of the poor and lower-middle class. The poor could be protected by giving them tax loopholes such as a standard deduction and personal exemptions for dependents.

constant, a flat-rate tax would reduce the tax burden on higher-income individuals while increasing the burden on the poor and lower-middle class. Because such an income redistribution is widely perceived as unfair, the proposals for a flat tax include some tax loopholes to protect the poor.

Proponents of a flat tax contend that it would simplify the tax system and thus reduce the cost of keeping records and filling out tax forms. The gains in simplicity would be immense: Families and businesses could file their returns on forms the size of postcards. The numbers entered on these forms would be clear and easy to calculate. Opportunities for cheating would be minimized.

Despite the advantages of a flat-rate income tax, several difficulties remain. One problem is the costly transition that it would involve. Individuals and corporations have made major decisions and investments designed to maximize income based on certain deductions and tax rates under the current tax structure. Thus, the introduction of a flat tax, and the elimination of tax loopholes, would alter long-standing tax rules sharply. A flat tax would also alter the distribution of income and wealth by increasing taxes on some income groups and decreasing taxes on others. The elimination of all deductions likely would encounter opposition from special interest groups representing churches, schools, state and local governments, housing industries, and the elderly who benefit from tax deductions.

A less extreme reform of the federal tax system would be to close tax loopholes while retaining the current progressive income tax. Advocates of this reform argue that there are plenty of loopholes that don't make economic sense. Tax breaks for second homes and lavish deductions for business expenses, for example, could be eliminated in order to cut taxes on working families. Nobody likes taxes. But if we are to have public services, doesn't it make sense to pay for them by taxing wealthy people at higher rates than the middle and working class?

Value-Added Tax

The U.S. government taxes its citizens mostly on the income they earn rather than on what they spend on consumption. However, many economists argue that this policy creates disincentives to earn income. Recall that a household that earns income and then invests that income for the future pays taxes twice: First on the original amount and next on any income earned from the investments. Therefore, a system that taxes households on their income rather than consumption provides them an incentive to spend their income today rather than to save and invest for the future. Yet, economists recognize that Americans need to save more for education expenses and retirement and investment is a source of economic growth. This underlies the rationale for a system that taxes consumption rather than a system that taxes income.

A **value-added tax (VAT)** is proposed by some as a substitute for current federal taxes: It would tax consumption instead of taxing income. A VAT operates like a national sales tax (which is collected when a good is sold at retail to consumers) except that it is collected in installments from businesses at every stage of production and carried through to the final price paid by consumers. For a loaf of bread, for example, the VAT would be collected from the farmer for wheat production, from the miller for flour production, from the baker at the cooking stage, and from the grocer at the retail sale stage. A VAT thus amounts to a national sales tax on consumer goods, that is, a consumption tax. Many European nations, such as Sweden and Germany, currently use the VAT as a source of revenue. By the time the VAT reaches the final consumer, it averages around 20 percent in Europe.

Proponents of VAT argue that Americans need to increase saving and investment and that VAT would help fulfill this objective. Also, a VAT would make tax avoidance extremely difficult. This is because tax-paying businesses leave a paper trail, which reduces the potential for tax evasion. However, the United States has not implemented a VAT for several reasons. Because the VAT is largely hidden, final customers may be unaware of the VAT included in the price of a product. Other objections are that the VAT generally has high administrative costs and that it is a regressive tax that takes a larger share of poor people's incomes than it takes from the rich.

National Sales Tax

Another alternative to the current federal income tax is a **national sales tax**. This system would entail a federal consumption tax collected only at the retail level by businesses: This is unlike a value-added tax that is applied at every stage of production and carried through to the final price paid by consumers. Used items would not be taxed. The national sales tax would equal a set percentage of the retail price of taxable goods and services. Retail businesses would collect the tax from individuals, and remit the tax revenues to the federal government.

Proponents argue that a national sales tax is a fair and simple alternative to the current federal income tax. The national sales tax is a voluntary consumption tax in which the more you buy, the more you pay in taxes; the less you buy, the less you pay in taxes. Also, this system would collect taxes from everyone living in the United States, including immigrants, illegal immigrants, and the underground cash economy, and thus add billions to the nation's treasury. To make sure that a national sales tax would not bear down excessively on low-income families, who spend almost every penny they earn on subsistence items, tax rebates would be provided on poverty-level expenditures. Moreover, as a tax on consumption rather than a tax on income, a national sales tax would better promote saving and investment than the current federal income tax.

However, critics maintain that the rates would be crushing if a national sales tax were established to generate the same amount of revenue that is generated under the current federal income tax. The national sales tax rate could be as much as 50 percent—or more—and be out of proportion with any existing state sales tax. The temptation to evade the national sales tax would thus become overwhelming, according to critics.

This chapter has examined the mixed economy of the United States. The next chapter will focus on how productivity influences the U.S. economy by considering its gross domestic product.

CHECK POINT

1 Do tax loopholes make the federal income tax more or less progressive? Why?
2 Why do critics of the current federal income tax system maintain that it is unfair and inefficient?
3 How does a flat-rate income tax differ from a progressive income tax?
4 Explain why a value-added tax is essentially a national sales tax.

CHAPTER SUMMARY

1 The way income is divided among members of society is known as the distribution of income. The personal distribution of income refers to the share of income received by poor, middle-income, and wealthy families.
2 Household income flows into consumption expenditures, taxes, and savings. The United States has a service-oriented economy with more than half of all household consumption expenditures used to pay for services.
3 A business firm can be organized in one of three ways: As a sole proprietorship, a partnership, or a corporation. Although sole proprietorships are numerically dominant in the United States, corporations account for the largest share of total business sales.
4 Government expenditures include federal, state, and local government purchases of goods and services as well as transfer payments. Transfer payments have been the main source of growth in government expenditures in the past four decades.
5 Social Security is the largest retirement and disability program in the United States. It is a pay-as-you-go system that is financed by payroll taxes levied on employees and their employers. Social Security is mandatory for most workers, who must belong whether they like it or not. Social Security's financial problems largely stem from liberal benefit increases and a declining number of workers paying into Social Security taxes compared to an increasing number of beneficiaries.
6 For the U.S. government, the personal income tax is the major source of revenue; income transfer programs—such as Social Security and Medicare—are the major expenditures. State and local governments rely primarily on sales taxes, excise taxes, and property taxes to raise revenues. Education is their major expenditure.
7 The U.S. tax system is founded upon the benefits-received and ability-to-pay principles. Taxes fit into one of three types of systems: Proportional taxation, progressive taxation, and regressive taxation. The federal tax system is somewhat progressive, whereas state and local tax systems tend to be regressive.
8 Tax loopholes—including exemptions, deductions, and credits—decrease the progressivity of the federal income tax. Critics of the federal income tax contend that it favors the rich, who can shelter much of their income by using tax loopholes. Proposed reforms

of the federal tax system include the flat-rate income tax, the value-added tax, and the national sales tax.

KEY TERMS AND CONCEPTS

human capital
sole proprietorship
partnership
corporation
mixed economy
government expenditures
government purchases
transfer payments
entitlement programs
unemployment compensation
Social Security
Medicare
cost-of-living adjustment (COLA)
average tax rate
benefits-received principle
ability-to-pay principle
marginal tax rate
taxable income
flat-rate income tax
value-added tax (VAT)
national sales tax
personal distribution of income

STUDY QUESTIONS AND PROBLEMS

1 Compare the advantages and disadvantages of a sole proprietorship, a partnership, and a corporation.

2 Distinguish between the benefits-received principle of taxation and the ability-to-pay principle of taxation. Which principle is more evident in the U.S. tax system?

3 Describe the progressivity, proportionality, or regressivity of the major taxes of the federal, state, and local governments.

4 The U.S. tax system alone is more progressive than the U.S. system of taxes and transfer payments combined. Do you agree with this statement?

5 Table 9.9 gives four levels of taxable income and the taxes to be paid at each of the income levels.

TABLE 9.9 Hypothetical Tax Data

Total Taxable Income (dollars)	*Total Taxes Paid (dollars)*	*Average Tax Rate (percent)*	*Marginal Tax Rate (percent)*
10,000	3,500		
20,000	6,000		
30,000	7,500		
40,000	8,000		

  a Calculate the average tax rate and the marginal tax rate at each level of taxable income.

  b Indicate whether the tax is progressive, proportional, or regressive.

6 Assume that the state of California levies an 8-percent sales tax on all consumption expenditures. Consumption expenditures for four income levels are illustrated in Table 9.10.

  a Calculate the sales tax paid at the four income levels.

  b Calculate the average tax rate at these incomes.

  c If income were used as the tax base, the sales tax would be classified as a ______ tax.

TABLE 9.10 Hypothetical Sales Tax Data

Income	*Consumption Expenditures (dollars)*	*Sales Tax Paid (dollars)*	*Average Tax Rate (percent)*
10,000	10,000		
11,000	10,800		
12,000	11,600		
13,000	12,400		

7 Would the proposed flat-rate income tax, value-added tax, or national sales tax lead to a more fair and efficient tax system than the current federal income tax?

NOTE

1 Joseph Stiglitz, *The Price of Inequality: How Today's Divided Society Endangers Our Future* (New York: W.W. Norton, 2012); and Thomas Edsall, "Separate and Unequal: The Price of Inequality by Joseph Stiglitz," Sunday Book Review, *New York Times*, August 3, 2012. See also Anthony Atkinson, Thomas Piketty, and Emmanuel Saez, "Top Incomes in the Long Run of History," *Journal of Economic Literature*, Vol. 49, No. 1, 2011, pp. 3–71; and Jill LePore, "Tax Time: Why We Pay," *The New Yorker*, November 26, 2012, pp. 24–29. See also Angus Deaton, "Inequalities in Income and Inequalities in Health," *The Causes and Consequences of Increasing Inequality* (Chicago: University of Chicago Press, 2001).

CHAPTER 10

Gross Domestic Product and Economic Growth

CHAPTER OBJECTIVES

After reading this chapter, you should be able to:

1 Discuss the nature of gross domestic product and explain how it is calculated.
2 Distinguish between nominal gross domestic product and real gross domestic product.
3 Describe the factors that underlie a nation's rate of economic growth in the long run.
4 Discuss the policies that a government might enact to speed up economic growth.
5 Distinguish between traditional growth theory and new growth theory.

DOI: 10.4324/9781003438571-13

ECONOMICS IN CONTEXT

Source: Monty Rakusen/DigitalVision/Getty Images®

Has the growth in technological innovation affected the economy as a whole? Yes, by increasing the productivity of the economy. Labor productivity in manufacturing, retail and wholesale trade, finance, business services, and other sectors of the economy has risen because of technological advances, improved organizational practices, and increased global competition. As we have learned, a more efficient economy can produce more output with a given number of resources.

The changes witnessed in the steel industry exemplify these updates in production processes and management practices. The fundamental processes of steelmaking remain much as they always were: Melting raw material, forming it into an intermediate product, and shaping and treating that product to produce the final good. But a number of technological advances, many incorporating computer technology to measure, monitor, and control these processes, have affected almost every step in the production of steel.

As recently as 1990, steelmaking involved extensive manual control and setup and relied heavily on operators' experience, observation, and intuition in determining how to control the process. Computer processing of data from sensors, using innovative software, has improved the ability to control the process, allowing for faster, more efficient operation.

For example, the availability of computing power to quickly process data has enabled steelmakers to reduce both energy consumption and wear and tear on the equipment. The setup for casting molten steel into an intermediate product has changed from a process in which several operators would "walk the line," setting the controls for every motor and pump, to one in which a single operator uses an automatic control system that synchronizes and sets the equipment. The rolling process now incorporates sensors that constantly inspect the steel for deviations from the desired shape, allowing operators to make corrections before material is wasted. Operators can remotely control the speed and clearance of the rolls using computer-controlled motors to correct problems as they occur.

The result of this computer integration into steelmaking has been a significant improvement in steelmaking performance. Together with other technological changes, such as larger furnaces and improvements in casting practices, as well as the closing of older, inefficient plants, the new technologies have contributed to higher product quality and productivity. Steelmakers today require fewer than four worker-hours to produce a ton of steel, down from six worker-hours in 1990. The best-performing mills can produce a ton of steel in less than one worker-hour.

In this chapter, we will learn how productivity influences the performance of not only a particular industry but also the entire economy. Just as a doctor gives a physical exam to determine how well a patient is, economists use statistics to get a quantitative measure of the economy's performance. This chapter will introduce the broadest measure of the total output of an economy—that is, gross domestic product—and discuss the factors that determine the long-run growth rate of an economy.

MEASURING AN ECONOMY'S OUTPUT

The output of an economy includes millions of different goods. We could tabulate how much of each product an economy produced in a given year: 3,600,224 houses, 2,436,789 radios, 40,987,345 apples, and so forth. Although such data may be useful for some purposes, they don't accurately measure an economy's output. Suppose that next year, the output of houses falls by 4 percent, the output of radios falls by 8 percent, and the output of apples rises by 2 percent. Has total output increased or decreased? By how much?

We need a single statistic to measure the output of an economy. But how do we add up all the houses, radios, apples, and millions of other goods produced in an economy? To make such a calculation, we compute what is known as **gross domestic product**, or **GDP**.

Gross Domestic Product

What exactly is GDP? GDP is the *market value of all final goods and services produced within a country in a given year.* All of the words in this definition are important.

GDP Is the Market Value

You have likely heard the expression, "You can't compare apples and oranges." However, GDP makes just such a comparison. GDP combines the different types of goods and services that an economy produced into a single measure of economic activity. To do this, it uses the total "market value" of the economy's output. Total market value means that we take the quantities of goods produced, multiply them by their respective prices, and add up the totals. For example, if an economy produced 200 apples at $0.20 an apple and 400 oranges at $0.15 an orange, the market value of these goods would be:

$$(200 \times \$0.20) + (400 \times \$0.15) = \$100$$

Adding the market value of all goods and services gives the total market value, or GDP. The reason we multiply the quantity of goods by their respective prices is that we cannot simply add the number of apples and the number of oranges. Using prices permits us to express everything in a common standard of value, in this case dollars.

Of All Final Goods and Services

GDP is a comprehensive measure of a nation's output. It measures the market value of not only apples and oranges but also many other goods, such as jetliners, calculators, and clothing. GDP also accounts for intangible services such as banking, engineering, medical, and legal services. When you purchase a video of your favorite rock concert, you are purchasing a good, and the purchase is part of GDP. When you go to a football game, you are buying a service, and the ticket price is also part of GDP.

Note that only "final" goods and services are included in GDP. Many goods and services are purchased for use as inputs in the production of other goods. For example, McDonald's buys ground beef to make Big Macs. If we counted the value of the ground beef and the value of the Big Mac, we would be counting the ground beef twice, thereby overstating the value of the production. Final goods therefore are finished goods and services that are produced for the end consumer.

Produced

GDP measures the current production of an economy. Many financial transactions take place, but they do not directly generate current output, and so they must be excluded from GDP. These transactions include transfer payments such as welfare payments and Social Security payments that the government makes to individuals. They also include a college student's yearly subsidy from their family to finance their college education. Moreover, purchases and sales of stocks and bonds are not part of GDP because they do not represent the production of new goods and services.

Within a Country

GDP includes the value of production within the boundaries of a country. When a Mexican citizen works temporarily in the United States, their production is part of U.S. GDP. When General Motors owns an assembly plant in Canada, the autos produced at that plant are part of Canada's GDP rather than U.S. GDP.

In a Given Year

Because GDP is expressed as a rate of current production, goods produced in previous years are not included in this year's GDP. If you sell your 2006 Honda Accord to a relative, this transaction would not be included in this year's GDP because no current production has occurred.

CHECK POINT

1 How do economists define gross domestic product (GDP)?
2 What is the significance of the following definitional characteristics of GDP?
  a Market value
  b Final goods and services
  c Produced within a country
  d In a given year

THE COMPONENTS OF GDP

The GDP of an economy can be calculated by totaling the expenditures on goods and services produced during the current year. National income accountants refer to this method of calculating GDP as the **expenditure approach**. When GDP is derived by the expenditure approach, its four components are (1) personal consumption expenditures, (2) gross private domestic investment, (3) government purchases of goods and services, and (4) net exports to foreigners. Table 10.1 shows the components of GDP for the United States in 2022. Let us examine each of these components.

Personal consumption expenditures (C) are purchases of final goods and services by households and individuals. Some items are durable goods, such as refrigerators, that last for several years. Nondurable goods are items that consumers use soon after purchase, such as gasoline and food. Services include intangible items such as the services of mechanics and engineers. For the United States, personal consumption expenditures typically account for two-thirds or more of GDP.

Gross private domestic investment (I), commonly known as gross investment, consists of all private-sector spending on investment. Gross investment includes the purchase of capital equipment and structures, such as a General Motors assembly plant, as well as purchases of new homes by households, a type of capital good. Moreover, gross investment includes changes in business inventories during the year. When General Motors' automobile inventories increase from one year to the next, they are added to investment. Increases in business inventories represent goods that have been produced during the current year that have not yet been sold to buyers in the market. Conversely, decreases in business inventories during the year are counted as negative investment.

Government purchases of goods and services (G) include spending on final output by federal, state, and local governments. Each tank, filing cabinet, calculator, and desk purchased

TABLE 10.1 Gross Domestic Product, 2022 (billions of dollars)

Component	*Amount*	*Percent of Total*
Personal consumption expenditures	17,360.4	68.2
Goods	5,939.6	
Services	11,420.8	
Gross private domestic investment	4,631.0	18.1
Fixed investment (plant, equipment)	4,472.0	
Business inventories	159.0	
Government purchases of goods and services	4,447.4	17.4
Federal	1,646.7	
State and local	2,800.7	
Net exports of goods and services	–974.3	–3.7
Exports	2,979.6	
Imports	–3,953.9	
Gross domestic product	25,464.5	100.0

Source: Data drawn from *Economic Report of the President*, 2023, Table B-3, available at https://www.whitehouse.gov/wp-content/uploads/2023/03/ERP-2023.pdf.

by government is part of the government purchases portion of GDP. Also included is the entire payroll of all governments, representing the purchases of labor services by governments. Recall that government purchases exclude transfer payments, such as welfare and Social Security payments, because they do not represent newly produced goods.

Net exports (X – M) are the last component of GDP. Sales of a country's goods and services to foreigners during a particular period represent its exports (X). For the United States, exports include the sale of a Dell computer to a Mexican buyer or the purchase of a ticket to Disneyland by a tourist from Germany. Purchases of foreign-produced goods and services by a country's residents constitute its imports (M). U.S. imports include the purchase of an Airbus jetliner by United Airlines, or a stay in a Toronto, Canada motel by the New York Yankees baseball team. Subtracting imports from exports yields net exports.

As shown in Table 10.1, in 2022 foreign buyers purchased $2,979.6 billion of goods and services from the United States. That same year, Americans purchased $3,953.9 billion of goods and services from foreign countries. The difference between these two figures, –974.3 billion, represents the net exports of the United States in 2022. Net exports were *negative* because imports exceeded exports. Conversely, net exports would be positive if exports exceed imports. In the past three decades, U.S. net exports have consistently been negative.

A Formula for GDP

GDP is the sum of purchases in the four sectors of the economy. Therefore, we can write the following equation for GDP:

$$GDP = C + I + G + (X - M)$$

Applying this formula to 2022, the U.S. GDP equaled \$25,464.5 billion.

$$\$25,464.5 = \$17,360.4 + \$4,631 + \$4,447.4 - \$974.3$$

This equation is a key element in analyzing macroeconomic problems and formulating macroeconomic policy. When economists analyze the economy at large, they apply this equation to predict the behavior of the major sectors of the economy: Households, business, government, and foreign commerce.

What GDP Does Not Measure

GDP is our best single measure of the value of output produced by an economy. Yet it is not a perfect measure. There are several flaws in the construction of GDP. First, GDP ignores transactions that do not take place in organized markets. If you grow your own vegetables, repair your car, paint your house, clean your apartment, or perform similar productive household activities, your labor services add nothing to GDP, because no market transaction is involved. Such nonmarket productive activities are sizable—10 percent of total GDP or more.

GDP also ignores the **underground economy** in which unreported barter and cash transactions take place outside recorded market channels. For example, owners of flea markets may make "under the table" cash transactions with their customers. The underground economy also includes transactions involving illegal goods and services, such as prostitution, gambling, and drugs. These illegal goods and services are final products that are not part of GDP. Estimates of the value of the transactions that take place in the underground economy are as high as one-third of GDP.

GDP does not value changes in the environment that arise through the production of output. Pollution and other aspects of industrial activity impose costs on society. However, these costs are not subtracted from the market value of final goods when GDP is calculated. For example, suppose that a chemical firm produces \$1 million worth of output but pollutes the water and decreases its value by \$2 million. Rather than indicating a loss to society, GDP will show a \$1 million increase.

GDP also excludes leisure, a good that is valuable to each of us. Suppose that Canada achieves a \$25,000 per-capita GDP, with an average workweek of 35 hours. Germany might achieve an identical per-capita GDP with a 40-hour workweek. Regarding economic well-being, Canada is better off, because it generates additional leisure time while producing the same output per person. However, GDP does not account for this fact.

Another problem of using GDP as a measure of well-being is that it does not show how much output is available per person. For example, suppose that Nigeria and Kuwait have the same GDP—say, $40 billion. Kuwait has a population of 2 million people, and Nigeria has a population of 124 million people. This suggests that people in Kuwait will have more than 60 times as many goods per person. In Kuwait, the $40 billion GDP must be divided among 2 million people, resulting in $20,000 worth of GDP per person ($40 billion / 2 million = $20,000). In Nigeria, however, there is just $323 worth of GDP per person ($40 billion / 124 million = $323). The people in Kuwait, on average, are better off than the people in Nigeria, even though the total value of GDP is the same for both nations.

The distribution of goods among different people in a nation also poses a problem for GDP. If most of a nation's GDP is consumed by a very small fraction of the people, there will be few rich people and many poor people. If a nation's GDP is more evenly distributed, however, the number of poor people will be smaller and the middle class will be larger. GDP is blind as to whether a small fraction of the citizenry consumes most of the nation's GDP or whether consumption is evenly divided.

Finally, GDP does not reflect the quality and kinds of goods that make up a nation's output. Today, new cars are safer and more fuel-efficient than the automobiles of 30 years ago. Dental procedures are usually less painful than they were 20 years ago. Moreover, the efficiency of the workplace has improved as a result of new products such as personal computers, scanners, fax machines, and the Internet. In short, GDP is a quantitative, rather than a qualitative, indicator of the output of goods and services.

Despite these limitations, GDP is a reasonable estimate of the rate of output in the economy. GDP was never intended to be a complete measure of economic well-being or the happiness of a nation's residents.

Why Are Some Countries Rich and Others Poor?

There are great discrepancies in living standards throughout the world, as Table 10.2 makes clear. If we ask a simple question, "Why are some economics rich and others poor?" we get a simple answer: Rich economies have greater resources per capita—that is, they have more human capital (skills), physical capital (machinery), and better technology. But this answer only begs another question: "Why do some economies have high levels of capital and technology, whereas others do not?"

A nation's choice of institutions greatly influences its wealth and development. What separates the economic "haves" from the "have-nots" is whether an economy's institutions, especially its public institutions, facilitate or confiscate the production of wealth.

What elements must a government put in place to allow an economy to take full advantage of the possible gains from specialization and trade? Economists note that a well-functioning economy requires a foundation of enforceable property rights, generally accepted accounting principles, sound financial institutions, a stable currency, and the like.

Throughout the world, there are great disparities in these institutions, which tend to promote differences in living standards. Therefore, a question naturally arises: How can a government create the sort of environment in which people find it worthwhile to accumulate human and physical capital and carry out technological development, thus creating economic prosperity?

TABLE 10.2 Comparisons of Living Standards Throughout the World

*Gross National Income per Person (U.S. dollars)**

Country	*2021*	*2015*	*2010*
Luxembourg	84,010	59,642	55,020
United States	70,930	55,860	48,880
Canada	52,390	43,400	39,280
Japan	43,740	37,920	34,650
Russia	32,170	24,710	19,860
Mexico	19,070	16,710	14,630
Ethiopia	2,530	1,500	1,060
Sierra Leone	1,750	1,830	1,330

*Measured at purchasing power parity.

Source: Data drawn from The World Bank, *World Development Indicators Database*, available at https://data.worldbank.org/indicator/NY.GNP.PCAP.PP.CD.

REAL GDP VERSUS NOMINAL GDP

We often want to compare GDP figures from year to year. Many people think that we are economically better off if GDP increases from one year to the next. However, we must exercise caution when making such a comparison.

So far, we have expressed GDP in terms of the prices existing in the year in which the goods and services were produced. Such an expression gives what is known as **nominal GDP**, or current-dollar GDP. To make comparisons over time when prices are changing, we must adjust nominal GDP so that it reflects only changes in output and not changes in prices.

Real GDP, or constant-dollar GDP, is nominal GDP adjusted to eliminate changes in prices. It measures actual (real) production and shows how actual production, rather than the prices of what is produced, has changed. Real GDP is thus superior to nominal GDP for assessing the performance of the economy, especially rates of economic growth.

Suppose, for example, that in 2022 a computer costs $2,000. The identical computer in 2023 costs $2,200. When the computer was counted as part of GDP in 2023, each computer added $200 more to GDP than it did in 2022. Even if the same number of computers were sold in 2023, GDP would have increased in 2023. The actual amount of goods available in the economy would not have increased, but the dollar value would have risen. The increase in the GDP would thus be the result of a rise in prices rather than an increase in output. When using GDP to assess growth, we must realize that part of the growth that we observe may be the result of rising prices.

To convert nominal GDP to real GDP, it is necessary to have a measure of price changes over the years. Economists use a **price index** to adjust GDP figures so that the figures show only changes in actual output. The broadest price index used to calculate real GDP is called the **GDP deflator**. It equals the ratio of the cost of buying all final goods and services in the current year to the cost of buying the identical goods at base-year prices. The GDP deflator is a weighted average of the prices of all final goods and services produced in an economy: Consumer goods, business investment, government purchases of goods and services, and net exports. It is a weighted average because the various goods and services are not of equal importance. In the base year, the GDP deflator has a value of 100. Currently, the base year for the GDP deflator is 2012.

Now let's calculate real GDP, or the GDP adjusted for price changes. To do so, we value the current-year output at the base-year prices. Thus, we divide the nominal GDP for a given year by the GDP deflator for that year, and then multiply that answer by 100.

$$\text{Real GDP for a given year} = \frac{\text{Nominal GDP for a given year}}{\text{GDP deflator for that year}} \times 100$$

Table 10.3 shows the nominal GDP, real GDP, and GDP deflator for the United States during the 2012–2022 period. Let us first calculate real GDP in 2012, the base year. To calculate real GDP, we divide nominal GDP in 2012 ($16,254 billion) by the GDP deflator in 2012 (100), and multiply that answer by 100, as follows:

$$\text{Real GDP} = \frac{\$16{,}254 \text{ billion}}{100.0} \times 100 = \$16{,}254 \text{ billion}$$

TABLE 10.3 Nominal Gross Domestic Product, Real Gross Domestic Product, and Gross Domestic Product Deflator, 2012–2022*

Year	*Nominal GDP (billions of dollars)*	*Real GDP (billions of dollars)*	*GDP Deflator (2012 = 100)*
2012	16,254	16,254	100.0
2018	20,533	18,616	110.3
2019	21,381	19,039	112.3
2020	21,060	18,506	113.8
2021	23,315	19,609	118.9
2022	25,463	20,018	127.2

*Chain-type price index for gross domestic product.

Source: Data drawn from Federal Reserve Bank of St. Louis, FRED Economic Data, *Real Gross Domestic Product*, March 30, 2023, available at https://fred.stlouisfed.org/series/GDPC1. See also *Economic Report of the President*, 2023, Table B-3, available at https://www.whitehouse.gov/wp-content/uploads/2023/03/ERP-2023.pdf.

Real GDP in 2012 was $16,254 billion, the same as nominal GDP in that year. In the base year, real GDP will always equal nominal GDP.

Now we will calculate real GDP in 2018. To compute real GDP, we divide nominal GDP in 2018 ($20,533 billion) by the GDP deflator in 2018 (110.3), and multiply that answer by 100. Therefore

$$\text{Real GDP} = \frac{\$20,533 \text{ billion}}{110.3} \times 100 = \$18,616 \text{ billion}$$

From 2012 to 2018, nominal GDP increased from $16,254 billion to $20,533 billion. However, the GDP deflator increased from 100.0 to 110.3 over this period, which suggests a 10.3 percent increase in prices. To calculate real GDP in 2018, therefore, we must thus subtract the increase in prices that occurred from 2012 to 2018. As a result, real GDP increased from $16,254 billion to only $18,616 billion over this period. This example illustrates the usefulness of real GDP as a measure of economic growth. It is apparent that real GDP grew between 2012 and 2018, but not by as much as suggested by the growth in nominal GDP suggested.

Productivity Gains: Working Smarter, Not Harder

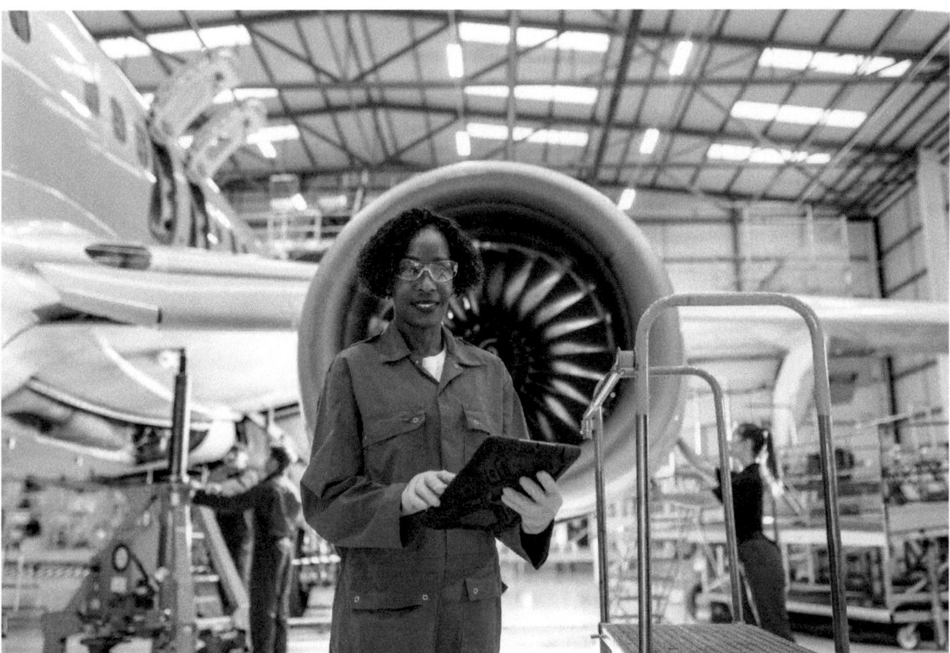

Source: Monty Rakusen/DigitalVision/Getty Images®

Compare America today with earlier times and one fact stands out: We live better. Give most of the credit to productivity. Through better productivity, we get more goods and services (GDP) from every bit of work. Through it, we secure economic progress and earn bigger paychecks. We've taken plenty of our added productivity as material gains—more cars, bigger and better-equipped houses, sophisticated computers, and the like. Also, we work less. Over the past few generations, the typical worker has gone from a six-day workweek with little vacation, to an average of 34 hours per workweek plus three weeks off. Indeed, the power of productivity has made the United States a rich nation. Consider these examples of productivity gains.

With ATMs, electronic fund transfers, and the Internet, banks can handle more transactions using fewer tellers and support staff. Output per hour in commercial banking has doubled since 1970. Electronic telephone switches have taken over much of the nation's long-distance and toll-call traffic. Calls per operator have risen from 17 per day in 1950 to about 2,100 today. Dr Pepper/Seven Up Bottling Group Inc. grew more productive by using huge machines that fill and package 800 bottles or 1,500 cans per minute, almost double the previous generation.

Day in and day out, markets encourage companies to push for greater output per hour. Do the job faster, reduce inputs, improve quality, and trim a few cents off the cost of production. The relentless march of productivity comes in myriad ways, limited only by technology and human ingenuity.

Indeed, as productivity reorganizes the economy, it changes how we use our innate skills and talents in the workplace. Each generation of inventions produces tools to take on more of the tasks once done by human beings. Americans adjust by taking jobs that put our other talents to work. Over time, our work moves up a hierarchy of human talents, focusing on new tasks that require higher-order skills, ones that machinery can't do as well. By redefining the way we work, the economy creates a new and more productive mix of technology and human talents. For example, workers once used muscle power to dig with picks and shovels. Over time, ever-larger digging and loading machines have allowed a single operator to do what once required legions of laborers.

This serves as a lesson for today's college students. Americans who want to prepare for the better jobs of the future should concentrate on developing skills that allow them to ascend the hierarchy of human talents. A college education is a window of opportunity that can help you improve your productivity.

CHECK POINT

1 How do economists calculate GDP according to the expenditure approach?

2 What are the major weaknesses of GDP as an indicator of economic well-being?

3 Distinguish between nominal GDP and real GDP. Which measure of GDP is superior for assessing the performance of the economy, especially rates of economic growth?

LONG-RUN ECONOMIC GROWTH

In the past 40 years, we have seen the development of many new products, such as personal computers and smartphones. Indeed, new products reflect our economic progress. Over time, we produce not only more goods and services but also new and better goods and services. As a result, our material standard of living increases.

A nation realizes **economic growth** when it increases its full production level of output over time. Recall from Chapter 1 that economic growth can be expressed in terms of the production possibilities model. When economic growth occurs, a nation's production possibilities curve shifts outward, or to the right. Economic growth is a *long-run* objective that can be achieved over a number of years.

Although economic growth suggests an increase in full production output over time, a more accurately definition is a rise in full production output *per person* over time. Suppose that output rises by 10 percent over time, but population grows at 12 percent over the same period. As a result, output per person would decrease. Even with more goods and services available, the average person would be worse off.

The Rate of Economic Growth

Let us now calculate the rate of growth in an economy. The **rate of economic growth** is the percentage change in the level of economic activity from one year to the next. Typically, analysts look at the rate of growth in an economy's real GDP.

The rate of economic growth is simply the change in real GDP between two periods divided by real GDP in the first period. To illustrate, suppose that in year 1 real GDP is $1,000 and in year 2 real GDP is $1,100. Hence, the rate of growth between years 1 and 2 would be:

$$\begin{aligned}\text{Rate of growth} &= \frac{\text{Year 2 real GDP} - \text{Year1 real GDP}}{\text{Year 1 real GDP}} \\ &= \frac{\$1{,}100 - \$1{,}000}{\$1{,}000} \\ &= 0.1\end{aligned}$$

Thus, the rate of growth for the economy between years 1 and 2 would be 10 percent.

A useful rule of thumb can help us appreciate the power of growth rates. Suppose that you know the constant rate of growth of real GDP, but you wanted to know the number of years it will take for the level of real GDP to double. The answer is given by the **rule of 70**:

$$\text{Year to double} = \frac{70}{\text{Percentage growth rate}}$$

As an example, suppose that real GDP grew at 3 percent a year. Thus, it would take about 23 years for the real GDP to double (70 / 3 = 23 1/3).

How fast can the U.S. economy grow on a sustainable basis? Most mainstream analysts believe that real GDP can grow about 2.5 percent per year. However, some analysts have asserted that much more rapid growth, possibly as much as 5 percent per year, may be sustainable. The answer to this question has profound implications for the future well-being of the American people. If the mainstream view is correct, real output will double only every 28 years or so according to the "rule of 70." But if the alternative view is correct, real output could double every 14 years.

WHAT DETERMINES ECONOMIC GROWTH?

The output level of an economy is determined by the level of inputs (land, labor, capital, and entrepreneurship) used and the production methods employed to convert the inputs into goods and services. Output can only be increased through additional inputs or more efficient use of the available inputs. How fast we can increase inputs is limited, however: Land is essentially fixed. Population growth and participation rates determine the size of the labor force.

In less-developed economies such as Ecuador or Honduras, a large fraction of inputs are underutilized and the level of capital is usually low. These economies can grow rapidly by increasing inputs and/or increasing production efficiency—for example, by moving toward state-of-the-art technology and raising the level of education. A developed economy, such as the United States or Germany, which is starting from a higher level of input use and efficiency, has more difficulty sustaining high rates of economic growth. Innovation and improvements in existing technology are the keys to increased growth rates.

In the final analysis, the keys to long-run economic growth are the incentives that induce individuals to work and firms to invest in production technology, within the limits imposed by demographics and the rate of technological advancement. Let us consider the major determinants of economic growth.

Natural Resources

The first pillar of economic growth is natural resources, which are gifts of nature that are usable in the production process. Resources such as mineral deposits, land, forests, and rivers come under this classification. Some natural resources, such as oil, are nonrenewable. Because it takes nature thousands of years to produce oil, there is a limited supply. When a barrel of oil is extracted from a well, it is impossible to produce more. Other natural resources, such as forests, are renewable. When we cut down a tree, we can replace it by planting a seedling in the ground to be harvested in the years ahead.

Although countries rely on natural resources as productive inputs, a domestic supply of natural resources is not crucial for an economy to produce goods and services. For example, Japan is a highly productive and wealthy nation, even though it has few natural resources. International trade allows Japan to be a productive nation. Japan imports natural resources, such as iron ore and oil, and transforms them into steel, automobiles, electronics, and other manufactured goods to be exported to nations that are abundant in natural resources.

You may wonder whether natural resources are a limit to growth. If the world has a fixed supply of nonrenewable resources, how can production, population, and standards of living continue to increase in the years ahead? Won't the supplies of resources eventually dry up, thus halting economic growth and causing living standards to decrease?

Although such arguments are appealing, most economists are optimistic about the economy's capacity to grow. They contend that technological progress often provides alternatives to the scarcity of resources. Comparing our current economy to that of years ago, we see many ways in which resources are better utilized. More productive oil rigs have increased the amount of oil harvested from wells. Modern automobiles have more efficient engines that allow them to run on less gasoline. New houses are better insulated and require less energy to cool or heat them. The recycling of oil, aluminum, tin, plastic, glass, cardboard, and paper permits the conservation of resources.

Technological progress has also allowed us to substitute abundant resources for scarce resources. For example, plastic has replaced tin as an input used to manufacture food containers, and telephone calls often travel over fiber-optic cables that are made from sand. In short, technological progress has contributed to the more efficient use of crucial resources.

Physical Capital

The second pillar of economic growth is increases in physical capital, which enable workers to produce more goods and services. No matter how educated workers are, they still need computers, machinery, and other equipment to produce goods and services. Capital investment is thus a key determinant of both productivity and growth. For example, when workers build a house, they use saws, hammers, electric drills, and other tools. Additional investment provides workers with more and better tools.

Productivity increases through capital investment have often involved exploiting economies of large-scale production. Industries such as electricity generation, food processing, and beverages are cases in point. In the beverage industry, for example, high-speed canning lines have raised productivity, but their contribution has been made possible in part by the development of large markets. To operate efficiently, these lines must produce nearly 500 million cans per year!

Of course, investment is not a free gift of nature; an opportunity cost is involved. When additional resources are used to produce equipment and manufacturing plants, fewer resources are available for the production of current-consumption goods such as hamburgers. However, those who save and invest will be able to produce more in the future.

Besides the economy's private sector, government is also a source of physical capital for the economy. Historically, investment in public capital such as roads, bridges, airports, and utilities has made a significant contribution to the nation's productivity growth. Such public capital is called **infrastructure**.

Human Capital

A third pillar of economic growth is **human capital**: the knowledge, experience, and skills of the workforce. As the economy has changed, the demands imposed on the brainpower of the American workforce have increased enormously. Increases in the hourly output of the average worker can reflect an improvement in the characteristics that allow workers to accomplish the same tasks in less time, to adapt to changing situations with greater flexibility, and to become engineers of change themselves.

The importance of human capital can be seen in the shipbuilding that took place during World War II. Between 1941 and 1944, U.S. shipyards produced more than 2,500 units of a cargo ship, known as the Liberty Ship, to a standardized design. In 1941, it required 1.2 million labor hours to construct a ship. By 1943, it required only 500,000. Thousands of workers learned from experience and attained human capital, more than doubling their productivity in two years.

Providing individuals with a formal education is one way to increase their human capital, thus contributing to aggregate productivity growth. Another way of increasing human capital is training workers on the job. Research has found that companies that offer more training enjoy higher rates of productivity growth.

Productivity

A fourth pillar of growth is greater **productivity**. Economists think of productivity as a ratio that measures the quantity of output produced relative to the amount of work required to produce it. Mathematically, it appears as follows:

$$\text{Productivity} = \frac{\text{Total output}}{\text{Hours worked}}$$

An increase in productivity occurs when total output increases faster than the amount of work required to produce it. For example, an increase in the quantity of output with no increase in hours worked would result in an increase in productivity.

Rearranging the terms can help us illustrate the significance of productivity for economic growth as follows:

$$\text{Total output} = \text{Productivity} \times \text{Hours worked}$$

This shows that total output depends on both work and productivity. Any increase in total output must come from an increase in either hours worked or productivity.

As seen in Table 10.4, U.S. productivity growth has been erratic. During the 1960s, productivity grew by 3.2 percent per year. But during the next five decades, productivity growth hovered around 2 percent per year. As Table 10.4 suggests, higher rates of productivity growth permit rising real compensation for labor. But when productivity growth rates decline, so does real compensation for labor.

What factors contribute to changes in productivity? Clearly, technological advancement has much to do with productivity gains. During the past century, the development

TABLE 10.4 Annual Rates of Growth in U.S. Labor Productivity and Real Compensation per Hour in the Business Sector, 1960–2021

Year	*Annual Labor Productivity Growth Rate (percent)*	*Annual Real Compensation Per Hour Growth Rate (percent)*
1960–1969	3.2%	2.9%
1970–1979	1.8	1.3
1980–1989	1.2	0.2
1990–1999	1.9	1.2
2000–2009	2.5	1.4
2010–2019	1.0	0.7
2020–2021	3.3	3.4

Source: Data drawn from *Economic Report of the President*, 2023, Table B-33, available at https://www.whitehouse.gov/wp-content/uploads/2023/03/ERP-2023.pdf.

of power-driven machines such as tractors, improvements in transportation such as railroads and airlines, and the growing stock of computers have increased the productivity of workers.

Obviously, technological advancement requires invention—that is, the discovery of a new process or product. Yet it also encompasses innovation—the successful introduction and adoption of a new process or product. Henry Ford did not invent the automobile; instead, he was an innovator who pioneered assembly-line production techniques that allowed workers to produce more automobiles in an hour, resulting in falling costs for each automobile produced.

Improving the productivity of the economy is not just a matter of improving technology. How the economy is organized plays an important role in creating incentives for firms to use their capital and labor as efficiently as possible. If the market economy is to deliver on its promise of growth and prosperity, markets have to be competitive, for it is competition that motivates firms to be efficient and innovative. Firms, however, often find it easier to increase profits by reducing competition than by improving efficiency in response to competition. Monopolies and oligopolies not only can charge inefficiently high prices and restrict output, but also may have a diminished drive to innovate.

Another source of increasing productivity in the economy is reorganization resulting from international trade. As competition forces producers to seek comparative advantage in the marketplace, resources shift to their best uses, creating a more efficient deployment of labor in the economy. As the economy reorganizes to produce more, it also lowers prices relative to wages, so that our paychecks buy more. Indeed, international trade can be every bit as powerful as technology in making us productive. Trade's productivity gains provide a strong justification for open markets. Economist widely agree that enormous benefits are lost when countries bow to their producers' narrow interests and enact protectionist measures that block imports or raise their prices.

Technological Innovation

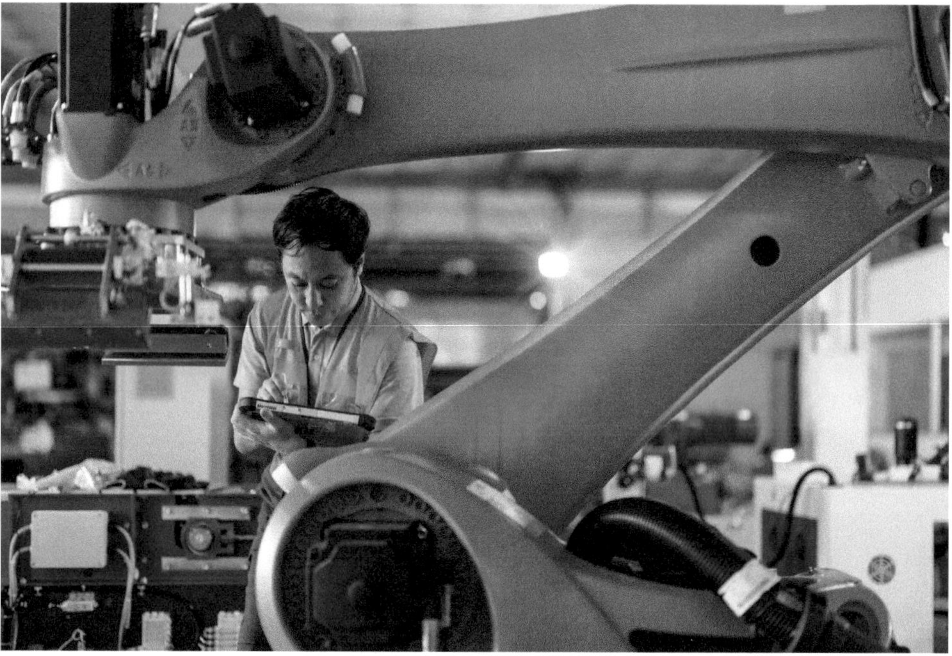

Source: PixeloneStocker/Moment/Getty Images®

We have learned how technological gains result in increased productivity. Over the long run, economic progress in advanced countries such as the United States hinges largely on technological progress. Each of the great industrial revolutions of the past was founded on innovation. The late 1800s and early 1900s, for example, witnessed the invention and general usage of electricity, the radio, the telephone, the internal combustion engine, the automobile, the factory assembly line, and the airplane. The surge of innovation that took place in the late 1900s was powered by the microprocessor, which gave rise to information technology and rapid growth in productivity.

Growth without technological advancement winds up becoming sluggish. If an economy continues to produce the same goods even with modest improvements, the result is stagnation. Without technological breakthroughs, the strategy of improving and refining existing production methods runs into diminishing returns and eventually fizzles out. Simply put, it's the jump to a new technology, such as computers or perhaps solar power, that radically improves people's lives.

If the pace of technological advance dwindles, there will be less need for college-educated workers. Jobs will be routinized, and companies will replace expensive college-educated workers with cheaper workers with associate degrees or even less education. Companies will also have greater incentives to outsource routine jobs to foreign workers, whose wages are a fraction of those of domestic workers. Advances in technology create better-paying jobs that require analytical reasoning, imagination, creativity, and people skills.

Economists often quote an old saying: "There is no such thing as a free lunch." The notion is that you generally get what you pay for. However, technological gains provide an exception to the free-lunch concept, furnishing a stimulus to growth and higher living standards. Simply put, rising productivity makes it easier to pay for things such as Social Security, better education, and other goods that improve our quality of life.

The Role of Government

The future rate of increase in an economy's productive capacity will largely be determined by the decisions of millions of individual businesses and households in the private sector of the economy. In addition, government can help promote the growth of an economy. Let us consider government policies that might speed up economic growth.

- **Boosting productivity by increasing domestic saving**. Historically, nations that have saved the most have also invested the most, and investment is strongly correlated with productivity. To stimulate national saving, government could reduce its spending, thus freeing resources to be used for investment. Government could also induce the private sector to save more by providing tax incentives.
- **Improving the skills of the workforce**. To help workers invest in skill acquisition, the government could adopt policies to promote lifelong learning. By funding basic education and by setting high standards in basic skills such as mathematics, science, and language, the government could improve the nation's production capabilities.
- **Stimulating research and development**. Increasing investment in research and development is one way to promote technological innovation and productivity growth. Since the 1800s, the U.S. government has sponsored research on agricultural practices and advised farmers how best to manage their land. The government has also supported aerospace research through NASA, and the U.S. Air Force and has provided tax breaks for firms practicing research and development.
- **Working to reduce trade barriers**. Economists have found that a country can raise its growth rate by increasing its openness to international trade, the education of its people, and its supply of telecommunications infrastructure. The impact on growth can be as much as 4 percentage points for a country that progresses from significantly below the average to significantly above the average on all of these indicators. As a result, economists generally argue for the reduction of trade barriers and the opening of markets to global competition.
- **Improving the efficiency of regulation**. In many cases, an improvement in government regulation can simultaneously promote the more effective attainment of policy

objectives and increase the efficiency of the economy. For example, a traditional approach to the problem of reducing pollution from the air might have entailed mandatory investment in costly new pollution-reduction equipment by all polluters. Instead, a system that is based on tradeable emissions certificates (see Chapter 8) can achieve the same results while encouraging the efficient allocation of pollution reduction among polluters.

Intel's Microprocessor and the Computer Revolution

The computer revolution of the late 1900s is often cited as a source of economic growth. Indeed, increased computing power has raised the productivity of households, businesses, and government.

What spurred the computer revolution was the development of the microprocessor by Intel Corporation. A microprocessor is a tiny electronic device that serves as an engine for computation. It consists of millions of transistors attached to a silicon chip as small as a fingernail. The microprocessor is often called a "computer on a chip." Intel's first microprocessor was produced in 1971 for use in handheld calculators. The chip contained 2,300 transistors and was capable of executing 60,000 operations a second.

These calculators were very expensive and few people could afford them. However, advanced manufacturing techniques soon decreased the cost of manufacturing microprocessors. The low cost, small size, and modest power requirements of microprocessors soon led to their use in hundreds of other products besides calculators. These products included microwave ovens, digital watches, telephones, sewing machines, and video games. Microprocessors also made possible the computerization of store checkout lines, bank records, gasoline pumps, medical instruments, and many other products that made the economy more productive. By the early 1980s, the microprocessor made possible the development of the personal computer.

Intel saw great potential for its technological breakthrough. If a bundle of transistors could be made to fit on a silicon chip, ways could be found to double the capacity of a single chip, and then quadruple it. Intel's goal has been to double the power of memory chips about every two years. Early microprocessors could execute up to 100,000 instructions per second. Today, microprocessors carry out more than 7 billion instructions per second.

Because Intel was the first firm to produce microprocessors, it could charge a premium price that resulted in large profit margins. By the 1980s, however, firms such as Motorola and Texas Instruments, as well as some Japanese companies, had developed their own microprocessors. Silicon chips thus became a commodity, with many different companies manufacturing them. This resulted in lower chip prices and falling profits for Intel.

The advent of competition has forced Intel to operate as if it were a research institution. The firm plows much of its profit into product development to stay ahead of the competition. Like a jogger running on an accelerating treadmill, Intel has to run faster just to maintain its position, and even faster to stay ahead of its competitors.[1]

CHECK POINT

1 Describe the concept of long-run economic growth. How do economists measure the rate of economic growth?
2 Of what significance is the "rule of 70" for economic growth?
3 Identify the major determinants of economic growth.
4 What policies might government enact to speed up economic growth?

THEORIES OF ECONOMIC GROWTH

The traditional theory of economic growth has its origins in the writings of Adam Smith, who wrote *The Wealth of Nations* in 1776.[2] According to Smith, larger markets encourage individuals to specialize in different parts of the production process and coordinate their labor. In turn, specialization is the chief engine of increased productivity. It fosters productivity gains by allowing workers to save time that would be lost in shifting from one type of work to another. In Smith's view, the inventive activity that improves production techniques is a by-product of specialization, because, as a worker concentrates attention on one activity, time-saving inventions often come to mind. Simply put, Smith's principles of economic growth emphasized two resources—labor and capital. Technology is discussed, but only in a superficial manner.

In the early 1900s, economists began formulating a different theory of economic growth. Considering technological progress to be within the scope of economic theory, they began to view innovation and creativity as economic activities. This perspective on economics found its foremost advocates in a Harvard professor named Joseph Schumpeter in 1942, and professor Paul Romer of Stanford University in the 1980s.[3]

Schumpeter constructed a theory of economic growth in which technological innovation is the prime source of growth in a modern economy and profits are the fuel. He argued that what is most important about a capitalist market system is precisely that it rewards change by allowing those who create new products and processes to capture some of the benefits of their creations in the form of monopoly profits. They provide entrepreneurs with the means to (1) fund creative activities in response to perceived opportunities; (2) override the natural conservatism of other parties who must cooperate with the new product's launch as well as the opposition of those whose markets may be harmed by the new products; and (3) widen and deepen their sales networks so that new products can be quickly made known to a large number of customers. Competition, if too vigorous, would deny these rewards to creators and instead pass them on to consumers, in which case firms would have scant reason to create new products.

The drive to temporarily capture monopoly profits promotes, in Schumpeter's words, **creative destruction**, as old technologies, goods, and livelihoods are replaced by new ones.

Thus, whereas Smith saw monopoly profits as an indication of economic inefficiency, Schumpeter saw them as evidence of valuable entrepreneurial activity in a healthy, dynamic economy. Indeed, in Schumpeter's view, new technologies and products are so valuable to consumers that governments of countries should encourage entrepreneurs by granting temporary monopolies over innovations and inventions.

Given that technological innovation tends to provide benefits to consumers, why are the forces opposing it so strong? One factor limiting technological innovation is that it puts existing products at risk. An example is the personal computer, whose power and speed have been rising at rapid rates for more than 20 years. In the competition to supply components of the personal computer, such as modems and memory, any firm that wants to play the game has to invest in creating new, faster, and smaller versions of the component. To earn profits and to justify this investment and its uncertainties, the resulting innovation must leapfrog the competition by creating a new generation. The first firm to market with the new generation can often grab the bulk of the entire market and, with it, almost all the profits to be had. Of course, this typically wipes out the profitability of the previous generation and sets the stage for the next leapfrogger, who will then destroy the profits of the current leader.

Also, being creative is inherently risky. You don't know what will work until you try it. Although successful new products may earn immense returns, others inevitably fail and create losses for their creators and supporters. An example of a product that was expected to fare well in the marketplace but did not was the Betamax, which looked like a technology winner to most experts when videocassette recorders were invented in the late 1970s. Beta was competing with VHS, and insiders knew that Sony had the opportunity to develop either Beta or VHS and had chosen Beta as the superior technology. But the corporations developing VHS were able to more rapidly lengthen videocassette playback times. Consumers who did adopt Beta eventually found that they had to switch to VHS, as Sony was forced to abandon the system as a result of the greater availability of prerecorded videocassettes on VHS. Simply put, when consumers choose one system, its rivals may suffer irreversible setbacks, as the Beta system did. Moreover, VHS was being replaced by DVD systems by 2000.

IS ECONOMIC GROWTH DESIRABLE?

Our analysis of economic growth in this chapter makes it appear to be beneficial. Is it?

The main justification for economic growth is that it allows a nation to realize rising material abundance and increased standards of living. Expanding output and rising incomes allow households to purchase additional medical care, education, recreation and travel, and higher-quality consumer goods. Growth is also an avenue for supporting more of the arts, including theater, music, and drama. The high living standard that growth permits increases our leisure and provides additional time for self-fulfillment.

Growth also helps generate more resources for national defense, police and fire protection, care of the disabled and sick, and improvements in our nation's infrastructure, such as roads and communications. In today's world, the additional jobs made possible by economic growth may be the only achievable method for decreasing poverty, given society's reluctance to increase the amount of national income that it shares with the poor.

Although economic growth may provide benefits, it can also entail costs. Some individuals maintain that additional economic growth results in more pollution, more crowded cities, excessive emphasis on materialism, and psychological problems that result in suicide and drug usage. They contend that the country would be better off with less growth rather than with more. What's wrong with a slower and more peaceful life?

Antigrowth advocates also contend that economic growth has not solved society's problems such as poverty, discrimination, and homelessness. According to the antigrowth view, poverty in the United States is largely attributable to the distribution of the nation's income, rather than the growth of production and income. To alleviate poverty, society must be willing to adopt policies to redistribute income and wealth in favor of the poor rather than making investments in new technologies more profitable for the rich.

Another concern is the relationship between economic growth and the availability of resources. Recall that many people argue that continued increases in population and the size of the economy will cause us to run out of scarce resources. At some point, the time will come when there is no more clean air and pure water, no more natural resources, and no more open space in which to live comfortably. As a result, the nation's living standard will decline. These people contend that we must reduce the rate of economic growth and conserve our scarce resources.

Others argue that economic growth does not cause these problems. They maintain that growth brings about favorable things such as higher real income, less poverty, and greater economic security. Moreover, if the government would strictly enforce environmental laws, pollution would not be a major problem. Finally, we are not running out of natural resources. If and when the scarcity of resources becomes a barrier to growth, the rising relative prices of these resources will force households to conserve them and develop alternative resources. As you can see, there are no simple answers to the question of the optimal rate of economic growth.

This chapter has considered the U.S. economy's gross domestic product and the role of economic growth. The next chapter will examine the impacts of the business cycle, unemployment, and inflation on the economy.

CHECK POINT

1 Distinguish between the traditional theory of economic growth and new growth theory.
2 Describe the principle of creative destruction. Why are the forces opposing creativity so strong?
3 Identify some of the disadvantages of economic growth.

CHAPTER SUMMARY

1 Economists have developed a single statistic to measure the output of an economy. This statistic is known as gross domestic product, or GDP. GDP is the market value of all final goods and services produced within a country in a given year.

2 The GDP of an economy can be calculated by totaling the expenditures on goods and services produced during the current year. When GDP is derived by the expenditure approach, it has four components: Personal consumption expenditures, gross private domestic investment, government purchases of goods and services, and net exports to foreigners. For the United States, personal consumption expenditures are the largest component of GDP, typically accounting for two-thirds or more of GDP.

3 Although GDP is our best single measure of the value of the output produced by an economy, it is not a perfect measure of economic well-being. For example, GDP ignores transactions that do not take place in organized markets. GDP also ignores the underground economy as well as changes in the environment that arise through the production of output. Furthermore, GDP does not account for leisure, nor does it show how much output is available per person. Finally, GDP does not reflect the quality and kinds of goods that compose a nation's output.

4 Nominal GDP, or current-dollar GDP, is expressed in terms of the prices existing in the year in which goods and services were produced. Real GDP, or constant-dollar GDP, is nominal GDP adjusted to eliminate changes in prices. It measures actual (real) production and shows how actual production—rather than the prices of what is produced—has changed. Real GDP is superior to nominal GDP for assessing rates of economic growth.

5 An economy realizes economic growth when it increases its full production level of output over time. The rate of economic growth is the percentage change in the level of economic activity from one year to the next. Typically, analysts look at the rate of growth in an economy's real GDP.

6 The keys to long-run economic growth are the incentives that induce individuals to work and firms to invest in production technology, within the limits imposed by demographics and the rate of technological advancement. Among the major determinants of economic growth are natural resources, physical capital, human capital, and economic efficiency. Government may enact policies to foster economic growth, such as boosting productivity by increasing domestic saving, stimulating research and development, working to reduce trade barriers, and improving the efficiency of regulation. Governments may also target and subsidize specific industries that might be especially important for technological progress.

7 According to the traditional theory of economic growth as pioneered by Adam Smith, economic efficiency is spurred by perfect competition. Traditional growth theory emphasizes two resources—labor and capital. Technological progress is viewed as being outside the scope of economic theory, and thus something that we accept as a given.

8 According to the new growth theory, pioneered by Joseph Schumpeter, technological progress is within the scope of economic theory, and creativity is an economic activity. According to Schumpeter, ideas and creativity are the prime sources of growth in a

modern economy and profits are the fuel. The drive to capture monopoly profits promotes creative destruction, as old goods and livelihoods are replaced by new ones. Thus, whereas Adam Smith saw monopoly profits as an indication of economic inefficiency, Schumpeter saw them as evidence of valuable entrepreneurial activity in a healthy, dynamic economy.

9 Although economic growth may provide benefits for a nation, it can also entail costs. Critics maintain that additional economic growth promotes more pollution, more crowded cities, excessive emphasis on materialism, and psychological problems that result in suicide and drug use. Economic growth may also cause the depletion of scarce resources, eventually resulting in a decline in the nation's standard of living. However, proponents argue that economic growth does not cause these problems; rather, it fosters higher real income, less poverty, and greater economic security.

KEY TERMS AND CONCEPTS

gross domestic product (GDP)
expenditure approach
personal consumption expenditures
gross private domestic investment
government purchases of goods and services
net exports
underground economy
nominal GDP
real GDP
price index
GDP deflator
economic growth
rate of economic growth
rule of 70
infrastructure
human capital
productivity
creative destruction

STUDY QUESTIONS AND PROBLEMS

1 Which of the following are included in calculating this year's GDP?
  a Interest received on a security of the U.S. government
  b The purchase of a new automobile
  c The services of a gardener in weeding a garden
  d The purchase of a life insurance policy
  e The money received by John when he sells his computer to Mary
  f The purchases of new office equipment by the U.S. government
  g Unemployment compensation benefits received by a former autoworker
  h A new apartment building built by a construction firm
  i Travel by people in Canada to the United States to visit Disneyland
2 Table 10.5 shows hypothetical GDP data for the United States. Based on this information, calculate GDP.

TABLE 10.5 Gross Domestic Product Data (billions of dollars)

Government purchases of goods and services	360
Compensation of employees	210
U.S. imports of goods and services	40
Interest and dividend income	23
Personal consumption expenditures	720
Social security earnings	13
Gross private domestic investment	77
Household saving	12
U.S. exports of goods and services	28
Household taxes	45

3 Table 10.6 shows the nominal GDP and the GDP price index for the United States for selected years. Based on this information, calculate real GDP.

TABLE 10.6 Calculation of Real Gross Domestic Product

Year	*Nominal GDP (billions of dollars)*	*Price Index*	*Real GDP (billions of dollars)*
2000	$6,139	93.6	
2001	6,079	97.3	
2002	6,244	100.0	
2003	6,386	102.6	
2004	6,609	105.0	

4 Assume that the average workweek declines by 20 percent because U.S. citizens decide to take life a little easier. How will this affect GDP for the United States? How will it affect the welfare of the United States?

5 Assume that the United States produces only radios and calculators. In 2001, it produced 100 radios at a price of $25 and 50 calculators at a price of $30. In 2005, the United States produced 120 radios at a price of $30 and 60 calculators at a price of $35. Calculate the nominal GDP for each year.

6 Why do economists prefer to compare real GDP figures for different years instead of nominal GDP figures?

7 If real GDP is $8,880 billion and nominal GDP is $9,988 billion, what does the GDP deflator equal?

8 Suppose that GDP for a given year equals $9,650 billion. What does this mean?

9 Why would removing a barrier to trade, such as a tariff, result in more rapid economic growth?

10 Explain how higher saving can promote a faster rate of economic growth.

NOTES

1 Tim Jackson, *Inside Intel* (New York: Plume Books, 1997); Andrew Grove, *Only the Paranoid Survive* (New York: Doubleday, 1996); T. R. Reid, *The Chip: How Two Americans Invented the Microchip and Launched a Revolution* (New York: Random House, 1985).

2 Adam Smith, *The Wealth of Nations* (New York: Modern Library, 1937).

3 Joseph Schumpeter, *Capitalism, Socialism, and Democracy* (New York: Harper, 1942); and Paul Romer, "Economic Growth," in David R. Henderson, ed., *The Fortune Encyclopedia* (New York: Warner Books, 1993).

CHAPTER 11

The Business Cycle, Unemployment, and Inflation

CHAPTER OBJECTIVES

After reading this chapter, you should be able to:

1 Discuss the four phases of the business cycle.
2 Explain what the unemployment rate means and how it is calculated.
3 Identify the various types of unemployment and their costs on the economy.
4 Discuss the importance of the consumer price index as a measure of inflation.
5 Identify who benefits from and who is hurt by inflation.
6 Describe the causes of inflation.

DOI: 10.4324/9781003438571-14

ECONOMICS IN CONTEXT

In the late 1990s, computer makers were boosting already robust sales by marketing elegant new hardware designs and faster processors. By the early 2000s, however, things had become ugly in the personal computer (PC) market: The PC market witnessed a brutal price war in which dealers rapidly slashed retail prices and provided generous rebates and lots of freebies. Dell Computer Corporation, which initiated the price battle, tossed in a free printer, free delivery, and free Internet access to customers who purchased a PC through its website.

Although that was good for customers, computer makers winced as the intensifying competition sliced into profits. Compaq Computer Corporation, the world's largest PC maker, downsized its operations and laid off workers to help compensate for the new price reductions. Other computer makers slashed jobs and warned investors of reduced sales. The focal point of the industry's problems was a dramatic slowdown in revenue growth. Fears of recession hurt sales as consumers and many companies held onto their computers longer. PC producers announced that if demand continued to decline and PC prices fell, the resulting squeeze could trigger a wave of consolidation among the biggest PC makers, as seen in the merger between Hewlett-Packard and Compaq in 2002.

Indeed, the history of the American economy is marked by recurrent periods of boom and bust. Sometimes business conditions are robust, with plenty of job vacancies, factories working near maximum capacity, and strong profits. At other times, goods are unsold and pile up as excess inventories, jobs become scarce, and profits are low. Sometimes a downturn is mild; at times, like the Great Depression of the 1930s, a downturn is prolonged and traumatic.

In this chapter, we will explore the nature and effects of macroeconomic instability. We will begin with an overview of the business cycle—the recurrent periods of recession and expansion that characterize our economy—and then we will examine the nature and causes of unemployment and inflation.

THE BUSINESS CYCLE

In an ideal economy, real gross domestic product (GDP) would increase over time at a smooth and steady pace. Moreover, the price level would remain constant or only increase slowly. However, economic history shows that the economy never grows in a smooth and steady pattern. Instead, it is interrupted by periods of economic instability, as shown in Figure 11.1.

The economy may realize several years of expansion and prosperity. Then national output declines, profits and real incomes decrease, and the unemployment rate increases to uncomfortably high levels as many workers lose their jobs. Eventually, the economic contraction vanishes and recovery begins. The recovery may be slow or fast. It may be partial, or it may be so strong that it results in a new era of prosperity. Or it may be characterized

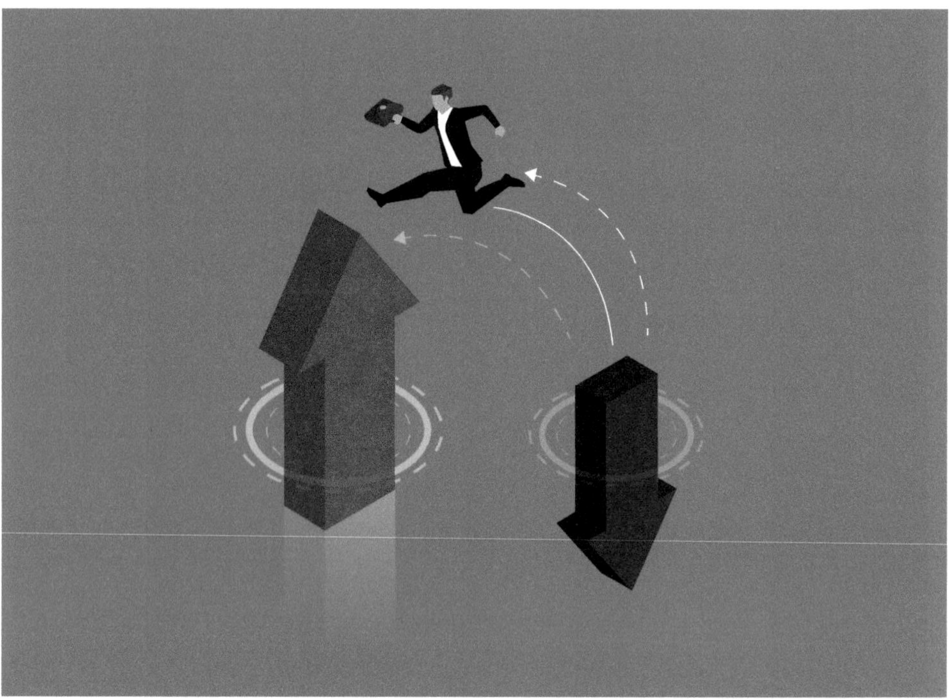

Source: sesame/DigitalVision Vectors/Getty Images®

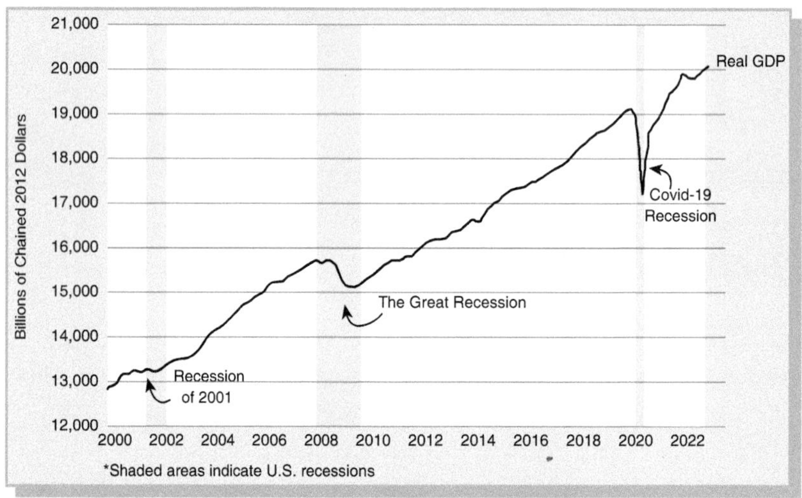

FIGURE 11.1 Historical Business Fluctuations in the United States

Source: Data taken from the *Economic Report of the President*, various issues

Although the long-run trend of the U.S. economy has been upward, occasional economic downturns have plagued the economy.

by escalating inflation, soon to be followed by another downturn. The upward and downward movements in output, employment, and inflation form the **business cycle** that characterizes all market economies.

Phases of the Business Cycle

The term **business cycle** refers to recurrent ups and downs in the level of economic activity over several years. Although business cycles may vary in intensity and duration, we can divide each into four phases, as shown in Figure 11.2.

- **Peak**. At the peak of a business cycle, real GDP is at its highest point. Employment and profits are usually strong.
- **Recession**. A recession is a period of significant decline in total output, income, employment, and trade, that usually lasts from 6 months to a year and is marked by widespread contraction in many sectors in the economy. A recession begins at a peak and ends at a trough. For example, the U.S. economy began the Great Recession in December 2007, which lasted until June 2009.
- **Trough**. The low point of real GDP, just before it begins to turn upward, is called the trough of a business cycle. At the trough, unemployment and idle productive capacity are at their highest levels relative to the previous recession. The trough may be short-lived or quite long.
- **Recovery**. Recovery is an upturn in the business cycle during which real GDP rises. During the recovery or expansion phase of the business cycle, industrial output expands, profits usually increase, and employment moves toward full employment.

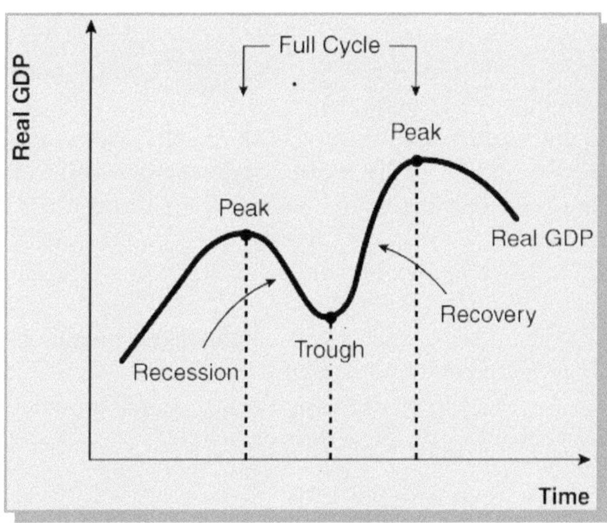

FIGURE 11.2 The Business Cycle

Over time, real GDP fluctuates around an overall upward trend. Such fluctuations are called the business cycle.

TABLE 11.1 Post-World War II Recessions for the United States

Period	*Duration (months)*	*Percentage Decline in Real Gross Domestic Product*
1940–1949	11	–2.0%
1953–1954	10	–3.7
1957–1958	8	–3.9
1960–1961	10	–1.6
1969–1970	11	–1.1
1973–1975	16	–4.9
1980	6	–2.4
1981–1982	16	–3.4
1990–1991	8	–1.8
2001	8	–0.5
2007–2009	18	–3.7
2020	2	–10.0
Average	10.3	3.3

Source: Drawn from National Bureau of Economic Research, *U.S. Business Cycle Expansions and Contractions*, March 14, 2023, available at https://www.nber.org/research/data/us-business-cycle-expansions-and-contractions.

Note that business cycles are erratic. Business cycles are like mountain ranges with different valleys and hills. Some valleys are deep and long, as in the Great Depression; others are shallow and narrow, as in the recession of 2001. We measure an entire business cycle from peak to peak. Usually, business cycles have averaged four to five years, although a few have been longer and some shorter. Since World War II, the average U.S. expansion has lasted about 3½ years; the average recession has lasted about 10 months, as shown in Table 11.1. During these recessions, U.S. real GDP has fallen by an average of 3.3 percent.

Despite these ups and downs, the U.S. economy has grown significantly over the long run, so the growth during expansions has more than offset the declines during recessions. Output has increased over the long run because of increases in the amount and quality of resources, better technology, and improvements in methods of production.

Recession Characteristics

Although no two recessions are alike, they do have similar characteristics. When the economy enters a period of recession, we can usually expect the following: First, consumer expenditures decrease abruptly while business inventories of steel, automobiles, and other durable goods rise unexpectedly. As businesses react by curtailing production, real GDP declines. Soon thereafter, business investment in plants and equipment falls. Second, the demand for labor decreases. This is first seen in a reduction in the average workweek, followed by layoffs and increased unemployment. Third, as output falls, the demand for materials, services, and labor decreases, which may result in a decline in prices or a slowdown in price rate increases. Finally, business profits decline during recessions. In anticipation of this, stock prices generally drop as investors become pessimistic about the decline in business activity. Moreover, because the demand for credit decreases, interest rates usually also decline during recessions. Simply put, a recession is a period of declining output and not just a period of slower economic growth.

Identifying the dates of beginnings and ends of recessions requires time. This is because analysts must look at a variety of economic data, such as industrial production and retail sales, to determine turning points in the economy. Compiling such data takes some time, which means they are only available after the events they describe. Also, because it takes time to discern changes in trends given the usual month-to-month volatility in economic data, it takes some time before analysts can agree that a recession began at a certain date. It can be a year or more after the fact that analysts announce the date a recession began.

What is the difference between a recession and a depression? Analysts generally describe a recession as a decrease in real GDP for at least two consecutive quarters. A **depression** is a very deep and prolonged recession. Because no subsequent recession has approached the severity of the Great Depression, the term *depression* is often used to refer to the long and pronounced recession of the 1930s. How severe was the Great Depression for the United States? During that slump, the unemployment rate skyrocketed to 25 percent, and industrial output fell by more than 40 percent over a three-year period, hampering business activity for more than a decade.

Most macroeconomic variables that measure some aspect of production, income, or spending fluctuate together throughout the business cycle. When real GDP decreases during a recession, so do national income, business profits, household expenditures, investment spending, industrial production, auto sales, retail sales, and the like. Also, fluctuations in the economy's output of goods and services correspond strongly to changes in the rate of unemployment. When real GDP decreases, unemployment rises, and vice versa.

THEORIES OF THE BUSINESS CYCLE: ECONOMIC SHOCKS

Over the years, economists have debated the sources of the business cycle. What causes the economy to turn downward or upward?

Many economists believe that a change in total spending (aggregate demand) is the immediate determinant of domestic output and employment. Recall that total spending in the economy includes expenditures for final goods by households, businesses, government, and foreign buyers. For example, if total spending decreases, businesses may find it unprofitable to produce the existing level of output. As they decrease production, they employ less land, labor, and capital. Thus, reductions in total spending result in decreases in national output, employment, and incomes. These decreases, in turn, can cause a recession in the economy. Conversely, an increase in total spending results in a rise in national output, employment, and incomes. These increases, in turn, promote economic expansion.

A leading theory is that business cycle fluctuations are the result of economic shocks. An **economic shock** is an unexpected change in fundamental macroeconomic variables that has a significant impact on the economy's real output, employment, and prices. Some shocks come from within the domestic economy, but many flow from outside an economic system; we call these external shocks.

Shocks influence the economy through either the demand side or supply side. Because markets and industries interact with each other, shocks to any sector of the economy can have a widespread effect. Economic shocks can be helpful (positive) or harmful (negative) to the economy. We will limit our discussion to negative shocks.

A **negative demand shock** occurs when there is an unanticipated and substantial decrease in the level of consumption spending or investment spending. Here are some examples of negative demand shocks.

- A technological advance (microcomputers) makes a previous technology (typewriters) antiquated and no longer in demand.
- A global pandemic (Covid-19) creates anxiety and leads to people becoming more inclined to save instead of consume.
- The bursting of asset bubbles, in which asset prices (stocks or homes) sharply decline. The confidence of households and businesses thus decreases, and they curtail their spending on consumption and investment, causing the economy to fall into recession.
- An economic downturn abroad results in declining foreign demand for imports and hence a decrease in investment spending for domestic export industries.

A **negative supply shock** is an unexpected occurrence that makes production throughout the economy more difficult, more costly, or unachievable for at least some industries. Here are some examples of negative supply shocks.

- Terrorism or wars can hinder the production of goods and services, as seen in the case of Russia's war against Ukraine in 2022.
- Pandemics such as Covid-19 can trigger the illness and death of workers, thus disrupting the production of goods.
- An increase in the cost of key products, such as natural gas or oil, can cause fuel prices to rise, making it more expensive to use for business production.
- Natural disasters or weather events, such as hurricanes, floods, or earthquakes, can disrupt production in the economy.

One question that has intrigued economists is whether each economic expansion contains the seeds of its own destruction. Is it true that the longer an expansion lasts, the more likely it is to end in the next quarter or the next year? Studies find no compelling evidence that expansions possess an inherent tendency to die of old age. Instead, they appear to fall victim to specific events related to economic shocks or government policies.

We will next consider how negative economic shocks contributed to two recessions for the United States—the Great Recession of 2007–2009 and the Covid-19 recession.

The Great Recession: 2007–2009: Negative Demand Shock

During the global financial crisis of 2007–2008, a negative demand shock in the U.S. economy was caused by factors that included falling house prices, a mortgage crisis, and decreased household wealth, which resulted in a decrease in consumer spending and business investment spending. Let us see how this occurred.

In 2007–2009, much of the industrialized world fell into a deep recession, known as the Great Recession. It was triggered by the disruptions in U.S. financial markets that began in 2007 and worsened to the point that the U.S. economy was in crisis in 2008. U.S. financial markets were disrupted by substantial declines in housing prices, rising default rates on residential mortgages, and a resulting sharp decline in the value of mortgages. These assets were held by banks and other financial institutions that play a vital role in the functioning of financial markets. Hundreds of billions of dollars in losses on these mortgages undermined the financial institutions that originated and invested in them.

The use of borrowed funds by these institutions made them vulnerable to large mortgage losses. Some financial institutions failed, such as Wachovia and Washington Mutual, and others were on the verge of failure. The remaining institutions pulled back from lending to each other, and the interest rates that they charged each other on a dwindling number of loans increased to unprecedented levels. This placed enormous stress on financial markets. Credit was frozen, and confidence in the financial system eroded.

Government also contributed to the financial crisis by pressuring banks to serve poor borrowers and poor regions of the country. This resulted in mortgages being made to many households who were unable to repay their loans. Also, poorly designed regulations resulted in banks not having sufficient safety cushions (capital) during periods of economic decline. Moreover, history shows that financial crises tend to occur when money is plentiful and inexpensive: Cheap money encourages excessive debt and risk taking. During the early 2000s, funds swept into the United States from high-saving countries such as China. Moreover, the Federal Reserve adopted a policy of providing abundant money to the U.S. economy. Simply put, there was plenty of blame to share concerning the origins of the financial crisis.

As default rates for American households rose, lenders became increasingly reluctant to make any but the least risky loans. Many banks tightened standards on mortgages and consumer debt. Therefore, consumers found it increasingly difficult to finance purchases of "big ticket" items, such as automobiles and houses. As the crisis continued, consumption spending and business investment declined, and layoffs of workers increased. By 2008, the U.S. economy was in a severe recession. This resulted in stimulative economic policies by the federal government and Federal Reserve, discussed later in this textbook.

McDonald's Hustles to Keep Its Burgers Sizzling in Lean Times

The Great Recession of 2007–2009 imposed economic hardship on many firms and workers. However, one firm that was able to perform relatively well during this era was

McDonald's Corporation. This is because many Americans flocked to the fast-food giant as an inexpensive substitute for sit-down meals. Similarly, Walmart's sales remained buoyant as households were attracted to the discounter's merchandise.

However, business was not so good for McDonald's in other parts of the world, such as Europe and Asia, from where about two-thirds of its revenues originate. Besides a worsening global economy that flattened sales, McDonald's suffered from a strengthening (appreciating) U.S. dollar that made its burgers, French fries, and shakes more expensive for foreign customers. Also soaring commodity costs pressured McDonald's bottom line. Restaurant outlets complained that the high cost of beef, cheese, buns, and other ingredients, combined with a rising minimum wage and high energy costs, were softening their profits.

How did McDonald's buoy its sales and profits during such lean times? By focusing on improving restaurant operations, lowering prices, and slashing costs. To reduce operating costs, McDonald's removed gas-guzzling automobiles from the firm's fleet and held meetings at the company's Hamburger University in suburban Chicago rather than at exotic and expensive locations. The firm also convinced media firms to negotiate decreased advertising rates for McDonald's' products, and it ceased constructing new restaurants in markets that showed economic weakness. Moreover, McDonald's increased investments in highly profitable coffee drinks that competed with Starbucks, and improved drive-through windows that increased sales and productivity.

As the Great Recession intensified, McDonald's increasingly encouraged restaurant managers across the world to scrutinize labor, food, and utility costs. Moreover, the food giant gave its restaurant managers more freedom to price items in line with weakening demand conditions. In particular, the firm shied away from increasing prices, and thus losing customers, at outlets in economically depressed areas of the country. Simply put, the strategy used by McDonald's to cope with the global recession was to cut costs and promote lower-priced items perceived as a good value. At the same time, franchise owners had to tolerate lower profit margins until the economy improved.

The Covid-19 Pandemic: Negative Supply Shock and Demand Shock

The Covid-19 pandemic provides another example of harmful negative economic shocks. The pandemic was a worldwide outbreak of coronavirus, an infectious disease that appeared in China in December, 2019. It caused the deaths of many people, the closure of businesses, falling trade and investment, and steeply rising unemployment rates.

Covid-19 resulted in large and widespread negative supply shocks and negative demand shocks throughout the world. The first shock wave started with a production shutdown (supply shock) in China in 2019, followed by a decline in domestic demand as affected people became unemployed, lost income, and decreased consumption spending (demand shock). The economic shocks then moved to Europe, whose businesses reduced production and laid off workers, who then decreased consumption spending. Finally, the pandemic pounded the United States and Canada, similar to the European episode. In all regions, the shocks were intensified by local transportation disruptions, such as slowdowns in shipping and airport closings, and a reduction in the workforce that resulted from illness and quarantine.

Supply chains were damaged in the United States because of Covid-19. For example, labor shortages due to the pandemic disrupted labor-intensive work, such as sowing and harvesting on farms. Many of these jobs were previously occupied by temporary or seasonal workers, and the absence of workers due to illness adversely affected agricultural supply chains. Similar disruptions occurred in other sectors of the economy, such as construction materials, triggering shortages of many products. The U.S. economy slid into a deep recession with real gross domestic product falling by 10 percent. However, the recession lasted only 2 months, the shortest recession on record.

Responding to the sharp downturn, the federal government and Federal Reserve enacted policies to stimulate the economy, which will be discussed later in this book.

CHECK POINT

1 Identify the four phases of the business cycle.
2 What factors cause the economy to turn upward or downward?
3 Describe the nature and operation of economic shocks.
4 What triggered the recession of 2007–2009 and the Covid-19 recession?

UNEMPLOYMENT

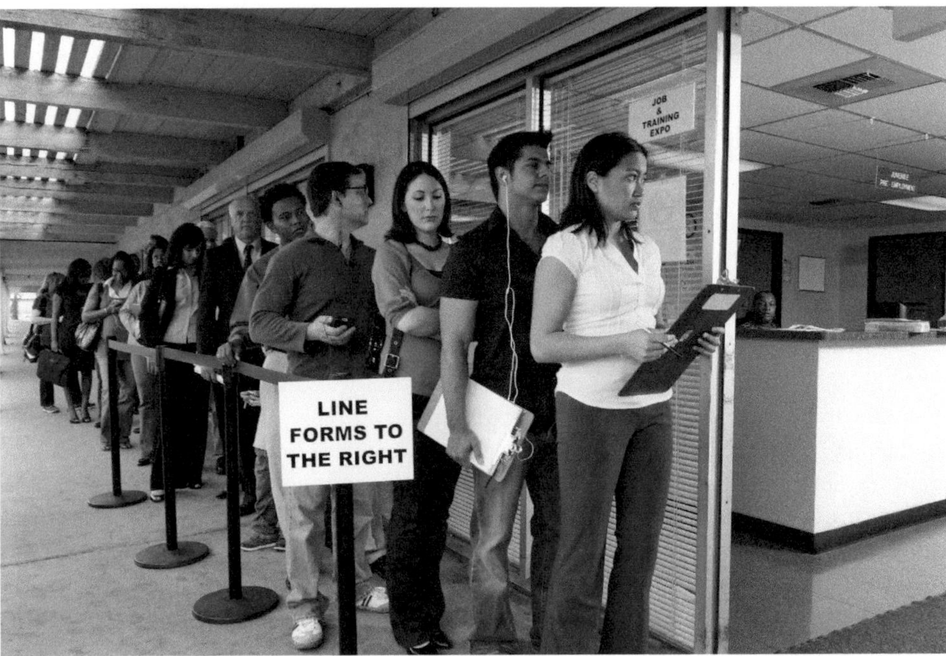

Source: Yellow Dog Productions/The Image Bank/Getty Images®

One reason we want to avoid recessions and depressions is that they cause hardship among individuals. During a recession, not only does real GDP decline, but also fewer people are able to find jobs. Economists define the **unemployed** as those individuals who do not have jobs but who are actively seeking work.

Besides imposing costs on individuals, unemployment generates a cost for the economy because it produces fewer goods and services. When the economy does not provide enough jobs to employ everyone who is seeking work, the productivity of that unemployed labor is forgone. This lost output, combined with the hardship that unemployment imposes on individuals and their families, is the real cost of unemployment.

Measuring Unemployment

The unemployment rate is a closely watched measure of an economy's health. How is the unemployment rate calculated, and what does it mean?

Every month, the U.S. Bureau of Labor Statistics conducts a random survey of about 60,000 households to gather information on labor market activities. The survey divides the adult (16 years old and over) population into three categories:

- Those who have jobs are classified as employed.
- Those who don't have jobs but are looking for them and are available for work are classified as unemployed.
- Those who don't have jobs and are not looking for work are not classified as members of the labor force.

The **unemployment rate** (known as "U-3") is the number of people who are unemployed divided by the civilian labor force (the number of people holding or seeking jobs).

$$\text{Unemployment rate} = \frac{\text{Number of persons unemployed}}{\text{Number of persons in the labor force}}$$

For example, in 2022, the unemployment rate was 3.6 percent:

$$\text{Unemployment rate} = \frac{5{,}999{,}600}{164{,}287{,}000} = 3.6 \text{ percent}$$

Although the overall unemployment rate in 2022 was 3.6 percent, the burdens of unemployment were not equally distributed. As seen in Table 11.2, unemployment rates tend to vary considerably among different groups in society. In particular, the unemployment rate among Blacks and African Americans has been roughly double the unemployment rate among whites. This may be the result of the concentration of Blacks and African Americans in less-skilled occupations or in the inner city, where job opportunities are negligible and there is discrimination in employment and education. Moreover, teenagers tend to have much higher unemployment rates than adults. This is largely because teenagers have relatively modest job skills, have little geographic mobility, and more frequently leave their jobs than adults.

TABLE 11.2 The Burden of Unemployment: Civilian Unemployment Rates, 2000–2022 (percent)

	2022	*2015*	*2010*	*2005*	*2000*
All civilian workers	3.6%	5.3%	9.6%	5.1%	4.0%
Men, 20 years and over	3.4	4.9	9.8	4.4	3.3
Women, 20 years and over	3.3	4.8	8.0	4.6	3.6
Both sexes, 16–19 years	10.8	16.9	25.9	16.6	13.1
White	3.2	4.6	8.7	4.4	3.5
Black or African American	6.1	9.6	16.0	10.0	7.6
Asian	2.8	3.8	7.5	4.0	3.6
Hispanic or Latino	4.3	5.8	12.5	6.0	5.7

Source: Data drawn from *Economic Report of the President*, 2023, Table B-27, available at https://www.whitehouse.gov/wp-content/uploads/2023/03/ERP-2023.pdf. See also Bureau of Labor Statistics, *The Employment Situation*, available at https://www.bls.gov/news.release/pdf/empsit.pdf.

Although the Bureau of Labor Statistics takes great care in calculating the unemployment rate, it suffers from several shortcomings. Part-time employment represents one problem. Although some part-time workers work less than a full week because they want to, others do so only because they cannot find a suitable full-time job. Nevertheless, a worker who has been cut back to part-time work is still counted as employed, even if that worker would prefer to work full-time. During a recession, workers may find their work hours reduced from 40 hours to 30 hours a week because of slack demand for the product their employer produces. Because the statistics don't measure the "underemployment" of these workers, they tend to *underestimate* the actual extent of unemployment in the economy.

Unemployment statistics also suffer from the problem of discouraged workers. A **discouraged worker** is a person who is out of work, would like to work, and is available for work but has stopped looking for work because of lack of success in finding a job. Discouraged workers also include people who have completely given up on finding a job. Discouraged workers are not considered part of the labor force because they are not actively seeking employment. As a result, we do not count them as unemployed. Because the official unemployment rate does not include discouraged workers, the actual degree of unemployment in the economy tends to be underestimated.

Table 11.3 adjusts the unemployment rate (U-3) for people who must settle for part-time work for economic reasons and those who are "discouraged workers." The revised unemployment rate is known as U-6 and is a broader measure of the unemployment situation in the United States. For example, during the Great Recession of 2007–2009, the unemployment rate as measured by U-6 was much higher than that measured by

TABLE 11.3 Civilian Unemployment Rate Adjusted for Part-time Workers and Discouraged Workers

Year	*Civilian Unemployment Rate, U-3 (percent)*	*Civilian Unemployment Rate Adjusted for Part-Time Workers and Discouraged Workers, U6 (percent)*
2008	5.8	10.5
2010	9.6	16.7
2012	8.1	14.7
2014	6.2	12.0
2016	4.9	9.6
2018	3.9	7.7
2020	8.1	13.6
2022	3.6	6.9

Source: Data drawn from *Economic Report of the President*, 2023, Table B-27, available at https://www.whitehouse.gov/wp-content/uploads/2023/03/ERP-2023.pdf. See also U.S. Bureau of Labor Statistics, *Alternative Measures of Labor Underutilization*.

U-3, as seen in the table. Indeed, the actual degree of unemployment in the economy was underestimated by U-3.

Three Kinds of Unemployment

Not everyone who is unemployed is unemployed for the same reason. Unemployment is classified into three types based on its causes. As you will see, some kinds of unemployment may not be as important as others.

Some people are unemployed because they cannot currently find work that matches their qualifications. For example, think of college students majoring in accounting or computer science. When they finish school, they will look for jobs that match their skills, but finding such jobs may take time. Yet the students will likely find jobs soon because their skills are marketable. This unemployment is temporary. Economists refer to this type of unemployment as frictional unemployment. **Frictional unemployment** is the unemployment that arises from normal labor turnover—that is, when people are "between jobs." Frictional unemployment is not of much concern when dealing with the national unemployment problem.

However, not all unemployment is short-lived. **Structural unemployment** is unemployment that occurs when individuals' skills do not match what employers require or when job seekers are geographically separated from job opportunities. Substantial structural unemployment is often found alongside job vacancies because the unemployed lack the skills required for newly created jobs. For example, there may be vacancies for electrical engineers while truck drivers are unemployed. Moreover, there may be worker shortages in the Southwestern states that are undergoing economic growth and unemployment in states that are suffering economic contraction, as in the Midwest during the era of weak demand for U.S. automobiles in the 1980s. Because both skill and location problems are usually of long duration, structural unemployment is perhaps the most serious type of unemployment.

Cyclical unemployment is the fluctuating unemployment that coincides with the business cycle. Cyclical unemployment is a repeating short-run problem. The amount of cyclical unemployment increases when the economy goes into a slump and decreases when the economy goes into an expansion. A steelworker who is laid off because the economy enters a recession and is rehired several months later when the upswing occurs experiences cyclical unemployment. Government policymakers are especially interested in decreasing both the frequency and extent of this type of unemployment by reducing the frequency and extent of the recessions that account for it. The government also attempts to lessen the impact of a recession by providing unemployment compensation for those who are temporarily laid off.

Mitigating the Costs of Unemployment

The U.S. government has policies and programs at its disposal to reduce the costs that unemployment imposes on some workers. The main policy instrument used to address the immediate needs of workers who lose their jobs is the **unemployment insurance** system. Other policies, such as mandatory advance notice of layoffs, may provide short-run benefits as well. Still other policies, such as education and training programs, attempt to improve the longer-term fortunes of those hurt by unemployment.

Unemployment insurance was established in the United States as part of the Social Security Act of 1935. This system helps support consumer spending during periods of job loss and provides economic security to workers through income maintenance. Another potential benefit of the unemployment insurance system is that it provides individuals with the financial resources to prolong their job search until they receive an offer that is appropriate to their skills. Although the federal government maintains control over the broad design of the unemployment insurance system, individual states have considerable autonomy in tailoring the program's features within their jurisdictions.

Unemployment insurance provides weekly benefits to workers who have been laid off or who have lost their jobs for reasons other than misconduct or a labor dispute. Only workers with a sufficiently long employment history—usually six months of significant employment—are eligible. Benefits are a fraction of the average weekly earnings on the job that was lost, up to a maximum dollar amount, and paid for up to 26 weeks in most states. This fraction is typically between 50 percent and 70 percent. Benefits are financed, in most states, by a payroll tax levied on firms.

Although the unemployment insurance system has benefited millions of workers over the years, these benefits do not come without costs. Some economists contend that higher unemployment benefits lead to longer unemployment spells. Providing benefits to unemployed workers reduces their incentive to search intensively for a new job.

What Is Full Employment?

Indeed, a high-employment economy provides benefits for society. But what do economists mean by full employment? Does full employment mean zero unemployment?

Recall that total unemployment in an economy consists of frictional, structural, and cyclical unemployment. We call the level of unemployment at which there is no cyclical unemployment the **natural rate of unemployment**. In other words, the natural rate of unemployment is the sum of frictional and structural unemployment, which economists consider as essentially unavoidable. The natural rate of unemployment is economists' notion of full employment. Therefore, we define **full employment** as something less than 100-percent employment of the labor force. In the United States today, most economists estimate that the natural rate of unemployment is around 4 percent.

Notice that the natural rate of unemployment can vary over time. Changes in the natural rate of unemployment occur in response to shifting demographics of the labor force or changes in society's customs and laws. In the early 1990s, for example, structural unemployment increased because of corporate downsizing and decreases in defense spending. These changes increased the natural rate of unemployment. However, the aging of the workforce in the 2000s will likely decrease the amount of frictional unemployment because older workers are less likely to quit their jobs than are younger workers. This will cause the natural rate of unemployment to decrease. Not only can the natural rate of unemployment change over time, but also it tends to differ among countries.

INFLEXIBLE LABOR MARKETS AND JOBS

We have learned how the business cycle can affect a country's unemployment rate. As the economy dips into recession, business sales and profits decrease, as does the demand for workers. This causes the unemployment rate to rise.

Another determinant of the unemployment rate is the degree of flexibility in a country's labor market. **Labor market flexibility** refers to how rapidly a company responds to changing conditions in the market by making changes to its workforce. If labor markets are flexible, companies have considerable leeway to make decisions regarding the hiring or firing of workers, the level of wages and benefits, and the prevailing working conditions. This allows companies to quickly adapt to evolving economic circumstances.

For example, during an economic downturn, an employer with flexibility can reduce wages or decrease the number of hours that employees will work. Conversely, when the economy rebounds, the employer may choose to give employees a raise or increase their hours.

However, employers do not have complete freedom to modify employees' compensation or working conditions because government has laws and regulations that protect workers. Also, workers may form unions to protect their jobs, compensation, and working conditions, thus making labor markets less flexible.

Proponents argue that increased flexibility in labor markets can lead to higher labor productivity and improved vitality for firms. They also maintain that countries with highly regulated and inflexible labor markets tend to have higher rates of unemployment and lower per-capita income. However, critics contend that flexibility puts all the economic power in the hands of the employer, potentially resulting in unfair conditions for workers. Therefore, the goal of promoting labor market flexibility may clash with the goal of preserving social standards for labor.

Europe's Labor Market Inflexibility

Prior to the 1990s, the labor markets of Western Europe were generally characterized as being inflexible. For example, Europe's approach to labor markets was to protect workers, especially low-skilled workers, which kept wages relatively high and penalized firms for firing them. Also, Europe was the birthplace of the welfare state, and countries such as Sweden legislated generous welfare benefits and unemployment insurance. This allowed people a longer period to conduct a job search, thus increasing the natural rate of unemployment. Moreover, European companies paid relatively high employment taxes to help finance the government, which added to the cost of hiring labor. Finally, a high percentage of Europe's labor force was unionized, and this detracted from labor market flexibility. Simply put, labor market rigidities, excessive regulation, and overly generous welfare policies were seen as factors contributing to economic sluggishness and high unemployment rates throughout Europe.

Figure 11.3 helps us understand the significance of labor market inflexibility. Assume that Europe has a relatively inflexible labor market, shown in Figure 11.3(*a*), while the

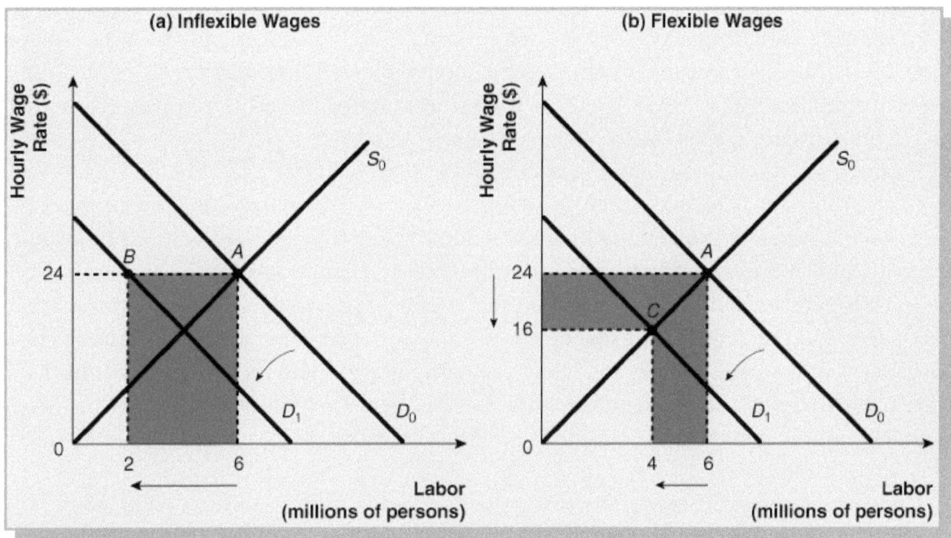

FIGURE 11.3 Rigid Wages Can Result in Involuntary Unemployment

During a business recession, market rigidities may prevent wages from decreasing, resulting in involuntary unemployment. In a flexible labor market, wages decrease during a recession. The wage reduction clears the market of involuntary unemployment. Many believe that Europe's labor market is more rigid, whereas the U.S. labor market is more flexible.

U.S. labor market is relatively flexible, shown in Figure 11.3(*b*). The labor market equilibrium is shown by point *A* in the figures, where the equilibrium wage is $24 per hour.

Due to an economic recession that results in falling sales and output for businesses, suppose that the demand for labor declines in the markets of Europe and the United States. The market rigidities of Europe prevent wages from declining to the new equilibrium at point C, resulting in a relatively large decrease in the quantity of labor demanded at point *B*, from 6 million persons to 2 million persons. In the more flexible U.S. market, however, wages fall during the recession. Although the quantity of labor demanded declines from 6 million persons to 4 million persons during the slump, it does not decrease as much as in Europe. Put simply, the rigidity of Europe's labor market causes a relatively large decline in the quantity of labor demanded and involuntary unemployment.

Many believed that the sluggishness and high unemployment of Western Europe's economy during the 1970s–1980s were caused by labor market rigidity, excessive government regulation, and overly generous welfare payments. The U.S. model of a more flexible labor market was thus seen as a possible solution to Western Europe's problem of high unemployment. During the 1990s and 2000s, the governments of Western Europe began allowing more worker mobility within their labor markets, and they improved the flexibility of regulations. These factors contributed to a more flexible economy that was moving toward openness and entrepreneurship.

PRODUCTIVITY, REAL WAGES, AND JOBS

In 2005, the *Washington Post* ran a story explaining that, a quarter-century ago, General Motors needed about 500,000 workers to turn out 5 million automobiles a year. By the early 2000s, however, improvements in productivity allowed the company to employ only a quarter of those workers to produce the same number of cars. Does this mean that strong productivity growth necessitates job losses?

Productivity is simply the amount of output for a given quantity of labor. Thus, increases in productivity must reflect either an increase in output for a fixed amount of employment or a decrease in the amount of labor required to produce a fixed amount of output. Of course, both the amount of labor and output could change at once.

Ask economists and they will tell you that faster productivity growth leads to higher real wages and improved living standards. Yet if higher productivity allows firms to shed workers, how can it raise wages and living standards? If productivity does lead to improved wages and living standards, why do workers often feel that productivity growth leaves them behind? To answer these questions, we must consider the short- and long-run effects of changes in productivity.

Concerning the short run, if firms see the demand for their products rising, they will respond by expanding production. If labor productivity is unchanged, then typically they will need to hire more workers to increase production. But if labor productivity increases, then it has the potential to reduce employment growth because firms can satisfy demand using fewer workers. Likewise, if the overall demand in the economy has not expanded, then an increase in labor productivity could lead to a fall in unemployment in the short run. In this case, faster productivity growth might lead to an increase in job losses without a corresponding increase in job creation in new and expanding industries. Eventually, employment catches up to the increased levels of output made possible by productivity growth. However, the problem can remain for some time.

In the long run, however, income and employment depend not on demand but instead on supply factors, including the economy's stock of capital, labor force, and technology. Whereas the short-run perspective emphasizes the impact of productivity on the number of workers needed to produce a given level of output, the long-run perspective emphasizes that an increase in labor productivity *increases* potential output. It does so directly by allowing more output to be produced with the same level of employment, but it also increases employment because it decreases the cost of labor to firms.[1] As new technological innovations boost productivity, new industries arise and new jobs are created. The increased demand for labor tends to boost wages as firms compete to hire additional workers and raises total employment.

There is little debate among economists about the long-run effect of productivity on employment: Faster productivity growth should translate into an increase in the overall demand for labor in the economy. This, in turn, will lead real wages to rise, just as an increase in the demand for a typical good or service acts to bid its price up.[2]

CHECK POINT

1. What is meant by the unemployment rate and how is it calculated?
2. Economists classify unemployment according to its causes. Explain.
3. What is meant by full employment and how is it measured?
4. What factors explain unemployment rate differences in the United States and Europe?
5. What is the connection between productivity, real wages, and jobs?

INFLATION

Since the end of World War II, the United States has experienced almost continuous inflation. We can define **inflation** as a sustained or continuous rise in the general price level. We should note several things about this definition. First, inflation refers to the movement in the general level of prices. However, some individual prices may fall. During the 1990s and 2000s, for example, the prices of computers fell, while the prices of many other goods increased. During an inflationary period, rising prices outweigh falling prices, causing the average level of prices to increase. Second, the rise in the price level must be substantial and continue over a period longer than a day, week, or month.

When there is inflation, the purchasing power of a given amount of money will decrease. Table 11.4 shows what would happen to the real value of $10,000, from January 1, 2010,

TABLE 11.4 The Impact of Inflation on the Real Value of $10,000, 2010–2020

	Annual Inflation Rate				
Year	*2 Percent*	*4 Percent*	*6 Percent*	*8 Percent*	*10 Percent*
2010	$10,000	$10,000	$10,000	$10,000	$10,000
2012	9,610	9,250	8,900	8,570	8,260
2014	9,240	8,550	7,920	7,350	6,830
2016	8,880	7,900	7,050	6,300	5,640
2018	8,530	7,310	6,270	5,400	4,670
2020	8,200	6,760	5,580	4,630	3,860

to January 1, 2020, at different rates of inflation. At 2-percent inflation, $10,000 would purchase only $8,200 of goods in 2020. At 10-percent inflation, that same $10,000 would be worth only $3,860.

The average price level may decrease or increase. We refer to a continuing decline in the average price level as **deflation**. It occurs when price reductions on some goods and services outweigh price increases on all others. The last deflation in the United States occurred during the Great Depression of the 1930s.

Measuring Inflation: The Consumer Price Index

The most frequently cited indicator of inflation is the **consumer price index (CPI)**. The CPI is calculated by the Bureau of Labor Statistics by sampling of thousands of households. When a news report says that the "cost of living" rose by, say, 3 percent, it is usually referring to the CPI.

To construct the CPI, the Bureau of Labor Statistics selects a "market basket" of goods and services that are assumed to be most crucial to the spending of the typical American consumer. Then it assigns weights to those goods and services according to past patterns of consumer expenditures. The major groups of product categories, examples of these categories, and their weights as of 2022 are summarized as:

- Housing (rent equivalent of primary residence, fuel oil, bedroom furniture), 32%
- Food and beverages (breakfast cereal, milk, chicken, wine, full service meals), 14%
- Transportation (new vehicles, airline fares, gasoline, motor vehicle insurance), 13%
- Medical care (prescription drugs, physicians, services, eyeglasses), 7%
- Education and communication (college tuition, postage, telephone services), 6%
- Apparel (men's shirts, women's dresses, jewelry), 3%
- Other goods and services (haircuts, funeral expenses), 25%

Every month, government data collectors visit or call thousands of retail stores, service establishments, rental units, and doctors' offices, all over the United States, to obtain information on the prices of the thousands of items used to track and measure price changes in the CPI. These collectors record the prices of about 80,000 items each month to compute the current cost of the market basket. Because buying patterns change, the market basket is revised about once each decade. Therefore, the CPI measures inflation as experienced by consumers in their day-to-day living expenses.

The Bureau of Labor Statistics arbitrarily sets the average value of the goods and services in the market basket for some base period (currently 1982–1984 = 100). Referring to Table 11.5, we see that the CPI was 296.8 in 2022. This means that prices in 2022 were 296.8 percent *higher* than the prices in the base period. A typical bundle of goods and services worth $1,000 in the base period would have cost $2,968 in 2022 ($1,000 X 2.968 = $2,968).

Once we have the CPI for selected years, we can calculate the rate of inflation between years. We use the following formula:

$$\text{Rate of inflation} = \frac{\text{CPI}_{\text{Given year}} - \text{CPI}_{\text{Previous year}}}{\text{CPI}_{\text{Previous year}}} \times 100$$

TABLE 11.5 Consumer Price Index and the Annual Rate of Inflation, 2013–2022

Year	*Consumer Price Index, December (1982–1984 = 100)*	*Yearly Percentage Change in Consumer Price Index*
2013	233.0	1.5
2014	234.8	0.8
2015	236.5	0.7
2016	241.1	1.9
2017	246.5	2.2
2018	251.2	1.9
2019	256.9	2.3
2020	260.5	1.4
2021	278.8	7.0
2022	296.8	6.5

Source: Data drawn from *Economic Report of the President*, 2023, Table B-38, available at https://www.whitehouse.gov/wp-content/uploads/2023/03/ERP-2023.pdf and U.S. Bureau of Labor Statistics, *Consumer Price Index Historical Tables for U.S. City Average*, April 2023, available at https://www.bls.gov/regions/mid-atlantic/data/consumerpriceindexhistorical_us_table.htm.

For example, suppose that we wanted to compute the rate of inflation between 2022 and 2021. Referring to Table 11.5, we see that the CPI equaled 296.8 in 2022 and 278.8 in 2021. The rate of inflation between the two years thus equals 6.5 percent, calculated as follows:

$$\text{Rate of inflation} = \frac{296.8 - 278.8}{278.8} \times 100 = 6.5 \text{ percent}$$

The CPI is the principal source of information concerning trends in consumer prices and inflation in the United States. The CPI is used as the basis for making cost-of-living adjustments to the wages paid to millions of union workers, payments to Social Security recipients and retirees of the federal government and military, and entitlement programs such as the Supplemental Nutrition Assistance Program. Also, many banks link the interest rates they charge on mortgages, automobile loans, and personal loans to the CPI. Moreover, individual income tax brackets and personal exemptions are adjusted upward to account for the rate of inflation. Finally, the Federal Reserve bases its monetary policy on the rate of inflation as measured by the CPI.

Although the CPI is used as a measure of the cost of living for a typical urban family, it is an imperfect measure. One weakness of the CPI is that people's buying patterns change, so that the change in what people spend on "living" deviates from measured increases in, say, bacon and eggs. As some prices rise, people switch to cheaper goods. Thus, the CPI overstates the actual cost of living.

Another problem with the CPI is that its fixed market basket fails to keep pace with the development of better products, such as computers offering greater memory and faster speeds. The price of a new computer may be higher, but its capabilities may be much better than those of an older model. Part of a price increase may reflect higher quality rather than simply a higher price for the same product. To the extent that product quality improves, the CPI overstates the rate of inflation.

Finally, the CPI ignores price discounting. New types of discount stores, such as Costco and Walmart, have gained an increased share of the market by offering lower prices than their competitors. Again, the CPI overstates the rate of inflation. For these reasons, most economists maintain that the CPI overstates inflation, but there is no consensus about the amount of overstatement.

Other measures of inflation include the producer price index, which looks at the cost of inputs into the production process, and the GDP price deflator, which considers all goods and services that are part of gross domestic product, which excludes imports and includes exports.

WHO BENEFITS FROM AND WHO IS HURT BY INFLATION?

Why are economists concerned about inflation? As we will see, inflation can greatly affect the national standard of living. It can also influence economic behavior and lead to significant impacts on the operation of the economy.

Inflation and the Purchasing Power of Income

No matter what the rate of inflation, it is interesting to know whether you are beating inflation or whether inflation is beating you. In other words, has your nominal income increased by a smaller percentage, the same percentage, or a greater percentage than the inflation rate?

To answer this question, we must adjust nominal income for changes in the price level. **Nominal income** is the actual number of dollars of income received during a year. **Real income** is the actual number of dollars received (nominal income) adjusted for any change in price. Real income, therefore, measures your real purchasing power—the amount of goods and services that can be purchased with your nominal income. Real income is computed as follows:

$$\text{Real income} = \frac{(\text{Nominal income})}{\text{CPI}} \times 100$$

This formula can help us determine whether we are beating inflation.

For example, assume that Emily's nominal income rises from $50,000 in 2021 to $56,000 in 2022, an increase of 12 percent. Also suppose the CPI rises from 278.8 in 2021 to 296.8 in 2022, an increase of 6.5 percent. Because Emily's nominal income rose by a greater percentage than the inflation rate, she has more than kept up with inflation. In other words, her real income rose from 2021 to 2022. Using the preceding formula, we can calculate her real income, stated in terms of the base year, for the two years, as follows:

$$\text{Realincome}_{2021} = (50{,}000 / 278.8) \times 100 = \$17{,}934$$
$$\text{Realincome}_{2022} = (56{,}000 / 296.8) \times 100 = \$18{,}868$$

Emily's real income has risen from $17,934 in 2021 to $18,868 in 2022.

The preceding example illustrates how inflation affects real purchasing power. Conclusion: If your nominal income increases by a greater percentage than the inflation rate, then your purchasing power rises. But if the inflation rate rises faster than your nominal income, then your purchasing power falls.

Concerning the purchasing power of income, have you ever wondered what a "Big Mac" hamburger sandwich, sold by McDonald's, costs throughout the world? Every year, *The Economist* publishes the so-called Big Mac Index, as shown in Table 11.6. For example, in January 2023, the cheapest burger on the chart was sold in Israel at $5.05, compared with an average American price of $5.15. American tourists traveling to Israel would find Big Macs a good buy, but not a good buy in Switzerland, where the price was $7.26.

Redistribution of Wealth from Lenders to Borrowers

What is the impact of inflation on lenders and borrowers? To the extent that inflation is unanticipated, it creates winners and losers among these groups. If inflation is higher than anticipated, the winners are those who agreed to borrow money at an interest rate that did

TABLE 11.6 The Price of a Big Mac, January 2023

Country	*Big Mac Price (in U.S. dollars)*
Switzerland	7.26
Uruguay	6.85
Norway	6.59
Argentina	5.31
Euro Area	5.29
United States	5.15
Australia	5.11
Lebanon	5.08
Saudi Arabia	5.05
Israel	5.05

Source: Data drawn from *Global Price of a Big Mac as of January 2023, by Country*, Statista, available at https://www.statista.com/statistics/274326/big-mac-index-global-prices-for-a-big-mac.

not reflect the higher inflation. The losers are all of those who lend money at that interest rate. In other words, unanticipated inflation benefits people who are in debt because the purchasing power of their dollars will decrease over the life of the loan. Borrowers thus pay back principal and interest using dollars that are less valuable than they were when they incurred the loan. As a result, unanticipated inflation results in a decrease in purchasing power for lenders.

The federal government is another debtor that has benefited from unanticipated inflation. Historically, the federal government has financed its budget deficits by borrowing from the public through the sales of Treasury bills and other securities. Unanticipated inflation has allowed the federal government to pay off its loans using dollars that have less purchasing power than the dollars it originally borrowed. Therefore, unanticipated inflation decreases the real burden of the public debt to the federal government.

Indeed, unanticipated inflation may cause a redistribution of wealth from lenders to borrowers. However, if inflation is steady and predictable, many people may correctly anticipate its effects on the purchasing power of money and thus can avoid the decline in real income that inflation causes. For example, if the lending officer at Wells Fargo Bank correctly anticipates inflation, they can avoid the unwanted impact on the bank's real income by attaching an inflation premium to the nominal interest rate they charge for new auto or real estate loans. The additional nominal interest rate compensates the bank for the loss in the purchasing power of money attributable to inflation.

Inflation and Real Interest Rates

Inflation may also hurt savers and investors. For example, suppose that you have a two-year certificate of deposit that yields 6 percent per year. If inflation is 10 percent per year, you will lose on your savings each year. Although you will receive interest payments of 6 percent, they will not keep pace with 10-percent inflation. The result will be a decline in your purchasing power.

The interest rate that the bank pays is called the **nominal interest rate**, and the interest rate that is adjusted for inflation is called the **real interest rate**. The relationship between the nominal interest rate and the real interest rate is given by the following formula:

$$\text{Real interest rate} = \text{Nominal interest rate} - \text{inflation rate}$$

The real interest rate is the difference between the nominal interest rate and the inflation rate. Although the nominal interest rate is positive, the real interest rate can be positive or negative. When the real interest rate is negative, savers and lenders are hurt because interest does not keep pace with inflation. Table 11.7 shows the real and nominal interest rates for the United States and other countries as of 2023.

Because inflation threatens people's financial well-being by reducing the purchasing power of their money, they take great pains to find investments for which returns exceed the inflation rate, such as stocks, bonds, and other financial instruments. When returns are corrected for inflation, however, investors sometimes see negative numbers.

TABLE 11.7 Nominal Interest Rates and Real Interest Rates Around the World, 2023 (percent)*

Country	*Nominal Interest Rate*	*Inflation Rate*	*Real Interest Rate*
Brazil	12.9%	5.6%	7.3%
South Africa	10.0	7.3	2.7
China	2.7	1.0	1.7
Mexico	9.2	7.6	1.6
Russia	10.8	11.0	–0.2
Philippines	6.3	8.6	–2.3
United States	3.5	6.0	–2.5
Great Britain	3.4	10.4	–7.0
Turkey	11.9	52.2	–40.3

* 10-year government bonds.

Source: Data drawn from *The Economist*, "Economic and Financial Indicators," March 25, 2023.

In 1997, the U.S. government made financial history by issuing the first U.S. security indexed to the rate of inflation, dubbed Treasury inflation-protection securities (TIPS). Now, U.S. investors can purchase a financial instrument that provides a guaranteed hedge against the loss of purchasing power that accompanies increases in the CPI. Another inflation-indexed security of the U.S. government is the I-Bond (Series I Savings Bond), introduced in 1998.

Inflation and Taxpayers

Before 1985, inflation hurt taxpayers because it pushed up tax bills without any explicit changes in the tax laws. The reason: Part of our country's tax system was based on nominal income instead of real income. During this era, the progressive structure of the individual income tax ensured that as incomes rose during a time of inflation, the average rate of tax paid by most taxpayers went up. In other words, tax bills didn't just rise as fast as inflation—they actually rose faster.

To illustrate, suppose that the average price level rises by 10 percent from year 1 to year 2. Suppose also that Alice has a cost-of-living provision in her labor contract that causes her nominal wages to increase by 10 percent from year 1 to year 2. On the surface, it appears that she broke even with inflation. Yet this does not account for the fact that a 10-percent rise in nominal income will push Alice into a higher tax bracket with a higher tax rate. Although Alice's nominal income keeps pace with inflation, her real income falls because she pays a higher tax rate because of inflation. Alice's real income is redistributed to the government and ultimately to those who benefit from government spending. Notice that Alice's tax rate increases without any congressional action to increase taxes. Critics refer to this situation as *taxation without representation*.

To prevent the redistribution of real income through the federal personal income tax system, in 1985, the U.S. government indexed the federal personal income tax. Each year, tax brackets and personal exemptions are now corrected to reflect the rate of inflation. Therefore, households are pushed into a higher tax bracket only if their real incomes increase, not by inflation alone.

EFFECTS OF SEVERE INFLATION

During periods of severe inflation, when the annual rate of inflation is 10 percent or higher, economic behavior may change. Many people feel discouraged because their income cannot keep up with rising prices. They cannot plan for future expenses because they do not know how much their money will buy later.

Some consumers fight the effects of inflation by purchasing more than usual during an inflationary period. Many consumers borrow money or use credit for large expenses instead of purchasing later when prices will probably have risen even further. Moreover, some consumers may barter their services, do their own home repairs, or make their own clothing.

Some people attempt to protect themselves against inflation by investing in items that quickly increase in value. Such items include gold bars, rare stamps, gold and silver coins, diamonds, and art objects. Many people purchase real estate during inflationary periods because the value of land and buildings tends to increase rapidly at such times.

Some businesses may prosper during periods of inflation. They include discount stores, credit card agencies, and agencies that collect overdue debts. Businesses that lease items such as large appliances and automobiles, which many people cannot afford to purchase, also thrive at these times.

It is possible for a country to experience **hyperinflation**, a rapid and uncontrolled inflation that destroys its economy. For example, hyperinflation caused the collapse of the German economy after World War I ended in 1918. The German government printed large amounts of currency to finance itself after the war. Therefore, prices in Germany increased more than 1 trillion percent from August 1922 to December 1923. In 1923, $1 in U.S. currency was worth more than 4 trillion marks! Many Germans took to burning their paper money because it was a cheaper source of fuel than firewood.

The hyperinflation left a traumatic impression on the German economy. Business owners discovered the impossibility of rational economic planning. Profits declined as employees demanded frequent increases in wages. Workers were often paid daily and sometimes two and three times a day, so that they could purchase goods in the morning before the inevitable afternoon increase in prices. Workers became demoralized and were reluctant to work as their money became worthless or virtually worthless. Also, patrons at restaurants found that they had to pay more for their meals than was listed on the menu when they ordered. Speculation became rampant, which disrupted production. The result was a 600-percent increase in unemployment between September 1 and December 15, 1923. As the hyperinflation intensified, people could not find goods on the shelves of retailers. Indeed, hyperinflation crushed the middle class of Germany and left an imprint on the country that affects its governmental policy to this day.

CAUSES OF INFLATION

Recall that inflation is an increase in the general level of prices and that prices are the result of the interaction of buyers' demand and sellers' supply decisions. Therefore, forces taking place on the buyers' side of the market or the sellers' side of the market may cause inflation. Inflation originating from upward pressure on the buyers' side of the market is called **demand-pull inflation**. Inflation caused by upward pressure on the sellers' side of the market is termed **cost-push inflation**.

The most familiar type of inflation is demand-pull inflation, which occurs when buyers' demands to purchase goods and services outrun sellers' capacities to supply them, thus forcing up prices on the goods and services that are available. Businesses cannot respond to this excess demand because all available resources are fully employed. Demand-pull inflation is often described as a situation in which "too much money chases too few goods."

However, some economists argue that inflation is caused on the sellers' side of the market. When businesses raise their prices in response to cost increases, the result is cost-push inflation. Workers then may demand higher wages to keep up with rising prices, and a wage-price spiral occurs. If wages and prices rise but production does not, the supply of goods and services cannot meet the demand for those items.

Cost-push inflation also occurs if a limited number of businesses control the supply of certain products. The increase in oil prices during the 1970s provides a good example. During this period, the Organization of Petroleum Exporting Countries limited the supply of oil in order to drive prices up and thus earn higher profits. Because oil is a resource that is used to make other goods, the cost of those items also rose, resulting in cost-push inflation.

This chapter has considered the impacts of the business cycle, unemployment, and inflation on the economy. In the next chapter, we will use aggregate demand curves and aggregate supply curves to analyze the causes of macroeconomic instability.

CHECK POINT

1 What is inflation and how is it measured?
2 Who is helped or hurt by inflation?
3 What are the sources of inflation?

CHAPTER SUMMARY

1 The business cycle refers to recurrent ups and downs in the level of economic activity extending over several years. Although business cycles may vary in intensity and duration, we can divide each into four phases: Peak, recession, trough, and recovery.

2 When real GDP decreases for at least two consecutive quarters, we say that the economy is in a recession. A depression is a very deep and prolonged recession. Because no subsequent recession has approached the severity of the Great Depression, the term depression is often used to refer to the slump of the 1930s.

3 Many economists believe that a change in total spending is the immediate determinant of domestic output and employment. However, other economists maintain that business cycles are caused by changes in the supply side of the market, such as the development of better technologies or decreases in natural resources.

4 The unemployment rate is the number of people who are unemployed divided by the number of people in the labor force. Although economists take great care in calculating the unemployment rate, it suffers from problems involving the measurement of part-time employment and discouraged workers.

5 Not everyone who is unemployed is unemployed for the same reason. In describing labor markets, economists refer to frictional unemployment, cyclical unemployment, and structural unemployment. To mitigate the costs of unemployment, government has many programs, such as education and training programs, and also unemployment insurance.

6 Economists call the level of unemployment at which there is no cyclical unemployment the "natural rate of unemployment." The natural rate of unemployment is the sum of frictional and structural unemployment, and it is the economist's notion of full employment.

7 Inflation is a sustained or continuous rise in the general price level; deflation is a continuing decline in the average price level. The most frequently cited indicator of inflation is the consumer price index.

8 Inflation results in a decrease in the purchasing power of a fixed amount of income, a redistribution of wealth from creditors to debtors, declining real interest rates on savings, and higher tax revenues for the government.

9 Inflation may be caused by forces taking place on the buyers' side of the market or the sellers' side of the market. Inflation originating from upward pressure on the buyers' side of the market is called demand-pull inflation. Conversely, cost-push inflation is caused by upward pressure on the sellers' side of the market.

KEY TERMS AND CONCEPTS

business cycle
peak
recession
trough
recovery
depression
economic shock
unemployed
unemployment rate
discouraged worker
frictional unemployment
structural unemployment
cyclical unemployment
unemployment insurance
natural rate of unemployment
full employment
inflation
deflation
consumer price index (CPI)
nominal income
real income
nominal interest rate
real interest rate
hyperinflation
demand-pull inflation
cost-push inflation

STUDY QUESTIONS AND PROBLEMS

1 Suppose that the Bureau of Labor Statistics announces that of all adult Americans, 129 million are employed, 7 million are unemployed, 3 million are not in the labor force, and 2 million are part-time workers looking for full-time jobs. What is the unemployment rate?

2 Discuss how the following individuals would be affected by inflation of 9 percent per year:

a A student who is heavily indebted with loans

b A retired nurse who is receiving a fixed pension

c An individual who has a savings account that pays an interest rate of 4 percent per year

d An autoworker who has a cost-of-living adjustment included in his labor contract

3 If the consumer price index was 155 last year and is 160 this year, what was this year's rate of inflation?

4 How can you realize an increase in nominal income and a decrease in real income at the same time?

5 Suppose that the interest rate on your passbook savings account is 4 percent per year and this year's inflation rate is 5 percent. Are you better off or worse off as a saver?

6 Assume that the consumer price index equaled 50 in 1960 and 150 in 1990. Suppose that you had $60 in 1990 to purchase goods and services. How much money would you have needed in 1960 to buy the same amount of goods and services?

7 In 1914, Henry Ford paid his employees $5 a day. If the consumer price index was 11 in 1914 and 161 in 1997, how much is the Ford paycheck worth in 1997 dollars?

8 In Table 11.8, compute the inflation rate for 2009–2012. Also compute the real wage in each year.

TABLE 11.8 Inflation and Real Wages

Year	*CPI*	*Inflation Rate*	*Nominal Wage*	*Real Wage*
2019	100		$12.00	
2020	106		14.00	
2021	110		15.00	
2022	112		15.50	

9 In Table 11.9, compute the real interest rate for 2010, 2011, and 2012. Assume that the CPI refers to the price level at the end of each year.

TABLE 11.9 Nominal and Real Interest Rates

Year	*Inflation Rate*	*Nominal Interest Rate*	*Real Interest Rate*
2020	6%	8%	
2021	3	3	
2022	5	4	

10 How can hyperinflation result in depression?

NOTES

1 For firms, the relevant cost of labor is not measured simply by the wages and benefits paid to the workers. Rather, it is measured by the costs of these wages and benefits *relative* to the output the workers can produce. Just as a rise in wages will increase labor costs if worker productivity remains constant, a rise in labor productivity will lower the cost of labor at a given level of wages and benefits. If higher productivity makes labor less costly, firms will find it profitable to expand employment.

2 Carl Walsh, "The Productivity and Jobs Connection: The Long and the Short Run of It," *Economic Letter*, Federal Reserve Bank of San Francisco, July 16, 2004; and Mark Schweitzer and Saeed Zaman, "Are We Engineering Ourselves Out of Manufacturing Jobs?" *Economic Commentary*, Federal Reserve Bank of Cleveland, January 1, 2006.

CHAPTER 12

Macroeconomic Instability: Aggregate Demand and Aggregate Supply

CHAPTER OBJECTIVES

After reading this chapter, you should be able to:

1 Explain why the classical economists felt that the economy would automatically move to full employment and why John Maynard Keynes argued that the market economy is inherently unstable.
2 Develop a macroeconomic model of aggregate demand and aggregate supply to understand how prices and output are determined in the short run.
3 Use the model of aggregate demand and aggregate supply to analyze the origins of recession and inflation.
4 Distinguish between demand-pull inflation and cost-push inflation.
5 Identify policies that the government might use to counteract recession or inflation.

DOI: 10.4324/9781003438571-15

ECONOMICS IN CONTEXT

For American consumers in the late 1990s, it couldn't get much better: Unemployment was down and real wages were growing. With higher incomes, consumers went on a spending spree.

Consider Mary Ann Turnquist, a typical American consumer. In 1999, she and her husband Fred purchased a four-bedroom home for $398,000 in Boulder, Colorado. They then spent $3,500 in cash on a new bedroom set and $7,000 on new kitchen and laundry appliances. The couple, she a clerk in the state court and he a truck mechanic, were not concerned about their job security or paying off their mortgage. With a strong economy in 1999, they had every right to feel secure. So did most Americans.

Indeed, consumers had plenty of cash to spend, which supported their spending sprees. For example, steady pay increases prompted Pam Miller of Pittsburgh to buy a new Ford Taurus to replace her Mercury Sable. Nothing was wrong with the five-year-old vehicle, but Pam Miller said that having extra cash gave her an itch for new wheels.

Paychecks went a lot further at the turn of the century, thanks to a low inflation rate that was reinforced by cheap imports from Asia because of its economic crisis. Also, low mortgage rates allowed more families to own homes. Furthermore, consumer installment debt as a percentage of take-home pay had declined, giving consumers more freedom to take out home-equity loans to use for computers, college tuition, and vacations. Finally, the stock market's "bull run" continued to increase household wealth.

However, the economy's dependence on consumers did have its risks. A sudden shock, such as a big decrease in stock prices, could cause consumers to feel less wealthy and snap shut their pocketbooks, leaving businesses with too much inventory and too many workers. Another risk was that all the consumer buying could become too much of a good thing. Excess spending could result in an overheated economy, in which more competition for workers could push labor costs above gains in productivity, resulting in inflation. If that trend continued and businesses started increasing prices, the Federal Reserve might slam on the monetary brakes, perhaps pushing the economy into recession.

Indeed, the growth performance of the U.S. economy has been uneven. In most years, the output of goods and services rises as a result of increases in the capital stock and labor force, and advances in technological knowledge. In some years, however, economic growth does not take place. Firms find themselves unable to sell the goods and services that they have produced, so they shut down factories and lay off workers. As a result, the economy's real gross domestic product (GDP) declines.

The central focus of macroeconomics is what causes short-run fluctuations in economic activity and what, if anything, the government can do to promote full employment without inflation. To answer these questions, we need a model of the macroeconomy. Most economists use the model of aggregate demand and aggregate supply. In this chapter, we will develop aggregate demand and aggregate supply curves that will help us analyze the problems of recession and inflation.

THE STABILITY OF THE MACROECONOMY

The stability of the macroeconomy is of concern to households, businesses, and government. Let us examine the classical and Keynesian views concerning this topic.

The Classical View

Prior to the Great Depression of the 1930s, a group of economists known as the classical economists dominated economic thinking. According to **classical economists**, the market economy automatically adjusts to ensure the full employment of its resources. Although an economic downturn might force producers to decrease their output and lay off workers, the downturn would be short-lived. Because the classical economists believed economic downturns to be temporary, they argued that the government should not interfere in economic affairs.

The optimism of the classical economists was founded on the assumption of freely flexible wages and flexible prices. If some workers become unemployed during an economic slump, they argued, they will make themselves attractive to employers by offering their services at lower wages. As wages fall, firms will find it more profitable to hire workers. As a result, the downward adjustment in wages would guarantee that everyone who wants a job can find one.

Flexible prices also help eliminate an economic downturn, according to the classical economists. During a recession, firms realize a decrease in demand for products. To clear the market of excess supply, they are willing to accept price reductions. If prices decline enough, all the output produced can be sold. Therefore, workers need not be laid off because of declining consumer demand.

The classical economists also contended that the economy would never suffer from a level of spending that would be inadequate to purchase the full-employment level of output. This contention was based on Say's Law, attributed to the 19th-century economist Jean-Baptiste Say. According to **Say's Law**, "supply creates its own demand." Whatever is produced (supplied) will create the income necessary to purchase that production. Say's Law thus suggests that there will always be enough spending to buy the full-employment output. Thus, overproduction is an impossibility according to classical economists. Simply put, the classical model attempted to explain the long-run behavior of the economy in terms of powerful forces that drive the economy to full employment.

The Great Depression

Although the classical economists advocated the impossibility of long-run unemployment, the Great Depression was a stunning blow to their theory. The depression was a global economic downturn that lasted for more than a decade. It was the worst and longest period of low business activity and high unemployment in modern times. It even caused some nations to change their leader and type of government.[1]

The Great Depression began in October, 1929, when stock values in the United States declined sharply. Thousands of stockholders lost huge amounts of money, and many went

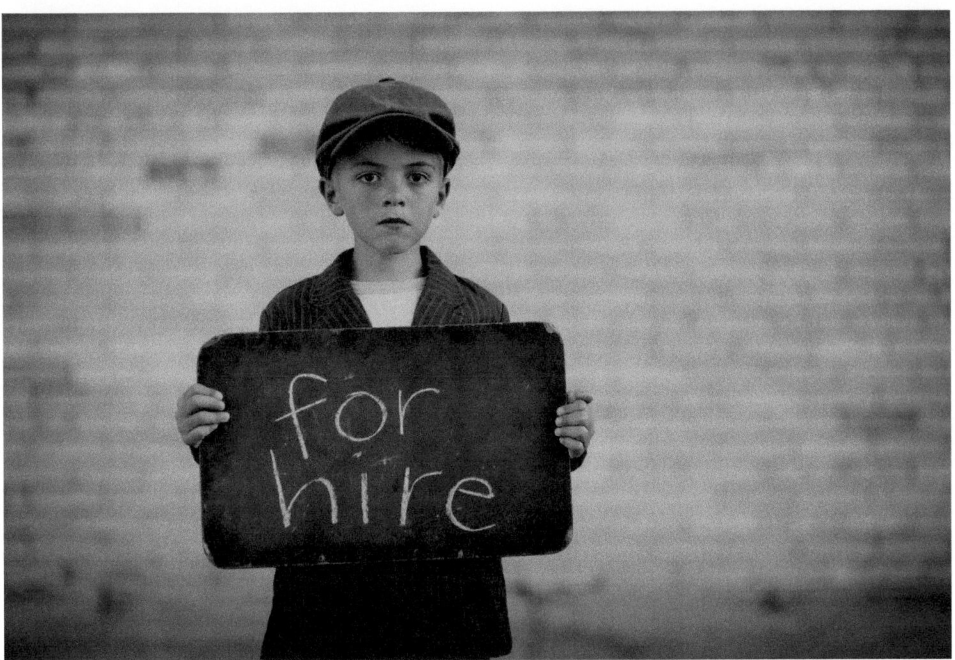

Source: RichVintage/E+/Getty Images®

bankrupt. Factories, banks, and stores shut down, leaving millions of people jobless and penniless. Many Americans had to depend on charity or the government for food and other basic necessities. The Great Depression affected almost every nation. It ended after nations increased their output of war goods at the beginning of World War II. The rising level of production provided jobs and put large sums of money back into circulation.

The depression was caused by several factors. During the 1920s, many bank failures, together with low incomes among farmers and factory workers, set the stage for the depression. Farmers were hit hard by slumping prices of agricultural goods. Although industrial production rose dramatically in the 1920s, the incomes of factory workers rose far more slowly. Thus, these workers could not purchase products as fast as industry produced them. Most economists agree that the stock market crash of 1929 triggered the depression. The crash was the result of rampant speculation, which prompted people to buy stocks in the hopes of making larger profits following future price increases. When stock values decreased dramatically in 1929, many investors panicked and sold huge amounts of stock at a loss.

In 1925, about 3 percent of the nation's workers were unemployed. The unemployment rate rose to 9 percent in 1930 and 25 percent in 1933. Many Americans who maintained or found jobs had to absorb wage reductions. In 1932, wage cuts averaged about 18 percent. Many people, including college graduates, felt lucky to find any job. In 1932, the New York City Police Department estimated that 8,000 people over the age of 17 sold pencils or shined shoes for a living. A popular song of the 1930s, "Brother, Can You Spare a Dime?" symbolized the despair of Americans.

Herbert Hoover was the president when the depression began. He thought that business, if left alone to operate without government regulation, would correct the economic downturn. He vetoed several bills intended to combat the depression because he believed they provided the federal government with too much power. Instead, he felt that it was the states' responsibility to provide assistance to the poor. Because most Americans thought that Hoover had performed inadequately in combating the depression, they elected Franklin D. Roosevelt as president in 1932.

Roosevelt thought the federal government had a major responsibility to combat the Great Depression. He called Congress to a special session to enact legislation to help the needy. Roosevelt called his program the New Deal. The new laws gave states money for the poor and provided jobs in the construction of such public projects as highways, parks, schools, bridges, and dams. The federal government also fostered recovery by spending large amounts of money and increased trade by lowering tariffs on imported goods, in return for which other nations agreed to lower tariffs on the products they purchased from the United States. Congress also created agencies to supervise banks, prevent unfair labor practices, and protect investors from purchasing unsafe stocks and bonds. In 1935, Congress passed the Social Security Act to provide money for retired and unemployed people. Although the New Deal did not end the depression, it did provide economic relief and renewed the confidence of Americans in the federal government.

The Great Depression altered the opinions of many Americans toward business and the federal government. Prior to the depression, most people considered bankers and business executives the nation's leaders. After the stock market crashed and these leaders could not promote prosperity, many Americans lost confidence in them. They thought that the government, not business, had the responsibility of stabilizing the economy. The stage was set for John Maynard Keynes, and his emphasis on an activist government, to influence economic thinking and policymaking.

The Keynesian View

In 1936, during the Great Depression, British economist **John Maynard Keynes** formed a theory that provided an explanation for prolonged depressed conditions.[2] According to Keynes and his followers, the market economy is inherently unstable, and the Great Depression was no accident: Adverse shocks that occur in one sector of the economy can quickly affect other sectors, causing reductions in total output and employment. Although the classical economists might have been able to explain the economy's operation in the long run, the long run could be a very long time in arriving according to Keynes. Keynes thus developed a macroeconomic model that focused on the causes of economic fluctuations in the short run.

Keynes's main disagreement with classical economists was that prices and wages, he believed, are not sufficiently flexible to guarantee the full employment of resources. According to Keynes, prices and wages are rather inflexible, or "sticky," in a downward direction. Even when demand is weak, Keynes argued, powerful labor unions and large businesses will resist wage and price reductions. Therefore, output and employment fall during economic downturns.

The essence of Keynesian economics is simple: The level of economic activity depends on the total spending of consumers, businesses, and government. If business expectations are pessimistic, investment spending will be reduced, resulting in a series of decreases in total spending. If this should occur, the economy can move into a depression and remain there.

Because the market economy is unstable, Keynes argued that an activist government must intervene to protect jobs and income. To avoid a depression, Keynes recommended that government increase spending, promote lower interest rates, and make more money available for loans. These actions, he maintained, would encourage investment and consumption spending, resulting in a greater increase in national output, employment, and income. Simply put, Keynes was a champion of the modern mixed economy in which government increases its spending during downturns to increase the overall level of demand and, thus, employment.

Keynes's ideas altered the thinking of many economists and became increasingly accepted in colleges and government agencies in the 1940s and 1950s. By the 1960s, most of the economics profession had adopted his theory. Macroeconomics became Keynesian economics, and the classical model was subsequently eliminated from most economics textbooks.

However, a counterrevolution to Keynesian economics emerged during the 1970s and 1980s. Today, many economists who find classical theory inadequate in explaining economic fluctuations in the short run find it useful in explaining long-run economic trends. The policy prescriptions of Keynesian economics will be discussed further in Chapters 13 and 15.

CHECK POINT

1 Why did the classical economists maintain that the market economy would automatically ensure the full employment of its resources?

2 According to John Maynard Keynes, the market economy is inherently unstable and the Great Depression was no accident. Explain.

3 What is the proper role for government in the economy according to the classical economists? According to John Maynard Keynes?

AGGREGATE DEMAND AND AGGREGATE SUPPLY

In the tradition of Keynes, let us develop a model of aggregate demand and aggregate supply that we can use to understand how output and prices are determined in the short run.

Just as we analyze an individual market with a market demand curve and a market supply curve, we analyze fluctuations in the entire economy using a model of aggregate demand and aggregate supply. This model is shown in Figure 12.1. On the vertical axis is

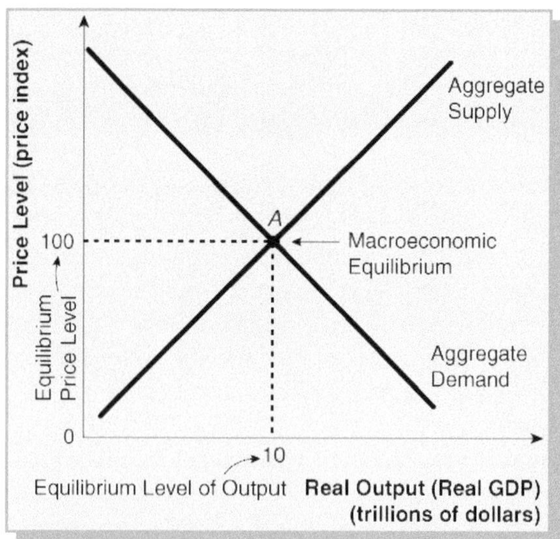

FIGURE 12.1 Macroeconomic Equilibrium

The economy is in equilibrium when aggregate supply equals aggregate demand. This intersection determines the equilibrium price level and output for the economy.

the average price level in the economy, as measured by the consumer price index. On the horizontal axis is the total quantity of goods and services. Because we are adding together many kinds of products, their dollar value is used to represent quantity in Figure 12.1. To keep out the effects of inflation, this quantity is given in *real* terms—that is, real GDP.

In Figure 12.1, the **aggregate demand curve** shows the total demand of all people for all final goods and services produced in an economy. The **aggregate supply curve** is the total supply of all final goods and services in an economy. The economy is in equilibrium when aggregate demand equals aggregate supply. This is where the two lines cross in Figure 12.1 at point *A*. To understand the nature of macroeconomic equilibrium, let us examine the forces that shape the aggregate demand and aggregate supply curves.

AGGREGATE DEMAND

The aggregate demand curve shows the total amount of final goods and services (real GDP) that buyers will purchase at alternative price levels during a given year. Recall that the total amount of final goods and services can be divided into the amounts spent for consumption, investment, government purchases, and net exports. The **aggregate quantity demanded** is the quantity of final output that buyers will purchase at a given price level.

As seen in Figure 12.1, the aggregate demand curve may look like a market demand curve, but it's different. Instead of showing the relationship between the price and quantity demanded of a single good—say, motorcycles—the aggregate demand curve describes the relationship between the price level and the aggregate quantity of all final goods and services demanded in the economy.

Movements Along the Aggregate Demand Curve

Referring to Figure 12.1, notice that the aggregate demand curve is downward-sloping. As the price level *falls*, all else being equal, the total amount of final goods and services purchased *rises*.

To understand this relationship, suppose that households maintain dollar deposits in their savings accounts at banks. The purchasing power of these deposits also depends on the prices of goods and services. For any given amount of deposits, say, $10,000, the purchasing power will rise as the price level falls, and people will demand more of the economy's output of goods and services. Therefore, a decrease in the price of output will result in an increase in the aggregate quantity demanded, and thus the aggregate demand curve is downward-sloping (inversely related to price).[3]

The downward slope of the aggregate demand curve suggests that, all else being equal, a decrease in the price level increases the aggregate quantity of goods and services demanded. Movements along the aggregate demand curve are thus caused by a change in the price level of the economy.

Shifts in the Aggregate Demand Curve

So far, we have found that changes in the price level induce changes in the level of spending by consumers, businesses, government, and foreigners. However, the spending patterns of these sectors are affected by factors other than the price level. If one or more of these other factors change, the aggregate demand curve shifts to a new location.

A change in aggregate demand is shown by a rightward or leftward shift in the aggregate demand curve. An *increase* in aggregate demand is represented by a *rightward* shift in the aggregate demand curve. When aggregate demand increases, a greater quantity of goods and services is demanded at each alternative price. Conversely, a *decrease* in aggregate demand is denoted by a *leftward* shift of the aggregate demand curve.

There are many possible events that can shift the aggregate demand curve. Here are a few examples:

- Because of expectations of a future economic recession, U.S. business firms do not think they can sell all their current output. Therefore, they decrease their purchases of machines and equipment, shifting the aggregate demand curve to the left.
- Economic weakness in Japan slows its economic growth, thereby depressing demand for U.S. exports of beef, lumber, and chemicals. As a result, the aggregate demand curve for the United States shifts to the left.
- Because of political tensions in the Middle East, Congress decides to increase purchases of new weapons systems. As the overall quantity of goods purchased increases, the aggregate demand curve shifts to the right.

THE MULTIPLIER EFFECT

Source: Stone/Chris Stein/Getty Images®

According to Keynesian economics, if an increase in demand occurs in the economy, then the final effect on national output will be much greater. In other words, there will be a multiple expansion of output, similar to the "ripple effect" that results from throwing a rock into a lake. How does this happen?

Suppose that the U.S. government purchases additional uniforms for members of the military. When clothing production increases, the demand for the textiles used in that production also rises. Increasing textile production then strengthens the demand for fibers, aiding the chemical manufacturer, cotton farmer, and sheep rancher alike. And when those producers are also able to sell their goods, the providers of production equipment, parts, fuel, and seed are able to sell theirs. Moreover, commercial support services also feel the prosperity: Software specialists, engineers, architects, bankers, insurance companies, truckers, railroaders, utilities, and construction workers. With U.S. factories in operation, countless small businesses then prosper: the car dealerships, dry cleaners, barbershops, and restaurants, among many local services. Simply put, an increase in one part of the economy moves throughout its length and breadth, aiding owners, workers, suppliers, distributors, communities, states, and ultimately the whole nation. In other words, an improvement in economic activity in one sector of the economy multiplies as it flows through the economy. But these forces also operate in reverse: A decline in one sector of the economy results in a magnified contractionary effect on the overall economy. Economists call this the **multiplier effect**.

To understand the multiplier effect, imagine someone throwing a rock into a pond: There is an initial splash (the increased spending on military uniforms), then additional ripples as the recipients of the initial money spend it, and so on, until the ripples decline in strength as they reach the bank.

The multiplier effect recognizes that all economies experience fluctuations in aggregate demand that can be caused by autonomous changes in spending on consumption, investment, government purchases, and net exports.[4] For example, a rise in aggregate demand of $100 million gives rise to further increases through the impact of higher incomes on consumer spending. This results in, say, a $300 million increase in national output. The **multiplier** is the ratio of the change in national output to the change in aggregate demand; in this example the multiplier equals 3 (300 / 100 = 3). It indicates the extent to which the change in aggregate demand is "multiplied" into changes in larger output. The mechanics of the multiplier effect are discussed in "Exploring Further 12.1" at the end of this chapter.

The multiplier effect is of great importance to economic policymakers. To combat a weak economy, policymakers may inject a stimulus by increasing government expenditures. Such a policy results in an increase in aggregate demand, which can lead to a magnified increase in the economy's output, employment, and income. Indeed, the multiplier effect is an integral part of economic policymaking, as discussed in the next chapter.

BOX ESSAY 12.1 ECONOMICS IN ACTION
The Great Recession and the Paradox of Thrift

Does Rachael Miller, a 93-year-old woman from Orlando, Florida, threaten American capitalism? The story began in 1964 when her husband bought her a car and Rachel began cruising the roadways in a new, $3,000 yellow Mercury Comet. Forty-eight years, and 567,000 miles later, the car was still on the road. Its longevity was aided by 8 replacement mufflers and 18 replacement batteries, all free because of lifetime guarantees. In 2012 Rachael retired from the road when she found that she could no longer read the daily newspaper. However, she refused to give the car to her relatives out of fear that they might break it. Indeed, Rachael Miller understood the principle of thrift.

Concerning thrift, during the recession of 2007–2009, American households devoted a larger portion of their income to savings and a smaller portion to consumption as they worried about decreased wealth, high debt, and possible job losses. But as Americans saved more, they were getting poorer. This is what some economists call the "paradox of thrift." It reasons that if everyone tries to save an increasingly larger portion of their income, they would become poorer instead of richer. This is because the economy will slow down from the reduction in spending and the very same people would lose their jobs, which drives down total income and the ability of households as a group to save as much as they did before their spending reduction. In other words, if we all individually reduce our spending in an attempt to increase individual savings, then our collective savings will paradoxically decline because one person's spending is another's income, the fountain from which savings flow.

So how do you get out of this situation? One possibility is for government to make up the shortfall of spending by spending more than it collects in the way of taxes—so that the total level of spending is unchanged. But fiscal stimulus is fraught with danger, not least of which is the current massive public debt faced by the United States and many European economies, as discussed later in this book.

It is important to note that the paradox of thrift is a theory, not a fact, and it is debated within the economics profession. One of the main arguments against the paradox of thrift is that when people increase savings in a bank, the bank has more money to lend, which tends to decrease the interest rate and promote lending and spending. Also, saving stimulates investment in capital goods, which brings prosperity in the long run. Thus, thriftiness is its own reward, just not right this second.

Source: Jonathan Kay, "How a Little Old 93-Year-Old Lady from Florida Threatens American Capitalism," *National Post*, April 12, 2012, available at www.nationalpost.com.

AGGREGATE SUPPLY

Now let's turn to the aggregate supply curve. The aggregate supply curve shows the relationship between the level of prices and the amount of final goods and services (real GDP) that will be produced by the economy each year. The **aggregate quantity supplied** is the quantity of final output that will be supplied by producers at a particular price level. Figure 12.2 shows the economy's aggregate supply curve. When drawing the aggregate supply curve, we assume that all resource prices and the availability of resources in the economy are constant. We also assume that the level of technology remains fixed during the current period. Thus, we consider the aggregate supply curve in the short run.

Movements along the Aggregate Supply Curve

Referring to Figure 12.2, notice that the aggregate supply curve has three segments: A horizontal range at price level 105, a positively sloped range from price level 105 to price level 110, and a vertical range from price level 110 and above.

Along the horizontal segment of the aggregate supply curve, the economy is assumed to be in recession. Notice that the full-employment level of real output is at $14 trillion, far beyond the output levels of the horizontal region of the aggregate supply curve. Recall that during a deep recession or depression there is much excess capacity and many unemployed resources in the economy. Therefore, producers are willing to sell additional output at current prices and workers are willing to work extra hours at current wages.

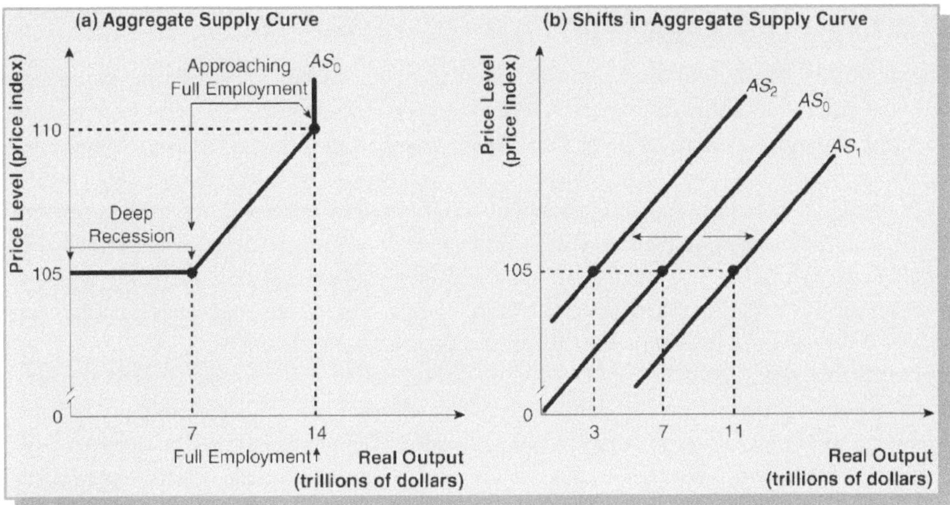

FIGURE 12.2 Aggregate Supply Curve

The aggregate supply curve has three distinct regions: (1) a horizontal region in which the economy is in deep recession or depression, (2) an upward-sloping region in which the economy approaches full employment, and (3) a vertical region in which the economy is at full employment. An increase (decrease) in aggregate supply is denoted by a rightward (leftward) shift of the aggregate supply curve.

Because excess capacity places no upward pressure on prices and wages, changes in aggregate demand cause changes in real output, but no change in the price level—along the horizontal segment of the aggregate supply curve.

Throughout the positively sloped region of the aggregate supply curve, higher price levels provide an incentive for companies to produce and sell additional real output, while lower price levels decrease real output. Therefore, the relationship between the price level and the amount of output that firms offer for sale is positive or direct. Consequently, as the price level rises from 105 to 110, firms find it profitable to increase real output from $7 trillion to $14 trillion. As companies increase production, they hire additional workers, which causes the unemployment rate to decline.

However, there is a physical limit to the amount of output that can be produced in a given year. Once the economy reaches its full-employment output level—$14 trillion in this illustration—the aggregate supply curve becomes vertical. At that point, it is impossible to hire the labor and other resources needed to expand output further. Any rise in the price level will not call forth extra output because the economy is already operating at maximum capacity. Individual companies may attempt to increase output by offering higher wages to attract workers from other companies. This will raise production costs and ultimately prices. However, the extra workers and output that one company gains will be forgone by other companies, which lose workers. Therefore, despite the increase in wage rates and price level, real output will not expand when the economy is at full employment.

Shifts in the Aggregate Supply Curve

The aggregate supply curve shows the quantity of goods and services that companies produce and sell at alternative price levels. However, the amount that firms will produce does not depend on the price level alone. Many events can induce shifts in the aggregate supply curve.

A change in aggregate supply is shown by a rightward or leftward shift in the aggregate supply curve. Referring to Figure 12.2(*b*), an *increase* in aggregate supply is represented by a *rightward* shift in the aggregate supply curve. When aggregate supply increases, a greater quantity of output is supplied at each possible price. Conversely, a *decrease* in aggregate supply is represented by a *leftward* shift in the aggregate supply curve.

Recall that the aggregate supply curve is drawn under the assumption that the level of all resource prices, the availability and quality of resources, and technology are fixed. A change in one or more of these factors will cause the aggregate supply curve to shift. Here are a few examples of events that can result in a shift in the aggregate supply curve.

- Wages and salaries are the largest expense for many companies, typically accounting for 70 to 75 percent of total costs. Therefore, an increase in wages and salaries can result in a significant cost increase. With unit costs rising, a firm cannot produce as much output at any given price. Therefore, a wage or salary increase causes the aggregate supply curve to shift to the left. A rise in the price of other resources will also cause the aggregate supply curve to shift to the left.
- To encourage the economy to increase its stock of capital goods, suppose that the government reduces taxes for businesses. Because the tax cut increases the profitability of investment, businesses purchase new, superior equipment, causing productivity to increase. By reducing per-unit production costs, the increase in productivity allows firms to offer more output at each price level, thus shifting the aggregate supply curve to the right.
- Suppose that entrepreneurs such as Bill Gates develop new technologies that increase the economy's productive capacity. This would decrease the per-unit cost of production and allow more output to be produced at each price. Therefore, the aggregate supply curve shifts to the right.

CHECK POINT

1 What factors account for the inverse relationship between the aggregate quantity demanded and the price level? What events might cause the aggregate demand curve to shift to the right or to the left?

2 What is the multiplier effect? What accounts for the size of the multiplier?

3 Why does the aggregate supply curve have a horizontal region, an upward-sloping region, and a vertical region? What events might cause the aggregate supply curve to shift to the right or to the left?

THE ORIGINS OF RECESSION: NEGATIVE ECONOMIC SHOCKS

Now that we have introduced the model of aggregate demand and aggregate supply, we have the tools we need to consider short-term fluctuations in economic activity. We will first apply the aggregate demand and aggregate supply model to the problem of recession by focusing on negative demand and supply shocks, and then to inflation.

Decreases in Aggregate Demand

Referring to Figure 12.3(*a*), assume that the economy is in equilibrium at point *A*, where the price level is 100 and real output is $12 trillion. Suppose that, for some reason, a wave of pessimism hits the U.S. economy. The source might be an economic crisis in East Asia, a war abroad, or a crash in the stock market. Because of this disturbance, many Americans lose confidence in the future and modify their behavior. Households curtail their purchases of dishwashers and furniture, and companies postpone purchases of new equipment and machinery.

How does this wave of pessimism affect the economy? Such an event decreases the aggregate demand for goods and services. This means that at any given price level, households and companies now desire to purchase a smaller quantity of goods and services. As aggregate demand shifts leftward from AD_0, to AD_1, in Figure 12.3(*a*), the economy

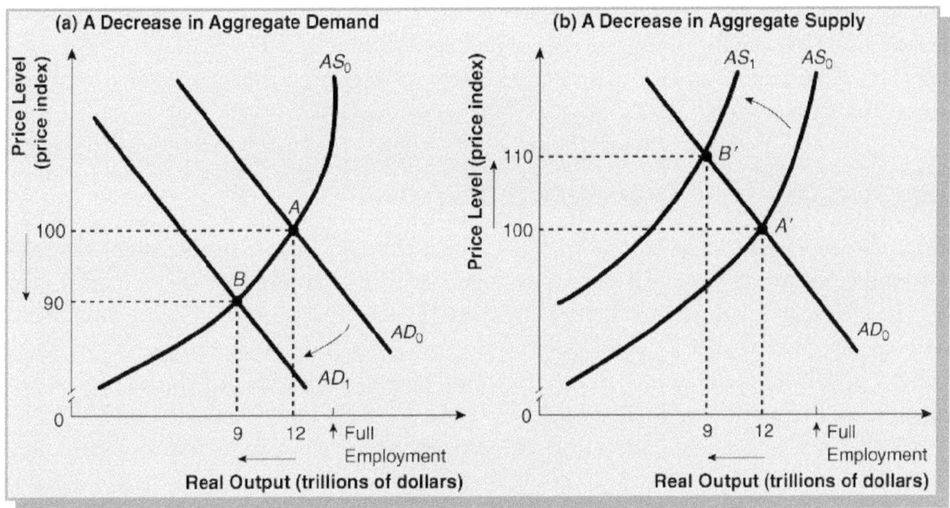

FIGURE 12.3 The Origins of Recession: Negative Economic Shocks

In the short run, a decrease in aggregate demand may cause the economy to move into recession. Government policymakers might attempt to offset the recession by increasing government spending in order to increase aggregate demand. A recession may also be caused by some event, say, rising oil prices, which leads to a decrease in aggregate supply. With a given aggregate demand curve, a decrease in aggregate supply can cause stagflation—a combination of recession and inflation.

moves to equilibrium at point *B*, whereby real output falls to $9 trillion and the price level declines to 90. As real output decreases, companies lay off workers and unemployment rises. The decrease in real output suggests that the economy moves into a contraction because of the reduction in aggregate demand. Therefore, the pessimism that triggered the reduction in aggregate demand is, to some degree, self-fulfilling: Pessimism about the future results in declining economic activity.

What should policymakers do when they are confronted with such a recession? According to John Maynard Keynes, policymakers should increase government spending or make more money available for loans. These actions would shift the aggregate demand curve to the right, thus causing an increase in output, employment, and income in the economy.

The recession of 2001 provides an example of a demand shock that plagued the U.S. economy. Prior to 2001, companies eagerly invested in equipment necessary to develop new technologies, including the Internet. New businesses were established to sell electronics, books, clothing, and prescription drugs on the Internet. They needed office space, capital equipment, and warehouses, which resulted in increased investment spending. By 2001, however, this investment had caught up with the needs of the market, and the level of investment spending began to decline. The terrorist attacks of September 11, 2001, contributed to the falling investment. The uncertainty and fear that gripped Americans following the attacks caused investment in jet airliners, hotels, and other goods to decrease. Although consumption spending continued to increase, partly because of a 10-year cut in income taxes that was implemented in June 2001, the decrease in investment more than offset the increase in consumption spending. This resulted in a decrease in the aggregate demand curve. As the negative multiplier effect kicked in, real GDP and employment declined, and the economy fell into recession. The recession lasted from March to November 2001. Chapters 13 and 15 will discuss the role of fiscal policy and monetary policy in counteracting recession.

Decreases in Aggregate Supply

Just as a decrease in aggregate demand can force the economy into recession, so can a decrease in aggregate supply. Referring to Figure 12.3(*b*), assume that the economy is in equilibrium at point *A'* where the price level is 100 and real output is $12 trillion. Now suppose that firms realize an increase in production costs. It might result from an increase in the level of wages that is not matched by productivity increases or from an increase in the price of a key resource such as oil.

What is the macroeconomic effect of such an increase in production costs? At any given price level, firms will be willing to offer a smaller quantity of goods to the market. Therefore, as Figure 12.3(*b*) shows, the aggregate supply curve shifts to the left, from AS_0 to AS_1. The decrease in aggregate supply moves the economy from its initial equilibrium at point *A'* to a new equilibrium at point *B'*. The real output of the economy decreases from $12 trillion to $9 trillion, and the price level rises from 100 to 110. The decline in aggregate supply is especially detrimental because it results in falling output, increased unemployment, and rising prices. Such an event is called **stagflation**, that is, recession (stagnation) with inflation.

The recession of 1990–1991 provides an example of a supply shock that burdened the U.S. economy. In 1990, Saddam Hussein and his Iraqi army invaded Kuwait, a major oil producer. Within 6 hours, Iraqi forces had occupied the entire country. Although the United States and its allies were able to oust the Iraqi army from Kuwait, during the conflict, the oil produced by both Kuwait and Iraq was taken off the world market. The decrease in the supply of oil caused oil prices to spike from $14 to $27 per barrel. Consistent with the prediction of the model of aggregate demand and aggregate supply, rising oil prices caused the aggregate supply curve to decrease, while the aggregate demand curve remained relatively constant. This resulted in a 1.5-percent decrease in real GDP during the first quarter of 1991, and a rise in the unemployment rate. Also, the consumer price index increased more rapidly as the recession gripped the nation.

THE ORIGINS OF INFLATION REVISITED

Source: Cemile Bingol/DigitalVision Vectors/Getty Images®

We will now apply the model of aggregate demand and aggregate supply to the types of inflation introduced in the previous chapter: demand-pull inflation and cost-push inflation.

Demand-Pull Inflation

Recall that *demand-pull inflation* is an increase in the average price level caused by an excess of total spending, that is, aggregate demand. The expression "too many dollars chasing too few goods" is often used to describe this type of inflation. "Too many dollars" suggests that the total spending in the economy is excessive. "Too few goods" suggests that the total supply of goods in the economy is too low relative to demand.

When firms cannot supply all the goods and services demanded by buyers, they respond by increasing prices. The average price level is thus pulled up by the total spending of buyers. A general increase in the availability of money and credit in the economy is a common cause of demand-pull inflation.

The degree to which an increase in aggregate demand pulls up the price level depends on how close the economy is to the level of real output that corresponds to full employment. Suppose that there is considerable unused capacity in the economy and significant unemployment during the year. Such a situation puts downward pressure on the prices charged by companies and on workers' wages. In this situation, the main effect of an increase in aggregate demand will be a rise in real output, with little or no upward pressure on the price level.

Now suppose that factories and offices are operating around the clock, and there is little, if any, slack capacity or unemployment. In this situation, the main effect of a rise in aggregate demand will be an increase in the price level; there will be little, if any, impact on real output. As seen in Figure 12.4(*a*), an increase in aggregate demand from AD_0 to AD_1 will pull up the price level from 105 to 110, a considerable increase. The price-level increase that is associated with the rise in aggregate demand indicates demand-pull inflation because the shift in aggregate demand pulls up the price level. To generate continuous demand-pull inflation, the aggregate demand curve would have to keep shifting out along a given aggregate supply curve.

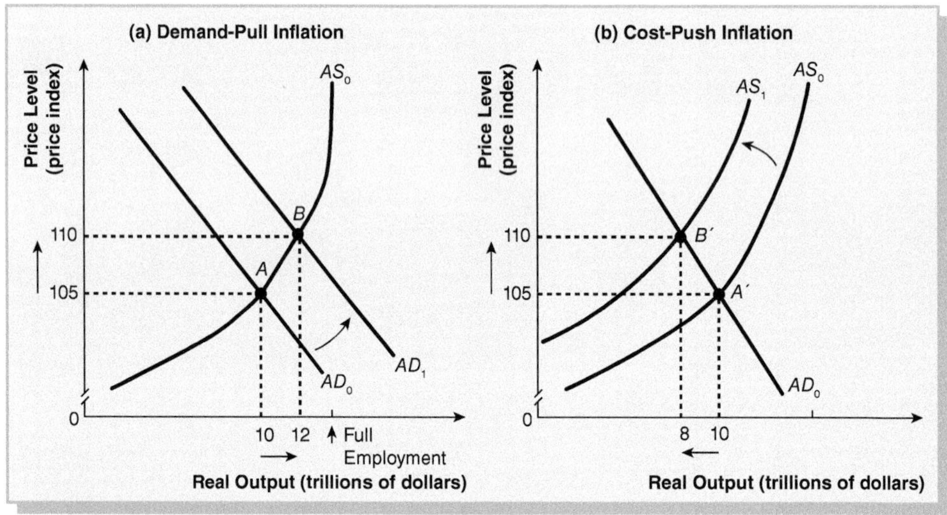

FIGURE 12.4 The Origins of Inflation

When buyers' demands to purchase goods and services exceed sellers' capacities to supply them, prices are driven up on available goods, and demand-pull inflation occurs. Demand-pull inflation arises when the economy is close to or at full employment. When price increases are caused by pressures from the sellers' side of the market, cost-push inflation occurs. Cost-push inflation can be caused by the bargaining power of resource owners, limited availability of resources, declining productivity, or chance events. It results in a higher price level and a lower level of real output and employment.

What should policymakers do when they are confronted with demand-pull inflation? To reduce inflation, policymakers must decrease the growth in aggregate demand by, for example, reducing the growth rate of the money supply or decreasing government spending. As aggregate supply grows over time, slower growth in aggregate demand will reduce the inflation rate.

However, a policy that reduces aggregate demand is not without problems. Although decreasing the growth rate of aggregate demand reduces the inflation rate, it is likely to be accompanied by a rise in unemployment in the short run because of companies' contractual obligations to pay higher wages. Such contracts were presumably signed when it seemed that inflation would accelerate. As inflation decreases, firms will see that the prices of their goods will rise less rapidly. Therefore, firms may have to lay off workers to fulfill their contractual obligations to those workers still employed. Such layoffs cause the unemployment rate to increase.

Increases in unemployment often accompany decreases in inflation. During the late 1970s, inflation accelerated in the United States, reaching a level of 13.5 percent in 1980. To reduce inflation, the Federal Reserve (see Chapter 15) sharply decreased the growth rate of the money supply in 1981. This policy reduced the growth rate of aggregate demand and resulted in a dramatic decline in the inflation rate. By 1983, the inflation rate was only 3.2 percent. However, the unemployment rate rose from 7.6 percent in 1981 to 9.6 percent in 1983, causing much hardship for many households. If the Federal Reserve had not pursued its anti-inflation policy in 1981, the inflation rate likely would have continued to accelerate. This would have required an even tougher anti-inflation policy, which would have caused more unemployment than occurred during 1981–1983.

Cost-Push Inflation

Although economists widely agree that inflation can be caused by demand-pull forces, some economists argue that inflation can also result from events on the supply side of the market. Recall that *cost-push inflation* arises from events that increase the cost of production at each price level. Two events that result in cost-push inflation are increases in wages and increases in the prices of non-labor inputs such as energy and raw materials. With an increase in the costs of production, the aggregate supply curve shifts to the left, while the aggregate demand curve remains unchanged. A decrease in aggregate supply usually leads not only to a higher price level but also to a falling level of output, a combination that is identified in Figure 12.4(*b*) as *stagflation.*

We can show the nature of cost-push inflation in Figure 12.4(*b*). The economy is initially assumed to be located at point *A'* where the price level is 105 and real output equals $10 trillion. Suppose that workers can secure increases in wages that exceed gains in productivity. As wages and unit production costs rise, the aggregate supply curve shifts leftward from AS_0 to AS_1. The price level therefore increases from 105 to 110, as shown by point *B'* in the figure. Also, the economy's real output falls from $10 trillion to $8 trillion because of the leftward shift in aggregate supply.

In economics, cost-push inflation is sometimes associated with the term **stagflation** or recession-inflation. This is a situation in which the inflation rate is high or rising, the economic growth rate slows or declines, and unemployment remains high.

Productivity Growth Dampens Inflation

During the late 1990s, economists struggled to apply traditional economic models to what was happening in the United States. Growth was robust, stocks were soaring, and job markets were tightening—yet inflation was negligible. Quarter after quarter, the pattern held. And try as they might, economists couldn't explain it using the old rules.

Instead, they considered a new view: The United States was in the midst of a technology-driven boom related to computers, the Internet, electronic commerce, and inventory management systems. This boom allowed the economy to grow faster than was once thought possible without igniting growth-inhibiting wages or price increases. Indeed, unemployment stood at a 29-year low, the economic expansion was robust, and the money supply was growing rapidly. But with inflation in check, these indicators could no longer be interpreted in the same manner.

The key to the new thinking was the belief that productivity growth, which had languished at 1 percent during the 1970s and 1980s, had taken a long-term leap to 2 percent or more as companies used technology to become more efficient. Economists pondered whether the adoption of productivity-enhancing technology had changed the way the economy operates. The possibilities of a long-term productivity rate of 2 percent were enormous for policymakers. It could mean that they could live with stronger growth without fearing resurgent inflation.

By 2001, however, the U.S. economy had returned to traditional economic principles. A sizable decline in investment spending caused aggregate demand to decrease, and the economy slumped into recession in March 2001. The recession was prolonged by declining private spending associated with the terrorist attacks of September 11, 2001. By 2002, the recession was over and economic expansion followed.

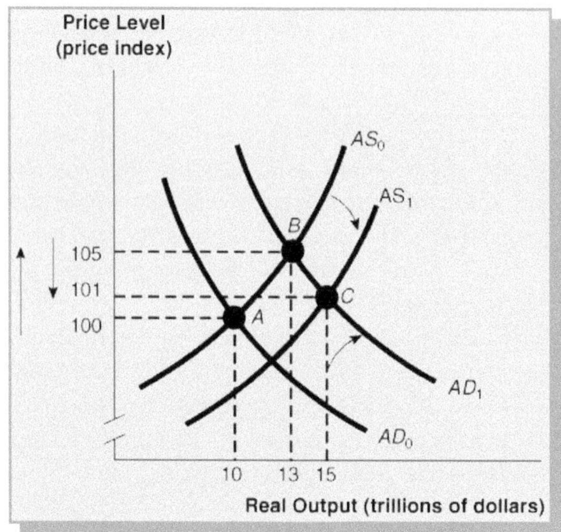

FIGURE 12.5 Productivity Growth Moderates Inflation

As seen in the experience of the U.S. economy during the late 1990s, an increase in productivity is a moderating influence on the economy's inflation rate.

Analysis. Traditional theory suggests that the relationship between the economy's price level and real output is such that as production increases, the price level increases more rapidly as full employment is approached. Figure 12.5 shows this relationship. Given aggregate supply curve AS_0, as aggregate demand increases from AD_0 to AD_1, the price level rises from 100 to 105. However, suppose that the increase in aggregate demand is accompanied by an increase in productivity. This results in a decrease in per-unit production cost and an increase in the aggregate supply curve from AS_0 to AS_1. Therefore, the price index decreases from 105 to 101 in the figure. Real output increases and the price level remains virtually unchanged as aggregate demand and aggregate supply increase. Simply put, productivity growth is a moderating influence on the economy's inflation rate.

Is Deflation Good or Bad?

During the Great Depression, the general price level in the United States fell 25 percent from 1929 to 1933. As prices declined, so did employment. By the time prices reached the bottom, a quarter of the labor force was out of work. Not surprisingly, the United States emerged from the Great Depression with much anxiety regarding falling prices.

Deflation is a sustained decrease in the general level of prices. It occurs when the annual inflation rate falls below zero percent, meaning a negative inflation rate. This should not be confused with disinflation, a slowdown in the inflation rate—such as when the inflation rate declines from 5 percent to 4 percent.

It would not be uncommon for prices to decrease in a particular sector because of rising productivity, falling costs, or weak demand relative to the wider economy. For example, although the overall price level of the U.S. economy increased about 34 percent during 1998–2008, the price of computers over the same period fell nearly 76 percent due to steadily falling production costs. Such declines are rarely a problem for the overall economy, and do not constitute deflation. Deflation occurs when price decreases are so widespread and sustained that they cause a broad-based price index such as the consumer price index to steadily decrease for more than one or two quarters.

Whether deflation is on balance good or bad depends on whether the force generating the falling price level is increasing aggregate supply or decreasing aggregate demand. Both forces exert downward pressure on the price level but they have opposite effects on the level of economic activity. For example, the U.S. deflation in the late 1800s occurred because aggregate supply was increasing faster than aggregate demand, exerting downward pressure on the price level but also causing output and employment to increase. Such positive supply-side shocks typically emanate from technological innovation, rising productivity, or trade liberalization.

Conversely, the U.S. deflation during the Great Depression and Japan's deflation during the 1990s occurred because of decreasing aggregate demand, exerting downward pressure on the price level, but also decreasing output and employment. Such a negative demand shock could be caused by a severe economic downturn, the bursting of an asset price bubble in the housing or stock markets, or overly tight macroeconomic policies.

There are several ways in which deflation from a negative demand shock contributes to economic downturn. First, falling prices cause consumers to postpone purchases in the hope of experiencing even lower prices in the future, thus causing decreases in output and employment. Also, decreasing prices increase the burden of debt because borrowers are now forced to repay their loans with dollars that now have greater purchasing power. Capital investment, purchases of new homes, and other types of spending decline, which worsens the economic downturn. Moreover, if product prices decline more rapidly than wages, profit margins decrease, which causes firms to reduce production and employment.

During the Great Recession of 2007–2009, policymakers attempted to offset the negative effects of a deflation caused by a negative demand shock. The tools that were used included an expansionary fiscal policy (increased government spending and reduced taxes) and an expansionary monetary policy (increased money supply and reductions in interest rates), as discussed in subsequent chapters.

CHECK POINT

1 Use the model of aggregate demand and aggregate supply to explain the origins of recession.
2 What do economists mean by "stagflation" and why is it a problem for economic policymakers?
3 Use the model of aggregate demand and aggregate supply to explain the origins of inflation.
4 If the government enacts policies to counteract demand-pull inflation, adverse side effects may ensue. Explain.
5 Why does cost-push inflation create a dilemma for economic policymakers?

CHAPTER SUMMARY

1 The growth performance of the U.S. economy has been uneven. Although the output of goods and services rises in most years, in some years economic growth does not occur. The central focus of macroeconomics is what causes short-run fluctuations in economic activity and what, if anything, the government can do to promote full employment without inflation.
2 Prior to the Great Depression of the 1930s, the classical economists dominated economic thinking. According to the classical economists, the market economy automatically ensures the full employment of all of its resources. The optimism of classical economists was largely based on the assumption of freely flexible wages and prices.
3 During the 1930s, John Maynard Keynes formed a theory that provided an explanation for the Great Depression. According to Keynes, the level of economic activity depends on the total spending of the economy. If business expectations are pessimistic, investment spending will be reduced, resulting in a series of decreases in total spending. If this should occur, the economy can move into a depression and remain there. Because the

market economy is inherently unstable, Keynes argued that government must intervene to protect jobs and income.

4 The model of aggregate demand and aggregate supply can be used to show how output and prices are determined in the short run. An economy is in equilibrium when aggregate demand equals aggregate supply.

5 The aggregate demand curve shows the total amount of real output that buyers will purchase at alternative price levels during a given year. Movements along an aggregate demand curve are caused by changes in the price level of the economy. Shifts in the aggregate demand curve are caused by changes in non-price factors that affect household consumption expenditures, business investment, government expenditures, and net exports of goods and services.

6 According to the multiplier effect, a change in any one of the components of aggregate demand (consumption, investment, government spending, or net exports) will have a magnified impact on national output and income. The size of the multiplier depends on the spending and saving habits of consumers and businesses.

7 The aggregate supply curve shows the relationship between the level of prices and amount of real output that will be produced by the economy in a given year. The aggregate supply curve is horizontal when the economy is in deep recession or depression, upward-sloping when the economy approaches full employment, and vertical when the economy achieves full employment. Changes in factors such as resource prices, resource availability, and the level of technology will cause the aggregate supply curve to shift.

8 The model of aggregate demand and aggregate supply can be applied to the problems of recession and inflation. According to this model, decreases in aggregate demand or aggregate supply can push the economy into recession; inflation may be the result of increases in aggregate demand or decreases in aggregate supply. An economy experiences "stagflation" when there is both recession and inflation.

KEY TERMS AND CONCEPTS

classical economists
Say's Law
John Maynard Keynes
aggregate demand curve
aggregate supply curve
aggregate quantity demanded
multiplier effect
multiplier
aggregate quantity supplied
stagflation
marginal propensity to consume
marginal propensity to save

STUDY QUESTIONS AND PROBLEMS

1 According to the classical economists, flexible prices and flexible wages guaranteed that all output produced can be sold and everyone who wants a job can find one.

Explain. Why did John Maynard Keynes believe that prices and wages are not sufficiently flexible to guarantee the full employment of resources?

2 What explains the inverse relationship between the aggregate quantity demanded and the price level?

3 What accounts for the shape of the aggregate supply curve?

4 Explain whether each of the following events would increase, decrease, or have no effect on the short-run aggregate demand curve:

- **a** Decrease in the U.S. price level makes American goods more attractive to foreign buyers.
- **b** Households decide to consume a larger share of their income.
- **c** Worsening profit expectations cause firms to decrease their expenditures on new machinery and equipment.
- **d** As the price level declines, the purchasing power of currency increases, and thus Americans increase their purchases of computers and office equipment.
- **e** Because of decreasing political tensions in North Korea, the U.S. Congress reduces purchases of jet fighters and tanks.
- **f** Economic expansion in Europe results in an increase in the European demand for Boeing jetliners.
- **g** Fearing a future economic downturn, households decide to save a larger fraction of their income.

5 Suppose that the marginal propensity to consume in the economy is 0.75. Assuming that prices are constant, what effect would a $50 million increase in investment spending have on the equilibrium real GDP?

6 Suppose that the marginal propensity to save in the economy is 0.1. Assuming that prices are constant, what effect would a $20 million decrease in net exports have on the equilibrium real GDP?

7 Explain whether the following events would increase, decrease, or have no effect on the short-run aggregate supply curve:

- **a** A tornado damages factories in Wisconsin and Minnesota.
- **b** Because of expectations of a booming economy, auto companies invest in more efficient machinery and equipment.
- **c** New technologies result in declining prices of crude oil.
- **d** The United Steel Workers Union wins a large increase in wages from domestic steel companies.
- **e** Workers participate in retraining programs that enhance their productivity.

8 Table 12.1 shows the short-run aggregate supply and aggregate demand schedules for a hypothetical economy.

TABLE 12.1 Aggregate Demand and Aggregate Supply Data

Real Domestic Output Demanded (billions of dollars)	*Price Level (price index)*	*Real Domestic Output Supplied (billions of dollars)*
$6,000	130	$16,000
8,000	120	16,000
10,000	110	14,000
12,000	100	12,000
14,000	90	10,000
16,000	90	8,000

- **a** What are the economy's equilibrium price and quantity of real output?
- **b** The full-employment segment of the economy's aggregate supply schedule is associated with what level of real output?
- **c** If the economy is in the horizontal segment of its aggregate supply schedule, what will be the impact of an increase in aggregate demand?
- **d** Given the initial data in the table, suppose that the quantity of real output supplied rises by $4,000 at each given price level. What will be the new equilibrium price level and real output?

9 Why is an increase in aggregate supply "doubly beneficial" and a decrease in aggregate supply "doubly detrimental"?

10 Use the model of aggregate demand and aggregate supply to show the differences between demand-pull inflation and cost-push inflation.

EXPLORING FURTHER 12.1: THE NATURE AND OPERATION OF THE MULTIPLIER EFFECT

According to the multiplier effect, an autonomous change in aggregate demand will have a magnified effect on the economy's income and output. Why is there a multiplier effect for the economy?

The basic idea is quite simple, as seen in Table 12.2. Suppose that General Electric constructs a factory in your town at a cost of $100 million. Also suppose that people spend 80 percent of their additional income and save 20 percent. According to the table, the increase in investment of $100 million, when spent, becomes income of $100 million for the owners of the construction firm and for the workers who build the factory. Suppose

TABLE 12.2 The Multiplier Process

Spending Rounds	*Increased Income and Output*	*Increased Consumption (spend 80%)*	*Increased Saving (s(save 20%)*
Original increase in investment	$100.0	$80.0	$20.0
Second round	80.0	64.0	16.0
Third round	64.0	51.2	12.8
Fourth round	51.2	41.0	11.2
	etc.	etc.	etc.
	500.0	400.0	100.0

that these people save 20 percent of their additional income, or $20 million, and use the rest, $80 million, to purchase new Ford automobiles. The $80 million becomes income to the owners of Ford Motor Co. and its workers. These people, in turn, spend 80 percent of the $80 million ($64 million) on food, and save the remaining $16 million. This results in $64 million in income for food producers. This process of receiving income and then respending the money, which generates income for others, continues until the original amount of money ($100 million) is all held in savings by the various individuals. At that point, no more income can be created. Through this process, the initial investment of $100 million results in an increase of $500 million in income and output. Therefore, in this example the multiplier has a value of 5.

The multiplier effect also works in reverse. Suppose that consumers become more thrifty and reduce their consumption spending. According to the multiplier effect, national output and income will decline by an amount greater than the initial decrease in consumption spending.

Calculating the Value of the Multiplier

As you examine Table 12.2, notice that the size of the multiplier depends on the spending and saving patterns of individuals and businesses in the economy. In the jargon of economists, the multiplier depends on the marginal propensity to consume and the marginal propensity to save.

The **marginal propensity to consume** (*MPC*) is the fraction of additional income that people spend. Referring to Table 12.2, we assume that people spend 80 percent of their additional income. This means that the *MPC* = 0.8. Similarly, the **marginal propensity to save** (*MPS*) is the fraction of additional income that is saved. Referring to the table, we assume that people save 20 percent of their additional income. Thus, the *MPS* = 0.2. Notice that the *MPS* and *MPC* always add up to 1 because all of the consumer income that is not spent on goods and services must be saved.

The formula for the multiplier is as follows:

$$\text{Multiplier} = 1/1(1 - MPC)$$

To illustrate this formula, if *MPC* = 0.8, then the multiplier is 1 / (1–0.8), or 5.

Because *MPC* + *MPS* = 1, it follows that *MPS* = (*1–MPC*). Therefore, we can restate the multiplier formula as

$$\text{Multiplier} = 1/MPS$$

To illustrate this formula, if *MPS* = 0.2, the multiplier is 1 / 0.2 = 5.

If aggregate demand changes, equilibrium income and output will change by the amount of the change in aggregate demand times the multiplier. This process can be summarized as follows:

$$\Delta Aggregatedemand \times Multiplier = \Delta Equilibrium\ income$$

For example, if investment spending rises by $100 million and the multiplier is 5, equilibrium output and income will rise by $500 million ($100 million × 5 = $500 million).

Graphical Illustration of the Multiplier Effect

Figure 12.6 shows the full multiplier effect of a $100 million increase in investment spending.

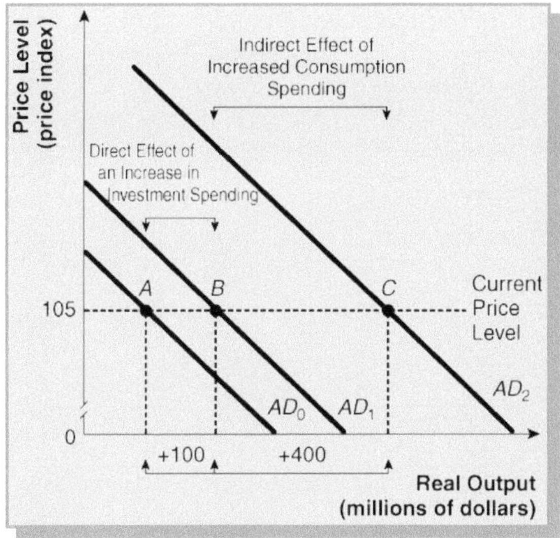

FIGURE 12.6 The Multiplier in Action

An increase in investment spending initially shifts aggregate demand rightward from AD_0 to AD_1. Aggregate demand gets an extra boost from the additional consumption resulting from increased income and respending. Because of the multiplier effect, aggregate demand increases from AD_1 to AD_2.

The direct effect of the increase in investment spending will be a $100 million increase (a rightward shift) in the aggregate demand curve from AD_0 to AD_1. Moreover, aggregate demand gets an additional boost from additional consumption that occurs as people receive income and then respend it. This causes aggregate demand to increase by $400 million (another rightward shift), from AD_1 to AD_2. In all, the $100 million increase in investment spending shifts aggregate demand from AD_0 *to* AD_2, causing national output to increase by $500 million.

For the full multiplier effect to occur, there must be some idle resources in the economy and a constant price level, as shown in Figure 12.6. If an increase in aggregate demand occurs when the economy is already at, or close to, full employment, consumers and others will bid up prices by attempting to purchase more output than the economy is capable of producing. This results in inflation, suggesting an increasing price level that offsets the multiplier effect. Therefore, without idle resources and a constant price level, the multiplier effect is impeded. Simply put, price-level increases weaken the multiplier.

NOTES

1 John K. Galbraith, *The Great Crash*, 1929 (New York: Houghton Mifflin, 1979); and Robert Stobel, "The Great Depression," *World Book Encyclopedia* (Chicago, IL: World Book, 1988), pp. 363–367.
2 John M. Keynes, *The General Theory of Employment, Interest, and Money* (New York: Harcourt, Brace and Company, 1936).
3 This explanation of the downward-sloping aggregate demand curve is known as the real-balances effect. Other explanations include the so-called interest rate effect and the foreign trade effect, which can be found in more advanced textbooks on macroeconomics.
4 An autonomous variable is one that is assumed not to depend on the state of the economy—that is, it does not change when the economy changes.

CHAPTER 13

Fiscal Policy and the Federal Budget

CHAPTER OBJECTIVES

After reading this chapter, you should be able to:

1 Discuss the operation of fiscal policy and the problems it encounters.
2 Explain how discretionary fiscal policy attempts to combat the problems of recession and inflation.
3 Describe how automatic stabilizers help cushion an economy during a recession.
4 Evaluate the strengths and weaknesses of supply-side fiscal policy.
5 Identify the potential effects of the federal debt.

DOI: 10.4324/9781003438571-16

ECONOMICS IN CONTEXT

Once upon a time, tax cuts commanded almost universal support among economists as the desired method of combating recessions. When Congress passed the Kennedy–Johnson tax cuts in 1964, such enthusiasm was at its peak. As time passed, however, changes in taxes and spending gradually lost favor to changes in interest rates by the Federal Reserve.

As the U.S. economy slowed in 2001, companies such as Hewlett-Packard, Nortel, and Cisco argued that the high-tech economy was so bad that they could not foresee profits that year. Moreover, job losses would likely occur for thousands of Americans. As a result, they lobbied for a fiscal boost in the form of a tax cut.

In response to the weakening economy, President George W. Bush assaulted the conventional wisdom by implementing a reduction in taxes in 2002. The United States needed a tax cut, he argued, because the federal government was pulling too much money out of the private economy, creating a drag on U.S. growth. This was followed by another tax cut in 2003.

Those who believe that the economy is inherently unstable often urge the government to intervene to protect jobs and income. The government can help stabilize the economy through its use of government spending and tax policies, as discussed in this chapter.

Before we proceed to government stabilization policies, recall that the federal budget consists of two components: Government expenditures, and tax revenues or receipts. When government spending exceeds tax revenues in a given year, a budget deficit occurs. When the budget is in deficit, the federal government must borrow funds by issuing securities, such as Treasury bills, notes, and bonds. If tax revenues exceed government spending, a budget surplus exists. When the federal government incurs a budget surplus, it can use the excess revenues to pay off some of its debt. Finally, when government spending equals tax revenues, we have a balanced budget. We will next examine the nature and operation of fiscal policy and the federal budget and their effects on the economy.

FISCAL POLICY

Recall from Chapter 12 that John Maynard Keynes believed that the Great Depression was caused by insufficient aggregate demand. Because he thought that prices and wages were inflexible in a downward direction, Keynes maintained that the classical economists' optimism that the economy would move automatically and quickly to full employment was incorrect. To Keynes and his followers, an activist government must increase aggregate demand to protect jobs and income. In other words, expansionary fiscal policy initiated by the federal government is the way to stabilize the economy.

Fiscal policy is the use of government expenditures and taxes to promote macroeconomic goals, such as full employment, stable prices, and economic growth. Government

TABLE 13.1 Examples of U.S. Fiscal Policies

Year	*Economic Problem*	*Policy*
1964	Recession	With the economy in a slump, Presidents Kennedy and Johnson enact permanent tax cuts for individuals and corporations. The top tax rate for individuals is cut from 91 percent to 70 percent.
1968	Inflation	To dampen inflationary pressures, President Johnson orders a temporary tax increase. This one-time surcharge of 10 percent is added to individual income tax liabilities.
1969	Inflation	Facing an overheated economy, President Nixon orders reductions in government spending
1975	Recession	Fearing a recession, President Ford orders a temporary tax reduction of 10 percent. The tax cut is enacted immediately by Congress.
1981	Recession	In response to a sluggish economy, President Reagan calls for a cut in individual income taxes and an increase in defense spending. The top rate for individuals is cut from 70 percent to 28 percent.
1992	Recession	President Bush orders a reduction in withholding rates to raise take-home pay and to increase consumption.
2007–2009	Recession	Presidents Bush and Obama convince Congress to cut income taxes and adopt increases in government spending.
2020	Recession	President Trump convinces Congress to increase government spending.

expenditures consist of purchases of goods and services, such as the procurement of jet aircraft from Boeing, and transfer payments, such as unemployment compensation and food stamps. In the United States, Congress and the president set fiscal policy: Therefore, it reflects a collective decision-making process. Table 13.1 shows examples of U.S. fiscal policies.

Fiscal policies may be expansionary or contractionary. An *expansionary fiscal policy* increases real output, employment, and income. Such a policy can be used to move the economy out of recession. A *contractionary fiscal policy* decreases real output, employment, and income. It can be used to combat the problem of inflation.

Fiscal policies are used to alter the economy's aggregate demand curve and aggregate supply curve to promote full employment and stable prices. Let us consider both possibilities, beginning with the use of fiscal policy to shift the aggregate demand curve.

DISCRETIONARY FISCAL POLICY AND AGGREGATE DEMAND: SHORT-RUN EFFECTS

Let us pick up where we left off in Chapter 12 by discussing the use of discretionary fiscal policy, as Keynes urged, to help stabilize the economy. **Discretionary fiscal policy** is the deliberate use of changes in government expenditures and taxation to affect aggregate demand and to influence the economy's performance in the short run, when its capacity to produce is fixed. This means that discretionary fiscal policy makes changes to the government's budget via changes to tax rates and/or levels of government spending.

Recall that aggregate demand has four components: consumption, investment, government spending, and net exports. In the short run, discretionary fiscal policy changes aggregate demand to affect the economy's business cycle by combating a recession or inflation.

Combating Recession

Source: dovate/E+/Getty Images®

Referring to Figure 13.1, suppose that the economy suffers from recession at equilibrium point *A*, where the aggregate demand curve intersects the aggregate supply curve. In equilibrium, the level of output is $700 billion, below the full-employment output of $900 billion. Here, the economy can be improved by following Keynesian economics and shifting the aggregate demand curve to the right—say, from AD_0 to AD_1. By doing so, the economy's output increases from $700 billion to $800 billion. Notice that the price level remains constant given the abundance of idle resources in the economy.

How can the government increase aggregate demand? It has three fiscal policy options: (1) Increase government spending, (2) cut taxes, or (3) combine the two in some manner. If the federal budget is initially balanced, fiscal policy should move toward a *budget deficit* (government spending more than tax revenues) in order to combat a recession.

Increased Government Spending. The simplest method would be to increase government spending. If government were to step up its purchases of jet planes, highways, and other goods, the increased spending would add directly to aggregate demand. According to the multiplier effect discussed in Chapter 12, aggregate demand will rise by more than just the added government spending.

If the government purchases, say, $25 billion of jet aircraft from Boeing, this sets the multiplier process in motion. The initial effect of the increased demand from the government is to stimulate employment and profits at Boeing. As Boeing workers realize fatter paychecks and the firm's owners realize higher dividends, they respond to the increased income by increasing their own spending on autos, appliances, and the like. Therefore, government purchases from Boeing increase the demand for the products of many other companies such as Ford, Whirlpool, and General Electric. Therefore, these firms hire more workers and realize higher profits. Higher earnings and profits lead to increased consumer spending once again, and so on. Each round of added spending increases aggregate demand a little more. When all of these effects are combined, the total impact on the quantity of goods and services demanded can be much larger than the initial stimulus from increased government expenditures. Referring to Figure 13.1, government purchases of $25 billion increase aggregate demand by $100 billion. See "Exploring Further 13.1" at the end of this chapter for additional information about fiscal policy and the multiplier effect.

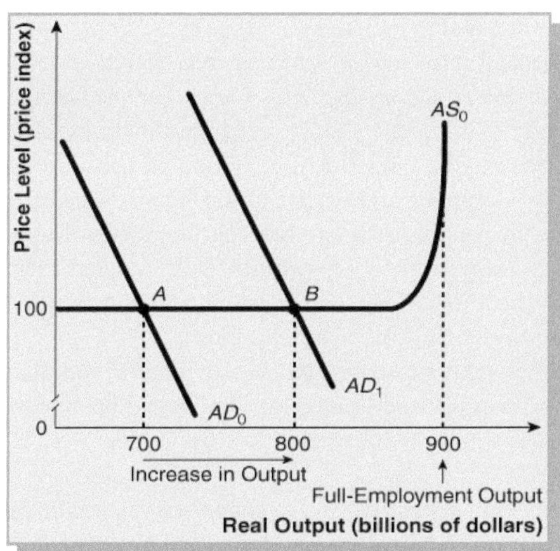

FIGURE 13.1 Expansionary Fiscal Policy

If the government wants to expand the economy, it can increase government spending or lower taxes. Either policy shifts the aggregate demand curve rightward, which results in an increase in real output and also an increase in prices as the economy approaches full employment.

Ever since the days of President Franklin D. Roosevelt, the federal government has implemented public-works projects to combat downturns in the economy and to create jobs. During the Great Depression of the 1930s, Roosevelt established the *Works Project Administration* (WPA). The WPA provided jobs building highways, streets, dams, bridges, schools, courthouses, parks, and other projects that were intended to have long-range value. It also created work for artists, writers, actors, and musicians. The WPA employed an average of 2 million workers annually between 1935 and 1941. Roosevelt also established the *Civilian Conservation Corps* (CCC) from 1933 until 1942. The CCC gave work and training to 2½ million young people. It achieved great success with its programs for flood control, forestry, and soil. These government projects cost a lot of money—much more than the government was collecting in taxes. The deficit was made up partly by raising taxes and partly by borrowing. As a result, the national debt rose higher than ever before.

In recent years, the federal government has provided public-works spending for mass transit, highways, and other transportation projects. When President George H.W. Bush signed a $151-billion transportation bill in 1991, he declared that the effect would be "jobs building roads, jobs building bridges, and jobs building railways."

Besides providing long-term public-works projects, the federal government has enacted public-employment projects. The notion underlying these programs is clear: If the economy suffers from high unemployment, why not create jobs directly? Public-employment projects are intended to hire unemployed workers for a limited period in public jobs, after which time those workers can take jobs in the economy's private sector. During the 1970s, for example, the *Comprehensive Employment and Training Act* provided public-service jobs for more than 700,000 hard-core unemployed and young people. These workers did everything from working in theaters and museums to raking leaves.

Decrease Taxes. Apart from increasing spending, is there another way the government could cause aggregate demand to increase? Another expansionary fiscal policy intended to increase aggregate demand is for the government to reduce taxes.

Lowering *taxes on personal income* increases the amount of take-home pay that people have. If take-home pay goes up, we can expect households to save more and consume more than they did prior to the tax reduction. The initial consumption spending induced by the tax cut sets the multiplier process in motion. The new consumer spending creates additional income for owners of firms and workers, who then use the additional income to increase their own consumption. This results in a cumulative increase in aggregate demand that exceeds the initial increase in consumption. Put simply, the multiplier effect makes tax reductions a powerful tool of fiscal policy.[1]

A reduction in the *tax rate on corporate profits* also tends to stimulate aggregate demand. After a tax reduction, firms have additional funds to spend on new machinery and equipment. They may also distribute more money to shareholders who, in turn, may spend at least a portion of it.

Another type of tax cut for businesses is an *investment tax credit*. Such a policy allows a company to decrease its tax liability by a fraction of the investment that it initiates during a particular period. Suppose that the investment tax credit is 10 percent. If Microsoft purchases $10-million worth of new equipment during a year, its tax liability will fall by $1 million for that year. The purpose of an investment tax credit is to make investment more profitable and thus to promote additional private-sector investment. As a result,

TABLE 13.2 Discretionary Fiscal Policies

Economic Problem and Solution	
Recession	*Inflation*
Expansionary Fiscal Policy	Contractionary Fiscal Policy
1. Increased government spending	1. Decreased government spending
2. Decreased taxes	2. Increased taxes

aggregate demand rises, causing an increase in real output, employment, and income. The investment tax credit was used during the 1960s to stimulate the sluggish economy.

As summarized in Table 13.2, government spending increases and tax reductions are expansionary fiscal policies. The levels of both government spending and taxation affect output and employment in the short run through their influence on the demand for goods and services in the economy. Simply put, the purpose of an expansionary fiscal policy is to provide short-term stimulus to the economy by generating enough demand to engage more of the economy's existing productive capacity. But which fiscal policy is most effective?

The goal of an expansionary fiscal policy is to increase spending, and fiscal policies can differ in the extent to which they induce spending. Whereas a fiscal stimulus delivered through a direct increase in government expenditures has a relatively straightforward effect, a fiscal stimulus delivered through a personal tax cut tends to have a more muted effect on the economy, because only part of it will be spent. The smaller the share spent, the smaller the stimulus. It is also possible that consumers who feel uncertainty about the future will not spend a tax cut. Therefore, a tax reduction must be somewhat larger than an increase in government expenditures if it is to yield an equal amount of stimulus to the economy.

Combating Inflation

The preceding example showed how expansionary fiscal policy moves an economy closer to full employment. Suppose, however, that aggregate demand exceeds the economy's capacity to produce, resulting in demand-pull inflation. In this case, a contractionary or restrictive fiscal policy may help control it.

Referring to Figure 13.2, suppose that a stock market boom boosts household wealth. This causes the aggregate demand curve to shift to the right, from AD_0 *to* AD_1, so that the economy operates at point *B* on the full-employment range of the aggregate supply curve, AS_0. The increase in aggregate demand raises the price level from 110 to 120. However, we want stable prices. If the government desires to combat this inflation, it may adopt a contractionary fiscal policy to reduce aggregate demand. The cost of doing so could be a lower level of real output and a higher rate of unemployment.

To decrease aggregate demand, the government has three fiscal options: (1) Cut government spending, (2) increase taxes, or (3) combine the two in some manner. When the

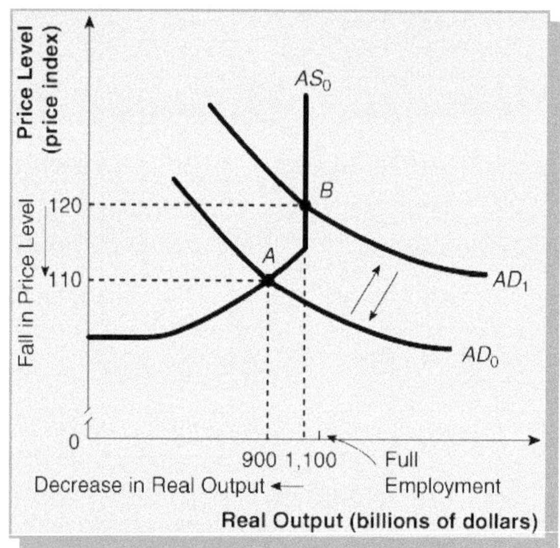

FIGURE 13.2 Contractionary Fiscal Policy

If the government wants to combat inflation, it can decrease government spending or increase taxes. Either policy shifts the aggregate demand curve leftward. Although inflation may decline as a result of a contractionary fiscal policy, real output may fall and unemployment may rise.

economy encounters demand-pull inflation, fiscal policy should move toward a *budget surplus* (tax revenues more than government spending).

AUTOMATIC STABILIZERS

Recall that discretionary fiscal policy entails an alteration in spending and taxes by the government to promote full employment, stable prices, and economic growth. "Discretionary" implies that changes in government spending programs and tax rates are made at the option of Congress and the White House.

Unlike discretionary fiscal policy, **automatic stabilizers** are changes in government spending and tax revenues that occur automatically as the economy fluctuates. This means that automatic stabilizers are built into government budgets, without any vote from legislators, that increase spending or reduce taxes as the economy slows. The automatic stabilizers prevent aggregate demand from decreasing too much in bad times and rising too much in good times, thus stabilizing the economy. It is important to note that automatic stabilizers operate silently in the background and do their job without requiring explicit policy changes by Congress or the White House.

The most important automatic stabilizer is the tax system. The personal income tax depends on the earnings of households; the corporate income tax depends on companies' profits; and the social security tax depends on workers' wages. When the economy goes into a recession, income, profits, and wages all decline, which results in a decrease in tax collections for the government. This automatic decline in tax revenues bolsters aggregate demand and reduces the severity of the recession.

Government transfer payments also serve as an automatic stabilizer. When the economy goes into recession and workers are laid off, they become eligible for unemployment insurance benefits, food stamps, and other welfare benefits. This automatic increase in transfer payments supports consumption spending and aggregate demand, which helps offset the decline in economic activity. The automatic stabilizers in the U.S. economy are not strong enough to eliminate recessions completely; however, they provide a cushion for the economy if it goes into a slump.

During times of economic prosperity, tax collections automatically rise and transfer payments automatically decline. The increase in tax collections and the decrease in transfer payments slow the growth of aggregate demand, thus controlling the upward pressure on the price level when the economy is expanding. In this manner, the automatic stabilizers help prevent an economy from overheating.

The Great Recession of 2007–2009 provides an example of how automatic stabilizers work, as summarized in Table 13.3.[2] As the U.S. economy plunged into recession, unemployment rose while declines occurred in income, profits, and workers' earnings. The result was a decrease in tax collections, including personal income taxes, corporate income taxes, and payroll taxes. Moreover, unemployment insurance and other forms of income support automatically increased as workers were laid off. The decreases in taxes and increases in transfer payments served to bolster aggregate demand and thus reduce the magnitude of the recession. However, the automatic stabilizers were not strong enough to eliminate the economic downturn, and thus discretionary fiscal policy and monetary policy were enacted to help stimulate the economy.

TABLE 13.3 Automatic Stabilizers during the Great Recession of 2007–2009

	Year	*Unemployment Rate*	*Individual Income Tax Receipts*	*Income Security Outlays**
	2007	4.6	$1,163.5	$365.9
	2008	5.8	1,145.7	431.3
Trough of Recession:	2009	9.3	915.3	533.2
	2010	9.6	898.5	622.2
	2011	8.9	1,091.5	597.4

* Includes unemployment insurance benefits, temporary assistance for needy families, housing and energy assistance to low-income families, supplemental nutrition assistance, and other income support payments.

Sources: Office of Management and Budget, *Budget of the U.S. Government, Historical Tables*; and *Economic Report of the President* 2012.

SUPPLY-SIDE FISCAL POLICY: DOES IT WORK?

According to John Maynard Keynes, increasing the demand for goods and services is the key driver of economic growth. That is, by shifting the aggregate demand curve rightward, an expansionary fiscal policy will cause output and employment to increase in the short run, when the economy's aggregate supply curve is fixed. Keynesian economics is known as **demand-side economics**.

Another theory in macroeconomics is **supply-side economics**, which asserts that increasing the supply of goods and services is the main engine of economic growth. That is, by increasing the economy's productive capacity, the aggregate supply curve will shift rightward, resulting in an increase in output and lower prices. Supply-side economics should be viewed as a long-run strategy to increase the economy's growth rate rather than a short-run strategy to end a recession.

Figure 13.3 illustrates the operation of supply-side economics. Assume that the economy is in equilibrium at point *A*, where aggregate demand curve AD_0 intersects aggregate supply curve AS_0. Suppose that the aggregate supply curve increases to AS_1. The result is an increase in the economy's output, from $12 trillion to $14 trillion, and a decrease in the price level from 100 to 90. Therefore, the increase in the supply of output is the driver of the economy's growth. But what causes the aggregate supply curve to shift to the right?

Recall that the aggregate supply curve's location is determined by the quantity of labor and capital, the state of technology, and government regulation of business. A change in any of these factors can cause a shift in the aggregate supply curve. According to supply-side economics, changes in governmental taxation and regulatory policies can lead to

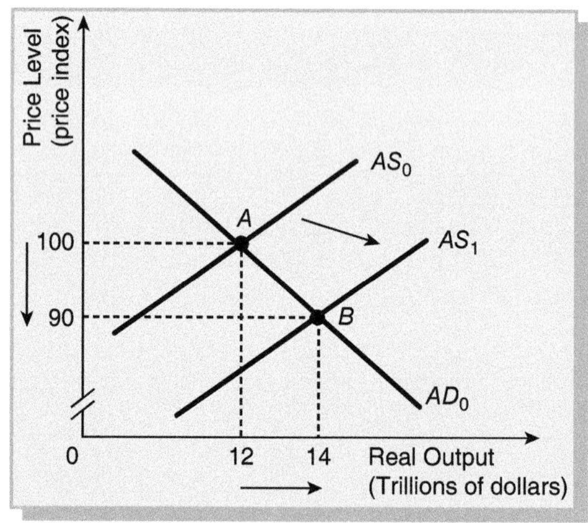

FIGURE 13.3 Supply-Side Fiscal Policy

Advocates of supply-side fiscal policy maintain that a decrease in tax rates or government regulations will provide an incentive for people to increase work, saving, and investment. This will result in an increase in the aggregate supply curve, causing real output to increase and the price level to decrease.

an increase in the economy's productive capacity and growth rate. Here are some policy recommendations of supply-side economists.

- Reduce marginal income tax rates to provide workers greater incentive to work, as opposed to leisure. The marginal tax rate is the amount of additional tax paid for each additional dollar earned as income.
- Reduce capital gains tax rates to induce investors to deploy capital productively. A capital gains tax is the tax on profits realized on the sale of an investment, such as stock.
- Reduce government regulations of business and thus encourage the operation of the free market.

Supply-side fiscal policy has been tried in the United States. For example, during the recession of the early 1980s, President Ronald Reagan thought that tax reductions for households, investors, and businesses would provide them incentives to work, save, and invest, yielding economic benefits that trickled down into the overall economy. Reagan also focused on deregulation of domestic markets and increases in military spending. So, with Reagan's signature, tax cuts and deregulation policies were approved by Congress. Also, the 2017 Tax Cuts and Jobs Act, advocated by President Donald Trump, was founded on the idea that lower business and corporate tax rates and new investment incentives would increase investment, make workers more productive, and ultimately increase output and wages.

Although supply-side economics has proponents, other economists disagree with its policies. Armed with evidence, critics argue that data shows that tax reductions and other policies to increase corporate profits don't always lead to more jobs, higher investment and productivity, and economic growth. Also, critics disagree that when the wealthy do well, their extra income trickles down to everybody else. The debate about supply-side economics will surely continue.

FISCAL POLICY IN ACTION

Although the basic elements of Keynesian fiscal policy were developed during the Great Depression, it took many years before these principals were accepted by politicians. In particular, they feared the consequences of large budget deficits that might result from an increase in government spending or a decrease in taxes, and this could lead to inflation. It was not until the 1960s that fiscal policy had become widely accepted as one of the country's main weapons for combating recession or inflation. Let us now discuss two cases of expansionary fiscal policy—the Great Recession of 2007–2009 and the Covid-19 pandemic.

Combating the Great Recession of 2007–2009

Following six consecutive years of expansion, the U.S. economy peaked in December 2007, beginning a recession that continued throughout 2008 and 2009. Policymakers moved quickly in 2008 to address the economic downturn. Although the Federal Reserve cut its key interest rate to help stimulate the economy, it was felt that monetary policy alone would not provide sufficient stimulus.

In February 2008, the Economic Stimulus Act was passed by Congress and signed into law by President George Bush. It was designed to provide temporary (one-time) tax rebates to those lower- and middle-income individuals and households who would immediately spend it. The Act also authorized businesses to deduct 50 percent of the cost of investment equipment installed during 2008 from their 2008 taxes.

The Bush administration hoped that the tax rebates would burn such a hole in peoples' pockets that they would not be able to resist spending it, therefore adding to aggregate demand. However, this optimism was unwarranted. It turned out that only 10–20 percent of the tax rebate dollars were spent: Most of the money went into household saving or for paying down past debt such as credit card bills, neither of which directly stimulated the economy. According to many economists, the Bush tax rebate was ineffective because it only provided a temporary increase to households' incomes, rather than a permanent increase in income.

When Barack Obama became president in 2009, he inherited an economy that was falling deeper into recession. Obama noted that decreases in consumption spending and investment spending continued to drag the economy downward. Thus, a massive increase in government spending was necessary to stimulate the economy.

In February of 2009, Obama signed into law a fiscal stimulus program of $825 billion, the most expansive unleashing of the government's fiscal firepower in the face of a recession since World War II. About two-thirds of the program took the form of government expenditures, and one-third took the form of tax reductions. The program was spread over a period of about four years. The primary intent of the program was to boost short-run aggregate demand: If more goods and services are being bought, whether cement for a new highway or groceries paid for with a household tax cut, there is less chance that decreasing demand will result in companies laying off workers, resulting in greater declines in demand and a deeper downturn.

Analysts generally agreed that the Obama fiscal stimulus yielded positive effects for the economy, although the recovery from the recession was very slow. Also, the fiscal stimulus was accompanied by an expansionary monetary policy of the Federal Reserve that made accurate measurement of the effects of fiscal stimulus very difficult.

Combating the Covid-19 Pandemic

The Covid-19 pandemic of 2020 and associated public health restrictions greatly disrupted economic activity in the United States and other countries. The pandemic resulted in a 10-percent decline in U.S. real GDP during the second quarter of 2020, the worst contraction in more than 70 years, and an unemployment rate exceeding 14 percent. Although the Covid-19 recession was sharp and pronounced, it lasted only 2 months as the economy quickly rebounded.

The pandemic affected both the supply side and demand side of the economy, impeding consumers' ability to consume goods and services and firms' ability to produce. The consumption of goods and services decreased dramatically and then began recovering slowly as Covid-19 containment policies eased and vaccines were made widely available.

However, industrial production was slow to rebound, creating an imbalance between supply and demand in the goods markets that contributed to rising prices.

To provide fiscal stimulus to the economy and relief to those harmed by the pandemic, the federal government increased its expenditures by an enormous $5.2 trillion. Direct cash payments were made to individuals, and grants and loans were provided to businesses and state and local governments. Also, the Federal Reserve enacted a series of monetary stimulus policies to complement the fiscal stimulus.

Although the fiscal support helped boost the consumption demand for goods, it did not have a significant impact on the supply of goods. Thus, the large increase in demand triggered by the fiscal and monetary stimulus policies, together with the slow increase in production, likely contributed to excess demand in the goods market. The result was a depletion of inventories, pronounced supply-chain bottlenecks, and ultimately inflation. The U.S. inflation rate surged from 1.8 percent in 2019 to about 8 percent in 2022. Critics questioned whether fiscal and monetary policy stimulus measures were too generous, triggering lasting inflation.

Despite the cost of higher inflation, proponents of the economic stimulus policies emphasized the positive role played by generous government support throughout this unprecedented crisis. The large spending supported a robust economic rebound, with both output and employment recovering at a remarkable pace, likely preventing worse outcomes despite the price pressures that may have resulted from the spending.

CHECK POINT

1. What are the tools of fiscal policy?
2. How does discretionary fiscal policy attempt to combat recession? How about inflation?
3. What impact does an expansionary fiscal policy have on the budget of the federal government? How about a contractionary fiscal policy?
4. How do automatic stabilizers help cushion the economy during a recession? What are some examples of automatic stabilizers?
5. How might cuts in individual income taxes or corporate income taxes encourage long-run economic growth?
6. Summarize the operation of fiscal policy during the Great Recession of 2007–2009 and the Covid-19 pandemic.

PROBLEMS OF FISCAL POLICY

Although Keynesian economists generally view fiscal policy as effective at combating recession and inflation, others have doubts about the effectiveness of fiscal policy. Let us examine some of these concerns.

Timing Lags

In theory, Congress and the president should work together to enact timely and effective fiscal policies. In practice, however, it can months or years for fiscal policies to be enacted and to have an impact on the economy. In particular, three timing lags constrain the operation of fiscal policy:

- **Recognition lag**. The recognition lag refers to the time between the beginning of inflation or recession and the recognition that it is occurring. For example, if the economy goes into a slump in March, the decline may not be apparent for three or four months. Once policymakers become aware of a problem in the economy, they rarely enact policies immediately. Instead, they want to be sure that the problem is more than a short-term disturbance.
- **Administrative lag**. The way Congress operates makes it difficult to get quick action on fiscal policy. Much debate occurs before a fiscal policy can be implemented. This process can take months.
- **Operational lag**. Once enacted, a fiscal policy measure takes time to have an impact on the economy. Government spending and taxation require some time to affect the economy's output, income, and employment.

Since the 1950s, most recessions in the U.S. economy have been short, lasting about 11 months on average. By the time a fiscal program begins to boost business and consumer demand—that is, once policymakers recognize that economic growth has slowed, propose a fiscal package, debate it, pass it, and send it to the president for their signature—the economy may be recovering. For this reason, discretionary fiscal policy in the United Sates is often viewed as too unwieldy for dealing with the typical, mild recessions experienced in recent decades.

For example, evidence appeared in late 2000 that the U.S. economy was slowing. Congress did pass a tax cut in 2001, but this had been part of President George W. Bush's legislative agenda before any hint of an economic slowdown. It took Congress until March 2002 to pass the Economic Recovery Act to provide further stimulus to the economy. Simply put, economists are often skeptical of fiscal policy as a stabilization tool, particularly through the mechanism of tax cuts. Because of lags in decision making and administrative lags in getting tax cuts to individuals, a fiscal stimulus enacted through a tax cut can be poorly timed.

Crowding-Out Effect

Another potential problem of expansionary fiscal policies is the **crowding-out effect**. With crowding out, private spending (consumption spending or investment) falls because of increased government expenditures and the subsequent budget deficits. The source of the decline in private spending is higher interest rates generated by budget deficits.

For example, suppose that the government enacts an expansionary fiscal policy—say, an increase in defense spending. The policy must be financed either by increased taxes or by borrowing funds to finance the enlarged federal deficit. If the government borrows funds to finance the deficit, the total demand for funds will increase as the government competes with the private sector to borrow the available supply of funds. The additional government borrowing thus increases the demand for funds and pushes up interest rates. Because of higher interest rates, businesses will delay or cancel purchases of machinery and equipment, residential housing construction will be postponed, and consumers will refrain from buying interest-sensitive goods, such as major appliances and automobiles. Therefore, the higher interest rates caused by government borrowing squeeze out private-sector borrowing. Thus, crowding out lessens the effectiveness of an expansionary fiscal policy.

Although economists see the logic of the crowding-out argument, they also recognize that government deficits don't necessarily squeeze out private spending. During recessions, the main problem is that people are not spending all of their available funds. Typically, consumers are saving more than businesses intend to invest. Such a shortage of spending is the main motivation for increased government spending. In this recessionary situation, deficit-financed government spending doesn't crowd out private spending. Moreover, when open international investment markets allow countries to draw on each other's savings, increases in one country's deficits may be offset by savings pulled into that country from abroad, with barely changed interest rates. This has been the situation for the United States, which has increasingly financed its deficits by borrowing funds from the Chinese, Japanese, and other global investors.

Offsetting State and Local Fiscal Policies

Balanced-budget requirements are used by most state and local governments, requiring them to balance projected tax revenue with expenditures. Strictly enforced balanced-budget requirements prohibit state and local government from carrying deficits into the following fiscal year.

During a recession and falling tax revenue, state and local governments are under pressure to cut expenditures to maintain a balanced budget. However, such action can work against an expansionary fiscal policy of the federal government that reduces taxes or increases expenditures, meaning that it is less effective in combating a recession.

For example, during the Great Depression of the 1930s, most of the increases in federal expenditures were offset by decreases in state and local expenditures. Also, during the Great Recession of 2007–2009, state and local governments sharply slashed expenditures to balance budgets. Some economists have argued that state and local contraction roughly canceled out federal expansion, so that overall government fiscal policy was roughly neutral.

However, not all state balanced-budget requirements are binding. For example, balanced budget-requirements typically apply to states' operating budgets, while capital expenditures and pension funds are exempt from these limitations. This may allow state policymakers to circumvent keeping their budgets in balance.

Negative Supply Shocks and Fiscal Policy Conflict

Considering the previously discussed complications, one must ask whether fiscal policy is useful as an economic stabilization tool. Some economists maintain that it is better not to use fiscal policy at all. Those holding that view usually consider monetary policy to be a more effective tool for combating unemployment and inflation, as discussed in Chapter 15.

However, many mainstream economists view fiscal policy to be an important economic tool. They feel that fiscal policy can help nudge an economy in a particular direction, although it cannot steer the economy to a precise macroeconomic outcome. Mainstream economists also contend that fiscal policy works best when the problem is deficiency of aggregate demand that can be corrected by increased government expenditures or tax cuts for households and businesses.

But suppose the economic problem is a "negative supply shock" that reduces the productivity of capital and labor, thus decreasing the economy's ability to produce goods and services. Examples of negative supply shocks include pandemics, wars, terrorist attacks, drought, and a decrease in the supply of oil. In this case, trying to stabilize the economy through increases or decreases in aggregate demand via fiscal policy does not work well, as a policy conflict arises.

To visualize this policy conflict, consider Figure 13.4, which shows the effects of a negative supply shock. The negative supply shock will cause the economy's aggregate supply curve to shift to the left, from AS_0 to AS_1. This will result in not only a decrease in real output, from \$120 trillion to \$110 trillion, but also an increase in inflation, from price level 100 to 105. These two effects (recession and inflation) will require opposite fiscal policies.

To reduce inflation, a contractionary fiscal policy could be enacted that reduces government spending or increases taxes, thus shifting the aggregate demand curve leftward; but

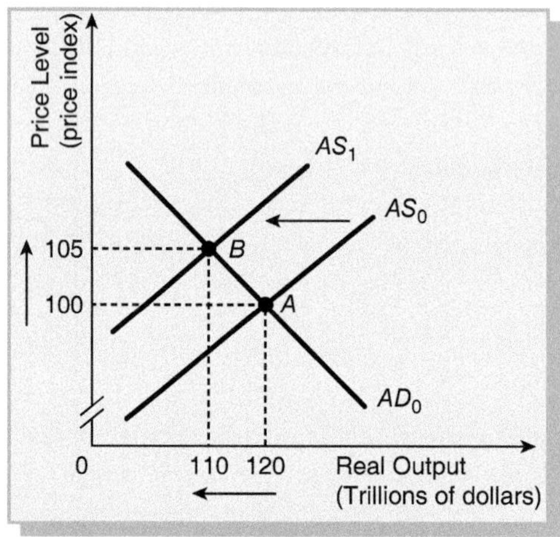

FIGURE 13.4 Fiscal Policy Conflict with a Negative Supply Shock

A negative supply shock will cause the aggregate supply curve to decrease, resulting in a decrease in real output and higher prices. To combat recession, the government might adopt an expansionary fiscal policy that increases aggregate demand; but this will likely increase inflation. Alternatively, to combat inflation the government might adopt a contractionary fiscal policy that decreases aggregate demand; but this will likely intensify the recession. A policy conflict thus exists.

that would only make the recession more severe. Or an expansionary fiscal policy could increase real output by increasing government spending or decreasing taxes, and thus stimulate aggregate demand; but that would likely promote even higher inflation. Thus, there is no easy answer to this policy conflict. Which fiscal policy should be used?

When Is Fiscal Policy Useful?

Considering the previously discussed complications, one must ask whether fiscal policy is useful as an economic stabilization tool. Some economists maintain that it is better not to use fiscal policy at all. Those holding that view consider monetary policy to be a more effective tool for combating unemployment and inflation, as discussed in Chapter 15.

However, most mainstream economists view fiscal policy as an important economic tool. They feel that fiscal policy can help nudge an economy in a particular direction, although it cannot steer the economy to a precise macroeconomic outcome. Mainstream economists also contend that fiscal policy works best when the problem is deficiency of aggregate demand that can be corrected by increased government expenditures or tax cuts for households and businesses.

But suppose the economic problem stems from a supply shock that reduces the productivity of capital and labor, thus decreasing the economy's ability to produce goods and services. In this case, increasing aggregate demand via an expansionary fiscal policy does not work well to pump prime the economy. Possible shocks that might harm an economy are wars, pandemic, terrorist attacks, drought, a decrease in the supply of oil, and the like.

THE FEDERAL DEFICIT AND NATIONAL DEBT

Recall that the goals of fiscal policy are to promote stable prices, maximum employment, and economic growth. To achieve these goals, fiscal policy uses the federal government's budget, which comprises the revenues and spending of the federal government.

Fiscal policy is expansionary when the government spends more on budget items, such as national defense or infrastructure, or when taxes are reduced. Such policies are generally used to stimulate the economy's output and employment. Conversely, fiscal policy is contractionary when government spending declines or taxes increase in order to combat rising inflation. Usually, expansionary fiscal policy results in higher budget deficits, and contractionary fiscal policy decreases budget deficits. Therefore, fiscal policy is often associated with an unbalanced budget for the federal government.

The Federal Deficit (Surplus)

The **federal deficit** (surplus) is the difference between total U.S. federal spending and revenue in a given fiscal year. Referring to Table 13.4, we see that in most fiscal years, the federal government's budget has been in deficit; the last period that the federal budget ran a surplus was 1999–2001.

TABLE 13.4. U.S. Federal Government Deficits and Surpluses, Fiscal Years 1980–2022 (billions of dollars)

Fiscal Year	*Deficit (-) or Surplus*
1980	–$73.8
1985	–212.3
1990	–221.0
1995	–164.0
1999	125.6
2000	236.2
2001	128.2
2005	–318.3
2010	–1,294.4
2015	–442.0
2020	–3,132.5
2022	–1,395.9

Source: Data drawn from Economic Report of the President, 2023, Table B-47, available at https://www.whitehouse.gov/wp-content/uploads/2023/03/ERP-2023.pdf.

To cover federal deficit, the U.S. government borrows through the sale of U.S. Treasury securities to the public, which includes individual American investors, pension funds, banks, insurance companies, the Federal Reserve, and also investors of foreign countries including individuals, central banks, and governments (especially Japan and China). Also, some Treasury securities are owned by other parts of the federal government, such as the trust funds of Social Security and Medicare. For example, the Social Security Trust Fund usually receives and spends money unevenly throughout the year. When the Social Security Trust Fund runs a surplus, the Treasury Department will borrow the funds by issuing Treasury securities; thus, the Social Security Trust Fund lends to the federal government. In 2022, 35 percent of the U.S. government's debt was owned by domestic private investors. Forty percent was owned by the Federal Reserve and U.S. government agencies, and 25 percent was owned by foreign investors.

The United States benefits from foreign purchases of U.S. Treasury securities because, as foreign investors fill part of America's borrowing needs, more domestic savings are available for private investment, and interest rates are lower than they otherwise would be. However, to service this foreign-owned debt, the U.S. government must send interest payments abroad, which adds to the income of citizens of other countries rather than American investors.

Most Treasury securities held by the public are marketable, meaning that once the government issues them, they can be resold by whoever owns them. These marketable securities consist of (1) Treasury bills, short-term securities that mature in 1 year or less); (2) Treasury notes, medium-term securities that mature between 2 and 10 years; and (3) Treasury bonds, which are issued in 20-year and 30-year maturities. Treasury securities pay a fixed amount of interest to their investors.

The mix of securities is important because it can have a significant impact on interest payments. For example, a long-term Treasury bond typically carries a higher interest rate than a short-term Treasury bill because of investors' perceptions that longer-term securities are subject to greater risks, such as higher inflation in the future. However, long-term bonds offer the certainty of knowing what your payments will be over a longer period.

The National (Federal) Debt

Source: erhui1979 / DigitalVision Vectors/Getty Images®

The **national debt** (federal debt) represents the total amount of outstanding borrowing by the U.S. federal government over the nation's history. The national debt then is the accumulation of this borrowing, and it represents what the U.S. government owes creditors. This means that the national debt equals the sum of all outstanding Treasury bills, notes, and bonds, and the associated interest payments. Thus, each yearly deficit adds to the amount of federal government debt. As the federal government experiences reoccurring yearly deficits, which is common, the national debt increases.

Simply put, the national debt is like using your Visa or Mastercard for purchases and not paying off the entire balance each month. The cost of purchases surpassing the amount paid off signifies a deficit, while accumulated deficits over time signify your overall debt.

The main measure of the U.S. national debt is the *debt held by the public.* This is the measure most used because it reflects how much of the nation's wealth is absorbed by the federal government to finance its obligations and, thus, best represents the current impact of past federal borrowing on the economy. As seen in Table 13.5, the federal debt held by the public was $24.3 trillion in 2022. In contrast, the federal debt was only $43 billion in 1940.

The amount of a borrower's debt by itself is not a particularly good indicator of the debt's burden. If size were the only thing that mattered, a wealthy individual with a large mortgage would be judged to have a greater debt burden than a person of modest means with a smaller mortgage. In other words, a borrower's income and wealth are also important in assessing the burden of debt. Therefore, to get a better sense of the burden represented by the federal debt, debt should be viewed in relation to the nation's income. A commonly used measure of national income is GDP. Comparing the debt to GDP provides a better indicator of the debt burden than the debt's dollar value, because it captures the capacity of the economy to sustain the debt.

As of 2022, the federal debt equaled 97 percent of GDP, as compared to 44 percent in 1940. This dramatic increase primarily reflected massive injections of fiscal stimulus into the economy, growth in spending for Medicare and Social Security, and increasing interest costs. The peak period in U.S. history occurred immediately after World War II,

TABLE 13.5 U.S. Government Debt Held by the Public, 1940–2022

Federal Debt Held by the Public

Year	*Billions of Dollars*	*Percent of Gross Domestic Product*
1940	$43	44%
1945	236	105
1955	227	57
1965	261	38
1975	395	25
1985	1,507	35
1995	3,604	48
2005	4,592	36
2015	13,117	73
2020	21,017	100
2022	24,252	97

Source: Data drawn from Economic Report of the President, 2023, Tables B-45 and B-46, available at https://www.whitehouse.gov/wp-content/uploads/2023/03/ERP-2023.pdf.

when, because of wartime borrowing, the federal debt was 106 percent of GDP, meaning that it exceeded the annual output of the economy. After the war, spurred by economic growth and inflation, this measure fell dramatically over the next three decades to a post-war low of 24 percent in 1974. Since the mid-1970s, the debt–GDP ratio has generally crept upward.

The federal government is not the only borrower to have increased its debt since the 1980s. The borrowing of individuals, businesses, and state and local governments have all risen significantly during this period, but not as much as the federal debt.

Debt Service and the Federal Government Debt

Being able to raise funds is an important task of the U.S. government. Beyond obtaining funds by levying taxes, the government borrows money by issuing securities, such as Treasury bills, notes, and bonds. However, obtaining debt and carrying it requires the government to make payments to the holders of bonds. The government's **debt service** refers to the cash required to pay back interest and principal on its debt obligations.

The cost of the U.S. government's debt service depends on both the amount of debt outstanding and the level of interest rates. For example, as interest rates decline, so too will the government's borrowing cost. Conversely, a rise in interest rates makes borrowing more expensive for the government.

Table 13.6 shows the net interest payments on U.S. government debt as a percentage of federal outlays during 1990–2022. U.S. government net interest payments

TABLE 13.6 Net Interest Payments on U.S. Government Debt as a Percentage of Federal Outlays, 1990–2022

Year	*Outlays (billions of dollars)*	*Net Interest Payments (billions of dollars)*	*Net Interest Payments as a Percentage of Outlays*	*Weighted Average Interest Rate on Treasury Securities (percent)*
1990	$1,253.0	$184.3	14.7%	8.63%
1995	1,515.7	232.1	15.3	7.09
2000	1,789.0	222.9	12.5	5.93
2005	2,472.0	184.0	7.4	4.87
2010	3,457.1	196.2	5.7	4.25
2015	3,691.9	223.2	6.0	3.13
2020	6,553.6	345.5	5.3	2.35
2022	6,273.3	475.9	7.6	2.38

Source: Data drawn from *Economic Report of the President*, 2023, Table B-47, available at https://www.whitehouse.gov/wp-content/uploads/2023/03/ERP-2023.pdf; Internal Revenue Service, *Weighted Average Interest Rate Table*, 1990–2023, available at https://www.irs.gov/retirement-plans/weighted-average-interest-rate-table.

increased from about 7 percent of total government outlays in the mid-1970s to over 15 percent of government outlays in the mid-1990s, reflecting higher interest rates and a higher amount of debt. This was followed by a decrease of debt payments as interest rates and federal government debt fell. By the early 2020s, net interest payments on the government's debt were again rising with the increase in interest rates. So what does this mean?

Rising levels of debt service can cause fiscal challenges for the government. As the cost of borrowing increases, the government will have to make the difficult choices to either increase taxes, decrease spending, or issue more debt to service its obligations. That is, every dollar that goes toward higher interest payments to bondholders means less funds are available for government to spend on the nation's infrastructure, national defense, or social welfare programs. And financing interest payments by issuing more debt can be problematic because eventually the bill will come due.

PROS AND CONS OF A BALANCED BUDGET

America's history of federal government debt dates to the American Revolution, when the Continental Congress borrowed from the governments of France and Spain and also from private Dutch lenders. The United States struggled to pay off its debts following the war, and it took until 1835 for President Andrew Jackson to pay off the national debt. Since that time, few issues in American politics are more controversial than federal government deficits and the national debt, and economists are divided on the issue. Let us consider the pros and cons of maintaining a balanced federal government budget.

Many believe that government borrowing is appropriate under certain circumstances. For example, some believe that the automatic increases in federal borrowing that occur during recessions can help the economy by maintaining income and spending levels. Wartime borrowing is also widely considered to be beneficial because it allows the government to increase defense spending without enacting large tax increases that could be disruptive to the economy. Moreover, federal borrowing may also be appropriate for investment spending, such as building roads, training workers, or conducting scientific research. If an investment is well chosen, it can ultimately boost worker productivity and economic growth in the long term, producing a larger economy from which to pay the interest on borrowed funds.

However, if federal borrowing is not used for any of the purposes mentioned earlier, many believe that the costs outweigh the benefits. In this case, the benefits of any increased federal spending are likely to be more concentrated in the short term, while the costs tend to occur mainly in the long term. This timing difference can have important implications for different generations. The impact of today's increased borrowing will be felt by tomorrow's workers and taxpayers, who may not fully share in the benefits of the additional spending made possible by the borrowing. To the extent that deficits reduce national investment, the economy's stock of capital decreases, which reduces labor productivity, the economy's production of goods and services, and real wages. Therefore, when the government increases its debt, future generations are born into an economy with lower incomes. Moreover, when the government's debts and accumulated interest come due, future generations will face the difficult decision of paying increased taxes, enjoying less government spending, or both, to free up resources to pay off the debt and accumulated interest.

Federal borrowing can reduce the funds that are available for private investment and put upward pressure on interest rates. Because the federal government competes with private investors for scarce capital, federal borrowing can reduce the amount that is available for other investors. Government borrowing can be large enough to affect the overall level of interest rates, making borrowing more expensive for individuals and families who take out loans for homes, cars, and college.

How does borrowing affect the federal budget? Although borrowing allows the government to provide more services today than it could otherwise afford, the cost is borne tomorrow in the form of interest payments. To make these payments while avoiding larger deficits, the government must forgo spending money on other national priorities. It also means less money is available for unexpected needs.

Simply put, proponents of balanced budgets fear that growing federal debt will result in harmful effects in the future. They also support restricting the power and scope of government. Others counter that although the debt might ultimately become problematic, it is not one that we need to face by balancing the budget right now. They cite historically low interest rates in the United States, which imply that investors don't see the government's debt as much of a problem. Also, U.S. government securities are still regarded as the safest in the world. Moreover, reducing the deficit would raise taxes. Ultimately, opponents of balanced budgets want the U.S. government to have the power to influence wide-reaching change if necessary.

APPROACHES FOR CONTROLLING BUDGET DEFICITS AND THE NATIONAL DEBT

Advocates of maintaining a balanced budget for the federal government maintain that future generations have the right to be defended from debts accumulated by previous generations. Because the president or Congress are unable or unwilling to control the debt through normal governance procedures, they argue that only a constitutional constraint will be strong enough to prevent lawmakers from acting in fiscally irresponsible ways. Let us consider three views on this issue.

Annually Balanced Budget

Proponents of responsible government finance often call for a budget rule to be added to the U.S. Constitution that would require federal spending not to exceed federal revenue. The amendment would make it unconstitutional for the federal government to run annual budget deficits. Most amendment proposals also include:

- A requirement that the president present a balanced budget to the Congress.
- Measures that permit some flexibility in times of war or economic downturn provided that a supermajority (three-fifths) of the members of Congress votes for a waiver.
- A measure mandating a supermajority vote of both houses of Congress in order to raise the federal government's debt ceiling.

Put simply, more than 40 state governments have balanced-budget requirements. Why not require the federal government to achieve what most states require for their own state governments?

Advocates of a balanced-budget amendment contend that regard for the Constitution will result in compelling political pressure for the president and Congress to curtail budget deficits. Because few elected officials would want to be part of a budget that violates the Constitution, opposing parties would be forced to compromise and pass legislation that would fulfill a balanced budget. Thus, only the power of a constitutional amendment could make the government operate within its means.

However, critics of a balanced-budget requirement argue that it could detract from the ability of fiscal policy to stabilize the economy during a recession when additional spending is required. This means that a balanced-budget requirement would make recessions longer and more painful, first by reducing the automatic fiscal stabilizers (unemployment insurance and supplemental nutrition assistance) that protect people during downturns, and, second, by instead requiring measures to cut spending or increase taxes during slowdowns when the economy is suffering from a lack of demand.

Also, critics of the balanced-budget amendment maintain that even if it were enacted Congress would figure out ways to escape its restrictive provisions. For example, Congress might use dubious accounting and budgeting gimmicks such as "off-budget" expenditures and unrealistic budget projections to avoid the amendment's discipline. Most mainstream economists maintain that although a balanced-budget amendment could impose a standard that most elected officials would not want to ignore, there are legitimate concerns about how it would operate in practice.

Cyclically Balanced Budget

Many mainstream economists maintain that balancing the federal government's budget annually is too extreme. Instead, they propose that the government should balance its budget over the course of the business cycle. Since the 1950s, the average business cycle for the United States has lasted about five to six years.

What is the rationale of maintaining a cyclically balanced budget? During the recession (depression) stage of the business cycle, government should reduce taxes and increase expenditures, thus incurring a deficit. This would result in an increase in aggregate demand that will help stimulate the economy. Conversely, during an inflationary upswing, the government should increase taxes and decrease expenditures, thus incurring a surplus. The resulting decrease in aggregate demand would dampen the rate of inflation. Moreover, fiscal integrity would be maintained, in that the budget would remain in balance over a complete business cycle—that is, cyclical deficits would be offset by prosperity surpluses. Therefore, over a complete business cycle, there would be no net increase in the national debt.

However, a cyclically balanced budget is not without challenges. One problem is that the expansions and contractions of the business cycle may not be of equal magnitude and duration. For example, a long and severe recession followed by a modest and short expansion would likely result in a large deficit during the recession, but little or no surplus during the expansion. Therefore, the budget would incur a deficit over the complete business cycle. Another problem is getting politicians not to spend revenue increases that occur during expansions.

Functional Finance

Other economists argue that the function of government finance should not simply be to balance the budget on a yearly basis or over the course of the business cycle. Instead, government should try to balance the economy at full employment without inflation.

The main rule of **functional finance** is that government should maintain a reasonable level of aggregate demand at all times. If there is inadequate spending and, thus, excessive unemployment, the government should decrease taxes or increase its own spending. If there is too much aggregate demand, the government should prevent inflation by decreasing its own expenditures or by raising taxes.

Advocates of the functional finance approach justify their position on the grounds that imbalances in the government's budget tend to be minor compared with prolonged recession or persistent inflation. However, critics note that the functional finance approach does not say what the non-inflation accelerating unemployment rate is or what should be done if both low levels of inflation and unemployment cannot be achieved.

The functional finance theory was developed in the 1940s, and it provided a set of rules for fiscal policy. By the early 2000s, the tenets of functional finance evolved into the development of a macroeconomic theory known as **modern monetary theory**. Like functional finance, Modern Monetary Theory asserts that government spending should not be restrained by fears of rising debt. Perhaps you will learn more about this theory in your advanced macroeconomics course.

This chapter discussed fiscal policy as a possible solution to macroeconomic instability. The next chapter will consider the roles of money and the economy's banking system.

CHECK POINT

1 Identify the major shortcomings of fiscal policy.
2 Why do proponents of supply-side fiscal policy consider it a painless remedy for our economic problems?
3 The federal debt entails both benefits and costs for the economy. Explain.
4 Identify advantages and disadvantages of a balanced-budget amendment for the federal government.

CHAPTER SUMMARY

1 Fiscal policy is the use of government expenditures and taxes to promote macroeconomic goals such as full employment, stable prices, and economic growth. In the United

States, fiscal policy is conducted by the Congress and the president. An expansionary fiscal policy attempts to nudge the economy out of a recession, whereas a contractionary fiscal policy attempts to combat inflation.

2 Discretionary fiscal policy is the deliberate use of changes in government expenditures and taxation to affect aggregate demand and to influence the economy's performance in the short run. To combat recession, the government can cut taxes and/or increase expenditures in order to boost aggregate demand. The government can combat inflation by increasing taxes and/or cutting expenditures, thus decreasing aggregate demand.

3 Automatic stabilizers are changes in government spending and tax revenues that occur automatically as the economy fluctuates. They prevent aggregate demand from decreasing too much in bad times and rising too much in good times, thus moderating fluctuations in economic activity. Automatic stabilizers include the personal income tax, the corporate income tax, and transfer payments such as unemployment insurance benefits, food stamps, and other welfare benefits.

4 Although Keynesian economists generally view fiscal policy as effective at combating recession and inflation, others are concerned about its shortcomings. Among the problems of discretionary fiscal policy are timing lags, inflationary bias, the crowding-out effect, and negative supply shocks to the economy.

5 Besides having potential effects on aggregate demand, fiscal policy can also influence the level of economic activity through its effect on aggregate supply. According to supply-side fiscal policy, a reduction in marginal tax rates will cause productivity to increase because individuals will work harder and longer, save more, and invest more. Therefore, the aggregate supply curve will shift to the right, which leads to higher real output.

6 During the early 1980s, supply-side economists argued that a cut in tax rates would enhance incentives to work, save, and invest, thus promoting an increase in economic activity and national income. In theory, the enlarged income would cause total tax revenues to rise even though tax rates would be lower. However, the evidence from the 1980s is weak on this outcome.

7 The federal deficit is the difference between total federal spending and tax revenue received in a given year. The federal debt represents the cumulative amount of outstanding borrowing from the public over the nation's history. The federal government borrows by issuing securities, mostly through the U.S. Treasury Department.

8 Federal borrowing entails both benefits and costs. Many believe that federal borrowing is beneficial when it helps the economy by supporting income and spending levels, when it is used to increase defense spending, and when it helps finance investment spending on roads, dams, bridges, and the like. Critics of federal borrowing fear that it will slow the growth in living standards for future generations and reduce private consumption and investment expenditures. As a result, critics often prefer laws that would force the federal government to refrain from deficit spending.

KEY TERMS AND CONCEPTS

fiscal policy
discretionary fiscal policy
automatic stabilizers
recognition lag
administrative lag
operational lag
crowding-out effect
federal deficit
national (federal) debt
functional finance
Modern Monetary Theory

STUDY QUESTIONS AND PROBLEMS

1 Explain how each of the following fiscal policies would affect aggregate demand.
   a The government increases its expenditures on highways and bridges by $10 billion.
   b Personal income tax rates are increased by 10 percent across the board.
   c Expenditures on the food-stamp program are increased by 15 percent in order to help the poor.
   d The government slashes national defense expenditures as peace spreads throughout the world.
2 In each of the following situations, explain whether discretionary fiscal policy is expansionary or contractionary.
   a The government increases tax rates for households and corporations.
   b The government increases funding for unemployment insurance benefits.
   c The government approves funding for highway improvements in the Pacific Northwest.
   d The government's budget shows a deficit because of increased expenditures.
3 Tax reductions tend to affect both aggregate demand and aggregate supply. Does it matter which is affected more? Use the model of aggregate demand and aggregate supply to explain your answer.
4 Some economists argue in favor of using discretionary fiscal policy to combat recession and inflation, whereas some argue against it. Discuss the advantages and disadvantages of using discretionary fiscal policy to stabilize the economy.
5 Explain how changes in government spending and taxes can have a multiplier effect on aggregate demand and real output.
6 The following questions are based on Table 13.7.
   a What two points indicate zero tax revenues? How can this occur?
   b What tax rate results in maximum tax revenues for the government?
   c Suppose that the economy imposes a tax rate of 25 percent, yielding tax revenues of $150 billion. What will happen to tax revenues if the tax rate rises to 30 percent? Why might this occur?

TABLE 13.7 Hypothetical Tax Data for the United States

Tax Rates (percent)	*Tax Revenues (billions of dollars)*
0	0
10	90
15	150
20	180
25	150
30	90
35	0

d Suppose that the economy imposes a tax rate of 10 percent, yielding tax revenues of $90 billion. What will happen to tax revenues if the tax rate rises to 15 percent? Why might this occur?

7 Using the model of aggregate demand and aggregate supply, describe the destabilizing effects of fiscal policy if a constitutional amendment mandating an annually balanced budget were enacted.

8 Keynesian economists emphasize the effects of fiscal policy on aggregate demand, whereas supply-side economists focus on the effects on aggregate supply. Discuss the process by which a tax reduction might result in an increase in real output and employment according to these two approaches. If tax reductions are beneficial for the economy, why doesn't the government slash taxes to zero?

9 Why is crowding out an important issue in the debate over the merits of discretionary fiscal policy? Is crowding out equally likely to occur during all phases of the business cycle?

10 If the government today decides that aggregate demand is deficient and is causing a recession, what is it likely to do? What if the government decides that aggregate demand is excessive and is causing inflation?

11 Expansionary fiscal policy can combat recessions, but it usually results in a cost in terms of higher inflation. This dilemma has sparked interest in "supply-side" tax cuts that are intended to stimulate aggregate supply. Use the model of aggregate demand and aggregate supply to explain the purpose of supply-side economics. Identify the problems associated with supply-side tax cuts.

12 Assume that the economy's marginal propensity to consume is 0.8. To combat a recession, suppose that the federal government increases its expenditures by $50 billion. If prices remain constant, what impact will this policy have on the economy's aggregate demand and real output? Instead, suppose that prices increase as the economy's aggregate demand increases. What effect would this have on your answer?

13 Assume that the economy's marginal propensity to consume is 0.67. To combat a recession, suppose that the federal government is considering whether to reduce personal income taxes by $40 billion or to increase government expenditures by $40 billion. Assuming a constant price level for the economy, what effect would each of these policies have on aggregate demand and real output? Which policy is more expansionary? Why?

EXPLORING FURTHER 13.1: FISCAL POLICY AND THE MULTIPLIER

Recall from Chapter 12 that the formula for the multiplier is 1 / (1 – *MPC*), where *MPC* is the economy's marginal propensity to consume. If *MPC* = 0.75, the value of the multiplier is 4: 1 / (1–0.75) = 4. In our example of an expansionary fiscal policy, we assume that government purchases increase by $25 billion. Given a multiplier of 4, the aggregate demand curve will shift to the right by four times the distance of the initial $25 billion increase in government purchases. Indeed, the multiplier makes government spending a very powerful policy tool for stimulating output and production.

To illustrate this multiplier effect, refer to Figure 13.5. The direct effect of the increase in government purchases is to shift the aggregate demand curve to the right by $25 billion, from AD_0 to AD_2. According to the multiplier process, the indirect effect of increased consumption spending is shown by a rightward shift in aggregate demand by an additional $75 billion, from AD_2 to AD_1. Altogether, the $25-billion increase in government purchases results in a $100-billion increase in aggregate demand, shown by the shift from AD_0 to AD_1. This fourfold increase in aggregate demand is attributable to the multiplier effect.

Notice that this increase in aggregate demand takes place within the horizontal region of the aggregate supply curve, where the economy's price level is constant. Thus, real

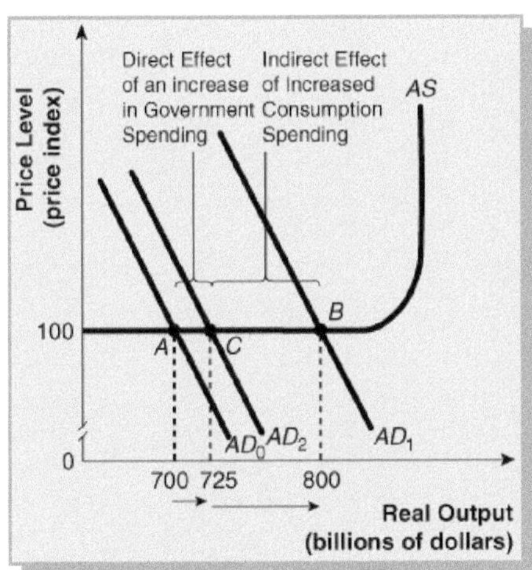

FIGURE 13.5 Fiscal Policy and the Multiplier Effect

output will increase by the full amount of the multiplier. Moreover, unemployment will decline as firms employ workers who were laid off during the recession.

In estimating the effects of fiscal policy, the multiplier is of crucial importance. Economists have debated the size of the multiplier for years. When J. M. Keynes and his colleagues first developed the concept of the multiplier in the 1930s, they estimated that the size of the government spending multiplier was as large as 10. This means that for every $100 increase in government spending, real GDP would increase by $1,000. More recent research indicates that the spending multiplier is much smaller than earlier analyses had assumed, reduced by the effect of a larger national debt on long-term interest rates, a crowding out of interest-sensitive spending caused by higher interest rates, and so on. Most researchers currently estimate the value of the government spending multiplier to be less than 2.

NOTES

1 However, the multiplier effect for a change in taxes is smaller than the effect for an equivalent change in government spending. For example, assume that the economy's marginal propensity to consume (*MPC*) is 0.75, which suggests that the expenditures multiplier is 4: Multiplier = 1 / (1 – *MPC*) = 1 / (1 – 0.75) = 4.

2 The Great Recession of 2007–2009 provides an approximate example of the impact of automatic stabilizers because tax rates and income-security programs were largely unchanged during this period. However, temporary tax cuts were granted to households in 2008 and, in 2009, payroll taxes were cut for workers, and tuition tax credits were provided to college students.

CHAPTER 14

Money and the Banking System

CHAPTER OBJECTIVES

After reading this chapter, you should be able to:

1 Define money and identify the functions of money.
2 Describe the collection process that a check goes through.
3 Describe the major depository institutions in our economy.
4 Explain how banks attempt to make a profit for their stockholders.
5 Discuss the process by which money is created in the banking system.
6 Identify the purposes of the Federal Deposit Insurance Corporation.

DOI: 10.4324/9781003438571-17

ECONOMICS IN CONTEXT

In 2000, the U.S. Mint issued its eighth dollar coin. The Golden Dollar coin, as it is known, bears the image of Sacagawea, the only woman on the Lewis and Clark Expedition. Proponents of the dollar coin point out that its widespread use would result in considerable savings for the government. On average, coins have a projected life of 30 years, compared with about 18 months for dollar bills. Although dollar bills cost about 7.5 cents to produce, compared to 10 cents for the dollar coin, the relatively short life of dollar bills makes them more expensive in the long run.

Dollar coins, however, have never been widely adopted for day-to-day transactions in the United States. One explanation is simply that people find coins inconvenient compared to paper currency. Accordingly, dollar coins would replace notes only if the public had no choice. Despite an ad campaign, approximately half the new coins remained in the vaults of the Federal Reserve Banks and the U.S. Mint a year after the coin was first introduced. The other half was in "circulation." However, many of these coins were apparently being hoarded, as few of them were observed in day-to-day transactions.

According to the adage, money makes the world go around. As far back as 300 B.C.E., Aristotle maintained that everything must be assessed in money because this allows people to exchange their services and so makes society possible. Indeed, money is an integral part of our everyday life.

In this chapter, we will examine money and the role that it plays in the economy. We will focus on the nature of money, the operation of our banking system, and the process by which money is created.

Throughout this chapter, we will refer to the Federal Reserve System (the Fed), which is the central banking system of the United States. The Federal Reserve supplies banks[1] with currency, operates a nationwide clearing mechanism for checks, serves as a lender of last resort for troubled banks, supervises and examines member banks for safety and soundness, provides checking accounts for the U.S. Treasury, issues and redeems government securities, and conducts monetary policy for the nation. We will discuss the nature and operations of the Federal Reserve System more fully in the next chapter.

THE MEANING OF MONEY

When you go to Pizza Hut to purchase a dinner, you obtain something of value—a pizza and a soft drink. To pay for these items, you might hand the waiter some cash or a personal check. The restaurant is happy to accept either of these pieces of paper, which, in themselves are worthless. Nevertheless, they are considered money.

We begin with a simple question: What is money? **Money** is the set of assets in the economy that people use regularly to purchase goods and services from others. Gold and

Source: We Are/DigitalVision/Getty Images®

silver were once the most common forms of money. But today, money consists primarily of paper bills, coins made of various metals, and checking account deposits.

Each country has its own system of money. In the United States, for example, the basic unit of money is the U.S. dollar. Canada uses the Canadian dollar, Mexico uses the peso, Japan uses the yen, and so on. We call the money in use in a country its **currency**.

Money has three functions in the economy: It is a medium of exchange, a unit of account, and a store of value. These functions distinguish money from other assets such as stocks, bonds, and real estate.

Medium of Exchange

First, money is a **medium of exchange**: It is something that people are willing to accept in payment for goods and services. In the United States, a penny, a dime, a quarter, and a $1 bill are media of exchange because people are willing to accept these items in payment, realizing that they can be used for other purchases. The transfer of money from the buyer to the seller allows the transaction to occur.

Without a medium of exchange, people would have to trade their goods and services directly for other goods and services. For example, if you wanted a motorcycle, you would have to find a motorcycle owner willing to trade. Suppose that the motorcycle owner wanted a computer in exchange for the motorcycle, and you did not own a computer. You would then have to find something that the owner of a computer wanted and trade it for a computer to give to the owner of the motorcycle.

Such trading, called *barter*, is inefficient because you could spend days running around looking for someone who has what you want and wants what you have. Also, some items, such as animals, simply are not divisible, and deals must be struck at uneven rates of exchange. Finally, barter restricts productive capacities. As societies become more sophisticated and produce a greater range of goods, the exchange process becomes too complicated for barter alone. However, a medium of exchange, or money, removes the problems of barter. Wants need not coincide because every person one deals with is willing to accept money in return for goods and services.

Unit of Account

A second function of money is that it serves as a **unit of account**. People state the prices of goods and services in terms of money. In the United States, people use dollars to specify prices. When you go shopping, you might observe that a pair of pants costs $40 and a 12-pack of Pepsi costs $4. The unit-of-account function of money allows us to compare the relative values of goods. If a pair of pants costs $40 and a 12-pack of Pepsi costs $4, then one pair of pants equals ten 12-packs of Pepsi ($40 / $4 = 10). Put simply, people use money to specify price, just as they use kilometers to measure distance or hours to express time.

Store of Value

A third function of money is that it provides a **store of value**. People can save money and then use it to make purchases in the future. Of course, money is not the only store of value in the economy. Other stores of value include gold, real estate, paintings, jewels, or even baseball cards. However, money has the advantage that it can be used immediately to meet financial obligations.

The store-of-value function of money helps us appreciate how severe and prolonged inflation can weaken an economy. With inflation, the ability of money to serve as a store of value deteriorates. Thus, people may be unwilling to save money if they expect that its future purchasing power will erode because of increasing prices. Moreover, borrowing money for productive investment may be hampered if lenders expect that the repaid loans will have less purchasing power.

Any object or substance that serves as a medium of exchange, a unit of account, and a store of value is considered money. To be convenient, however, money should have several other characteristics. It should be portable so that people can carry enough money to purchase what they need. It should come in pieces of standard value so that it does not have to be weighed or measured every time it is used. It should be durable and hold up over time. Finally, it should be divisible into smaller units so that people can make small purchases and receive change.

Are Credit Cards Money?

Most people think of credit cards, such as Mastercard and Visa, as "plastic money." After all, credit cards serve as a convenient form of financing transactions.

Are credit cards money? Not at all! Mastercard may be accepted as readily as money, but the reason that merchants honor these cards is that they expect to be paid by the financial institution that gave you the card. Eventually, you must pay off your bill by writing a check to the financial institution that issued the card. Yet, without an adequate amount of funds in your checking account, Mastercard would soon discover that the credit receipt that it received with your signature on it is virtually worthless. Put simply, if you use your Mastercard to make a purchase, you obtain a short-term loan from the financial institution that issued the card. Credit cards are thus a method of postponing payment for a brief period.

Often, credit cards are more convenient than writing checks or making payments in cash. People who have credit cards can pay many of their bills all at once at the end of the month, instead of sporadically as they make purchases. Therefore, people who have credit cards tend to hold less cash on average than people who do not have credit cards. Thus, the increased usage of credit cards may decrease the amount of money that people desire to hold.

SHOPPING FOR A CREDIT CARD: WHY RATES ARE SO HIGH

This year, you may receive a few invitations to get a new credit card. Card companies mail billions of unsolicited credit offers to U.S. households during a year and make tens of millions of telephone calls to sell their cards. Today, some large issuers, such as First USA Bank, which has 12 million cards in circulation, are banks in name only. Credit cards are their primary business. The business can be highly profitable if cardholders stay in debt. Today, the typical U.S. adult has a credit card account with a balance of more than $1,800.

Credit associations, such as Visa and Mastercard, sign up banks that offer cards to consumers; firms such as Discover and American Express offer cards directly to consumers. How does the amount on your charge slip end up on your monthly statement, and how does it get paid along the way?

Suppose that you go to Walmart and purchase a phone case with your Visa card. The cashier runs the card through an electronic approval machine to see whether the card is valid and whether you have enough credit to make the purchase. You sign the receipt, which becomes your agreement to repay. Within five business days, Walmart sends the receipt to Visa, which serves as a clearinghouse for all sales receipts. Visa contacts Walmart's bank, which pays the store the sales price minus a fee, which is generally around 3 percent, depending on the store's monthly sales volume and other considerations. Merchants can't increase prices to consumers to cover the bank's fees, but they can offer discounts to customers who pay by cash or check. Then, Visa clears the receipt from its books by charging the bank that issued the card. Your bank immediately pays Walmart's bank the entire amount. Your bank then mails you a statement for the full amount of the purchase and for any other purchases you made during the period.

No credit card will serve all the needs and usage patterns of every consumer. You'll have to do some homework if you want to take advantage of the best available terms. For example, in the disclosure provided by the credit card issuer, a key credit term to consider is the *annual percentage rate* (APR). A low APR can make a big difference if you often carry a balance from month to month. Unfortunately, credit card issuers with low APRs (around 10 percent) are very particular about whom they extend credit to; they may turn down people with sizable credit card debts—the very folks who would benefit the most from a lower rate.

Equally important is the *grace period*—the time between when you make purchases and when you must pay to avoid finance charges. Also remember that if you exceed your credit line, the bank may charge an *over-limit* fee of, say, $15. If your minimum payment is overdue, there is often a *late-payment fee* as well. Moreover, most banks also charge *cash advance fees* for money that is withdrawn from an automatic teller with your credit card. Don't forget that you begin paying interest on cash advances immediately—there is no grace period. Table 14.1 shows features of selected credit card plans.

Table 14.2 provides a comparison of average interest rates on household loans. Notice that rates on bank credit cards are relatively high. Why? Generally, credit card

TABLE 14.1 How Bank Credit Cards Compare, 2022

Card Issuer	*Annual Percentage Rate*	*Type of Interest Rate*	*Grace Period (days)*	*Annual Fee (dollars)*	*Late Fee (dollars)*
Boeing Employees Credit Union (Visa)	14.7	Variable	23	0	25
Cortrust Bank (Mastercard)	29.9	Fixed	25	75	27
First National Bank (Mastercard)	13.9	Fixed	25	0	25
Central Bank (Visa)	16.5	Fixed	25	20	5
OneUnited Bank (Visa)	17.99	Fixed	25	39	10

Source: Data drawn from Consumer Finance Protection Bureau, *Terms of Credit Card Plans (TCCP) Survey*, March 31, 2023, available at https://www.consumerfinance.gov/data-research/credit-card-data/terms-credit-card-plans-survey.

TABLE 14.2 Interest Rates on Household Loans (percentage)

Loan Type	*2022*	*2020*	*2018*
Bank credit card	16.26%	14.71%	14.22%
Personal loan (24 months)	9.87	9.51	10.32
30-year conventional mortgage (fixed rate)	6.27	2.71	4.81
New car loan (60 month)	5.36	5.02	5.02

Source: Data drawn from Board of Governors of the Federal Reserve System, *Consumer Credit-G.19* and *Selected Interest Rates-H.15*. Available at https://www.federalreserve.gov/releases/g19/current. See also Federal Reserve Bank of St. Louis, *FRED Economic Data*, available at https://fred.stlouisfed.org.

rates will be higher than those of other loan types because credit card debt is unsecured. Mortgages are backed by houses, and auto loans are secured by cars. That means a lender can take the house or the car if the borrower fails to make payments. However, credit card issuers don't have that option. Defaults and charge-offs are typically higher on credit cards than on secured loans, too. So, the risk that the issuer could lose out is higher than for a mortgage lender or auto lender. Also, interest rates are relatively high on credit cards because they are determined by what the market will bear. Credit card companies are not bound to any specific limits with their interest rates. Thus, they can essentially charge whatever they want if their rate is competitive with other credit card companies. Finally, high interest rates on credit cards encourage you to make your payments on time. The longer you allow your account to sit, the more interest penalties you will have to pay. If you feel the burden of a high interest rate on your account balance, the odds are you will be more likely to make your payments back to the issuing bank.

How can you get a better rate on your credit card? It might sound unlikely, but experts say consumers should just ask for one. Experience and consumer studies show that credit card issuers are often willing to negotiate with their best customers in order to keep them from switching to a rival. As a word of caution, if you call a bank and say that you've gotten a better credit card offer elsewhere, be prepared for the issuer to call your bluff. The wisest use of a credit card, by far, is to pay off your debt every month and avoid high interest costs. Consider making it your top financial priority.

CHECK POINT

1. What is money?
2. Identify the functions of money.
3. Why are credit cards not considered a form of money?
4. As a consumer, what factors should you weigh when comparing credit cards?

THE U.S. MONEY SUPPLY

Money is anything that people agree to accept in exchange for the things they sell or the work they do. Gold and silver were once the most common types of money. Today, however, money consists mainly of currency and checking account deposits. Let us first examine the currency of the United States.

U.S. currency consists of coins and paper money. Under federal law, only the Federal Reserve System can issue paper currency and only the U.S. Treasury can issue coins. The Federal Reserve issues paper currency called *Federal Reserve notes*. All U.S. currency carries the nation's official motto, "In God We Trust."

Source: Yevgen Romanenko/Moment/Getty Images®

Coins

Coins come in six denominations: pennies (1 cent), nickels (5 cents), dimes (10 cents), quarters (25 cents), half-dollars (50 cents), and $1.

The U.S. Mint—with satellites in Philadelphia, Denver, West Point, and San Francisco—produces coins for circulation. All U.S. coins typically bear a mint mark showing which mint produced them. Coins minted in Philadelphia bear a *P* or no mint mark; those minted in Denver, a *D*; in San Francisco, an *S*; and in West Point, a W. All the U.S. coins currently minted portray past U.S. presidents.

All coins are made from alloys (mixtures of metals). Pennies are copper-coated zinc alloyed with less than 3 percent copper. Nickels are a mixture of copper and nickel. Dimes, quarters, half-dollars, and dollars consist of three layers of metal. The core is pure copper, and the outer layers are an alloy of copper and nickel. Federal law requires that coins be dated with the year that they were made. Coins also must bear the word *Liberty* and the Latin motto *E Pluribus Unum*, meaning "out of many, one." This motto refers to the formation of the United States from the original 13 colonies.

When producing coins, the U.S. Mint rolls ingots of metal alloys into flat sheets of proper thickness. Blanks are punched from the metal sheets, and the good blanks are sorted from the scrap. After being softened and washed, blanks are put into a machine that gives them a raised edge. Blanks are then weighed and inspected before stamping. The front and back are stamped simultaneously at pressures exceeding 40 tons. Finally, the coins are weighed, counted, and shipped to the Federal Reserve Banks for distribution.

Why do coins have ridges? When coins were made of gold and silver, subtle cheating was a common occurrence. People would shave the edges of their coins before spending them, eventually collecting enough shavings to use as money. Milled edges, the ridges, were devised to discourage these cheaters. Today, gold and silver are no longer used to make coins, but the style still remains. Placing ridges on coins also helps visually impaired people recognize certain denominations. For example, the ridges on a dime distinguish it from a penny, which has a smooth edge.

Paper Money

Federal Reserve notes make up all the paper money issued in the United States today.[2] They come in seven denominations: $1, $2, $5, $10, $20, $50, and $100. The notes are issued by the 12 Federal Reserve Banks in the Federal Reserve System. Each note has a letter, number, and seal, identifying the bank that issued it. Moreover, each note bears the words *Federal Reserve Note* and a green Treasury seal. It costs about 5.5 cents to produce a Federal Reserve note.

The Bureau of Engraving and Printing in Washington, D.C., is responsible for designing and printing our paper currency. There is also a satellite production facility in Fort Worth, Texas. All notes bear the words *Washington, D.C.*, below the upper-right serial number on the face of the note. Notes printed in Fort Worth also show the letters *FW* immediately to the left of the plate serial number in the lower-right corner of the note's face.

New paper money is shipped to the 12 Federal Reserve Banks, which pay it out to commercial banks, savings and loan associations, and other depository institutions. Customers of these institutions withdraw cash as they need it. Once people spend their money at grocery stores, department stores, and so on, the money is redeposited in depository institutions. As notes wear out or become dirty or damaged, depository institutions redeposit them at the 12 Federal Reserve Banks.

Money wears out from handling, and it is sometimes accidentally damaged or destroyed. The average life of a $1 bill, for example, is about 18 months. For a $5 bill, the average life is 15 months; for a $20 bill, two years. The $10 bill has about the same life as a $1 bill. The larger bills, $50s and $100s, last longer than the smaller denominations because they don't circulate as often. A $50 bill usually lasts five years, and a $100, eight and a half years.

Banks send old, worn, torn, or soiled notes to a Federal Reserve Bank to be exchanged for new bills. The Federal Reserve Banks sort the money they receive from commercial banks to determine if it is "fit" or "unfit." Fit (reusable) money is stored in their vaults until it goes out again through the commercial banking system. The Federal Reserve Banks destroy worn-out paper money in shredding machines and burn the shredded paper into a mulch; they return damaged and worn coins to the U.S. Treasury.

Paper money that is mutilated or partially destroyed may be redeemable at full face value. Any badly soiled, dirtied, defaced, disintegrated, limp, torn, or worn-out currency that is clearly more than half the original note can be exchanged at a commercial bank, which processes the note through a Federal Reserve Bank. More seriously damaged notes, those with not clearly more than half the original surface, or those requiring special examination to determine their value, must be sent to the U.S. Treasury for redemption.

The Dollar Bill

Have you ever stopped to examine the features of the dollar bill, as shown in Figure 14.1? It's more than a piece of paper printed with green and black ink. Look at a dollar bill—it probably is a Federal Reserve note. To the left of the portrait of George Washington is a seal of the Federal Reserve Bank that issued the note. The seal bears the name and the code letter of that bank. Which Federal Reserve Bank issued your currency? To the right of the portrait is the Treasury seal, which is printed over the face of each note. The dollar bill also contains the signatures of the treasurer of the United States and the secretary of the Treasury, as well as the expression that the dollar bill is, "legal tender for all debts, public and private."

A serial number appears in the upper-right and lower-left corners of a dollar bill. Each dollar bill has a different serial number. Counterfeiters can be caught when they make batches of a bill bearing the same serial number. Businesses and banks may have lists of dollar bills with certain serial numbers that are known to be counterfeit.

The Great Seal of the United States, adopted in 1782, appears on the back of a dollar bill. The face of the seal, on the right-hand side of the bill, shows the American bald eagle with wings and claws outstretched. Above the eagle's head is a "glory," or burst of light, containing 13 stars. The number "13" represents the original 13 colonies. The eagle's right claw holds an olive branch with 13 leaves, representing peace; in the left, a bundle of 13 arrows, symbolizing war. The eagle's head is turned toward the olive branch, indicating a desire for peace. The shield (with 13 stripes) covering the eagle's breast symbolizes a

FIGURE 14.1 The Dollar Bill

united nation. The top of the shield represents Congress; the head of the eagle, the executive branch; and the nine tail feathers, the Supreme Court. A ribbon held in the eagle's beak bears the Latin motto *E Pluribus Unum* (13 letters), which means "out of many, one."

The back of the Great Seal, on the left-hand side of the dollar bill, depicts a pyramid, a symbol of material strength and endurance. The pyramid is unfinished, symbolizing the nation's striving toward growth and a goal of perfection. Above the pyramid, a glory, with an eye inside a triangle, represents the benevolent gaze of God, placing the spiritual above the material. At the top edge is the 13-letter Latin motto *Annuit Coeptis*, meaning "He has favored our undertakings." The base of the pyramid bears the year 1776 in Roman numerals. Below is the motto *Novus Ordo Seclorum*, meaning "a new order of the ages."

Checking Accounts

In the U.S. economy, the supply of money includes more than dollar bills and coins. Many people choose to pay for goods using a check instead of currency. The "money balances" that you have in your checking account can be used to purchase goods and services and to pay debts, or they can be retained for future use. Because checking accounts perform the same functions as currency, we must include checking account balances in our notion of money.

With a checking account, you use checks to withdraw money from the account in which you have deposited it. Therefore, you have quick, convenient and, if needed, frequent access to your money. Typically, you can make deposits into a checking account as often as you choose. Many institutions allow you to withdraw or deposit funds at an automated teller machine (ATM) and to pay for purchases at stores using your ATM card.

Some checking accounts pay interest; others do not. A regular checking account, frequently called a **demand deposit account**, does not pay interest. The money in the account is available to the account holder "on demand" by writing a check, making a withdrawal, or transferring funds. Another type of checking account is a **negotiable order of withdrawal (NOW) account**, which does pay interest but typically requires a larger minimum balance. Credit unions offer accounts that are similar to checking accounts at other depository institutions, but have different names.

Credit union members have **share draft accounts** rather than checking accounts. A credit union is a membership organization in which each member owns a share. Therefore, a share account represents an individual's ownership in the credit union. Share accounts can be either checking accounts or savings accounts.

Financial institutions may impose fees on checking accounts, in addition to the charge for the checks you order. Fees vary among institutions. Some institutions charge a maintenance or flat monthly fee regardless of the balance in your account. Other institutions charge a monthly fee if the minimum balance in your account drops below a certain amount. Some charge a fee for every transaction, such as for each check you write or for each withdrawal you make at an ATM. Many institutions impose a combination of these fees.

Although a checking account that pays interest may appear more attractive than one that does not, it is important to look at fees for both types of accounts. Often, checking

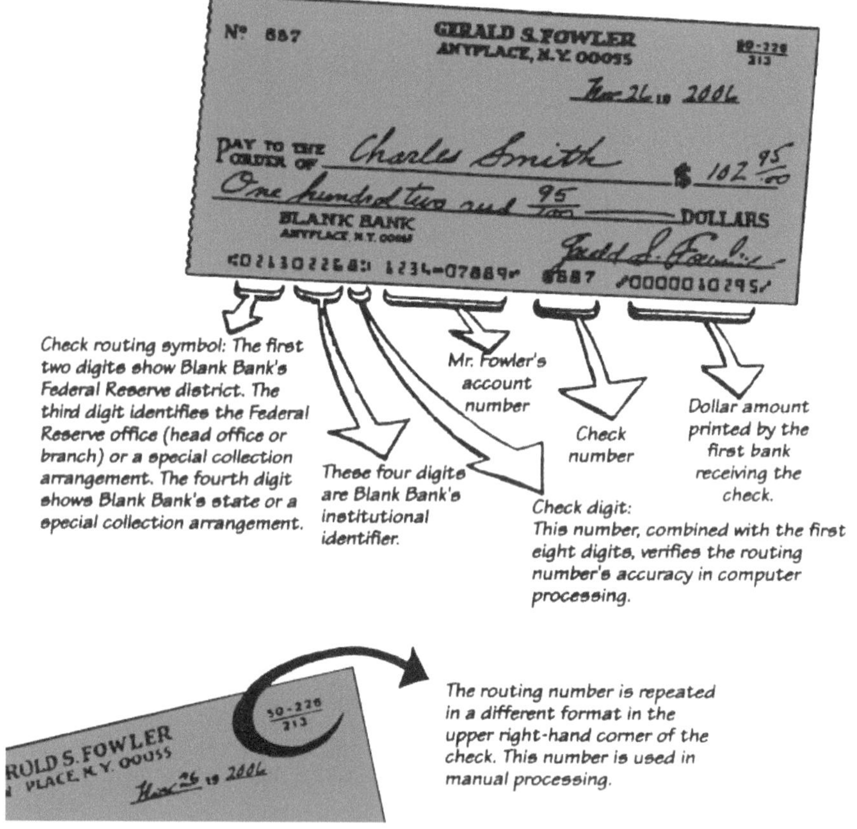
Check processing is automated. High-speed electronic machines sort checks by "reading" the sorting instructions printed in magnetic ink characters along the bottom of checks . . . at a speed surpassing 100,000 checks an hour.
Check routing symbol: The first two digits show Blank Bank's Federal Reserve district. The third digit identifies the Federal Reserve office (head office or branch) or a special collection arrangement. The fourth digit shows Blank Bank's state or a special collection arrangement.
These four digits are Blank Bank's institutional identifier.
Mr. Fowler's account number
Check number
Dollar amount printed by the first bank receiving the check.
Check digit:
This number, combined with the first eight digits, verifies the routing number's accuracy in computer processing.
The routing number is repeated in a different format in the upper right-hand corner of the check. This number is used in manual processing.

FIGURE 14.2 Electronic Codes on a Check

Source: Federal Reserve Bank of New York, The Story of Checks and Electronic Payment, 1983, p. 15.

accounts that pay interest charge higher fees than do regular checking accounts, so you could end up paying more in fees than you earn in interest.

The next time you write a check, take a close look at the electronic codes that appear on the face of the check. Do you know what these numbers stand for? Figure 14.2 gives you the answer.

Special Types of Checks

For most personal financial transactions, a check drawn on a personal checking account is an acceptable form of payment. In certain situations, though, a special type of check that carries a greater guarantee of payment may be needed.

A **certified check** is usually used when it is called for by a legal contract, such as a real estate or automobile sale agreement. Certified checks are considered less risky than personal checks because the bank on which they are drawn certifies that the funds are available to the payee. To certify a check, a bank uses the following procedure: First, a bank officer or other authorized employee verifies the check writer's signature and determines that there are sufficient funds in the checking account to pay the check. Then, the authorized employee signs the check and certifies it by marking, stamping, or perforating it so that it is less likely to be altered. By certifying the check, the bank guarantees payment and becomes liable for the amount certified, and the check writer no longer has access to the funds.

A less expensive alternative to a certified check is a **cashier's check**. The purchaser of a cashier's check does not need to have a checking account. They merely go to the bank, request a cashier's check for a certain amount, and pay the bank that amount plus a service charge. For some financial transactions, the payee may prefer a cashier's check to a personal check. A cashier's check has a better guarantee of payment because it is drawn by a bank against itself.

For people who do not maintain a checking account or who prefer not to make payments with cash, a money order often serves the same function as a personal check. **Money orders** can be purchased at banks, some retail establishments, and the U.S. Postal Service. They are usually issued in smaller amounts and are cheaper than cashier's checks. Often, only the amount is filled in at the time the money order is issued. Until the blanks for the payee's name, the date, and the purchaser's signatures are filled in, the money order is as risky as cash to the purchaser. For this reason, some banks require that the blank spaces be filled in when the money order is issued.

Travelers who want to protect their money against loss or theft can purchase traveler's checks through banks and travel companies. **Traveler's checks** are usually issued in $20, $50, $100, and $500 denominations. The usual cost is the check's face value plus a small percentage. Widely accepted both in the United States and abroad, traveler's checks are nearly as convenient to use as cash. The purchaser of a traveler's check signs the check at the time of purchase and again when it is cashed. This practice protects both the user and the cashing party. The issuing company will replace lost or stolen traveler's checks.

Check Processing and Collection

Each year, billions of checks are processed in the United States. How does the check processing and collection system work? As seen in Figure 14.3, assume that Mrs. Henderson lives in Albany, New York, and conducts her banking with an Albany bank. Suppose that she buys a painting from a Sacramento, California, art dealer. The first place the check goes is to the art dealer's bank, where it is deposited. But the funds may not be immediately available to the art dealer unless Mrs. Henderson and the art dealer use the same bank, in which the processing (clearing) of the check is handled internally. In practice, about 30 percent of checks are drawn on and deposited into the same bank.

However, an internally cleared check does not apply to our example. Instead, the art dealer's Sacramento bank will likely desire to verify the check with Mrs. Henderson's Albany bank, the paying bank, before it converts the check value to cash. However, banks

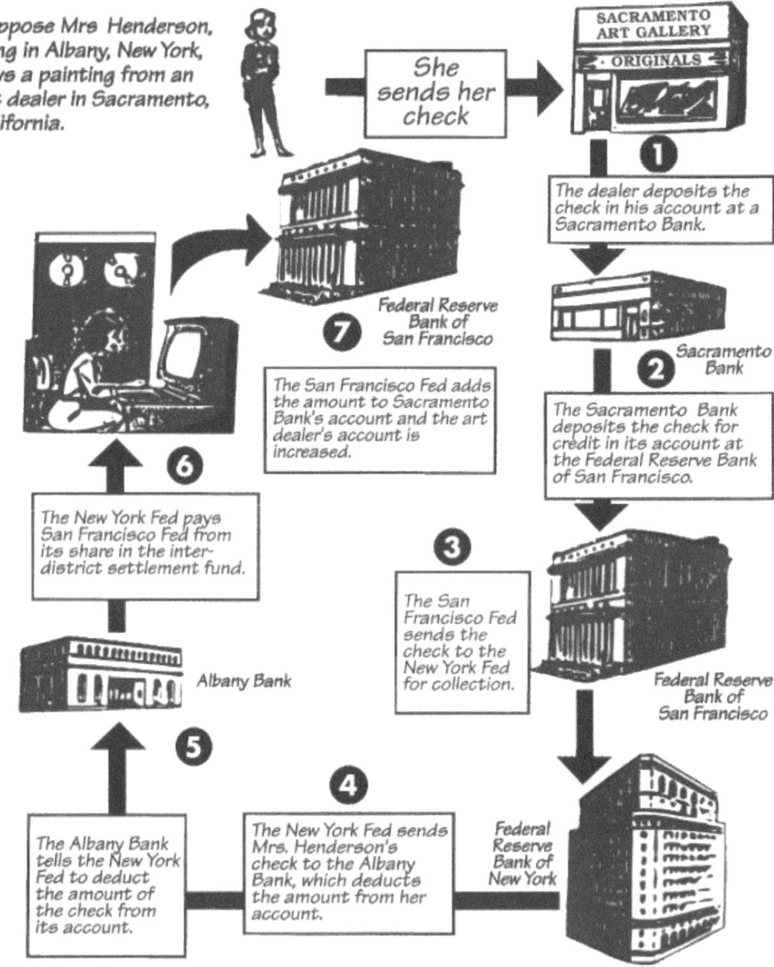
Suppose Mrs Henderson, living in Albany, New York, buys a painting from an art dealer in Sacramento, California.
She sends her check
SACRAMENTO ART GALLERY
ORIGINALS
1
The dealer deposits the check in his account at a Sacramento Bank.
Sacramento Bank
2
The Sacramento Bank deposits the check for credit in its account at the Federal Reserve Bank of San Francisco.
3
The San Francisco Fed sends the check to the New York Fed for collection.
Federal Reserve Bank of San Francisco
4
The New York Fed sends Mrs. Henderson's check to the Albany Bank, which deducts the amount from her account.
Federal Reserve Bank of New York
5
The Albany Bank tells the New York Fed to deduct the amount of the check from its account.
Albany Bank
6
The New York Fed pays San Francisco Fed from its share in the inter-district settlement fund.
7
Federal Reserve Bank of San Francisco
The San Francisco Fed adds the amount to Sacramento Bank's account and the art dealer's account is increased.

FIGURE 14.3 How the Payment System Works

Source: Federal Reserve Bank of New York, *The Story of Checks and Electronic Payment*, 1983, p. 13.

People and organizations move money among themselves by using depository institutions, such as commercial banks, as their switching mechanism. Depository institutions, in turn, use clearinghouses, correspondent banks, or Federal Reserve Banks as their switching mechanism. Federal Reserve Banks use the Interdistrict Settlement Fund in Washington, D.C., as their switching mechanism. The fund settles net amounts due between Federal Reserve Banks daily. Let's trace a check through the Federal Reserve System's clearing and collection facilities to see how the Fed links the payments system.

do not generally conduct business with each other directly; instead, they go through an "intermediary bank" which serves as a middleman. There are three types of intermediary banks.

The **Federal Reserve** is the central bank of the United States. Regional branches of the Federal Reserve handle check processing for banks that hold accounts with them, and they charge a fee for their services. Such services include check collection, air transportation of checks to the Federal Reserve Bank, and delivery of checks to paying banks. All financial institutions that accept deposits can purchase Federal Reserve check collection and payment services. Federal Reserve Banks handle about 27 percent of all checks processed in the United States.

Correspondent banks are banks that form partnerships with other banks in order to exchange checks and payments directly, bypassing the Federal Reserve and its check-processing fee. Outside banks may go through a correspondent bank to exchange checks and payments with one of its partners. For example, Mrs. Henderson's Albany bank and the art dealer's Sacramento bank may form a partnership with Citibank of New York, which serves as the correspondent bank.

Correspondent banks form a clearinghouse corporation, in which members exchange checks and payments in bulk, instead of on a check-by-check basis, which can be inefficient when each bank might receive thousands of checks in a day. The clearinghouse banks save up the checks drawn on other members and exchange them on a daily basis. The net payments for these checks are generally settled through Fedwire, an electronic funds transfer system that handles large-scale check settlement between U.S. banks. Correspondent banks and clearinghouse corporations make up the private sector of check clearing, and together they handle about 43 percent of U.S. checks.[3]

Returning to our check-clearing example, suppose that the Sacramento art dealer's bank uses the check-clearing services of the Federal Reserve. Assume that the Sacramento bank deposits Mrs. Henderson's check in its account at the Federal Reserve Bank of San Francisco. The San Francisco Federal Reserve Bank sends the check to the New York Federal Reserve Bank for collection. The New York Federal Reserve Bank then sends Mrs. Henderson's check to the Albany Bank, which deducts the amount from her account. The Albany bank then tells the New York Federal Reserve Bank to deduct the amount of the check from its account. The New York Federal Reserve Bank then pays the San Francisco Federal Reserve Bank from its share in the Interdistrict Settlement Fund of the Federal Reserve, which is in Washington, D.C. The San Francisco Federal Reserve Bank then adds the amount to the Sacramento bank's account and the art dealer's account is increased. These are the steps in the settlement process of a check that is cleared through the Federal Reserve System and are summarized in Figure 14.3.

Although the Federal Reserve is a major processor of checks, the number of checks that it processes has been declining since the mid-1990s. This is because of the use of ATMs and electronic payment methods, such as funds transfers and debit cards, which reduce the need to write paper checks. In the future, the use of checks will likely decrease as electronic payment methods become less expensive and more accessible and familiar to consumers.

Holds on Checking Accounts

Have you ever deposited a check at your bank only to find that you do not have immediate access to your money? Welcome to the world of check holds.

Opening a bank account and making deposits does not necessarily mean that those funds are immediately available for use. When you deposit a check into a bank, a holding period is often placed on the funds. The reason for the hold is that a bank wants to make sure that it receives the funds from the other bank against which the check is written, before you spend it all. The waiting period is the approximate number of days it takes for a bank to collect funds from the other bank. Simply put, check holds are intended to protect banks from fraud or insufficient funds.

Under federal law, certain deposits must be available by the next business day, such as checks payable by the U.S. Treasury or a Federal Reserve Bank, U.S. Postal Service money orders, state or local government checks, or electronic payments received by the bank for deposit in an account. Other deposits can be subject to a check hold of one to five business days, depending on whether the check is drawn on a local or non-local bank, and the size of the deposit.

Federal law establishes maximum hold periods—a bank is free to hold a deposit for less time than the regulation stipulates, but never for a longer time. Also, a bank is free to count days based on how it defines its business hours. This means that a deposit you make at 3:00 P.M. at one bank might be considered as deposited on that day, but that same deposit at another bank might be added to the next day's activity.

As with most government regulations, the rules are complicated, so be sure you do your own research regarding check holds. Banks are required to make sure you know the rules.

What Backs the Money Supply?

If you ask your friends "What backs our money supply?" you may get answers such as "Gold or silver backs our money." No! Gold and silver were removed from our monetary system decades ago. We must look elsewhere to see what backs our money supply.

Recall that the major components of our money supply—paper currency and checking deposits—are promises to pay, or debts. Paper currency is the circulating debt of the Federal Reserve System, and checking deposits represent the debt of depository institutions. These items have no intrinsic value. A $20 bill is simply a piece of paper; a checking account is an accounting entry; and a 25-cent piece has less value as metal than its face value.

What underlies the value of a $10 bill or a $500 balance in a checking account? Currency and checking accounts are considered money because we widely accept them in return for goods and services. We accept money in exchange because we are confident that others will be willing to accept our money when we spend it. Put simply, money is anything that we generally accept as a medium of exchange.

The law reinforces our confidence in the acceptability of currency. All U.S. currency, including paper money and coins, is designated as **legal tender**—that is, the federal government mandates its acceptance in transactions and requires that dollars be used in the payment of taxes. However, this does not mean that a particular type of currency must always be accepted. For example, a convenience store may legally refuse to accept bills in denominations of more than $20, or an automobile dealer may refuse to be paid only in pennies.

Although the legal tender pledge reinforces the general acceptability of currency, it does not apply to other types of money. For example, the government does not mandate that checks be legal tender. Nevertheless, checking accounts are an important component of the basic money supply. Although checks are a generally accepted medium of exchange, we may legally turn them down as payments for goods and services. Perhaps you have attempted to buy gasoline from an establishment that has a sign next to the cash register saying "No out-of-town checks!"

Does the Penny Make Sense?

For years, a debate has existed within the United States over whether the 1-cent coin, commonly known as the penny, should be abolished as a unit of currency in the United States. Although several bills have been introduced in Congress to eliminate the penny, none of them have been approved. These bills would leave the nickel, at 5 cents, as the lowest-value coin. Why the fuss?

Critics of the penny note that its production results in a loss to the U.S. government. As of 2022, it cost about 2.7 cents to mint a penny that is worth only a cent because of the cost of materials, production, and distribution; pennies are made of zinc coated with copper. Critics also note that the penny fails to achieve a major purpose of our monetary system, the facilitation of exchange. When people start leaving a monetary unit at the cash register for the next customer, the unit is too small to be useful. Simply put, the penny is a waste of people's time. Moreover, pennies are not accepted by all vending machines or many toll booths, and pennies are not accepted in bulk.

The experience of Canada offers lessons for those who advocate eliminating pennies in the United States. In 2013, Canada joined the ranks of other countries that have removed their lowest-denomination coin from circulation, including Switzerland, Norway, Australia, and the United Kingdom. Citing low purchasing power and rising production costs (1.6 cents to produce every penny), the Canadian government estimated that it would save $11 million a year by eliminating the penny. The government estimated that it would take some 4–5 years for pennies to become extinct in Canada. During this period, businesses are expected to apply rounding to the nearest 5-cent mark for cash transactions. For example, if the total price of a soft drink and a sandwich is $7.92, a customer that was paying in cash would owe $7.90. But those using another method of payment, say, a credit card, would pay $7.92, and the pennies would be tallied electronically.

However, defenders of the American penny maintain that its abolishment would result in problems. They fear that if the penny is eliminated, consumers would be hit with a rounding tax, since merchants would tend to round upward rather than downward. They also note that the penny aids causes in raising hundreds of millions of dollars each year for important charities like Ronald McDonald House Charities, School and Youth Programs, and the like. Moreover, the U.S. Mint's fixed costs would continue to be incurred whether or not the mint produces the penny; these costs would be absorbed by the remaining denominations of circulating coins, without the penny adding to their production costs. Finally, if pennies were eliminated, Americans would switch to using the nickel, which cost about 9 cents to manufacture in 2015. Would the government really be saving money by eliminating the penny?

To date, the U.S. government has said that it needs more research before it can make a decision to either change the composition of the penny so as to include cheaper metals than zinc or copper or do away with the penny altogether.[4]

BOX ESSAY 14.1
Will Bitcoin Be Adopted as a Main National Currency?

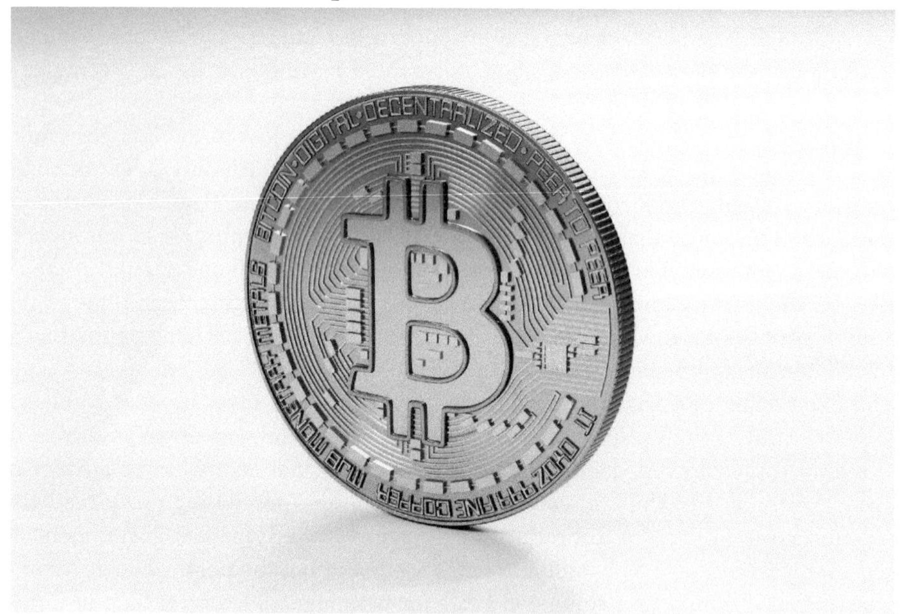

Source: Westend61 / Getty Images®

Another type of money is Bitcoin, a digital currency that was created in 2009 by an unknown person using the alias Satoshi Nakamoto. Bitcoin operates free of any central control or oversight of banks or governments. You can send Bitcoin through the Internet to make payments to merchants and retailers that are willing to accept them. Some people purchase Bitcoin as an investment, anticipating that it will rise in value.

To obtain Bitcoin, you can exchange money, such as the dollar, on an online exchange, such as Coinbase or Okcoin. The exchange fee declines as the size of the transaction increases, ranging from 0.5 percent for small transactions to 0.2 percent for large transactions.

Proponents maintain that Bitcoin serves as a better store of value than traditional fiat money like the dollar. They note that unlike government-issued money that can easily be inflated, the supply of Bitcoin is limited to 21 million Bitcoins, and that quantity can never change. Since there is only a fixed number of Bitcoins that can be released into circulation, there is no loss of purchasing power due to inflation—too much money chasing too few goods. Thus, Bitcoin becomes a superior store of value than the dollar. Yet skeptics question Bitcoin for its lack of intrinsic value because it is not backed by gold or silver.

Proponents also maintain that Bitcoin entails relatively low transaction costs because sellers and buyers of Bitcoin deal directly with each other, thus eliminating any middleman fees. Also, Bitcoin provides a high degree of privacy for users since the names of Bitcoin sellers and buyers are never revealed.

However, critics express concerns about Bitcoin's not serving as legal tender, and therefore it does not have to be accepted in payment of debt. Also, since Bitcoin's creation in 2009, its price instability has prevented its serving as an effective medium of exchange. For example, in November 2021, Bitcoin rose to a record value of 1 Bitcoin equal to $67,802, only to crash to $20,111 in June 2022. This 70-percent decline in the value of Bitcoin (and other cryptocurrencies) resulted in about $2 trillion of wealth being eliminated. Finally, critics contend that the market for Bitcoin tends to be governed by speculators, thus providing people the incentive to hoard Bitcoins rather than spend them.

Several countries allow Bitcoin to be used in transactions, such as Australia, Canada, Germany, Switzerland, and the United States. Yet other countries consider Bitcoin a threat to their monetary systems and are concerned about its use to support illicit activities like terrorism and drug trafficking. China, Qatar, and Saudi Arabia are among the countries that have declared Bitcoin illegal.

As the Bob Dylan song of 1964 stated, "The Times They Are a-Changin," and the nature of money is evolving. Today, central banks around the world, including the Federal Reserve, are contemplating whether they should offer regulated digital currencies to the public.

MEASURING THE MONEY SUPPLY; THE M1 MONEY SUPPLY

So far in this chapter, we have discussed many forms of money. Let us now consider how the money supply is measured in the United States.

There are two approaches to defining and measuring money: The *narrow* definition of the money supply, which emphasizes the role of money as a *medium of exchange*, and the *broader* definition of the money supply, which emphasizes the role of money as a *store of value*.

Table 14.3 lists the components of the U.S. money supply according to its narrowest definition, the **M1 money supply**. This measure of the money supply includes currency in the hands of the public, demand deposits at commercial banks, and other liquid assets, such as savings accounts and other checkable deposits. Therefore, M1 includes the most liquid (immediately spendable) components of the money supply because it contains

TABLE 14.3 The M1 Measure of the Money Supply, 2023

Component	*In Billions of Dollars ($)*	*Percent of Total*
Currency	2,215.6	11.4
Demand deposits	5,043.1	26.1
Other liquid deposits*	12,078.0	62.5
Total	19,336.7	100.0

* Other liquid deposits consist of savings deposits, negotiable order of withdrawal (NOW) and automatic transfer service (ATS) balances at depository institutions, share draft accounts at credit unions, demand deposits at thrift institutions, and savings deposits, including money market deposit accounts.

Source: Board of Governors of the Federal Reserve System, *Money Stock Measures-H.6 Release*, March 28, 2023, available at https://www.federalreserve.gov/releases/h6/current/default.htm.

currency and assets that either are or can be quickly converted into cash. M1 is expressed by the following formula:

$$M1 = \text{Currency} + \text{Demand deposits} + \text{Savings deposits} + \text{Other checkable deposits}$$

In our definition of money, we include currency only if it is *in the hands of the public.* Some cash is kept in bank vaults and is released only when customers withdraw cash from their vaults. Other cash is kept on deposit at a Federal Reserve Bank, which stores the funds for future use. Until this cash is released by banks or a Federal Reserve Bank, it is not considered part of the money supply.

As seen in Table 14.3, the M1 money supply equaled $19,336.7 billion in 2022. Of this amount, 11.4 percent was issued by the U.S. Treasury and the Federal Reserve Banks as coins and paper currency; 26.1 percent was issued by our commercial banking system as demand deposits, and 62.5 percent came from other highly liquid assets issued by financial institutions such as savings and loan associations, mutual savings bank, credit unions, and commercial banks.

Why are checking accounts (demand deposits) a widely used type of money? First, making large payments by check is convenient. Imagine how much paper money—say, $20 bills—you would need to purchase a new house! Second, checks provide a record of payment, thus making it unnecessary to keep receipts for purchases of goods and services. Finally, checking accounts provide an element of safety. If you lose your checkbook, you can instruct your bank to stop payment on any future checks that are written on your account.

The **M2 money supply** is a broader measure of the money supply that includes all components of M1 and several less liquid assets—small-denomination time certificates of deposit (amounts less than $100,000) and shares in retail money market funds, which are less liquid and not suitable as a medium of exchange. Although components of the M2 money supply can be converted into cash or checking deposits, their convertibility is not as quick as the components of the M1 money supply.

For many, the measurement of the money supply showed a close relationship between the money supply and economic variables, such as gross domestic product and inflation.

But in recent decades, this relationship became uncertain. Therefore, the significance of the money supply's acting as a guide for the formation of the monetary policy the Federal Reserve substantially declined.

CHECK POINT

1. In the United States, who issues coins? How about paper currency?
2. How do checks clear from one bank to another?
3. What "backs" the U.S. money supply?
4. Identify the components of the U.S. money supply according to the M1 and M2 money supply.

HOW YOUR MONEY GROWS OVER TIME: COMPOUND INTEREST

As a saver, do you realize that **compound interest** is one of your best friends?

When you add to your savings account at a bank, you will receive repayment of the principal amount saved as well as interest payments. By not spending a dollar today and saving it, you obtain more than a dollar to spend in the future. The interest rate is the percentage of your money that is added to your account each time you are paid interest. Simply put, the interest rate is the reward for saving. To a saver, the key is whether the interest is compounded and how it is compounded.

Suppose that you have just won $10,000 in a lottery. You would like to save the winnings so that you can eventually purchase a house. You place the money in a savings account at your bank, which offers you 5-percent interest each year. After one year, you will have a total of $10,500; your original $10,000 plus interest of $500 ($10,000 × 1.05 = $10,500).

What happens if you hold your savings deposit for two years? If the interest rate remains constant at 5 percent and you reinvest your principal and accumulated interest, you will earn 5-percent interest on your accumulated savings each year. This process of earning interest on the interest, as well as on the principal, is known as *compounding*. At the end of two years, you will have $11,025 ($10,500 × 1.05 = $11,025). Notice that your interest increases to $525 in the second year ($11,025 – $10,500 = $525), which is $25 more than the $500 interest that you earned during the first year. Why do you earn more interest during the second year than in the first? Simply because you can now earn interest on the sum of the original principal and the interest you earned in the first year. You are now earning interest on interest, which is the concept of compound interest.

It is easy to use the concept of compound interest to calculate the value of your savings for any number of years. As seen in Figure 14.4, at the end of three years the value of your

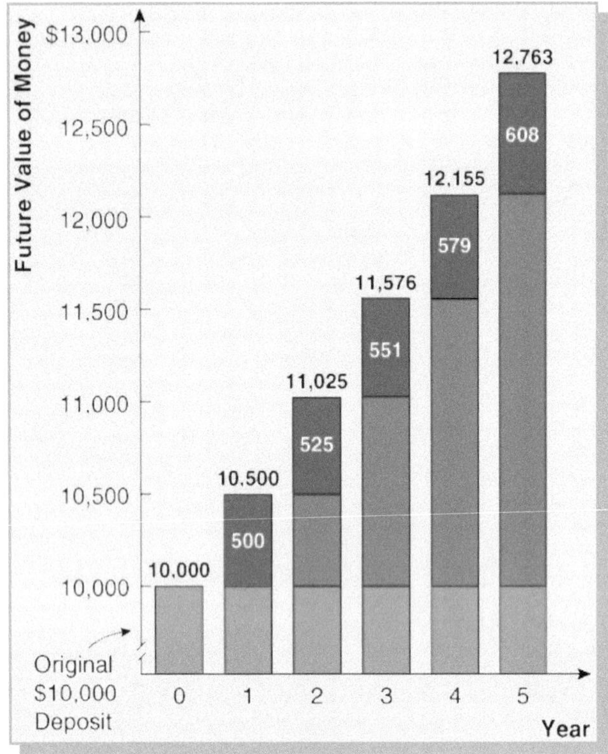

FIGURE 14.4 The Future Value of $10,000 Compounded Annually at an Interest Rate of 5 Percent

According to the concept of compound interest, a savings deposit earns "interest on interest." This means that interest earned in earlier periods is reinvested to earn interest in future periods. In this manner, the amount of interest you earn grows, or compounds. As seen in the figure, a $10,000 savings deposit compounded annually at an interest rate of 5 percent will have a future value of $12,763 at the end of the fifth year.

savings will have grown to $11,576; at the end of four years, the value of your savings will have grown to $12,155; and at the end of five years, the value of your savings will have grown to $12,763. Indeed, compound interest really does make a difference.

Until now we have assumed that the compounding period is always annual. However, banks sometimes compound interest on a quarterly or daily basis. What happens to the future value of your money when the compounding period is less than a year? You earn more money faster. The sooner your interest is paid, the sooner you start earning interest on it, and the sooner you realize the benefits of compound interest. For example, if a bank decided to switch from paying interest annually to paying interest daily, the number of compounding periods per year increases from one period to 365 periods. Your money grows faster as the number of compounding periods increases. For a given interest rate and identical saving period, the more frequent the compounding, the larger the future value of money. This explains why banks like to advertise daily compounding rather than annual or quarterly compounding. Also, it's not just time that adds to the future value of money—it's also the interest rate. Obviously, a higher interest rate will earn you more money.

THE BUSINESS OF BANKING

A commercial bank is a corporation that seeks to make a profit for its stockholders. How does a bank operate? To understand the business of banking more clearly, we can look at a bank's balance sheet, a tool that is used by accountants.

A Bank's Balance Sheet

A **balance sheet** is a two-column list that shows the financial position of a bank at a specific date. It shows everything of value that the bank owns (assets), the debts that it owes (liabilities), and the amount of the owners' investment (net worth) in the bank. The difference between a bank's assets and liabilities is its net worth. When a bank is established, its owners must place their own funds into the bank. These funds are the bank's initial net worth. If a bank makes profits, its net worth will rise. Conversely, the bank's net worth will fall if it incurs losses.

Table 14.4 shows the consolidated balance sheet for all commercial banks in the United States as of March 2023. We will use this picture of the entire banking system to get an idea of what a commercial bank does and the importance of the various assets and liabilities to an average or typical commercial bank in this country.

Let us consider the assets of the commercial banking system, which we see on the left side of Table 14.4. First are banks' reserves, which total $3,334.2 billion. **Reserves** are deposits that banks have received but have not lent out. Reserves can be kept either in vault cash or as deposits at a Federal Reserve Bank. One reason to hold reserves is that on a particular day, some of a bank's customers might want to withdraw more cash than other customers are depositing. The bank must be able to fulfill its obligation for withdrawals, so it must have cash on hand to meet this commitment.

TABLE 14.4 Consolidated Balance Sheet for All U.S. Commercial Banks (billions of dollars), March, 2023

Assets	*Liabilities and Net Worth*
Cash assets (reserves) $3,334.2	Deposits $17,446.3
Loans 12,062.4	Borrowings 2,338.4
Securities 5,370.7	Other liabilities 1,117.9
Other assets 2,305.3	Total 20,902.6
Total 23,072.6	Net worth (assets – 2,170.0 liabilities)

Source: Data drawn from Board of Governors of the Federal Reserve System, *Assets and Liabilities of Commercial Banks in the United States-H.8*, April 14, 2023, available at https://www.federalreserve.gov/releases/h8/current.

Next come the $12,062.4 billion of loans and $5,370.7 billion of securities owned by the commercial banking system. Loans are IOUs signed by households and businesses. Examples include commercial and industrial loans, real estate loans, and consumer loans for automobiles and other durable goods. Securities are IOUs issued by the U.S. Treasury or other government agencies when they borrow money. Both loans and securities provide interest income for banks. Finally, banks have "other" assets such as the value of their office buildings and equipment.

On the right side of the balance sheet are banks' liabilities. The major liability is deposits, which equal $17,446.3 billion and include both checking deposits and a variety of savings deposits and time deposits. Why are deposits considered liabilities? Because bank customers have the right to withdraw funds from their deposit accounts. Until they do, the banks owe them these funds. Another liability is bank borrowings. At a particular point in time, a bank may find that its reserves are inadequate to fulfill the withdrawal of deposits by its customers, and thus they may borrow reserves. A bank may borrow reserves from another bank or from a Federal Reserve Bank.

Also on the right side of the balance sheet is the banks' net worth, $2,170 billion, which represents the difference between assets ($23,072.6 billion) and liabilities ($20,902.6 billion). If a bank were to go out of business, selling all its assets and using the proceeds to pay off all of its liabilities, the excess would go to the bank's stockholders—its owners.

The Reserve Requirement

By law, all banks are required to hold a certain percentage of their checking deposits on reserve either in the form of vault cash or as deposits at the Federal Reserve. **Required reserves** represent the minimum amount of vault cash and deposits at the Federal Reserve that a bank must maintain. **Actual reserves** are the amount that a bank is holding. If a bank is holding more than the law requires, it has **excess reserves**, which can be used to make loans or purchase government securities. Therefore, actual reserves are the sum of a bank's required and excess reserves, calculated as follows:

$$\text{Actual reserves} = \text{Required reserves} + \text{Excess reserves}$$

For example, U.S. Bank may have $80 million of actual reserves, of which $8 million must be held in required reserves. The remainder, $72 million, is the bank's excess reserves.

The **required reserve ratio** is a specific percentage of checking deposits that must be kept either as vault cash or as deposits at a local Federal Reserve Bank. It is established by the Federal Reserve System and directly limits the ability of banks to grant new loans. For example, a required reserve ratio of 10 percent on checking deposits means that a bank must have an amount on reserve equal to 10 percent of the value of the checking deposits it is holding. For example, if Bank of America has $50 million in checking accounts and a 10-percent required reserve ratio, it must maintain at least $5 million in actual reserves ($50,000,000 × 0.10 = $5,000,000).[5]

THE PROCESS OF MONEY CREATION

If you were to ask your friends where our money comes from, they might have a simple answer: "The government prints it." They might even have toured the U.S. Mint in Philadelphia or Denver and seen pennies and nickels being stamped, or they may have visited the Bureau of Engraving and Printing in Washington, D.C., and seen dollar bills being printed. As we have learned, however, most of our money comes from checking accounts issued by banks rather than from the government. Let us examine how banks create money.

Suppose that you walk into Wells Fargo Bank and deposit $1,000 cash into your checking account. The deposit of cash, which the bank keeps in its vault, results in a $1,000 decrease in the money supply (recall that the currency held by a bank is not part of the economy's money supply). However, the checking account component of the money supply rises by $1,000 because of the deposit. Thus, the total supply of money does not change. However, Wells Fargo Bank will not earn a profit by keeping all of the cash that it receives in its vault. It wants to make loans to the public.

Let's suppose that the required reserve ratio is 10 percent, indicating that a bank must keep 10 percent of its checking deposits as required reserves. Thus, Wells Fargo Bank will keep $100 in required reserves ($1,000 × 0.10 = $100) and make loans of $900. When Wells Fargo Bank makes these loans, the supply of money increases. Why? As a depositor, you still have your checking account of $1,000, but now the borrowers hold $900 in their checking accounts. Therefore, the money supply equals $1,900. Figure 14.5(*a*) shows the change in the balance sheet of Wells Fargo Bank after it has made the loan.

Suppose that Wells Fargo Bank makes a loan to a computer software company that wants to purchase some equipment. The company buys $900 of equipment from another

(a) Wells Fargo Bank

Assets		Liabilities
Required Reserves =	$100	Checking Deposits = $1,000
Loans =	$900	

(b) U.S. Bank

Assets		Liabilities
Required Reserves =	$90	Checking Deposits = $900
Loans =	$810	

(c) Rainier Bank

Assets		Liabilities
Required Reserves =	$81	Checking Deposits = $810
Loans =	$729	

FIGURE 14.5 The Process of Money Creation

firm, which deposits the check in its account at U.S. Bank. Figure 14.5(*b*) shows what happens to the balance sheet of U.S. Bank. Its checking deposits increase by $900 because of the deposit. The bank must maintain $90 of required reserves ($900 × 0.10 = $90) and it can lend out $810. Suppose that the bank lends $810 to the owner of an espresso stand and opens a checking account for him. In this way, U.S. Bank creates an additional $810 of money. The espresso stand owner then purchases supplies from a wholesaler who deposits the check in her account at Rainier Bank, which keeps $81 in reserve ($810 × 0.010 = $81) and makes $729 in loans. Figure 14.5(*c*) shows what happens to the balance sheet of Rainier Bank.

The process goes on and on. Each time we deposit a check and a bank makes a loan, more money is created. We can determine how much money is eventually created by the banking system by adding the money created by each bank:

Original checking deposit	=	$1,000
Wells Fargo Bank loan	=	900
U.S. Bank loan	=	720
Total money supply	=	$10,000

The process of money creation can continue forever. If we added the infinite sequence of numbers in our example, we find that the initial checking deposit of $1,000 results in a total money supply of $10,000. Put simply, the money supply of the banking system can be increased by a *multiple* of the initial checking deposit.[6]

We call the maximum amount of money that the banking system can generate with each dollar of reserves the **money multiplier**. In our example, the initial $1,000 of reserves leads to a money supply totaling $10,000; the money multiplier is 10.

What determines the size of the money multiplier? The money multiplier is the reciprocal of the required reserve ratio, calculated as follows:

$$\text{Money multiplier} = 1 / \text{required reserve ratio}$$

In our example, the required reserve ratio is 10 percent, so the money multiplier is 10 (1 / 0.10 = 10). If the required reserve ratio is 20 percent, the money multiplier is 5 (1 / 0.20 = 5).

Notice that the formula tells us the *maximum* amount of money that the banking system can generate with each dollar of reserves. In the real world, however, the ability of the banking system to create money is smaller than the formula suggests. The main reason is that the formula assumes that all loans make their way directly into checking accounts. In reality, people may hold part of their loans as currency. The currency kept in a person's purse or wallet or safe-deposit box remains outside the banking system and cannot be held by banks as reserves from which to make loans. The greater the currency holdings, the smaller the actual money expansion multiplier.

THE FEDERAL DEPOSIT INSURANCE CORPORATION

Although we expect our banks and other depository institutions to engage in sound financial practices, sometimes banks are perceived as being unsound and likely to fail. This can trigger a run on a bank in which depositors rush to withdraw their deposits before the bank fails. If too many depositors withdraw from their accounts at the same time, a bank can fail. And bank failure can create a confidence crisis in the nation's banking system.

To promote public confidence in banking and prevent runs on banks, the **Federal Deposit Insurance Corporation (FDIC)** has been insuring deposits and regulating banks since 1933. The FDIC sign, posted at insured commercial banks, mutual savings banks, and savings and loan associations across the country, has become a symbol of confidence. In similar fashion, the National Credit Union Administration (NCUA) insures deposits and regulates credit unions. It's important to verify that your depository institution is insured by the FDIC (or NCUA) prior to making a deposit there.

Why Was the FDIC Created?

The Great Depression of the 1930s caused financial chaos in the United States. More than 9,000 banks closed between the stock market crash of October 1929 and March 1933, when President Franklin D. Roosevelt took office. For all practical purposes, the nation's banking system had shut down completely even before Roosevelt (less than 48 hours after his inauguration) declared a "banking holiday," suspending all banking activities until stability could be restored.

Among the actions taken by Congress to bring order to the system was the creation of the FDIC in June 1933. The intent was to provide a federal government guarantee of deposits so that customers' funds, within certain limits, would be safe and available to them on demand. After the introduction of federal deposit insurance, the number of bank failures declined sharply. Since the creation of the FDIC, not one depositor has lost a cent of insured funds because of bank failure.

Breaking Down the FDIC

The FDIC doesn't just wait for a bank to fail before taking action. As a government regulatory body, the FDIC conducts bank examinations to promote and maintain the safety and soundness of banks. Through bank examinations, the FDIC determines the financial condition of insured banks and obtains a better understanding of the risks that it assumes in insuring a bank's deposits. Bank examinations help the FDIC identify potential problems early so it can work with the bank's staff to resolve problems with them before they escalate.

If the FDIC has reason to believe that a bank practices unsafe and unsound banking, it may issue a cease-and-desist order, which stops bank employees from engaging in some activity. Also, the FDIC may levy civil money penalties on bank employees, and it may remove them from their banking positions. Moreover, the FDIC can terminate deposit insurance for banks judged to be unsound.

The FDIC also provides for a system of deposit insurance. FDIC insurance covers all types of deposits received at an insured bank, such as checking deposits, savings deposits, time certificates of deposit (CDs), and money market deposits. The standard deposit insurance amount is $250,000 per depositor, per insured bank, for each account ownership category.

Insured banks pay premiums to the FDIC to cover the cost of their deposit insurance. This money is placed into the Deposit Insurance Fund of the FDIC, which is used to insure people's deposits and allow the FDIC to resolve bank failures. Also, the FDIC earns interest on its funds invested in U.S. government securities. Moreover, the FDIC is backed by the full faith and credit of the U.S. government. This means that the resources of the U.S. government stand behind FDIC-insured depositors.

Is $250,000 the maximum amount of insurance coverage that you can receive from the FDIC? No. If you have more than $250,000 deposited in an account with a single bank, you can spread your funds among multiple banks to ensure that you are fully protected by the FDIC. For example, if you have $500,000, you might open a savings account at Wells Fargo Bank for $250,000 and a savings account at U.S. Bank for $250,000, thus receiving $500,000 of insurance coverage by the FDIC.

Another way to increase your FDIC deposit insurance coverage beyond $250,000 is to open accounts in *different categories of legal ownership* at your bank, such as a single account and a joint account. For example, suppose that Susan and Tim Miller bank at Capital One Financial Corporation.

- They can have a total of $500,000 FDIC insurance coverage if they each open a *single account* (say, a checking account) that is insured up to the FDIC limit of $250,000.
- Also, suppose that Susan and Tim combine funds into a *joint checking account* at Capital One. This account is in a different legal ownership category than their single accounts, and it is insured up to a maximum of $250,000 per owner, or $500,000 for both Susan and Tim.

With these two accounts of different legal ownership categories, Susan and Tim can receive a total of $1,000,000 insurance coverage from the FDIC ($500,000 + $500,000 = $1,000,000).

How the FDIC Resolves Bank Failures

The unlikely event of a bank's failure results in the closing of an insolvent bank by a federal or state regulator. A bank can be closed when it does not have enough liquid assets (cash) to meet its financial obligations to depositors and creditors. When a bank is closed, the FDIC is appointed as receiver and the closed bank is placed into receivership. This means that the FDIC has the responsibility to sell the failed bank to another bank or liquidate the failed bank's assets to pay depositors and creditors.

When a bank fails, the FDIC will typically try to find a healthy bank that is willing merge with the failed bank. This means that the healthy bank purchases assets (loans, government securities) and assumes all insured deposits from the failed bank. Insured depositors of the failed bank immediately become depositors of the healthy bank, and they have access to their insured funds. Therefore, all depositors, even those having accounts more than the $250,000 insurance limit, are fully protected. This is generally the preferred and most widely used method of the FDIC in resolving bank failure, as banking customers can continue their banking without disruption.

Deposit payoffs are another approach used by the FDIC to resolve bank failure. When a bank fails, the FDIC mails a check to insured depositors, within a few days after the bank closing, subject to the $250,000 limit on insurance coverage. The failed bank closes, and there is no successor bank. Depositors with accounts greater than the $250,000 insurance cap become creditors of the failed bank, for the amount that their deposits exceed the insurance limit. This means that as the receiver of the failed bank, the FDIC assumes the responsibility of selling the assets of the failed bank, such as owned real estate, equipment, loans, and securities. With these proceeds, the FDIC then settles the bank's debts, including claims for deposits that exceed the insured limit. To the extent that funds become available as the FDIC sells the failed bank's assets, the uninsured depositors are paid by the FDIC according to their pro-rata claim on these funds. In practice, not all depositors may be fully reimbursed by the FDIC.

Resolving Bank Failures: Three Case Studies

The timely and effective resolution of failed insured banks is an important part of the FDIC's mission. When a bank fails, the FDIC will seek the least costly resolution method, which may include selling the bank to another institution or paying off insured depositors directly. Let us consider three cases of bank failure.

Failure of Heritage Community Bank. In 2006, Heritage Community Bank was one of the nation's most profitable small lenders. But on February 27, 2009, the Glenwood Illinois bank was closed by the FDIC.

When the FDIC became receiver of Heritage Community Bank, it arranged a merger between the bank and Chicago-based MB Financial Inc, who purchased Heritage's deposits and loans. On the next day, the newly merged Heritage Community Bank reopened on time, with the same staff and banking products, but with a new owner and a new name.

When times were good, construction lending provided high levels of income for Heritage. But when the housing market crashed in 2007, Heritage's reliance on construction loans proved unprofitable, leading to the bank's failure.

Because Heritage was bought by MB Financial, the FDIC did not have to pay off Heritage depositors. Even depositors with funds over the FDIC's insurance limit of $250,000 were fully protected. However, arranging the merger between Heritage and MB Financial cost the FDIC's Deposit Insurance Fund about $42 million. FDIC officials stated that the merger of Heritage and MB Financial Bank's was the least costly resolution method for the FDIC's Deposit Insurance Fund compared to alternatives.

Failure of Washington Mutual Bank. The origins of Washington Mutual Bank (WaMu) date back to 1889, when it was established after the Great Fire of Seattle, Washington. WaMu was originally a regional savings bank that grew to become a bank with branch offices in 15 states and $188 billion in deposits. Yet on September 25, 2008, WaMu declared bankruptcy, and it was bought by JPMorgan Chase.

The failure of Washington Mutual was primarily because of the subprime mortgage crisis of 2007–2008, which resulted in a surplus quantity of unsold homes and decreasing home prices. Many of WaMu's mortgages were made to unqualified buyers, and the bank couldn't sell them to raise cash. As WaMu wrote down defaulted mortgages, depositors panicked and quickly withdrew funds from the bank, which resulted in its failure.

As it became clear that WaMu was about to fail, the FDIC shopped for a merger partner for the bank. The winning bid was made by JPMorgan Chase, and WaMu's branches were soon renamed as Chase branches. All of WaMu's depositors were fully protected by the merger of WaMu and JPMorgan Chase. The failure of WaMu was the largest bank failure in U.S. history.

Failure of Silicon Valley Bank. Silicon Valley Bank (SVB) was founded as a regional bank in 1983, headquartered in Santa Clara, California. By 2022, it became the 16th largest lender in the United States. SVB specialized in providing financial services to venture capital and technology startup companies. However, on March 10, 2023, after a run on its deposits, the bank failed and was taken into receivership by the FDIC.

SVB's financial problems began on March 8, 2023, when the bank surprised investors with news that it needed to raise $2.25 billion to shore up its balance sheet. This news prompted a panic for the venture capital and technology companies that SVB served, and it resulted in depositors withdrawing a staggering $42 billion within 48 hours. Nearly 90 percent of the bank's deposits exceeded the FDIC insurance cap of $250,000, making them more subject to withdrawal in times of trouble because the FDIC doesn't stand behind them.

When the FDIC took control of SVB, it stated that the bank's failure was a "systemic risk" that could lead to the collapse of the nation's banking system. This action allowed the FDIC to guarantee all insured and uninsured depositors immediate access to their funds, rather than the standard $250,000. The policy was intended to minimize any lack of public confidence in the banking system, thus preventing widespread runs on bank deposits. The FDIC then sold SVB to First Citizens Bank, based in Raleigh, North Carolina.

The failure of SVB cost the FDIC's deposit insurance fund about $20 billion. To recoup this sum, the FDIC raised insurance premiums paid by banks for deposit insurance, especially the nation's largest banks.

WHY WERE BIG BANKS BAILED OUT DURING THE FINANCIAL CRISIS OF 2007–2008?

The financial crisis of 2007–2008 has been described as the worst financial crisis since the Great Depression of the 1930s. It resulted in the threat of total collapse of large financial institutions and downturns in stock markets throughout the world. In many areas, the housing market suffered, resulting in evictions, foreclosures, and prolonged unemployment.

An initial response of the U.S. Treasury and the Federal Reserve to this crisis was to stabilize the financial system through bailouts of banks and other financial services firms such as JPMorgan Chase, Citigroup Inc., Bank of America, Wells Fargo and Company, U.S. Bancorp, and the like. Why the bailouts?

The general issue involving bailouts is known as "systemic risk," which means that the failure of one bank can result in the failure of many other banks, just as a chain of dominoes are collapsing. Have you heard the old joke: "If you owe your banker a thousand dollars, and can't pay, then it's your problem. But if you owe your banker a million dollars and can't pay, then your banker has a problem"? The government feared that if major banks failed and defaulted, the losses suffered by other banks, firms, and households would be catastrophic for the entire economy. Simply put, the government felt that some big banks were too important to fail and that it had to rescue them.

However, critics pointed out a problem. When the government enacts policies to reduce systemic risk, it protects at least some banks from the consequences of their bad decisions. For example, a bank that lent too much money to, say, Bank of America now realizes that it does not have to worry in the future because the government will step in to bail out Bank of America. Thus, the bank can continue taking on too much risk because it has an implied guarantee: Heads the bank wins, tails the taxpayer bails out the bank. Indeed, the bailout of some of America's biggest financial institutions has sparked sharp criticism from politicians and the public, who feel that the greed and excessive risk taking by these institutions have been a major source of their problems.

CHECK POINT

1. Identify the major assets and liabilities of a typical commercial bank.
2. How do banks create money? Why does the banking system have a money multiplier?
3. How does the Federal Deposit Insurance Corporation promote stability in the nation's banking system?

CHAPTER SUMMARY

1. Money is the set of assets in the economy that people use regularly to purchase goods and services from others. Money has three functions in the economy: It is a medium of exchange, a unit of account, and a store of value. These functions distinguish money from other assets such as stocks, bonds, and real estate.
2. Are credit cards money? Not at all! When you use a credit card to make a purchase, you obtain a short-term loan from the financial institution that issued the card. Credit cards are thus a method of postponing payment for a brief period. In shopping for a credit card, it is important to consider features such as the card's annual percentage rate, the grace period, fees such as an over-limit fee or late-payment fee, and the annual cost of the card.
3. The basic money supply (M1) in the United States consists of coins, paper money, savings accounts, checking accounts, and traveler's checks. Under federal law, only the

Federal Reserve System can issue paper currency, and only the U.S. Treasury can issue coins. Checking accounts and savings accounts are issued by the banking system.

4 The check collection system in the United States is efficient, but the collection process that a check goes through may be complicated. The check processing system is conducted by local clearinghouses, correspondent banks, and the Federal Reserve System's check collection network.

5 The U.S. economy has an array of banks, including commercial banks, savings and loan associations, mutual savings banks, and credit unions. We call these depository institutions because they accept deposits from people and provide checking accounts that are part of the money supply.

6 If you save money in a bank, you have alternatives to checking accounts, such as money market deposit accounts, savings accounts, and certificates of deposit. In shopping for an account, it is important to look at features such as the interest rate, the method of interest compounding, the annual percentage yield, the timing of interest payments, and fees.

7 A commercial bank is a corporation that seeks to make a profit for its stockholders. Among the most important assets of a bank are its reserves, loans, and government securities. Deposits and borrowings are a bank's major liabilities.

8 Most of our money comes from checking accounts issued by banks, rather than currency. Through the process of lending reserves, banks create money. The money multiplier is used to calculate the maximum amount of money that the banking system can generate with each dollar of reserves. The money multiplier is the reciprocal of the required reserve ratio.

9 The FDIC has insured deposits and promoted safe and sound banking practices since 1933. The FDIC insures deposits up to $250,000 at virtually all U.S. banks. Since the formation of the FDIC, not one depositor has lost a cent of insured funds because of bank failure.

KEY TERMS AND CONCEPTS

money
currency
medium of exchange
unit of account
store of value
demand deposit account
negotiable order of withdrawal (NOW) account
share draft account
certified check
cashier's check
money order
traveler's checks
Federal Reserve
correspondent bank
clearinghouse corporation
legal tender
M1 money supply
M2 money supply
compound interest
balance sheet
reserves
required reserves
actual reserves
excess reserves
required reserve ratio
money multiplier
Federal Deposit Insurance Corporation (FDIC)

STUDY QUESTIONS AND PROBLEMS

1 Analyze each of the following assets in terms of their potential use as a medium of exchange, a unit of account, and a store of value. Which use is most appropriately associated with each asset?

- **a** A Visa credit card
- **b** A $20 Federal Reserve note
- **c** 10 shares of Microsoft stock
- **d** A 90-day Treasury bill
- **e** A certificate of deposit at a commercial bank
- **f** A checking account at a savings and loan association
- **g** $20 worth of dimes

2 Table 14.5 shows hypothetical money supply data for the United States. Compute the basic (M1) money supply.

TABLE 14.5 Hypothetical Money Supply Data (billions of dollars)

Money market deposit accounts	20
Checking deposits	150
Coin	10
Paper currency	90
Certificates of deposit	25
Traveler's checks	5
Mutual funds	15

3 For a commercial bank, which of the following items represent assets and which represent liabilities?

- **a** Certificates of deposit
- **b** Borrowings from a Federal Reserve Bank
- **c** Bank office equipment
- **d** Loans to businesses and households
- **e** Holdings of government securities
- **f** Checking deposits
- **g** Deposits with a district Federal Reserve Bank

4 If borrowers take a portion of their loans as cash rather than checkable deposits, what happens to the money multiplier of the commercial banking system?

5 If Jennifer Gray deposits a $100 bill into her checking account, and her bank has a required reserve ratio of 5 percent, how much will the bank's required reserves increase? What happens to excess reserves?

6 Suppose that the Federal Reserve sets the required reserve ratio at 15 percent. If the banking system has $10 million in excess reserves, how many checkable deposits can be created?

7 American National Bank has reserves of $100,000 and checking deposits of $500,000. The required reserve ratio is 20 percent. Suppose that households deposit $50,000 cash into their checking deposits at American National Bank, which then adds this amount to its reserves. How much excess reserves does the bank now have?

8 Suppose that the banking system has reserves totaling $50 billion. Also assume that required reserves are 25 percent of checking deposits and that banks hold no excess reserves and households hold no cash. What is the money multiplier?

9 Assume that you take $2,000 cash and deposit it in your bank checking account. If this $2,000 remains in the banking system as reserves and if banks hold reserves equal to 20 percent of checking deposits, how much will the total amount of checking deposits in the banking system increase?

10 Table 14.6 shows the hypothetical balance sheet of the Bank of Ohio. Assuming that the required reserve ratio on checkable deposits is 10 percent, answer the following questions:

TABLE 14.6 Balance Sheet of the Bank of Ohio

Assets		*Liabilities*	
Reserves	$55,000	Checkable deposits	$110,000
Loans	90,000	Savings deposits	75,000
Securities	28,000	Borrowings from other banks	8,000
Other	20,000		

a The Bank of Ohio must maintain required reserves of ______.

b The Bank of Ohio has excess reserves in the amount of ______.

c The maximum that the Bank of Ohio can increase the money supply by lending is ______. If the Bank of Ohio lends the maximum amount that it can lend, what will happen to its excess reserves?

d Instead, suppose that the balance sheet pertains to the entire commercial banking system. The maximum that the banking system can increase the money supply by lending is ______.

NOTES

1 The U.S. economy has an array of banks, including commercial banks, savings and loan associations, mutual savings banks, and credit unions. We call these *depository institutions*: They accept deposits from people and provide checking accounts that are part of the money supply.

2 The other small part of paper currency consists of *U.S. notes*, which are still in circulation but are no longer issued. The notes, which were issued in the denomination of $100, are the descendants of Civil War *greenbacks*.

3 "When I Pay for My Groceries by Check, Where Does That Check Go?" *How Stuff Works*, 2013, available at http://money.howstuffworks.com/personal-finance/budgeting/check-processing.htm.

4 U.S. Mint, *Annual Report*, 2015; "Canada Drops Penny from its Currency," *Chicago Tribune*, February 5, 2013; "Canadian Penny Discontinued," *The Huffington Post*, February 4, 2013.

5 America's banking system has traditionally operated under a system of fractional reserve banking, in which actual reserves equal required reserves plus excess reserves, and the required reserve ratios are positive across all tiers of checkable deposits. But during the Covid-19 pandemic, the Federal Reserve decreased the required reserve ratio to zero percent, effective March 26, 2020. Why? Because the banking system had abundant reserves at that time, the required reserve ratio did not play a significant role in the implementation of monetary policy, and thus it was set to zero percent. **According to the Federal Reserve's website, this change of policy will likely apply to the longer term, which means there are currently no plans to reinstate the reserve requirement. However, the Federal Reserve left open the possibility of changing required reserve ratios if future conditions warrant. Therefore, in this textbook, we will assume that the required reserve ratio is set at a positive amount.**

6 The basic money supply (M1) is the sum of currency held by the public plus savings deposits and checking accounts issued by banks. Thus, the *change* in the money supply equals the change in currency held by the public plus the change in checking accounts. Although in our example of money creation checking accounts increased by $10,000, the public now has $1,000 less currency because they deposited the currency in the bank. The money supply thus *increased* by $9,000 ($10,000 – $1,000 = $9,000).

CHAPTER 15

The Federal Reserve and Monetary Policy

CHAPTER OBJECTIVES

After reading this chapter, you should be able to:

1 Describe the structure and operation of the Federal Reserve System.
2 Identify the services that the Federal Reserve System provides for the U.S. economy.
3 Explain the purpose and operation of monetary policy.
4 Assess the advantages and disadvantages of monetary policy.
5 Evaluate whether Congress should reduce the independence of the Federal Reserve.

DOI: 10.4324/9781003438571-18

ECONOMICS IN CONTEXT

In 2008 and 2009, developing gloom lay heavy and thick on the U.S. economy like smog in the air. Consumers, who account for about 70 percent of all economic activity, had lost a significant amount of their wealth as the value of their stocks fell in a sagging market. Increasingly, consumers put off their purchases, causing sales to fall and business profitability to decline. Economists feared that eroding profit expectations would dampen capital spending. Add in the slower growth in much of the world economy, and the prospects for U.S. exporters also looked grim.

To bolster the weakening economy, the Federal Reserve cut its interest rates. Its actions were aimed at Americans like Jim Riley, who owned a small construction firm in Fort Collins, Colorado. Mr. Riley was contemplating starting a new business that wouldn't experience the winter downturns that construction does. He thought about manufacturing new homes using an indoor facility; these homes could then be transported to a building site, in any season. By 2008, however, his enthusiasm for the project dwindled as the economy waned.

Indeed, few issues in economics evoke more emotion than the conduct of monetary policy. Critics have maintained that the Federal Reserve System—also known as the Fed—has sometimes destabilized the economy by causing inflation or recession. However, proponents of the Fed argue that it has done a credible job of promoting economic stability. They maintain that severe economic shocks—such as stock market crashes, wars, rising oil prices, and foreign competition—have unsettled the economy, and that the Fed has done its best to maintain a stable economy.

In this chapter, we will examine the nature and operation of the Fed. We will begin by considering its structure and how it attempts to control the money supply and interest rates in order to stabilize the economy.

THE FEDERAL RESERVE SYSTEM

The **Federal Reserve System (Fed)** is the central bank of the United States. It was legislated by Congress and signed into law by President Woodrow Wilson in 1913 to provide the nation with a safer, more flexible, and more stable monetary and financial system. All major countries have a central bank whose functions are broadly like those of the Fed. These central banks include the Bank of England, the Bank of Canada, and the Bank of Japan.

Before Congress created the Fed, periodic financial panics had plagued the nation. These panics had contributed to many bank failures, business bankruptcies, and general economic downturns. A particularly severe crisis in 1907 prompted the eventual passage of the Federal Reserve Act in 1913.

Source: Rudy Sulgan/The Image Bank/Getty Images®

STRUCTURE OF THE FEDERAL RESERVE SYSTEM

The Fed's structure was designed by Congress to give it a broad perspective on the economy and on economic activity in all parts of the nation. At the head of its formal organization is the Board of Governors, located in Washington, D.C. The 12 regional Federal Reserve Banks make up the next level. The organization of the Fed also includes the Federal Open Market Committee and three advisory councils. These bodies and other policymaking committees provide additional avenues for regional and private-sector participation in the Fed's activities.

Board of Governors

The **Board of Governors** administers the Fed. The board consists of seven members who are appointed by the president and confirmed by the Senate to serve 14-year terms of office. Members may serve only one full term, but a member who has been appointed to complete an unexpired term may later be reappointed to a full term. These long terms help insulate the decisions of the board from day-to-day political pressures. The president designates, and the Senate confirms, two members of the Board of Governors to serve as chair and vice chair, for four-year terms. Only one member of the board may be selected from any one of the 12 Federal Reserve districts. In making appointments, the president is directed by law to select a fair representation of the financial, agricultural, industrial, and commercial interests and geographic divisions of the country.

As head of the nation's central bank, the chair appears before Congress to report on Federal Reserve policies, the Federal Reserve System's views about the economy, financial developments, and other matters. The chair also meets from time to time with the president of the United States and regularly confers with the secretary of the Treasury and the chair of the Council of Economic Advisers.

Board members usually meet several times a week. As they carry out their duties, members of the board routinely confer with officials of other government agencies, representatives of banking industry groups, officials of the central banks of other countries, members of Congress, and academicians.

Federal Open Market Committee

The **Federal Open Market Committee (FOMC)** is the Fed's most important policymaking body for controlling the growth of the money supply. To do so, the FOMC oversees the purchases and sales of U.S. government securities. These operations are conducted by the Federal Reserve Bank of New York, which serves as the agent for the FOMC. The FOMC members include the seven members of the Board of Governors, the president of the Federal Reserve Bank of New York, and four other Reserve Bank presidents who serve one-year terms on a rotating basis.

The Reserve Banks

The day-to-day operations of the Fed are carried out by the 12 Federal Reserve Banks. As seen in Figure 15.1, each of the Federal Reserve Banks serves a certain region of the country and is named for the location of its headquarters—Atlanta, Boston, Chicago, Cleveland, Dallas, Kansas City, Minneapolis, New York, Philadelphia, Richmond, San Francisco, and St. Louis. Also, there are 25 Federal Reserve branch banks located throughout the country.

Although the Federal Reserve Banks are not motivated by profit, they generally earn substantial revenues on the Fed's large holdings of income-producing government securities acquired in the process of implementing monetary policy. Also, the Federal Reserve Banks charge financial institutions for their check collection and other services. Most of these revenues are turned over to the U.S. Treasury. Moreover, the Fed receives no funding from the government.

The Federal Reserve Banks are owned by the banks that are members of the Federal Reserve System. That is, the member banks are the stockholders of the Fed. Each Federal Reserve Bank has its own board of nine directors chosen from outside the Bank.

Finally, at the bottom of the Fed's organizational structure is the U.S. banking system, which consists of commercial banks, mutual savings banks, savings and loan associations, and credit unions.

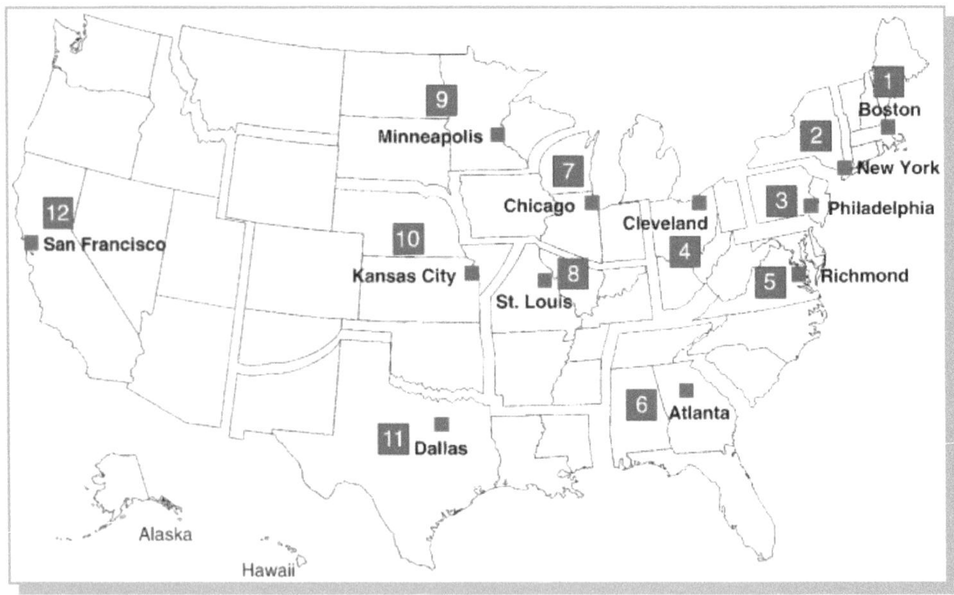

FIGURE 15.1 The Twelve Federal Reserve Districts

The day-to-day operations of the Federal Reserve are carried out by the 12 Federal Reserve Banks, which are located throughout the United States.

The Functions of the Federal Reserve System: The Dual Mandate

The Federal Reserve, as the overseer of the nation's monetary system, has a variety of important duties. Some of the important functions of the Fed include:

- Controlling the money supply through policies that affect the quantity of reserves that banks use to make loans.
- Acting as a lender of last resort to banks to forestall financial panics.
- Regulating and supervising banks to maintain financial responsibility.
- Supplying services to banks such as check processing and electronic transfers of funds.
- Supplying services to the government, such as the transportation of currency, the issuance and redemption of Treasury securities, and the maintenance of the Treasury's checking account.

Although some of these functions are routine activities or have a service aspect, the major task of the Fed is to manage the availability and cost of money and credit to promote a healthy economy.

Congress has given the Fed a **dual mandate**, which includes two coequal goals for monetary policy: First, maximum employment, and, second, stable prices which implies low, stable inflation. The dual mandate also suggests another, lesser-known goal of moderate long-term interest rates.

Fed officials consider that a 2-percent inflation rate is most consistent over the long run with its mandate for stable prices. This means that the Fed should aim to achieve an inflation rate that averages 2 percent over time, rather than striving for 2-percent inflation at any given time. Therefore, following eras when inflation has continued below 2 percent, the Fed strives for inflation to be moderately above 2 percent for some time.

The Independence of the Fed

Congress structured the Fed so that it would be independent within the government—that is, although the Fed is accountable to Congress, it is insulated from day-to-day political pressures. This reflects the conviction that the people who control the country's money supply should be independent of the people who make the government's spending decisions. Most studies of central bank independence rank the Fed among the most independent in the world. Three structural features make the Fed independent: The appointment procedure for governors, the appointment procedure for Reserve Bank presidents, and funding.

The seven members of the Board of Governors are appointed by the president of the United States and confirmed by the Senate. The Fed's independence derives from several factors. First, the appointments are staggered to reduce the chance that a single U.S. president could "stack" the board with appointees. Second, their terms of office are 14 years—much longer than elected officials' terms.

Also, each Reserve Bank president is appointed to a five-year term by that Bank's Board of Directors, subject to final approval by the Board of Governors. This procedure adds to the Fed's independence because the directors of each Reserve Bank are not chosen by politicians but are selected to represent a cross-section of interests within the region—including banks, businesses, labor, and the public.

Finally, the Fed is structured to be self-sufficient in the sense that it meets its operating expenses primarily from the interest earnings on its holdings of government securities. Thus, it is independent of congressional decisions about appropriations.

Although the Fed is independent of congressional funding and administrative control, it is ultimately accountable to Congress and comes under government audit and review. The chair, other governors, and Reserve Bank presidents report regularly to Congress on monetary policy and regulatory policy, and they meet with government officials to discuss the economic programs of the Federal Reserve and the federal government. Let us next consider the nature and operation of monetary policy.

CHECK POINT

1 What is the Fed, and why was it established?
2 Describe the organizational structure of the Fed.
3 Which committee is the Fed's most important policymaking body for controlling the growth of the money supply?
4 What are the major functions of the Fed?

TRADITIONAL TOOLS OF MONETARY POLICY

The Federal Reserve conducts **monetary policy** by changing the economy's money and credit to help the economy achieve maximum employment and stable prices. The aim of monetary policy is to balance the flow of money and credit with the needs of the economy. Too much money and credit in the economy can result in inflation; too little can stifle economic activity. The Fed seeks to strike a balance between these two extremes.

To begin, it is important to understand what monetary policy can and cannot accomplish. The Fed has little or no control over an economy's long-term economic fundamentals—the skills of the workforce, the energy and vision of entrepreneurs, and the rate at which new technologies are developed and implemented for commercial use. However, what the Fed can achieve are two things. First, by reducing the severity of recessions, monetary policy can help ensure that the economy makes full use of its resources, notably the workforce. Second, by keeping inflation low and stable, monetary policy can help the market economy operate better and make it easier for people to plan for the future.

The Fed has traditionally used three tools to conduct monetary policy: Open market operations, the discount rate, and reserve requirements. Let us examine each of these policy tools.

Open Market Operations

Open market operations refer to the purchase or sale of U.S. government securities on the open market by the Fed. When the Fed conducts an open market operation, it makes a transaction with a bank or some other business or individual, but it does not initiate a transaction directly with the federal government. The Trading Desk of the Federal Reserve Bank of New York conducts open market operations on behalf of the Federal Reserve.

Each purchase or sale of securities by the Fed directly affects the volume of reserves in the banking system and, in the process, the overall economy. When the Fed wants to increase the flow of money and credit, it buys government securities from banks and businesses; when it wants to restrict the flow of money and credit, it sells government securities.

Open market operations occur largely through auctions in which security dealers are asked to submit bids to buy or offers to sell securities of the type and maturity that the Fed has elected to sell or to buy. The dealers' bids or offers are arranged according to price, and the Fed accepts amounts bid or offered in sequence, taking the highest prices bid for its sales and the lowest prices offered for its purchases, until the desired size of the whole transaction is reached.

When the Fed buys securities from a bank, the Fed pays for the securities by increasing the bank's deposits at the Fed (its reserves). The bank's excess reserves increase by the full amount of the transaction. With more excess reserves, the bank can make more loans and increase its checking deposits.

The Fed's purchase of government securities can be illustrated by using balance sheets. Referring to Figure 15.2, suppose the Fed buys $10 million of securities from U.S. Bank.

Federal Reserve				U.S. Bank			
Assets		**Liabilities**		**Assets**		**Liabilities**	
Government Securities	+ $10 million	Deposits of U.S. Bank	+ $10 million	Reserves with Fed	+ $10 million		
				Government Securities	− $10 million		

FIGURE 15.2 Open Market Operations: Purchase of Securities from a Commercial Bank

When the Fed buys securities from a bank, the Fed pays for the securities by increasing the bank's deposits at the Fed (its reserves). The bank's excess reserves increase by the full amount of the transaction. With more excess reserves, the bank can make more loans and increase its checking deposits.

The Fed will pay for the securities by increasing U.S. Bank's deposits at the Fed—its reserves—by $10 million. U.S. Bank's excess reserves increase by the full amount of the transaction.[1] With more excess reserves, it can make more loans and increase its checking deposits.

The process does not stop here. As deposit holders spend their newly acquired funds, the deposits will move to other banks. These institutions will set aside part of their new funds as reserves to back their new deposits, but they can lend the remainder. The resulting loans create additional new deposits, which move, in part, to other depository institutions, expanding loans and deposits in the same manner. By the time the process ends, checking deposits usually will have risen by several times the amount of reserves created by the Fed's original action. Put simply, a purchase of securities by the Fed results in a multiple expansion of money and credit.

We saw in Chapter 14 that a change in bank reserves can result in a multiplied change in the money supply. If the required reserve ratio is 20 percent, the $10 million purchase of securities from banks will result in a $50 million increase in the economy's money supply. Virtually the same result can be achieved if the Fed purchases securities from businesses or individuals, as these sellers generally deposit the money received from the sale of securities in banks. Conversely, if the Fed wanted to decrease the money supply, it would sell securities to banks, businesses, or individuals.

As we have learned, the Federal Open Market Committee oversees the purchases and sales of U.S. government securities by the Trading Desk of the Federal Reserve Bank of New York. The FOMC meets about every six weeks, more often if necessary, to establish policy. The FOMC meetings generally are broken into four parts—A review of recent actions by the managers of the Fed accounts, a discussion of general economic conditions, a discussion of financial conditions and monetary policy alternatives, and finally, a vote on monetary policy by FOMC members. Discussion is quite free, and often there is considerable diversity of opinion. Twice each year, in accordance with the law, the FOMC establishes its long-term goals for monetary policy and reports them to Congress. Between meetings, the various members of the FOMC stay in touch through written and electronic correspondence. Zoom meetings of the entire FOMC may be called on very short notice, if necessary.

The Discount Rate

Another policy tool of the Fed is the discount rate—the rate that Federal Reserve Banks charge for loans to banks. An important purpose of the Fed is to serve as a "lender of last resort" to banks that are in need. By lending funds to banks through its discount window, the Fed can help protect the safety and soundness of the nation's financial system.[2]

Financially sound banks can borrow from the Fed with few restrictions. Such loans are often made to banks that experience unexpected withdrawals of deposits or spikes in loan demand. However, the Fed expects that banks will not rely on the discount window as a regular source of funding. Discount window loans can also be made to help troubled banks on the verge of bankruptcy. The Fed closely monitors such loans, and troubled banks must demonstrate that they are conforming to the Fed's regulatory requirements.

Changes in the discount rate are initiated by the individual Federal Reserve Banks and must be approved by the Board of Governors. This coordination generally results in simultaneous changes at all 12 Federal Reserve Banks.

Discount rate changes have important effects on bank credit conditions. An increase in the discount rate, for example, makes it more costly for banks to borrow from Federal Reserve Banks. The higher cost may encourage banks to obtain funds by selling government securities rather than using the discount window. Also, it may force banks to screen their customers' loan applications more carefully and slow the growth of their loans. Thus, if the Fed raises the discount rate, banks are discouraged from borrowing reserves because borrowing becomes more costly. Conversely, lowering the discount rate will induce banks to borrow additional reserves.

In principle, the Fed can use the discount rate as a tool of monetary policy: Reducing the discount rate to increase bank reserves and the money supply and increasing the discount rate to decrease bank reserves and the money supply. In practice, changes in the discount rate have only minor effects on bank borrowing and the money supply. This is because the Fed expects that banks will not rely on the discount window as a regular source of funding.

The Reserve Requirement

Changing reserve requirements can also affect bank lending and the money supply. Recall that banks are required to maintain a fraction of their checking deposits in reserve, either as cash in their vaults or as deposits at a local Federal Reserve Bank. This fraction is known as the required reserve ratio, and it is applied to a bank's total checking deposit liabilities to determine the dollar amount of reserve assets that must be held. For example, a bank whose depositors' own checking accounts equal $100 million would need to have cash plus reserve accounts at the Fed equal to $10 million if the required reserve ratio were 10 percent.

As we learned in the previous chapter, the ability of the banking system to create checking deposit money depends on the required reserve ratio. A required reserve ratio of 10 percent requires a bank that receives a $100 deposit to maintain $10 in required reserves and thus lend out only $90 of that deposit. If the borrower then writes a check to someone who deposits the $90, the bank receiving that deposit will receive reserves of $90 when the check clears through the system. It can then lend $81 and must keep $9 in reserve. As the process continues, the banking system will expand the initial deposit of $100 into a maximum of $1,000 ($100 + $90 + $81 + $72.90 + ... = $1,000). If the required reserve ratio were 20 percent, the banking system would be able to expand the initial $100 deposit into a maximum of $500 ($100 + $80 + $64 + $51.20 + ... = $500). Therefore, a lower required reserve ratio should result in an increase in the money supply; a higher required reserve ratio should result in a decrease in the money supply.

In principle, changes in required reserve ratios can be a useful tool of monetary policy. However, required reserve ratios currently play a relatively limited role in money creation in the United States. Why? Because even small changes in the required reserve ratio can substantially affect required reserves; adjustments to required reserve ratios are not well suited to the day-to-day implementation of monetary policy. Also, because required reserve ratios are an important factor in banks' business calculations, frequent changes in them would unnecessarily complicate these institutions' financial planning. Therefore, the Fed has changed required reserve ratios only infrequently.

As will be discussed later in this chapter, during the 2007–2008 financial crisis, the Fed dramatically increased the level of reserves in the banking system to increase the supply of money and credit and thus stimulate the economy. Since that time, monetary policy has operated in an environment of abundant (ample) reserves, where banks have many more reserves on hand than are needed to meet their reserve requirements. In this environment of abundant reserves, reserve requirements do not serve to contribute to the enactment of monetary policy through open market operations. Therefore, in 2020, the Fed decreased reserve requirement percentages for all depository institutions to zero.

Federal Funds Rate

Another part of monetary policy is the federal funds rate. Banks such as Bank of America and JPMorgan Chase actively trade reserves held at Federal Reserve Banks among themselves. This market for reserves is called the **federal funds market**. Banks with surplus balances in their accounts transfer reserves to those needing to boost their balances. The actual interest rate charged by a lending bank will be determined through negotiations between the two banks. That is, the Fed cannot force banks to charge a precise federal funds rate.

Typically, a federal funds transaction takes the form of an uncollateralized, overnight loan of millions of dollars. Arrangements are agreed upon between the lending bank and the borrowing bank and confirmed later by mail. The actual transfer of the reserves is accomplished by a communication from the lending bank to the Federal Reserve Bank, instructing the latter to transfer the agreed-upon amount from its reserve account to that of the borrower.

The Federal Reserve focuses monetary policy on the interest rate that it can best influence: The **federal funds rate**. The Federal Reserve targets the federal funds rate by controlling the amount of reserves supplied to the federal funds market. For example, an increase in the amount of reserves supplied to the federal funds market causes the funds rate to fall; a decrease in the supply of reserves raises that rate. Indeed, the federal funds rate closely reflects the basic supply and demand conditions in the market for bank reserves that are influenced by the Fed's monetary policies.

Rather than mandating a precise number for the federal funds rate, the Fed sets a target range that has an upper limit and lower limit as a guide for financial institutions to follow when they make loans in the federal funds market. Therefore, an increase in the Fed's target range tends to cause the federal funds rate to increase, while a decrease in the Fed's target range tends to cause the federal funds rate to decline.

The significance of the federal funds rate is its impact on other market interest rates. This means that the federal funds rate affects the prime rate, the interest rate that banks charge their best business customers. In turn, the prime rate affects many consumer interest rates, including savings deposits, bank loans, credit cards, and adjustable-rate mortgages. Therefore, analysts pay close attention to the federal funds rate for signals of change in monetary policy.

NONTRADITIONAL TOOLS OF MONETARY POLICY

The Federal Reserve has traditionally used open market operations, the discount rate, and reserve requirements for achieving maximum employment and stable prices. As we will learn, these policy tools influence short-term interest rates, which affect spending and the level of economic activity.

However, during the financial crisis and Great Recession of 2007–2009, the Federal Reserve pushed short-term interest rates to virtually zero. Unfortunately, even near-zero interest rates could not significantly revive the economy, and it seemed as if traditional monetary policy was "out of ammunition." Therefore, the Federal Reserve turned to nontraditional monetary policy tools, such as quantitative easing, forward guidance, and interest on bank reserves held at local Federal Reserve Banks. Let us examine these nontraditional tools of monetary policy.

Quantitative Easing

Quantitative easing (QE) is a nontraditional monetary policy of the Fed when traditional monetary policy is ineffective at stimulating the economy. The Fed implements quantitative easing by buying long-term securities from banks and other financial institutions, therefore injecting a pre-determined amount of money and credit into the economy. The aim is to push long-term interest rates down and thus make borrowing more attractive for mortgages and businesses to finance investment in equipment and factories.

During 2008–2014, the Fed engaged in several rounds of quantitative easing to help stimulate a sluggish economy, in particular a weak mortgage market. The Fed implemented quantitative easing by purchasing long-maturity U.S. government securities and mortgage-backed securities to reduce long-term interest rates. This was designed to aid the sagging housing market: By reducing long-term interest rates, quantitative easing made mortgage loans more affordable, thus stimulating the demand for houses and the construction industry. Also, the Fed engaged in quantitative easing to stimulate the economy during the Covid-19 pandemic.

Forward Guidance

Forward guidance is a nontraditional tool that the Fed uses to communicate to the public about the likely future course of monetary policy. It can come in forms such as speeches and press releases. Forward guidance aims to affect the financial decisions of households, businesses, and investors by providing a yardstick for the anticipated path of interest rates. The theory behind forward guidance is that by clarifying its view of the future economy, the Fed can affect financial and economic conditions today.

For example, in March 2022, the Fed started raising interest rates to reduce the rate of inflation. Fed officials indicated that they were prepared to increase interest rates further if high inflation continued, which it did. Therefore, the Federal Reserve used forward guidance to provide communication to the public about the likely course of monetary policy.

However, critics maintain that forward guidance can result in policy failure. For example, destabilizing monetary policy occurred in 2013 when a failed attempt to explain the Fed's intention to reduce purchases of government securities triggered more market instability, instead of less.

Interest on Bank Reserves

In 2008, the Federal Reserve began paying interest on the reserves of banks held at local Federal Reserve Banks, which provided the Fed another tool of monetary policy. For example, if the Fed aims to stimulate a weak economy, it can decrease the interest rate that it pays on bank holdings of reserves at Federal Reserve Banks. The lower rate will make it less attractive for banks to hold reserves, thus increasing the incentive for them to increase lending to households and businesses that stimulates spending and the economy. In fact, in the environment of superabundant reserves, the interest rate on bank reserves became the main tool of monetary policy for influencing other short-term interest rates. This topic is appropriate for an upper-level course in money and banking, so it will not be further discussed in this book.

MONETARY POLICY: PURSUING THE DUAL MANDATE

In pursuing its dual mandate of maximum employment and stable prices, the Fed implements monetary policy mainly by influencing the federal funds rate. Recall that the **federal funds rate** is the interest rate at which a bank lends reserve balances located at local Federal Reserve Banks to another bank. Let us consider how the federal funds rate relates to the transmission of monetary policy.

Transmission of Monetary Policy

The flowchart in Figure 15.3 shows the chain reaction of how the stance of monetary policy is transmitted through financial markets and ultimately affects economic activity.

Federal funds rate	→	Market interest rates	→	Consumption, investment, and aggregate demand	→	Progress made toward maximum employment and stable prices

FIGURE 15.3 How Monetary Policy Affects Economic Activity

The Fed starts the process by using its monetary tools to influence the federal funds rate, which is then transmitted to market interest rates throughout the economy, such as rates for credit cards, automobile loans, and mortgages. As market interest rates change, the cost of borrowing for households and businesses changes, which impacts their decisions regarding consumption and investment spending. And changes in consumption and investment spending will cause changes in aggregate demand, which ultimately affect employment and inflation (prices). Let us next apply this sequence of events to the Fed's pursuit of maximum employment and stable prices.

Expansionary Monetary Policy: Combating Recession

Suppose that the economy is in recession, producing less than its full-employment potential. This situation is seen at point A in Figure 15.4(*a*), where the economy's equilibrium output is $60 trillion. The goal of the Fed in this situation is to stimulate the economy and increase output to $70 trillion.

To combat recession, the Fed can use its monetary policy tools to lower the federal funds rate. This means that monetary policy becomes more expansionary or stimulative. The lower federal funds rate will be transmitted through financial markets into reductions in market interest rates on consumer and business loans throughout the economy, making it cheaper to get credit. Lower interest rates will encourage consumers to purchase goods that are sensitive to interest rates, such as large household appliances and automobiles. Also, businesses will be encouraged by lower interest rates to invest more in equipment and factories. Therefore, the expansionary monetary policy will cause a rightward shift in the aggregate demand curve to AD_1 in the figure, and the economy will move toward the full-employment level of output. Simply put, the Fed's cutting the federal funds rate is consistent with an expansionary monetary policy that is intended to stimulate a weak economy.

Although the short-run effect of the expansionary monetary policy will be to stimulate output and employment, the action can also have long-term consequences. In the long run, an expansionary monetary policy may result in expectations of higher future inflation, as too many dollars chase too few goods. The higher the expected inflation rate, the more likely it will be for interest rates to increase. This occurs because lenders will demand higher interest rates as compensation for the decline in purchasing power of the dollars they are paid in the future.

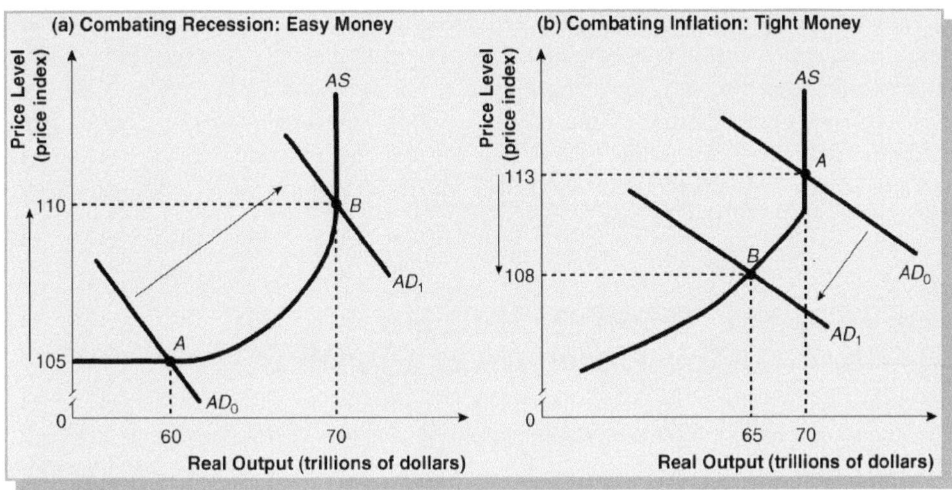

FIGURE 15.4 Effects of Monetary Policy on the Economy

To combat recession, the Fed will reduce the target federal funds rate, which leads to a reduction in market interest rates, an increase in consumption and business investment spending, an increase in aggregate demand, and an increase in economic activity. Combating demand-pull inflation implies an opposite chain of events for the Fed.

Contractionary Monetary Policy: Combating Inflation

Monetary policy can also be used to combat demand-pull inflation. Recall that demand-pull inflation occurs when buyers' demands for goods and services outpace sellers' capacities to supply them, forcing up prices on the goods and services that are available.

The objective of monetary policy in this situation is to decrease aggregate demand from curve AD_0 to AD_1, as shown in Figure 15.4(*b*). The decrease in aggregate demand will eliminate the excess spending and demand-pull inflation.

Thus, the Fed will initiate a contractionary or restrictive monetary policy by using its monetary tools to increase the federal funds rate. A higher federal funds rate will be transmitted through financial markets into an increase in market interest rates, a rise in the cost of borrowing for households and businesses, a decrease in interest-rate-sensitive consumption and business investment spending, and a decline in aggregate demand.

When the Fed implements a contractionary monetary policy, the intended outcome is price stability over the long run. In the short run, however, the contractionary monetary policy causes a decline in aggregate demand and a fall in output and employment. This is why the Fed may be criticized when it attempts to combat inflation: Nobody wants to have their business shut down or be thrown out of work because of a restrictive monetary policy. Over time, however, price stability contributes to low interest rates and increases the confidence of consumers, savers, and investors, and thus it tends to promote economic expansion. Therefore, the Fed must consider whether the short-run side effects of combating inflation, which are adverse, are outweighed by the long-run benefits of price stability.

For example, in the early 1980s, the Fed successfully used a contractionary monetary policy to fight an inflation rate running above 11 percent annually. As a result, short-term interest rates spiked to an astonishing 17 percent in 1980 and 19 percent in 1981. The monetary policy helped bring inflation down to 3.2 percent three years later, thus building the Fed's credibility as an inflation fighter. But lowering the inflation rate was not painless, as the economy fell into recession in 1981–1982, during which the unemployment rate rose to 9.7 percent of the civilian labor force.

THE FEDERAL RESERVE AND ECONOMIC STABILIZATION: THREE CASE STUDIES

Economists generally view monetary policy as the first line of defense against economic instability, be it recession or inflation. This is because the Federal Reserve can alter monetary policy quickly in response to changes in the economy. Because most recessions last for only a few quarters, the timeliness of the response of monetary policy is crucial. In some cases, however, monetary policy may be insufficient to stabilize the economy, hence the need for fiscal policy. Let us consider some examples of how the Federal Reserve has attempted to stabilize the economy.

The Great Recession of 2007–2009

Following six years of continuous expansion, the U.S. economy entered a recession at the end of 2007. The immediate cause of the recession was a collapse of the financial system due to the downward turn of the housing cycle and the rise in delinquencies on mortgages which resulted in substantial losses for many banks. Breakdowns in lending regulations and oversight, increased reliance on complex financial instruments that proved fragile under stress, and excessive risk taking by home buyers and bank lenders contributed to the financial crisis. Also, the Fed may have nurtured this problem. Beginning in 2001, the Fed cut interest rates to stimulate growth. With interest rates so low, many people felt mortgages were affordable and rushed to purchase homes that they could not afford. The Fed never saw the housing market as an overvalued "asset bubble" and thus did nothing to prevent it.

Because many banks also made risky gambles on the values of mortgages, many lost enough money to be close to failure, so people no longer trusted banks. This further harmed the economy because it reduced the credit available, and the expectation of a severe recession and declining profits caused the stock market to crash. Loss of confidence in the economy caused decreases in consumption and investment, which resulted in declining aggregate demand and economic contraction. Simply put, policymakers were confronted by two major economic problems: A collapse of the financial system and a downturn in the economy at large.

As the crisis worsened throughout 2008 and 2009, the Fed took extraordinary steps to stabilize the economy. For example, the Fed injected hundreds of billions of dollars in new liquidity into the banking system to prevent the failure of several large, interconnected banks. To provide liquidity to businesses and households, the Fed initiated measures to reduce interest rates to make loans for mortgages and business investment more affordable, including the use of its quantitative easing policy. However, it became clear to many economists that monetary policy, by itself, would not be able to bring the economy back to full employment. Therefore, the federal government enacted an expansionary fiscal policy as discussed in Chapter 13 of this text.

Figure 15.5 illustrates this situation. Initially, the economy was at point *A*, with output equaling, say, $92 trillion in 2008. The Fed worried that if it refrained from action, decreases in consumption and investment would cause the aggregate demand curve to decrease from AD_0 to AD_2; this would move the economy to equilibrium point C, where output equals, say, $88 trillion. When the Fed enacted an expansionary monetary policy, aggregate demand instead fell to AD_1 and the decline in output was smaller. Although the Fed's aggressive monetary policy could not completely offset the recession, it reduced its depth. However, policymakers felt that monetary policy by itself was insufficient to prevent the economy from undergoing sizable contraction. Therefore, expansionary fiscal policies, consisting of increased government expenditures and tax cuts, were initiated to supplement monetary policy's effort to bolster aggregate demand.

But what about the effect of the Fed's actions on the price level? Here, we must realize that there is a discrepancy between what Figure 15.5 shows and what occurred. According to the figure, the price level should decline following a decrease in aggregate demand. During the 2007–2009 recession, however, prices actually rose. One reason is that inflation tends to have momentum: When inflation has been increasing at some rate for a period of time then, left alone, it will proceed at that same rate. Although prices rose during that period, the decrease in aggregate demand moderated their rate of increase, as the model of aggregate demand and aggregate supply would suggest.

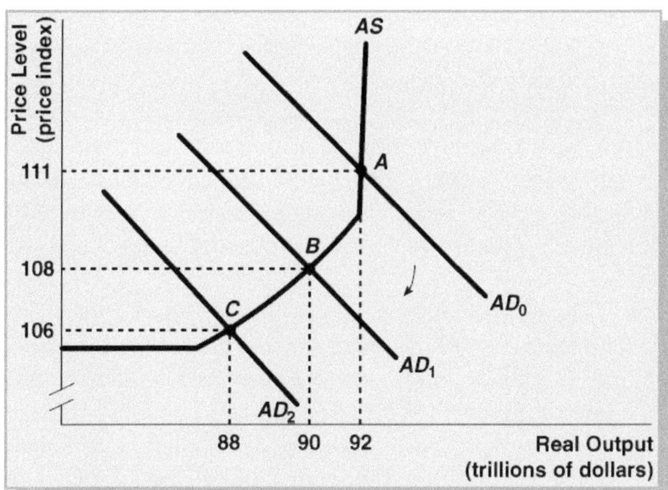

FIGURE 15.5 The Fed and the Great Recession of 2007–2009

To combat the recession, the Fed initiated an expansionary monetary policy. Although the policy could not eliminate the recession, it made it less severe. Because of the expansionary policy, the economy moved from *A* to *B* rather than from *A* to *C*, and the decline in output was smaller.

Following the bottoming-out of the U.S. economy in 2009, the economy began to recover, although at a very slow rate. By 2015, the economy appeared strong enough to warrant a return to a more normal interest rate policy. Therefore, in December, 2015, the Fed announced that it was raising interest rates, for the first time in nearly a decade.

2001 Attack on America

Besides combating recession and inflation, the Fed also attempts to stabilize the economy during times of national emergency. Consider how the Fed defended the U.S. financial system following the terrorist attacks on the United States in 2001.

It was a day like no other in U.S. history. September 11, 2001, marked the end of American global innocence, the onset of recession, and perhaps even the demise of the country's anything-is-possible economic exuberance. A devastating terrorist attack hit at the heart of the nation's economic and military power: The World Trade Center near Wall Street in New York City and the Pentagon in Washington, D.C., just miles from the White House.

In addition to causing thousands of lives to be lost, the attacks forced immediate changes in the way the nation conducted business. Following the attack, travel was suspended, sporting events were canceled, business offices were closed, and financial markets were shut down. Corporations, such as United Airlines and Boeing, announced layoffs of thousands of employees as sales plummeted. Indeed, the attack seriously shook the nation's confidence and economists feared that it could throw the United States into despair and recession.

Officials at the Fed realized that the future economic outlook depended on the behavior of U.S. consumers and businesses. Typically, consumers respond to a crisis by freezing—spending stops, and decisions about the future are put on hold. If fear and uncertainty prevail, how can people be expected to spend and invest for the future? If hijackers can steal commercial jets and crash them into high-profile buildings, how can people feel safe flying or working in ordinary skyscrapers?

While efforts were made to rescue the victims of the attack, the immediate job ahead for the Federal Reserve was clear: It must address this national crisis and restore confidence as quickly as possible. As news spread about the nation's catastrophe, banks faced soaring demand for cash as nervous depositors began to pull money out of their accounts. The Fed quickly announced that it would keep its discount window open to any bank that needed it.

The provision of liquidity following September 11 was unprecedented in Federal Reserve history. On September 12, discount window borrowing by financial institutions peaked at more than $45 billion, compared to around $100 million on a typical day. On the same day, the Federal Reserve injected $38 billion in liquidity through open market operations, as opposed to a typical daily action of $3.5 billion. The Federal Reserve also extended swap lines of credit with the European Central Bank, the Bank of England, and the Bank of Canada to provide liquidity to international markets. Simply put, the Fed sent a clear message to financial markets that it would provide sufficient liquidity to keep them operating in an orderly fashion.

Having restored confidence in the financial system, the Fed turned its attention to the disaster's impact on the economy. The Fed quickly cut the federal funds rate, its target for short-term interest rates, by 0.5 percentage point. Several large U.S. commercial banks responded to the Fed rate by reducing their lending rates to business and household customers.

As the situation eased, the Fed kept the financial system flush with cash but at much lower levels than in previous days. Although the United States had suffered a major blow, the financial system proved to be quite resilient, with markets and companies functioning better than one might expect.

Covid-19 Pandemic

Source: Constantine Johnny/Moment/Getty Images®

The 2020 coronavirus pandemic in the United States resulted in event cancelations, business closures, and work-from-home policies that triggered a sharp economic downturn and rising unemployment. Uncertainty about the course of the virus and economy led to the desire of Americans to hold only the most liquid financial assets, such as checking deposits and savings deposits. The result was a disruption to financial markets.

To stabilize the economy, the Federal Reserve enacted a wide range of policies to keep credit flowing. These included lending to support households, businesses, financial market participants, and state and local governments. Among the policies of the Federal Reserve were:

- **Federal Funds Rate.** A 1.5 percentage point reduction in the federal funds rate, which serves as a benchmark for other interest rates. The policy was intended to support spending by reducing borrowing costs for businesses and households.
- **Discount Rate.** To provide liquidity to banks, the Fed lowered the rate that it charges for loans from its discount window by 2 percentage points.

- **Quantitative Easing**. The Fed resumed purchases of massive amounts of long-term securities to reduce long-term interest rates.
- **Forward guidance**. In policy statements and press releases, the Fed signaled the future path of interest rates. The Fed stated that it would keep interest rates near zero until it was confident that the economy had weathered the adverse effects of the pandemic and was on track to achieve its goals of maximum employment and price stability.

The Fed's actions ensured that credit continued to flow to businesses and households, thus limiting the economic damage caused by the pandemic. In addition to the expansionary monetary policies of the Federal Reserve, the federal government implemented expansionary fiscal policy, including an increase in government spending of about $5.2 trillion. The stimulative policies during the pandemic helped boost economic activity and shorten the recession. However, they came at the cost of rising inflation, which reached over 7 percent in 2021.

MONETARY POLICY: ADVANTAGES AND DISADVANTAGES

Most economists consider monetary policy to be an important tool for stabilizing the economy. Let us evaluate how well monetary policy works.

Advantages of Monetary Policy

One strength of monetary policy is that it interferes very little with the freedom of the market, although market imperfections sometimes intensify the effects of policy upon particular sectors of the economy. For example, a restrictive monetary policy cuts down the rate at which total spending can increase, but it does not dictate which expenditures must be slowed or reduced. If a restrictive monetary policy forces interest rates up from 6 percent to 8 percent, for example, you, the typical consumer, still have the option of borrowing money to purchase a new home, a car, or a major appliance. The expenditures that you cut in response to higher borrowing costs are the ones to which you attach the lowest priorities. Similarly, an expansionary monetary policy stimulates total spending, but the market also dictates its form.

Another strength is that monetary policy is flexible. The FOMC usually meets about every six weeks, reaches a decision regarding the buying or selling of government securities by the Trading Desk of the Federal Reserve Bank of New York, and acts on that decision immediately. Moreover, the FOMC can call extraordinary meetings if economic events require it. In contrast, the application of fiscal policy may be postponed for many months by congressional deliberations.

However, businesses do not usually change their spending plans immediately upon an interest rate change initiated by the Fed. Businesses must re-evaluate, make new decisions, and order reductions or expansions in production and expenditures. This suggests that months may pass before spending is significantly affected by a change in monetary policy.

Economists note that it can take 18–24 months or more for monetary policy to substantially affect the economy and prices (inflation). And this lag can vary considerably. Therefore, when the Fed changes interest rates today, its policy will affect economic conditions in about one and a half years or more.

Finally, and perhaps most important, Congress has carefully insulated the Fed from day-to-day political pressures so that it may act in the best interests of the economy. As a result, the Fed can base its policy actions almost entirely upon economic considerations rather than political ones. This allows the Fed to engage in policies that might be unpopular but necessary for the long-term health of the economy. Of course, it also empowers the Fed to pursue correct policies despite pressures to do otherwise.

Disadvantages of Monetary Policy

Formulating monetary policy is a difficult task, and policies have definite limitations. Promoting economic stability requires not only wise monetary policy, but sound fiscal policy, as well. It also requires sufficient competition throughout the economy so that individual prices are free to move up and down. Obviously, trouble can develop in all three areas, so it is difficult to achieve perfect stability.

Policy trade-offs present another problem for the Fed. Consider the goals of price stability and full employment. As we have learned, combating inflation requires the Fed to adopt a contractionary monetary policy by increasing the target range of the federal funds rate, which will lead to higher market interest rates. However, a contractionary monetary policy also results in declining economic activity and rising unemployment. Conversely, combating unemployment calls for an expansionary monetary policy, which may intensify inflation. Indeed, the short-run trade-offs between price stability and full employment can make it difficult for the Fed to formulate policy.

Moreover, the extent to which monetary policy can revive a sagging economy has long been debated. Some sectors of the economy, such as manufacturing and construction of houses and apartment buildings, are more sensitive to changes in the interest rate than other sectors, such as retail trade and services. With lower interest rates, companies will often undertake large projects, such as building a factory or buying equipment, that they had been pondering, because lower rates decrease the costs of such projects. But that is untrue for service and retail sectors because these industries generally do not initiate the type of long-term projects that are sensitive to changes in interest rates. Although a change in monetary policy can affect these less-interest-rate-sensitive sectors, the impact on these sectors tends to be slower and less pronounced than in construction and manufacturing. Simply put, a change in monetary policy does not affect everybody in the same manner.

Finally, some economists question whether monetary policy can revive economic activity after a downturn. Recall that during a downturn the Fed will adopt an expansionary monetary policy by reducing interest rates. However, this does not guarantee that banks will make loans and spending will increase. If businesses or households are pessimistic about future profits or incomes, they may be unwilling to borrow, thus frustrating the expansionary monetary policy.

Discretion or Rules for Monetary Policy

The weaknesses of monetary policy highlight a debate concerning the conduct of monetary policy. Should the Fed be free to use its own discretion to stabilize the economy, or should it be limited to following a set of rules? And if the Fed should follow rules, what kind of rules?

The case for discretionary monetary policy is founded on the notion that the economy is constantly affected by recessionary or expansionary forces. Without an active monetary policy, based on the judgments of the Fed about the current needs of the economy, it is feared that the economy would oscillate in unacceptably wide swings. To decrease such instability, proponents maintain that the Fed can stimulate the economy when it becomes sluggish or restrain the economy when it overheats.

However, critics say that discretionary changes in monetary policy may destabilize the economy. They note that the Fed does not have up-to-the-minute, reliable information about the state of the economy and prices. Information is limited because of lags in the publication of data. Also, the Fed has a less-than-perfect understanding of the way the economy works, including the knowledge of when and to what extent policy actions will affect aggregate demand. These limitations add to uncertainties in the policy process and make determining the appropriate setting of monetary policy instruments more difficult.

Rather than using its own discretion to conduct monetary policy, the Fed might adopt a fixed-rule policy that is independent of the state of the economy. One fixed-rule policy would be for the Fed to keep the quantity of money growing at a constant annual rate that is consistent with the average growth in the economy's productivity. The Fed's only purpose would be to use its monetary tools to make sure that the money supply increased steadily by, say, 3 percent per year. Proponents maintain that this approach would eliminate inappropriate monetary policy as a source of macroeconomic instability. However, critics contend that such a policy would limit the Fed's flexibility in responding to extraordinary circumstances, such as the September 11 terrorist attacks or Covid-19 pandemic. They also note that the quantity of money in the economy is difficult to measure, and its relationship to overall spending—which drives prices up or down—tends to be erratic and unreliable.

Some proponents of a fixed-rule policy have called for the Fed to implement *inflation targeting*, a policy that is used by Canada, Australia, New Zealand, and the United Kingdom. According to this policy, the Fed would be required to announce a target for the inflation rate. It would then be expected to use its monetary tools to keep inflation at the target. If the Fed failed to achieve its target, it would have to explain what went wrong. Thus, inflation targeting would make monetary policy more predictable and accountable to the public.

In 2012, the Fed announced an explicit inflation target to the public for the first time in its history. The Fed set the inflation target at a rate of 2 percent as measured by the annual change in the price index for personal consumption expenditures. In 2020 the Fed loosened its inflation target policy by adopting average inflation targeting. This strategy allows inflation to rise and fall such that it averages 2 percent over time.

CHECK POINT

1. Describe the nature and operation of monetary policy.
2. Identify the instruments that the Fed uses to control the money supply.
3. Discuss how changes in the money supply by the Fed can result in changes in output, employment, and prices.
4. How would the Fed combat a recession in the economy? How about inflation?

SHOULD CONGRESS REDUCE THE INDEPENDENCE OF THE FEDERAL RESERVE?

Recall that when the Federal Reserve was created, Congress carefully insulated it from day-to-day political pressures so that it could act in the best interest of the country. Congress made the Fed responsible to itself rather than to the president or the political party in power. The Fed is governmental, but it is independent within government.

The primary argument for Fed independence is that monetary policy—which affects inflation, employment, and economic growth—is too important to be determined by politicians. Because elections occur frequently, politicians may be more concerned with the short-run benefits rather than the long-run costs of their economic policies. Put simply, politicians may put re-election, rather than the long-run health of the economy, first in their decision making.

The most sensitive aspect of the economy over which short- and long-run interests clash is inflation. Supporters of the Fed's independence maintain that monetary policy tends to become too expansionary if it is left to policymakers with short-run horizons, thus intensifying inflationary pressures. However, the Fed cannot assume that the goals of politicians reflect public sentiment. The public may prefer that monetary policy is formulated by officials at the Fed, rather than politicians.

However, critics of the Fed's independence contend that, in a democracy, elected officials should formulate public policy. Because the voting public holds elected officials responsible for their economic policies, the president and Congress should exercise more control over monetary policy. Moreover, critics also maintain that placing the Fed under the control of elected officials could reap benefits by coordinating monetary policy with the government's fiscal policy. Finally, critics argue that the Fed has not always used its independence well. For example, they note that monetary policy was too expansionary during the inflationary era of the 1970s and too restrictive during the recessionary era of the early 1990s.

This chapter has considered the Federal Reserve and monetary policy as a possible solution to macroeconomic instability. The next chapter will broaden our focus by discussing the United States in the global economy.

CHECK POINT

1 Identify the major strengths and weaknesses of monetary policy.
2 Why do some economists argue that the Fed should keep the money supply growing at a steady rate rather than actively manage the money supply in order to fine-tune the economy?
3 Why was the Fed structured so as to have a high degree of independence from the federal government? Discuss the advantages and disadvantages of the Fed's independence.

CHAPTER SUMMARY

1 The Federal Reserve System, often simply called the Fed, is the central bank of the United States. It was legislated by Congress and signed into law by President Woodrow Wilson in 1913 to provide the nation with a safer, more flexible, and more stable monetary and financial system.

2 The Fed's structure was designed by Congress to give it a broad perspective on the economy. At the head of the Fed's formal organization is the Board of Governors. The 12 regional Federal Reserve Banks make up the next level. The organization of the Fed also includes the Federal Open Market Committee and three advisory councils. The Federal Reserve's stockholders are commercial banks that are members of the Fed.

3 The Fed, as the overseer of the nation's monetary system, has many important duties: Acting as the lender of last resort, regulating and supervising banks, supplying services to banks and to the government, conducting foreign exchange operations, and controlling the money supply and interest rates.

4 The Fed's main responsibility is to formulate and implement monetary policy, which is conducted by changing the economy's money supply in order to help the economy achieve maximum output and employment, as well as stable prices. The Fed uses three policy instruments to influence the money supply: Open market operations, the discount rate, and the reserve requirement.

5 In the short run, when prices are temporarily fixed, the Fed has the ability to affect the level of interest rates in the economy. When the Fed increases the money supply to reduce interest rates, aggregate demand increases, which results in an increase in output and employment. Conversely, a decrease in the money supply will reduce aggregate demand, output, and employment. In the long run, a change in the money supply by the Fed affects only prices and not the level of output and employment.

6 One strength of monetary policy is that it is highly impersonal: Monetary policy interferes very little with the freedom of the market. Monetary policy is also flexible and can be implemented quickly in response to changing economic circumstances. Finally, the

Fed is insulated from day-to-day political pressures, so it can act in the best interests of the economy. This allows the Fed to engage in policies that might be unpopular but necessary for the long-run health of the economy.

7 However, critics of the Fed argue that active changes in the money supply by the Fed can and do destabilize the economy. They note that the Fed does not have up-to-the-minute, reliable information about the state of the economy and prices. Timing lags also limit the effectiveness of monetary policy. As a result, critics call for the elimination of activism in monetary policy in favor of a law requiring a fixed rate of increase in money each year.

KEY TERMS AND CONCEPTS

Federal Reserve System (Fed)
Board of Governors
Federal Open Market Committee (FOMC)
monetary policy
open market operations
discount rate
discount window
federal funds market
federal funds rate

STUDY QUESTIONS AND PROBLEMS

1 Who is the current chair of the Board of Governors of the Federal Reserve System? Why has the chair of the Board of Governors been characterized as the second most powerful person in Washington, D.C., next to the president?

2 If the Fed's independence were restricted so that it became subordinate to the president and Congress, would this affect the ability of monetary policy to combat recession or inflation?

3 When the Fed purchases government securities from commercial banks, businesses, or individuals, the nation's money supply increases. Explain how this works.

4 What is the discount rate and how can the Fed use it to influence the nation's supply of money?

5 How can a decrease in the reserve requirement by the Fed result in an increase in the money supply?

6 Which is the Fed's most frequently used monetary instrument? Why?

7 If the Fed wants to increase the value of the dollar in terms of other currencies, what should it do? What should the Fed do if it wants to decrease the foreign exchange value of the dollar?

8 Suppose that the economy is suffering from a prolonged and deep recession. What changes in open market operations, the discount rate, and the reserve requirement would the Fed likely enact? Explain how each change would affect bank reserves, the money supply, interest rates, and aggregate demand.

9 Suppose that the Fed adopts a restrictive monetary policy in order to combat demand-pull inflation. Assuming that the economy is closed to international trade, use the model of aggregate demand and aggregate supply to show the effects of the Fed's policy. Assume that the economy is open to international trade. How will changes in the international value of the dollar affect the performance of the economy? Now, answer the same set of questions by assuming that the Fed adopts an expansionary monetary policy to combat recession.

10 Why do some economists maintain that an active monetary policy by the Fed is counterproductive?

11 Explain how the Fed is structured to have certain checks and balances that limit the power any one group inside or outside the Fed can wield.

12 Why do critics argue that the Fed has aggravated the income gap between the rich and the poor?

13 Suppose that the required reserve ratio on checking deposits is 15 percent and the Fed purchases $10 million of U.S. securities from the commercial banking system. What is the maximum amount of new money that the banking system could create?

14 Pioneer Bank has checking deposits of $10 million and total reserves of $7.5 million; the required reserve ratio is 10 percent. If the Fed sells $1.5 million of government securities to the bank, what will happen to its total reserves and excess reserves?

15 Figure 15.6 shows the balance sheet for the commercial banking system. Answer the following questions based on this information:

Assets		Liabilities	
Cash in vault	$ 300	Checking deposits	$3,600
Reserves with Federal Reserve Banks	150	Due to other banks and Fed	850
Loans	3,000		
Government securities	1,000		

FIGURE 15.6 Consolidated Balance Sheet of All Commercial Banks (billions of dollars)

a If the Fed set the required reserve ratio at 10 percent, the banks would have required reserves of _____ and excess reserves of _____; the money multiplier would equal _____ and the maximum amount of new money that the banking system could create would equal _____.

b If the Fed decreased the required reserve ratio to 5 percent, banks would have _____ of excess reserves; the money multiplier would equal _____ and the maximum amount of new money that the banking system could create would equal _____.

16 Figure 15.7 shows the balance sheet of Wisconsin National Bank. Assume that the Fed has set the required reserve ratio at 10 percent.

Assets		Liabilities	
Reserves with Fed	$90	Checking deposits	$120
Loans	10		
Government securities	20		

FIGURE 15.7 Wisconsin National Bank's Balance Sheet (millions of dollars)

- **a** Wisconsin National Bank would have required reserves of _____ and excess reserves of _____. The maximum amount of new money that the bank could create would equal _____.
- **b** Suppose that the Fed sells $10 million in government securities to Wisconsin National Bank. After the sale, the bank would have _____ of required reserves and _____of excess reserves. As a result of this transaction, Wisconsin National Bank's ability to create additional money would increase/decrease by _____.
- **c** Instead, suppose that the Fed buys $10 million in government securities from Wisconsin National Bank. As a result of this transaction, Wisconsin National Bank's ability to create additional money would increase/decrease by_____.

NOTES

1 Because the transaction does not affect U.S. Bank's checking deposits, against which the reserve requirement applies, its required reserves do not change. As a result, the bank's total reserves and excess reserves change by the same amount.

2 Banks historically borrowed from Federal Reserve Banks by bringing securities and other asset documents to a teller's cage, or window. The amount loaned equaled the face value of the security, minus a discount. At maturity, the full value of the security was paid by the bank to the Federal Reserve Bank. Thus, the terms "discount loan" and "discount window" applied to these loans. However, when banks currently borrow from Federal Reserve Banks, they obtain advances of funds. This means that the bank receives a given amount of money from the Federal Reserve Bank and repays the principal and interest at maturity. Government securities typically serve as collateral for a loan advance.

PART 4

The International Economy

CHAPTER 16

International Trade and the Global Economy

CHAPTER OBJECTIVES

After reading this chapter, you should be able to:

1 Explain how the United States is an open economy.
2 Discuss the advantages of specialization and trade.
3 Explain why free trade is controversial.
4 Identify the effects of import tariffs and summarize the arguments for trade restrictions.
5 Assess the advantages and disadvantages of the World Trade Organization, the U.S.–Mexico–Canada Agreement, and the European Union.

DOI: 10.4324/9781003438571-20

ECONOMICS IN CONTEXT

U.S. sheep producers have long been dependent on the government. Burdened with high costs and inefficiencies, and facing domestic competition from beef, chicken, and pork, sheep producers attempted to limit foreign competition by petitioning the U.S. government for import restrictions at the beginning of the new millennium.

Almost all U.S. lamb imports come from producers in New Zealand and Australia, who provide strong competition for U.S. producers. These producers have invested substantial resources in new technology and effective marketing, making them among the most efficient producers in the world. These cost savings were passed on to American consumers in the form of low-priced lamb.

In response to increasing imports of lamb, the American Sheep Industry Association complained that domestic producers were being seriously injured by foreign competition. As a result, the U.S. government levied restrictions on lamb imports. This policy outraged farmers in Australia and New Zealand, who relied on exports to the United States for their livelihood. Moreover, American consumers complained that the trade restrictions prevented them from purchasing low-priced foreign lamb. Simply put, consumers felt that they were being "fleeced" by the import restrictions on lamb.

The United States has generally recognized that open domestic markets and an open global trading system are superior to trade protection and isolationism when it comes to promoting broad-based growth and prosperity. For decades, our open economy has generated important benefits for the American people in the form of stronger growth and improved employment opportunities. The opportunity to acquire goods and services from abroad both encourages us as producers to stay competitive and allows us as consumers to raise our standard of living.

Although most people benefit from an open global trading system, some do not. To mitigate the unequal distribution of benefits and burdens in an open global system, some nations impose restrictions on international trade.

In this chapter, we will examine the benefits and costs of an open trading system. We will consider the effects of trade on consumers, producers in exporting industries, and on producers in import-competing industries.

THE UNITED STATES AS AN OPEN ECONOMY

Throughout the 1900s–2000s, the U.S. economy has become increasingly integrated into the world economy—that is, it has become an open economy. This integration has involved trade in goods and services, financial markets, the labor force, ownership of production facilities, and dependence on imported materials.

As a measure of the importance of international trade in a nation's economy, we can look at the nation's exports plus imports as a percentage of its gross domestic product

Source: Richard Ross/The Image Bank/Getty Images®

TABLE 16.1 Top Trading Partners of the United States, 2022

Country	*Value of U.S. Exports (in billions of dollars)*	*Value of U.S. Imports (in billions of dollars)*	*Balance (in billions of dollars)*
China	$153.8	$536.8	–$383.0
Canada	356.1	437.7	–81.6
Mexico	324.4	454.9	–130.5
Japan	80.3	148.3	–68.0
Germany	72.9	146.6	–73.7
United Kingdom	77.3	64.0	13.3
South Korea	71.4	115.3	–43.9
France	45.8	57.4	–11.6
Australia	30.2	16.2	14.0

Source: Data drawn from U.S. Department of Commerce, U.S. Census Bureau, *Foreign Trade: U.S. Trade in Goods by Country*, April 2023, available at https://www.census.gov/foreign-trade/balance/c6021.html.

TABLE 16.2 The Fruits of Global Trade

On a trip to the grocery store, consumers can find goods from all over the globe.	
Apples from New Zealand	Limes from El Salvador
Apricots from China	Oranges from Australia
Bananas from Ecuador	Pears from South Korea
Blackberries from Canada	Pineapples from Costa Rica
Blueberries from Chile	Plums from Guatemala
Coconuts from Philippines	Raspberries from Mexico
Grapefruit from Bahamas	Strawberries from Poland
Grapes from Peru	Tangerines from South Africa

Source: Data drawn from "The Fruits of Free Trade," *Annual Report*, Federal Reserve Bank of Dallas, 2002, p. 3.

(GDP). In 2022, the United States exported about 12 percent of its GDP, while imports were about 16 percent of GDP; the U.S. economy's openness to trade thus equaled 28 percent. The relative importance of international trade in the U.S. economy has increased by about 50 percent during the past century.

The United States exports a variety of goods, including grain, chemicals, scientific equipment, machinery, automobiles, computers, and commercial aircraft. It also imports many goods such as steel, oil, automobiles, textiles, shoes, rubber, and foodstuffs such as bananas, tea, and coffee. Among the United States' biggest trade partners are Canada, Japan, Mexico, and China, as seen in Table 16.1.

The significance of international trade for the U.S. economy is even more apparent when we consider certain products. For example, we would have no chrome bumpers for automobiles if we did not import chromium, no tin cans without imported tin, and fewer personal computers without imported components such as memory chips. Students taking a 9:00 a.m. course in economic principles might doze off if we did not import tea and coffee. Moreover, many of the goods that we purchase from foreigners would be much more expensive if we depended on American production. Table 16.2 provides examples of fruits that the United States imports.

THE ADVANTAGES OF SPECIALIZATION AND TRADE

The notion of being self-sufficient may be appealing. You might even desire to live by yourself in an isolated area such as northern Alaska. However, living on your own would mean you could only consume the goods that you produce. The food that you eat, the clothing that you sew, and the house that you build would be nothing like the goods that you are currently able to buy. You would not be able to obtain many products, such as cell phones, medicines, and automobiles. Because of the constraints of self-sufficiency, most people prefer to specialize and trade with others.

Specialization and trade pertain not only to individuals but also to groups of individuals. Consider what would happen if the people of your state desired to be self-sufficient and refused to trade with people in other states throughout the country. Residents in the state of Montana, for example, could produce their own lumber and wheat, but where would they get grapefruit and cotton? Conceivably, they could grow grapefruit in greenhouses, but grapefruit would come at great cost. Therefore, it is not practical for each of the 50 states to be self-sufficient. The founders of the United States realized this, and thus they banned the enacting of trade barriers on interstate commerce. What is true for states is also true for countries. National specialization and trade can result in a more efficient use of the world's resources.

Specialization increases productivity in several ways. First, specialization saves time because workers focus only on one job rather than on switching from one task to another. Also, specialization allows production processes to be divided so that workers can practice and perfect a particular skill; this process is called the **division of labor**. People who practice a particular activity, such as hitting a golf ball or solving mathematical equations, tend to become much better at that activity than those who do not practice. Likewise, a country that specializes in the production of, say, computers tends to become highly productive in this activity. Finally, the division of labor promotes innovation and invention. As workers learn a task very well, they may figure out ways to perform it better—perhaps by inventing a new technology or a means to do it. Specialization and invention thus reinforce one another. However, the very nature of specialization can also limit its benefits because repetitive jobs may cause workers to become bored and unproductive.

Indeed, the degree to which specialization can be practiced is limited by the size of the market. For many mass-produced items, producing for the vast world market provides a greater scope for specialization than producing for the smaller domestic market. Boeing is an example: It has sold about 70 percent of its jet planes overseas in recent years. Without export revenue, Boeing would have found it difficult to cover the enormous design and tooling costs of its planes, and the planes might not have been produced at all.

The production of the Boeing Dreamliner (787), which began in 2009, is one of the most advanced processes within the aviation industry. The firm assembles the Dreamliner at its plant in Charleston, South Carolina. To produce the Dreamliner as cheaply and efficiently as possible, Boeing has taken advantage of specialization by outsourcing a large part of the process: Boeing by itself does not have the expertise to produce all of the plane's components.

The Dreamliner's components are produced at about 135 sites by 50 subcontractors. Also, more than 40 percent of the plane's components come from overseas producers, including Japan, Italy, Sweden, France, and the United Kingdom, as seen in Table 16.3. However, outsourcing has come with challenges to Boeing, which found out that some of the components manufactured from far-away suppliers did not always fit together. Also, relying on foreign suppliers has meant that Boeing has had to believe their word on the quality of components. Simply put, taking advantage of international specialization is not always easy.

TABLE 16.3 The Boeing Dreamliner (787): Selected Components

Country	*Component*
South Korea	Wing tips
Australia	Movable trailing edge
Italy	Horizontal stabilizer
United States	Tail fin, forward fuselage
Sweden	Cargo door
United Kingdom	Engine, landing gear
Japan	Wing
France	Entry doors

Source: Data drawn from the Boeing Company, press releases.

COMPARATIVE ADVANTAGE AND INTERNATIONAL TRADE

To illustrate the advantages of specialization and trade, let us consider a world of only two countries—the United States and France—that each produce only two goods—automobiles and computers. Also assume that the resources in each country are equally suited to producing autos or computers. As a result, the production possibilities schedule of each country appears as a straight line in Figure 16.1.[1]

Comparing the production possibilities schedules of the two countries, we see that the United States can produce more autos and more computers than France. If the United States devotes all of its resources to auto production, it can produce 100 autos a day. France, on the other hand, can produce a maximum of 80 autos a day because it has less efficient production skills than the United States. Similarly, by devoting all of its resources to producing a single good, the United States can produce a maximum of 200 computers a day, whereas France can produce only 80 computers a day. Again, the United States can out-produce France in computers because of its superior production skills.

Production and Consumption without Specialization and Trade

Without trade, the production possibilities schedule of each country defines the maximum amount of two goods that are available for consumption. In other words, a country can consume only what it produces when there is no trade. Without trade, suppose that the United States decides to produce and consume 120 computers and 40 autos, shown by point *A* in Figure 16.1(a). Also suppose that France decides to produce and consume 60 computers and 20 autos, shown by point *A′* in Figure 16.1(b). Because we assume that

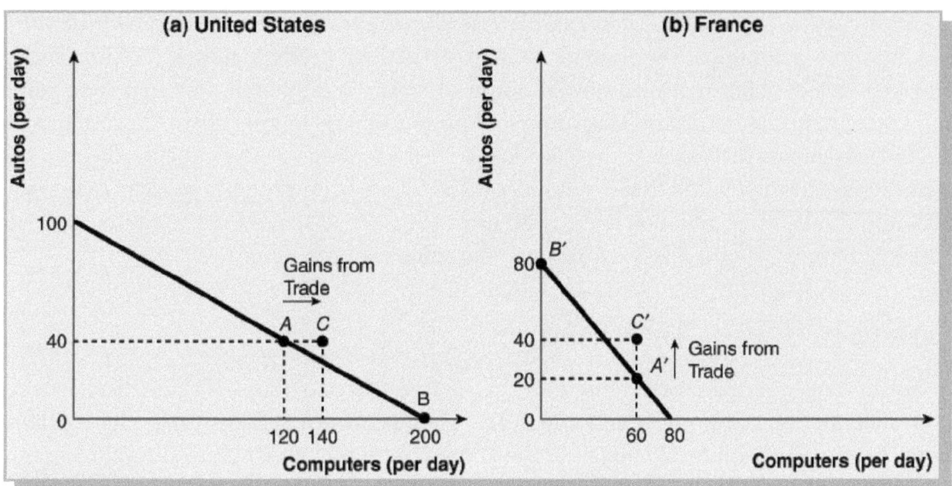

Figure 16.1 Comparative Advantage and International Trade

According to the principle of comparative advantage, countries should specialize in producing those goods in which they are relatively more efficient. Such specialization allows countries to realize gains in production and consumption.

the United States and France are the only two countries in the world, the world output of these goods totals 180 computers (120 + 60 =180) and 60 autos (40 + 20 = 60).

Production and Consumption with Specialization and Trade

Now assume that the United States specializes in the production of computers and France specializes in the production of autos. As seen in Figure 16.1(a), the United States moves down along its production possibilities schedule until it produces 200 computers, shown by point *B*. Similarly, France slides upward along its production possibilities schedule until it produces 80 autos, shown by point *B'* in Figure 16.1(b). Comparing the total world output that occurs before and after specialization, we see that specialization increases output by 20 computers (200–180 = 20) and 20 autos (80–60 = 20). Clearly, specialization is desirable because it allows resources to be used more efficiently.

Because specialization entails more efficient production, larger quantities of output are available to both countries. Referring to Figure 16.1(a), assume that the United States specializes in computer production at point *B* and agrees to import 40 autos from France in exchange for 60 of its computers. Are consumers in the United States better off with trade? Yes. At point *B*, the United States produces 200 computers. Subtracting the 60 computers that it exports to France leaves the United States with 140 computers; however, the United States imports 40 autos from France. The United States winds up consuming at point C in the figure. Comparing points *A* and C, we see that the United States can consume the same number of autos and 20 more computers because of trade. Clearly, U.S. consumers are better off with trade.

France also gains from trade. After exchanging 40 of its autos for 60 computers, France moves from point *A'* to point C' in Figure 16.1(b). French consumers thus have the same number of computers, but 20 more autos than they had without trade.

Trade between the United States and France allows both countries to gain because they can consume a combination of goods that exceeds their production possibilities schedules.[2] The effect of international specialization and trade is thus equivalent to having more and better resources or discovering improved production techniques. By reallocating production assignments so that France produces 60 more autos at the expense of only 60 computers, and the United States produces 80 additional computers in exchange for only 40 autos, total auto production rises by 20 units (60–40 = 20) and total computer output rises by 20 units (80–60 = 20)—a win–win outcome for both countries.

Comparative Advantage

In our trading example, we assume that the United States is more efficient than France at producing both computers and autos. The possession of superior production skills is called having an **absolute advantage**. If the United States has an absolute advantage in the production of both goods, why does it specialize in the production of computers? Why does France, with absolute disadvantages in both goods, specialize in auto production? The answer lies in the principle of **comparative advantage**, which states that individuals and countries should specialize in producing those goods in which they are relatively, not absolutely, more efficient. In other words, comparative advantage is the relative ability of one country to produce a good at a lower opportunity cost than some other country.

Let us return to our trading example in Figure 16.1 to determine the opportunity costs of producing computers and autos for the United States and France. Because workers in the United States can produce 200 computers or 100 autos, the opportunity cost of one computer is 0.5 auto (100 / 200 = 0.5). In France, because workers can produce 80 computers or 80 autos, the opportunity cost of one computer is one auto (80 / 80 = 1). Thus, the opportunity cost of computers is lower in the United States than in France. Therefore, the United States has a comparative advantage in the production of computers because it has a lower opportunity cost—that is, producing computers "costs" fewer autos. Similarly, France has a comparative advantage in the production of autos because its opportunity cost in that industry is lower.

According to the principle of comparative advantage, mutually beneficial trade between any two countries is possible whenever one country is relatively better at producing an item than the other country. Being "relatively better" suggests that one country can produce an item at a lower opportunity cost—that is, at a lower sacrifice of other items forgone.

There are many examples of comparative advantage. Brazil, for instance, is a major exporter of coffee because its soil and climate are relatively better suited to the cultivation of coffee. China, with its abundance of low-skilled labor, has a comparative advantage in the production of shirts that require much handiwork. Saudi Arabia has a comparative advantage in the production of oil because its vast oil reserves can be harvested at low cost. Canada is a major exporter of lumber because its forested land is relatively unproductive in non-forest crops. Table 16.4 provides other examples of comparative advantage.

But endowments of natural resources are not the only source of comparative advantage. For example, Japan has few natural resources, yet it is a major exporter of autos, steel, and electronics. The basic materials used in the production of autos, such as iron ore, are imported by the Japanese. Japan's auto industry highlights the importance of acquiring

TABLE 16.4 Comparative Advantages in the Global Economy

Country	*Product*
Israel	Citrus fruit
Japan	Automobiles
Canada	Lumber
Italy	Wine
Saudi Arabia	Oil
South Korea	Steel, ships
China	Textiles
Mexico	Tomatoes
United Kingdom	Financial services

comparative advantage by saving and accumulating capital and by constructing efficient factories. Moreover, countries can develop comparative advantages in goods that require a skilled labor force, such as scientific instruments, by channeling resources to education.

Superior knowledge also results in comparative advantage. Many years ago, Switzerland developed a comparative advantage in watches because the people of that country have superior knowledge and expertise in manufacturing watches. Similarly, semiconductor equipment is an export product of the United States because of the technical expertise of firms such as Intel Corp.

CHECK POINT

1. How does specialization promote increases in productivity?
2. How does the principle of comparative advantage explain the pattern of world trade?
3. What determines comparative advantage?
4. Discuss the argument for free trade.

WHY IS FREE TRADE CONTROVERSIAL?

Given that all nations can benefit from specialization and trade, why do some people object to free trade? The answer is not hard to find. Despite the gains to the overall economy, some groups within the economy are likely to lose from free trade, whereas others gain much more.

Clearly those industries that produce goods in which the home country has a comparative advantage gain from free trade. For example, Boeing's production of jetliners expands when orders increase from foreign airline companies. Also, Boeing's workers find that the demand for their labor increases along with the level of production. Moreover, firms that supply engines, landing gears, and other parts used to produce Boeing jetliners realize increased sales and employment. Indeed, people in the states of Washington and South Carolina, who account for a significant portion of the production of Boeing jetliners, benefit from international trade.

The consumer is another beneficiary of free trade. We have learned that competition among firms leads to increased output and lower prices. This also pertains to competition between domestic and foreign firms. Because international trade prevents markets from being dominated by one or a few domestic firms, there is more competition. This forces domestic firms to charge lower prices and to produce higher-quality goods—factors that consumers value. Clearly, American Airlines and its passengers are better off when Boeing and Airbus compete for its jetliner purchases. Also, trade can increase the diversity of products available to consumers. U.S. auto buyers, for example, can purchase Ford and Chevrolet models as well as Toyotas, Hondas, and Mitsubishis.

Reducing restrictions on trade, however, does not benefit everyone. Firms and their workers in import-competing industries face declining sales, profits, and employment levels as foreign-produced goods displace domestic goods. Many workers who lose their jobs in import-competing industries do not have the skills they need to be easily reemployed at a comparable wage level. Also, firms and workers who supply inputs to these industries suffer because of foreign competition. Both management and labor in these industries are likely to oppose free trade and seek government protection against imports. Seekers of protectionism are often established firms in aging industries that have lost their comparative advantage. High costs may be attributable to a lack of modern technology, inefficient management procedures, outmoded work rules, or high wages paid to domestic workers. In the United States, industries that have sought protectionism have included shoes, textiles, steel, oil, and automobiles.

Government officials must balance the opposing interests of consumers and firms and workers in exporting industries against firms and workers in import-competing industries when setting a course for changes in international trade policy.

LIMITING FOREIGN COMPETITION: TARIFFS

For centuries, governments have used tariffs to raise revenues and protect domestic producers from foreign competition. A **tariff** is a tax that is imposed on imports. For example, the United States imposes a tariff of 2.5 percent on autos. If a foreign car costs \$60,000, the amount of the tariff will equal \$1,740 (\$60,000 × 0.025 = \$1,500) and the domestic price including the tariff will be \$61,500. Table 16.5 shows average import tariffs of selected countries in 2020.[3]

We can use demand and supply analysis to understand the economic effects of tariffs. Figure 16.2 shows the steel market of the United States. The domestic demand and supply

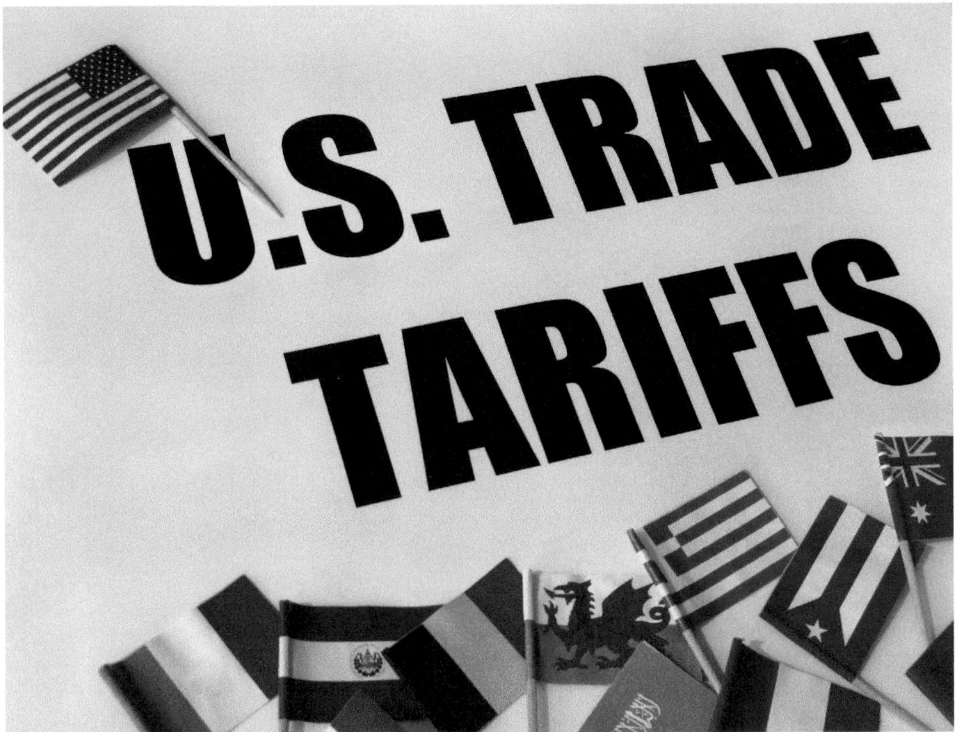

Source: Marie Hickman/Stone/Getty Images®

TABLE 16.5 Average Import Tariff Rates for Selected Countries, All Products, 2020

Country	*Percentage*	*Country*	*Percentage*
Bermuda	24.1	South Korea	5.5
Belize	18.1	Norway	2.8
Chad	16.4	Japan	2.2
Venezuela	14.1	Austria	1.5
Ethiopia	12.1	Canada	1.5
Grenada	10.8	United States	1.5
Brazil	8.8	Germany	1.4
Cuba	8.8	United Kingdom	1.3
India	6.2	Mexico	1.2

Source: Data drawn from The World Bank, *Tariff Rate, Applied, Weighted Mean, All Products*, available at https://data.worldbank.org/indicator/TM.TAX.MRCH.WM.AR.ZS.

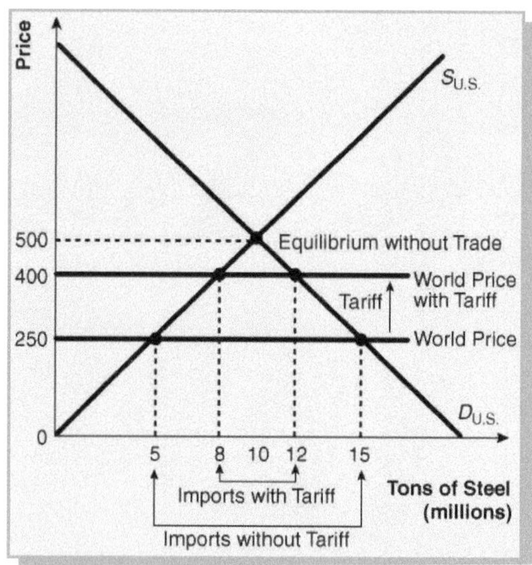

Figure 16.2 Economic Effects of a Tariff

A tariff placed on an imported good is shifted to the domestic consumer via a higher product price. As a result, imports of the product decrease from their pre-tariff level. This reduction can be attributed to falling domestic consumption and rising domestic production. The effect of a tariff is to protect domestic producers from foreign competition.

curves for steel are denoted by $D_{U.S.}$ and $S_{U.S.}$, respectively. In the absence of international trade, the equilibrium price of steel is $500 per ton, the quantity of steel supplied by U.S. producers is 10 million tons, and the quantity of steel demanded by U.S. consumers is 10 million tons.

Suppose that the U.S. economy is opened to international trade, and the rest of the world has a comparative advantage in steel. Assume that the world price of steel is $250 per ton. For simplicity, we will also assume that the United States takes the world price of steel as given.[4] At a price of $250, domestic consumption is 15 million tons and domestic production is 5 million tons. The quantity of imported steel, 10 million tons, reflects the horizontal difference between the U.S. demand curve and U.S. supply curve at a price of $250.

Free trade causes the domestic price of steel to fall from $500 to $250. As a result, consumers increase their purchases from 10 million tons to 15 million tons. Clearly, domestic consumers are better off because they can buy more steel at a lower price. However, domestic producers now sell less steel at a lower price than they did before trade. As production falls from 10 million tons to 5 million tons for domestic steel firms, profits decline and unemployment rises for domestic steelworkers.

In response to the domestic steel industry's pleas for protection against imports, assume that the U.S. government imposes a tariff of $150 per ton on steel that is imported into the United States. This increases the price of steel from $250 to $400 per ton. Therefore, domestic consumption will decline from the 15 million tons in the free-trade equilibrium to 12 million tons after the tariff is imposed. Also, domestic production increases from 5 million tons to 8 million tons and the quantity of imports falls from 10 million tons to 4 million tons. Thus, a tariff tends to raise the price, lower the amounts consumed and imported, and increase domestic production.

Clearly, the tariff benefits domestic steel firms and their workers at the expense of domestic consumers. Because of the tariff, consumers pay more for farm equipment, refrigerators, and other steel-using products. Steel-using firms such as Ford (autos) and Caterpillar (tractors) will realize higher costs and lower sales because of the tariff on steel. As production declines for these firms, they will lay off some of their workers.

Another effect of tariffs is the revenue that they raise for the government. In our example, we assume that the tariff equals $150 per ton of imported steel. Multiplying this amount by the quantity of imports—4 million tons—gives tariff revenues of $600 million. This tariff revenue is a transfer of income from U.S. steel consumers to the U.S. government.

Also, U.S. exporters are indirectly impeded by a tariff. Because a tariff causes sales of imported steel to decline in the United States, the rest of the world has fewer dollars to purchase U.S. exports of computers, chemicals, and wheat. U.S. export industries, which have a comparative advantage, will thus decrease production. Also, if the imposition of an import tariff by the United States causes foreign nations to retaliate and impose tariffs on imports from the United States, U.S. export industries will suffer. Simply put, tariffs foster the growth of inefficient industries that do not have a comparative advantage and promote the decline of efficient industries that do have a comparative advantage. By causing resources to move from high-efficiency industries to low-efficiency industries, tariffs reduce the standard of living.

The Regressive Nature of U.S. Tariffs

Does the burden of U.S. import tariffs fall on all consumers in the same manner? No. Economists have shown that on balance, U.S. tariffs are regressive because they disproportionately increase the relative price of goods consumed by lower-income Americans. Some of the most restrictive tariffs are levied on everyday consumer products such as footwear, textiles, and apparel items.

Tariffs disproportionately affect the poor in two ways. First, many tariffs are highest on products that represent higher shares of income expenditures for lower-income households. Staple consumer products such as shoes and clothing face import taxes of more than 30 percent, some of the highest tariffs in the U.S. tariff schedule. Footwear represents 1.3 percent of income expenditures for lower-income households compared to just 0.5 percent for higher-income households. Second, products that are more commonly purchased by lower-income consumers are subject to higher import taxes than are those commonly purchased by upper-income consumers.

For government officials, a legitimate concern is whether the costs of a tax are shared uniformly by all people in a country, or whether some income groups bear a disproportionate share of the cost. For tariffs, the cost tends to be disproportionately absorbed by the poor.

LIMITING FOREIGN COMPETITION: IMPORT QUOTA

Another instrument for limiting imports is a quota. An **import quota** is a restriction on the quantity of a product that is imported during some period. Once a quota is filled, no more of the product can be imported. A quota is more successful in limiting imports than a tariff. With a tariff, a product can be imported, although it will be more expensive as the tariff raises its price. However, once a quota is filled, all imports are banned.

Once again, refer to Figure 16.2, which shows the steel market of the United States. With free trade, the world price is assumed to be $250 per ton of steel, and the United States produces 5 tons, consumes 15 tons, and imports 10 tons. Instead of imposing a tariff, suppose the U.S. government imposes an import quota of 4 tons of steel; this means that any imports of steel exceeding 4 tons are prohibited.

As steel becomes scarcer in the United States under the quota, its price rises from $250 to $400 per ton. Therefore, domestic consumption falls from the 15 million tons in the free-trade equilibrium to 12 million tons after the quota is imposed. Also, domestic production rises from 5 million tons to 8 million tons and the quantity of imports falls from 10 million tons to 4 million tons. Thus, an import quota tends to raise the price, lower the amounts consumed and imported, and increase domestic production.

Simply put, an import quota is a device that is used to protect a domestic industry from foreign competition. Although an import quota provides gains for domestic producers, it entails costs for domestic consumers, who must pay higher prices because import competition has decreased.

INDUSTRIAL POLICY AND SUBSIDIES

The United States has a long history concerning **industrial policy**, in which government intervenes in the private sector to support domestic strategic industries. In 1791, Alexander Hamilton, the first Secretary of the U.S. Treasury, formulated a strategy to develop America's manufacturing sector to catch up with Britain and establish the material base for a strong military. His strategy included government subsidies to targeted industries, protective import tariffs, government procurement contracts, tax exemptions for manufacturing inputs, and government support for infrastructure improvements.

In recent years, the U.S. government has provided cash payments and tax credits to American producers of alternative energies, such as wind and solar power, as well as producers of fossil fuels. Subsidies have also been granted to vital manufacturers such as Boeing, which produces jetliners, and Tesla, which produces electric vehicles. Moreover, firms considered too big to fail have received government assistance, such as U.S. Steel Corporation, and General Motors. Finally, American exporting companies can receive financial assistance from the Export-Import Bank of the United States. The bank provides loan guarantees, loans, and insurance to help foreign companies purchase U.S. goods when private banks will not lend. This is especially prevalent in industries such as manufacturing, energy, and aerospace. Therefore, the notion of industrial policy is part of America's business environment.

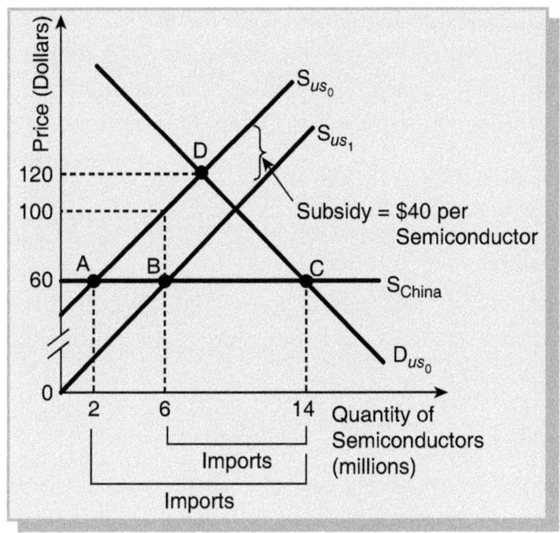

Figure 16.3 Industrial Policy: Effects of a Production Subsidy

A government production subsidy granted to an import-competing producer will result in a cost reduction, a rightward shift in its supply curve, and an improvement in its competitiveness. This allows the producer to capture a larger share of the domestic market. However, the subsidy must be financed by the domestic government, and thus the domestic taxpayer.

In 2022, President Joe Biden launched a massive industrial policy to outcompete China in semiconductor manufacturing, offering $39 billion in funding incentives for companies seeking to build manufacturing plants in the United States. He cited the importance of semiconductors to America's security as a main justification for his policy. Figure 16.3 will help us understand the operation of a production subsidy granted to a U.S. semiconductor manufacturer.

Assume that America's supply and demand schedules for semiconductors are shown by curves $S_{U.S.0}$ and $D_{U.S.0}$ in Figure 16.3. Market equilibrium occurs at point *D*, where the price of semiconductors equals $120 per unit. Suppose that China represents the rest of the world's supplier of semiconductors, and its supply price to the United States is $60 per unit. With free trade, the price of semiconductors will equal $60 and 14 million semiconductors will be purchased by Americans, shown at point C in the figure. American manufacturers will produce 2 million semiconductors, and imports from China will equal 12 million semiconductors.

To partially insulate American semiconductor production from Chinese competition, suppose the U.S. government grants a production subsidy of $40 per semiconductor to American manufacturers. The cost reduction made possible by the subsidy results in the U.S. supply curve of semiconductors shifting rightward to $S_{U.S.1}$, as shown in the figure. With the price of semiconductors remaining at $60, American production will increase from 2 million semiconductors to 6 million semiconductors, and American imports will fall from 12 million semiconductors to 8 million semiconductors. Therefore, the production subsidy results in an improvement in the competitiveness of American manufacturers and their capturing a larger share of the domestic market for semiconductors.

However, the production subsidy entails costs for the U.S. government, and thus the American taxpayer. The total cost of the subsidy equals $240 million, found by multiplying the per-unit subsidy ($40) times the quantity of semiconductors produced by American manufacturers resulting from the subsidy (6 million semiconductors).

ARGUMENTS FOR TRADE RESTRICTIONS

Although the free-trade argument is very influential, almost all nations have imposed restrictions on international trade. Let us consider the main arguments for trade restrictions.

Job Protection

The issue of jobs has been a major factor in motivating government officials to impose trade restrictions on imported goods. During periods of economic recession, workers are especially eager to point out that cheap foreign goods undercut domestic production, resulting in a loss of domestic jobs to foreign workers. Alleged job losses to foreign competition have historically been a major force behind the desire of most U.S. labor leaders to reject free-trade policies.

This view, however, has a limitation: It does not recognize the dual nature of international trade. Changes in a nation's imports of goods and services are closely linked to changes in its exports. Nations export goods because they want to import products from other nations. When the United States imports goods, foreigners gain buying power in dollars that will eventually be spent on U.S. goods, services, or financial assets. U.S. export industries then realize increases in sales and employment, whereas the opposite happens in U.S. import-competing industries. Rather than fostering overall unemployment, imports tend to promote job opportunities in some industries as part of the process by which they reduce employment in other industries. However, the job increases that result from open trade policies tend to be less visible to the public than the readily observable job losses stemming from foreign competition. The more conspicuous losses have enabled many U.S. business and labor leaders in import-competing industries to combine forces in their opposition to free trade.

Protection against Cheap Foreign Labor

One of the most vocal arguments used to justify trade restrictions is that tariffs are needed to protect domestic jobs against cheap foreign labor. For example, manufacturing workers in the United States are paid higher wages, in terms of the U.S. dollar, than workers in countries such as Brazil and Mexico. Thus, it can be argued that low wages abroad make it hard for American producers to compete with producers using cheap foreign labor, and, unless American producers are protected from imports, domestic output and employment levels will decline.

Indeed, a widely held view maintains that competition from goods produced in low-wage countries is unfair and harmful to American workers. A solution: Impose a tariff on goods brought into the United States to make up for the wage differential between foreign workers and American workers in the same industry. That way, competition would be based on who makes the best product, not who works for the least amount of money. Therefore, if an American firm desires to produce sweatshirts in Malaysia, the firm would be charged a tariff equal to the cost difference between the earnings of a Malaysian worker and a U.S. apparel worker.

Although this viewpoint may be appealing, it fails to account for the links among efficiency, wages, and labor. Labor cost per unit of output reflects not only the wage rate, but also the productivity of labor. Even if American wages are, say, twice that of foreign wages, if the productivity of American labor is more than twice as much as the productivity of foreign labor, American unit labor costs will be lower.

Fairness in Trade: A Level Playing Field

Fairness in trade is another argument for protectionism. Business firms and workers often maintain that foreign governments adhere to a different set of rules than the home government, allowing foreign firms an unfair competitive advantage. Domestic producers contend that import restrictions should be imposed to offset these foreign advantages, thus creating a **level playing field** on which all producers could compete on equal terms.

For example, American companies sometimes contend that foreign firms do not face the same government regulations regarding pollution control and worker safety that American companies must follow; this is especially true in many developing nations (such as South Korea and Mexico), where anti-pollution enforcement has been lax. Moreover, foreign firms may not pay as much in corporate taxes or have to comply with employment regulations such as affirmative action, minimum wage, and overtime pay. Also, foreign governments may establish high trade barriers that close their markets to imports, or they may subsidize their producers to enhance their competitiveness in world markets.

Infant Industry

One of the more commonly accepted cases for tariff protection is the **infant industry argument**. This argument does not deny the importance of free trade. However, it maintains that in order for free trade to be meaningful, trading nations should temporarily shield their newly developing industries from foreign competition. Otherwise, mature and efficient foreign businesses could eliminate young domestic businesses from the market. Only after the young firms have had time to become efficient producers should the tariff barriers be lifted and free trade occur.

Although there is some truth to the infant industry argument, it must be qualified in several respects. First, once a protective tariff is enacted, it tends to be difficult to eliminate, even after an industry has achieved maturity. Special interest groups can often convince policymakers that further protection is warranted. Second, it is hard to determine which industries will be capable of realizing their comparative advantage, and thus merit protection. Third, the infant industry argument generally is not valid for mature, industrialized nations such as the United States, Germany, and Japan.

National Security

Noneconomic considerations are among the arguments for protectionism. One such consideration is national security. The national security argument maintains that a country may be put in jeopardy in the event of an international crisis or war if it depends on foreign suppliers. Even though domestic producers may not be as efficient, tariff protection should be granted to ensure their continued existence. In the United States, oil and steel producers have argued for protection against imports on the grounds that they are essential for national defense. The problem, however, is deciding what constitutes an "essential industry." Are the watch and shoe industries essential for national security? If the term is defined broadly, many industries may be able to win import protection, and the argument loses its meaning.

BOX ESSAY 16.1 ECONOMICS IN ACTION
Should America's Steel Industry be Protected from Foreign Competition?

Trade protection for the U.S. steel industry is hardly new. It began in the 1790s as iron forges, the predecessor of the modern steel industry, were emerging in Pennsylvania. Tariffs were levied on imported nails, horseshoes, and rifle barrels to protect the infant industry from foreign competition.

Tariffs and other protections for America's steel producers almost disappeared following World War II. As the war destroyed steel production in Japan and Europe, American steel producers prospered, so there was no need for trade protection. However, the domestic industry weakened in the 1970s as foreign steel companies were reconstructed with the latest technology, and U.S. producers failed to invest in modern equipment. The United States lost its technological advantage, and cheaper foreign steel surged into the country. Obsolete U.S. plants were thus closed, and more than 100,000 steel workers lost their jobs, thus devastating their communities.

Since the 1970s, the U.S. steel industry has been a consistent beneficiary of trade protection by the U.S. government, much of it stemming from the industry's political strength. Such strength has come from a coalition of American steel companies, the steelworkers' union, and members of Congress from steel-producing regions. Another factor that has contributed to the steel industry's political success is the relative lack of cohesiveness among domestic steel-using manufacturing industries.

In 2018, President Donald Trump levied a tariff of 25 percent on steel imported from many foreign countries. Trump indicated that America's steel industry was dying and that a strong steel industry was vital to the nation's security. Therefore, tariffs were implemented to increase the demand for domestic steel, thus protecting the jobs of American steelworkers.

However, critics maintained that although the tariffs may have led to some increase in domestic steel sales and jobs, they resulted in higher steel prices that adversely affected other U.S. manufacturing industries that purchase steel as an input, such as automobiles and tractors. This resulted in higher production costs, falling sales, and job losses in these industries. Moreover, the increase in the cost of steel in the United States placed U.S. exporters at a disadvantage, as they competed against foreign rivals who paid a lower price in the global market when buying steel for production.

Critics also noted that there are two components of the U.S. steel industry. First, there are the traditional blast-furnace-based mills, which produce steel from iron ore and that Trump was supporting with tariffs. Second, there are the growing and thriving steel mini-mills, which use electricity to melt recycled scrap steel. By 2003, mini-mills overtook the traditional blast furnace mills for domestic steel production. Therefore, the U.S. steel industry overall was far from dead, and its evolution is a classic story of "creative destruction," according to tariff critics.

PURSUING TRADE LIBERALIZATION

Since World War II, advanced nations have generally lowered their trade restrictions. Such trade liberalization has stemmed from two approaches.

The first is a reciprocal reduction of trade barriers on a non-discriminatory basis. For example, the members of the World Trade Organization acknowledge that tariff reductions agreed to by any two nations will be extended to all other members. Such an international approach encourages a gradual relaxation of tariffs throughout the world.

A second approach to trade liberalization occurs when a relatively small group of nations, typically those in a geographic region, forms a regional trading arrangement. Under this system, member nations agree to impose lower trade barriers on nations within the group than on non-members. The U.S.–Mexico–Canada Agreement is an example of a regional trading arrangement.

Proponents of regional trading arrangements maintain that small blocs of nations with many similar interests are more likely to liberalize trade dramatically than the vast number of dissimilar nations. Critics, however, maintain that the members of a regional trading arrangement may not be greatly interested in global liberalization, but only in liberalization among themselves. Let us examine three trading arrangements—the World Trade Organization and U.S.–Mexico–Canada Agreement, and the European Union.

World Trade Organization

Established in 1995, the **World Trade Organization (WTO)** is headquartered in Geneva, Switzerland. Having 164 member countries as of 2023, the WTO strives to promote freer international trade. It does this by administering international trade agreements, facilitating trade negotiations of lower tariffs and quotas, resolving trade disputes, and providing technical assistance and training to developing countries. The WTO is not a government; individual nations are free to set their own appropriate levels of environment, labor, health, and safety protections. One of the most useful roles of the WTO is the settlement of trade disputes. The

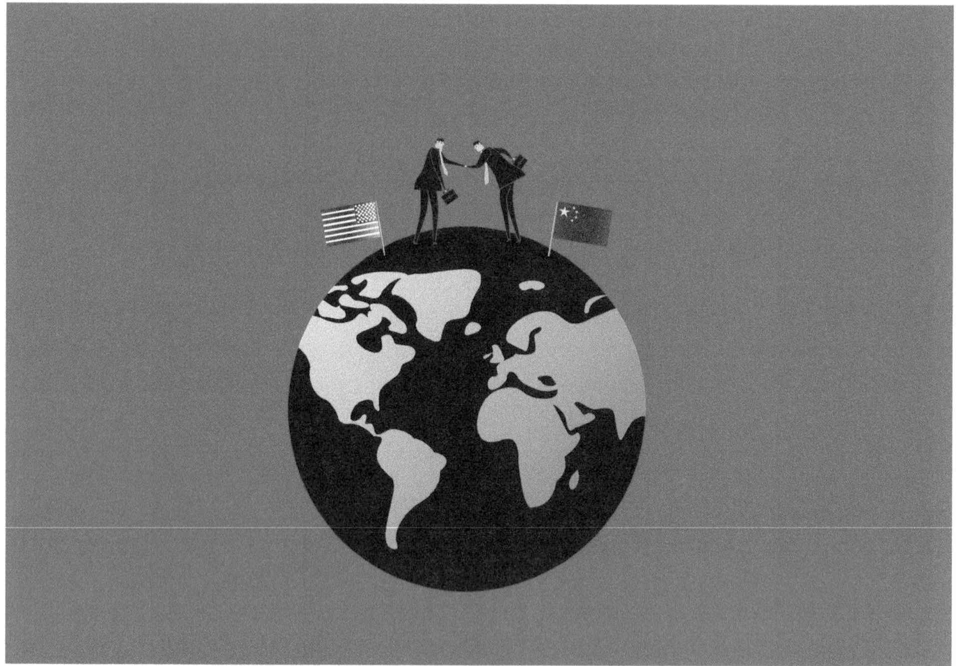

Source: wenjin chen/DigitalVision Vectors/Getty Images®

dispute-settlement mechanism of the WTO provides for the formation of a dispute panel once a case is brought and sets time limits for each stage of the process. The decision of the panel may be taken to an appellate body, but the accused party cannot block the final decision.

For example, during the 1990s, the United States complained that governments in Europe were preventing U.S. producers from selling their beef in Europe. After consulting with experts, the WTO found that Europe had engaged in unfair trade. The European nations, therefore, had the choice of halting this practice or facing retaliation from the United States. As things turned out, the United States imposed 100-percent tariffs on imports of selected European goods to pressure Europe to open its markets to U.S. beef.

Although the WTO attempts to promote freer international trade, it has become a magnet for resistance to globalization by protectionists and critics of free trade. Protectionists include American steelworkers who complain that the free-trade policies of the WTO allow cheap South Korean steel to flood the U.S. market, with the result that South Korean workers take away their jobs. Also, critics of free trade are incensed that, as economies become more closely intertwined, trade policy increasingly impinges on such sensitive issues as social justice, product safety, and the environment.

For example, American environmentalists were unhappy during the 1990s when the WTO ruled against a U.S. ban on imports of Malaysian shrimp from countries using nets that trap turtles and a ban on imports of Mexican tuna caught in ways that drown dolphins. Also, U.S. labor unions insist that Indonesian firms must pay liveable wages to their workers and improve the working conditions in their "sweatshop" factories if they are to sell their goods in the United States. Finally, some church leaders have declared that the international debts of poor nations should be forgiven.

Despite pressure for reform, the WTO has remained a centerpiece of the world trading system. Its policies are based on the idea that when countries can trade freely with each other, without import tariffs or other measures aimed at protecting the domestic market from competition, the world economy grows and everyone in general benefits. However, free trade can impose costs on firms and workers in import-competing industries. The protesters of the WTO are a reminder that its policies must be weighed in a broader context of the world community and social justice, not just increased economic growth.

The U.S.–Mexico–Canada Agreement (USMCA)

The idea of a free-trade area among the United States, Canada, and Mexico has a long tradition. During the 1900s, the three nations considered the free-trade issue several times. However, because of the urgency of nation building and apprehensions concerning political sovereignty, the nations chose not to integrate their economies.

This outlook had changed by the 1990s. In 1993, the North American Free Trade Agreement (NAFTA) was approved by the governments of the United States, Mexico, and Canada. The pact went into effect in 1994. By removing trade restrictions among themselves, the members hoped to gain better access to the others' markets, technology, labor, and expertise. In many respects, there were remarkable fits between the nations: The United States would benefit from Mexico's endowment of inexpensive and increasingly skilled labor, while Mexico would benefit from U.S. investment and expertise. Moreover, trade between the United States and Canada was also expected to increase because of free trade. After much discussion, a modernized NAFTA agreement was approved in 2020 by the three governments under a new name, the **U.S.–Mexico–Canada Agreement (USMCA)**.

Proponents maintain that the USMCA agreement has benefited the United States by expanding trade opportunities, reducing prices, increasing competition, and enhancing the ability of U.S. firms to attain economies of large-scale production. The United States produces more goods that benefit from large amounts of physical capital and a highly skilled workforce, including chemicals, plastics, cement, and sophisticated electronics. Moreover, USMCA has allowed the United States and Mexico to form closer political ties.

But most analysts acknowledge that USMCA has also had a harmful effect on some sectors of the American economy. For example, the losers have included industries such as sugar and citrus growers, which rely on trade restrictions to limit imports of low-priced Mexican goods. Other losers have included lower-skilled workers, such as those in the apparel industry, whose jobs are most vulnerable to competition from low-paid workers abroad. Simply put, although USMCA has provided economic benefits to the participating countries, it has also raised some concerns.

Mexico Stews over Tomato Dispute

The implementation of the NAFTA agreement in 1994 eliminated U.S. import tariffs on Mexican tomatoes and many other products. Almost immediately, U.S. tomato producers accused Mexican producers of dumping tomatoes at low prices and driving them out of business. Therefore, they demanded that antidumping tariffs be imposed on Mexican tomatoes. However, the Mexican government maintained that Mexican tomatoes were not being sold in the United States at prices below fair value: Mexican-grown tomatoes were more competitive because of lower labor costs, good weather, and more than a decade of greenhouse technology. It would be inappropriate to punish Mexican producers for being efficient, according to the Mexican government.

To resolve this conflict, an accord was reached in 1996 in which Mexico's largest producers agreed to ship their tomatoes to the United States at a minimum price, ensuring that they could not sell tomatoes at prices that might undercut U.S. producers. The price floor for Mexican tomatoes was set at 17 cents per pound in summer months and 21 cents per pound in the winter. For the price agreement to hold, producers representing 85 percent of Mexico's tomato exports agreed to be bound by the minimum. In return, the United States agreed to refrain from implementing antidumping tariffs.

The voluntary floor price on Mexican fresh tomato exports fulfilled the American producers' goal of preventing some Mexican tomato exports when prices were low. But did the agreement really protect American producers from import competition? Economists who studied this matter found that when the price floor was in effect, Mexico exported more tomatoes to Canada, while Canada and the rest of the world increased their exports to the United States. This behavior sharply reduced the protectionist effect of the border measure in the United States.

During 2012–2013, U.S. tomato producers lobbied for the abolishment of the minimum price agreement, arguing that they could not compete at those prices. If the agreement would be abolished, they would be free to again petition the U.S. government to impose more restrictive antidumping tariffs against cheap Mexican tomatoes.

In 2013 the United States and Mexico reached an agreement on cross-border trade in tomatoes. The agreement raised the minimum sales price for Mexican tomatoes in the United States from 21.69 cents a pound to 31 cents for winter tomatoes, and for summer tomatoes from 17.20 cents per pound to 24.58 cents. Also, the agreement increased the types of tomatoes governed by the pact to include all Mexican growers and exporters as well as strengthening compliance and enforcement. Although the highly competitive tomato producers of Mexico were not thrilled to see the price floor increased, they recognized that the agreement restored stability and confidence to the U.S. tomato market and thus avoided a more costly trade war.

The European Union (EU)

At the end of World War II, several western European nations desired closer economic, social, and political ties to attain economic growth and military security, and to foster lasting peace between France and Germany. These nations wanted to put an end to the devastating wars that had inflicted much harm to Europeans for centuries. It was also apparent that a united Europe would provide more economic and political power than the individual nations in years following World War II.

To this end, the leaders of six countries—Belgium, France, Italy, Luxembourg, the Netherlands, and West Germany—formed the European Economic Community (EEC) in 1957. By 1992, the EEC had evolved into the so-called **European Union (EU)**, which created a common market that featured the elimination of most barriers to the movement of goods, services, capital, and labor, the prohibition of most policies that inhibit market competition, a common agricultural policy, and a common external trade policy.

Also, membership in the EU increased from the original 6 nations to 28 nations, although Great Britain left the EU in 2020, bringing the current membership to 27 nations. These members include nations of both Western and Eastern Europe. Twenty members of the EU share a common currency, known as the euro, and a common monetary policy.

The EU has achieved increased regional specialization, greater productivity and output, and faster rates of economic growth. The free flow of goods and services has also created large markets for European industries, allowing them to benefit from economies of large-scale production and lower costs than what could have been achieved in their small single-nation markets. Moreover, the increased competition occurring through economic integration has helped keep prices down. Finally, the economies of the EU have been stimulated by higher levels of investment spending that have come about through economic integration. However, these benefits must be measured against the loss of sovereignty of countries when they become members of the EU.

CHECK POINT

1 Why do tariffs result in benefits for domestic producers but costs for domestic consumers?

2 Describe the nature and operation of industrial policy.

3 What are the major arguments for trade restrictions? Explain the limitation of each argument.

4 How does the World Trade Organization attempt to improve the efficiency of the world trading system?

5 What are the objectives of the U.S.–Mexico–Canada Agreement and the European Union?

CHAPTER SUMMARY

1 In recent decades, the U.S. economy has become increasingly integrated into the world economy. This integration has involved trade in goods and services, financial markets, the labor force, ownership of production facilities, and dependence on imported materials.

2 Specialization and trade pertain not only to individuals but also to groups of individuals. By increasing productivity, specialization can result in a more efficient use of resources and an increase in output. However, the nature of specialization can limit its benefits because repetitive jobs may cause workers to become bored and unproductive.

3 Proponents of free trade contend that if each country produces what it can best create and allows trade, over the long run, all countries will enjoy lower costs and prices as well as higher levels of output, income, and consumption, than could be achieved in isolation. A free market compels firms and their workers to adjust to forces such as shifts in technologies, input productivities, and consumer tastes and preferences.

4 The principle of comparative advantage underlies patterns of world trade. This principle states that countries should specialize in producing those goods in which they are relatively, not absolutely, more efficient. In other words, comparative advantage is the relative ability of one country to produce a good at a lower opportunity cost than some other country. Among the sources of comparative advantage are natural endowments of resources, a skilled labor force, and superior knowledge.

5 Although economies can benefit from specialization and free trade, some people object to free trade. This is because some groups in the economy lose from free trade, while others gain. Consumers and firms and workers that produce goods in which the home country has a comparative advantage gain from free trade. However, firms and their workers in import-competing industries suffer. Government officials must consider the opposing interests of these groups when setting a course for international trade policy.

6 To protect firms and workers from foreign competition, governments can impose tariffs, subsidies, and other trade restrictions. These devices, however, tend to foster the growth of inefficient industries that do not have a comparative advantage and promote the decline of efficient industries that do have a comparative advantage, thus reducing the standard of living for the nation.

7 Among the arguments for trade restrictions are job protection, protection against cheap foreign labor, fairness in trade, infant industry, national security, and preservation of culture.

8 Since World War II, advanced nations have significantly lowered their trade barriers. Such trade liberalization has stemmed from the World Trade Organization and regional trading arrangements such as the U.S.–Mexico–Canada Agreement and the European Union.

KEY TERMS AND CONCEPTS

division of labor
absolute advantage
comparative advantage
tariff
subsidy
level playing field
infant industry argument
World Trade Organization (WTO)
U.S.–Mexico–Canada Agreement (USMCA)
European Union (EU)

STUDY QUESTIONS AND PROBLEMS

1 Table 16.6 shows the hypothetical production possibilities tables of Japan and South Korea. Use this information to answer the following questions:

TABLE 16.6 Production Possibilities Schedules of Japan and South Korea

	Japan TVs	*Phone Cases*		*South Korea TVs*	*Phone Cases*
A	0	80	*A′*	0	120
B	8	64	*B′*	6	96
C	16	48	*C′*	12	72
D	24	32	*D′*	18	48
E	32	16	*E′*	24	24
F	40	0	*F′*	30	0

- **a** What is the opportunity cost of producing a TV for Japan and for South Korea?
- **b** Which country has a comparative advantage in the production of TVs?
- **c** In the absence of trade and specialization, suppose that Japan produces and consumes at combination *B* and South Korea produces and consumes at combination *E′*. If these countries specialize according to the principle of comparative advantage, how much will total output increase?
- **d** Show how consumers in each country can share the gains in total output that result from specialization.

2 The United States tends to have a comparative advantage over other nations in the production of high-technology goods. What are the likely sources of this advantage?

3 Which individuals might gain from a tariff placed on imported textiles? Who might lose?

4 Why do economists maintain that trade barriers lead to a misallocation of resources in the world economy?

5 Although people may grow grapefruit in Idaho, why do they purchase most of their grapefruit from California and Florida?

6 Suppose that the U.S. government imposes a quota on cheese imported from Europe. Who would likely be helped and hurt?

7 What is the purpose of the European Union and the U.S.–Mexico–Canada Agreement?

8 Explain how trade with low-wage countries affects jobs in the United States. How can the United States pay its workers higher wages than foreign nations and still be competitive in foreign markets?

9 Suppose that Canada can produce 160 machine tools by using all of its resources to produce machine tools and 120 calculators by devoting all of its resources to calculators. Comparative figures for Brazil are 120 machine tools and 120 calculators. According to the principle of comparative advantage, in which product should each country specialize?

10 Draw a demand and supply diagram for autos in the United States, a product in which the United States has a comparative disadvantage. Show the effect of Japanese imports on the domestic price and quantity. Now show a tariff that cuts the level of auto imports in half. Show the effects of the tariff on U.S. producers and consumers.

11 Table 16.7 shows the demand and supply schedules for computers in Australia. On the basis of this information, answer the following questions:

TABLE 16.7 Australia's Computer Market

Price of Computers	*Quantity Demanded*	*Quantity Supplied*
$4,000	10	40
3,500	15	35
3,000	20	30
2,500	25	25
2,000	30	20
1,500	35	15
1,000	40	10

a In the absence of trade, what are the equilibrium price and quantity of computers for Australia?

b Suppose that the world price of computers is $1,500 per unit and that Australia takes this price as given. How many computers will Australia produce, consume, and import?

c To protect its producers from world competition, suppose that the Australian government imposes a tariff of $500 per unit on computer imports. What effect will the tariff have on the price of computers in Australia, the quantity of computers supplied by Australian producers, the quantity of computers demanded by Australian consumers, and the quantity of imports? How much revenue will the Australian government gain because of the tariff?

NOTES

1 A straight-line production possibilities curve implies that the law of increasing costs, as discussed in Chapter 1, is replaced with the assumption of constant costs.
2 How much each country gains from trade depends on the rate at which autos exchange for computers. The United States gains more from trade when a given quantity of its computers exchanges for larger quantities of French autos. In contrast, France gains more from trade when a given quantity of its autos trades for larger quantities of U.S. computers. Demand and supply conditions in the two countries determine the rate of exchange and thus the distribution of the gains from trade.
3 Another way to restrict foreign competition is to impose a quota. A **quota** is a physical restriction on the quantity of goods traded each year. For example, a quota might state that no more than 1 million kilograms of cheese or 2 million kilograms of ice cream can be imported during a year.
4 This assumption implies that the United States is a small economy compared to the rest of the world. Although the small-economy assumption is not necessary to analyze the effects of international trade, it greatly simplifies the analysis.

CHAPTER 17

International Finance

CHAPTER OBJECTIVES

After reading this chapter, you should be able to:

1 Explain what a current account deficit or surplus means.
2 Understand the foreign exchange quotations as presented in major newspapers.
3 Identify the factors that determine the dollar's exchange rate.
4 Discuss the features of the major exchange rate systems of the world.

DOI: 10.4324/9781003438571-21

ECONOMICS IN CONTEXT

During the early 2000s, the U.S. balance of payments (current account) reached record deficits, sparking fears of a flight from the dollar with wrenching consequences for U.S. economic prosperity. Nothing is intrinsically wrong with a country running such a deficit, but the United States has run a string of deficits for decades, and foreign countries now hold unprecedented financial claims on the United States. At some point, they might become reluctant to hold these dollars and set in motion a series of corrective economic adjustments that would result in sharply rising interest rates and recession for the U.S. economy.

Although international trade is an important component of the global economy, it is just one part of the picture; international finance is another part. The balance of payments is an important dimension of international finance, as is the financing of international trade.

In this chapter, we will examine the U.S. balance of payments and the markets in which Americans exchange dollars for other currencies. We will also expand our understanding of foreign currency markets by considering the advantages and disadvantages of various exchange rate systems.

THE BALANCE OF PAYMENTS

Every year, Americans conduct many transactions with residents of other countries. Some examples include the following:

- Walmart imports shirts from Hong Kong.
- General Motors exports minivans to Brazil.
- Holiday Inn supplies rooms to German tourists visiting San Francisco.
- Ayako Ozawa, a student at Stanford University, receives gifts from her family in Japan.
- American investors receive dividends from their investments in Germany.
- Edgar Valdez, a resident of Mexico, purchases U.S. Treasury bills.
- George Thomas, who lives in Philadelphia, purchases stock in Sony Corp. of Japan.

The U.S. government compiles a statistical record of these and other transactions. This record is called the balance of payments. The **balance of payments** is a record of a country's international trading, borrowing, and lending. In the balance of payments, *inflows* of funds from residents of other countries to the United States are noted as *receipts*, with a plus sign. *Outflows* of funds from the United States to residents of other countries are noted as *payments*, with a minus sign. The balance of payments has two components, the current account and the capital and financial account, which we will now examine.

The Current Account

The first component of the balance of payments is the **current account**, which represents, as the name suggests, the dollar value of U.S. transactions in currently produced goods and services, investment income, and unilateral transfers.

The most widely reported component of the current account is the **balance of trade**, also known as the **trade balance**. This balance includes all of the goods (merchandise) that the United States exports or imports: Agricultural products, machinery, autos, petroleum, electronics, computer software, jetliners, textiles, and the like. Combining the exports and imports of goods gives the balance of trade. When exports exceed imports, the trade balance is a *surplus*; when imports exceed exports, the trade balance is a *deficit*.

Another component of the current account is exports and imports of **services**. Examples of internationally traded services include tourism, airline and shipping transportation, construction, architecture, engineering, consulting, information management, banking, insurance, medical, and legal. When exports exceed imports, the services balance is a *surplus*; when imports exceed exports, the services balance is a *deficit*.

Broadening the current account, we also include flows of **income**. This item consists of the net earnings (dividends and interest) on U.S. investments abroad—that is, earnings on U.S. investments abroad less payments on foreign investments in the United States. It also includes the net compensation of employees.

Finally, the current account includes **unilateral transfers**. These items or gifts include transfers of goods and services or money between the United States and the rest of the world for which nothing is given in exchange—hence, they are unilateral. Examples of private transfers are gifts that Americans make to their families in Europe or living allowances that Japanese families send to their sons and daughters who attend college in the United States. The economic and military aid that the U.S. government provides to other governments is an example of a governmental unilateral transfer.

The **current account balance** is the sum of the trade balance, the services balance, net investment income, and net unilateral transfers. If the monetary inflows on these accounts exceed the monetary outflows, the current account balance is a *surplus*. But if the monetary outflows on these accounts exceed the monetary inflows, the current account balance is a *deficit*.

The Capital and Financial Account

The second component of the balance of payments is the **capital and financial account**. Capital and financial transactions in the balance of payments represent all international purchases or sales of assets such as real estate, corporate stocks and bonds, and government securities. Changes in foreign asset holdings by governments and central banks are also included in the capital and financial account.

When an American sells an asset (such as a golf course, a share of stock, or a bond) to a Japanese investor, the transaction is recorded in the capital and financial account as an inflow, because funds flow into the United States to purchase the asset. When an American purchases a skyscraper in Switzerland, the transaction is recorded in the capital and financial account as an outflow because funds flow from the United States to purchase the asset.

The **capital and financial account balance** is the amount of inflows minus outflows. The capital and financial account balance is a *surplus* if those in the United States sell more assets to residents of other countries than they purchase from residents of other countries. The capital and financial account balance is a *deficit* if those in the United States buy more assets from residents of other countries than they sell to residents of other countries.

What Does a Current Account Deficit (Surplus) Mean?

The current account and the capital and financial account are not unrelated; they are essentially reflections of one another. Recall that each international transaction represents an exchange of goods, services, or assets among households, businesses, or governments. Thus, the two sides of the exchange must always balance. This means that the current account balance equals the capital and financial account balance, as shown in the following equation:

Current account balance = Capital and financial account balance

It follows that any current account *deficit* must be balanced by a capital and financial account *surplus*. Conversely, any current account *surplus* must be balanced by a capital and financial account *deficit*.

To better understand this notion, assume that in a particular year your spending is greater than your income. How will you finance your deficit? By borrowing or by selling some of your assets. You might liquidate some real assets (for example, sell your personal computer) or perhaps some financial assets (sell a U.S. government security that you own). In like manner, when a nation experiences a current account deficit, its expenditures for foreign goods and services are greater than the income that it receives from the international sales of its own goods and services, after making allowances for investment income flows and gifts to and from residents of other countries. The nation must somehow finance its current account deficit. But how? By borrowing or by selling assets. In other words, a nation's current account *deficit* is financed essentially by a net *inflow* of capital in its capital and financial account. Conversely, a nation's current account *surplus* is financed by a net *outflow* of capital in its capital and financial account.

Although the current account balance always equals the capital and financial account balance, the figures gathered on international transactions are not 100-percent accurate or complete. Consequently, an adjustment for measurement errors, the **statistical discrepancy**, is reported in the capital and financial account component of the balance of payments. Economists generally believe that the statistical discrepancy is primarily the result of large hidden capital and financial flows (for example, unidentified borrowing from the rest of the world or tax evasion), and so the item is placed in the capital and financial account component of the balance of payments.

THE U.S. BALANCE OF PAYMENTS

Table 17.1 shows the balance of payments for the United States during 1980–2021. Items that result in flows of funds from the United States to other nations have a minus sign.

Let us consider the U.S. balance of payments for 2021. As seen in the table, the United States had a merchandise trade deficit of –$1,090.2 billion, resulting from the difference between U.S. merchandise exports and U.S. merchandise imports. The United States was thus a net importer of merchandise. The table also shows that the United States has consistently realized merchandise trade deficits since 1980.

Discussions of U.S. competitiveness in merchandise trade sometimes give the impression that the United States has consistently performed poorly relative to other nations. However, the merchandise trade deficit is a narrow concept because goods are only part of what the world trades. Another part of trade is services. Table 17.1 shows that in 2021, the United States realized a surplus of $245.2 billion on services transactions with residents of other countries. In recent decades, the United States has consistently generated a surplus in its services account. The United States has been especially competitive in transportation, construction, engineering, finance, and certain health care services.

Next, we adjust the merchandise trade balance and the services balance for net income flows ($139.5 billion) and net unilateral transfers (–$140.8 billion). This gives the balance on the current account. The United States had a current account deficit of –$846.3 billion in 2021, as seen in the table. Because U.S. exports were insufficient to pay for U.S. imports, the country either borrowed from residents of other countries or sold them assets such as corporate stock, golf courses, real estate, and skyscrapers to make up the difference. The capital and financial account tells us how much was borrowed and sold. In 2021, the

TABLE 17.1 U.S. International Transactions, 1980–2021 (billions of dollars)

Year	*Merchandise Trade Balance*	*Services Balance*	*Primary Income Balance*	*Unilateral Transfers Balance*	*Current Account Balance*	*Capital and Financial Account Balance*
1980	-$25.5	$6.1	$30.0	-$8.3	$2.3	-$2.3
1990	-111.0	30.2	28.5	-26.6	-78.9	78.9
2000	-446.8	77.1	14.6	-46.7	-401.8	401.8
2010	-648.7	145.6	169.9	-98.8	-432.0	432.0
2021	-1,090.2	245.2	139.5	-140.8	-846.3	846.3

Source: Data from Department of Commerce (Bureau of Economic Analysis), from *Economic Report of the President*, 2023, Table B-57, available at https://www.whitehouse.gov/wp-content/uploads/2023/03/ERP-2023.pdf.

net borrowing and sale of assets by the United States was $846.3 billion. Since 1982, the United States has realized continuous current account deficits.

Indeed, Americans buy more from residents of other countries than they buy from Americans. Therefore, residents of other countries lend or give Americans the funds to make up the difference between its imports and exports. It would not be an overstatement to say that, by borrowing from residents of other countries to finance its current account deficits, the country sells them pieces of America, so to speak. Those pieces consist primarily of real estate and corporate stock. However, residents of other countries also lend Americans billions of dollars each year in the form of purchases of government and corporate securities and other debt instruments.

Are U.S. Current Account Deficits Bad?

In both the media and popular opinion, current account deficits are often portrayed negatively, blamed on either the unfair practices of our trading partners or a lack of U.S. competitiveness in world markets. Some have even suggested that growing current account deficits will eventually interfere with the expansion of the U.S. economy.

When a nation realizes a current account deficit, it becomes a net borrower of funds from the rest of the world. Is this bad? Not necessarily. The advantage of a current account deficit is that it allows current spending to exceed current production. However, the cost is the debt service that must be paid on the associated borrowing from the rest of the world.

Is it problematic for a country to incur debt? The answer depends on what the country does with the money. If it is being used to finance an increase in domestic investment, the burden could be modest. This is because investment spending increases a nation's stock of capital, and increases an economy's ability to produce goods and services, thus increasing the country's standard of living. However, if foreign borrowing is used to finance an increase in domestic consumption, there is no stimulus given to future productive capacity. Therefore, to fulfill the cost of debt service, future consumption must decrease. Such a decrease represents the burden of borrowing.

In the past two decades, the United States has realized continuous deficits in its current account. Can the United States realize deficits indefinitely? Since the current account deficit arises mainly because residents of other countries desire to purchase American assets, there is no economic reason why the deficits cannot continue indefinitely. As long as the investment opportunities are large enough to provide foreign investors with competitive rates of return, they will be willing to continue investing in the United States.

However, the consequence of a current account deficit is increasing foreign ownership of the capital stock of the United States and an increasing share of U.S. income that must be shifted abroad in the form of interest and dividends to residents of other countries. Whether the United States can sustain its current account deficit over the foreseeable future depends on whether residents of other countries are willing to increase their investments in U.S. assets. The current account deficit puts the economic fortunes of the United States partially in the hands of foreign investors.

CHECK POINT

1. What is the balance of payments?
2. The balance of payments includes the current account and the capital and financial account. Identify the components of each.
3. What does a current account deficit mean? How about a current account surplus?
4. What are the advantages and disadvantages of a current account deficit for the United States?

FOREIGN EXCHANGE MARKET

Now that we have learned about international flows of exports, imports, income, and unilateral transfers, let us consider how these transactions are financed. Financing these transactions involves the purchase and sale of foreign currencies, such as the Mexican peso and Japanese yen.

In most cases, the buying and selling of currencies takes place in the **foreign exchange market**. The foreign exchange market does not involve sending large loads of currency from one country to another. Typically, it involves electronic transfers of money. Computer-housed dollar-denominated balances in the United States or other countries are traded for computer-housed balances around the world that are denominated in Canadian dollars, British pounds, Japanese yen, or any of the dozens of other commonly traded monies. In short, when "currency" is traded, paper and metal are not the usual media of exchange. Foreign exchange exists mainly in the world of cyberspace.

The **exchange rate** is the rate at which one currency will be exchanged for another—for example, the number of dollars required to purchase one British pound. The dollar price of the pound may be, say, \$2 = 1 pound. We can also define the exchange rate as the number of units of foreign currency required to purchase one unit of domestic currency. For example, the pound price of the dollar may be 0.5 pound = \$1. Of course, the pound price of the dollar is the reciprocal of the dollar price of the pound, calculated as shown:

$$\text{Pound price of the dollar} = 1 / \text{Dollar price of the pound}$$

Therefore, if \$2 is required to buy 1 pound, 0.5 pound is required to buy \$1—that is, $1 / 2 = 0.5$, or 0.5 pound per dollar.

Table 17.2 shows examples of exchange rates during 2020–2022. The table indicates how many U.S. dollars were required to purchase one unit of a given foreign currency. For example, the 2022 quote for the United Kingdom pound was 0.8083 dollars. This means that it took $0.8083 (about 81 cents) to buy one pound. To calculate the number of pounds required to buy one dollar, you would divide 1 by the current exchange rate of 0.8083 dollars per pound—that is, 1 / 0.8083 = 1.2372, or 1.24 pounds per dollar.

In a system of market-determined exchange rates, the exchange rate between two currencies can change frequently, usually within a narrow range. When the dollar price of the pound increases—for example, from $2 = 1 pound to $2.01 = 1 pound—the dollar has depreciated (weakened) relative to the pound. Currency **depreciation** means that it takes *more* units of a nation's currency to purchase a unit of some foreign currency. As a result, the prices of foreign goods increase for domestic consumers, and imports decline. Conversely, when the dollar price of a pound decreases—say, from $2 = 1 pound to $1.99 = 1 pound—the value of the dollar has appreciated (strengthened) relative to the pound. Currency **appreciation** means that it takes *fewer* units of a nation's currency to purchase a unit of some foreign currency. Because foreign goods become more attractive to domestic consumers, imports tend to increase.

Referring to Table 17.2, let us consider examples of changes of exchange rates from 2021 to 2022. During this period, the exchange rate between the U.S. dollar and the European euro went from $0.8453 per euro to $0.9493 per euro—the dollar depreciated against the euro. During the same period, the exchange rate between the U.S. dollar and the Swiss franc went from $1.0936 per franc to $1.0471 per franc—the dollar appreciated against the franc.

TABLE 17.2 Foreign Exchange Quotations in U.S. Dollars (annual)

U.S. Dollars Per Unit of Foreign Currency

Currency	*2022*	*2021*	*2020*
Canada (dollar)	$0.7684	$0.7978	$0.7450
Europe (euro)	0.9493	0.8453	0.8764
Japan (yen)	0.0076	0.0091	0.0093
Mexico (peso)	0.0496	0.0492	0.0464
Norway (krone)	0.1040	0.1163	0.1060
Sweden (krona)	0.9883	0.1165	0.1085
Switzerland (franc)	1.0471	1.0936	1.0650
United Kingdom (pound)	0.8083	0.7596	0.7795

Source: Data drawn from Federal Reserve Bank of New York, *Foreign Exchange Rates*—G.5A Annual, January 9, 2023, available at https://www.federalreserve.gov/releases/g5a/current.

BOX ESSAY 17.1 ECONOMICS IN ACTION

How to Save Money When Exchanging Foreign Currency

When traveling abroad, you may need to obtain foreign currency. How can you get the best exchange rate, while limiting the fees that you must pay, when exchanging foreign currency? Here are a few tips.

- To usually get the best exchange rate, obtain foreign currency at your bank or credit union before you travel internationally. Most major U.S banks have foreign currency available to sell their customers, with a checking or savings account, without charging an extra fee beyond the exchange rate.
- Avoid currency exchanges at airports. If you cannot obtain foreign currency at your bank before traveling abroad, it may be convenient to purchase it from an airport kiosk. However, kiosks generally have the worst exchange rates and charge some of the highest transaction fees.
- Once abroad, you may want to conserve your foreign banknotes and pay with your debit card or credit card. However, your debit card or credit card may carry a foreign transaction fee of up to 3 percent on each foreign purchase.
- If you need foreign currency while traveling internationally, often the best option for exchanging foreign currency and saving fees is to use your bank's ATM overseas or a foreign ATM. However, you will wish to know the types of transaction fees your bank charges and the restrictions imposed on daily withdrawals.
- When you return from your trip, see if your bank or credit union will buy back any foreign currency that you have. If not, you can exchange it at an airport kiosk, although you likely won't receive the best rate.

Sources: Drawn from Ellen Chang, "Where is the Best Place to Exchange Foreign Currency?" *U.S News*, June 11, 2021 at https://money.usnews.com/banking/articles/where-is-the-best-place-to-exchange-foreign-currency; E. Napoletano, "Where to Exchange Currency Without Paying Huge Fees," *Fortune*, October 19, 2022 at https://www.forbes.com/advisor/money-transfer/money-transfer-where-to-exchange-currency.

EXCHANGE RATE DETERMINATION

What determines the equilibrium exchange value of a currency in a free market? The exchange rate is determined by both demand and supply conditions.

Figure 17.1 shows the market for the British pound. The demand curve for pounds, depicted by D_0, stems from the desire of Americans to purchase British goods, services, and assets. Like most demand schedules, the U.S. demand for pounds varies inversely with price. As the dollar price of the pound decreases, British goods become less expensive for Americans, who thus purchase greater quantities. Therefore, more pounds are demanded in the foreign exchange market.

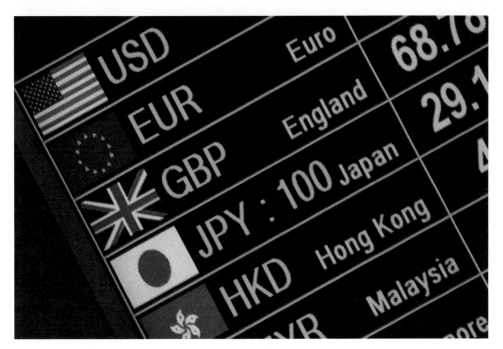

Source: Jeremy Horner/Corbis Documentary/Getty Images®

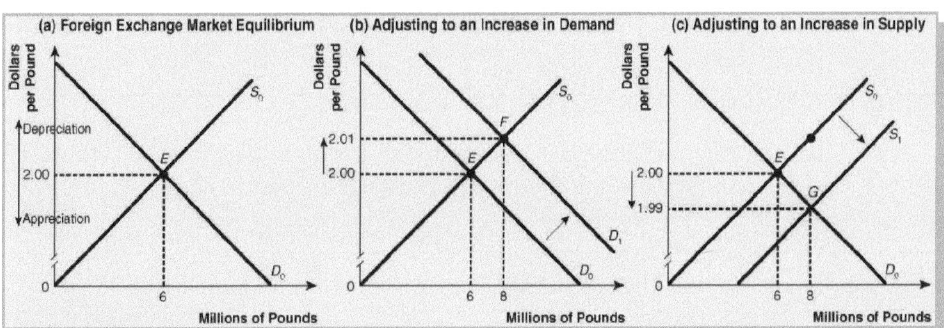

Figure 17.1 Exchange Rate Determination

In a free market, the equilibrium exchange rate is determined by the market forces of supply and demand. In the figure, market equilibrium occurs at point *E*, where S_0 and D_0 intersect. All else being equal, an increase in the demand for foreign currency causes a depreciation of the dollar; an increase in the supply of foreign currency results in an appreciation of the dollar.

The supply curve for pounds, depicted by S_0 in the figure, shows the quantity of pounds that will be offered to the market at various exchange rates. The British supply pounds to the market to purchase American goods, services, and assets. As the dollar price of the pound increases, and the pound price of the dollar decreases, American goods become cheaper to the British, who are induced to purchase additional quantities. Therefore, more pounds are offered in the foreign exchange market to purchase dollars with which to pay American exporters.

The **equilibrium exchange rate** is determined by the market forces of demand and supply. In Figure 17.1(*a*), exchange market equilibrium occurs at point *E*, where S_0 and D_0 intersect. A total of 6 million pounds will be traded at a price of $2 per pound. The foreign exchange market is precisely cleared, leaving neither an excess demand for, nor an excess supply of, pounds.

With given demand and supply schedules for pounds, the pound's exchange rate will remain at the equilibrium level. However, it is unlikely that the equilibrium exchange rate will remain at the existing level for long. This is because the determinants that underlie the location of the demand and supply schedules tend to change frequently, causing shifts in the schedules.

Referring to Figure 17.1(*b*), suppose that a rise in the quantity of British goods demanded by Americans causes the demand for pounds to increase. Therefore, the dollar price of the pound increases, meaning that the dollar *depreciates* against the pound. Conversely, a *decrease* in the demand for pounds causes the dollar to *appreciate.*

Now we will consider the effect of a change in the supply of pounds on the equilibrium exchange rate. Referring to Figure 17.1(*c*), suppose that rising American exports to the United Kingdom result in an *increase* in the supply of pounds on the foreign exchange market. This results in a decrease in the dollar price of the pound, suggesting that the dollar *appreciates* against the pound. Conversely, a *decrease* in the supply of pounds causes the dollar to *depreciate.*

We have learned that a shift in the demand or supply curve of a currency causes changes in the equilibrium price of the currency. What factors will induce shifts in these curves, causing the currency to depreciate or appreciate? We can analyze exchange rate movements over two time periods, the long run and the short run.

Long-Run Determinants of Exchange Rates

Changes in the long-run value (one, two, or even five years) of the exchange rate are attributable to the reactions of traders in the foreign exchange market to changes in four key factors: Relative price levels, relative productivity levels, consumer preferences for domestic or foreign goods, and trade barriers. Note that these factors underlie trade in domestic and foreign goods and thus changes in the demand for exports and imports.

- **Relative prices**. Suppose that the domestic price level increases rapidly in Mexico, but remains constant in the United States. Mexican consumers will desire low-priced tractors produced by Caterpillar Inc., thereby increasing the supply of pesos. At the same time, U.S. consumers will buy fewer tomatoes from Mexico, reducing the demand for pesos. The combination of an increase in the supply of pesos and a decrease in the demand for pesos will cause the dollar price of the peso to fall—that is, the dollar will appreciate.
- **Relative productivity levels**. If German CD manufacturers become more productive than Canadian manufacturers, they can produce CDs more cheaply than their Canadian competitors. Thus, Germany's exports of CDs to Canada will increase and its imports from Canada will decrease. This results in an appreciation of Germany's euro against Canada's dollar.

- **Consumer preferences**. If the preferences of Americans change in favor of Swiss watches, the demand for the Swiss franc will increase as Americans import more watches, causing a depreciation of the dollar against the franc.
- **Trade barriers**. Suppose that the U.S. government imposes tariffs on Toyota automobiles. By making Toyotas more expensive, the tariff will discourage Americans from purchasing them. This results in a decrease in the demand for Japanese yen and an appreciation of the dollar against the yen.

Short-Run Determinants of Exchange Rates

Economists believe that the determinants of exchange rate fluctuations are rather different in the short run (a few weeks or even days) than in the long run (a year or more). Thus, we will consider the short-run time frame when analyzing exchange rates. In the short run, foreign exchange transactions are dominated by transfers of investment funds (bank deposits and Treasury securities), which respond to differences in interest rates and to shifting expectations of future exchange rates; such transactions have a major influence on short-run exchange rates.

- **Relative interest rates**. A country with relatively *high* interest rates tends to find its currency's exchange value *appreciating*. You've already learned that a rise in interest rates makes an asset, such as a Treasury bill, more attractive to investors. Suppose that a tight monetary policy causes interest rates to be high in the United States, while an easy monetary policy causes interest rates to be low in Switzerland. Therefore, Swiss investors will find the United States an attractive place to purchase Treasury bills. The increase in the demand for U.S. Treasury bills results in an increase in the supply of Swiss francs and thus a decrease in the dollar price of the franc. The dollar therefore appreciates against the franc.
- **Expectations of Future Exchange Rates**. Suppose that an unanticipated rise in the growth rate of the U.S. money supply is interpreted as a signal that the U.S. inflation rate will rise, which in turn signals a possible depreciation in the dollar's exchange rate. This set of expectations causes Americans who intend to make purchases in Sweden to obtain krona prior to the anticipated depreciation of the dollar (when the krona would become more expensive in dollars). Accordingly, the demand for krona increases in the foreign exchange market. The increased demand for krona results in a depreciation of the dollar.
- **Safe Haven**. Market psychology also affects currency values in the short run. Unsettling international events can lead to a flight to quality, whereby investors move their assets to a perceived "safe haven" whose value is reliable and dependable. There will be a greater demand, thus a higher price, for currencies perceived as stronger over their relatively weaker counterparts. The U.S. dollar, Swiss franc, and gold have been traditional safe havens during times of political or economic uncertainty.

EXCHANGE RATE SYSTEMS

We have learned that exchange rates are determined by the actions of the investors, exporters, tourists, and importers who participate in the foreign exchange market. However, governments can also affect exchange rates. The extent and nature of government participation in foreign exchange markets define the various exchange rate systems. These systems include floating exchange rates and fixed exchange rates.

Floating Exchange Rates

In a **floating exchange rate system**, governments and central banks do not participate in the foreign exchange market. Instead, currency values are established daily in the foreign exchange market by demand and supply conditions. With floating exchange rates, an equilibrium exchange rate equates the demand for and supply of the home currency. The exchange rate depends on relative income levels among nations, relative interest rates, relative prices, and the like.

Proponents defend floating exchange rates on the grounds of their adjustment efficiency. They maintain that floating exchange rates respond quickly to changing demand and supply conditions, clearing the market of shortages or surpluses of a given currency. Thus, governments do not have to restore balance in international payments through painful adjustments in fiscal policy or monetary policy. Instead, they can use these policies to combat domestic unemployment and inflation.

However, floating exchange rates are sometimes considered to be of limited usefulness to bankers and businesspeople. Critics maintain that an unregulated market may lead to wide fluctuations in currency values, discouraging foreign trade and investment. Moreover, the greater freedom that domestic policymakers provide may cause them to be more inclined to overspend, which contributes to inflation.

Fixed Exchange Rates

Rather than allowing exchange rates to be determined by market forces, governments sometimes attempt to maintain fixed exchange rates.[1] Today, **fixed exchange rates** are used primarily by developing nations that have ties to a key currency such as the U.S. dollar. A key currency is one that is widely traded on world money markets, demonstrates a relatively stable value over time, and is accepted as a means of international settlement.

Maintaining links to a key currency provides several benefits for developing nations. First, the prices of many developing nations' traded products are determined mainly in the markets of industrialized nations such as the United States. By tying their currencies to, say, the dollar, these nations can stabilize the domestic currency prices of their imports and exports. Second, many developing nations with high inflation link to the dollar (the United States has relatively low inflation) in order to exert restraint on domestic prices and reduce inflation. By making the commitment to stabilize their exchange rates against the dollar, governments hope to convince their citizens that they are willing to adopt the responsible monetary policies that are necessary to achieve low inflation.

The exchange rate system used by the United States is a combination of fixed and floating exchange rates. Known as **managed floating exchange rates**, the system allows the dollar to generally float in the foreign exchange market according to the market forces of demand and supply. However, governmental intervention may be used to stabilize the dollar's value when the foreign exchange market becomes disorderly and disruptive to international trade and investment.

IS CHINA A CURRENCY MANIPULATOR?

Trade relationships between the United States and China have been tense during the 2000s. The U.S. government has repeatedly restated its long-held view that China's efforts to manipulate its currency (the yuan) harm the U.S. economy. The U.S. government notes that China has deliberately lowered (depreciated) the value of the yuan so its exports are cheaper, and this undercuts American workers, especially in manufacturing. The U.S. government has considered China as the most flagrant currency-manipulating country, although it has regarded Japan, South Korea, and India as occasional or questionable manipulators.

How does China manipulate the yuan, according to the U.S. Treasury Department? The People's Bank of China sells yuan and buys dollar-denominated assets such as U.S. Treasury securities, thus causing a depreciation of the yuan against the dollar. The U.S. government cites China's large trade surplus with the United States and its sizable accumulation of dollar reserves as evidence that China has manipulated the value of its yuan against the dollar for competitive advantage. To pressure China and other countries to refrain from manipulating their currencies, the U.S. government might threaten to undertake offsetting currency interventions, levy countervailing tariffs on goods imported from currency manipulators, and the like.

However, other analysts question the connection between the yuan and the competitiveness of U.S. manufacturing. They note that if currency movements were the major factor in determining trade patterns, one would expect that China's exports to the United States would be closely related to currency movements. But the evidence does not support this conclusion.

For example, although the dollar–yuan exchange rate did not change during 1995–2005, China's exports to the United States expanded about 19.6 percent per year during this period. The only period during which China's exports to the United States significantly decreased was during the Great Recession, when they declined by about 33 percent during 2008–2010, a period when the dollar–yuan exchange rate was constant. The explanation for the decrease in China's exports to the United States was the fall in America's demand for consumption goods in general. Therefore, exchange rates are not the most important determinant of trade, although they do have some impact on trade flows in the short run.

Indeed, the topic of currency manipulation is controversial. It has plagued the United States and other countries for more than half a century.

MONETARY INTEGRATION IN EUROPE: THE EURO

Source: Formatoriginal / 500px/Getty Images®

The globalization of economies has promoted opportunities and challenges for the international monetary system. Let us consider the case of the European Monetary Union and its euro.

One important challenge for the international monetary system is the development of the European Union. Recall that the European Union (EU) is a regional economic bloc consisting of 27 European nations. The main goal of the EU has been to create an economic bloc in which trade and other transactions take place freely among member nations. From the 1950s to the 1990s, the EU succeeded in eliminating trade restrictions among member countries, allowing for the free movement of labor and capital within the union, and adopting common policies toward competition and agriculture.

In 1991, the EU agreed to establish monetary unification in 1999 for those nations eligible to participate. Participation in the monetary unification would require nations to fulfill economic goals concerning inflation, public finances, interest rates, and exchange rates. The nations participating in the EU would have a common currency, a single exchange rate, a single monetary policy, and a single central bank to oversee the monetary policy.

In 2002, 11 European countries united to form the **European Monetary Union (EMU)**, also called the eurozone, and replaced their individual currencies, such as the German mark and the Spanish peseta, with a single currency, the **euro**. At that point, the euro became the single currency in circulation throughout the monetary union.

The EMU also created a new **European Central Bank** to take control of monetary policy and exchange rate policy for the member countries. This central bank alone controls the supply of euros, sets the euro interest rate, and maintains permanently fixed exchange rates for the member countries. With a common central bank, the central bank of each participating nation performs operations like those of the 12 regional Federal Reserve Banks in the United States. As of 2023, 20 of the 27 members of the European Union were members of the European Monetary Union.

For Americans, the benefits of a common currency are apparent. Americans know that they can walk into a Wendy's or McDonald's anywhere in the United States and purchase a hamburger with dollar bills in their purses and wallets. Before the adoption of the euro, this was not the case in European countries. Because each nation had its own currency, an Italian could not purchase an item at a French store without first exchanging Italian lira for French francs. This would be like someone from Arizona having to exchange Arizona currency for Pennsylvania currency each time they visit Philadelphia. By replacing the various European currencies with a single currency—the euro—the eurozone has avoided such costs.

To be included in the eurozone, countries were supposed to fulfill certain economic criteria—a budget deficit of less than 3 percent of their GDP, a debt ratio of less than 60 percent of GDP, low inflation, and interest rates close to the eurozone's average. However, these standards were often ignored once countries became members of the eurozone. Also, some countries, such as Greece, did not appear to meet the standards when they were applying for membership, although they were accepted into the organization. This put the eurozone on unsound financial footing.

While the eurozone is open to all EU member states to join once they meet the criteria, the agreement is silent on the matter of members leaving the eurozone. Likewise, there is no provision for a member to be expelled from the eurozone. Some, however, including the Dutch government, favor such a provision being created if a heavily indebted member in the eurozone refuses to comply with a eurozone economic reform policy.

Another eurozone problem has been the integration of very different economies into a monetary union without a way to adjust their economies. For example, during 1999–2012, productivity in the northern member nations (notably Germany) increased rapidly while wages remained stagnant. In the southern nations (Greece and Italy), productivity remained sluggish. Therefore, labor cost per unit of output in Germany decreased about 25 percent compared to the southern nations and France. Normally, exchange rate adjustments would shrink this discrepancy: That is, Germany's exchange rate would appreciate relative to the currencies of the southern nations, thus increasing the competitiveness of the southern nations. However, within the eurozone there are no exchange rates to change since there is only one currency, the euro. Without an exchange rate as an adjustment mechanism, rebalancing economies would require workers to move freely to high-growth areas, prices to rise in productive countries, wealthy nations to subsidize poorer nations, workers of poorer nations to accept decades of unemployment to grind down wages, and so on. However, it is very difficult to achieve these adjustments in practice, as political barriers abound.

Therefore, without the normal adjustment mechanisms to keep economic imbalances from destroying the eurozone, some analysts have pushed for the concept of fiscal union. This would result in the integration of the fiscal policies of the eurozone countries, including taxation and government spending programs. The idea would be to impose budget discipline on the laggard, deficit countries. However, control over fiscal policy has been regarded as essential to national sovereignty, and in the world today eurozone members have not been willing to give up their fiscal independence. Simply put, the eurozone has a monetary union but it does not have a fiscal union. The future success of the eurozone remains an open question.

CHECK POINT

1 What is the foreign exchange rate? What does it mean when a currency depreciates (appreciates) in the foreign exchange market?
2 Identify the major factors that determine the exchange value of the dollar in the long run and in the short run.
3 Discuss the major features of floating exchange rates and fixed exchange rates.
4 Why would a country "manipulate" its exchange rate?
5 What are the advantages and disadvantages of the European Monetary Union's adoption of the euro?

CHAPTER SUMMARY

1 The balance of payments is a record of a country's international trading, borrowing, and lending. In the balance of payments, inflows of funds from residents of other countries to the United States are noted as receipts; outflows of funds from the United States to residents of other countries are noted as payments.
2 The balance of payments has two components, the current account and the capital and financial account. The current account represents the dollar value of transactions in currently produced goods and services, investment income, and unilateral transfers. If the monetary inflows on these accounts are greater (less) than monetary outflows, the current account balance is a surplus (deficit). The second component of the balance of payments is the capital and financial account, which represents international purchases or sales of assets such as real estate, corporate stocks and bonds, and government securities. The capital and financial account balance is a surplus (deficit) if domestic residents sell more (fewer) assets to residents of other countries than they purchase from them. Because the current account balance and capital and financial account balance always equal each other, any current account deficit (surplus) must be balanced by a capital and financial account surplus (deficit).
3 Since the 1980s, the United States has run continuous deficits in its current account. Thus, residents of other countries lend or give us the funds to make up the difference between our imports and our exports. It would not be an overstatement to say that we

borrow so much from residents of other countries to finance our current account deficits that we sell them pieces of America. Those pieces consist primarily of real estate and corporate stock. However, residents of other countries also lend us billions of dollars each year in the form of purchases of government and corporate securities and other debt instruments.

4 The buying and selling of currencies generally takes place in the foreign exchange market. This market does not involve sending large loads of currency from one country to another. Typically, it involves electronic balances. Dollar-denominated balances in computers in the United States or other countries are traded for computer-housed balances around the world that are denominated in yen, pounds, francs, and the like. In short, when currency is traded, paper and metal are not the usual media of exchange.

5 Most daily newspapers publish foreign exchange rates for major currencies. The exchange rate is the price of one currency in terms of another. Currency depreciation (appreciation) means that it takes more (fewer) units of a nation's currency to purchase a unit of some foreign currency. The major factors that determine the equilibrium exchange rate in a free market are relative prices, relative productivity levels, consumer preferences, trade barriers, relative interest rates, and expectations of future exchange rates.

6 Although exchange rates are determined by demand and supply, governments can also affect exchange rates. The extent and nature of government participation in foreign exchange markets define the various exchange rate systems. These systems include floating exchange rates and fixed exchange rates.

7 As part of its strategy for forming a regional economic bloc, the European Union has pursued monetary integration. For participating nations, monetary integration implies a common currency, a single exchange rate, a single monetary policy, and a single central bank to oversee the monetary policy.

KEY TERMS AND CONCEPTS

balance of payments
current account
balance of trade (trade balance)
services
income
unilateral transfers
current account balance
capital and financial account
capital and financial account balance
statistical discrepancy
foreign exchange market
exchange rate
depreciation
appreciation
equilibrium exchange rate
floating exchange rate system
fixed exchange rates
managed floating exchange rates
European Union (EU)
European Monetary Union (EMU)
euro
European Central Bank

STUDY QUESTIONS AND PROBLEMS

1 Indicate whether each of the following items represents a monetary inflow or outflow on the U.S. balance of payments:

a A U.S. importer purchases a shipload of French wine.

b A Japanese automobile firm builds an assembly plant in Kentucky.

c A British manufacturer exports machinery to Taiwan on a U.S. vessel.

d A U.S. college student spends a year studying in Switzerland.

e U.S. charities donate food to people in drought-plagued Africa.

f Japanese investors collect interest income on their holdings of U.S. government securities.

g A German resident sends money to her relatives in the United States.

h Lloyds of London sells an insurance policy to a U.S. firm.

i A Swiss resident receives dividends on his IBM stock.

2 Concerning a country's balance of payments, when would its current account be in surplus (deficit)? What would a current account surplus (deficit) imply for the capital and financial account? Is a current account deficit necessarily bad?

3 Why are some economists concerned that the United States borrows too much from abroad?

4 Table 17.3 summarizes hypothetical transactions, in billions of U.S. dollars, that took place during a given year.

TABLE 17.3 International Transactions of the United States (billions of dollars)

U.S. capital inflows	100
Merchandise exports	375
Services imports	–20
Income receipts from abroad	35
Statistical discrepancy	30
Merchandise imports	–450
Net unilateral transfers	–45
Services exports	55
Income payments abroad	–25
U.S. capital outflows	–55

- **a** Calculate the U.S. merchandise trade and current account balances.
- **b** Which of these balances pertains to the net borrowing (lending) position of the United States? How would you describe that position?

5 Table 17.4 shows supply and demand schedules for the British pound. Assume that exchange rates are flexible.

TABLE 17.4 Supply of and Demand for British Pounds

Quantity of Pounds Supplied	*Dollars per Pound*	*Quantity of Pounds Demanded*
50	$2.50	10
40	2.00	20
30	1.50	30
20	1.00	40
10	0.50	50

- **a** The equilibrium exchange rate equals ____. At this exchange rate, how many pounds will be purchased, and at what cost in terms of dollars?
- **b** Suppose that the exchange rate is $2.00 per pound. At this exchange rate, there is an excess (supply/demand) of pounds. This imbalance causes (an increase/a decrease) in the dollar price of the pound, which leads to (a/an) ____ in the quantity of pounds supplied and (a/an) ____ in the quantity of pounds demanded.
- **c** Suppose that the exchange rate is $1.00 per pound. At this exchange rate, there is an excess (supply/demand) for pounds. This imbalance causes (an increase/a decrease) in the price of the pound, which leads to (a/an) ____ in the quantity of pounds supplied and (a/an) ____ in the quantity of pounds demanded.

6 If the exchange rate changes from $1.70 = 1 pound to $1.68 = 1 pound, what does this mean for the dollar? For the pound? What if the exchange rate changes from $1.70 = 1 pound to $1.72 = 1 pound?

7 Table 17.5 gives hypothetical dollar/franc exchange values for Wednesday, May 1, 2023.

TABLE 17.5 Dollar/Franc Exchange Values

	U.S. $ Equivalent		*Currency per U.S.$*	
	Wed.	Tue.	Wed.	Tue.
Switzerland (franc)	0.7207	0.7225		

a Fill in the last two columns of the table with the reciprocal price of the dollar in terms of the franc.

b On Wednesday, the price of the two currencies was _____ dollars per franc, or ____ francs per dollar.

c From Tuesday to Wednesday, the dollar (appreciated/depreciated) against the franc; the franc (appreciated/depreciated) against the dollar.

d On Wednesday, the cost of buying 100 francs was ____ dollars; the cost of buying 100 dollars was ____francs.

8 Assuming market-determined exchange rates, use demand and supply schedules for pounds to analyze the effect on the exchange rate (dollars per pound) between the U.S. dollar and the British pound under each of the following circumstances:

a Voter polls suggest that Britain's conservative government will be replaced by radicals who pledge to nationalize all foreign-owned assets.

b The British economy and U.S. economy slide into recession, but the British recession is less severe than the U.S. recession.

c The Federal Reserve adopts a tight monetary policy that dramatically increases U.S. interest rates.

d The United Kingdom encounters severe inflation, while the United States experiences price stability.

e Fears of terrorism reduce U.S. tourism in the United Kingdom.

f The British government invites U.S. firms to invest in oil in British fields.

g The rate of productivity growth in the United Kingdom decreases sharply.

h An economic boom occurs in the United Kingdom, which induces the British to purchase more U.S.-made autos, trucks, and computers.

i Both the United Kingdom and the United States experience 10-percent inflation.

9 Explain why you agree or disagree with each of the following statements:

a "A nation's currency will depreciate if its inflation rate is less than that of its trading partners."

b "A nation whose interest rate falls more rapidly than that of other nations can expect the exchange value of its currency to depreciate."

c "A nation whose economy grows more slowly than its major trading partners can expect the exchange value of its currency to appreciate."

d "A nation's currency will appreciate if its interest rate rises relative to that of its trading partners and its income level falls relative to that of its trading partners."

10 Suppose that the United States has a system of managed floating exchange rates. What policies could the Federal Reserve implement to prevent the dollar from depreciating below acceptable levels? How about appreciating beyond acceptable levels? What are the weaknesses of these policies?

NOTE

1 How do central banks attempt to maintain fixed exchange rates? For example, to prevent the dollar from depreciating against the euro, the Federal Reserve could purchase dollars on the foreign exchange market, drawing on its holdings of euros. The increase in the demand for the dollar thus promotes an increase in the exchange value of the dollar against the euro. Instead, the Fed could adopt a contractionary monetary policy that will increase domestic interest rates and attract European purchases of American securities. As more dollars are demanded by Europeans, the value of the dollar will rise against the euro.

CHAPTER 18

Economic Systems and Developing Countries

CHAPTER OBJECTIVES

After reading this chapter, you should be able to:

1. Discuss how a market economy, command economy, and mixed economy answer the so-called fundamental economic questions.
2. Explain why transition economies began moving toward capitalism in the 1990s.
3. Discuss the obstacles to economic growth faced by developing nations.
4. Identify sources of aid for developing countries.

DOI: 10.4324/9781003438571-22

ECONOMICS IN CONTEXT

Integration into the global economy has offered a powerful means for countries to achieve economic growth, development, and poverty reduction. Most developing countries have shared in this progress, although in different amounts. As a group, developing countries have become more prominent in international trade, and they have considerably increased their exports of manufactured products and services relative to traditional commodity exports, such as bananas, sugar, and bauxite.

However, the progress of integration has remained unbalanced in recent decades. Progress has been very significant for several developing countries in Asia, such as China and India, and to a lesser extent in Latin America. These countries have attained success because they have partaken in global trade, helping them to attract sizable amounts of foreign investment. However, progress has been less rapid for many other countries, especially in the Middle East and Africa. The reasons for their lack of success are complicated, including structural economic problems, weak institutions and policy frameworks, and protectionism from global competition.

In this chapter, we will discuss the various economic systems that nations prefer to implement and what underlies their choices. We will also examine why some nations are rich and others are poor, consider obstacles that have prevented poor nations from developing, and identify policies that might help impoverished nations increase their growth rates.

ECONOMIC SYSTEMS AND THE FUNDAMENTAL ECONOMIC QUESTIONS

Every society, regardless of its wealth and power, must make certain decisions about the production and distribution of its goods and services: (1) *What* goods will be produced, and in what quantities? (2) *How* will these goods be produced? (3) *For whom* will these goods be produced? These questions are known as the **fundamental economic questions**.

The first economic decision—what goods to produce—is influenced by the problem of scarcity, which means that a society cannot have all the goods that it would like to have. Producing more of one good requires producing less of another good. In the United States, most production is geared toward consumer goods, whereas less effort is devoted to the production of military goods. In the former Soviet Union, a relatively large share of national output went to military goods, causing Soviet consumers to become frustrated. Japan has emphasized investment in plants and equipment to produce goods such as autos and consumer electronics while allocating a negligible share of national output to military equipment.

After deciding what goods to produce, a society must determine how to combine scarce resources and technology to produce these goods. For example, a shoe can be manufactured primarily by hand (labor), primarily by machine (capital), or partially by hand

Source: traffic_analyzer/DigitalVision Vectors/Getty Images®

and partially by machine. Which production method uses society's scarce resources most efficiently? Should college students be taught in large classes by professors (highly skilled labor) or in small sections by graduate teaching assistants (less-skilled labor)?

Another business decision involves the location of production. The growth of the global economy, coupled with technological advancement, has enabled many companies to move production easily around the world. For example, Toyota Motor Co. shifts the assembly of its autos between its plants in Japan and the United States in response to changing market conditions. Also, The Kellogg Co. of Battle Creek, Michigan, produces breakfast cereals in more than 20 countries and sells them in more than 150 countries. U.S. companies haven't made televisions for years. The last U.S. producer, Zenith Inc., shifted its television assembly to Mexico in the 1980s to cut labor costs. By deciding to close its U.S. factories, Zenith admitted that its U.S.-made televisions could not compete against lower-cost foreign competitors.

The final decision—for whom goods will be produced—refers to the distribution of output among different groups within society. Who should receive the computers, automobiles, and other goods produced by the economy? Should the distribution of goods and services among households be based on their ability to buy them? For example, students majoring in engineering generally find jobs that pay much higher incomes than students majoring in education or sociology. Thus, engineers can buy more goods and services than teachers, who earn less.

Although there are significant exceptions, whites tend to earn more than minorities; men tend to earn more than women; and college graduates tend to earn more than high school graduates. Moreover, Americans generally earn more than Africans and Asians. The income inequality around the world contributes to greatly different standards of living. Instead of distributing goods based on ability to pay, would "need" be a better criterion?

The way these decisions are made depends on a society's economic system. There are three broad types of economies: The market economy, the command economy, and the mixed economy. Let us consider the main features of each type of economy.

Market Economy

A **market economy**, also called **capitalism**, is a free-enterprise system that is rooted in private property and markets. Individuals and businesses have the freedom to possess and dispose of goods, services, and resources as they choose. Buyers and sellers are brought together in markets. Buyers come to markets expressing their desire to purchase property in the form of goods, services, and resources at various prices. Sellers come to markets expressing their desire to supply property in the form of goods, services, and resources at various prices. In this manner, property is exchanged at freely negotiated prices.

Because the market system leads to production efficiency, high employment, and economic growth, proponents contend, the need for governmental control is small. The extreme case of a market economy—one in which the government has almost no economic role—is called a **laissez-faire economy**; in this case, the main purpose of the government is to protect private property and provide a legal system that allows free markets.

In a market economy, goods and services are produced and resources are supplied in competitive markets consisting of many sellers and buyers. This means that economic power is decentralized because it is widely distributed. A system of prices and markets, with profits and losses, determines *what, how,* and *for whom* goods will be produced. Because suppliers are self-interested and attempt to maximize profits, they tend to combine resources in such a manner as to produce a good or service at the lowest cost. Suppliers also make production decisions according to the dollar expenditures of consumers, who decide what goods will be produced. Goods and services are distributed to consumers who have the income to purchase them. Households that have more income—because they possess more valuable resources—can afford to purchase more goods and services.

Although a market economy recognizes economic freedom and human initiative, it is not without problems. For example, the motivation to manufacture goods at the lowest cost could cause business firms to make production decisions with little regard for the safety of workers or the quality of the environment. Firms might be able to cut costs by adopting unsafe working procedures for employees or by dumping hazardous wastes into the environment. Also, the ability of individual consumers to determine what goods and services should be produced is weakened if a small number of firms dominate a market. Furthermore, the operation of a market economy does not guarantee full employment for workers or the absence of poverty; it also does not ensure that firms will produce goods that are safe for use by consumers.

Command Economy

By contrast, a **command economy** (also termed a planned economy or communism) is one in which government makes all the decisions concerning production and distribution. In a command economy, the government owns virtually all the means of production, including land and capital. Business firms are also government-owned. Economic decisions regarding the organization of production, the use of resources, and the prices of goods and services are made by government planners. Individual production units receive detailed plans and orders that carry the weight of law. The government also establishes the composition and distribution of output as well as wage levels for workers. In short, in a command economy, the government answers the fundamental questions of *what*, *how*, and *for whom* goods will be produced through its control of resources and its power to enforce decisions.

Central planning was the primary method of organization in the former Soviet Union, in other nations in Eastern Europe, and in China prior to their movement toward market economies in the 1980s. By the 1990s, command economies were disappearing rapidly. Cuba and North Korea, however, still make extensive use of central planning.

Advocates of a command economy contend that the system is superior to a market economy in achieving a fair distribution of income. Because the government owns the means of production, small groups of people are prevented from acquiring a disproportionate fraction of a nation's wealth. It is also argued that central planning can help decrease unemployment by channeling additional labor into production processes. For example, farming can be carried out by labor using hand tools or capital equipment such as tractors. If planners desire to keep agricultural workers employed, they will mandate that less equipment and more labor be used in farming. Finally, it is maintained that national goals can be easily formulated and pursued by a small number of central planners.

Central planning, however, can be criticized on the grounds that it is inconsistent with economic freedom and that it creates an elite class of government bureaucrats. Central planning can also suffer from the problem of overproduction of some goods and underproduction of other goods. This is because the decisions of planners regarding the types and amounts of output produced may not coincide with the preferences of consumers. Moreover, the absence of a profit motive for innovation and entrepreneurship may lead to inferior product quality, production inefficiencies, and reduced economic growth. Finally, in an economy in which central planners are distant from the actual production operations, long-term environmental damage may occur. As witnessed in Eastern Europe, serious water and air pollution have been a consequence of the failure of central planners to include environmental quality in many of their decisions.

Mixed Economy

No modern economy exactly fits the description of the polar categories of a market economy and a command economy. Instead, all economies are **mixed economies**, with elements of both market and command economies.

In a mixed economy, the most important decision mechanism is the market that provides answers to *what*, *how*, and *for whom* goods will be produced. However, the government plays an important role in modifying the operation of the market. The government establishes laws and rules that regulate economic behavior, provides public services such as education and national defense, regulates pollution and product safety, initiates policies to combat unemployment and inflation, modifies the distribution of income, and the like. In short, the objective of a mixed economy is to leave economic decisions to the market when it is operating well, but to intervene in the economy when market outcomes become unacceptable.

Indeed, the blend of market and command varies among mixed economies. Today, most economic decisions in the United States are made in the marketplace, although the government often modifies the operation of the market. However, governments are more heavily involved in the economy in Sweden and Denmark than in the United States. These nations embrace **socialism** as an economic system.

Socialists believe that a country's resources should be used according to an overall economic plan that is formulated by manufacturers, farmers, workers, and government officials working together. Through such planning, socialists hope to adjust production to the needs of the people. Although the forces of demand and supply may influence production and prices under the socialist economic plan, many decisions regarding how much to produce and what to charge are made by political authorities. Many socialists also call for the redistribution of wealth through taxation. They favor laws to help the aged, the unemployed, the disabled, and other people in need. Moreover, many socialists believe that the government should provide free education and medical services to everyone and should help all citizens obtain safe and sanitary housing at rents that they can afford. Indeed, implementing socialist goals calls for a relatively large amount of government activity in a mixed economy.

MARKET CAPITALISM VERSUS STATE CAPITALISM: WHICH WORKS BETTER?

From the 1980s to 2008, the debate about the merits of market capitalism versus state-directed capitalism appeared settled. The strong performance of the American economy, based on free trade, deregulation, and globalization combined with the abrupt decline of the Soviet Union and China's movement toward capitalism attested to the weakness of state-controlled economies. Simply put, free-market capitalism appeared to be the winner.

However, the Great Recession of 2007–2009 reopened the debate about the role of government in the economy. The severity of this recession exposed the inadequacies of the systems of the advanced economies and caused many to wonder whether the market capitalism model had broken down. In the United States, Democrats called for a more active government policy to create jobs and nurture new industries, like solar power, to help America compete with China. At the same time, Republicans proposed a smaller government to foster economic recovery. In Europe, debate focused on how to develop competitiveness through liberalized economic policies while preserving their public welfare systems.

However, state assistance to promote economic development has been less controversial for developing countries. Countries such as China, Brazil, Russia, and Malaysia have embraced "state capitalism," which attempts to combine the powers of the state with the powers of capitalism. In this system, governments use various types of state-owned businesses to manage the exploitation of resources that they consider of key importance to the state and to create large numbers of jobs.

Examples of state-owned businesses include natural gas companies in Russia, oil companies in Malaysia, and television companies in China. Also, governments influence bank lending, own large and important segments of the economy, and freely guide the economy through bureaucratic mandates. Although state capitalism is a type of capitalism, it is one in which the government acts as the dominant economic player and uses markets mainly for political gain, especially the leadership's chances of survival. The success of state-capitalistic nations like China in maintaining their growth during the Great Recession has caused analysts to ask if this combination of state control and market forces can foster better economic results than the free-market models favored in the United States.

The significance of state capitalism is striking. For example, the Chinese state is the largest shareholder of the country's 150 largest companies. Also, state companies make up about 80 percent of the value of the stock market in China, 62 percent in Russia, and 38 percent in Brazil. Moreover, the 13 largest oil companies, which between them control more than 75 percent of the world's oil reserves, are all state-backed.

Although state capitalism is a formidable foe of market capitalism, it has its weaknesses. When the government favors some companies, the others suffer. State giants soak up talent and capital that might have been better used by private companies. Also, although state companies are successful at imitating others, partly because they can use the government's influence to get access to technology, they tend to be less successful in fostering new technological innovations. Finally, state capitalism works well only when directed by a competent state. However, the model can result in favoritism, inequality, and discontent, as seen in Russia and Egypt. Simply put, the future success of state capitalism remains an open question.

China

For more than 2,000 years, China maintained a policy of self-reliance that eventually caused its economy to trail advanced countries. China implemented policies that kept its economy centrally controlled, inefficient, stagnant, and relatively isolated from the global economy. Then in 1979, China initiated new economic reforms that transformed one of the poorest economies in the world into one of the fastest-growing nations. What accounts for this transformation?

Modern China began in 1949, when a revolutionary communist movement captured control of the nation. Soon after the communist takeover, China instituted a Soviet model of central planning with an emphasis on rapid industrial growth. The state took over urban manufacturing industry, collectivized agriculture, eliminated household farming, and established compulsory production quotas.

By the 1970s, China saw its formerly poor neighbors realizing rapid economic growth and prosperity—Japan, Singapore, Taiwan, South Korea, and Hong Kong. Therefore, China began "marketizing" its economy through small, incremental changes. In industry and

Source: wenjin chen/DigitalVision Vectors/Getty Images®

agriculture, reforms were enacted to increase individual incentives and to decrease the importance of government planners. Most goods were sold for market-determined, rather than government-controlled, prices. Greater competition was allowed, both between private-sector firms and between new private firms and state-owned businesses. The Chinese government's monopoly over foreign trade was also terminated. Instead, economic zones appeared in which firms could keep foreign exchange earnings and hire and fire workers.

After opening to foreign trade and investment and enacting free-market reforms in 1979, China became among the world's fastest-growing economies, with real GDP growing at an average annual rate of 9.5 percent through 2018. Such growth allowed China to double its real output every 8 years and helped raise some 800 million people out of poverty. Also, China became the world's largest economy, manufacturer, trader of merchandise, and holder of foreign exchange reserves. Therefore, China became a major commercial partner of the United States.

By the early 2000s, China had made many of the relatively easy economic adjustments in its transition toward a market economy: Letting farmers sell their own produce and opening its doors to foreign investors and salespeople. Other reforms, however, have still needed to be addressed: (1) The massive restructuring of state-owned industries, which have lost money; (2) the clean-up of bankrupt state banks; (3) the creation of a social security system in a society that once guaranteed a job for life; and (4) the establishment of a monetary system with a central bank free of Communist Party or government control.

As China's economy has matured, its economic growth rate has slowed significantly, from 14.2 percent in 2007 to 5.2 percent in 2022. The Chinese government has acknowledged slower economic growth, describing it as the "new normal." China's government also has recognized the need to implement a new growth model that relies less on fixed investment and exporting, and more on private consumption, services, and innovation to drive economic growth. Such reforms are essential for China to avoid achieving a certain economic level but realizing diminishing economic growth rates because it is unable to tap new sources of economic growth, such as innovation. Therefore, the Chinese government has made innovation a top priority in its economic planning through high-profile initiatives, such as "Made in China 2025," a plan formulated in 2015 to upgrade and modernize China's manufacturing in 10 key sectors through widespread government support.

China's expanding global economic influence and the economic and trade policies it pursues have important implications for the United States. While China has become a large and growing market for American companies, its incomplete transition to a free-market economy has led to economic policies that are widely considered harmful to American economic interests, such as the theft of U.S. intellectual property and industrial policies. Moreover, political freedoms have not increased in China, as seen in the Chinese government's use of military force to end a pro-democracy demonstration in Beijing's Tiananmen Square in 1989 and the takeover of Hong Kong in 2022. Today, China describes itself as a *socialist market economy*.

India

India is another example of an economy that has improved its standard of living following the enactment of more open markets. The economy of India is broad, including manufacturing, agriculture, handicrafts, and many services. The advent of the computer and the large number of educated Indians fluent in English have contributed to India's becoming an important destination for global outsourcing of customer services and technical support.

India and China have followed different avenues of economic development. China has traveled the traditional development route of countries like South Korea and Japan, becoming a center for low-wage manufacturing of goods. Knowing that it could not compete with China in manufacturing, India decided that its best opportunity was in exporting services that embodied its abundance of highly educated workers.

After achieving independence from Britain in 1947, India initially engaged in socialism and adopted tariffs and quotas to protect its infant industries. It also enacted prohibitions on foreign investment to lessen competition, tight controls over private companies and financial institutions, and a large governmental sector. This resulted in India's shutting itself off from much of the world during the 1950s to 1980s. During this era, India's economy realized sluggish growth and poverty was prevalent.

By 1991, India realized that its system of state regulation hampered economic growth, and that change was needed. The result was a movement toward a market-based economy. The policy that government must approve industrial investment expenditures was eliminated, quotas on imports were terminated, export subsidies were slashed, and import tariffs were cut. These reforms helped India evolve from an agriculture-based, closed economy into a more open one which promotes foreign investment and emphasizes industry and services. The result was more rapid growth and a decrease in India's poverty rate. It remains to be seen how far up the ladder of economic development India will proceed in the future.

BOX ESSAY 18.1 ECONOMICS IN ACTION
Bono, U2, and the Developing Countries

The next time you hear a song by Bono, keep in mind that he is a friend of the developing countries. Paul David Hewson, known by his stage name Bono, is a singer, musician, and humanitarian best known for being the main vocalist of U2, an Irish rock band.

Bono was born in 1960 and raised in Dublin, Ireland, where he met the future members of U2. Bono writes almost all the lyrics for U2's songs, often using political, social, and religious themes. During the band's early years, Bono's lyrics contributed to U2's rebellious and spiritual tone. As the band matured, his lyrics were influenced more by personal experiences shared with members of U2. In 2005, the U2 band members were inducted into the Rock and Roll Hall of Fame, in their first year of eligibility. In 2008, *Rolling Stone* ranked Bono the 32nd greatest singer of all time.

Bono is also widely known for his humanitarian work. He has organized and played in numerous government, religious, and philanthropic organizations, and the business world in order to develop organizations that combine humanitarian relief with global activism and corporate commercial enterprise. Since 1999, Bono has been actively involved in campaigning to end poverty and hunger in developing countries. He has especially attempted to raise awareness of the economic and social problems of Africa and the need for debt relief.

Bono has been nominated for the Nobel Peace Prize, was granted an honorary knighthood by Queen Elizabeth II of the United Kingdom, was named Person of the Year by *Time* magazine, among numerous other awards. In 2007, Bono received the Philadelphia Liberty Medal for his work to end world poverty. In accepting this medal, Bono said, "When you are trapped by poverty, you are not free. When trade laws prevent you from selling the food you grew, you are not free…" Bona donated the $100,000 prize to assist debt relief and the prevention of AIDS in Africa.

Sources: "Bono Gets Medal for His Work in Africa," *Huffington Post*, September 27, 2007. See also Michka Assayas, *Bono in Conversation with Michka Assayas* (New York, NY: Riverhead Books, 2005); Sheelagh Matthews, *Bono: Remarkable People* (New York, NY: Weigl Publishers, 2008); Steve Stockman, *Walk On: The Spiritual Journey* of *U2* (Lake Mary, FL: Relevant Books, 2001).

THE ECONOMICS OF DEVELOPING COUNTRIES

We have learned that no one economic system can fulfill the objectives of all nations. As a result, nations embrace a variety of economic systems that embody elements of capitalism and central planning. Similarly, not all nations use the same strategy for promoting economic development. Thus, some nations, such as the United States, have advanced economies and high standards of living for many, but not all, of their citizens. Yet other developing nations, such as Bangladesh and Ethiopia, remain poor. What accounts for these differences?

A widely used technique is to rank all nations according to income and then to draw a dividing line between the advanced and developing ones. Included in the category of **advanced nations** are those of Western Europe and North America, plus Japan, New Zealand, and Australia. Most nations of the world are referred to as developing, or less-developed, nations. **Developing nations** include most of those in Latin America, Asia, Africa, and the Middle East.

Table 18.1 includes economic and social indicators for selected nations as of 2021. Usually, advanced nations are characterized by high levels of income per person, longer life expectancies, and higher levels of adult literacy. Today, the richest 20 percent of the world's population receives more than 80 percent of the world's income, suggesting that there is considerable income inequality among nations.

TABLE 18.1 Basic Economic and Social Indicators for Selected Countries, 2021

Country	*Gross Domestic Product per Person (in U.S. dollars)**	*Life Expectancy (years)*	*Adult Illiteracy (percent)*
Switzerland	77,121	83	Under 5 percent
United States	69,288	78	"
Germany	58,276	81	"
Japan	43,140	85	"
Mexico	19,585	70	10
India	7,242	71	21
Guinea	2,901	54	76
Mozambique	1,348	50	59

* At purchasing power parity.

Source: Data drawn from The World Bank, *Country Data*, available at www.worldbank.org/data.

CHECK POINT

1 Identify the fundamental economic questions that all economies must answer.
2 How do a market economy, a command economy, and a mixed economy answer the fundamental economic questions?
3 Why are all contemporary economies of the world best classified as mixed economies?
4 Describe the economic development paths of China and India.

OBSTACLES TO ECONOMIC DEVELOPMENT

The economic development criteria are identical for developing countries and countries with advanced economies. Both must use their existing supplies of resources more efficiently and must also increase their available supplies of resources. All developing countries are aware of these criteria for economic development, so why have some of them experienced economic growth while others have lagged far behind? The economic, institutional, and cultural conditions in these nations are the reasons why they experience different rates of economic growth. Consider the following obstacles to economic development:

- Many developing countries possess inadequate natural resources such as mineral deposits, arable land, and sources of power.
- There are problems with human resources in developing countries. Developing countries tend to be overpopulated and have high rates of population growth. These growing populations decrease the developing countries' capacities to save, invest, and increase productivity. Developing countries often experience both high levels of unemployment and underemployment.
- Developing countries generally have shortages of capital goods such as public utilities, machinery, and factories. These shortages stem from a lack of saving and investment because the nations are too poor to save. Insufficient amounts of capital goods contribute to low levels of labor productivity. Moreover, technological advancement is slow in developing countries, which retards economic development.
- The economies of many developing countries are non-diversified, and emphasize the production of primary products such as bauxite, copper, and agricultural goods. Developing countries would generally prefer to diversify their economies by fostering manufacturing industries.
- Besides economic factors, institutional and cultural factors can hinder economic development. For example, political corruption and bribery are common in many

developing countries. Also, economic growth depends partly on the desire to develop. Are people in developing countries willing to make the necessary changes in their ways of doing things to promote growth?

Another problem of developing countries is limited access to foreign markets. If we examine the characteristics of trade among developing nations, we find that developing nations are highly dependent on advanced nations. Most developing-nation exports go to advanced nations, and most developing-nation imports originate in advanced nations. Trade among developing nations is relatively minor.

Although developing countries have generally improved their penetration of world markets in recent years, global protectionism has been a hindrance to their market access. This is especially true for agricultural products and labor-intensive manufactured products, such as clothing and textiles. These products are important to the world's poor because they represent more than half of low-income countries' exports.

However, developing countries themselves contribute to the problem. As seen in Table 18.2, developing countries tend to impose tariffs that are higher than those imposed by advanced countries.

Simply put, developing countries have often experienced a **vicious circle of poverty**. They save little and thus invest little in physical and human capital because they are poor, and because they do not invest, their outputs per capita remain low and they remain poor. Even if the vicious circle were to be broken, a rapid increase in population would leave the standard of living unchanged.

TABLE 18.2 Average Tariff Rates of Selected Advanced Countries and Developing Countries, All Products, 2021

Advanced Countries		*Developing Countries*	
Country	*Tariff Rate (percent)*	*Country*	*Tariff Rate (percent)*
Australia	2.4	Algeria	19.1
Canada	4.0	Botswana	13.7
European Union	5.2	El Salvador	6.0
Japan	4.2	India	18.3
Norway	5.9	Morocco	14.2
Switzerland	5.6	Nepal	12.7
United Kingdom	3.9	Panama	5.1
United States	3.4	Sri Lanka	5.9
New Zealand	1.9	Viet Nam	9.6

Source: Data drawn from World Trade Organization, *World Tariff Profiles*, 2022, available at https://www.wto.org/english/res_e/booksp_e/world_tariff_profiles22_e.pdf.

THE LADDER OF ECONOMIC DEVELOPMENT AND TRADE CONFLICTS

Despite the economic problems of poor, developing countries, most economists today maintain that it is beneficial for them to participate in international trade. And yet, ironically, despite the support that economists have given to open markets, the advanced world has sometimes restricted its markets to imports from developing countries. Why has this occurred?

Imagine that the global economy is a ladder. On the top steps are the United States, Germany, and other advanced countries, which produce sophisticated airplanes and pharmaceuticals. On the bottom steps are the developing countries that produce mainly labor-intensive, low-technology goods, such as shirts. Up and down the middle steps are all the other nations, producing everything from aluminum to autos. From this viewpoint, economic development implies that everyone tries to climb to a higher step on the ladder. This works best if advanced countries at the top can create new industries and products, thus adding another step to the ladder. But if innovation stagnates at the highest step, then that's bad news for Americans who must compete with lower-wage workers in less-developed countries who are creeping upward.

Developing countries face a dilemma: To achieve progress, they must displace producers of the least sophisticated goods that are still being produced in the advanced countries. For example, if Laos is going to produce sneakers and trousers, it must compete against American and European producers of these goods. As producers in advanced countries are threatened by import competition, they often seek trade barriers to avoid this competition. However, this protection prevents developing countries from having access to the markets of advanced countries, thus offsetting their efforts to grow.

People in advanced countries who are sheltered from the competition with developing countries often consist of those who are already near the bottom of the advanced countries' income ladder. Many of these people work in labor-intensive industries and have modest skills and low wages.

FAIRTRADE INTERNATIONAL AND COFFEE GROWERS

The next time that you drink a cup of coffee or tea, you might consider whether it is a "fair trade" beverage. The same applies to goods such as cocoa, fruits, vegetables, herbs, spices, sugar, honey, wine, flowers, grains, and rubber products.

Fairtrade International is a nonprofit organization that began modestly in the 1940s when a few small European and North American organizations reached out to poverty-stricken farmers in developing nations to sell their products to well-off markets. Today, Fairtrade International is a global organization that is owned by about 1.8 million farmers and operates in 24 nations throughout the world.

Regarding coffee, the goal of Fairtrade International is to increase the incomes of poor coffee farmers by implementing a system where the farmers can sell their beans directly to roasters and retailers, bypassing the traditional practice of selling to middlemen in their own

Source: Luca Sage/Photodisc/Getty Images®

countries. This arrangement allows farmers to earn a higher price for their beans, compared to the price they would have received from middlemen. Fairtrade International coffee carries a logo identifying it as such. Other fair-trade products include cocoa, sugar, flowers, and plants.

Fairtrade International has realized much success in Europe, where Fairtrade coffee sells in more than 35,000 stores and has sales of about $300 million a year. In some countries like Switzerland and the Netherlands, Fairtrade coffee accounts for as much as 5 percent of total coffee sales. But Fairtrade proponents admit that selling Americans on the idea of buying coffee with a social theme has been more challenging than it was in Europe. Nevertheless, some retailers, such as Safeway supermarket chain and Starbucks Coffee Co., sell Fairtrade International coffee to their American customers.

Yet critics question the degree to which "fairly traded" coffee helps. They note that the biggest winners may not be the farmers, but rather the retailers that sometimes charge large markups on fairly traded coffee while advertising themselves as corporate citizens. They can get away with it because consumers often have little or no information about how much of a product's price goes to farmers.

STRATEGIES FOR ECONOMIC GROWTH

In attempting to achieve economic development, poor countries have pursued two competing strategies. Let us examine these strategies.

During the 1950s and 1960s, the growth strategy of **import substitution** was widely used in developing nations such as Mexico and Brazil; some countries use this strategy today. Import substitution is an economic policy that advocates replacing foreign imports with domestic production. It rests on the notion that a country should attempt to decrease its foreign dependency through the domestic production of manufactured goods. Import substitution operates by having the government promote economic development through nationalization, subsidization of key industries, and highly restrictive trade barriers to protect domestic producers from import competition. For example, if a nation imports textiles, import substitution would result in the establishment of a domestic textile industry to produce replacements for the imports.

However, import substitution does not imply complete import elimination; as a country industrializes, it begins to import other types of goods that become needed for its industries, such as chemicals, petroleum, and the raw materials it may lack. Simply put, import substitution is founded on the infant industry argument for protectionism—that backward producers of a developing country require temporary protection in order to become competitive against highly advanced producers in foreign countries.

An alternative growth is **export-led growth**. This strategy is outward-oriented because it links the domestic economy to the world economy. Rather than attempting to grow by protecting inefficient domestic industries, this strategy promotes growth through the export of manufactured goods. Export-led growth implies opening domestic markets to foreign competition in exchange for market access to other countries. Therefore, trade restrictions are either nonexistent or very low. By the 1980s, many developing countries had abandoned their import-substitution strategies and shifted to export-led growth. Among the countries that have benefited from export-led growth are China, Singapore, Hong Kong, South Korea, and Taiwan.

What is the evidence concerning these growth strategies? Researchers generally have concluded that nations enacting export-led growth policies have superior economic performance compared to those using import-substitution policies. This is because export-led growth policies result in global competition for domestic producers, which encourages them to become more productive if they are to survive. Instead, import-substitution policies have often created industries that are inefficient and obsolete as they are not exposed to rival, internationally competitive industries.

ASSISTING THE DEVELOPING COUNTRIES

Unhappy about their poverty and hunger, and convinced that many of their problems are the result of limitations on the existing world trading system, developing nations have pressured the advanced nations for institutions and policies to improve the climate for their economic development. Among the institutions and policies that have been established to assist developing countries are the World Bank, the International Monetary Fund, and the Generalized System of Preferences.

World Bank

During the 1940s, two international institutions were created to assist the transition from a wartime to a peacetime environment and to help prevent a recurrence of the disruptive economic conditions of the Great Depression era. The World Bank and the International Monetary Fund were founded in July 1944.

The **World Bank** is an international organization that makes loans to developing countries intended to reduce poverty and foster economic development. Headquartered in Washington, D.C., it makes loans to member governments and their agencies, as well as private firms in the member nations. Rather than being a "bank" in the common sense, the World Bank is an agency of the United Nations, having 189 member countries as of 2023. Together, these countries finance the institution and decide how its money is spent. The World Bank receives its funds from contributions of wealthy advanced countries.

The World Bank lends money to developing members that cannot obtain loans from other sources at reasonable terms. These loans are granted for development projects, such as schools, highways, hospitals, and dams. The World Bank is involved in projects as diverse as raising Covid-19 awareness in Nigeria, assisting the education of children in Costa Rica, improving health care delivery in Peru, and assisting India to rebuild after a tumultuous earthquake. The World Bank provides low-interest-rate loans, and sometimes interest-free loans, to developing countries that have little or no ability to borrow on market terms. The World Bank has funded the debt-refinancing activities of some of the most heavily indebted developing nations.

International Monetary Fund

Another source of assistance to developing countries (as well as advanced countries) is the **International Monetary Fund (IMF)**, headquartered in Washington, D.C. Representing 190 nations as of 2023, the IMF is a bank for the central banks of member nations. Over a given period, some nations will realize balance-of-payments deficits, and others will face surpluses. A nation with a deficit initially draws on its supply of foreign currencies, such as the yen or dollar, that are accepted in payment by other nations. However, the deficit nation may encounter inadequate amounts of currency. That is when other nations, through the IMF, can provide aid. By making currencies available to the IMF, the surplus nations send funds to nations with temporary deficits. Over the long run, the deficits need to be eliminated, and the IMF attempts to make certain that this adjustment is as timely as possible.

Most of the funds of the IMF come from subscriptions. The size of a member's subscription depends on its economic and financial importance in the world; nations with larger economic importance have larger subscriptions. The subscriptions are increased periodically to increase the IMF's resources. The IMF also obtains funds through loans from member nations. The IMF has lines of credit with major advanced nations as well as with Saudi Arabia.

All IMF loans are subject to some degree of *conditionality*. This means that to borrow money from the IMF, a deficit nation must agree to enact economic policies as mandated by the IMF. These policies are intended to correct the member's balance-of-payments deficit and to foster non-inflationary economic growth. However, the conditionality requirement to IMF loans has often met opposition from deficit nations, which maintain that these programs impose excessive hardships on their people. How much "tough love" should the IMF require for its loans?

Generalized System of Preferences

Given insufficient access to the markets of advanced countries, less-developed countries have pressured advanced countries to lower their tariff barriers. To assist developing nations in improving their global competitiveness, many advanced nations have granted tariff reductions (preferences) to the exports of developing nations. Under this **Generalized System of Preferences (GSP)**, advanced nations temporarily decrease tariffs on selected imports from developing nations below the levels applied to imports from other advanced nations. The GSP is not a uniform system, however, because it includes many individual schemes that differ in the types of products covered and the degree of tariff cuts.

The trade preferences extended by industrial countries are voluntary. Granting nations establish the eligibility criteria, the product coverage, the size of tariff reductions, and the duration of the tariff reductions. Generally, advanced countries do not grant tariff reductions in products in which developing countries have a sizable export potential. The main reason for these modest preferences is that in some industries there is strong domestic opposition to tariff reductions in advanced countries.

CHECK POINT

1 Identify the obstacles to development that poor countries face.
2 Describe the "ladder of economic development."
3 Concerning economic growth strategies, what is meant by import substitution and export-led growth?
4 What policies and institutions have been created to aid developing countries?

CHAPTER SUMMARY

1 Every society must make certain decisions regarding the production and distribution of goods and services: (1) *What* goods will be produced and in what quantities? (2) *How* will these goods be produced? (3) *For whom* will these goods be produced? These questions are known as the fundamental economic questions.

2 The way the fundamental economic questions are answered depends on a society's economic system. There are three broad types of economies: The market economy, the command economy, and the mixed economy. The United States has a mixed economy.

3 By the 1990s, the centrally planned economies in the former Soviet Union and Eastern Europe had collapsed and began switching to capitalism. Also, the Chinese economy started embracing capitalism. These nations are known as transition economies.

4 The advanced nations are those of North America and Western Europe, plus Australia, New Zealand, and Japan. Most nations of the world are classified as developing nations. These nations include most of those in Africa, Asia, Latin America, and the Middle East. Compared to advanced countries, developing countries generally have lower levels of real GDP per capita, shorter life expectancies, and lower levels of adult literacy.

5 For developing nations, obstacles to economic growth include inadequate natural resources, low rates of saving and investment, shortages of capital goods, low productivity levels, modest technological advancement, and lack of access to the markets of advanced countries. Many developing nations experience a vicious circle of poverty: They save little and thus invest little in physical and human capital because they are poor, and because they do not invest, their outputs per capita remain low and they remain poor.

6 In attempting to achieve economic development, poor countries have pursued two competing strategies, import substitution and export-led growth. Researchers have generally found that developing countries have benefited the most from export-led growth strategies.

7 Among the institutions and policies that have been created to support developing countries are the World Bank, the International Monetary Fund, and the Generalized System of Preferences.

KEY TERMS AND CONCEPTS

fundamental economic questions
market economy
capitalism
laissez-faire economy
command economy
mixed economies
socialism
advanced nations
developing nations
vicious circle of poverty
import substitution
export-led growth
World Bank
International Monetary Fund (IMF)
generalized system of preferences (GSP)

STUDY QUESTIONS AND PROBLEMS

1 Why do incentive and coordination problems arise in economies that embrace central planning? How are those problems dealt with in a market economy?

2 Why do nations such as Sweden and Norway prefer socialism to capitalism?

3 Evaluate the prospects for the transformation of the Chinese and Eastern European economies into market economies.
4 Why are some nations rich and other nations poor?
5 In what ways do advanced nations help developing nations?
6 Suppose that you are the manager of an automobile assembly plant. Explain how you might attain production goals under a communistic system and under a capitalist system.
7 Describe the merits of import substitution versus export-led growth as strategies for economic development.

Glossary

A

ability-to-pay principle The principle that people with greater income and wealth should be taxed at a higher rate because their ability to pay is presumably greater. *(Chapter 9)*

absolute advantage The ability of an individual or group to carry out an activity more productively than another individual or group. *(Chapter 16)*

accounting profit Total revenue minus explicit costs; costs that are payable to others, such as wages, materials, and interest. *(Chapter 4)*

actual reserves The amount of vault cash and Federal Reserve deposits that a bank is actually holding; the sum of a bank's required and excess reserves. *(Chapter 14)*

administrative lag The inability to get quick action on fiscal policy because of the way Congress operates. *(Chapter 13)*

advanced nations Nations with relatively high per-capita income and standards of living, such as those in North America and Western Europe, as well as Australia, New Zealand, and Japan. *(Chapter 18)*

aggregate demand curve A graphical representation of the total demand of all people for all final goods and services produced in an economy. *(Chapter 12)*

aggregate quantity demanded The quantity of final output that buyers will purchase at a given price level. *(Chapter 12)*

aggregate quantity supplied The quantity of final output that will be supplied by producers at a particular price level. *(Chapter 12)*

aggregate supply curve A graphical representation of the total supply of all final goods and services in an economy. *(Chapter 12)*

antitrust policy The attempt to foster a market structure that will lead to increased competition and curb anticompetitive behavior that harms consumers; laws designed to prevent unfair business practices. *(Chapter 8)*

appreciation The strengthening of a currency; fewer units of a nation's currency are needed to purchase a unit of some foreign currency. *(Chapter 17)*

arbitration A process whereby a person called an arbitrator listens to both sides of a labor dispute and makes a decision that is binding on both sides. *(Chapter 7)*

artificial intelligence The ability of computer systems to carry out tasks that normally involve human intelligence, such as decision making. *(Chapter 4)*

automatic stabilizers Changes in government spending and tax revenues that occur automatically as the economy fluctuates; they prevent aggregate demand from decreasing too much in bad times and rising too much in good times, thus stabilizing the economy. *(Chapter 13)*

average fixed cost The total fixed cost per unit of output; total fixed cost divided by output. *(Chapter 4)*
average tax rate The average tax rate is the total amount of taxes paid by an individual or business divided by taxable income. *(Chapter 9)*
average total cost The total cost per unit of output; total cost divided by output. *(Chapter 4)*
average variable cost The total variable cost per unit of output; total variable cost divided by output. *(Chapter 4)*

B

balance of payments A record of a country's international trading, borrowing, and lending. *(Chapter 17)*
balance of trade (trade balance) A component of the current account that includes all the goods (merchandise) that a country exports or imports. *(Chapter 17)*
balance sheet A two-column list that shows the financial position of a bank at a specific date. *(Chapter 14)*
barriers to entry Impediments created by the government or by the firm or firms already in the market that protect an established firm from potential competition. *(Chapter 5)*
benefits-received principle The principle that taxes should be paid in proportion to the benefits that taxpayers derive from public expenditures. *(Chapter 9)*
Board of Governors A seven-member board appointed by the president and confirmed by the Senate to serve 14-year terms of office; administers the Federal Reserve System. *(Chapter 15)*
business cycle Recurrent ups and downs in the level of economic activity extending over several years. *(Chapter 11)*

C

cap and trade system Under a cap and trade program, a limit (or "cap") on pollutions is set, and companies are permitted to sell (or "trade") the unused portion of their limits to other companies that are struggling to comply. *(Chapter 8)*
capacity utilization rate The ratio of an industry's production to its capacity. *(Chapter 1)*
capital and financial account A component of the balance of payments that includes all international purchases or sales of assets such as real estate, corporate stocks and bonds, and government securities. *(Chapter 17)*
capital and financial account balance The amount of capital and financial inflows minus capital and financial outflows. *(Chapter 17)*
capital goods Goods used to produce other goods and services in the future, such as factories and machines; a source of economic growth potential. *(Chapter 1)*
capitalism A free-enterprise system that is rooted in private property and markets; also called a market economy. *(Chapter 18)*
carbon tax A tax imposed on carbon emissions required to produce goods and services. *(Chapter 8)*
cartel A formal organization of firms that attempts to act as if there were only one firm in the industry (monopoly); the purpose of a cartel is to reduce output and increase price in order to increase the joint profits of its members. *(Chapter 6)*
cashier's check A type of check purchased by someone who does not necessarily have a checking account; issued by a bank for a fee plus the amount of the check. *(Chapter 14)*
certified check A type of check that may be called for by a legal contract, such as a real estate or automobile sale agreement; considered less risky than a personal

check because the bank on which it is drawn certifies that the funds are available. *(Chapter 14)*

change in demand A shift in a demand curve caused by a demand shifter. *(Chapter 2)*

change in quantity demanded A movement along a demand curve caused by a change in the price of the good under consideration. *(Chapter 2)*

change in supply A shift in a supply curve induced by a supply shifter. *(Chapter 2)*

classical economists A group of economists who dominated economic thinking prior to the Great Depression; they believed that the market economy automatically adjusts to ensure the full employment of its resources and that economic downturns are temporary, so government should not interfere in economic affairs. *(Chapter 12)*

Clayton Act of 1914 Federal legislation enacted to make explicit the intent of the Sherman Act of 1890; broadened federal antitrust powers to outlaw price discrimination, some mergers, exclusive contracts between supplier and buyer, and to prohibit interlocking boards of directors among competing firms. *(Chapter 8)*

collective bargaining A process whereby unions act on behalf of workers to bargain with employers on matters relating to employment; allows one negotiator to act as the workers' agent rather than having each worker negotiate their own labor contract. *(Chapter 7)*

command-and-control regulations Government-imposed restrictions or mandates on the spillover costs of production. *(Chapter 8)*

command economy An economy in which the government makes all decisions concerning production and distribution; also called planned economy or communism. *(Chapter 18)*

comparative advantage The principle that individuals and countries should specialize in producing goods in which they are relatively—not absolutely—more efficient. *(Chapter 16)*

complementary goods Goods that are used in conjunction with one another. A decrease in the price of one good will increase the demand for another good; conversely, an increase in the price of one good will decrease the demand for another good. *(Chapter 2)*

compound interest The increase in the value of savings that is the result of earning interest on interest. *(Chapter 14)*

concentration ratio The percentage of an industry's sales that are accounted for by the four largest firms in an industry; a low concentration ratio suggests a high degree of competition, whereas a high concentration ratio implies an absence of competition. *(Chapter 6)*

congestion pricing An attempt to decrease traffic and pollution by charging higher prices to travel in certain areas of a city. *(Chapter 2)*

conglomerate merger A merger that brings together two firms producing in different industries. *(Chapter 6)*

constant returns to scale A situation that occurs when a firm's output changes by the same percentage as that of all inputs. *(Chapter 4)*

consumer goods Goods that are available for immediate use by households and do not contribute to future production in the economy, such as food, electricity, and clothing. *(Chapter 1)*

consumer price index (CPI) An indicator of inflation that is calculated by the U.S. Bureau of Labor Statistics by sampling households and businesses; a monitoring of consumer expenditures on specified goods and services. *(Chapter 11)*

corporate average fuel economy (CAFE) Government-enacted standards that apply to all cars and light trucks sold in the United States; originally enacted in 1975, CAFE represents the foundation of U.S. energy conservation policy. *(Chapter 8)*
corporation A "legal person" that conducts business just as an individual does; corporations are owned by stockholders, who receive profits in the form of dividends. *(Chapter 9)*
correspondent banks Banks that form partnerships with other banks in order to exchange checks and payments directly, bypassing the Federal Reserve and its check-processing fee. *(Chapter 14)*
cost-of-living adjustment (COLA) The annual adjustment of Social Security benefits to reflect inflation. *(Chapter 9)*
cost-push inflation Inflation caused by upward pressure on the sellers' side of the market. *(Chapter 11)*
creative destruction According to economist Joseph Schumpeter, in a dynamic economy, the drive to temporarily capture monopoly profits results in old technologies, goods, and livelihoods being replaced by new ones; ideas and creativity are the prime sources of growth in a capitalist economy, and profits are the fuel. *(Chapter 10)*
crowding-out effect A situation that occurs when private spending (consumption or investment) falls as a result of increased government expenditures and subsequent budget deficits. *(Chapter 13)*
currency The money in use in a country. *(Chapter 14)*
current account A component of the balance of payments; the value of transactions in currently produced goods and services, income flows, and unilateral transfers. *(Chapter 17)*
current account balance The sum of the trade balance, the services balance, net income, and net unilateral transfers. *(Chapter 17)*
cyclical unemployment Fluctuating unemployment that coincides with the business cycle and is a repeating short-run problem. *(Chapter 11)*

D

debt service The cash necessary to pay the required principal and interest of a loan during a given period. *(Chapter 13)*
deflation A continuing fall in the average price level that occurs when price reductions on some goods and services outweigh price increases on all others. *(Chapter 11)*
demand A schedule showing the amount of a good or service that a buyer is willing and able to purchase at each possible price during a particular period. *(Chapter 2)*
demand curve A graphical representation of a market demand schedule. *(Chapter 2)*
demand curve for labor The value of the marginal product of labor curve; on a graph, a representation of the wage rate and the amount of labor that a firm is willing to hire at each rate. *(Chapter 7)*
demand deposit account A regular checking account that does not pay interest; the money in the account is available to the account holder "on demand" by writing a check, making a withdrawal, or transferring funds. *(Chapter 14)*
demand-pull inflation Inflation originating from upward pressure on the buyers' side of the market; a situation in which "too much money chases too few goods." *(Chapter 11)*
demand shifter A change in a variable that causes a shift in a demand curve. *(Chapter 2)*
demand-side economics The theory that the demand for goods and services drives economic activity. *(Chapter 13)*

dependent variable A variable that is functionally dependent on another variable. *(Chapter 1)*

depreciation The weakening of a currency; more units of one nation's currency are needed to purchase a unit of another's currency. *(Chapter 17)*

depression A very deep and prolonged recession. *(Chapter 11)*

deregulation The federal dismantling of regulations in industries (such as airlines, trucking, and railroads) in which the existing regulations have outlived their usefulness; an attempt by the government to increase price competition and provide incentives for companies to introduce new products and services. *(Chapter 8)*

derived demand Demand for an input that arises from, and varies with, the demand for the product it helps produce. *(Chapter 7)*

developing nations Nations with relatively low levels of industrialization and low standards of living; these include most of the nations of Africa, Asia, Latin America, and the Middle East. *(Chapter 18)*

diminishing marginal returns The addition of more workers continues to increase output, but by successively smaller increments. *(Chapter 4)*

diminishing marginal utility As a person consumes additional units of a particular good, each additional unit provides less and less additional utility (satisfaction). *(Chapter 2)*

direct relationship A relationship in which two variables show a positive relationship to each other—that is, as one variable increases (decreases), the other also increases (decreases). *(Chapter 1)*

discount rate The rate that Federal Reserve Banks charge for loans to banks. *(Chapter 15)*

discount window An expression for Federal Reserve loans that are repaid with interest at maturity, arranged by telephone, and recorded along with pledged collateral such as U.S. government securities. *(Chapter 15)*

discouraged worker A person who is out of work, would like to work, and is available for work but has stopped looking for work because of lack of success in finding a job. *(Chapter 11)*

discretionary fiscal policy The deliberate use of changes in government expenditures and taxation to affect aggregate demand and to influence the economy's performance in the short run. *(Chapter 13)*

diseconomies of scale A situation in which a firm's unit cost increases and its long-run average total cost curve turns upward. *(Chapter 4)*

division of labor The process of dividing production processes so that workers can practice and perfect a particular skill. *(Chapter 16)*

dual mandate The monetary policy goals of the Federal Reserve to promote economic conditions that achieve both stable prices and maximum sustainable employment. *(Chapter 15)*

dynamic pricing Results in firms adjusting price in response to changing demand conditions. *(Chapter 3)*

E

economic growth The increased productive capabilities of an economy that are made possible by either an increasing resource base or technological advancement. *(Chapter 1 and Chapter 10)*

economic profit Total revenue minus the sum of explicit and implicit costs. *(Chapter 4)*

economic regulation Federal legislation enacted to control the prices, wages, conditions of entry, standards of service, or other important economic characteristics of particular industries. *(Chapter 8)*

economic sanctions Government-imposed limitations, or complete bans, placed on customary trade or financial relations between nations. *(Chapter 1)*

economic shock An unexpected or unpredictable event that affects an economy, either positively or negatively. *(Chapter 11)*

economics The study of choice under conditions of scarcity. *(Chapter 1)*

economies of scale A situation in which a firm's long-run average total cost curve slopes downward, showing an increase in scale and production, which results in a decline in cost per unit. *(Chapter 4)*

economies of scope A reduction in cost when producing two or more distinct goods, when the cost of doing so is less than that of producing each good separately. *(Chapter 4)*

efficiency The point at which an economy is operating along its production possibilities curve, thereby realizing its output potential. *(Chapter 1)*

elastic demand The percentage change in quantity demanded is greater than the percentage change in price. *(Chapter 3)*

entitlement programs A government program guaranteeing certain benefits to a segment of the population. *(Chapter 9)*

equilibrium exchange rate The rate determined by the market forces of demand and supply; central bankers do not attempt to influence the exchange rate. *(Chapter 17)*

equilibrium price The price at which buyers' intentions are equal to sellers' intentions. *(Chapter 2)*

euro The common currency that was introduced by the European Monetary Union in 2002. *(Chapter 17)*

European Central Bank Central bank created by the European Monetary Union to take control of monetary policy and exchange rate policy for member countries; the bank controls the supply of euros, sets the euro interest rate, and maintains permanently fixed exchange rates for member countries. *(Chapter 17)*

European Monetary Union (EMU) A system in which European countries united to replace their individual currencies with a single currency, the euro. *(Chapter 17)*

European Union (EU) A regional economic bloc consisting of 27 European nations; its primary objective has been to create an economic bloc in which trade and other transactions take place freely among member nations. *(Chapter 17)*

excess capacity The difference between the output corresponding to minimum average total cost and the output produced by a monopolistically competitive firm in the long run. *(Chapter 6)*

excess reserves Extra reserves that a bank is holding; can be used to make loans or purchase government securities. *(Chapter 14)*

exchange rate The price of one currency in terms of another. *(Chapter 17)*

expenditure approach A method of calculating GDP by totaling the expenditures on goods and services produced during the current year. *(Chapter 10)*

explicit costs Payments made to others as a cost of running a business. *(Chapter 4)*

export-led growth Growth based on exporting in foreign markets. *(Chapter 18)*

externality A cost or benefit imposed on people other than the producers and consumers of a good or service; also called a spillover. *(Chapter 8)*

F

factors of production Inputs used in the production of goods and services. *(Chapter 1)*

fair-return price A price that is just high enough to cover a regulated firm's average total cost. *(Chapter 8)*

federal debt The cumulative amount of outstanding borrowing from the public over the nation's history. *(Chapter 13)*

federal deficit The difference between total federal spending and revenues in a given year; the annual amount of government borrowing. *(Chapter 13)*

Federal Deposit Insurance Corporation (FDIC) The organization that insures deposits and promotes safe and sound banking practices, conducts examinations and audits, insures deposits up to $250,000 at U.S. banks, and arranges for the disposition of assets and deposit liabilities of insured banks that fail; established by Congress in 1933. *(Chapter 14)*

federal funds market Trading market for reserves held at the Federal Reserve; banks with surplus balances in their accounts transfer reserves to those needing to boost their balances. *(Chapter 15)*

federal funds rate The benchmark rate of interest charged for the short-term use of reserve funds; a market-determined rate. *(Chapter 15)*

Federal Open Market Committee (FOMC) The policymaking body of the Federal Reserve that oversees the purchase and sale of U.S. government securities. *(Chapter 15)*

Federal Reserve System (Fed) The central bank of the United States; legislated by Congress and signed into law by President Wilson in 1913 to provide the nation with a safe, flexible, and stable monetary and financial system. *(Chapter 14 and Chapter 15)*

fiscal policy The use of government expenditures and taxes to promote particular macroeconomic goals, such as full employment, stable prices, and economic growth. *(Chapter 13)*

fixed exchange rates Rates that are used primarily by small, developing nations to maintain ties to a key currency, such as the U.S. dollar. *(Chapter 17)*

fixed input Any resource for which the quantity cannot be varied during the period under consideration. *(Chapter 4)*

flat-rate income tax A proposed substitute for the current federal tax system; such a system would do away with the existing tax rates on personal income and replace them with a single tax rate; exemptions, deductions, and credits would be abolished. *(Chapter 9)*

floating exchange rate system A system in which governments and central banks do not participate in the foreign exchange market; an equilibrium exchange rate equates the demand for and supply of the home currency. *(Chapter 17)*

foreign exchange market A market in which currencies are bought and sold. *(Chapter 17)*

forward guidance The Federal Reserve's communication about the likely future course of monetary policy. *(Chapter 15)*

free-rider problem A situation that exists when it is impossible to exclude a consumer from the consumption of a public good, regardless of whether the consumer pays for it; others pay for the consumer's use of a good. *(Chapter 8)*

frictional unemployment Unemployment that arises from normal labor turnover. *(Chapter 11)*

full employment To an economist, the natural rate of unemployment; something less than 100-percent employment of the labor force. *(Chapter 11)*

functional finance A theory that suggests that government should finance itself to fulfill explicit goals, such as achieving full employment, ensuring growth, and low inflation. *(Chapter 13)*

fundamental economic questions All societies must answer the following questions: What goods will be produced? How will these goods be produced? For whom will these goods be produced? *(Chapter 18)*

G

game theory A method of studying oligopolistic behavior by analyzing a series of strategies and payoffs among rival firms. *(Chapter 6)*

GDP deflator The broadest price index used to calculate real GDP; the ratio of the cost of buying all final goods and services in the current year to the cost of buying the identical goods at base-year prices. *(Chapter 10)*

Generalized System of Preferences (GSP) A system in which the major industrial nations temporarily reduce tariffs on designated manufactured imports from developing nations below the levels applied to imports from other industrial nations. *(Chapter 18)*

government expenditures Federal, state, and local government outlays of funds. *(Chapter 9)*

government purchases Expenditures by federal, state, and local governments on goods and services such as street lighting, sewage systems, national parks, fire trucks, engineers, teachers, and the like. *(Chapter 9)*

government purchases of goods and services Spending on final output by federal, state, and local governments, including the entire payroll of all governments. *(Chapter 10)*

gross domestic product (GDP) The market value of all final goods and services produced within a country in a given year. *(Chapter 10)*

gross private domestic investment All private-sector spending on investment; also known as gross investment. *(Chapter 10)*

H

horizontal merger A merger in which one firm combines with another firm that sells similar products in the same market. *(Chapter 6)*

human capital The knowledge, experience, and skills of the labor force. *(Chapter 9 and Chapter 10)*

hyperinflation A rapid and uncontrolled inflation that destroys an economy. *(Chapter 11)*

I

imperfect competition A market in which more than one seller competes for sales with many other sellers, each of which has some price-making ability. *(Chapter 6)*

implicit costs Costs that represent the value of resources used in production for which no monetary payment is made. *(Chapter 4)*

import quota A limit on the amount of imports that can enter a country. *(Chapter 16)*

import substitution A strategy in which countries protect their import-competing industries by imposing tariffs on imported goods. *(Chapter 18)*

incentive-based regulations Government attempts to control the spillover costs of production; these regulations are flexible because they allow producers to find ways to achieve the objective. *(Chapter 8)*

income Earnings on U.S. investments abroad less payments on foreign investments in the United States; also includes the net compensation of employees. *(Chapter 17)*

income effect A decrease in the price of a good creates an increase in the purchasing power of consumers' money incomes. *(Chapter 2)*

increasing marginal returns The marginal product of an added worker increases the marginal product of the first worker, thereby increasing returns to the firm. *(Chapter 4)*

independent variable A variable that initiates change in other variables. *(Chapter 1)*
industrial policy A government's attempt to influence the economy by targeting specific industries, firms, or economic activities. *(Chapter 16)*
inefficiency The failure of an economy to realize the output potential of its production possibilities curve. *(Chapter 1)*
inelastic demand The percentage change in quantity demanded is smaller than the percentage change in price. *(Chapter 3)*
infant industry argument An argument for tariff protection contending that in order for free trade to be meaningful, trading nations should temporarily shield their newly developing industries from foreign competition. *(Chapter 16)*
inferior good A good for which demand falls as consumer income rises, such as second-hand appliances or inexpensive cuts of meat. *(Chapter 2)*
inflation A sustained or continuous rise in the general price level. *(Chapter 11)*
infrastructure Public capital, including roads, bridges, airports, and utilities. *(Chapter 10)*
International Monetary Fund (IMF) A source of aid to developing countries; a bank for the central banks of member nations. *(Chapter 18)*
inverse relationship A relationship in which two variables show a negative relationship to each other—that is, as one variable increases (decreases), the other decreases (increases). *(Chapter 1)*

K

Keynes, John Maynard British economist who theorized that the market economy is inherently unstable; the level of economic activity depends on the total spending of consumers, businesses, and government; the government must intervene to protect jobs and income. *(Chapter 12)*

L

labor market flexibility Permits firms to enact changes such as employee hiring and firing, compensation and benefits, and working hours and conditions. *(Chapter 11)*
laissez-faire economy The extreme case of a market economy in which the government has almost no economic role except to protect private property and provide a legal system that allows free markets. *(Chapter 18)*
law of demand The principle that price and quantity demanded are inversely (negatively) related, assuming that all other factors affecting the quantity demanded remain the same. *(Chapter 2)*
law of diminishing marginal returns The principle that explains the decline in the marginal product curve; after some point, the marginal product diminishes as additional units of a variable resource are added to a fixed resource. *(Chapter 4)*
law of increasing opportunity cost The principle that opportunity costs increase as more of a good is produced. *(Chapter 1)*
law of supply The principle that, in general, sellers are willing and able to make more of their product available at a higher price than at a lower price, all other determinants of supply being constant. *(Chapter 2)*
legal tender All U.S. currency, including paper money and coins; the federal government mandates its acceptance in transactions and requires that dollars be used in the payment of taxes. *(Chapter 14)*
level playing field The contention of domestic producers that import restrictions should be enacted to offset foreign advantages; all producers should compete on equal terms. *(Chapter 16)*

long run Period during which all inputs are considered to be variable in amount; there are no fixed inputs. *(Chapter 4)*

long-run average total cost curve A curve that shows the minimum cost per unit of producing each output level when any desired size of factory can be constructed. *(Chapter 4)*

losses Negative profit, achieved when costs are greater than revenues. *(Chapter 4)*

M

M1 money supply Money supply consisting of currency in the hands of the public, demand deposits, other checkable deposits, and traveler's checks; the narrowest definition of the U.S. money supply. *(Chapter 14)*

macroeconomics The branch of economics that is concerned with the overall performance of the economy. *(Chapter 1)*

managed floating exchange rates A system that allows the dollar to float in the foreign exchange market according to the market forces of demand and supply; central banks may try to stabilize exchange rates in the short run to provide financial security. *(Chapter 17)*

marginal cost The change in total cost when one more unit of output is produced. *(Chapter 4)*

marginal product The change in output that results from increasing the amount of labor by one unit, holding all other inputs fixed. *(Chapter 4)*

marginal product of labor The additional output produced by hiring one more unit of labor. *(Chapter 7)*

marginal propensity to consume The fraction of additional income that people spend. *(Chapter 12)*

marginal propensity to save The fraction of additional income that is saved. *(Chapter 12)*

marginal revenue The increase in total revenue resulting from the sale of another unit of output, calculated as total revenue divided by the change in quantity between any two points on the total revenue schedule. *(Chapter 5)*

marginal revenue = marginal cost rule Total profit is maximized when marginal revenue is equal to marginal cost. *(Chapter 5)*

marginal tax rate The fraction of additional income paid in taxes, calculated as the change in taxes due divided by the change in income. *(Chapter 9)*

market Mechanism through which buyers (demanders) and sellers (suppliers) communicate in order to trade goods and services. *(Chapter 2)*

market economy A free-enterprise system that is rooted in private property and markets; also called capitalism. *(Chapter 18)*

market equilibrium A situation that occurs when the price of a product adjusts so that the quantity consumers will purchase at that price is identical to the quantity suppliers will sell; the point at which the forces of demand and supply are balanced. *(Chapter 2)*

market failure A situation that occurs when a market fails to allocate resources efficiently. *(Chapter 8)*

mediation A process whereby an outside party is called in to help resolve disagreements between labor and management. *(Chapter 7)*

Medicare A federal government health insurance program whose objective is to reduce the financial burden of illness on the elderly. *(Chapter 9)*

medium of exchange A function of money; something that people are willing to accept in payment for goods and services. *(Chapter 14)*

merger A practice in which firms combine under a single ownership or control; the merged firm is larger, and therefore it may realize economies of scale as output expands, and usually has a greater ability to control the market price of its product. *(Chapter 6)*

microeconomics The branch of economics that focuses on the choices made by households and firms and the effects those choices have on particular markets. *(Chapter 1)*

minimum wage The smallest amount of money per hour that an employer can legally pay a worker. *(Chapter 7)*

mixed economy An economy that has elements of both market and command economics. *(Chapter 9 and Chapter 18)*

models Simplified representations of the real world that we use to help us understand, explain, and predict economic phenomena in the real world; also called theories. *(Chapter 1)*

modern monetary theory A macroeconomic theory that asserts that government spending should not be restrained by fears of rising debt. *(Chapter 13)*

monetary policy Changing the economy's money supply in order to help the economy achieve maximum output and employment and stable prices; carried out by the Federal Reserve. *(Chapter 15)*

money The set of assets in the economy that people use regularly to purchase goods and services from other people; functions as a medium of exchange, a unit of account, and a store of value. *(Chapter 14)*

money multiplier The maximum amount of money that the banking system can generate with each dollar of reserves; the reciprocal of the required reserve ratio. *(Chapter 14)*

money order A form of payment that serves the same function as a personal check; can be issued by businesses other than banks; usually issued in smaller amounts and at a lower cost than cashier's checks. *(Chapter 14)*

monopolistic competition The market structure that is closest to perfect competition; this structure is based on a large number of firms, each firm having a relatively small share of the total market. *(Chapter 6)*

monopoly A market structure characterized by a single supplier of a good or service for which there is no close substitute. *(Chapter 5)*

multiplier The ratio of the change in national output to the change in aggregate demand; indicates the extent to which the change in aggregate demand is "multiplied" into changes in larger output and income. *(Chapter 12)*

multiplier effect The result of changes in aggregate demand caused by the multiplier; an improvement in economic activity in one sector of the economy multiplies as it flows through the economy. *(Chapter 12)*

N

national debt The total amount of outstanding borrowing by the federal government accumulated over the nation's history. *(Chapter 13)*

national sales tax A proposed alternative to the current federal income tax system; this system would entail a federal consumption tax collected at the retail level by businesses. *(Chapter 9)*

natural monopoly A market structure in which one firm can supply a product to the entire market at a lower cost per unit than could be achieved by two or more firms each supplying only some of it. *(Chapter 5)*

natural rate of unemployment The level of unemployment at which there is no cyclical unemployment; the sum of frictional unemployment and structural unemployment. *(Chapter 11)*

negative demand shock A sudden economic event that reduces aggregate demand. *(Chapter 11)*

negative supply shock A sudden economic event that reduces aggregate supply. *(Chapter 11)*

negotiable order of withdrawal (NOW) account A type of checking account that pays interest but typically requires a larger minimum balance. *(Chapter 14)*

net exports Sales of a country's goods and services to foreigners during a particular time period minus purchases of foreign-produced goods and services by that country's residents—in other words, exports minus imports. *(Chapter 10)*

nominal GDP Gross domestic product expressed in terms of the prices existing in the year in which the goods and services were produced; also known as current-dollar GDP. *(Chapter 10)*

nominal income The actual number of dollars of income received during a year. *(Chapter 11)*

nominal interest rate The interest rate that a bank pays. *(Chapter 11)*

normal good A good that is purchased more often as consumer income rises, such as a ski trip or a new car. *(Chapter 2)*

normal profit The minimum profit necessary to keep a firm in operation; normal profit occurs when total revenue just covers the sum of explicit and implicit costs; zero economic profit. *(Chapter 4)*

normative economics A term used to describe economic value judgments that cannot be tested empirically. *(Chapter 1)*

North American Free Trade Agreement (NAFTA) A pact approved in 1993 by the governments of the United States, Canada, and Mexico to remove trade restrictions among them. *(Chapter 16)*

O

oligopoly A form of imperfect competition in which a small number of firms compete with one another, and each firm has significant price-making ability. *(Chapter 6)*

open market operations The purchase or sale of securities by the Federal Reserve; transactions made with a bank or some other business or individual but not directly with the federal government; the most useful and important policy tool of the Fed. *(Chapter 15)*

operational lag The time it takes for a fiscal policy, once enacted, to be put into operation. *(Chapter 13)*

opportunity cost The value of the best alternative sacrificed; the cost of any particular economic choice. *(Chapter 1)*

Organization of Petroleum Exporting Countries (OPEC) A group of nations that sells oil on the world market; the best-known cartel. *(Chapter 6)*

outsourcing Contracting out functions that once were done in-house. *(Chapter 7)*

P

partnership A form of business organization in which two or more owners pool their financial resources and business skills. *(Chapter 9)*

peak The phase of a business cycle when real GDP is at a temporary high and employment and profits are strong. *(Chapter 11)*

peak-load pricing A pricing strategy whereby consumers pay more for electricity used during periods of peak energy demand and less for electricity used during off-peak periods. *(Chapter 8)*

perfect competition A market characterized by insignificant barriers to entry or exit, many sellers and buyers, a standardized product produced by firms in the industry, and perfect information; the most competitive market structure. *(Chapter 5)*

personal consumption expenditures Purchases of final goods and services by households and individuals. *(Chapter 10)*

personal distribution of income Distribution showing how the nation's income is shared by households; it indicates the share of before-tax annual money income received. *(Chapter 9)*

positive economics A term used to describe the facts of the economy, dealing with the way in which the economy works. *(Chapter 1)*

price ceiling The government-imposed maximum legal price that a seller may charge for a product. *(Chapter 3)*

price discrimination The practice of charging some customers a lower price than others for an identical good, even though there is no difference in the cost to the firm for supplying these consumers. *(Chapter 6)*

price elasticity of demand A formula that measures how responsive, or sensitive, buyers are to a change in price. *(Chapter 3)*

price floor A government-imposed price that prevents prices from falling below a legally mandated level. *(Chapter 3)*

price index A mechanism used to adjust GDP figures so that the figures only show changes in actual output. *(Chapter 10)*

price taker A firm that has to "take," or accept, the price established by the market; a perfectly competitive firm. *(Chapter 5)*

private goods Goods that are produced through the market system; private goods are divisible subject to the exclusion principle and to the principle of rival consumption. *(Chapter 8)*

product differentiation The fundamental characteristic of monopolistic competition; the assumption that the product of each firm is not a perfect substitute for the products of competing firms. *(Chapter 6)*

production The use of resources to make outputs of goods and services available for human wants. *(Chapter 4)*

production function The relationship between physical output and the quantity of resources used in the production process. *(Chapter 4)*

production possibilities curve A graphical illustration of the maximum combinations of two goods that an economy can produce, given its available resources and technology. *(Chapter 1)*

productivity A ratio that measures the quantity of output produced relative to the amount of work required to produce it; total output divided by hours worked. *(Chapter 10)*

profit The difference between the amount of revenues a firm takes in (total revenue) and the amount it spends for wages, materials, electricity, and so on (total cost). *(Chapter 4)*

public goods Goods such as national defense, highways, lighthouses, and air-traffic control; goods that are indivisible and are not subject to the exclusion principle. *(Chapter 8)*

Q

quantity supplied The quantity of a good that is available at any given time or price, assuming that all of the other determinants of supply remain unchanged; a single point on a supply schedule. *(Chapter 2)*

quota A physical restriction on the quantity of goods traded each year. *(Chapter 16)*

R

rate of economic growth The percentage change in the level of economic activity from one year to the next. *(Chapter 10)*

real GDP Nominal GDP adjusted to reflect only changes in output, not changes in prices; real GDP measures actual (real) production and shows how actual production—rather than the prices of what is produced—has changed; also known as constant-dollar GDP. *(Chapter 10)*

real income The actual number of dollars received (nominal income) adjusted for any change in price; measures real purchasing power—that is, the amount of goods and services that can be purchased with nominal income. *(Chapter 11)*

real interest rate The interest rate that is adjusted for inflation, calculated as the nominal interest rate minus the inflation rate. *(Chapter 11)*

recession A period of significant decline in total output, income, employment, and trade that lasts from 6 months to a year and is marked by widespread contraction in many sectors in the economy; the phase of the business cycle that begins at a peak and ends at a trough. *(Chapter 11)*

recognition lag The time between the beginning of inflation or recession and the recognition that it is actually occurring. *(Chapter 13)*

recovery The phase of the business cycle when real GDP rises, industrial output expands, profits increase, and employment moves toward full employment; also called expansion. *(Chapter 11)*

rent controls A mechanism used to protect low-income households from escalating rents caused by perceived housing shortages and to make housing more affordable to the poor. *(Chapter 3)*

required reserve ratio A specific percentage of checking deposits that must be kept either as vault cash or as deposits at the Federal Reserve; directly limits the ability of banks to grant new loans; established by the Federal Reserve System. *(Chapter 14)*

required reserves The minimum amount of vault cash and deposits at the Federal Reserve that a bank must maintain. *(Chapter 14)*

reserves Deposits that banks have received but have not lent out; can be kept either in vault cash or as deposits at a Federal Reserve Bank. *(Chapter 14)*

right-to-work law A right-to-work law guarantees that no person can be compelled, as a condition of employment, to join or not to join, nor to pay dues to, a labor union. *(Chapter 7)*

rule of 70 An indicator of the power of growth rates, determined by dividing 70 by the growth rate; indicates the number of years it will take for the level of real GDP to double. *(Chapter 10)*

S

Say's Law A law attributed to 19th-century economist Jean-Baptiste Say according to which supply creates its own demand; whatever is produced (supplied) will create the income necessary to purchase the product; therefore, overproduction is not possible. *(Chapter 12)*

scarcity The principle that there are not enough—nor can there ever be enough—goods and services to satisfy the wants and needs of everyone. *(Chapter 1)*

services Work done by doctors, dentists, lawyers, engineers, accountants, and the like for consumers. *(Chapter 17)*

share draft account A credit union account that is like a bank's checking account, except that it results in the purchase of a share in the credit union. *(Chapter 14)*

Sherman Act of 1890 The cornerstone of federal antitrust law; the act prohibits contracts and conspiracies in the restraint of trade, as well as monopolization and the threat of monopolization of an industry. *(Chapter 8)*

shock effect An assumption whereby the minimum wage leads to an increase in the demand for labor, thus moderating some unemployment. *(Chapter 7)*

short run Period during which the quantity of at least one input is fixed and the quantities of other inputs can be varied. *(Chapter 4)*

shortage The amount by which the quantity demanded exceeds the quantity supplied; excess demand. *(Chapter 2)*

shut-down rule In the short run, a firm should continue to produce if total revenue exceeds total variable cost; otherwise, it should shut down. *(Chapter 5)*

slope On a graph, the vertical distance between two points (the "rise") divided by the horizontal distance between the two points (the "run"). *(Chapter 1)*

social regulation Government regulation that is intended to correct a variety of undesirable side effects in a market economy that relate to health, safety, and the environment; examples include the regulations imposed by the Environmental Protection Agency, the Food and Drug Administration, and the Occupational Safety and Health Administration. *(Chapter 8)*

Social Security The largest retirement and disability program in the United States, created as a means of providing income security upon retirement to people who would not otherwise have that form of security; also known as Old-Age, Survivors, and Disability Insurance. *(Chapter 9)*

socialism An economic system in which the government is actively involved in the economy and an overall economic plan is formulated by manufacturers, farmers, workers, and government officials working together. *(Chapter 18)*

sole proprietorship A firm that is owned and operated by one individual. *(Chapter 9)*

spillover A cost or benefit imposed on people other than the producers and consumers of a good or service; also called an externality. *(Chapter 8)*

spillover benefit A desirable spillover or externality; a benefit imposed on people other than the producers and consumers of a good. *(Chapter 8)*

spillover cost An undesirable spillover or externality; a cost imposed on people other than the producers and consumers of a good. *(Chapter 8)*

stagflation A decline in aggregate supply that results in falling output, increased unemployment, and rising prices; recession (stagnation) with inflation. *(Chapter 12)*

statistical discrepancy An adjustment for measurement errors that is reported in the capital account component of the balance of payments. *(Chapter 17)*

store of value A function of money; the ability to save money and then use it to make future purchases. *(Chapter 14)*

strikes Work stoppages called by a majority of the voting members of a union; strikes occur when workers feel that stopping work is the best way to pressure their employer into granting their demands. *(Chapter 7)*

structural unemployment Unemployment that occurs when individuals' skills do not match what employers require or when job seekers are geographically separated from job opportunities. *(Chapter 11)*

substitute goods Goods for which a reduction in the price of one good will decrease the demand for the other good; conversely, an increase in the price of one good will increase the demand for the other good. *(Chapter 2)*

substitution effect When the price of a good falls—and all other determinants of demand remain the same—the price falls relative to the prices of all other similar goods. *(Chapter 2)*

supply A schedule that shows the amount of a good or service that a firm or household is willing and able to sell at each possible price during a particular period. *(Chapter 2)*

supply curve A graphical representation of a market supply schedule; a line showing the quantities of a good or service that are supplied at various prices. *(Chapter 2)*
supply shifter A change in a variable that causes a shift in a supply curve. *(Chapter 2)*
supply-side economics A macroeconomic theory asserting that economic growth can be most effectively promoted by reducing taxes, decreasing regulation, and allowing free trade. *(Chapter 13)*
surplus The amount by which the quantity supplied exceeds the quantity demanded; excess supply. *(Chapter 2)*

T

tariff A tax imposed on imports. *(Chapter 16)*
taxable income Gross income minus exemptions, deductions, and credits. *(Chapter 9)*
theories Simplified representations of the real world that we use to help us understand, explain, and predict economic phenomena in the real world; also called models. *(Chapter 1)*
total cost The sum of the value of all resources used over a given period to manufacture a good; the sum of total fixed cost and total variable cost. *(Chapter 4)*
total fixed cost The sum of all costs that do not vary with output; also called overhead cost. *(Chapter 4)*
total product The maximum quantity of output that can be produced from a given amount of inputs. *(Chapter 4)*
total revenue Dollars earned by sellers of a product, calculated by multiplying the quantity sold over a period by the price. *(Chapter 3 and Chapter 5)*
total variable cost The sum of all costs that change as the rate of output varies; total variable cost depends on weekly or monthly output. *(Chapter 4)*
tradeable gasoline rights (TGRs) Individuals with more TGRs than they need could sell the excess, while those who want to use more gallons than their allocation would have to buy extra TGRs. *(Chapter 2)*
transfer payments Payments of income (such as unemployment compensation or Medicaid) from taxpayers to individuals who make no contribution to current output for these payments. *(Chapter 9)*
traveler's checks Checks that are usually issued in $20, $50, $100, and $500 denominations; they are used by travelers to protect against loss or theft and are widely accepted both in the United States and abroad. *(Chapter 14)*
trough The phase of the business cycle when real GDP is at a low point, just before it begins to turn upward, and unemployment and idle productive capacity are at their highest levels. *(Chapter 11)*

U

underground economy Unreported barter and cash transactions that take place outside recorded market channels. *(Chapter 10)*
unemployed Individuals who do not have jobs but are actively seeking work. *(Chapter 11)*
unemployment compensation Funds paid by the state to unemployed workers who have lost their jobs due to layoffs or retrenchment. *(Chapter 9)*
unemployment insurance The system that helps support consumer spending during periods of job loss and provides economic security to workers through income maintenance; established as part of the Social Security Act of 1935. *(Chapter 11)*
unemployment rate The number of people unemployed divided by the labor force (the number of people holding or seeking jobs). *(Chapter 11)*

unilateral transfers A component of the current account; gifts that include transfers of goods and services or money between the United States and the rest of the world for which nothing is given in exchange. *(Chapter 17)*

union shop A workplace in which employees are required to join the recognized union within a specified length of time after their employment with the firm begins; each state may accept or reject union shops. *(Chapter 7)*

unions Organizations that allow their members to sell their services collectively, thus giving the members more bargaining power than they would have if they acted individually. *(Chapter 7)*

unit elastic demand The percentage change in quantity demanded equals the percentage change in price. *(Chapter 3)*

unit of account A function of money; allows consumers to compare the relative values of goods; a measure that specifies price. *(Chapter 14)*

U.S.–Mexico–Canada Agreement (USMCA) A free trade agreement between the United States, Mexico, and Canada. *(Chapter 16)*

value of the marginal product of a worker The increase in revenue that results from hiring an additional worker; the dollar value of a worker's contribution to production. *(Chapter 7)*

value-added tax (VAT) A proposed substitute for the current federal tax system; a tax that would be collected at the various stages of production of goods and services. *(Chapter 9)*

variable input Resources (such as labor and materials) whose quantities can be altered in the short run. *(Chapter 4)*

vertical merger A merger between firms that are in the same industry but at different stages in the production process. *(Chapter 6)*

vicious circle of poverty A cycle in which developing nations cannot break out of low standards of living. *(Chapter 18)*

World Bank An international organization that provides loans to developing countries aimed toward poverty reduction and economic development. *(Chapter 18)*

World Trade Organization (WTO) An organization whose 164 members acknowledge that tariff reductions agreed to by any two nations will be extended to all other members; encourages a gradual relaxation of tariffs throughout the world. *(Chapter 16)*

Index

Note: Information in figures and tables is indicated by page numbers in *italics* and **bold**.